Copyright © 1974, by John Wiley & Sons Ltd.

All rights reserved.

No part of this book may be reproduced by any means,
nor transmitted, nor translated into a machine language
without the written permission of the publisher.

*Library of Congress Cataloging in Publication Data:*
Main entry under title:

Conservation in practice.

1. Nature conservation. 2. Ecology. I. Warren, Andrew,
ed. II. Goldsmith, Frank Barrie, ed.

QH75.C67          333.7'2          73–9281
ISBN 0 471 92114 9 Cloth bound
ISBN 0 471 92105 X Paper bound

Printed in Great Britain by Aberdeen University Press, Aberdeen

# Conservation in Practice

Edited by

A. WARREN
*Department of Geography*
*University College London*

F. B. GOLDSMITH
*Department of Botany and Microbiology*
*University College London*

**JOHN WILEY & SONS**
London · New York · Sydney · Toronto

# Foreword

It took a long time for public opinion to grasp both the necessity for taking care of the environment, and the fact that this could only be done by the practical application of ecology, which is one definition of conservation, and not a bad one. When Sir Julian Huxley, Sir Arthur Tansley and their colleagues (of whom I was one) were appointed at the end of World War II to make recommendations to the British Government on this subject they accepted and spelt out Tansley's view that the Government should take formal responsibility for conservation through a new specialist service, and that this would necessitate countrywide research on fundamental ecological problems to make possible scientific management of Nature Reserves and other areas. That view, supported by the British Ecological Society, the Society for the Promotion of Nature Reserves, and indirectly by the Royal Society, had implications much more revolutionary and far-reaching than most of its sponsors then appreciated.

The idea that nothing more was needed than finding allegedly 'natural' areas and putting a ringfence round them died hard. Passions soon ran high between the older *laissez faire* school of conservationists and those who insisted that, in Britain at least, there hardly survived any habitats sufficiently untouched and ecologically viable to be able to do without at least some measure of interventionist management, based not upon hunches and impulses, but on comprehensive controlled field experiments. The official reports (Cmd 7022 and Cmd 6784, of 1947 and 1949, for England and Wales and Scotland respectively) were full of wise words, but when it came to carrying them into effect most ecologists and conservationists shrank back, either from irrational distaste or from a rational appraisal of their technical unpreparedness for such responsibilities.

For this hesitation plenty of excuses can be found. Professional ecologists were still very few, with narrow training and experience and negligible resources. Much of the steam behind the movement came from laymen whose sentiments for nature were predominantly romantic or escapist. Apart from certain glaring examples such as oil pollution at sea and systematic drainage of wetlands it had not yet become widely evident that the impact of the technosphere would demand so many complex appraisals and interventions – indeed the term technosphere was only invented twenty years after the Nature Conservancy's charter.

The fact remains that the publicly accepted prospectus called for widespread scientific research and management. Had the strong reaction in favour of reliance on empirical and *laissez-faire* approaches prevailed, as it came near to doing around 1951, the Nature Conservancy would inevitably have failed and would probably have been abolished, as some influential figures at the time thought it should be. After all, no other country on earth had embraced so integral a fusion of science and conservation as the Nature Conservancy (ranking as fourth official Research Council) embodied. No lesser status and resources would have sufficed to attract enough recruits of adequate calibre into this still largely unexplored region of research and management.

Even so, many biologists, many teachers and many universities and other institutions took their time to consider whether the bandwagon was worth mounting. The studentships offered by the Conservancy were taken up in many cases for researches which suited the Departments better than they contributed towards the building of an infrastructure for conservation in practice. As the Conservancy's scientific staff increased slowly, from some half-dozen at the opening of the 1950s to over seventy at their close, the lack of university teaching and training in applied ecology became increasingly serious.

Through the influence of Professor W. H. Pearsall, then Chairman of the Conservancy's Scientific Policy Committee, and the helpfulness both of Lord Murray of Newhaven, then Chairman of the University Grants Committee, and of Sir Ifor Evans, then Provost of University College London, it proved possible in 1960 to establish a formal post-graduate interdisciplinary Course in Conservation at the College, whose success quickly demonstrated to a number of other universities what they had been missing. It is from that Course that this book has sprung, and in addition to its obvious value as a most comprehensive and authoritative review of the state of the science and art it should stimulate further effort and thinking on wider aspects.

An immediate reflection, which may not so readily occur to readers unfamiliar with conservation in other countries, is how strongly it demonstrates and vindicates the peculiar modern British approach to the subject. Perhaps nowhere else would one expect to find a work entitled *Conservation in Practice* written almost entirely by administrators, planners and official and university scientists, without a park superintendent, a forester, or a land manager among them. We have come, in this country, to accept almost unquestioningly Tansley's thesis that true conservation of nature and the environment flows naturally from full ecological understanding. This implies that the strategy, the principles, and the standards of practice in conservation must come from a new breed of field scientists, while the old-style ground staff at all levels become essentially technicians and executives engaged in applying the scientific doctrines and knowledge.

We should pause to note that such an outlook is still quite new in Britain and has probably yet to win acceptance elsewhere. To what extent it is valid can best be put to the test by a critical reading of what follows. Different ecologists would no doubt have made a somewhat different presentation from the contributors to this volume, but all would probably agree that this interdisciplinary spectrum of information and interpretation offers a fair sample of the new approach to conservation as applied ecology.

It is not only the conservationists from whom adaptation is demanded. Until the launching a decade ago of the International Biological Programme a number of leading biologists clung to the belief that some benign spirit from on high would whisper to each new recruit what research mission he should adopt as his own Holy Grail, and that no impious fellows should presume to intrude on these mysteries with such sacrilegious heresies as organized programmes of study. In the earlier days too much public money was wasted in irrelevant or abortive doctorate exercises in deference to this mystique. It took time to demonstrate in practice that the biosphere itself, and its conflicts with the technosphere, would clearly delineate research topics of the highest relevance to both scientific advances and conservation requirements, and that those who focus on such great issues are thereby better qualified to interpret research needs than inheritors of the previous *laissez-faire* tradition. A parallel path had been charted earlier by the Medical Research Council, with widespread acceptance and great success. What was unique to the Nature Conservancy was the combination, in one organization and through a unified staff, of every kind of research, fundamental, applied and survey, with the acquisition and management of land all over Britain for a national network of nature reserves and outdoor laboratories, and with the conduct not merely of advisory and educational services but of related administrative functions such as scientific licensing and enforcement of bylaws.

The Nature Conservancy Council Act of 1973 formally disrupts this unity, in face of a record of success and progress which few other governmental agencies have matched since World War II. I must confess to a bias in favour of the idea that Westminster and Whitehall should let alone the few organizations which work and concentrate on putting right the many which do not. I am sure also that that great administrator Herbert Morrison who gave the Nature Conservancy its charter would deprecate the inability to let well alone, even at a titular level by adding the entirely superfluous 'Council' to the good simple English of his 'Nature Conservancy'.

I am on record as having in my day strongly and effectively resisted successive ill-judged efforts to separate the research functions from the conservation functions, as the new Act largely does, despite the Cranbrook amendment. Nevertheless I did not feel called upon to reiterate my previously stated view on this occasion, for reasons it may be desirable briefly to summarize here. First, as I have shown above, the transformation of the conservation movement from a sentiment-based to a scientifically-based activity could not have been achieved, as this book shows it to have been, without the capability for training and funding a new generation of picked scientists on the only lines calculated to validate that approach. Nobody but the Conservancy would or could have seen this task through with the necessary sincerity, vigour and realism. It has however now been near enough completed.

Given reasonable goodwill at the top, those Conservancy scientists so sadly divorced from their conservation colleagues by being brigaded under the Institute of Terrestrial Ecology in the Natural Environment Research Council should not find it impossible to continue to work on the well-tried team basis. I must in fairness add that having struggled against odds for the inclusion of the then strange word 'Environment' in the title of the Natural Environment Research Council I could not properly support a new deal which left N.E.R.C. bereft of terrestrial ecologists.

My friendly neutrality towards the new dispensation is mainly based however on two factors new during the past decade. I was opposed to the supersession of the old informal Lord President's Office by a Department of Education and Science which among its other disabilities, is very badly educated and does not begin to understand science. I welcomed the merger of the local government and planning, works and transport ministries in a comprehensive Department of the Environment, and its promising start under Peter Walker. Given such a new approach it no longer made sense for the Nature Conservancy to be tied to D.E.S. It was clear that both the public image and the backroom work at the Department of the Environment would greatly benefit by bringing the Nature Conservancy within the family, always provided that (as the new statute at least theoretically assures) the Conservancy reverts to the degree of autonomy of Whitehall which it had from the outset.

These considerations are reinforced by one further weighty factor. When I was negotiating the original status of the Conservancy as one of the official Research Councils, these were the bodies, clothed with the then magical prestige of science, which could count on getting the most public money with the fewest stupid questions asked from its bumbling custodians. Recently the reverse has become true. The kind of divine-right ivory-tower scientists who, if not neutralized, would have frustrated nearly everything that this book enshrines so overplayed their hand in other directions that money for science is now exceedingly tight. Clearly had the Nature Conservancy remained on the Science vote under N.E.R.C. it would have been doubly penalized in future, first by this overall stringency and again by the bottom priority assigned by rival scientific interests to the funding of its conservation activities. By contrast, linked to the Department of the Environment, it enjoys a share in an immense total vote of which an embarrassingly minute part has hitherto been assigned to research and development. It can therefore confidently expect far better financial backing than under N.E.R.C. or as a separate Research Council under D.E.S. I have always maintained that conservationists, whatever their personal preferences, must be realists and opportunists if they are to fulfil their obligations to the biosphere, and on that ground the new order has my reluctant and provisional blessing. I reserve the right to judge it further by its results.

I close by most warmly commending a book which was as badly needed as it has been well done.

MAX NICHOLSON

London, October 1973

# Preface

The Conservation Course at University College London, upon which this collection of essays is focused, was initiated in 1960 as a result of the initiatives of Professor Pearsall and Mr. Max Nicholson, then Director of the Nature Conservancy. It is very appropriate, therefore, that Mr. Nicholson has written a Foreword to a book which represents the range of interests and responsibilities of the many British scientists, administrators and planners who have lectured to the course over the years. Our lecturers have included the botanists, zoologists, geographers, archaeologists, engineers, geneticists, hydrologists, national and local planners, and administrators who have written these essays. In addition to our usual lecturers, Mr. Blackmore, Dr. Coddington and Lord Kennet have widened our horizons with chapters on The Nature Conservancy and on economic and political implications.

The essays exhibit some important common features. There is the universal concern to base action on as much sound research as possible, an approach which contrasts with the wilder suggestions of some environmentalists. There is a desire that there should be cooperation between planners and natural scientists which springs from the close professional association many of the contributors have experienced (some as members of the Conservation Course itself). Above all there is the constructive belief, which prompts our title, that it is possible to evolve sensible management strategies for conservation problems.

We are conscious of gaps in our coverage both of natural environments and of planning approaches, and for these we can only plead lack of space. Marine conservation is probably the most serious omission although we would argue that it is a somewhat distinct field. Topics that we would particularly like to have covered but have not been able to, include freshwater ecology, the work of international and voluntary groups, forestry and landscape evaluation.

We have extended our own knowledge about conservation in editing this volume, and we hope that the results will also enlighten others. In order that our audience should be as wide as possible, we asked the contributors to write for informed laymen as well as for students, planners, and land managers by explaining their technical jargon where necessary and by including selected biographies to guide the interested reader to the specialist literature.

Another recent development which will undoubtedly have profound effects on all of the environmental problems discussed in these chapters is the escalating energy famine. If, for example, private cars are to become more expensive to operate, many countryside planning policies will have to be reappraised. But if we have read the signs correctly and based our conclusions on sound research, they will be of no less use in planning for the challenges of the last half of this century.

It is inevitable, in a field in which change is rapid, that some of these essays became dated almost as soon as they were written. Of the many important developments, the most far-reaching has been the replacement of the Nature Conservancy by the Nature Conservancy Council and the Institute of Terrestrial Ecology. Where possible we have tried to update essays in the proof stage.

We must thank many people (apart from our contributors) who have helped the preparation of this collection. In particular we are indebted to Dr. Brian O'Connor, The Director of the Conservation Course, and to our colleagues Dr. Carolyn Harrison and Dr. Richard Munton, and our former colleagues Professor Peter Jewell and Professor Palmer Newbould who have helped to develop the course on which these papers are based. The entire staff of the drawing office in the Department of Geography helped to prepare the diagrams and we must thank them all, but Miss Margaret Thomas in particular deserves thanks for her patience and research into some of the figures. Finally, Miss Sylvia New deserves our thanks for her patient and cheerful work in typing many parts of the collection.

We hope that this voume will help to stimulate the development of conservation in a rational and scientific manner and that readers will be motivated to extend their own conservation activities.

ANDREW WARREN
BARRIE GOLDSMITH
University College London, October 1973

# Contributors

R. J. BERRY
Department of Biology, Royal Free Hospital School of Medicine, 8 Hunter Street, Brunswick Square, London WC1N 1BP.

M. BLACKMORE
Nature Conservancy Council, 19 and 20 Belgrave Square, London SW1X 8PY.

T. J. CHANDLER
Department of Geography, University of Manchester, Manchester M13 9PL.

A. CODDINGTON
Department of Economics, Queen Mary College, Mile End Road, London E1 4NS.

JOAN DAVIDSON
School of Environmental Studies, University College London, Flaxman House, 16 Flaxman Terrace, London WC1H 9AT.

J. M. DAVIDSON
The Countryside Commission, 1 Cambridge Gate, London NW1 4JY.

G. W. DIMBLEBY
Institute of Archaeology, University of London, 31-34 Gordon Square, London WC1 0PY.

E. A. G. DUFFEY
Natural Environment Research Council, Monks Wood Experimental Station, Abbot's Ripton, Huntingdon PE17 2LS.

F. B. GOLDSMITH
Department of Botany and Microbiology, University College London, Gower Street, London WC1E 6BT.

G. T. GOODMAN
Department of Applied Biology, Chelsea College of Science and Technology, Hortensia Road, London SW10 0QX.

CAROLYN M. HARRISON
Department of Geography, University College London, Gower Street, London WC1E 6BT.

G. E. HOLLIS         *Department of Geography, University College London, Gower Street, London WC1E, 6BT.*

T. HUXLEY            *Countryside Commission for Scotland, Battleby, Redgorton, Perth PH1 3EW, Scotland.*

P. G. JAMES          *Department of Agricultural Economics, University of New England, Armidale, New South Wales 2351, Australia.*

P. A. JEWELL         *Department of Zoology, Royal Holloway College, Englefield Green, Egham, TW20 0EX, Surrey.*

P. H. KEMP           *Department of Civil Engineering, University College London, Gower Street, London WC1E 6BT.*

LORD KENNET          *100 Bayswater Road, London W2 3HJ.*

CELIA KIRBY          *Institute of Hydrology, MacLean Building, Crowmarsh Gifford, Wallingford, Berks OX10 8BB.*

I. MERCER            *Devon County Council, County Hall, Exeter EX2 4QH.*

G. R. MILLER         *Natural Environment Research Council, Hill of Brathens, Glassel, Banchory, Kincardineshire AB3 4BY, Scotland.*

N. W. MOORE          *Natural Environment Research Council, Monks Wood Experimental Station, Abbot's Ripton, Huntingdon PE17 2LS.*

R. J. C. MUNTON      *Department of Geography, University College London, Gower Street, London WC1E 6BT.*

P. J. NEWBOULD       *School of Environmental Sciences, New University of Ulster, Coleraine, County Londonderry, Northern Ireland BT52 15A.*

E. M. NICHOLSON      *Land Use Consultants, 139 Sloane Street, London SW1X 1AY.*

F. B. O'CONNOR       *Department of Botany and Microbiology, University College London, Gower Street, London WC1E 6BT.*

J. C. RODDA          *Department of the Environment, 2 Marsham Street, London SW1 3EB.*

J. SHEAIL            *Natural Environment Research Council, Monks Wood Experimental Station, Abbot's Ripton, Huntingdon PE17 2LS.*

Contributors                                                          XV

I. G. SIMMONS        *Department of Geography, Science Laboratories, University of Durham, South Road, Durham DH1 3LE.*

C. R. TUBBS         *The Nature Conservancy Council, Shrubbs Hill Road, Lyndhurst, Hampshire SO4 7DJ.*

C. VITA-FINZI       *Department of Geography, University College London, Gower Street, London WC1E 6BT.*

A. WARREN           *Department of Geography, University College London, Gower Street, London WC1E 6BT.*

A. WATSON           *Natural Environment Research Council, Hill of Brathens, Glassel, Banchory, Kincardineshire AB3 4BY, Scotland.*

# Contents

Contents

# CHAPTER I

# An Introduction to Conservation in the Natural Environment

A. WARREN and F. B. GOLDSMITH

More minds are constructively thinking about conservation than in any period in history. Although they are concerned with many facets of our environment, from its works of art and old buildings to its wildlife, natural resources are most commonly associated with the term ' conservation ', and their long term management has received more thought than any other field. Moreover they are widely recognized to be in need of urgent attention.

Conservation seen as a responsible attitude to natural resources has a long history in the philosophy of many cultures, and has expressed itself in many different ways. In the industrial West increases in lifespans, material investments and leisure time have induced a greater concern for the future of an environment which is threatened by material shortages and decreasing quality. This concern is usually traced to the early nineteenth century, when Malthus wrote of the evidently inevitable conflict between increasing human population and fixed or decreasing resources. To most conservationists this concern for the imbalance between population and resources is only a part, albeit a major part, of a wider motivation which is an amalgam of interest in, and enjoyment of, the natural world. The conservationist sees his role as the custodian of natural resources where these are interpreted in the broadest sense to mean the whole of the non-cultural world.

## THE DEVELOPMENT OF THE CONSERVATION MOVEMENT

Although this interpretation of conservation is now widely accepted, the movement has had different histories in different parts of the world. Concern for the environment in North America, for example, was clear in the work of early scholars such as Marsh (1874) and in the popular political movements for environmental management at the turn of the century to

1

whom we owe many valuable institutions such as National Parks (Simmons, Chapter 25, Burton and Kates, 1965; Barnet and Morse, 1963). These movements, whose aims were initially environmental, later dissipated their efforts over many areas of national and social concern, and the more specific theme of environmental management was not revived until Bennett's campaign for soil conservation in the 1930s, and the writings of resource economists such as Ciriacy-Wantrup (1952). Another element, always strong in North American conservation, is an ecological and aesthetic interest in nature which is well expressed in the essays of Aldo Leopold (1949).

In Britain conservation has had a more biological and preservationist patrimony (Stamp, 1969; Nicholson, 1970). The concern for biological nature grew from protectionist movements amongst natural historians in the late nineteenth century and was evident in the writings of the early ecologists, among them Sir Arthur Tansley, who perceived that many semi-natural habitats were threatened in these crowded and highly industrialized islands. Three main themes came to characterize British conservation, the first concerned with the maintenance of sites of scientific or educational interest, the second with the amenity and recreation potential of the countryside and the third with the application of ecological principles to land use, particularly in the uplands. The Nature Conservancy and the National Parks Commission were jointly instituted in 1949 to administer to these interests. The Nature Conservancy is now divided between the Nature Conservancy Council in the Department of the Environment and the Institute of Terrestrial Ecology under the Natural Environment Research Council; the National Parks Commission has become the Countryside Commission (Davidson, Chapter 24; Blackmore, Chapter 27). There are, of course, many other Government and voluntary agencies in Britain concerned with conservation, notably the Forestry Commission, the Fisheries Research Establishments, the Freshwater Pollution Laboratories, the Royal Society for the Protection of Birds and the Council for Nature. Concern for the physical environment has not been as prominent in Britain as in the United States, but there has nonetheless been valuable work in this field by the Water Resources Board, the river conservancies, the Alkali Inspectorate, various coastal protection committees and the Institute of Hydrology (Chandler, Chapter 2; Kirby and Rodda, Chapter 5).

The physical and biological, economic and political, scientific and aesthetic approaches and the various national traditions have converged over the last decade as the complexity of natural and social processes as well as their universality have become apparent and as new techniques for their analysis have been evolved. The new approaches are referred to as systems analysis or systems management, for it is realized that only within some such unifying concept can problems be solved satisfactorily (Watt, 1968).

## THE SCOPE OF CONSERVATION

The systems which are the concern of conservationists lie at the meeting-point of cultural, social and economic systems on the one hand and natural systems on the other. Conservation aims at the planned, harmonious interlocking of the two sets of systems and requires a knowledge of both. On the cultural side it is necessary to understand the nature of demands, the forces leading to change, the methods, modes of operation and adaptability of individuals, groups and institutions, and the economic constraints on action. Of natural systems it is desirable to know the choices they present, and these depend on structural characteristics, paths of flow and storage of energy and matter, homeostatic mechanisms, yields and thresholds of tolerance to different forms of use.

Fields of knowledge that are concerned only with the separate functioning of the two systems are therefore excluded from conservation, but the concept is, by this description, still too vague to be useful for research or action. Bearing in mind that conservation problems need a holistic treatment, there are areas of activity and study which can be isolated using two criteria: dimensions and demands.

### Dimensions

The ideas of many earlier conservationists were formalized by Ciriacy-Wantrup (1952) when he distinguished two types of resource using a time-dimensional criterion: renewable (flow) and non-renewable (stock) resources. The precise antithesis of these two is undesirable since some resources are intermediate in character, and the actual use of resources may embrace both types in a single process, but the distinction is useful because the conservation programme for distinctly non-renewable resources differs fundamentally from that for renewable resources.

Non-renewable resources are defined as materials that are concentrated or created at rates that are very much slower than their rate of consumption. The idea is best applied to the minerals or the fossil fuels such as oil which although it is being created in modern marine sediments and concentrated in currently forming geological structures, has a rate of production which is at least $10^6$ times slower than the current rate of extraction. There have been many acrimonious arguments about the nature of the economic problems created by this situation (Coddington, Chapter 29), but whatever the solutions may be, they can implicate only technical, economic and social adjustments, and not adjustments of the natural systems that provide the resource, since these are virtually unmanageable, whereas the very process by which the renewable resources are produced can be manipulated.

Renewable resources are, in modern parlance, parts of functioning natural systems that are turning over at rates which are approximately comparable to their rates of use. Here the limitations to use are not set by fixed quantities but by rates of flow. The paths and sometimes the rates of these flows and the loci of their concentrations can be materially altered by man, and their conservation therefore amounts to the marrying of these natural systems and social demands to maintain stability or 'sustained yield'. A population of wild game can be regulated with a knowledge of its population dynamics and physiology, but planned use of the resource should also consider the demand for meat or other products, the system of pricing, preparation and marketing, the demand for recreation, sport or amenity, and the other uses to which the land might be put. It is these mutual adjustments of the supply-and-demand equation that are the crux of this kind of conservation.

One of the fundamental characteristics of the conservation of flow resources is that it is concerned with wider spatial and temporal horizons than is the environmental management associated with closely controlled systems such as is practised by agriculturalists or engineers. The difference is illustrated in the discussion of soil conservation by Held and Clawson (1965), who contrast the short accounting periods used by most agricultural activities in the United States which result in slowly declining returns with soil conservation programmes whose aim is a steady flow of agricultural products over indefinite periods achieved by the maintenance of basic productive capacity. The former method seeks to maximize profits for the near future whereas the latter means investment in the future and may lead to temporarily or even permanently reduced annual yields (Figure 1.1). The arguments applied to agriculture could be equally applied to many other systems. Thus short-term engineering solutions to localized coastal erosion can be contrasted with longer-term conservation of an entire coast in which slow erosion, movement or accretion may have to be accepted. Moreover long-term planning differs from short-term management in that the extended time perspectives mean that more extreme events have to be catered for (Warren, Chapter 3; Hollis, Chapter 13).

An extension of the time scale in a study usually brings an extension of the space scale as well, since the two are linked in the management of ecological and physical systems (Harrison and Warren, 1970). In coastal control an increase in the time dimension of a plan must mean a corresponding increase in its spatial scale: instead of a local beach profile a whole sedimentary cell, involving supply, perhaps from a river mouth, movement and storage in a series of beaches, and abstraction to dunes or marine deeps, must be examined (Kemp, Chapter 4). The same is true in the management of a predominantly agricultural landscape where the desire to maintain a wild population of predatory birds over extended time-scales, either for

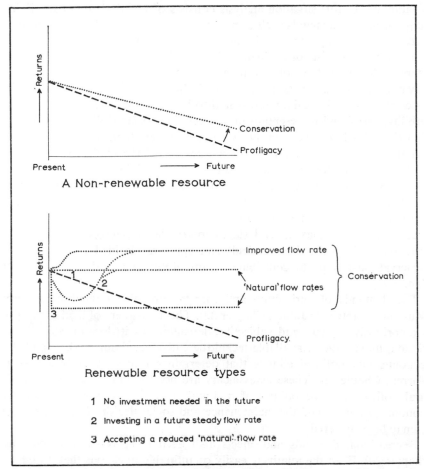

**Figure 1.1.** Types of conservation for renewable and non-renewable resources. (Adapted from Held and Clawson, 1965, *inter alia*.)

scientific interest or for pest control, cannot be accomplished with only a few isolated nature reserves but requires a whole network of protected areas.

In their view of wide spatial and temporal horizons conservationists have much in common with planners. Planners approach natural resource problems with a cultural (demand) bias whereas most conservationists, being natural scientists at heart, are more interested in resources.

## Demands on resources

Although the accommodation of demands is at least as difficult a problem as the recognition of appropriate dimensions for study or management, as clear a statement as possible about the demands is vital to any conservation programme. In this situation analysis consists of identifying and specifying major groups of demands such as nature conservation, agriculture, forestry, recreation, landscape or amenity and the ways in which each is changing, and synthesis consists of evaluating the demands and assessing the choices offered. The aim is to resolve conflicts and to conserve the resource.

Nature conservationists have found it hard to specify their demands. Assessment of biological interest is said to be based on concepts of diversity, stability, rarity and representativeness (Ratcliffe, 1971; Helliwell, 1973), but high diversity is not necessarily of greater interest than low diversity; the definition of stability is very much a question of the choice of time-scale (Goldsmith, Chapter 14); rarity is no more easy to define, for it too depends on the area and scale which is considered, for some plants that are rare in Britain are common if the whole of Europe is considered; and finally representativeness is an even more difficult concept: do we want representatives of natural climaxes, seral stages, particular species or balanced ecosystems? Only when these difficult concepts are clarified can the nature conservationist hope to contribute meaningfully to a wider conservation plan.

The demands of agriculture and forestry are also difficult to specify (Munton, Chapter 21; James, Chapter 22). The assessment of land capability is notoriously difficult and subjective depending as it does on soil, slope, climate, management, available techniques, distance from markets and the economic and political climate that determines prices and subsidies (e.g. Warren, Chapter 3). These assessments are not the only basis for agricultural policy since the politics of national strategic security, international economic alliances and the maintenance and social health of rural life have often to be considered.

Recreational demands and effects also need close research (Davidson, Chapter 20). Even the relatively easily quantifiable questions that centre on visitor numbers are linked to factors such as the nature and periodicity of visits, accessibility, age structure of the population and the ecological character of the sites. When demands for wilderness and good landscapes are considered, an understanding of a range of disciplines from physical geography to psychology and philosophy is required (Huxley, Chapter 23).

The demand for improved environmental quality receives the greatest attention in the press. It embraces a spectrum of concerns within which, however, some distinctions can be made: where largely man-made environments have replaced relatively natural ones there are the problems of noise, chemical pollution or of urban renewal, but whereas the solutions to these problems may need major social or economic changes they usually require relatively minor adjustments to natural systems. At the other end of the spectrum there is a maximum of involvement with natural systems where there are the problems of the maintenance of ecological or geomorphological balance (Warren, Chapter 3), the study and control of movements of pollutants and pesticides in food-chains (Moore, Chapter 15), eutrophication of freshwaters, or overtramping of ecologically interesting swards (Goldsmith, Chapter 14). It is with this end of the spectrum that natural resource conservation is most concerned.

A clear statement of demands is only a preliminary step in the preparation of plans for conservation. The next step is the attachment of relative values to the demands so that they can be compared. Value and utility are always likely to be controversial though vital questions, and they have eluded precise definition since the birth of economics (Robinson, 1964). In conservation the problem of value is compounded since it must be assigned to intangibles such as stability, interest, peace, quiet and beauty, and since discounting must be over long and ill-defined periods. It is probable that the goal of being able to allot market values to such variables in conservation will remain elusive.

The most popular method of comparing alternative schemes is cost-benefit analysis, where the costs of schemes (usually intangible conservation demands that have to go unsatisfied) are compared with tangible benefits, such as electric power, housing or faster travel (James, Chapter 22; Sewell, 1973). Although environmentalists are increasingly speaking out against cost-benefit analysis particularly for its short-sightedness (Adams, 1971) they have offered few tangible alternatives. The methods of analysis used in these comparisons are very much the field of the economist and are bound up with the whole question of other economic goals (Mishan, 1967; Coddington, Chapter 29).

This discussion has assumed that most demands can be satisfied, whereas many conservationists hold the neo-Malthusian view that management of the environment must ultimately hinge on containment of our own demands or numbers (Ehrlich and Ehrlich, 1970). The control of human numbers is a vital area of concern but it is not management of nature in the stricter sense and is therefore disinct from the view of conservation presented here.


## THE STRATEGY FOR CONSERVATION

The conservation of natural resources has been and will continue to be achieved by co-operation between planners, administrators and natural scientists operating within voluntary or governmental frameworks who can use a range of tactics such as protection, management, economic incentive, legislative restriction, or education. Research and monitoring need to accompany these moves, and in a democratic society the whole process must be publicly accountable.

Planners and administrators approach the natural environment having identified a social demand and knowing the economic or administrative bases for action. Ideally they should then consult natural scientists about the possibilities for resource manipulation, but this is probably the weakest link in the whole process of conservationist action. Planners have been criticized both for their imperfect perception of the environment which has resulted in some notable blunders (e.g. Hollis, Chapter 13; Sewell, 1973), and for their inability to 'ask the right questions'.

For their part the natural scientists have been berated for their poor appreciation of social and economic realities (e.g. Kennet, Chapter 30). The scientist starts by constructing and testing a model of the funtioning of a natural system (O'Connor, Chapter 6), a process which is central to the approach to conservation outlined in this chapter, but his subsequent suggestions for cropping or manipulation have often been said to be naïve in terms of economic survival or social need.

These misunderstandings between executives and scientists may well be the most critical obstacle to constructive environmental management (O'Riordan, 1971). Their amelioration can come firstly from mere recognition, and then from the intelligent application of the results of careful research into the administrative process and the consequences of individual and group perception, but they are not a problem that will ever disappear since there will always be a fundamental and probably fruitful conflict between aims and means (or possibilities and demands). Although this problem is critical it is shared with every field of executive action whether social, technical or environmental, and its study is the field more of the pure social scientist than of the conservationist.

In most parts of the world voluntary pressure groups initiated and continue to stimulate conservation. It is the work of individuals, small groups such as the British Naturalists Trusts, better funded specialist national or international groups such as the Royal Society for the Protection of Birds or the World Wildlife Fund, or more political groups with global concerns such as the Friends of the Earth. Voluntary organizations can use a range of tactics, but they seldom have the finance or permanence for major research or action, they sometimes suffer from their isolation from the public, and they can never enjoy the power of legislation.

Government activity may be slow and difficult to initiate, but the powers of restrictive legislation, taxation and its access to large funds make it ultimately the most effective. In Britain real government interest in the environment dates only from 1949, but subsequent legislation and administrative adjustment now allow it a wide range of involvement although still only a modest budget (Davidson, Chapter 24; Blackmore, Chapter 27; Kennet, Chapter 30). Action has usually originated with central government, but local government has taken an increasing interest in the environment (Mercer, Chapter 26). Much of the potentially fruitful conflict about conservation can now come from within and between the various environmental agencies of the government, although voluntary stimulus will always play an important role because of its greater freedom of action.

Both voluntary and governmental conservation movements began with the belief that their task was primarily the protection of limited areas such as Nature Reserves (Blackmore, Chapter 27), wilderness areas (Huxley, Chapter 23), National Parks (Simmons, Chapter 25), or a range of zones with lesser protection such as Areas of Outstanding Natural Beauty or Sites of Special Scientific Interest. At first it was envisaged that mere protection would ensure continued existence of the resource, and that each area should be reserved for only one kind of purpose such as scientific research, education, recreation, or amenity, but the complexity and changeability of both social demands and ecological systems has brought the realization that they need continuing positive management often for a multiplicity of uses.

Where the statutory protection of reserves is a spatially restricted approach, emergency programmes such as the rehabilitation of swards damaged by visitors (Goldsmith, Chapter 14), the revegetation of industrial tip-heads (Goodman, Chapter 16) or the dispersion of marine oil slicks are restricted in time.

The need for reserves and for emergency programmes will undoubtedly continue, if not increase, but many conservationists are now realizing that the broader dimensions of conservation problems mentioned above require the environmental management of whole landscapes, if not of the whole planet. Renewable resource systems have been so thoroughly altered by men that they can seldom be left to themselves to produce, or even to remain in a stable condition (e.g. Jewell, Chapter 12), so that management is constantly needed. Management of this kind is central to the concept of conservation discussed here.

Environmental management, as well as protection and emergency action, can be encouraged by a variety of administrative tactics. The Government could use fiscal policy very effectively to encourage waste recycling, or to discourage pollution (Coddington, Chapter 29), to optimize soil use or to channel recreation into less environmentally damaging areas or activities. Both official and private bodies could use pricing to similar ends (e.g. James, Chapter 22), and the government could also use economic disincentives by way of punitive fines.

A longer term tactic, and therefore one that is more in tune with conservation thinking as a whole, is education. Environmental education should be at all levels of decision making, to all age groups, and should be about problems of local to global scale. It is probably the single most important weapon in the conservationist's armoury (Newbould, Chapter 28).

The research to support and direct all these activities and bodies is the real substance of this volume, although the essays can only cover a small part of the huge research effort that is being mounted. Research is needed not only into the detailed functioning of ecological and physical environmental systems, but also into the longer term aspects of variability and secular change; it needs to elucidate the best methods of social management, and the problem of improving our perception of the world around us; and it needs to look at the past to show the extent and kind of human involvement with the environment in history (Dimbleby, Chapter 18; Sheail, Chapter 19), and the kinds of errors that can be made if we wrongly interpret the evidence of the past (Vita-Finzi, Chapter 17).

Finally there must always be in the management of the environment, as in any other major problem, a continuous accountability and reassessment whose maintenance is the function of the politician (Kennet, Chapter 30).


## ACKNOWLEDGMENTS

We would like to thank Dr. Carolyn Harrison, Mrs. Joan Davidson, Dr. R. J. C. Munton, Dr. F. B. O'Connor, Dr. I. G. Simmons and Dr. J. G. U. Adams for the constructive criticism of and suggested changes to the earlier drafts of this chapter.


## BIBLIOGRAPHY AND REFERENCES

The subject of this introduction has been covered by so much literature that it is difficult to select works for specific reference. This bibliography should therefore be regarded as a mere outline for further reading.

### The history of conservation thought

Barnett, J. J. (1960). Malthusianism and Conservation: their role as origins of the doctrine of increasing economic scarcity of natural resources; in *Demographic and Economic Change in Developed Countries*, Universities National Bureau Committee for Economic Research, Special Conference Series No. 11, Princeton University Press, Princeton, N.J., pp. 423–56.

Barnett, H. J., and Morse, C. (1963). *Scarcity and Growth: The Economics of Natural Resource Availability*, Johns Hopkins University Press for Resources for the Future Inc., Baltimore, 288 pp.

Burton, H. J., and Kates, R. W. (Eds) (1965). *Readings in Resource Management and Conservation*, University of Chicago Press, Chicago, 609 pp.

Ciriacy-Wantrup, S. V. (1952). *Resource Conservation, Economics and Policies*, University of California Press, Berkeley, 395 pp.

Darling, F. F. (1955). *West Highland Survey: An Essay in Human Ecology,* Oxford University Press, London, 438 pp.

Douglas, M. (1966). *Purity and Danger: An Analysis of Concepts of Pollution and Taboo,* Penguin, London, 220 pp.

Glacken, C. (1967). *Traces on the Rhodian Shore, Nature and Culture in Western Thought from Ancient Times to the end of the Eighteenth Century.* University of California Press, Berkeley, 763 pp.

Held, R. B., and Clawson, M. (1965). *Soil Conservation in Perspective,* Johns Hopkins University Press for Resources for the Future Inc., Baltimore, 344 pp.

Jarrett, H. (1958). *Perspectives on Conservation,* Johns Hopkins University Press for Resources for the Future Inc., Baltimore, 271 pp.

Leopold, A. (1949). *A Sand-Country Almanac,* Sierra Club/Ballantine, New York, 295 pp.

MacConnel, G. (1954). The conservation movement, past and present, *Western Political Quarterly,* **7,** 463–78. Also in *Readings in Resource Management and Conservation,* Ed. I. Burton and R. W. Kates, University of Chicago Press, Chicago, 189–220.

Marsh, G. P. (1874). *The Earth as Modified by Human Actions,* Sampson Low, Marston Low and Searl, London, 656 pp.

Nicholson, M. (1970). *The Environmental Revolution: A Guide for the New Masters of the World,* Hodder and Stoughton, London 366 pp.

Raup, H. M. (1964). Ecological theory and conservation, *J. Ecology,* **52,** (Suppl.), 39–45.

Schyltz, A. M. (1967). The ecosystem as a conceptual tool in the management of natural resources, in: *Natural Resources, Quality and Quantity,* Ed. S. V. Ciriacy-Wantrup and J. J. Parsons, University of California Press, Berkeley, 139–61.

Stamp, D. (1969). *Nature Conservation in Britain,* Collins, Glasgow, 273 pp.

Watt, K. E. F. (1968). *Ecology and Resource Management a Quantitative Approach,* McGraw-Hill, New York, 450 pp.

## The Scope of Conservation

Adams, J. G. U. (1971). London's third airport. *Geog J.* **137,** 468–504.

Ash, M. (1972). Planners and ecologists, *Town and Country Planning,* **40,** 219–21.

Coddington, A. (1971). The new utilitarians, *The Political Quarterly,* **42,** 320–25.

Ehrlich, P. R., and Ehrlich, A. H. (1970). *Population, Pollution and Resources,* Freeman, San Francisco, 383 pp.

Harrison, C. M., and Warren, A. (1970). Conservation, stability and management, *Area,* **2,** 26–32.

Helliwell, D. R. (1973). Priorities and values in nature conservation. *J. Environmental Management,* **1,** 85–127.

Her Majesty's Government (1972). *Framework for Government Research and Development,* HMSO, Cmnd. 5046, London, 45 pp.

Hubbert, M. K. (1969). Energy resources, in: *Resources and Man,* Committee on Resources and Man, National Academy of Sciences, Freeman, San Francisco, 157–242.

Lovering, T. S. (1969). Mineral resources from the land, in: *Resources and Man,* Committee on Resources and Man, National Academy of Sciences, Freeman, San Francisco, 109–34.

Meadows, D. H., Meadows, D. L., Randers, J., and Behrens, W. W. III (1972). *The Limits to Growth*, Potomac Earth Island, London, 205 pp.

Mishan, E. J. (1967). *The Costs of Economic Growth*, Penguin, London, 240 pp.

Moore, N. W. (1969). Experience with pesticides and the theory of conservation, *Biological Conservation*, **1**, 201-8.

O'Riordan, T. (1971). Environmental management, *Progress in Geography*, **3**, 171–231.

Ratcliffe, D. A. (1971). Criteria for selection of nature reserves, *Advancement of Science*, **27**, 294–6.

Robinson, J. (1964). *Economic Philosophy*, Penguin, London, 104 pp.

Sewell, W. R. D. (1973). Broadening the approach to evaluation in resource management decision-making, *J. Evironmental Management*, **1**, 33–60.

# Part I. The Constraints and Opportunities of Some Semi-Natural Systems

## A, Physical Systems

# The Management of Climatic Resources

T. J. CHANDLER

One of the main reasons for man's relative success in competition with other forms of life on this earth has been his ability not only to capitalize upon the advantages of natural conditions but deliberately to control the physical attributes of parts of his environment to his own ends.

Control of the natural environment is an intoxicating pursuit, but in spite of successes in other areas, the enormous energies and complexities of the atmosphere have so far resisted most of man's attempts to shape its properties. And yet, though only relatively minor changes have been deliberately won, much greater modifications have followed accidentally in the train of man's multifarious activities.

For most of the time that man has inhabited the earth his numbers have been small and his technical powers, apart from fire, limited. Damage to his environment was mainly local and often, though by no means always, subject to the regenerative powers of nature. Even in AD 1600 the world's population was no more than perhaps 500 million and much of the earth was uninhabited or little affected by man's activity. It took several hundred thousand years to reach the first billion of human beings around 1800, but a mere 130 years more were needed to add the second billion, and less than 30 years for the third by about 1960. Today, we are two-thirds of the way to the fourth billion and the expectation is that well over two billions more will be added in the last quarter of this century.

Such enormous increases of population cannot help but extend and intensify climatological changes in the planetary boundary layer (the lower 600 m or so of the atmosphere) and possibly, directly or indirectly, in the atmosphere as a whole. This is because the properties of the atmosphere are closely controlled by physical and chemical exchanges at the earth–air interface and these are a function of surface conditions such as the shape and surface cover of the land which will be increasingly changed as populations grow. The intensity of the meteorological consequences will depend on a number of factors, including the prevailing areal, volumetric and time scales controlling the earth–air exchanges of heat, moisture and momentum, and so the particular character of the earth's surface, whether or not this is in whole or part the outcome of man's activities, will often exert its strongest influence upon micrometeorological conditions of the atmosphere at times of inversions in the surface boundary layer (the lowest 100 to 200 m of the planetary boundary layer). On the other hand, it is quite feasible that the heat balance of the whole earth–atmosphere system could be affected by a variety of human activities ranging from widespread forest clearance to stratospheric flights.

As far as we can see, man will never match the solar energies which drive the earth–atmosphere system, and his aspirations for weather control will for ever be sharply constrained by the limitations of his power potential. The daily input of solar energy to the earth–atmosphere system is approximately 70,000 times man's daily energy consumption, although the direct comparison of natural and man-made energies, by themselves, may be rather misleading, for only 70 per cent of the incident solar energy is used in the internal workings of the earth–atmosphere system, more particularly of the lower 15 km or so of air, whilst under not infrequent though temporary circumstances, heat from combustion and other terrestrial energy sources will affect only a shallow layer, perhaps no more than 100 m deep.

But man's influence upon the atmosphere stems much less from a direct energy input to the system than from a modification of those surface conditions relevant to natural energy exchanges at the earth–atmosphere interface. Seventy-five per cent of the atmosphere's heat input and 100 per cent of its moisture comes by way of the earth's surface, and surface friction accounts for the dissipation of about 40 per cent of the atmosphere's kinetic energy, so that surface and near-surface conditions and man's changes to these are of paramount importance in the atmosphere's various energy budgets. But the amounts of these changes are difficult to quantify, and there is no doubt that many scientifically uninformed, even irresponsible, statements have been made suggesting far greater and more extensive effects than now seem likely. George P. Marsh, for instance, in his well-known book *Man and Nature, or Physical Geography as Modified by Human Action,* published in 1864, was concerned with the thesis of man's very substantial and widespread modification of weather and climate by his interference with surface conditions; but he clearly overstated his case, even for the time he was writing. One of his main interests was the influence of forests upon meteorological and pedological conditions as exemplified through the particular study of forest planting and clearance.

## CLIMATIC CONSEQUENCES OF FOREST CLEARANCE
## AND TREE PLANTING

There is little doubt that forest clearance and tree planting represent two of man's greatest changes of conditions at the earth's surface, resulting in very considerable modifications of the local ecology and affecting meteorological, pedologiocal and hydrological conditions within and around the forest. Albedo, roughness length, height of the active surface, evapotranspiration rates and sensible heat transfers are all changed locally, and these could trigger off a chain of secondary effects, some of which could be quite serious. Losses to the surface through the interception of precipitation in the crown layer of forests, particularly coniferous forests, can amount to more than 90 per cent at times of light rains, and even in heavy storms they are of the order of 15 per cent (Food and Agricultural Organization of the United Nations, 1962). In consequence, the wisdom of afforestation in water catchment areas, such as parts of upland Wales, has been seriously questioned and field investigations have been set up in this country and elsewhere to better quantify the hydrological parameters of wooded areas (Kirby and Rodda, Chapter 5).

One of the most fascinating aspects of forest meteorology is the question of the possible effects of forests and forest clearance upon local precipitation, but it is a very complex and controversial subject. There is a good deal of field evidence that precipitation above and immediately downwind of extensive forests is greater than falls over nearby unforested but otherwise topographically similar country: reported excesses of annual rainfall vary from 7 to 25 per cent (Food and Agricultural Organization of the United Nations, 1962). Meteorologically, however, the explanations are very uncertain and more probably related to intensified thermal turbulence than to any increase in the humidity of the overlying air, for the latter is almost certain to be relatively small and meteorologically unimportant. The most one can say is that the widespread deforestation which has accompanied the increase in world population may have been associated with reduced precipitation, but amounts, except perhaps in central continental areas (Flohn, 1961), are likely to be small. Changes in the other terms of the water budget are clearly much more important than any effect upon precipitation, and they are like to include increased run-off followed by accelerated soil erosion and decreased ground water, thus leading to hydrological rather than a meteorological drought.

The relationships between forests and airflow are much more certain. Forest clearance will inevitably lead to stronger near-surface winds in the cleared area and in a surrounding belt whose width will depend upon the extent of the former forest and the form, height and density of the trees, although it is unlikely to be more than one or two kilometres wide. This is because the wind near the ground adjusts itself over a relatively short fetch to changes of surface roughness. Because of the stronger winds, deforestation has frequently been followed by wind erosion of the soil, and attention has been drawn for example to the danger of accelerated soil erosion in eastern England following the removal of hedges and the enlargement of fields (Warren, Chapter 3).

The deliberate planting of trees to provide shelter is the related, positive approach to the atmospheric environment. Initially developed as an empirical art, tree planting has now become a fairly precise science following the work of such people as Jensen (1954) and Caborn (1965). The practice has a long history in Britain, being decreed by the Scottish Parliament as long ago as 1457 (Caborn, 1965); It was achieved accidentally by the eighteenth-century landscape gardeners and was deliberately planned by the agricultural improvers. But shelter is only one aspect of the improvement. A well-designed windbreak brings with it not only protection from damaging winds, but as a consequence of this higher humidities, reduced evapo-transpiration, and raised day-time and reduced night-time temperatures. In consequence, there is normally an increased crop yield in areas sheltered from the wind.

There are, of course, those who believe that broad and laterally extensive belts of trees serve not only to reduce winds in their vicinity but, in the manner described, to increase local precipitation. The Russians attached great importance to these ideas: one of the main features of the so-called 'Stalin Plan' was the struggle against aridity, including the planting of gigantic windbreaks across the Steppes. In the United States the Timber Culture Act of 1873 was passed in the belief that if trees were planted in the Great Plains and prairie states, rainfall would be increased sufficiently to eliminate one of the local climatic hazards to agriculture. Something of the same pious hope was evident in the Shelter-Belt Project for tree planting on the Great Plains authorized by President Roosevelt in 1934 (Thornthwaite, 1956).

All surface changes must alter the properties of the overlying air, but many of the modifications in rural areas are small and environmentally unimportant. This is not to say that the unintentional modification of climate on the regional and possibly global scale is necessarily restricted to essentially urban activities. The clearing of coniferous forest in high latitudes will materially alter the average albedo of these areas during winter and perhaps more especially during spring, for snow readily falls through the crown layer of coniferous forests, keeping their albedo well below that of snow-covered open country (Sawyer, 1971). Destructive agricultural activities resulting in wind erosion and an increase in atmospheric turbidity might also affect the heat balance, whilst the firing of vegetation and crop waste had been shown, under certain circumstances, to affect precipitation in neighbouring areas (Schaefer, 1969). But changes in the heat and water balances of areas affected by agricultural activities are too detailed to be presently capable of simulation in our still rather crude numerical models of atmospheric behaviour. They constitute one of many outstanding problems of human interference with meteorological processes the solution to which depends upon an improved understanding of fundamental meteorological processes, more particularly in the atmospheric boundary layer. Nevertheless, it is generally true that in the majority of cases farming has brought no particular or permanent atmospheric problems; indeed in some areas, following land drainage in the Fenlands of England, for instance, climates will, if anything, have improved. But it is generally difficult to quantify the changes, and there is clearly somewhat confused evidence and theory for the precise manner and degree to which rural atmospheres have been accidentally modified by man. There is much less uncertainty about urban atmospheres.

## URBAN CLIMATES

One of the primary purposes of man's shelter is protection against adverse or undesirable climatic environments, but when buildings are congregated in villages, towns and conurbations, the result is a degree of modification of local boundary layer conditions which amounts to the creation of a distinctive and often far from pleasant climate.

All over the world, urban areas are expanding by in-migration and natural population increase: already 30 per cent of the world's population live in towns of 5,000 or more persons and the proportion is increasing fast. In almost every country, towns are expanding like hungry amoebae, consuming more and more land. Almost everywhere in the developed and developing world, brick, stone, concrete and macadam are replacing field, farm and forest. Already about 12 per cent of the surface area of England and Wales is built upon, and Best (1968) has estimated that by the year 2000 this coverage will have increased to 15·4 per cent.

In built-up areas, the aerodynamic roughness parameters, the thermal and hydrological properties of the surface, the heat from metabolism and the various combustion processes, and the chemical composition of the atmosphere create a climate which is quite distinct from that of extra-urban areas. Strong winds are decelerated and light winds accelerated as they move into towns; turbulence is increased; relative humidities are reduced; the chemical composition of the air is changed; receipts and losses of radiation are both reduced; temperatures are raised; fogs are made thicker, more frequent and more persistent; and rainfall is sometimes increased (Chandler, 1965; World Meteorological Organization, 1970).

### Air Pollution

Undoubtedly the best known aspect of urban atmospheres is their generally high levels of pollution. Man has always treated the atmosphere as an open sewer, commonly loading it beyond its natural self-cleansing capacities. There has in the past been a curious contradiction in attitudes between a militant concern for the purity of the 3 lb of food and the 5 lb of water that we consume daily and a general apathy towards the fouling of the 38 lb of air we breathe each day by a miasma of assorted and generally unwholesome pollutants.

But it must not be fogotten that man, much less urbanized man, is not solely responsible for the contamination of his atmospheric environment. In the sparsely settled parts of the globe most of the air pollutants are the products of natural processes, being comprised mainly of pollen, mineral dust and the smoke from forest and bush fires. Even so, the concentration of Aitken nuclei (particles having a radius of less than 0·2 $\mu$m) in cities is, on average, sixteen times greater than that over inland rural areas and 160 times greater than over the oceans (Table 2.1). The increasing pace of urbanization serves only to highlight the much higher concentrations of aerosols* in towns.

**Table 2.1.** Number of Aitken nuclei per cubic centimetre

| Locality | No. of observations | Average count | Extreme count |
|---|---|---|---|
| Cities (population 100,000 or more) | 2,500 | 147,000 | 4,000,000 |
| Towns (population less than 100,000) | 4,700 | 34,000 | 400,000 |
| Country, inland | 3,500 | 9,500 | 336,000 |
| Country, seashore | 2,700 | 9,500 | 150,000 |
| Mountain    500–1,000 m | 870 | 6,000 | 155,000 |
| 1,000–2,000 m | 1,000 | 2,130 | 37,000 |
| 2,000 m | 190 | 950 | 27,000 |
| Islands | 480 | 9,200 | 109,000 |
| Ocean | 600 | 940 | 39,800 |

(After Landsberg, 1938)

Atmospheric pollution has therefore been with us since the Creation; but it became much worse with the Garden of Eden and infinitely worse following the mechanical ingenuity of James Watt.

* An aggregation of minute solid or liquid particles suspended in the atmosphere.

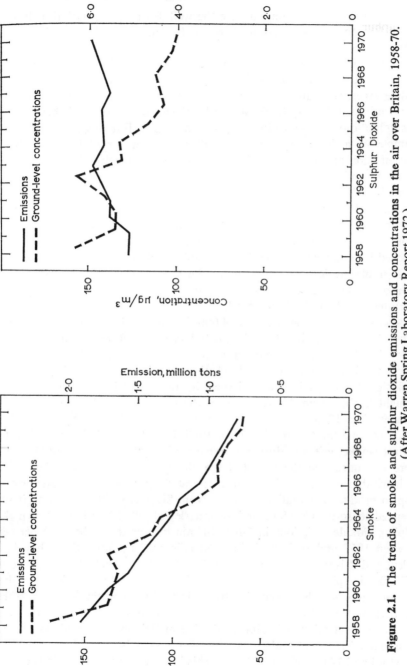

**Figure 2.1.** The trends of smoke and sulphur dioxide emissions and concentrations in the air over Britain, 1958-70. (After Warren Spring Laboratory Report 1972.)

For many centuries, London bore the well-deserved reputation of having one of the most polluted atmospheres to be found anywhere in the world, although it was certainly not the first or only polluted city. Seneca reviled 'the heavy air of Rome and the stench of its smoky chimneys', and Roman patricians complained about the soot that soiled their togas. During the Middle Ages, the substitution of soft coal for Europe's dwindling timber supply initiated the very thick palls of black smoke and the invisible shrouds of sulphur dioxide that still plague many cities. But despite the horrific example of a fourteenth-century artificer hanged for violating a Royal Proclamation against the burning of sea-coal, the black pall over London thickened and the sky darkened. In 1578, we are told, Queen Elizabeth I found herself 'greatly grieved and annoyed with the taste and smoke of the sea coals'—to which discomfiture she was, of course, one of the chief contributors. 'Hell is a city much like London, a populous and smoky city', wrote Shelley at the beginning of the Industrial Revolution; and Blake couched his comment in magnificent words (dark, satanic mills, etc.) which, set to noble music, now form one of the flag-waving highlights of the last night of the Proms, heard, appropriately enough, in the until recently soot-encrusted cupola of the Albert Hall.

However, it was the death of 4,000 Londoners in the December 1952 smog, following similar though much less severe disasters in the Meuse valley in 1930 and the Donora valley of Pennsylvania in 1948, which shocked Britain into action. In 1954, the committee set up under the chairmanship of Sir Hugh Beaver issued its report, and in 1956 Parliament brought in the Clean Air Act, one of the great social milestones of recent decades. The 1956 Act was later strengthened by Robert Maxwell's bill, which became the Clean Air Act of 1968. In both, legislation was directed against smoke, grit and dust, but not directly against sulphur dioxide, and there was unease at the time lest the changeover from coal to heavy oil, an inevitable power development accelerated by the Clean Air Act, would help to produce a pollution menace (from $SO_2$) as great as the one it was intended to solve. Craxford and Weatherley (1968; 1971) have shown that sulphur dioxide emissions in Great Britain increased by about 12 per cent between 1957 and their peak in 1963 (Figure 2.1). Since then they have fallen, and it is expected that the 1957 level will be reached again in about 1975. But in spite of the greater total emission of sulphur dioxide now than ten years ago—much of it coming from electricity generating stations—there has been a steady fall in average low-level concentrations of this gas. Near-surface concentrations of sulphur dioxide in Britain decreased on average by about 35 per cent and smoke by 57 per cent between 1960 and 1970 Craxford and Weatherley (1971), and this in spite of an increase in the gross energy consumption of about one-third. The main reason for the remarkable reduction in $SO_2$ concentrations is the dominance of domestic sources in the make-up of low-level pollution and the steady decline in domestic emissions because of the increasing popularity of gas, electricity and light oil fuels instead of sulphur-rich coal and coke. Domestic sources now account for about 83 per cent of the total emission of smoke in Great Britain and more than 90 per cent of the average near-surface concentrations, but in the case of sulphur dioxide only 15 per cent of total emissions are from domestic sources, although these are responsible for 75 per cent of the near-surface concentrations. Domestic sources are therefore by far the most serious overall offenders against clean air in Great Britain as a whole, although locally one must recognize the possible dominance of other sources.

There is no doubt that the widespread but by no means uniform implementation of the provisions of the Clean Air Act has resulted in improvements in general air quality in the United Kingdom which are nothing less than spectacular and the envy of many other countries. But the Act came at a time of social and industrial change with a swing away from solid fuels which even by itself would have resulted in a lowering of smoke levels. Concentrations of smoke in London were already falling in the 1930s, and more recently several towns having no smoke control regulations have nevertheless recorded less and less smoke in their atmospheres (Aulieiems and Burton, 1972).

In many parts of the world, then, the battle against the contamination of the air by smoke and sulphur dioxide is being won at the local level, frequently by raising chimneys so that the pollutants are more efficiently diffused away from their source at lower average concentrations, but these pollutants may travel great distances and pollution recognizes no international or other administrative boundaries. Radioactive pollutants circulate in the upper atmosphere for many months before being brought down to earth to contaminate the land and impair the health of people living thousands of miles from the source, and although the tall industrial and power station chimneys in this country may help to preserve the relative purity of our air, this is being achieved in part by exporting sulphur dioxide to the Continent, thus contributing to the acidity of Continental rain. It has been alleged that between 15 and 50 per cent of the sulphur dioxide in the air over Sweden originates in other countries, including Britain, and rather alarming increases in the sulphuric acid content of their rain have been recorded (Anon, 1972; Greenberg, 1969). It is argued that because of this and the limited ability of the shallow soils to neutralize the acidity, surface waters have become very contaminated, with consequent damage to fish and plant life. Atmospheric sulphates are also a major cause of plant damage and of the leaching of nutrient ions from the soils of forest eco-systems. Clearly, the SO$_2$ cycle through the earth–atmosphere system needs to be much better understood than it is at present, for until we know the terms more accurately we cannot assess the significance of man's contribution, which some estimates (Kellogg *et al.*, 1972) put as high as one-half of that in nature, with the prospect of equalling natural emissions by the end of the century. Sulphur dioxide along with all the other so-called atmospheric pollutants (except for a few radioactive materials) are not exotic but exist naturally in the atmosphere, so that the problems stem not from the introduction of alien materials into the air but from man's disturbance of the natural balance of these substances.

Smoke and sulphur dioxide might be called the traditional pollutants, more particularly of industrial societies, but in recent years there have emerged the ecological amenity and health problems of a far more modern and diabolical brew of toxic and irritant gases produced by complex photochemical reactions upon the enormous quantities of oxides of nitrogen and polycyclic hydrocarbons (including known carcinogens like 3:4 benz-pyrene) released into the air from automobile fuel tanks, carburettors and vehicle exhausts, and from innumerable other sources such as domestic garbage incinerators. Petrol engines also emit poisons in significant quantities such as carbon monoxide and inorganic lead bromides and chlorides. The archetype of this modern pollution menace is Los Angeles, though the situation has improved a good deal in recent years: because of these gases, the high frequency of stable atmospheric conditions, the intense solar radiation and the amphitheatre form of the local topography, the city had all the essential ingredients of this chemical cauldron, one of the most serious photochemical products of which was ozone which, contrary to popular opinion, is toxic not tonic. Other urban areas such as Mexico City are now seriously troubled by these same problems which are, indeed, faced to some extent by all modern cities. In Britain, the accepted maximum allowable industrial concentration of carbon monoxide for an exposure period of 8 hours is 100 parts per million. By and large, street concentrations are well below this and petrol engines are, in fact, much less serious sources of carbon monoxide in the blood than are cigarettes. Proportions of the gas can, however, be very much greater in the bottom of deep urban chasms congested by slow-moving traffic: roadside measurements in London, for instance, have shown that concentrations of carbon monoxide of more than 200 p.p.m. exist for very short periods and that mean values over a 10-minute period may exceed 50 p.p.m. (Reed, 1966). The diesel engine produces virtually no carbon monoxide, although when overloaded or badly maintained it does, of course, generate clouds of malodorous black smoke.

The United States has already taken strong legislative action against pollution from road vehicles, and in France and Germany there are somewhat weaker anti-emission laws. Other countries, including Great Britain, are beginning to follow suit. The medical case against vehicle emissions is admittedly uncertain, but while any doubt exists it would be foolhardy to remain unconcerned and, in any case, the fumes are highly objectionable on straightforward amenity grounds alone.

But atmospheric pollutants are not confined to the unburnt by-products of various fossil fuels. Among other polluters of the atmospheric environment are industries such as oil refining, cement and abestos manufacture and brick making, where the most serious pollutants come from the materials of manufacture rather than the fuels of combustion. The chemical compositions of their emissions are frequently complex, and although many gases are present in concentrations of only a few parts per million, they sometimes give rise to strong, objectionable odours such as the pungent smell, reminiscent of burning rubber, which spreads downwind from the chimneys of the Bedfordshire and Buckinghamshire brickfields. The exact chemistry of this particular offending smell is presently unknown, although it is probably made up of a variety of sulphur compounds. These same chimneys also emit many other gases, including various fluorines, particularly serious since they are taken up by grass and so lead to fluorosis in cattle. In consequence, grazing is officially discouraged in the vicinity of the brickworks.

Lord Ritchie-Calder (1970) has described pollution as 'a crime, compounded of ignorance and avarice', and careful and urgent management is clearly needed if we are to contain and reduce air pollution so that healthy and attractive atmospheric environments can be achieved and maintained. Action is required on a variety of fronts: technical, planning, legislative and social.

Substantial technical progress has already been made in reducing the pollutant content of fuels, exhausts and chimney plumes and in the use of more efficient combustion processes, but costs are often high and sometimes prohibitive. In the field of clean air legislation Great Britain has already made very substantial progress, about half the acreage of the so-called 'black areas' being covered by smoke control orders either confirmed or awaiting decision; but there is clearly a long way to go before we can claim complete success for the Clean Air Acts. Steady legislative progress towards cleaner air is also being made in many other countries.

## ACCIDENTAL MODIFICATION OF REGIONAL AND GLOBAL CLIMATES

Damage to plants and animals, to property and to environmental quality are not the only detrimental effects of air pollution. Unless we apply effective

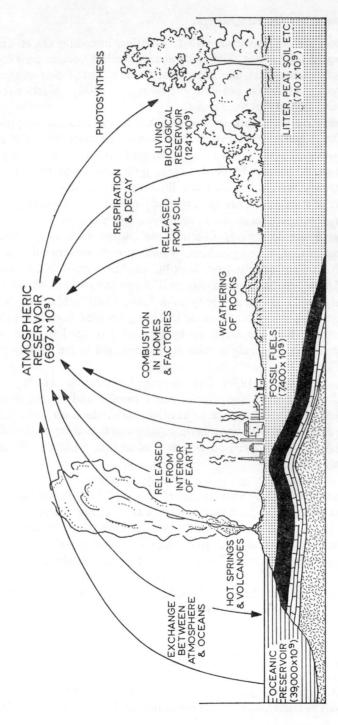

**Figure 2.2.** Sources and sinks of atmospheric carbon dioxide. The latest available statistics from Hare (1971) have been used. Levels of $CO_2$ in the atmosphere have been rising in recent years.

controls to limit changes in the composition of the air, inadvertent modifications of climate may easily follow. Depending on the source, type and concentrations of pollutants, this can happen on a local, regional or even global scale.

**The Increase in Carbon Dioxide Levels**

This can be illustrated by the almost worldwide increase in the concentration of carbon dioxide in the air caused, in part, by the burning of fossil fuels, the firing of vegetation and the operation of certain industries such as cement plants (Figure 2.2). The destruction of woodlands, especially tropical forests, further favours the concentration of carbon dioxide in the air by weakening one of the mechanisms by which gas is cycled, in this case with the carbon stored in the biomass, although the effects are unlikely to be as important as those of fossil fuel burning (Hare, 1971). In this century alone, atmospheric levels of carbon dioxide have risen from 300 to 330 p.p.m., and on the reasonable assumption that 50 per cent of the input will remain in the atmosphere, are expected to reach 375 p.p.m. by the end of the century. These increases have for many years been under suspicion as a factor of climatic change on a near-global scale, because carbon dioxide strongly absorbs outgoing terrestrial radiation in the infrared waveband from 12 to 16·3 $\mu$m. But calculations by Manabe and Strickler (1964) showed that even a doubling of the $CO_2$ content of the atmosphere would probably raise the near-surface temperature of the earth's atmosphere by only 2·3°C, and the predicted 25 per cent increase in $CO_2$ from AD 1900 to AD 2000 would result in a 0·8°C warming. In any case, the increased concentrations of carbon dioxide in the atmosphere could, in part at least, be a consequence as well as a cause of higher temperatures during the first half of this century, for there is a complex, cyclic exchange of $CO_2$ between the atmosphere and the oceans which is influenced by sea temperatures. But the rather sharp global cooling which has taken place since about 1940 indicates there are many other factors of long-term temperature change which are presently more influential than the atmosphere's increasing amounts of carbon dioxide.

It has been shown, too, that an increase in photosynthetic production consequent upon raised $CO_2$ concentrations should, by the end of the century, be almost exactly balanced by a reduction following the increase in atmospheric turbidity which is inevitably associated with increased combustion of fossil fuels (Monteith, 1970).

For several decades now, records from a number of stations throughout the world have shown an almost continuous upward trend in atmospheric turbidity, and it has been suggested (McCormick and Ludwig, 1967; Bryson, 1968) that the increase in the dust content of the atmosphere is mainly the result of man's domestic, industrial and agricultural activities. Many of the records are, however, suspect as representative of general background conditions. The frequently quoted Mauna Loa record, for instance, has been shown to be seriously affected by local tropospheric disturbances (Ellis and Pueschel, 1971), and those taken at Washington DC and Davos are still fairly close to local sources. We need far more measures from truly remote areas of the world before we can be sure that the average dust content of the atmosphere is increasing. We must also better understand the effect of atmospheric aerosols on both incoming and outgoing radiation before we can accurately assess the consequences of any additional atmospheric dust load (Sawyer, 1971). Meanwhile, probably the most reasonable estimates are those of Ångström (1962), who calculated that if cloud amount remained unchanged, a 10 per cent increase in turbidity would result in a 0·8 per cent decrease in the solar energy absorbed into the earth–atmosphere system.

The warming influence of carbon dioxide must therefore be balanced against the cooling effect of increased particulate loading, both being, in part at least, the consequence of human activity. Some authorities (Budyko, 1969) believe the point of balance has already been passed, thus explaining the sharp fall of temperatures since 1940 following a long period of warming since the late nineteenth century; others calculate that the cross-over point is still to come (Mitchell, 1970).

The effect of increasing atmospheric turbidity upon total radiation receipts at the earth will of course vary with latitude, and it is therefore noteworthy that since 1940 temperatures have fallen particularly sharply in high latitudes, with more extensive pack ice than for many decades. Associated with these changes, the hemispheric temperature gradient has increased and meridional transports have intensified through a strengthening of the circulation and of waves in the mid-latitude Westerlies, so that the frequency of warm, westerly winds has declined sharply (Lamb, 1966; Perry, 1970). If these changes are even partly the consequence of increases in atmospheric pollution, then mankind faces an even more urgent need for sensible and effective climatic management.

There is also some evidence (Schaefer, 1969) that the pollution from cities, vehicles, particular industries and the firing of growing vegetation and crop waste contains condensation and freezing nuclei which can, under special meteorological circumstances, lead to cloud formation and to increased or decreased precipitation downwind of the source (Changnon, 1969).

### The Effects of High-Flying Aircraft

The thin veils of cirrus clouds produced in the upper troposphere by the spreading of contrails from high-flying jet aircraft have also been cited as constituting a climatic hazard. The average cloud coverage along the main flight routes between North America and Europe has, according to one estimate, increased by 5 to 10 per cent, but the effect of such a relatively small increase in cirrus cloud upon radiation receipts at and heat losses from the ground is probably, for the present, small and limited to quite small areas (Manabe, 1970). Nevertheless, the phenomenon needs careful watching (Reinking, 1968), although given the almost universally subjective methods for estimating cloud cover, it is inherently difficult to establish conclusively any regional trends in the amounts of cirrus clouds.

But the effect of water vapour injected by supersonic aircraft into the very dry stratosphere is potentially much more serious were this type of transport to become common. Because of the very low water content of the stratosphere, and the weak vertical diffusion in the lower stratosphere, even quite modest discharges of water vapour by aircraft flying at these levels could perhaps materially change local water and heat balances. It is calculated that 400 supersonic transports making four flights each per day would inject 150 million kg of water into the lower stratosphere (Sawyer, 1971) and, assuming the exchange time between the stratosphere and troposphere is 10 years (much longer than is generally believed), then the water vapour content of the stratosphere could be doubled. This might so change the radiation exchanges in the earth–atmosphere system as to raise near-surface temperatures by about $0.6°C$, which is quite substantial and of the same order as the warming between the 1890s and 1940s.

A great deal has been written lately about the effects of exotic chemicals injected into the atmosphere by rockets and high-flying aircraft. Much of the controversy as related to supersonic transports was triggered off by the chemist Dr. Harold Johnson (1971). He claims that the oxides of nitrogen in the exhausts of supersonic transports could lead to important chemical changes in the ozone layer, which lies between about 15 and 45 km above the earth's surface with a maximum ozone concentration at 25 km. The ozone filters out the dangerous short wavebands of solar radiation and Johnson has suggested, though this is strongly contested by others, that the layer might be sufficiently eroded to affect its efficiency as a radiation shield and even endanger life on earth. Controversy still rages around these ideas (Harrison, 1970; SCEP, 1970; SMIC, 1971; Crutzen, 1972; Johnson, 1972), and it is clear that there is sufficient scientific uncertainty to engender unease which can only be resolved by further enquiry.

### 'Heat Pollution'

With regard to so-called heat pollution, although the yearly production of man-made energy is presently only about 1:2,500 of the net radiation balance at the earth's surface, Budyko (1969) has stated that it could increase to equal the surface radiation balance if compounded at 4 per cent (a conservative estimate) for 200 years. Higher temperatures in cities, caused in part by the use of fuel for space heating and by industry, have been recognized for many years, but when averaged over substantial areas, then the liberated heat of combustion is clearly a small fraction of natural energies. But much depends upon the assumed rates of diffusion, and these we know much less accurately than we need before we can be certain of the significance of our calculations. We can, for instance, calculate that by the year 2000 the Boston to Washington DC megalopolis and the eastern United States will release heat into the atmosphere at the rate of about 65 calories per square centimetre per day, which in winter represents about 50 per cent and in summer about 15 per cent of the heat of solar radiation on a horizontal surface (Landsberg, 1970). But of the effects of this upon mean temperatures we cannot presently be sure.

It could, of course, be argued that not all changes of climate accidentally induced by man's various activities need necessarily be regarded as detrimental to his general wellbeing; indeed, some might be thought of as positively beneficial. Whatever their cause, and we cannot be absolutely sure that it is anything more than some natural, in-built periodicity, the unusually warm, moist and equable climates which characterized the first four decades of the present century in middle and high latitudes were generally favourable to life in these areas. In this country, for instance, grass yields were unusually high, especially in the early part of the period (Smith, 1963), and many species of plants and animals colonized more northerly latitudes than for many centuries (Perring, 1965; Crisp, 1965). Unfortunately, many of our present socio-economic organizations have been adjusted to this most unusual period in our recent climatic history, and the present swing towards generally harsher conditions has sometimes left us ill-prepared. Indications are that our power, building and transport industries might wisely adapt themselves to a much higher frequency of severe winters than that to which they have become accustomed and adjusted in the past.

But perhaps the main reason for concern lies in man's fragmentary knowledge of his inherent abilities to inadvertently modify climate, coupled with his incomplete understanding of the sizes of the terms involved in the climatological chain reactions unintentionally triggered off by his activities. There is also the fear, born of uncertainty, that some point of no return might be reached beyond which some changes of climate would be self-developing and perhaps irreversible.

## PURPOSEFUL WEATHER MODIFICATION

Clearly, man must move very cautiously and knowingly in his dealings with the climatically linked aspects of his environment, and the need for care is even more obvious in relation to the purposeful, intentional management of climatic resources.

It has, of course, been one of man's oldest environment-oriented dreams to influence the weather, and since the Second World War there has been a great deal of talk, much of it uninformed, about weather and climate control. But apart from measures to improve the night-time microclimate of plants by such devices as heaters and fans, only a relatively few techniques have met with any success. Among these attempts are those to augment precipitation by the introduction into clouds of freezing nuclei, salt particles or water droplets, processes known as cloud seeding. There is no doubt that solid carbon dioxide pellets (dry ice) and silver iodide smoke can induce certain clouds to grow and precipitate by triggering off the freezing stage of the so-called Bergeron–Findeisen process. But the techniques are clearly more complicated, less productive and less certain of success than was thought in the years of wildcat empiricism following the experiments of Langmuir and Schaefer in 1946 (Neiburger, 1970). Nevertheless, modest increases of precipitation of between 10 and 20 per cent during individual operations have been fairly widely reported. Equally, however, several field experiments, including the recently highly organized Project Whitetop in the United States, have resulted in a widespread decrease in rain. In this particular investigation, precipitation over the central portion of the target area was more than 32 per cent less on seeded than on unseeded days, and the estimated average loss of rain within the 100,000 square miles affected by the seeding was 21 per cent. This reduction represents a tremendous loss of water as a result of attempts to increase it (Neyman *et al.*, 1969; Neiburger, 1970). The amount of seeding material used and the prevailing meteorological conditions are clearly very critical to success, but in the weather business one can never win, for in 1950 claims totalling some $2 million were made in New York by people seeking compensation for the alleged harm resulting from artificially induced rainfall (Bowen, 1969).

Cloud seeding is also being used in experiments on lightning suppression and, in the West Indies, to see if it can change the structure and movement of hurricanes. These experiments are incomplete, and no one is yet sure if we can significantly modify the properties of such a large and powerful meteorological system.

The suppression or mitigation of hail damage by the use of small rockets fitted with silver iodide nose-cones is a highly organized system of weather control operated in a number of countries: for instance, more than 50,000 rockets are fired annually into storms in northern Italy. If the system really works, and this is by no means proven, it probably does so through the use of the explosion to shatter hailstones along planes of natural weakness and by the diffusion of ice nuclei to freeze many of the supercooled droplets essential for hailstone growth. In consequence, a large number of small rather than a few large hailstones are produced and these often melt before reaching the ground.

Fog clearance is another avenue of current research and limited practice. Many techniques have been tried (Stewart, 1960) but only a few have had even moderate success, the most effective using some source of heat to raise the temperature of the foggy air above the dew point. This method was first used, successfully but expensively, during the Second World War under the code name FIDO. Supercooled fogs are relatively easy to treat and can be efficiently cleared by spraying them with the ubiquitous philosopher's stone of the weather controller, silver iodide smoke, whereupon some of the droplets change into ice crystals; they then grow at the expense of the water droplets and fall to the ground.

On the scale of true climatic control, one must remember the enormity of natural energies compared with man's capabilities, so that frequently the only possibilities are to find means whereby relatively small energy inputs can be used to trigger off natural instabilities in a desired manner. (This, indeed, is precisely what happens, on a smaller scale, in cloud seeding.) Many speculative schemes have been proposed. These include spreading sheets of black plastic over Arctic pack ice to reduce the albedo and raise local temperatures; altering the courses of certain ocean currents by, for instance, damming the Bering Straits; and the creation of vast inland seas in Siberia and central Africa. These are wild, speculative schemes, more often than not as uncertain in method as aim and almost completely unknowing of consequences. Before we can so rashly tamper with climate, we must observe and theorize in order to understand the exact weather science, we must understand before we can predict, and we must be able to predict with a high degree of accuracy before, with discretion and sensitivity, we can safely experiment with the atmosphere (Rand Corporation, 1969).

## CONCLUSION

In man's dealings with climate, as in so many other fields, past pragmatism, ignorance and indifference have caused us to drift into a series of local, regional and global problems, sometimes amounting to disasters. Environmental scientists must be given the means to accelerate their research and be encouraged, in conjunction with others, to apply their findings to the real world. Many alarmist, partially or wholly misinformed statements have been made, particularly in the popular press, but there are nonetheless sufficient and varied grounds for concern to justify concerted international scientific investigation of the management and mismanagement of climatic resources. Man must clearly learn to make the best use of his environment, conserving its main form and using purposeful modification only where the benefits are clear and the ill effects can be shown to be negligible. These surely should be the primary aims of climate management.

## REFERENCES

Ångström, A. (1962). Atmospheric turbidity, global illumination and planetary albedo of the earth, *Tellus*, **14**, 435–50.

Anon (1972). Sulphur pollution across national boundaries, *Ambio*, **1**, 15–20.

Auliciems, A., and Burton, I. (1972). Trends in smoke concentrations before and after the Clean Air Act 1956, Paper presented to the Commission on *Man and Environment* Symposium, International Geographical Union, Calgary, 23–31 July 1972.

Best, R. H. (1968). Extent of urban growth and agriculture displacement in postwar Britain, *Urban Studies*, **5**, 1–23.

Bowen, D. (1969). *Britain's Weather*, David and Charles, Newton Abbot, England, 310 pp.

Bryson, R. A. (1968). All other factors being constant, *Weatherwise*, **21**, 56–61.

Budyko, M. I. (1969). Climatic change, *Soviet Geography: Review and Translation*, **10**, 429–57.

Caborn, J. M. (1965). *Shelterbelts and Windbreaks*, Faber, London, 288 pp.

Chandler, T. J. (1965). *The Climate of London*, Hutchinson, London, 292 pp.

Changnon, S. A. (1969). Recent studies of urban effects on precipitation in the United States, *Bull. Amer. Meteorological Soc.*, **50**, 411–21.

Craxford, S. R., and Weatherley, M-L. P. M. (1968). *Air Pollution in Great Britain*, Warren Spring Laboratory, Stevenage, 17 pp.

Craxford, S. R., and Weatherley, M-L. P. M. (1971). The national survey of smoke and sulphur dioxide: the first ten years, *Proceedings of the Clean Air Conference, Folkestone, 2–5 November 1971*, National Society for Clean Air, Brighton, England, pp. 114–24.

Crisp, D. J. (1965). Observations on the effects of climate and weather on marine communities, *The Biological Significance of Climatic Changes in Britain*, ed. C. G. Johnson, and L. P. Smith, Academic Press, London, 63–78.

Crutzen, P. J. (1972). SST's—threat to the earth's ozone shield, *Ambio*, **1**, 41–51.

Ellis, H. T., and Pueschel, R. F. (1971). Solar radiation: absence of air pollution trends at Mauna Loa, *Science*, **172**, 845–6.

Flohn, H. (1961). Man's activity as a factor in climatic change, *Ann. New York Acad. Sci.*, **95**, 27–81.

Food and Agricultural Organization of the United Nations (1962). *Forest Influence*, Rome, 110 pp.

Greenberg, D. S. (1969). Pollution control: Sweden sets up an ambitious new program, *Science*, **166**, 200–1.

Hare, F. K. (1971). Future climates and future environments, *Bull. Amer. Meteorological Soc.*, **52**, 451–6.

Harrison, H. (1970). Stratospheric ozone with added water vapour: influence of high altitude aircraft, *Science*, **170**, 734–6.

Jensen, M. (1954). *Shelter Effect*, Danish Technical Press, Copenhagen, 264 pp.

Johnson, H. (1972). The Concorde, oxides of nitrogen and stratospheric ozone, *Search*, **3**, 276–82.

Johnson, H. S. (1971). Reduction of stratospheric ozone by nitrogen oxide catalysts from supersonic transport exhaust, *Science*, **173**, 517–22.

Kellogg, W. W., Cadel, R. D., Allen, E. R., Lazurs, A. L., and Martell, E. A. (1972). The sulfur cycle, *Science*, **175**, 587–96.

Lamb, H. H. (1966). *The Changing Climate*, Methuen, London, 236 pp.

Landsberg, H. E. (1938). Atmospheric condensation nuclei, *Ergebnisse Rosm. Physik.*, **3**, 155.

Landsberg, H. E. (1970). Man-made climatic changes, *Science*, **170**, 1265–74.

McCormick, R. A., and Ludwig, J. H. (1967). Climate modification by atmospheric aerosols, *Science*, **156**, 1358.

Manabe, S. (1970). The dependence of atmospheric temperature on the concentration of carbon dioxide *Global Effects of Environmental Pollution*, ed. S. F. Singer, Reidel, Dordrecht, 218 pp.

Manabe, S., and Strickler, R. F. (1964). Thermal equilibrium of the atmosphere with a convective adjustment, *J. Atmospheric Sci.*, **21**, 361–85.

Mitchell, J. M. (1970). A preliminary evaluation of atmospheric pollution as a cause of the global temperature fluctuation of the past century, *Global Effects of Environmental Pollution*, ed. S. F. Singer, Reidel, Dordrecht, 218 pp.

Monteith, J. L. (1970). Prospects for photosynthesis from A.D. 1970 to A.D. 2000, *Weather*, **25**, 456–62.

Neiburger, M. (1970). Present status of precipitation control, *W.M.O. Bull.*, **19**, 21–4.

Neyman, J., Scott, E., and Smith, J. A. (1969). Areal spread of the effect of cloud seeding at the Whitetop Experiment, *Science*, **163**, 1445–8.

Perring, F. H. (1965). The advance and retreat of the British Flora, *The Biological Significance of Climatic Changes in Britain*, ed. C. G. Johnson, and L. P. Smith, Academic Press, London, 51–62.

Perry, A. H. (1970). Changes in duration and frequency of synoptic types over the British Isles, *Weather*, **25**, 123–6.

Plass, G. M. (1959). Carbon dioxide and climate, *Sci. American*, **201**, 41–7.

Rand Corporation, Weather Modification Research Project (1969). Weather modification progress and the need for interactive research, *Bull. Amer. Meteorological Soc.*, **50**, 216–46.

Reed, L. E. (1966). Vehicle exhausts in relation to public health, *The Royal Society of Health J.*, **86**, 227–38.

Reinking, R. F. (1968). Insolation reduction by contrails, *Weather*, **23**, 171–3.

Ritchie-Calder, Lord (1970). Mortgaging the old homestead, *Foreign Affairs*, **48**, 207-20.

Sawyer, J. S. (1971). Possible effects of human activity on the world climate, *Weather*, **26**, 251–62.

Schaefer, V. J. (1969). The inadvertent modification of the atmosphere by air pollution, *Bull. Amer. Meteorological Soc.*, **50**, 199–206.

Smith, L. P. (1963). The significance of climatic variations in Britain, *UNESCO, Arid Zone Research 20, Proceedings of the Rome Symposium October 1961*, 457–68.

Stewart, K. H. (1960). Recent work on artificial dispersal of fog, *Meteorological Mag.*, **89**, 311–19.

Study of Critical Environmental Problems (SCEP) (1970). *Man's Impact on the Global Environment, MIT Press*, Cambridge, Mass., 319 pp.

*Study of Man's Impact on Climate* (SMIC) (1971). MIT Press, Cambridge, Mass., 594 pp.

Thornthwaite, C. W. (1956). Modification of rural microclimates, *Man's Role in Changing the Face of the Earth*, ed. W. L. Thomas, University of Chicago Press, Chicago, 567-83.

Warren Spring Laboratory (1972). *Review 1971-72*, WSL, Stevenage, Herts, 37 pp.

World Meteorological Organization (1970). *Urban Climates*, Geneva, 390 pp.

# CHAPTER 3

# Managing the Land

A. WARREN

## INTRODUCTION

The popular image of the soil has never been as dynamic as that of some other resources. Whereas the seas, weather, streams and life have always been symbols of change, flow or decay, the soil has been synonymous with stability. Although the soil is a dynamic system it needs a disaster such as the dust bowl in America forty years ago to translate this idea into literature and so to public consciousness.

The novels of the dust-bowl years, such as those of John Steinbeck (1939), were part of a massive scientific, administrative and political response to the soil erosion of the period. Because earlier conservation campaigns had never been as extensive, nor had involved such a vital national asset, the soil was the first conservation issue to be massively funded by a central government, and because of this soil conservationists came to pioneer some of the many difficult issues that occur in any serious forward planning that involves nature: the distinctions between production and productive capacity, economic and moral motives, private and public responsibilities, short- and long-term accounting, concentrated and dispersed effort, and research and action. It was the first programme to attempt to influence public attitudes on a really large scale, and it is the first, forty years after its foundation, to be able to appraise its achievements in depth.

Many of these important considerations have been explored by Held and Clawson (1965), and they are only briefly discussed here, for the principal purpose of this chapter is to discuss the ways in which conservationists should plan for the long-term use of a natural system.

## MANAGING SOIL PROCESSES

Soil conservation is an attempt to balance the inputs and outputs in two series of stores. The first series, at the larger scale, concerns the budgets of what Kubiena (1938) called the *soil skeleton* (the larger, mostly chemically inert particles); this is a part of the sedimentary budget in geomorphological systems. The second series, at the smaller scale, concerns transfers and budgets of what Kubiena called the *soil plasma* (the fine-grained chemically active material), or in other words the more truly pedological processes.

Conservation of both these processes is necessary since they are easily disturbed even under primitive land use (Dimbleby, Chapter 18), but because the disturbance of the skeleton results in more serious destruction it was the first problem to receive concerted attention from conservationists, and it will be the first and principal topic to be discussed here.

## Managing the Soil Skeleton

The volume of soil on a slope between a watershed and a stream-line (Figure 3.1) is a reflection of the balance between inputs of weathered rock

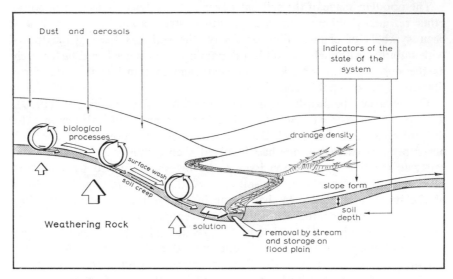

**Figure 3.1.** Inputs and outputs from the dynamic soil system; some of the indicators of homeostasis in the system are also shown.

from beneath and of atmospheric dust and organic litter from above and outputs to streams by mass soil movement, surface wash and solution (outputs removed by the wind will be discussed later). It is necessary to maintain a usable depth of fertile soil in this dynamic situation, and to be able to do this the conservationist must know about the nature and volume of the fluxes of material and about the controls on their redistribution.

Although in most cases it is evident that the largest volume of *inputs* to the soil is from the underlying rock, it is seldom easy to quantify them. The usual method of arriving at an estimate assumes that the system is in dynamic equilibrium, in which case the simpler measure of outgoing material (minus atmospheric inputs) can be substituted for the more difficult measure of weathering (e.g. Johnson *et al.,* 1966). But meaningful results can only come from relatively undisturbed sites, and it is difficult, if not impossible, to find these in the kinds of agricultural areas for which the information is usually needed. For this reason, and for others to be explained below, the figures in Table 3.1 should be treated with very great caution as estimates of input into agricultural soils. Another method of estimating inputs is to measure the amount of dissolved load in water draining from soil profiles and by comparing these figures with the proportions of soluble and insoluble material in the parent rock, arrive at a figure for the amount of insoluble residue being released to the soil. By suitably correcting this calculation for the bulk density of the soil and the amount of undissolved soluble residue, Perrin (1965) estimated that 1 cm depth was being added to soils over the Cambridgeshire chalk every 5,200 years (about 0·003 tonnes per hectare per year). He noted that this estimate, in spite of many dubious assumptions, gives a figure that appears to be about the right order of magnitude. Several other methods of estimating weathering rates are reviewed by Smith and Stamey (1965).

There are many different controls on the rate of weathering. If world regions are compared, the largest differences can be attributed to climatic controls, although much of the range occurs in zones where agriculture is impossible. At the local scale, variation is controlled by factors such as rock type, and, more importantly, by a homeostatic mechanism operating through soil depth: the shallower a soil, the nearer is the parent material to the surface, where climatic fluctuations and organic activity, are more active in rock breakdown; but the more intense this activity the deeper the soil becomes. Thus the depth of a soil is an expression of an equilibrium between removal and renewal. Of course, if erosion is very much slower than weathering the depth of weathered material may continue to increase this in itself can present problems which will be discussed below.

Weathering may be the principal, but it is not the sole, source of inputs to the soil. In humid areas plant litter is the most important subsidiary source of additions, although much of it is either returned to the air as carbon dioxide or is recycled through the vegetation. In the mixed deciduous woodland at Meathop in Lancashire approximately 3·77 tonnes per hectare per year are added to soil surfaces (Satchell, 1969). Atmospheric dust is another important source of inputs, although in humid climates it is mostly 'plasma' rather than 'skeleton', and the additions are very variable in space and time. Only in semi-arid areas is the rate really measurable; in Kansas 17·9 tonnes per hectare per year of dust have been reported, although common rates are probably about 3·4 (Smith and Stamey, 1965). A third source, on low-lying sites is from flood waters; these can be important to agriculture in old irrigation systems as along the Nile.

The most important mechanism of *removal* from soils in humid climates is undoubtedly by solution (in other words it is removal of 'plasma'), since flow across the soil surface is volumetrically much less than sub-surface flow through it. Up to 80 per cent of total outputs can be in the dissolved form in temperate areas and surfaces are lowered on average by about 0·03 mm per year (roughly 0·04 tonnes per hectare per year) by solution in climates with rainfall of about 750 mm (Carson and Kirkby, 1972).

Soil creep and surface wash are the two important mechanisms which remove skeletal material from soils, and some figures for these in British situations are shown in Table 3.1. Although most of the figures are for

**Table 3.1.** Some estimated and measured erosion rates in Britain

| Site | Rate as quoted | Approx. rate in tonnes/ ha/yr | Source |
|---|---|---|---|
| A. *Surface-wash from slopes* | | | |
| Upper Derwent Valley | 0·08 cm³/cm/yr | 0·010 | Young (1960) |
| Water of Deugh, Dumfriesshire | 0·09 cm³/cm/yr | 0·011 | Young (1972) |
| | | | |
| B. *Soil creep on slopes* | | | |
| Upper Derwent Valley | 0·60 cm³/cm/yr | 0·078 | Young (1960) |
| Water of Deugh, Dumfriesshire | 2·10 cm³/cm/yr | 0·273 | Carson and Kirkby |
| Upper Wye Valley, Mid-Wales | | | (1972) |
| undercut slopes | 3·86 cm³/cm/yr | 0·502 | Slaymaker (1972) |
| slopes not undercut | 1·06 cm³/cm/yr | 0·138 | Slaymaker (1972) |
| | | | |
| C. *From reservoir siltation and other 'total basin' studies* | | | |
| Strines Reservoir, Yorkshire | 0·005 in/yr | 0·066 | Young (1958) |
| (catchment area *c*.11 sq. km) | | | |
| Upper Wye Valley, Mid-Wales | 367 m³/km²/yr | 0·048 | Slaymaker (1972) |
| (catchment areas c.10–15 sq. km) | | | |
| Cropston Reservoir, Leicestershire | 7590 ft³/yr | 0·001 | Cummins and Potter |
| (catchment 17 sq. km) | | | (1967) |

Note: Numerous assumptions are involved in converting volume to weight measurements. The assumptions used here are similar to the ones used by Smith and Stamey (1965). The measurements in cm³/cm/yr have been converted using the assumption that a hectare would discharge sediment across a 100 m length of slope.

relatively undisturbed sites, they cannot be taken as good examples of natural rates on agricultural land for several reasons. Firstly, there are very few sites in Britain on which the vegetation can be regarded as undisturbed even over short periods. Some of Slaymaker's (1972) results indicate a degree of balance in mid-Wales, though others do not, and many other studies have shown that sites in upland Britain suffer accelerated erosion (e.g. Bryan, 1969; Imeson, 1971). Secondly, few of the figures, if any, refer to areas with slope angles below 11°, which is the accepted upper limit for mechanized agriculture (Bibby and Mackney, 1969); the erosion rates shown may therefore be higher than on gentler slopes, although this need not necessarily be so (see, for example, Slaymaker, 1972).

Rates of creep and rainwash are subject, like weathering rates, to climatic controls on a world scale, and to rock type and perhaps topographic controls locally, but the most critical and vulnerable control is undoubtedly the vegetation cover. A covering of vegetation virtually eliminates damaging rainsplash and overland flow, and its clearance lays the soil bare to these attacks. The removal of vegetation, as has so often been observed, may lead to enormous local increases in erosion rates. Agricultural land *commonly* has rates at least five times the 'natural' level, and increases of 10,000 times have been observed. It has been estimated that human disturbance of vegetation has increased the world denudation rate from 20 to 54,000 million tonnes per year (Gregor, 1970). The plant cover is thus a vital part of the whole geomorphological process.

Soil erosion by water is generally thought to be unimportant on agricultural land in Britain, and various reasons have been advanced to explain this, such as gentle rainfall, dense vegetation, or generally good topsoil structure. But erosion does occur in Britain on soils with an inherently poor structure such as sandy soils which are cropped in such a way as to leave the soil bare at some seasons. In the West Midlands near Kidderminster and Ross-on-Wye, for example, soils have suffered bad erosion (e.g. Hodgson and Palmer, 1971) and the soils of the Lower Greensand are also known to be vulnerable. In upland areas accelerated erosion has been noted by several authorities, including Bryan (1969), Imeson (1971) and several others mentioned by Evans (1971) and peat erosion is another serious problem (e.g. Tallis, 1964). Soil erosion in the uplands was undoubtedly more serious in the past. The erosion of peats and mineral soils is usually attributed to burning or overgrazing by sheep.

Erosion by rainsplash and overland flow has been one of the principal studies of soil conservation organizations. The United States Soil Conservation Service has evolved an empirical 'soil loss equation' which is used to calculate losses under proposed cropping regimes and so to attempt to limit losses. Many publications contain descriptions of this equation (e.g. Task Committee on Preparation of Sedimentation Manual, 1970); the brief discussion that follows is intended to introduce the factors that are thought to be important.

The equation ($E=RKLSCP$) relates soil loss in tons per acre per annum ($E$) to six factors: rainfall erosion potential ($R$), inherent soil erodibility ($K$), slope length ($L$), slope angle ($S$), cropping management ($C$) and conservation practice ($P$). In the predictive use of the equation, empirical values which have been derived from a very large number of observations are given to each factor for each site. The value of $R$ includes measures of the kinetic energy and intensity of the rain for the site as calculated from the nearest available climatic records; $K$ is intended as a measure of the inherent cohesion and strength of the soil aggregates to resist rainsplash, although actual values are derived from experimental plots on soils similar to the one under consideration; $S$ and $L$ have been related empirically to a 'soil loss ratio', which is read off from standard graphs; $C$ is the ratio of soil loss under a proposed crop to loss from clean fallow and is calculated by crop stages over an entire rotation, relating crops and tillage methods to seasonal figures for the eroding power of the rainfall; and finally, $P$ too is given empirical values such as 0·6 for contour ploughing or 1 for straight-row farming.

By manipulating $K$, $S$, $L$ and $C$, soil losses have been considerably reduced. $K$ is kept low by adding lime and organic matter to the soil and by careful tillage, $S$ and $L$ are changed by contouring or terracing, and $C$ is kept low with crops which give good ground cover, especially in the dangerous early stages of growth. A very large body of experience has been built up and is applied widely in the United States and elsewhere, much of which is summarized by Hudson (1971). Whereas the lowest figures for soil skeleton loss are invariably found under grass, and indeed, they are lower under grass than under the climax oakwood in the Peak District (Bryan, 1969), the nutrient (plasmic) turnover under grassland is probably much faster than under woodland (Malmer, 1969).

Most soil conservation aims only to stem the outputs of skeletal material, but there is a long history of soil management practices in which attempts are made to increase the inputs. Most soil additions are to the plasma, but skeletal material has been added to the soil in labour-intensive systems as in the west of Ireland, in Egypt, or more generally in gardens and parks, and marling, which is another example of the practice, survived in England until the middle of this century when it became too expensive. Inputs can, of course, be inadvertently increased when tillage leads to increased erosion and so to a decrease in the depth of soil, for, as has been explained, this may increase the inputs from weathering. This would mean that there would be a faster rate of turnover and a different kind of homeostatic equilibrium than under 'natural' conditions (Stamey and Smith, 1964).

The selection of a figure for a stable turnover rate at which soil conserva-tion should aim is not therefore a simple matter, and tends still to be somewhat rule-of-thumb. Several thousand carefully monitored grass plots have been set up all over the United States in an attempt to produce precise values, but actual target values must depend on the nature of the material beneath the soil or the presence or absence of unsuitable sub-soil conditions such as hard pans. In a review of turnover rates, Smith and Stamey (1965) noted that whereas the available data indicated natural turnover rates of between 0·2 and 1·3 tonnes per hectare per year in the United States, target rates were commonly 11·2 and ranged from 1·1 over hard rock to 13·4 or even higher in the deep loess soils of the Mid-West. These are, however, a very considerable reduction from the maximum rate of over 284,000 tonnes per hectare per year that has been recorded in this last area. The danger in selecting an incorrect target is usually thought to be overestimation, but it will be shown below that underestimation can also cause problems, for if erosion rates are cut below renewal rates, great depths of unstable soil can sometimes accumulate.

Apparently successful though this approach may seem it begs profound questions concerning the spatial patterns of erosion and the relations between the time periods used for planning and the variability of climatic controls.

**The Spatial Distribution of Erosion**

One of the many platforms on which the early soil conservationists such as Bennett (1939) based their campaigns was the communality of the erosion problem: one farmer's disregard for the soil would become the concern not only of his neighbours but also of his fellow citizens many miles downstream or downwind.

The most obvious, and least disputable, spatially variable aspects of accelerated erosion is the development of gullies. The concentration of run-off into narrow channels is part of any normal fluvial system, and like many other patterns of fluid flow in nature (leaves, trees, arteries) it adopts a regular branching pattern. The length of stream channel or the number of streams per unit area is a reflection of the amount of water to be disposed of, and this in turn is in part a reflection of soil permeability, slope angles, and above all of the vegetation cover.

The clearance of natural vegetation involved in agriculture changes the water balance and this increases stream density, the actual change usually following an intense shower: new streams appear and cut deeply into the friable soil and a gully system is formed (Strahler, 1956; Task Committee on Preparation of Sedimentation Manual, 1970). Although this is a common cause of gullying it is not always accurate to attribute gullying only to agricultural or pastoral misuse of the land, since intense showers with long return periods or even phases of climatic change can also initiate it (Vita-Finzi, Chapter 16). Although gullying does not account for as much soil removal as surface wash (Task Committee) 1970) it does create serious problems for agriculture, and 'induced' (and perhaps even 'natural') gullying can be avoided by simple management practices such as terracing, grassing possible gully paths, and avoiding the overuse of pathways by animals.

Gullying appears to be even less of a menace in Britain today than erosion by surface wash although it may well have been serious at certain periods in the past. In the New Forest intense showers often initiate small gullies on disturbed ground with slope angles over 5°; the gullies grow slowly by headward erosion but as their slide-slopes are cut back they are graded by frost weathering and are eventually stabilized by plant colonization. Old stabilized gullies are quite common, and many may be very ancient, but here too they contribute little to the overall erosion of the area (Tuckfield, 1964). Local activity by heavy vehicles in forestry operations or by military manoeuvres may create favourable conditions for gullies but the effects are usually short-lived (White, 1963).

Sediment redistribution is a more controversial aspect of the spatial pattern of soil erosion. Bennett (1939) raised many millions of dollars for soil conservation in the belief that the great amounts of soil and run-off known to be leaving agricultural fields would be taken downstream and would both clog waterways and reservoirs and lead to serious flooding. There was undoubtedly an element of political shrewdness in his campaign, since waterways are a federal responsibility in the United States, and only the federal government had the funds and inclination to finance schemes as extensive as Bennett wanted. But he also had a strong belief in the truth of the relationship, although it was founded on very little scientific knowledge; recent research has, in fact, questioned the severity of the problem.

Corey Creek and Elk Run are two fourth-order streams in Pennsylvania draining agricultural areas each of about 6 km by 6 km in size. In 1954 the Corey Creek basin was very thoroughly laid out with a number of conservation practices (strip-cropping, terraces, afforestation, putting land down to grass, building farm ponds, etc.). Elk Run was virtually untouched, becoming a 'control' in a useful experiment which was carefully monitored by the U.S. Geological Survey (Jones, 1966). The measured effects of conservation in the Corey Creek Basin between 1954 and 1967 in terms of stream flow and sediment discharge (Reed, 1971) might have appalled Bennett. The flooding characteristics of the streams were not changed in any significant way, but this effect is discussed elsewhere in this volume and will not be expanded here (Kirby and Rodda, Chapter 5). Although the sediment discharge was reduced by 47 per cent during the growing season, only 6 per cent of the annual load is lost in this period; there was no significant increase in the 94 per cent of the annual load lost between November and April.

There are several ways in which these figures might be explained, and, of course, they are for only one drainage basin. But they may be taken to illustrate an important general principle about sediment movement: there is no simple throughput from slopes to streams, since the sediment released from slopes tarries in a series of 'stores' as it passes through a drainage basin. It is said that the delivery ratio of sediment is high for small-order valleys* (Task Committee, 1970), sediment often being trapped high up the system. One explanation of the Corey Creek results could be that when erosion was taking place in Corey Creek before conservation, or Elk Run at any time, it was being moved only a short distance to nearby fields or flood plains and little was reaching the main stream. The conservation measures therefore only stopped the replenishment of these local stores, so that they benefited the local farmers but did little for the navigation and reservoir engineers. Sediment from severe erosion of bare soil patches in the Pennines and in Mid-Wales similarly moves only a short distance downslope (Evans, 1971; Slaymaker, 1972). The calculation of erosion rates based on one output figure is therefore highly dependent on the size of the area involved, and this should be borne in mind in reading Table 3.1.

Of course, there are many, well-documented instances in which careful management has cut sediment yields, particularly in small watersheds on semi-arid rangeland (Kirby and Rodda, Chapter 5). In larger streams, on the other hand, there are ways other than soil erosion in which sediment can be brought into traction, for interference with the 'natural' pattern of a channel, for example by building training walls, can increase bank erosion.

### Wind Erosion and other Problems

In Britain the loss of topsoil in 'blows' is probably a more serious problem than its removal by water. Soil erosion by the wind presents the conservationist with a somewhat different problem to soil erosion by water, since under undisturbed conditions in humid climates it is likely that losses to the wind are very small indeed and thus control of wind erosion is an attempt to cut losses to a minimum, and not balance them with inputs.

The United States Soil Conservation Service has evolved a 'wind erosion equation' which is similar to that for water erosion. It involves measures of soil erodibility, ground roughness, local wind conditions, fetch and vegetative cover (Task Committee, 1965). Wind erosion is controlled by maintaining a good soil structure, by ridging fields at dangerous periods,

---

* Delivery ratio = ratio of sediment yield at a given point in a stream in tonnes per hectare per year to the total material eroded from the watershed upstream in tonnes per hectare per year, given as a percentage. If all the material eroded were to enter the stream, the ratio would be 100 per cent.

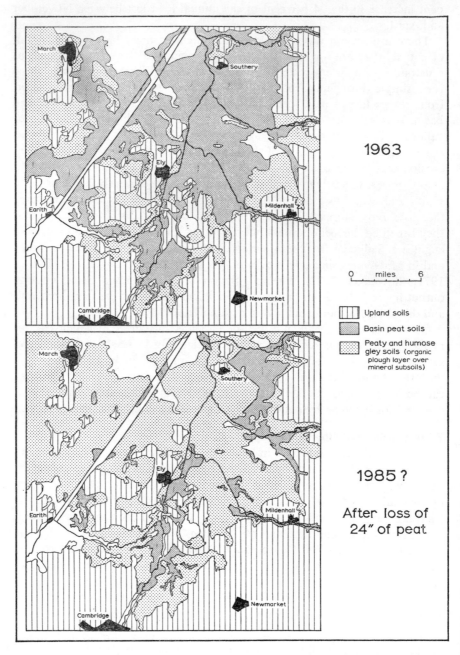

**Figure 3.2.** The probable pattern of peat loss in the Black Fen areas of East
Anglia. (Adapted from Perrin and Hodge, 1965.)

by making fields short in the direction of prevailing storm winds, and by maintaining a maximum plant cover during vulnerable periods.

In England there are several factors which control the time and place of wind erosion on agricultural land, but the most important concerns the soil itself, for it is the light sandy soils in East Anglia, Lincolnshire, and East Yorkshire, and the light Fen peats which suffer most (Pollard and Miller, 1968; Wilkinson *et al.,* 1968). It is the inherent lack of good structure of the sandy (usually podzolic) soils and the feathery lightness of the peats which renders them liable to blowing when cleared of vegetation. Although there is evidence that some blowing occurred as far back as the sixteenth century, there is a belief that the problem has become more severe in the last few years. This is said to be because soil structure has deteriorated due to the change from the use of farmyard manure to inorganic fertilizers on the mineral soils, the heavy mechanical cultivation of some crops, and hedgerow grubbing which has given the wind a longer fetch. When the soils do blow, up to 2 cm of intensely fertilized topsoil with its seeds may be removed, remaining crops can be damaged by blasting, and large sums of money may be needed for resowing and ditch and road clearance (Robinson, 1969; Radley and Simms, 1967).

Serious blows are said to occur every three to five years, although almost every year brings reports of blows somewhere; 1973 was a particularly bad year. It seems to need a wind of over 20 knots (37 km/hr) to start a blow (e.g. Spence, 1957) although the published research on this is scanty, as is the research on the return periods of these winds and the relationship between wind velocities and soil losses. Conservation measures such as hedges, subsoiling and surface-stabilizing sprays are now being adopted by Fen farmers, for the peat is now visibly wasting (Figure 3.2; Sneesby, 1966).

In the Fen peatlands there are other wastage problems which are probably more important than wind erosion. The Fens are a non-renewing asset, for no more peat is being formed, and with the inevitable disappearance of most of the peat, the underlying, often heavy, soils may not be as productive of high-value crops such as celery and carrots and they will certainly not provide the same flexibility for cropping. The land will fall from Class 1 to Class 2 land on the Ministry of Agriculture scale (see Griffiths, 1972). A reduction in the rate of peat wastage would seem to be a sensible conservation policy.

When the English Fen peats are first drained there is a very rapid shrinkage as water (often three times the solid volume is lost). The remaining denser peat shrinks at the much slower rate of about 2·5 cm/year, mainly by biochemical oxidation in the now aerobic conditions, but also by occasional burning, by blowing or by compaction. Eventually the layer of peat shrinks to within the plough depth and the underlying soil is mixed in with the peat. Most of the Fen peats are very near to this stage today. The rate of loss then declines to about 1·8 cm/year and then to 0·5 cm/year as more and more mineral matter is mixed in. Finally, the losses tail off as they are balanced by additions of organic matter. It is estimated from the present distribution of peat thicknesses that very large areas will be changed from black peat fen to 'skirtland' in the next 10 or 15 years (Figure 3.2 and e.g. Richardson and Caldwell, 1972).

The peat can be conserved in a number of ways: for example, blows can be controlled; water tables can be kept at a level where they do not inhibit crops but where they minimize losses by aerobic decomposition; stubble burning can be stopped; and marling might be reintroduced (Richardson and Caldwell, 1972). The most hopeful method seems to be subsoiling with a 90 cm plough which mixes the mineral soil and peat (Smith *et al.*, 1971).

### Long-Term Problems

The principal controls on the rates of erosion are climatic, and these are highly variable in time: rainfall and windspeeds (the most important factors) vary widely about mean values, with the extremes (drought, hurricanes or floods) occurring rarely but with a calculable probability. The greater the extremity of a climatic event the lower its probability, so that extreme events are said to have long 'return periods'.

The concept of the return period of extreme events is of considerable importance to conservation. In plant communities, for example, rare hurricanes or fires may be important in rejuvenating or opening up gaps in woodland in which light-demanding species can survive. In soil conservation the importance of extreme events is not only that they can do spectacular damage, but also that the 'natural' geomorphology of an area appears to be adjusted to them. Stream channels in England, for example, are said to adjust their form to floods which occur on average every 2·2 years (Nixon, 1959). The relationship between extreme events and the form of the slopes which are so critical to agriculture has received far less attention, but Kirkby has made some interesting calculations for slopes in southwestern England: for grassland slopes he estimated that the return period of the event which determined slope form was 100 years, and for oak woodland slopes it was probably much longer (Carson and Kirkby, 1972). If significant events are so far apart, terracing, which considerably modifies the form of slopes, might be successful in the short run, but would present the significant storm with a situation far from equilibrium. Indeed this appears to be the case in Kansas, where terracing can reduce soil loss in the short term from 56 tonnes per hectare per year to 22 or even 2 under grass, but during extremely heavy storms the losses from terraced land are very high (Moldenhauer and

Wischmeier, 1960). And in Corey Creek (referred to above), Reed (1971) found terracing to be far less successful in reducing soil loss over the period from 1954 to 1967.

The reduction of surface soil losses leads to a greater depth of loose soil, and this, with the increased infiltration on unnaturally low-angle terrace surfaces, may introduce the additional problem of soil instability and slippage. Serious slippage following terracing has been noted, for example, in the Rif Mountains of northern Morocco (Beaudet, 1962). It can be seen that while terraces, which were Bennett's principal answer to many soil conservation problems, may sometimes have been successful, they have often been a liability.

As well as rare extreme events, long perspectives into the future include the probability of secular climatic change. There is an immense amount of evidence for climatic change even in the period since cultivation began some 10,000 years ago (Vita-Finzi, Chapter 17), and there is no reason to think that changes will not happen in the future. Each change will bring about new slope equilibria to which agriculture will have to adapt.

These observations raise difficult questions about the length of time span with which conservationists should be concerned. Should the Mid-Western farmer terrace his land and so gamble with the weather for a short-term gain, or should he avoid terraces and protect his land with an unprofitable crop such as grass, so reducing his present income but ensuring it in the long term? Should a Fen or sandland farmer in Britain put up hedges and reduce his acreage, or allow the soil to blow occasionally? The choice is not always simple, since the farmer must decide not only on the significant return period of destructive events, but also on the discounting period he should adopt for his borrowed capital (see below). As for climatic change, its probability means that planning should look no further forward than a hundred years at the most.

### Managing the Soil Plasma

As with the skeleton, the soil plasma under natural conditions is part of a dynamic homeostatic process in which material is added from weathered rock, from biota and from the atmosphere, and is lost to streams.

The plasma is, by definition, more mobile than the skeleton, and much of it is recycled through the soil and vegetation on an annual or even a monthly cycle. In spite of the fact that solution losses are often volumetrically larger than losses of skeletal material, replacement of the plasma removed either by crops or by leaching is an easier task than the replacement of soil skeleton since many plasmic materials can be manufactured. Although for this reason the conservation problems of plasma may seem less severe, they are nonetheless considerable.

Some of the evidence underlying the case for long-term plasma management comes from soils which have a long history of use. Dimbleby (e.g. Chapter 18) has shown how soils which once supported relatively productive deciduous woodlands were so altered by early cultivation that they now only support *Calluna*-dominated heath. This was brought about by the removal of plasma at a faster rate than its replacement, and eventually by an alteration in the type of semi-natural vegetation which maintained the supply of plasma.

The evidence that long-term soil use can materially alter the soil is not all negative. Phosphorus is supplied by most soils in only small amounts, but in natural plant communities it is fairly efficiently recycled and the very small losses by leaching are probably made up from rock weathering and from dust. Cropping removes phosphorus faster than it is supplied and it is often the first nutrient to make its deficiency felt in crop yields. During the Middle Ages in North Germany and Holland phosphorus deficiencies were made up by collecting forest litter, peats or turves from uncultivated land, using them as bedding for cattle in the winter, and then spreading the mixture of turf and dung on the fields in spring (Pape, 1970); in Ireland and northern and western Scotland seaweed and sand were used for the same purpose. Over many years a quite distinctive soil profile (a 'plaggen' soil) resulted which, though poor in other nutrients, had a good response to phosphatic fertilizer.

Since the revolution in agriculture of the 1840s in which Liebig and Lawes discovered the value of artificial phosphatic fertilizers, phosphorus has come mostly from mineral sources. But a serious problem has been discovered: soils which have not been cultivated for long periods 'fix' phosphorus in enormous quantities, and render it virtually unavailable to plants. In many 'new' agricultural soils three or four times more phosphorus is added than is removed. There are many ways in which fixation happens (e.g. Kardos, 1964; Cooke, 1967), but there are two processes which dominate: at low pH phosphates combine with iron or aluminium and at high pH with calcium. Only when the pH is 6 to 7 are phosphates moderately available, although even then there is fixation. The positive aspect of the phosphorus problem concerns the plaggen soils, since their appetite for phosphorus appears to be nearly satisfied. As cultivation continues, more and more soils will need less and less phosphorus.

The case for concern with long perspectives in the management of the soil plasma rests mainly on the observation that 'artificial' plasma comes from non-renewable sources and must be manufactured with increasingly scarce energy. The three main nutrients supplied to crops in fertilizers are nitrogen, phosphorus and potassium: nitrogen fertilizers come mostly from the atmosphere; phosphorus comes from mineral supplies—mainly in

Morocco—which are not in great quantity; potassium, though relatively abundant in mineral deposits (there are often world gluts of potassium), needs, like nitrogen and phosphorus, scarce energy to make it available to crops as a fertilizer. All these fertilizers, therefore, will be faced with increasing prices and perhaps real scarcity in the future.

The tactics of nutrient conservation involve the intelligent use of the storage and supply system within the soil. Nutrients are held as mobile cations or anions or in crystal lattices. Only as cations or anions are they available to plants, but as such they are also liable to be washed through the soil by percolating rain water. Some soils have the property of holding some nutrients loosely in crystal lattice stores from whence they can be fed via the soil solution, or directly, to plants as they need them. This is particularly the case with potassium (e.g. Cooke, 1967).

Conservation of the nutrients requires firstly that they are not fed to the soil either to be fixed almost irrevocably in firm lattices (as in the case of phosphorus) or to be washed out of the soil (as when more nutrient is added than can be taken up either by the plants or the mineral stores). If this were avoided some problems of stream eutrophication in agricultural areas might also be avoided although it is said that this situation is not yet serious in Britain (Tomlinson, 1971). Secondly, only soils with good storage capacities for nutrients should be used: the sandy soils of the Dorset heaths which require huge additions of potassium because of their small storage capacity should not be used, whereas the 'cover loams' of East Anglia which have excellent potassium-holding capacities are the soils on which cultivation should be concentrated.

There are two further areas of concern in the conservation of soil plasma. The first, the maintenance of soil structure, is discussed in more detail by Munton (Chapter 21). Although soil structure is not thought to be a long-term problem, one of the recommendations that emerged from the recent report on soil structure mentioned by Munton was that unsuitable soils for arable cropping, particularly wet clays, should be avoided. This underlines the principal theme in long-term plasma management, namely, the fitting of crops to soil, which will be discussed briefly in a broader context in the next section. Lastly, there is a concern for the ecology and function of the soil organisms which manufacture the organic matter of soils, since these can be endangered by pollution particularly from agricultural pesticides. This aspect of soil conservation is expanded in the chapter by Moore (Chapter 15).

## THE ALTERNATIVES OFFERED BY THE LAND

Like any resource, the land offers a number of choices to its users: the alternatives are between short-term gain and long-term stability, and between

various levels of productivity and investment. Some of these choices have
been discussed elsewhere (e.g. Hendricks, 1969) and only one aspect can
be elaborated here.

A recurring theme in this chapter, and indeed in much of the soil conservation literature, is the concept of land capability, since many conservation problems might be avoided if crops were grown only on the soils most
suited to their production. Only crops with low sediment yields, for example,
should be planted on steep erodible land. Although land capability is a
relative concept, depending as it does on the technology of the time, and the
choice of a viable level of investment to combat erosion or nutrient loss,
(which may itself depend on the market for crops and on the climate
of taxation or subsidy at a particular time) the use of scarce resources
on the most suitable land at any one time has many clear advantages and
is being shown to be feasible. In the United States, for example, production
has not been jeopardized by the concentration of arable cropping on deep,
fertile, level soils. The loss of arable acreage equal in area to about half of
France over the last 30 years has been accompanied by an enormous increase
in production in spite of a vigorous policy of subsidizing against overproduction (Held and Clawson, 1965). The underdeveloped countries are
being advised to concentrate scarce capital and resources on to the better
land since their limitations to agricultural growth are cultural rather than
environmental (e.g. Mohammed, 1965). Thus there may well be a growth
in production despite a declining acreage, and this would contradict the
simpler assumptions of Malthus, Ricardo and Meadows alike (Meadows
*et al.*, 1972) although this is not to say, of course, that there are no environmental or energy limits to production.

In Britain the withdrawal from upland soils, from sandy soils which have
poor nutrient response and are erosion-prone and from clay soils which
are prone to waterlogging and so to both structure deterioration and nitrogen loss would mean the release of land to recreation, wildlife or water
catchment (Kirby and Rodda, Chapter 5; James, Chapter 22).

## SOME ECONOMIC AND SOCIAL IMPLICATIONS

The land cannot, of itself, be productive, since modern agriculture also
needs capital, labour and management to yield crops. The soil has been
having less and less control over production, and conservation programmes
are concerned increasingly with manipulating factors other than the land
itself. The implications of these trends are the principal theme of Held and
Clawson (1965), and only a few points can be mentioned here.

Held and Clawson adopted a definition of conservation based on Figure
1.1(b) (p. 5). Soil conservation by that definition is an attempt to hold

the trend of expected income steady over a long period, or to maintain or improve basic productive capacity, goals known to biological conservationists as 'sustained yield'. Some simple conservation methods, such as liming, may show almost immediate return on investment (Curve 1 in the figure), but most methods involve a pattern as in Curve 2 in which a relatively large investment, as in terracing, leads to a drop in immediate income in anticipation of steadying in the future; the conservation of poor land may even require a permanent drop in income, as when it has to be put down to grass (Curve 3).

Because few farmers can hope to live to see a return on their investment in conservation or hope themselves to receive a proportional return from the benefits to their neighbours or to the community, soil conservation programmes are seldom justifiable on economic grounds (see Dumsday, 1971). To most farmers erosion is an 'externality' to their business (Coddington, Chapter 29); these and other problems faced by farmers in their approach to conservation are discussed more fully by Munton (Chapter 21). The constraints on conservation at the level of the individual farm imply that conservation must be a national rather than an individual concern, and this is indeed what has happened in the United States, where the Soil Conservation Service with its huge system of government expertise and democratically run local organizations is a model for other conservation programmes (Simms, 1970).

Many investigations have shown that in the current climate of economic reasoning, particularly its short accounting periods and its emphasis on the individual, no real economic arguments can be made for conservation. But while it may be difficult to justify soil conservation on these grounds, it can be supported by real arguments: its fundamental aim is to conserve basic productive capacity, or where its decline is inevitable, as in the case of the Fen peats, to slow the rate of decline. Farmers who have adopted a conservation attitude have done so for non-economic reasons such as these, which express a deep belief in the good husbandry of their land.

## CONCLUSIONS

The land presents a number of choices to its users, but the selection of a policy is complicated by the absence of clear criteria for judgment, since soil conservation can seldom be justified on simple economic grounds, and a suitable time period for planning is difficult to discover. If conservation is chosen as an approach, and there are good arguments for doing so, there are some important corollaries: it must be a communal rather than an individual activity, for individuals cannot enjoy the necessary perspectives in time or space; and conservation, especially in a democracy, cannot be a static, rigid programme for all time, for experience over the last forty years has shown that not only will our evaluation of problems change but so will the problems themselves.

## ACKNOWLEDGMENT

I would like to thank Drs. R. U. Cooke and F. B. Goldsmith for reading earlier drafts of this chapter and for their helpful suggestions.

## REFERENCES

Beaudet, G. (1962). Types d'évolution actuelle des vertants dans le Rif occidental, *Rév. de Géog. du Maroc*, **1–2,** 41–7.
Bennett, H. H. (1939). *Soil Conservation,* McGraw-Hill, New York, 993 pp.
Bibby, J. S., and Mackney, D. (1969). Land Use Capability Classification, *Soil Survey of England and Wales, Tech. Mem. No. 1,* 27 pp.
Bryan, R. B. (1969). The relative erodibility of soils developed in the Peak District of Derbyshire, *Geog. Annaler,* **51** Ser. A, 145–59.
Carson, M. A., and Kirkby, M. J. (1972). *Hillslope Form and Process,* Cambridge University Press, Cambridge, 475 pp.
Cooke, G. W. (1967). *The Control of Soil Fertility,* Crossby Lockwood, London, 526 pp.
Cummins, W. A., and Potter, H. R. (1967). Rate of sedimentation in Cropston Reservoir, Charnwood Forest, Leicestershire, *The Mercian Geologist,* **2,** 31–9.
Dumsday, R. G. (1971). Evaluation of soil conservation policies by systems analysis, in *Systems Analysis in Agricultural Management,* eds. J. B. Dent and J. R. Anderson, John Wiley, Sydney, 152–172.
Evans, R. (1971). The need for soil conservation, *Area,* **3,** 20–3.
Gregor, B. (1970). Denudation of the continents, *Nature,* **228,** 273–5.
Griffiths, D. J. (1972). Agricultural land classification in England and Wales, *Agriculture,* **79,** 479–83.
Held, R. B., and Clawson, M. (1965). *Soil Conservation in Perspective,* Johns Hopkins University Press for Resources for the Future Inc., Baltimore, 344 pp.
Hendricks, S. B. (1969). Food from the land, in *Man and Resources,* National Research Council, Washington, D.C., Freeman, San Francisco, 65–85.
Hodgson, M., and Palmer, R. C. (1971). Soils in Herefordshire I, Sheet SO 53 (Hereford South), *Soil Survey of England and Wales, Survey Record No. 2,* 81 pp.
Hudson, N. W. (1971). *Soil Conservation,* Batsford, London, 352 pp.
Imeson, A. C. (1971). Heather burning and soil erosion on the North Yorkshire Moors, *J. Appl. Ecol.,* **8,** 537–42.
Johnson, M. M., Likens, G. E., Bormann, F. H., and Pierce, R. J. (1966). Bulk chemical changes and rate of chemical weathering in central New Hampshire, *Trans. Amer. Geophys. Union,* **47,** 83–4.
Jones, B. L. (1966). Effects of agricultural conservation practices on the hydrology of Corey Creek basin, Pennsylvania, *U.S. Geol. Survey, Water Supply Paper, 1532–C,* 55 pp.
Kardos, L. T. (1964). Soil fixation of plant nutrients, in: *Chemistry of the Soil,* 2 edn., ed. F. E. Bear, Van Nostrand Reinhold, New York, pp. 369–444.

Kubiena, W. L. (1938). *Micropedology,* Collegiate Press, Ames, Iowa, 243 pp.

Malmer, N. (1969). Organic matter and cycling of minerals in virgin and present ecosystems, *Oikos, Suppl.,* **12,** 79–86.

Meadows, D. H., Meadows, D. L., Randers, J., and Behrens, W. W. III (1972). *The Limits to Growth,* Potomac Associates, Earth Island, London, 205 pp.

Mohammed, Ghulam (1965). Waterlogging and salinity in the Indus Plain, *Pakistan Development Review,* **5,** 393–407.

Moldenhauer, W. C., and Wischmeier, W. H. (1960). Soil and water losses and infiltration rates on Ida silt-loam as influenced by cropping systems, tillage practices and rainfall characteristics, *Proc. Soil Sci. Soc. Amer.,* **24,** 409–13.

Nixon, M. (1959). A study of the bankfull discharges of rivers in England and Wales, *Inst. of Civil Engr. Proc.,* **12,** 157–74.

Pape, J. C. (1970). Plaggen soils in the Netherlands, *Geoderma,* **4,** 229–55.

Perrin, R. M. S. (1965). The use of drainage water analysis in soil studies, in: *Experimental Pedology,* eds. E. G. Hallsworth and D. V. Crawford, Butterworth, London, pp. 40–92.

Perrin, R. M. S., and Hodge, C. A. H. (1965). Soils, in: *The Cambridge Region,* ed. J. A. Steers, British Association for the Advancement of Science, Cambridge, pp. 68–84.

Pollard, E., and Miller, A. (1968). Wind erosion in the East Anglian Fens, *Weather,* **23,** 415–17.

Radley, J., and Simms, C. (1967). Wind erosion in East Yorkshire, *Nature,* **216,** 20–2.

Reed, L. A. (1971). Hydrology and sedimentation of Corey Creek and Elk Run basins, north-central Pennsylvania, *United States Geol. Survey. Water Supply Paper, 1532–E,* 27 pp.

Richardson, S. J., and Caldwell, T. H. (1972). Lowland peats and organic soils, *Min. of Ag., Fish, and Food, A.D.A.S., Open Conf. of Advisory Soil Scientists,* Soil Physical Condition and Crop Production, SS/0/72/6, 19 pp.

Robinson, D. N. (1969). Soil erosion by wind in Lincolnshire, March 1968, *Geography,* **54,** 351–62.

Satchell, J. E. (1969). Feasibility study of an energy budget for Meathop Wood, *Symp. on the Productivity of the Forest Ecosystems of the World,* Brussels, 21 pp.

Simms, D. H. (1970). *The Soil Conservation Service,* Pall Mall, London, 238 pp.

Slaymaker, H. O. (1972). Patterns of present sub-aerial erosion and landforms in Mid-Wales, *Trans. Inst. British Geographers,* **55,** 47–68.

Smith, J., Wickens, R., and Richardson, S J. (1971). Soil mixing in the fens, *Arthur Rockwood Exp. Husbandry Fm. 6th Report,* pp. 24–31.

Smith, R. M., and Stamey, W. D. (1965). Determining the range of tolerable erosion, *Soil Sci.,* **100,** 414–24.

Sneesby, N. J. (1966). Erosion control in the Black Fens. *Agric. J.,* **73,** 39–4.

Spence, M. T. (1957). Soil blowing in the Fens in 1956, *Met. Mag.,* **86,** 21–2.

Stamey, W. L., and Smith, R. M. (1964). A conservation definition of erosion tolerance, *Soil Sci.,* **97,** 183–6.

Steinbeck, J. (1939). *The Grapes of Wrath,* Heinemann, London, 416 pp.

Strahler, A. N. (1956). The nature of induced erosion and aggradation, Wenner-Gren Internat. Symp. on *Man's role in Changing the Face of the Earth,* ed. W. L. Thomas, Jr., University of Chicago Press, Chicago, pp. 621–38.

Tallis, J. H. (1964). Studies of South Pennine peats, II. Patterns of erosion, *J. Ecol.,* **52,** 333–44.

Task Committee on Preparation of Sedimentation Manual (1965). Chapter II, Sediment transport mechanics: wind erosion and transportation, *J. Hydrol. Div., Proc. Amer. Soc. Civil Eng.,* **91,** 267–81.

Task Committee on Preparation of Sedimentation Manual (1970). Chapter IV, Sediment sources and sediment yields, *J. Hydrol. Div., Proc. Amer. Soc. Civil Eng.,* **96,** 1283–329.

Tomlinson, T. E. (1971). Nutrient losses from agricultural land, *Outlook on Agriculture,* **6,** 272–8.

Tuckfield, C. G. (1964). Gully erosion in the New Forest, Hampshire. *Amer. J. Sci.,* **262,** 795–807.

White, D. A. (1963). *A study of contemporary erosion with particular reference to gullys on various heathlands in southern England in relation to geomorphology, ecology and land-use,* unpublished M.Sc. thesis, University of London.

Wilkinson, B., Broughton, W., and Jean Parker-Sutton (1968). Survey of wind erosion on sandy soils in the E. Midlands, *Experim. Husbandry,* **18,** Min. of Ag., Fish and Food, H.M.S.O., 53–9.

Young, A. (1958). A record of the rate of erosion on Millstone Grit, *Proc. Yorks. Geol. Soc.,* **31,** 149–56.

Young, A. (1960). Soil movement by denudational processes on slopes, *Nature,* **188,** 120–2.

Young, A. (1972). *Slopes,* Oliver and Boyd, Edinburgh, 288 pp.

CHAPTER 4

# Shoreline Management

P. H. KEMP

## INTRODUCTION

The shoreline is the visible line of discontinuity between land and water. It is a meeting place of many diverse interests and disciplines. It is here that the dynamic forces of the wind, waves and tide are confronted by the comparatively static defences of beaches, cliffs and harbours. The normal processes of weathering are as active in this zone as elsewhere on land. Shoreline management must be largely concerned with the identification and evaluation of the many forces acting on the coast, and the effects which these forces produce. The objective may be to attempt to interpret past changes, to identify the processes currently at work, or to predict and control future trends both in the absence of or as a result of man's intervention.

The contexts within which the need for coastal control may arise are many and varied. They include the preservation of life, land or property in the immediate vicinity of the coast, the prevention of inundation of low-lying areas further inland, the maintenance or improvement of beaches for recreation, or the construction of yacht marinas or commercial harbours. Correct diagnosis of the causes of beach erosion can help to minimize future losses and maximize the benefit of remedial measures. Accurate prediction of the effects of proposed works on the coastal regime can likewise enable detrimental effects to be avoided, and can eliminate the implementation of schemes which would be ineffective. The cost of engineering works may be considerable, and it is essential, wherever possible, to work with nature by encouraging natural processes, rather than to confront the forces acting on the coast with rigid structures.

Where the coastline is characterized by the existence of sand or shingle beaches, these not only provide a valuable natural amenity, but perform the vital function of a barrier against attack by the sea. Waves dissipate their tremendous energy by breaking in shallow water and running up the beach until friction, turbulence and percolation bring the uprush to rest.

The greater the incident energy, the greater the uprush distance required. Beaches change their slope and profile with changes in wave action, flattening under the action of storm waves to provide a longer run-up, and steepening again as the energy diminishes. As described by Kemp (1961; 1962), the ability of a beach to adjust itself in this way to the prevailing forces makes it the most effective and efficient method of defence. The flattening of the beach under storm attack must not be confused with erosion, which implies a permanent loss of foreshore material. Providing that the volume of beach material on a stretch of stable coast does not diminish, the coast will not degrade. When beach material is in movement as littoral drift under the action of longshore currents, the beach volume will remain constant if the inflow of material into a given section is equal to the outflow. This assumes that there is no long-term loss of material in the offshore direction. It is important to note that if this continuity of flow of material is interrupted, dramatic or even disastrous effects may result.

Changes in littoral drift may be due to a local cause such as the construction of a groyne or breakwater, or to interference with the supply of material a great distance away, possibly at its source. Examples are not hard to find. According to Gagliano *et al.* (1970), recent measures of flood control, navigation improvement and road building have virtually eliminated overtopping of the banks of the channels of the Mississippi River Delta, and have altered the natural process of sedimentation which has been taking place for over 5,000 years. Most of the river-transported sediment is now deposited offshore in the deep Gulf of Mexico. Salt-water encroachment has occurred and has been detrimental to the flora and fauna. There has been a net loss of land. Measures have had to be taken to divert some of the sediment-laden water to encourage the formation of new sub-deltas. A similar situation appears to have arisen in the Nile Delta as a result of the construction of barrages across the Nile, with a consequent reduction in the quantity of sediment reaching the Delta area. A number of localities are now subject to coast erosion and recession. In some cases, even today, material is removed from beaches on a commercial basis, a practice which was condemned by the Royal Commission on Coast Erosion as long ago as 1911. It is the first rule of shoreline management that beach material should be conserved.

## National and Regional Responsibility

In several countries it has long been recognized that the planning and management of coastal areas should be subject to control at both local and national levels. In addition, it was appreciated that the high costs associated with coast protection works should be borne at least in part by the government or local authority. The scope and powers of the authority designated to control coastal development vary widely. In the Netherlands most aspects of hydraulic engineering and water resources are coordinated. This is clearly necessary in a country where nearly half the land area is below sea level. Responsibility largely rests with the Rijkswaterstaat Board of the Ministry of Transport, Hydraulics and Public Works, and far-reaching and imaginative schemes have been carried out in recent years. Wemelsfelder (1954) describes the exceptional tidal levels which resulted from the North Sea surge in 1953 and inundated nearly 5 per cent of the land area of the Netherlands with salt or brackish water. This was accompanied by heavy loss of life, property and livestock. The main damage occurred in the area of the Rhine Delta, where the country is intersected by many inlets or arms of the sea. The resulting Delta Plan has closed off the major inlets at their seaward ends, thus shortening the vulnerable coastline by 700 km, reducing the saltwater intrusion, and providing freshwater areas, recreational facilities and better communications. The 1953 surge also caused considerable damage in the United Kingdom, and as a result new standards of coastal protection were laid down. Residential and industrial areas or large areas of agricultural land must be given a standard of protection sufficient to withstand a flood of the magnitude of the one of 1953. This is equivalent to protection against a flood with a return period of 200 to 300 years. Where conditions are such that flooding would produce disastrous effects, a 1,000 year period is recommended. In general, responsibility in the United Kingdom for coastal protection outside urban areas rests with the Ministry of Agriculture if the land area is liable to inundation. The River Authorities have powers under the 1930 Land Drainage Act for the construction or improvement of coastal protection works. These responsibilities may in the future be taken over by Regional Water Authorities.

In the United States, Public Law 520 of the 71st Congress was approved in 1930, placing responsibility for investigations and studies of coastal erosion on the Chief of Engineers of the United States Army. The Beach Erosion Board set up at that time was redesignated the Coastal Engineering Research Center (C.E.R.C.) in 1963. The Corps of Engineers works in close collaboration with local agencies in the preparation of projects. Up to 70 per cent of the cost of protecting publicly owned shores may come from Federal funds if certain conservation, development and use requirements are satisfied. Contributions to the protection of private property may also be made if such protection would result in public benefits.

One further case of public control may be cited from Australia, where, for instance, the Beach Protection Act (1968) set up the Beach Protection Authority, Queensland, to formulate measures necessary and practicable for the preservation and restoration of beaches, and to control and prevent, where necessary, acts damaging to beaches.

The need for conservation and control has, therefore, been recognized. Many problems need solutions on a regional rather than a local basis. The demands on the coast are increasing, and, as in the case of rivers, often conflict with one another. Access to dune areas by the public may be desirable but can considerably reduce their protective value. The disposal of waste material in the sea, or the abstraction of sand and gravel from inshore banks, are economically advantageous but need careful consideration. The evaluation of the effects which such measures produce can only be made in the knowledge of the natural processes at work, and in the light of data relating to each local and regional area. Coastal management must rest on an understanding of the physical background to coastal dynamics, for it is only in the knowledge of what is possible or feasible that decisions involving questions of amenity and economics can be made. Reference should be made to the Bibliography for information in depth, as only the salient features can be mentioned in the present context.

## Erosion

The forces acting on the coast become relevant when they produce changes in the shoreline. These changes may be beneficial or detrimental. Both are of interest, the beneficial because they can be exploited to effect improvements, and the detrimental because action is often necessary to stabilize the situation. The detrimental effects are usually associated with erosion, although the siltation of navigation channels and harbours may be economically more serious. The coastline is subjected to the erosive influences of wind, rain, frost, waves and currents. These forces break down the land into particulate matter, and it then becomes part of the beach or of the sea bed. The protection of the coast necessitates the study of the history of this material, its behaviour under the action of waves and currents and, finally, the effect of protective works on its movement, deposition and configuration.

Some areas appear to have been subjected to progressive erosion as far back as records go. Matthews, giving evidence before the Royal Commission on Coast Erosion (1907), reported erosion at the rate of 3 m per year and a loss of twelve towns and villages between the fourteenth and twentieth centuries in the area between Bridlington and Spurn Point on the East Coast of England. The Royal Commission in its final report estimated that so far as the area of the British Isles was concerned, there had been a net gain of approximately 15,000 hectares in the 35-year period preceding the inquiry. This figure was based on a comparison of Ordnance Survey maps. Whereas most of the losses of land occurred on the coast, the majority of the accretion took place in estuaries. The Report of the Departmental Committee on Coastal Flooding (1954) reaffirms the net gain, but in less specific terms. Duvivier (1947) has estimated that 33 per cent of the English coast-line is subject to erosion, mainly on the south and east coasts. In the United States, Mason (1948) estimates that there is a net annual loss of land equivalent to a strip 0·3 m wide along the total coastline.

The configuration and orientation of the coastline and its exposure to wave action broadly determine its liability to erosion, and the extent of erosion is influenced by the type of beach and local geology. Instances have been cited of clay foreshores which have eroded 2 m vertically in two tides.

Carey (1907), Owens and Case (1908), Hutchinson (1971) and Kemp (1972a) draw attention to the fact that cliffs are particularly vulnerable to attack by rain and frost, and poor drainage is blamed for many cliff falls. Cliff erosion may be accelerated by the transport of material into deep water or its lateral transport by waves breaking obliquely to the shore.

Farquharson (1953) remarks that exceptional high tides and the surges resulting from high winds or barometric pressure enable waves to attack areas normally free from wave action, and severe erosion often occurs.

Headlands may cause the diversion of beach material, as indeed may harbours, piers, jetties and groynes. Hall (1952) maintains that the effect of such structures may be felt for distances of 16 km or more in the downdrift direction. The question of injury caused by groynes to the foreshore at a distance was the subject of early enquiry by the Royal Commission, and 'disastrous effects' are mentioned. The legal or common law right of any man to interrupt the flow of shingle was also discussed, together with the advisability of enforcing the lowering of groynes to allow shingle to pass. The removal of beach material for aggregate was recognized as a fundamental cause of erosion, and this has largely ceased.

The profile of the beach is being continually remoulded to a shape characteristic of the waves acting upon it at any given time. Cornish (1898) emphasized that when this adjustment involves the flattening of the foreshore there is an apparent loss of material which must not be mistaken for erosion. Eaton (1951) pointed out that the effectiveness of a newly constructed system of groynes on a sandy coast may be overrated should their erection coincide with the shoreward migration of a sand bar, which under favourable conditions can advance the high water mark a hundred feet or so in a few days.

Regulation of erosion may be preferable to complete protection. A fall of cliff in one place may well replenish the natural defences of another. The cost of protection works must be judged against the value of the land which is threatened, and on the possible effect which a recession would have on adjoining areas. The degree of protection which can be economically provided undoubtedly influences the design of coast protection works.

## COASTAL DYNAMICS

### Tides and Surges

From the point of view of coastal dynamics there are two dominant factors associated with the tide, viz. (a) the variations in water level, and (b) the velocity, duration and phase of the tidal currents. In the majority of cases it is unnecessary to understand the influence of the tide-raising forces of the sun and moon. In a given area, the predicted tide is usually known, or if not, local observations can be made to establish the tidal pattern. If, however, as Dronkers and Schoenfeld (1955) point out, a substantial interference with the movement of the tides is contemplated, it will be necessary to investigate thoroughly the mechanism of the tidal motion in order to predict correctly the effect of the intended interference. For this purpose recourse can be made to computations or to research on an hydraulic model of the area. In shallow water, effects such as bed friction become appreciable, and as a result the tide is distorted. There is then a difference in the shape of the tidal curve and the associated velocities between the flood and the ebb. This tidal asymmetry is most important, for when bed material is subjected to alternating flow conditions it is the net movement or difference between the ebb and flood which determines the net transport of the material.

The effect of the tidal range is to move the level of action of waves up and down the beach. Exceptionally high tides can enable waves to attack areas normally beyond their range.

The damage caused by storm surges in the Netherlands and England in 1953 referred to by Wemelsfelder (1954) and Farquharson (1953) has already been mentioned. These surges are characterized by a rise in water level in addition to the normal tidal variation. They are meteorological in origin and can be induced by the passage of a low pressure area, or by high winds piling the water against the coast under the action of surface wind stress. If a depression moves across a sea area at a speed approximately equal to the natural velocity of a long wave in the local depth of water, then a wave is generated which accentuates the rise in water level. Fluctuations of up to 1 m are common in the North Sea in any year. Gale force winds may produce elevations of up to 5 m. Negative surges also occur when the conditions are reversed. They have little significance in the present context, although they may produce navigational difficulties due to the reduction in the predicted depth of dredged or natural channels.

To summarize, tides and surges change the level of wave attack. In addition, exceptional rises in sea level may result in overtopping of sea walls, which may then fail due to erosion on their landward sides. The currents associated with the flood and ebb are often sufficient to move sand offshore of the breakers. The sand or shingle in this area is also liable to disturbance by wave action, as calculated by Rance and Warren (1968), and the disturbed sand may then be transplanted by the tidal current. Wave action, in fact, plays the dominant role in coastal dynamics.

## Waves

The study of shoreline processes and coastal conservation is ultimately concerned with the characteristics of the waves generated in the open sea, and with their behaviour as they approach and finally expend their energy on the shore. The range of oscillations in the sea is more or less continuous, from the shortest ripples, through swell and longer period waves, up to the largest known tidal period, which depends on the variation of the angular distance of the moon from the ecliptic and lasts nearly 19 years.

The waves observed breaking on the shore commonly have periods of about 5 to 15 sec. The shorter periods down to 1 sec and the longer periods of up to, say, 25 sec are less easily identified, as they are largely masked by the middle period waves.

These waves derive their energy from the wind, and their periods vary over the entire range mentioned in the previous paragraph. If the sea area is large enough, the component waves eventually segregate so that the longest waves arrive at the coast first, followed by shorter and shorter period waves as time goes by. In the generating area, therefore, the sea is random and confused. Outside this area the segregated waves are smoother and more regular, and are known as swell. Many observations have enabled wave forecasting diagrams to be prepared from which heights and periods can be deduced, of which those by Bretschneider (1952) and Darbyshire and Draper (1963) are representative. The wave periods forecast in this way do not change as the waves approach the shore, but variations in the bed contours offshore have the effect of retarding the wave crests where they are travelling over shallower water, and the wave wheels in the direction of the retarded zone. This refraction effect is similar to the refraction of light through a lens. A shallow underwater bank tends to make the waves converge, thus increasing their height, whereas an offshore trench produces divergence and height reduction. This concentration or diffusion of wave energy is most marked at bays and headlands. The resultant beneficial or detrimental effects on the shoreline can be inferred from refraction diagrams.

From the standpoint of beach changes, the nature of wave motion shoreward of the break point is by far the most important. However, just as the asymmetry of tidal motion has been identified as of great significance, so in the case of waves approaching the shore the asymmetry of water motion associated with the passage of the wave is of equal importance. In shallow water, waves tend to resemble a series of comparatively isolated crests, connected by long flat troughs. The forward component of orbital motion associated with the passage of the crest is of high velocity but short duration, and the backward motion due to the trough is of longer duration and lower velocity. This asymmetry tends to move bed material shoreward, especially if the material is coarse sand or shingle.

Waves finally dissipate much of their energy in breaking. The manner in which they break depends on the breaker height, wave period and beach slope, as described by Galvin (1968). The breaker height is the dominant characteristic of the wave in the nearshore zone. After breaking the wave runs up the beach, dissipating more energy in friction and turbulence, and after reaching the limit of its uprush or swash, it runs back as backwash. The way in which the uprush and backwash influence the beach has been the subject of a number of papers by Kemp (1961; 1963) and Kemp and Plinston (1968).

The height to which waves will run up a beach or structure depends on the nature of the surface, and on the wave period, the wave height from trough to crest and the slope of the surface. Kemp (1963) has shown that on permeable shingle beaches this height is approximately equal to the height of the breaking wave. The run-up of waves on impermeable slopes is dealt with in papers by Saville (1958) and Hunt (1961). An example of application to a shore platform and cliff situation is given by Kemp (1972a).

If the waves break obliquely to the shoreline, the longshore component of the wave energy generates a longshore current, and this is the main mechanism by which sand and shingle are transported along the coast. Illustrations of this process are given by Caldwell (1966), Fairchild (1966) and Galvin (1967).


## Wind

The wind acts in three ways. Firstly, it generates the waves. Secondly, it acts on the water surface to produce a current in the same direction as the wind. Francis (1953) and Reid (1956) investigated the shear stress and velocity distribution associated with wind-driven water currents. Rance (1966) showed the relevance of these currents to the design of sea outfalls. These currents are confined to the upper layers of the water, to a depth perhaps of 6 or 7 m, and thus produce their maximum effect in shallow water. An onshore wind induces an onshore current at the surface and a seaward flowing return current at the bed, and vice versa. The consequent effects on bed material can be inferred. The third effect of the wind is to transport beach sand, and with an onshore wind, dunes may result.

**Beaches**

By attenuating and dissipating wave energy, beaches form the main defence against erosion or flooding by the sea. Beaches must, therefore, be conserved at all costs. It was for this reason that the fundamental part played by beaches was emphasized at the beginning of the chapter. Reference should, therefore, be made to the introduction on beach adjustment.

The most important characteristic of a beach is the size of the material of which it is composed. This influences the behaviour of the beach in three main ways: (a) the ability of waves and currents to move the material; (b) the permeability of the beach and thus its ability to absorb the wave uprush; (c) the speed with which material is returned to the beach after being moved offshore by storm action. Shingle returns more quickly than sand. The larger material can withstand wave attack most readily. It therefore forms steeper beaches, since it can attenuate wave attack over a shorter uprush distance.

Shoreline structures such as groynes create turbulence and seaward flowing currents. Shingle is little affected by these associated effects, but fine sand is easily put into suspension and scouring is likely to occur.

Dunes at the back of a beach provide excellent defence in depth. They will erode under storm wave action, but a sufficient volume of sand in the dunes will enable them to outlast the transient wave attack, and the sea will restore the sand under calmer conditions. Reference will be made below to the use of dunes in shoreline protection.

## SHORELINE CONTROL

Problems are as varied as the local geology, topography, dynamic forces, shore utilization and other variables concerned. However, by collecting data for a given region or locality, and by assessing the relative importance of the factors relating to the area, guidelines can be laid down or plans drawn up which will conserve or improve the coastal area. In this section reference will be made to typical areas of interest. The serious student of coastline management will need to follow up the literature quoted, and the references given in individual publications. However, apart from the references at the end of the chapter, many introductions to various aspects of the subject exist, a few of which are included under the heading 'Bibliography'.

**Data collection**

The type of data to be collected and observations to be made depend on an initial evaluation of the problem. In particular, the time scale is important. If a stretch of coast is rapidly deteriorating, then an immediate assessment of the littoral drift, wave climate, cliff stability or dune erosion must be made. The effect of a single storm or exceptional high tide is of importance. On the other hand, if the long-term stability or recession of the shoreline is to be assessed, then it may be that annual measurements could be sufficient. Wherever possible, it is desirable to make a coastal survey whether or not there is an immediate problem. In this way, a background of information is built up which may not only be useful if protection works become necessary, but which can lead to the development of projects for improvement, especially in relation to recreational use of the coast. According to Kemp (1972a), such surveys can be carried out in a reasonably short time and can still be comprehensive in nature. The general character of the coast, and the history of erosion or accretion, can often be obtained from maps, charts or aerial photographs. Tidal information can be interpolated from published tables. Wave refraction patterns can be seen on aerial photographs or inferred or constructed from charts. Beach materials are easily measured by sieving, and beach contours measured. The wave climate is of great importance, and here recordings may have to be made; these can supplement and control values obtained from forecasts based on wind data. From the wave data, an assessment of the littoral transport and the run-up on the beach can be made. The type and quantity of beach material necessary to improve or nourish the beach can also be assessed.

Examples of systematic and continuous collection of data are given by Edelman (1966) in relation to the Netherlands, Berg (1968) in the U.S., Zwamborn *et al.* (In Press) in South Africa, and in various publications of the Beach Protection Authority of Queensland. In Queensland, for instance, survey observations are analysed by computer, and the information fed to a flat-bed plotter. Up to fifty stations record observations of wave characteristics, wind velocity and direction, beach dimensions, vegetation movement and tidal variations. In many cases, field observations are used to provide information necessary for the correct design and control of hydraulic models, as quoted by Jordaan (1970) in the case of erosion and silting in the area of Durban Harbour. Bakker and Joustra (1970) report investigations in the Netherlands which provide examples of systematic data collection going back over a period of many years. Such records give information on erosion and accretion of the dunes, the effects of groynes and harbours, periodic climatological changes, and determinations of the quantity of littoral drift.

The advent of space photography has helped to identify seaward tongues of sediment which Nichols (1970) describes as extending up to 22 km offshore.

**Wave Data**

The systematic collection of wave data should enable different wave properties to be evaluated. The estimation of the quantity of sand transported as littoral drift can be based on the component of wave energy along the coast, its duration, direction, and incidence throughout the year. The overtopping of a sea wall requires data on the exceptionally large waves which may occur very occasionally over many years. Wave measuring instruments vary from simple optical types described by Kemp (1972b) to sophisticated accelerometer systems referred to in the National Institute of Oceanography Conference of 1961. Whatever method is used, the records must be systematically analysed. This is a comparatively simple process, and the presentation of the data is now becoming standardized along the lines suggested by Draper (1966). The combination of wave forecasting methods and instrumentally measured wave data has been used by Draper (in press) to obtain a general picture of extreme wave conditions likely to occur once in 50 years.

### Littoral Drift and Beach Replenishment

The importance of the littoral drift of sand and shingle has already been emphasized, and the relationship between wave power and wave obliquity indicated. This transport of material is related to the longshore currents generated by the waves, which has been the subject of a recent publication by Longuet-Higgins (1970). However, according to Fairchild (1966), variations in beach material type, beach slope and tidal range also appear to affect the total transport of material.

If an obstacle such as a groyne interferes with the flow of material, then the shoreline will build out on the updrift side. The rate of progression and final shape can be estimated along the lines suggested by Pelnard-Considère (1956). Price *et al.* (in press) describe a similar procedure covering the case when the incident wave energy is affected by, say, offshore dredging.

Where, as mentioned in the introduction, there is a net loss of material, sand or shingle can be imported to replenish or nourish the beach. The main point to be observed is that the material should be similar in size or grading to the existing beach, or preferably larger, otherwise it is likely to be lost seaward. Many projects of this type have been carried out, and they suffer from none of the drawbacks associated with groynes. Hall (1952), Taylor (in press) and Kramer (in press), all cite recent examples of beach replenishment, although examples could be quoted going back nearly 100 years. The use of marine-dredged sand is quoted in *Hydrospace* (Anon, 1972).

### Groynes

Groynes have been used for over 100 years to prevent beach material from being moved along the coast under the action of waves and currents. The main drawback to their use is that the coastal areas downdrift are starved of littoral drift material and suffer increased erosion. However, groynes can be used in conjunction with artificial replenishment. In areas where the beach material is trapped, as in an indented bay, groynes are used to maintain an equal distribution of material. There have been many publications on groynes, including the report of model studies by Kemp (1962), and recent papers by Hale (in press) and Balsillie and Berg (in press). The design and application of groyne systems is still a matter for investigation and judgment.

## Sea Walls

With regard to walls, it has been stated that 'the mistake which is so often made is to erect a barrier, designed as a direct obstruction. The mechanical effect of a heavy sea striking a cliff or sea wall is to set up a scouring action at the base of the obstruction '. Where walls are the only answer to threats of flooding or the destruction of property Carey (1967) goes on to point out that 'the great feature is to put the embankment well in the rear of the foreshore'. The design of the walls themselves is as controversial as the design of groynes, and is not considered here. However, the two design weaknesses of walls are, firstly, the liability of the wall to be undermined at the toe, unless protected by an apron or sheet-piling, and, secondly, the failure which is likely to occur in a sloping revetment, once it is broken. The sea washes out the supporting filling, and the whole wall collapses. Such sloping revetments should be secured by the provision of tranverse bulkheads.

References to the design of walls will be found in *Shore Protection, Planning and Design* (Anon., 1966) and *Shore Management Guidelines* (Anon., 1971).

## Dunes

Where the wind is the agent which transports the sand, the general processes of sand movement are similar on beaches and in deserts. Bagnold (1941) and Kadib (1964) may be consulted on sand transport. The value of dunes as a barrier against wave attack has already been emphasized. Every effort must therefore be made to conserve dune areas both from winds, waves and currents and from man.

Savage and Woodhouse (1968) discuss the use of both sand fences and vegetation to encourage the growth of dunes and to prevent their erosion. Experiments have been carried out by the Beach Protection Authority of Queensland and others to determine the best type of vegetation for a given area, and to study the ways in which growth can be stimulated by the use of fertilizers. Dune grasses have proved extremely successful, and again illustrate the advantage of using natural methods of conservation. Unhappily, dune areas can be damaged by people using or crossing the dunes (see Goldsmith, Chapter 14). Vegetation is destroyed and wind erosion takes place. In addition, tracks through the dunes gradually form gullies which allow the sea to penetrate during times of storm, with resultant flooding. The remedy is to provide solid paths or planked walkways.

## Cliffs

In general, cliffs provide an effective barrier against short-term erosion. The material of which they are composed varies from soft easily eroded deposits to resistant rock. Several aspects of cliff erosion were discussed at a meeting chaired by Irving (1962). In many cases cliffs fail due to the hydrostatic pressures induced by water draining to the cliffs from the landward side. Fissured rocks may also fail due to frost action. A discussion of these aspects in relation to chalk cliffs may be found in Hutchinson (1971). Kemp (1972a) demonstrates that wave action must be carefully assessed in each case.

## CONTROL OF DEVELOPMENT

The attraction of the coast for recreation has resulted in many coastal areas being used for holiday residences. The fluctuating position of the shoreline from year to year or over longer periods of time has not always been recognized, and buildings have been erected on areas which are eventually overrun by the sea with consequent damage and loss. At this stage the erection of expensive sea walls and barriers is demanded, which often produce additional adverse effects. Just as rivers should be allowed to overrun their banks in times of flood, so should coastal areas be zoned to preclude urban development on the backshore. An estimate of the position of the set-back line is imperative, and could be based on the work of Purpura (in press).

## CONCLUSION

Coastal management requires an understanding of the processes at work, control of development, conservation of beach material and regional or national funds to implement both remedial measures and plans for future improvements.

## BIBLIOGRAPHY

Anon (1966). Shore Protection, Planning and Design (Third edition), U.S. Army Coastal Eng. Res. Center, Washington DC, *Tech. Rep. No.* 4, 40 pp.

Anon (1971). *Shore Management Guidelines* (1971). Dept. of the U.S. Army Corps of Engrs. Washington DC, 56 pp.

Anon (1971). *Shore Protection Guidelines* (1971). Dept. of the U.S. Army Corps of Engrs. Washington DC, 59 pp.

Caldwell, J. M. (1965). Coastal processes and beach erosion, *J. Boston Soc. Civ. Eng.*, **53**, 142–57 (also in the U.S. Army C.E.R.C. Report AD 652 025).

Deacon, G. E. R. (1964). Review of recent advances in physical oceanography, *Trans. Roy. Inst. Naval Arch.*, **106**, 27–38.

Ippen, A. T. (1966). *Estuary and Coastline Hydrodynamics*, McGraw-Hill, New York, 744 pp.

King, C. A. M. (1972). *Beaches and Coasts*, Second edn., Arnold, London, 570 pp.

Muir Wood, A. M. (1969). *Coastal Hydraulics*, Macmillan, London, 187 pp.

*Proceedings of the Coastal Engineering Conferences*, 1951—to date.

Rayner, A. C. (1964). *Land against the sea*, Dept. of the U.S. Army Corps of Engrs. Washington DC, *Rept. AD 453 227*, 43 pp.

Russell, R. C. H. (1960). Coast erosion and defence: nine questions and answers, *Hydraulic Research Stn. Paper* **3**, H.M.S.O., London, 14 pp.

Russell, R. C. H., and Macmillan, D. H. (1952). *Waves and Tides*, Hutchinson, London, 348 pp.

Wiegel, R. L. (1964). *Oceanographical Engineering*, Prentice Hall, Englewood Cliffs, 532 pp.

# REFERENCES

Anon (1972). Marine dredged sand for new beach, *Hydrospace,* August, Spearhead Publications, 1 p.

Bagnold, R. A. (1941). *The Physics of Blown Sand and Desert Dunes*, Methuen, London, 265 pp.

Bakker, W. T., and Joustra, Sj. D. (1970). The history of the Dutch coast in the last century, *Proc. 12th Coastal Eng. Conf.* **2**, Washington DC, 641–7.

Balsillie, J. H., and Berg, D. W. (In Press). State of groyne design and effectiveness, *Proc. 13th Coastal Eng. Conf.*, Vancouver, Paper T–26.

*Beach Conservation* (1971). Nos. 5 and 6, Beach Protection Authority of Queensland, Australia, 4 pp.

*Beach Conservation* (1972). No. 7, Beach Protection Authority of Queensland, Australia, 6 pp.

Beach Protection Authority (1969). *Annual Report*, Beach Protection Authority of Queensland, Australia, 12 pp.

Berg, D. W. (1968). Systematic collection of beach data, *Proc. 11th Coastal Eng. Conf.*, London, 273–97.

Bretschneider, C. L. (1952). The generation and decay of wind waves in deep water, *Trans. Amer. Geophys. Un.*, **33**, 381–9.

Caldwell, J. M. (1966). Coastal processes and beach erosion, *J. Boston Soc. Civ. Eng.*, **53**, 142–57 (also in the U.S. Army C.E.R.C. Report AD 652 025).

Carey, A. E. (1907). *The Protection of Sea Shores from Erosion*, Greening, London, 35 pp.

Cornish, Vaughan (1898). On sea beaches and sand banks, *Geog. J.* **11**, 528–43, 628–51.

Darbyshire, Mollie, and Draper, L. (1963). Forecasting wind-generated sea waves, *Engineering* (London), **195**, 482–4.

Deacon, G. E. R., Russell, R. C. H., and Palmer, J. E. G. (1957). Origin of long period waves in ports, *19th Intl. Navign. Congr. Paper 4*, C.L., London, 20 pp.

Draper, L. (1966). The analysis and presentation of wave data—a plea for uniformity, *Proc. 10th Coastal Eng. Conf.*, Tokyo, **1**, 1–11.

Draper, L. (In Press). Extreme wave conditions in waters surrounding the British Isles, *Proc. 13th Coastal Eng. Conf.*, Vancouver, BC, 1972, Paper T–15.

Dronkers, J. J., and Schoenfeld, J. C. (1955). Tidal computations in shallow water, *Proc. Amer. Soc. Civ. Eng.*, **81**, (WWI) separate paper 714, 48 pp.

Duvivier, J. (1947). Coast erosion, *Public Works, Roads and Transport Congr.*, London, 20 pp.

Eaton, R. O. (1951). Littoral processes on sandy coasts, *Proc. 1st Coastal Eng. Conf.*, Long Beach, Calif., 140–54.

Edelman, T. (1966). Systematic measurements along the Dutch coast, *Proc. 10th Coastal Eng. Conf.* Tokyo, **1**, 489–501.

Fairchild, J. C. (1966). Correlation of littoral transport with wave energy along the shores of New York and New Jersey, *U.S. Army Coastal Eng. Res. Center, Tech. Memo.* **18**, 35 pp.

Farquharson, W. I. (1953). Storm surges on the East Coast of England, *Inst. Civ. Eng. Conf. on the North Sea Floods*, I.C.E., London, 8 pp.

Francis, J. R. D. (1953). A note on the velocity distribution and bottom stress in a wind-driven water current system, *J. Marine Res.*, **12**, 93–8.

Gagliano, S. M., Kroon, H. J., and van Beck, J. L. (1970). Deterioration and restoration of coastal wetlands, *Proc. 12th Coastal Eng. Conf.*, Washington DC, pp. 1767–79.

Galvin, C. J. (1967). Longshore current velocity: a review of theory and data, *Rev. Geophys.*, **5**, 287–304.

Galvin, C. J. (1968). Breaker-type classification on three laboratory beaches, *J. Geophys. Res.*, **73**, 3651–9.

Hale, J. S. (In Press). Calculated sand fills and groyne systems, *Proc. 13th Coastal Eng. Conf.*, Vancouver, BC, 1972, Paper T–28.

Hall, J. V. (1952). Artificially nourished and constructed beaches, *Proc. 3rd Coastal Eng. Conf.* Cambridge, Mass., 119–36.

Hunt, I. A. (1961). Design of sea walls and breakwaters, *Trans. Amer. Soc. Civ. Eng.*, **126**, 542–70.

Hutchinson, J. N. (1971). Field and laboratory studies of a fall in Upper Chalk cliffs at Joss Bay, Isle of Thanet, *Proc. Roscoe Mem. Symp.*, Cambridge University, 692–3.

Inman, D. L., Komar, P. D., and Bowen, A. U. (1968). Longshore transport of sand, *Proc. 11th Coastal Eng. Conf.*, London, **1**, 298–306.

Irving, E. G. (Chairman) (1962). Coastal cliffs: Report of a symposium, *Geog. J.*, **128**, 303–20.

Jordaan, J. M. (1970). Study of Durban Harbour silting and beach erosion, *Proc. 12th Coastal Eng. Conf.*, Washington, DC, 1097–116.

Kadib, A.-L. (1964). Calculation procedure for sand transport by wind on natural beaches, *U.S. Army Coastal Eng. Res. Center, Misc. Paper* **2–64**, 25 pp.

Kemp, P. H. (1961). The relationship between wave action and beach profile characteristics, *7th Coastal Eng. Conf.*, The Hague, 262–77.

Kemp, P. H. (1962). A model study of the behaviour of beaches and groynes, *Proc. Instn. Civ. Engrs.*, **22**, 191–210.

Kemp, P. H. (1963). A field study of wave action on natural beaches, *Proc. 10th Int. Assn. Hydraul. Res. Congr.*, London, 131–7.

Kemp, P. H. (1972a). A coastal engineering survey in Kent, *J. Instn. Municipal Engrs.*, **99**, 289–95.

Kemp, P. H. (1972b). Optical wave recorders, *Dock & Harbour Auth.*, **53**, 177–8.

Kemp, P. H., and Plinston, D. T. (1968). Beaches produced by waves of low phase difference, *J. Hydraul. Div. (HY5) Proc. Amer. Soc. Civ. Eng.*, **94**, 1183–95.

Kramer, J. (In Press). Coastal protection by beach nourishment, *Proc. 13th Coastal Eng. Conf.*, Vancouver, BC, 1972, Paper T–31.

Longuet-Higgins, M. S. (1970). Longshore currents generated by obliquely incident sea waves, *J. Geophys. Res.*, **75**, 6778–801.

Mason, M. A. (1948). Ocean wave research and its engineering applications, *Ann. N.Y. Acad. Sci.*, **51**, 523–32.

Nichols, M. A. (1970). Coastal processes from space photography, *Proc. 12th Coastal Eng. Conf.*, Washington, DC, **2**, 641–7.

Owens, J. S., and Case, G. O. (1908). *Coast Erosion and Foreshore Protection*, St. Brides Press, London, 144 pp.

Pelnard-Considère, R. (1956). Essai de théorie de l'évolution des formes de rivage en plages de sable et de galets. Les energies de la mer, *Quatr. Journées de l'Hydralique*, **2**, 289–98.

Price, W. A., Tomlinson, K. W., and Willis, D. H. (In Press). Predicting the changes in the plan shape of beaches, *Proc. 13th Coastal Eng. Conf.*, Vancouver, Paper W–42.

Purpura, J. A. (In Press). Establishment of a coastal setback line, *Proc. 13th Coastal Eng. Conf.*, Vancouver, BC, Paper B–29.

Rance, R. J. (1966). Investigation of wind-induced currents and their effects on the performance of sea outfalls, *Proc. Instn. Civ. Engrs.*, **33**, 231–60.

Rance, P. J., and Warren, N. F. (1968). The threshold of movement of coarse materials in oscillating flow, *Proc. 11th Coastal Eng. Conf.*, London, **1**, 487–91.

Reid, R. O. (1956). Modification of the quadratic bottom stress law for turbulent channel flow in the presence of surface wind stress, *U.S. Army Beach Erosion Board. Tech Mem. 93*, 40 pp.

*Report of the Departmental Committee on Coastal Flooding* (1954). H.M.S.O., London.

*Royal Commission on Coast Erosion* (1907–11). H.M.S.O., London, 500 pp.

Savage, R. P., and Woodhouse, W. W. (1968). Creation and stabilisation of coastal barrier dunes, *Proc. 11th Coastal Eng. Conf.*, London, **1**, 671–700.

Saville, T. Jr. (1958). Wave run-up on shore structures, *Trans. Amer. Soc. Civ. Eng.*, **123**, 139–50.

*Shore Protection Programme* (1970). Dept. of the U.S. Army Office of Chief of Engrs., Washington DC, 10 pp.

Taylor, J. I. (In Press). Artificial beach nourishment in south-east England, *Proc. 13th Coastal Eng. Conf.*, Vancouver, BC, 1972, Paper T–30.

Wemelsfelder, P. J. (1954). The disaster in the Netherlands caused by the storm flood of February 1 1953, *Proc. 4th Coastal Eng. Conf.*, Berkeley, California, 256–71.

Zwamborn, J. A., Russel, K. S., and Nicholson, J. (In Press). Coastal engineering B.C. measurements, *Proc. 13th Coastal Eng. Conf.*, Vancouver, BC, 1972, Paper B–33.

# CHAPTER 5

# Managing the Hydrological Cycle

CELIA KIRBY and JOHN C. RODDA

Water supply and flood control are central issues in many resource management problems, but the management of water is far from a simple matter. Every year we find more and more uses for water, but until economic ways are found of converting salt to fresh water we have only a finite quantity to use, since there is no known way of increasing total precipitation.

Water arrives on the land surface as rain, hail, snow or one of the other forms of precipitation and then, by way of several intermediate processes, it is taken to the sea. The surface streams and underground channels flowing into the sea are not feeding an ultimate sink, since water evaporates from the sea to migrate again over the land masses as clouds. The cycle is complicated because water is evaporated from all surfaces, and water infiltrating down through the soil may become trapped in rock fissures, may enter the deep-lying water table before ultimately finding its way to the surface channels, or may be drawn up to the surface under the action of transpiration.

There are now parts of Britain where the increasing demand for water for domestic, industrial and agricultural purposes has reached the limits of local resources. To overcome this problem, local regional and indeed national water management has to consider what factors affect the water balance and how they operate. These factors need detailed and long-term investigation. Precipitation, evaporation, infiltration, surface run-off and storage in lakes and reservoirs both above and below ground have to be studied, not just to collect complete sets of records, but rather to investigate how the different phases of the hydrological cycle interact with each other and to determine the controlling or limiting factors. This is the essence of hydrology, the science of water as it occurs and moves in that part of the natural environment contained within the land masses. Climatic and geological influences mean that any studies of natural water movements are inevitably long term and inter-disciplinary.

In addition to problems of water supply, the hydrologist is periodically faced with problems of an unwanted surplus. The United Kingdom, with its plentiful but spatially unevenly distributed rainfall, has suffered so much from flooding that flood prediction still remains one of the most pressing problems facing British hydrologists (Hollis, Chapter 13). On a world scale, however, and certainly by the end of the century in this country, the main problem will be one of water shortage.

Water resource management is complicated not only by the variation in supplies and demands from day to day and season to season but also by the fact that water is available from several different sources—rivers, wells and reservoirs. Decisions have to be made about utilizing supplementary supplies when the demand cannot be met by one source alone, and this may involve the siting of new wells and reservoirs. Proposals for new reservoirs bring problems of choosing between alternative methods of land use as well as sociological problems. Hydrologists have to be involved in these issues since their findings about different hydrological responses should influence the choice of different land uses. In conjunction with agriculturalists, they can help to answer fundamental questions of how to determine the appropriate crop for a particular area.

Although few studies of the hydrological effects of land-use changes have been carried out in the United Kingdom, results from other parts of the world give some indication of the kind of answers to expect. For example, it is clearly established that the hydrological changes caused by converting a previously uninhabited region to subsistence farming can take place very rapidly and that they are difficult to reverse (UNESCO, 1972). The magnitude and distribution of river flows as well as the quality of the water can be altered radically. One of the most widely-known experiments on the effects of land-use change is the experiment at Coweeta in the United States reported by Hewlett and Hibbert (1965). Clear-felling of complete catchments, repeated after an interval of 23 years to allow the forest to regenerate, gave each time a much more irregular (flashier) river regime with a greatly increased sediment load.

Because this type of hydrological research is obviously long term, it is necessary to start the work well in advance of the demand for results. Careful planning and some degree of foresight are needed to anticipate gaps in knowledge about the effects of land-use change in hydrological terms.

The actual relations between changes in river flow and land use are difficult to establish, because records of climate, quality and quantity of river flows and details of land-use changes do not usually exist side by side. When available they are often incomplete because they have been obtained by different authorities with different objectives, and it is most unusual to find that a complete basin has been affected by a single land-use change. Standard hydrological information in the United Kingdom is at present collected from a countrywide network of rain gauges, river gauges, wells and climatic stations, the measurements being acquired by river authorities, water companies, the Meteorological Office and the Water Resources Board. This network gives a good background but can hardly answer fundamental questions such as what governs a basin's response to rainfall, or what are the factors that control the shape and magnitude of a stream flow hydrograph.* The quantity and quality of run-off vary in response to a number of environmental controls. For example, run-off response is related to the geomorphological characteristics of a basin, as has been shown quite frequently (Lull and Sopper, 1965), although the relationship is certainly not fully understood. For many years hydrologists have been mainly concerned to collect the information necessary to understand these processes by studying complete catchment areas of drainage basins. From this type of experiment it is hoped to define the processes involved in the relationships between such basic characteristics as area, slope and proportion of permeable and impermeable strata and the hydrological variables of precipitation, run-off, evaporation, transpiration and soil moisture storage.

The basic aim of a catchment experiment is to establish a water balance: to measure what comes in and what goes out, the differences between the two values being the amount of water stored or lost to evaporation. The Institute of Hydrology's experiment at Plynlimon in Mid-Wales (see Figure 5.1) is the most intensive catchment experiment in the United Kingdom at present. The headwater river basins of the Wye and the Severn are essentially identical in geological and geomorphological terms, but one is covered by extensive coniferous forest while virtually all of the other is used as sheep pasture. By instrumenting the two valleys intensively to record the variations in rainfall and other meteorological conditions and by monitoring very accurately the outflow in the two rivers, a precise water balance can be drawn up. The numerous problems invoved in studying this very wet and almost inaccessible area have unfortunately meant that the very early years of this experiment were largely concerned with overcoming the difficulties of instrumentation. To get the accuracy needed to detect the likely differences between the two valleys with their different vegetation cover (not expected to exceed a 20 per cent difference in run-off) meant that the instrumentation had to be refined and in some cases specially designed. The instrument networks are still being modified in the light of the early experimental results. A more detailed account of this experiment can be found in the Institute's annual reports (Institute of Hydrology, 1971; 1972).

Observations recorded in a natural system like a river basin can be no better than the instruments that are employed; there are few devices that can be matched to absolute standards since, for example, a polythene sheet cannot be spread over the whole basin to catch all the rain for measurement,

* The trace of volume against time.

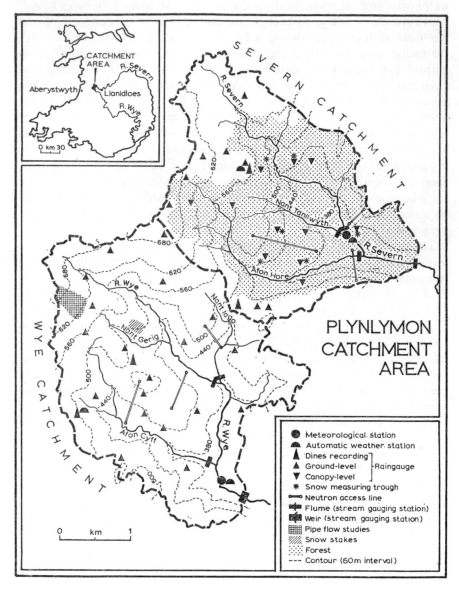

**Figure 5.1.** Map of the Institute of Hydrology's experimental catchments at Plynlimon in central Wales.

neither can all the water in a stream be caught. The measurement problems are minimized if attention is paid to adequate sampling patterns for rainfall and if streamflow measurements can be checked by independent methods. There will always remain the doubt as to whether or not the recorded values from a river basin contain a large range of experimental error.

Until a few years ago soil moisture was estimated as a 'by-difference' calculation in a water balance equation. This approach, forced upon hydrologists because of the lack of a measuring technique, neglected the role of the soil as the regulating mechanism between the input and output of a catchment. Now, with the refinement of the neutron scattering technique for determining soil moisture, this term in the water balance can be measured directly and seasonal and even daily fluctuations studied. Although used only as a research tool, the technique is particularly suitable for routine soil moisture measurements. Fast neutrons emitted from a radioactive source are slowed down in the soil by elastic collisions with the atomic nuclei in the soil matrix, predominantly by the hydrogen of the soil water, to produce 'slow' neutrons which can be counted. In dry soil the probability of collision is less and therefore the count rate is less (Bell and McCulloch, 1966).

The assessment of evaporation from a simple physical system such as the surface of a lake is a complex task, and to determine evaporation and transpiration from plants is even more difficult. Penman (1948) provided one of the most widely used methods for estimating both open-water evaporation and transpiration from well-watered growing vegetation. The method uses routine meteorological observations to estimate evaporation from open water and the ability of air to remove the water vapour thus produced. The result, modified by seasonal factors, provides an estimate of the sum of transpiration through plants and evaporation from the surface of the soil and wet foliage.

Streamflow is what is left after the evaporation demand and the soil deficit have been satisfied. A number of factors influence the possible precision of streamflow measurement, such as the hydraulic characteristics of the stream and the nature of the load it carries, the range of flows to be measured and the technique used to obtain the measurement. In addition to measuring flow by structures such as weirs and flumes, it is now possible to use chemical measuring techniques. Samples taken downstream of the injection point of a suitable dye of known concentration can be analysed and their dilution used to work out the flow of the stream (Water Research Association, 1970).

Field experiments in hydrology are not easy; the physical size of an experimental catchment, the problem of adequate and reliable data collection, coupled with the length of time necessary before valid conclusions can

4

be reached, combine to present hydrologists with a challenging task. Catchment* experiments are designed to evaluate the effects of land-use changes on water budgets, but strictly speaking all they can do is to give quantitative answers for a particular catchment from which it is reasonable to make qualitative statements about similar areas elsewhere; they cannot usually identify the detail of the processes involved nor the variables which exert the most influence in any given situation. To reach an understanding of these aspects, the hydrological cycle must be broken down into its components. The rate of evaporation from different surfaces, the part played by plants taking up water from the soil and releasing it to the atmosphere through transpiration, the rate of infiltration into the soil, the long-term storage and movement of water in underground aquifers and in the soil, are all areas where detailed study is still required. These kinds of questions are at last receiving the attention they deserve, as is shown by the complex experiment in Thetford forest in which the energetics of evaporation from a pine forest are being examined (Stewart and Oliver, 1972).

To be of use to society the hydrologist must try to apply the results of his field experiments to the prediction and forecasting of future river flows during both flood and drought conditions. The construction of mathematical models for this purpose is vital to better resource valuation. One difficulty with the mathematical modelling of natural systems is to avoid the assumption that the system is a closed one, in which the hydrograph is made up simply of a direct storm response† and base flow‡ and in which the intermediate processes are ignored. One can sympathize with those tempted to keep to this simple concept, for if no assumptions are made then the problem of prediction is virtually insolvable. The more assumptions that are made, the easier is the solution of the problem but also the greater the risk of failure of the model to reflect the true situation (Dooge, 1968). Nevertheless, even with its necessary assumptions, the mathematical model is one of the most useful tools that the scientist can offer, as several papers recording progress in modelling experimental catchments show (Edwards and Rodda, 1970; Mandeville *et al.*, 1970; Dickinson and Douglas, 1972). However, to make these models more flexible in operation in space and time, parameters with real physical meaning must be introduced. This is where the growing emphasis on studies of actual processes is relevant. The essence of hydrological modelling technique is constantly to refine the description of the relation between the inputs and outputs of hydrological systems.

---

* Areas draining to streams.

† Storm response is the effect of fairly intense rain falling in excess of the filtration capacity of the catchment.

‡ Base flow is the gravity discharge of groundwater to river channels.

## CURRENT STATE OF KNOWLEDGE ABOUT THE EFFECTS OF DIFFERENT LAND USES

### Forests

There is no scientific evidence for the widespread belief that the presence of forests is a direct cause of increased precipitation (Chandler, Chapter 2). The chief effect of forest cover from a hydrological point of view is that of increasing the interception of incoming precipitation (Leyton and Rodda, In press).

Compared with shorter vegetation, forest has a greater surface area for interception and evaporation of water and offers a better mechanism for the absorption of solar radiation and for the exchange of water vapour between foliage and the atmosphere. Where the soil is deep, it is likely that the trees will have a deep root network in which soil water can be stored and withdrawn for transpiration. The total annual water use is very dependent on the duration of growth and transpiration, so that where water is freely supplied, evergreen forests use substantially more water than deciduous forests, short season grasses or annual crops. If water is scarce and the soil is shallow, trees and other plants with similar rooting depth will reach wilting point at more or less the same time and there is obviously little difference in their use of water. There seems to be little doubt that forests have an important regulating effect on the pattern of streamflow, as is shown by the large number of papers making this point and a considerable amount of evidence summarized in a report on the influence of man on the hydrological cycle (UNESCO, 1972). When water is abundant, the free infiltration and temporary retention of water in the porous leaf litter and upper root zone have a major effect in reducing peak flows and recharging aquifers from which dry season flow is maintained. In most situations, however, it is the steepness of the terrain far more than the vegetation cover that exerts the major effect on the hydrological regime of an area. Where there is a surplus of water over requirements, the effect of forest on water yield of a catchment remains one merely of scientific interest. But if demands become more urgent, as is expected in the United Kingdom by the end of the century, then decisions will have to be taken on the relative merits of the economic and amenity values of forests as against their hydrological effects.

### Grasslands

In temperate climates, grass roots exploit only a half metre or less of the total soil depth; consequently, they are unable to produce a seasonal soil moisture deficit that extends to considerable depth in the profile. In modern agriculture, grass is treated as an important crop and is fed, grazed and cut for maximum yield. Grass-covered land has a high infiltration capacity and can give the soil a high degree of protection against erosion. There has been little study of the hydrological effects of grass in the United Kingdom, but experiments have been carried out in Georgia in the United States (Agricultural Research Service, 1963) and in New Zealand (Toebes *et al.*, 1968) on the difference in storm run-off from managed and unmanaged grazed grasslands. In the New Zealand experiment the control area (unmanaged) had the standard heavy sheep stocking typical of the district but no other treatment, while the treated pasture was contour furrowed and seeded with rye-grass and clover, and given a heavy application of fertilizer. Over a period of 18 years the treated pasture supported five times the number of sheep but produced no measurable storm flows. On the other hand, extreme storm events did produce flows from the control area, which over the years gave 30 times the total water yield, 500 times the total soil loss and one-fifth the number of sheep-grazing days. In Western Colorado, where the mean annual rainfall is eight inches, Lusby (1965) reports that the effect of excluding stock from grazing land was to decrease run-off by 20 per cent and decrease sediment flow by 18–54 per cent. Vegetation was not increased appreciably as a result of this protection, and the differences were thought to be due to the cessation of trampling by livestock; this was confirmed by penetrometer tests.

**Arable Lands**

The effect of replacing trees and shrubs with lower vegetation and with a shorter season of water use is to decrease evapotranspiration and consequently to increase run-off. Since the ecological climax vegetation usually consists of those species best adapted to make full use of whatever water supplies are available, the general effect of clearing for agriculture to produce such crops as cereals and roots is to create a surplus of water available as streamflow. When all the vegetation is removed for the preparation of a seed bed it can mean a loss in regulation of streamflow, and heavy rains can then produce immediate overland run-off (UNESCO, 1972). This is probably not important in the United Kingdom, but where it is a problem it can be avoided by cultivating along the contour. The adverse effects of arable farming on the hydrological behaviour of a basin, arising from the periodic removal of vegetation and sometimes excessive cultivation techniques, decreases as the standard of farming rises, for the dense foliage of a heavy crop stand provides excellent cover to protect the soil from rain, sun and wind, while the high volume of roots adds organic matter to the soil and this assists in the infiltration of rainfall.

The aim of good land use from both the agricultural productivity and the hydrological viewpoint is to increase soil moisture by encouraging good tilth, reducing surface run-off by maintaining high infiltration capacity and by preventing excessive soil erosion (Warren, Chapter 3).

## Urbanization

Replacing natural vegetation or farmland with the massive construction of a city or the more gradual advance of the urban front around an existing conurbation is perhaps the most drastic of all changes in land use. This subject is treated in some detail elsewhere in this volume (Hollis, Chapter 13).

In many countries rivers draining urban areas have become open sewers, a charge that still applies to many in Britain. While some may think this statement somewhat excessive, it is true that the dry weather flow of many British rivers consists largely of effluent from sewage works. The problem of water quality has been pushed into the limelight with growing public concern over the amenity value of our waterways. Apart from the public health and amenity problems of sewage dispersal, there is also the danger of eutrophication in slow-moving channels. The blame for this is usually laid at the door of agriculture because of its increasing use of nitrogenous fertilizers as demanded by modern intensive farming, much of which must surely find their way into the rivers—or so it has been suggested (*The Ecologist*, 1971). For their part, the agriculturalists point out that a fair quantity of nitrogen is present in normal seepage from uncultivated land and that the ploughing and cultivation of land would release more nitrogen even if no fertilizer was to be applied. What probably tips the balance towards eutrophication is the growing percentage of phosphates coming from sewage treatment plants, since phosphorus is an important limiting factor in the growth of the algal blooms which are the principal problem that arises from eutrophication.

## Groundwater

Half of the world's freshwater, excluding that bound up in the icecaps and glaciers, is to be found in the deep underground supplies. Although wells and springs have been used for generations, much of the technology of water supply has in Britain been concentrated on open water storage such as upland reservoirs or more recently as estuarine barrage schemes. Unfortunately, this has meant that deep aquifers have not received the attention they deserve, although recent studies have done much to reverse this position. Groundwater in large aquifers moves very slowly, so that water tables can be seen to represent a long-term equilibrium with the climate, in contrast to surface flows which respond to immediate weather conditions.

The general effects of land-use changes on groundwater levels arise from the changes in the use of water by the vegetation cover and from the deterioration of the rate of acceptance by the soil surface of infiltrating rainwater.

Thus in Australia (UNESCO, 1972) there has been a rise in the groundwater level following the clear-felling of forest and, conversely, trees planted in marshy areas tend to lower the water table, an effect which has been used successfully in Uganda for malaria control. There are also instances where over-grazing of hill slopes has produced semi-permanent flooding in valley bottoms because of the consequent rise in the water table.

In this country, the most serious concern with groundwater is over-pumping from boreholes which means that water is extracted faster than it can be replaced by natural recharge. This has already happened with extraction from the chalk aquifers below the London Basin, the water table having been lowered appreciably in several areas. It is now not uncommon for water extracted from some wells in East Anglia to be contaminated with salt, showing that the aquifers are being exploited to such an extent that the seawater/groundwater interface has moved inland (Guiver, 1972). Understanding the extent and movement of groundwater resources will become critical in the future as demand increases.

## PROBLEMS FOR THE FUTURE

Public water supply in this country has largely been dependent on water diverted out of the river system at upland storage sites and conveyed from there in aqueducts. Improved treatment techniques have made it possible to abstract water from much lower down the river channels and this has helped to meet the increased demands of recent years (Rydz, 1972). Some rivers, however, are still too polluted for use as a source of potable water. It is this aspect of water resource management that is receiving so much political attention at present because pollution problems can only be overcome at high cost and with the support of strong public opinion to secure the enactment and enforcement of legislation.

Inevitably we shall continue to compromise by using some 'new' and some 'second-hand' water; by both storing and re-use. This is because there is still insufficient knowledge of the extent and precise location of much of our natural water, and although we know in general terms the hydrological impact of specific land-use practices, we are still only groping towards an understanding of how these interact in real situations to affect sediment load, peak discharges and surface run-off.

Many administrators, already concerned about the difficulties of meeting existing water demands, suggest that the future demand for supplies will only be met if the current price of water to the consumer is increased tenfold. Meanwhile, the awareness of the threat to water supplies has at last provoked intensive study of the hydrological cycle, the main outcome of which has been to reveal that it is much more involved than might have been thought. One thing is clear: this type of research has considerable significance for engineers concerned with water and for planners and conservationists, since the results of research may be translated into conclusions and predictions which can provide the basis for management decisions in the future.

## BIBLIOGRAPHY AND REFERENCES

Agricultural Research Service (1963). Hydrologic data for experimental agricultural watersheds in the United States 1956–59, *U.S. Dept. of Agric., Misc. Publication, No.* **945,** 611 pp.

Bell, J. P., and McCulloch, J. S. G. (1966). Soil moisture estimation by the neutron scattering method in Britain, *J. Hydrology,* **4,** 254–63.

Chorley, R. J. (ed.) (1969). *Water, Earth and Man,* Methuen, London, 588 pp.

Dickinson, W. T., and Douglas, J. R. (1972). A conceptual runoff model for the Cam catchment, *Inst. of Hydrol. Report,* **17,** 44pp.

Dooge, J. C. I. (1968). The hydrologic cycle as a closed system, *Bull. Int. Ass. sci. Hydrol.,* **13,** 58–68.

*The Ecologist* (1971). Blueprint for survival, *The Ecologist,* **2,** 44 pp.

Edwards, K. A., and Rodda, J. C. (1970). A preliminary study of the water balance of a small clay catchment, *J. Hydrology (NZ),* **9,** 202–18.

Guiver, K. (1972). Chemical characteristics of underground chalk water in Essex and Suffolk. *J. Soc. Water Treatment and Examination,* **21,** 30–40.

Hewlett, J. D., and Hibbert, A. R. (1965). Factors affecting response of small watersheds to precipitation in humid areas, *Proc. Inter. Symp. on Forest Hydrol.,* National Science Foundation, Pennsylvania State Univ., 279–90.

Institute of Hydrology (1971). *Record of Research 1970–71,* Institute of Hydrology, Wallingford, Berks., 54 pp.

Institute of Hydrology (1972). *Research 1971–72,* Institute of Hydrology, Wallingford, Berks., 67 pp.

Leyton, L., and Rodda, J. C. (In Press). Precipitation and forests, *Forest Influences and Watershed Management,* Paper presented at FAO/USSR International Symposium, Moscow.

Lull, H. W., and Sopper, W. E. (1965). Predictions of average annual and seasonal streamflow of physiographic units in the northeast, *Proc. Inter. Symp. on Forest Hydrology,* National Science Foundation, Pennsylvania State Univ., 507–20.

Lusby, G. C. (1965). Causes of variations in runoff and sediment yield from small drainage basins in Western Colorado, *USDA Agricultural Research Service, Misc. Publications,* **970,** 94–8.

Mandeville, A. N., O'Connell, P. E., Sutcliffe, J. V., and Nash, J. E. (1970). River flow forecasting through conceptual models: part III, the Ray Catchment at Grendon Underwood, *J. Hydrology,* **2,** 109–28.

More, W. L., and Morgan, C. W. (eds.) (1969). Effects of watershed changes in streamflow, *Water Resources Symp. No. 2,* US Center for Research in Water Resources, Texas, 289 pp.

Penman, H. L. (1948). Natural evaporation from open water, bare soil and grass, *Proc. Roy. Soc. (A),* **193,** 120–48.

Rydz, B. (1972). New water—or second-hand, *J. Soc. Water Treatment and Examination,* **21,** 182–6.

Smith, K. (1972). *Water in Britain*, Macmillan, London, 241 pp.

Stewart, J. B., and Oliver, Sylvia (1972). Evaporation studies at Thetford, Norfolk, in: Taylor, J. A. (ed.), *Research Papers in Forest Hydrology*, Aberystwyth Symp. 91–9.

UNESCO (1972). Influence of man on the hydrological cycle: guidelines to policies for safe development of land and water resources, in: *Status and Trends of Research in Hydrology 1965–74*, UNESCO, Paris, 31–70.

Toebes, C., Scar, F., and Yates, M. F. (1968). Effects of cultural changes on Makara Experimental Basin, *Bull. Int. Ass. Sci. Hydrol.*, **13,** 95–122.

Water Research Association (1970). River flow measurement by dilution gauging, *Water Research Assoc. Technical Paper*, **74,** 85 pp.

# B Biological Systems

# CHAPTER 6

# The Ecological Basis for Conservation

F. B. O'Connor

## ATTITUDES AND AIMS IN CONSERVATION

Pollution and despoliation of the environment are becoming of increasing concern to our society; private individuals, industry and public bodies are becoming aware of some of the dangers in an economic system based on the exploitive use of resources and of the possibility that human population growth might outstrip the capacity of food production systems.

Ecologists and conservationists are increasingly in demand as specialists who can advise on how to protect the environment. The boards of nationalized industry, statutory bodies, new town authorities, local government authorities as well as private industry and developers are actively seeking advice on an increasing scale for the conservation or restoration of natural systems. Both the developed and developing countries are considering production systems based upon so-called ecological principles and are concerned for the stability of the environment in the face of the increasing needs of human populations for space, food and recreation.

Demands upon conservationists and ecologists have led to a pressing need for a precise statement of what ecologists can and cannot do and a clearer definition of the basic aims of conservation. There is a considerable lack of appreciation in the minds of the public both about the potential of ecologists to give useful advice and about the potential and limitations of natural systems for a range of uses. There is also a degree of suspicion about the aims of conservationists: they are all too frequently regarded as a minority sectarian interest concerned with protection rather than progress (Moore, 1968).

It is hardly a matter for surprise that problems of communication exist when, for many years, practical conservationists have avoided the definition of their basic aims, both in terms of what should be conserved and in terms of an organized management philosophy. It is worth examining some of the reasons for this imprecision. In Britain, but less so in America, the conservationist movement was founded on a basis of concern about the disappearance of natural habitats and the increasing rarity of interesting and beautiful species of plants and animals. This history has had two consequences. Firstly, there has been a failure to separate either the objectives or the methodology of species conservation from those of habitat conservation. Secondly, the concentration of effort upon the acquisition and protection of rare or restricted species or areas of land has given conservationists an image of self-indulgence in at least some sectors of the public mind.

This introduction to the management of biological systems will attempt to formulate a more precise statement of the aims and philosophy of conservation and to arrive at useable working hypotheses upon which the management of biological systems can be based.

The development of attitudes underlying the practice of conservation has paralleled the development of ecology. In the early part of this century ecologists were mainly concerned with describing events at the level of individual plants or animals and with their distribution in relation to environmental factors. From this, at least in the field of animal ecology, grew a concern with numbers and their regulation. Only a few ecologists (Clements, 1928; Tansley, 1929, 1935; Elton, 1935) were concerned primarily with the community or ecosystem as a structural and functional ecological unit. These, and other workers, progressed towards an appreciation of the ecosystem (or community) as the highest unit in ecological study and as a central theme within which ecological knowledge of the individual or species populations could be integrated. Two main schools of thought about the study of ecosystems have emerged: the system may be regarded as the result of interactions between its component parts and as being capable of study by a divisive approach (Lindemann, 1942); or it is possible to regard the ecosystem as a single entity, reacting as a whole to external impacts (Margalef, 1969).

From the point of view of the conservationist it is important to consider which level of ecological study is the most useful guide to the practical management of biological systems. In order to do this, it is necessary first to consider the aims of conservation. Four main categories of aim are apparent.

(i) *Species conservation.* This stems from the early foundations of ecology, and is a concern for the protection of rare, interesting or beautiful species.

(ii) *Habitat conservation.* The maintenance of representative habitat types over a range of climatic and edaphic conditions has gained considerable importance in the minds of conservationists during the last twenty years or so. A range of habitats provides reference points against which changes imposed by man can be measured, a set of sites where research into the functioning of natural systems can be carried out, and, incidentally, it often provides sites where rare species can survive. Within the framework of habitat conservation populations of single species may be the object of management when their numbers become either too low for successful breeding or too high in relation to the resources of the environment.

(iii) *Conservation as an attitude to land use.* Few areas of natural habitat remain in developed countries, where most of the land surface has been or is being used. In this context, the aim is to provide an input to land-use planning and management so that the demands of people upon natural systems can be balanced against their ability to support them. In the context of the national need for a viable agricultural economy, and the inevitability of urban and industrial development, the conservationist must seek to influence the direction of change and the choice of sites in order to minimize the disruption or destruction of natural systems. The conservationist has a positive role to play in planning and management for less intensive uses of the countryside such as nature conservation, forestry and recreation. In these spheres the matching of sites with demands is more amenable to influence by ecological considerations than in urban or intensive agricultural settings, where economic considerations are often of overriding importance.

It is in the field of land-use planning and management that ecologists are called upon to make judgments about the responses of biological systems to a range of kinds and intensities of use, and it is also in this field that ecologists are most frequently at the limits of their own knowledge. This is the field of greatest opportunity and greatest challenge.

(iv) *Creative conservation.* Large-scale modification of the landscape by, for example, reclamation of land from the sea, motorway construction and extractive mineral workings provides new and unusual opportunities for conservation.

## THE RELATIONSHIPS BETWEEN ECOLOGY AND CONSERVATION

Having identified the main classes of aim in conservation, and the main levels of ecological enquiry, the two can now be related.

(i) *Species conservation.* Management at this level requires a detailed knowledge of the environmental factors which determine the occurrence and distribution of the species concerned. For example its requirements for light, minerals, water, temperature and space need to be defined for each stage in its life-cycle. Deductions can then be made about the vulnerability of the species to external influences in terms of its physical and biotic environment. Species conservation can be sub-divided into a concern for rare species as such, or for the greatest possible variety of species. Both attitudes lead to a management policy based upon habitat fragmentation. Areas of often only a few square feet in extent may be set aside for the benefit of a particular orchid or butterfly. A corollary of this is that the area may become fragile and readily subject to change, generated both internally by successional progress and externally by immigrations of plants and animals or by human activities. Because of this susceptibility, management costs are high and restriction of access may become necessary. Valid arguments in favour of this approach to conservation include the maintenance of a 'gene pool' of potentially useful species (Berry, Chapter 7), the educational or aesthetic value of an area of diverse habitats, or the supposed right of all species to survive. Most of these requirements are, however, better satisfied within a framework of habitat conservation.

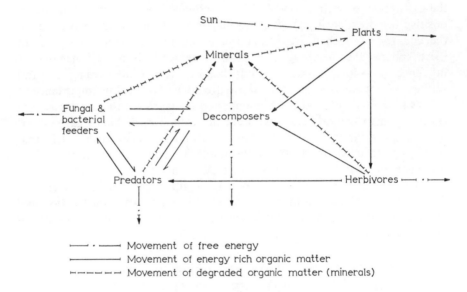

**Figure 6. 1.** Generalized energy and organic matter paths in ecosystems. Ideally, knowledge such as this should form the basis for management; but the knowledge is difficult and time consuming to collect.

(ii) *Habitat conservation.* The development of ecological thinking from autecological studies of species towards an holistic approach to the eco‑ system combined with the notions of vegetational succession have led to a swing of attitudes towards habitat conservation. The mainstay of the Nature Conservancy's Nature Reserve acquisition policy has been, and still is, the creation and maintenance of a series of habitats which represent the range of naturally occurring ecosystem types in Britain (Blackmore, Chapter 27).

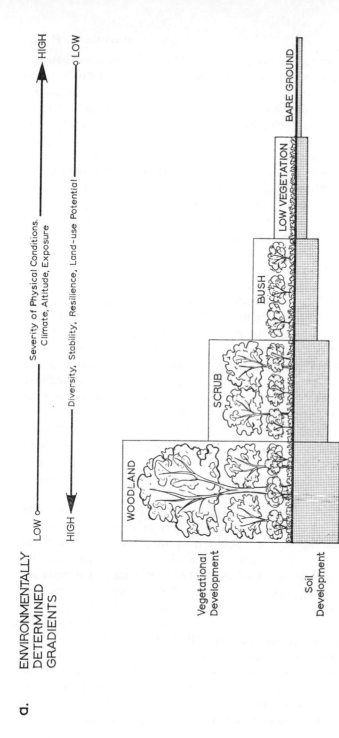

**Figure 6. 2.** Gradients of environmental severity and land-use intensity related to various ecosystem properties along a successional sequence. Generalized knowledge about these processes can be used effectively when management is urgently needed.

Because of the relative paucity of truly natural biological systems in Britain, an important major aim of management policy must be to assist natural processes towards a reconstruction of characteristic climatic or edaptic climaxes. In parallel with this notion, and in some cases confused with it, is a desire to conserve a number of biological systems which reflect the interaction between land-use practices and natural phenomena, notably on chalk grassland and lowland heaths. Habitat conservation is based upon a knowledge of the direction, rate and nature of energy flow and of the cycles of building and decay which underlie seral change. The ecosystem can be regarded from two points of view. Firstly, it is possible to consider events within a particular system in terms of processes indicated in Figure 6.1. This implies a divisive approach in which the various components of the system are examined separately and a view of the ecosystem constructed from a knowledge of events within and between its component parts. The alternative view, derived from successional theory, is concerned with the response of whole ecosystems to internally or externally generated changes in environmental conditions. Figure 6.2 illustrates the main kinds and directions of such changes. Two distinct kinds of gradient are apparent. Figure 6.2, legend a, indicates a sequence of vegetative types in which the structural characteristics are determined by the interaction between environmental conditions and biological phenomena. Figure 6.2, legend b, illustrates a sequence which, though similar in structural characteristics, results from the interaction of imposed land-use systems and the biological properties of climax vegetation.

Embodied in Figures 6.1 and 6.2 are two distinct approaches to the conservation and practical management of biological systems. The philosophy underlying Figure 6.1 is that a sufficiently detailed knowledge of the nature, direction and rates of the processes of energy flow and mineral cycling will enable the informed ecologist to predict the effects upon the whole system of changes imposed upon any part of it. While this notion is academically satisfying and no doubt true, there are severe practical difficulties involved in its realization. The work of the International Biological Programme for the study of productivity and human welfare has involved the detailed investigation of a range of ecosystems in many parts of the world along these lines. It is a salutary thought that some forty or so people have now devoted about five years, equivalent to 200 man-years, to the study of a single hectare of mixed deciduous woodland in the English Lake District. It is now possible, for this wood, to put quantitative values to most of the pathways in Figure 6.1, and we are within sight of a static, descriptive model of events in this wood. However, there is no basis yet for any statements of a predictive kind upon which a management policy for this or other woodlands could be based. Thus, although the model in Figure

6.1 has the great virtue that it provides a framework within which most kinds of ecological knowledge can be integrated and used to contribute to an understanding of ecosystem function, it does not contribute much towards the informed management of biological systems. Were the objective simply to provide and maintain a set of representative community types, primarily for their wildlife interest, this might not matter for here the main concern of the conservationist is to allow natural phenomena to take their course, and management intervention is either unnecessary or desirable only insofar as it assists in the restoration of a system to its natural state. But when the objective is to maintain land-use systems for their biological interest, or more importantly as a basis for advice on the kinds and levels of use which a given system can sustain, the deficiencies of the approach implied in Figure 6.1 become apparent. These deficiencies stem firstly from the inadequacy of present knowledge, and secondly from the length of time required for research to provide the knowledge.

The alternative approach is based upon the more readily observable response of whole ecosystems to external pressures. Responses can be studied at any level of detail, ranging from the simple structural description of the vegetation, through various levels of complexity in terms of the species composition of both plants and animals, to measures of relative or absolute abundance of populations. Several important characteristics of ecosystems underlie this approach to conservation or management based upon an holistic view. Figure 6.2, legend a, indicates the well-known phenomenon of structural simplification and reduction in species diversity in response to increasing severity of environmental conditions. This is a matter for observation and is well documented by Tansley (1929; 1935) for example. A number of important phenomena are associated with this sequence of structural and species diversity. Elton (1958; Elton and Miller, 1954) has gathered together a variety of evidence indicating that a high degree of diversity is associated with high internal stability. Structurally diverse systems also appear to be more resilient and to have a greater capacity for self-restoration following damage than do naturally simpler ones. Consequently, the range of opportunity for a variety of land uses is greater at the diverse end of the sequence and the probability of irreversible damage through over-intensive or inappropriate use least. The response of a structurally diverse system to a gradient in intensity of use is illustrated in Figure 6.2, legend b. There are close parallels between the characteristics of a naturally occurring climatic or altitudinal gradient and a land-use gradient. The main difference lies in the capacity of the simplified land-use systems to restore themselves to a state of increased diversity when management is relaxed.

In applying these ideas, it is necessary to distinguish between management for wildlife interest and ecologically based land management for other purposes. In the former case, the emphasis will be upon the management cost incurred in maintaining a structurally simple system against the natural tendency to return to a more complex state, while in the latter, the main concern will be with the dynamic relationships between the intensity of use and the ability of the system to sustain that use. In both cases, land management can be based on an empirical approach in which a particular treatment can be applied with broadly predictable results, though the details of processes involved in the response may be imperfectly understood. This has been, and still is in many cases, the basis of much agricultural practice. Its greatest virtue is that it is capable of producing results quickly.

Such an approach, whether applied to wildlife management or to the more general aspects of conservation, sets a considerable premium upon the definition of the desired result. Thus, for example, the development of methods for maintaining a chalk grassland sward by cutting instead of grazing requires a definition of the valued characteristics of chalk grassland and a means of measuring the extent to which a given management regime achieves the desired result. Similar problems exist in estimating the capacity of a biological system for recreational use. While it is clear in general terms that the system will change towards simplicity in response to increasing intensity of use, the question of how far it should be allowed to go is not easily answered from ecological principles alone.

In spite of difficulties of this kind, the approach based upon ecosystem response provides a set of hypotheses which are readily subject to experimental testing and which are capable of providing predictive models of a kind which land managers can apply. Regression models, derived from experimental studies, can be used to relate the degree of attainment of a particular result with the intensity of a use or treatment.

The foregoing discussion has distinguished between two approaches to habitat conservation. The first, involving a detailed knowledge of the internal functioning of ecosystems, is unlikely to provide solutions to management problems in the very near future. The alternative, based upon an empirical evaluation of the results of management practices, is less satisfying academically but seems more likely to provide usable pragmatic solutions in the short term.

Embodied in the whole concept of habitat conservation outlined above is a notion that, provided the habitat is correctly managed, the species complex normally associated with it is also likely to be favoured. There is, however, a field in which the object of management is legitimately a single species population, and there are a number of well-known cases where management at the population level is a necessary device for ensuring habitat stability. Notable examples are to be found amongst grazing animals such as red deer in this country and a range of herbivorous mammals in

Africa (Jewell, Chapter 12). The large herbivores seem to lack innate mechanisms for population regulation, and when external controls such as predators are removed, their numbers tend to increase to pest proportions and habitat destruction follows as an inevitable consequence. At this level of conservation management, the ecological information required is at the population rather than the ecosystem level.

A further caveat to the holistic approach to ecosystem response arises in relation to the effect of pollutants. It is a matter for debate which of the two kinds of models indicated above is most appropriate for an analysis of the qualitative and quantitative effects of pollutants and, more importantly, which approach can best be used to indicate acceptable levels of pollution (Moore, Chapter 15). While the effects of a pollutant can clearly be measured in terms of structural simplification of biological systems, this is less clearly so when the toxicity of a pesticide residue in the soil is considered. The effect may be in terms of changes in numbers of one or a few species, and its seriousness can only be judged in terms of the contribution of that species to the overall functioning of the system. It appears that, at this level, there is no substitute for a detailed knowledge of the internal functioning of the system.

(iii) *Conservation as an attitude to land use.* In a situation, common to most of Western Europe, where much of the land surface is intensively used, there is a shortage of land upon which wildlife conservation can be practised for its own sake. It is therefore necessary to consider how conservation interests can be incorporated into other activities or, in an extreme case, how land or water of low present value can be modified to create or re-create ecological interest.

Within land used for upland grazing, forestry, agriculture or recreation, there is scope for the maintenance and development of wildlife interest as a secondary land use. Even in urban and industrial areas, there is scope for wildlife conservation in parks and recreational areas and on land reclaimed from industrial dereliction (Goodman, Chapter 16).

The ecological basis for conservation as a secondary land use is similar to that for habitat conservation outlined above, but some problems of a social kind are also involved. Here the aim is to conserve wildlife as a component of a land-use system, or in the fragmentary remains of semi-natural systems amidst highly modified derivatives.

All biological systems, however severely modified or however small, will have some interesting wildlife content. In evolving a policy for maintaining or enhancing such interest, it is important to attribute a value to ecologically interesting features. At least some land managers are sympathetic towards the ideas of wildlife conservation and are prepared to make concessions in this direction. However, ecologists are frequently unable to make an objective statement of either the relative or still less the absolute value of ecological features. It would, for example be useful to assess the value of conifer plantations thinned at different ages or of hedges, copses and ponds amidst intensive agriculture. Research in this field of evaluation is limited and no clear methodology exists. It is not the intention here to examine those attempts which have been made in any detail, but rather to consider some general problems in development of a workable methodology.

There are both conceptual and methodological advantages in making the clearest distinction between ecological and conservation value. The former can be based upon the observable characteristics of a particular site of biological system, while the latter must include information about demands, economic and social benefits and about ecological value in relation to value for other purposes. While these two kinds of evaluation are complementary in application, the former is more clearly the concern of the ecologist, and hence the present discussion will be limited to the problems of ecological evaluation. The aim of an ecological evaluation is presumably to provide, in a concise and generally comprehensible way, a quantitative statement of the worth which a competent ecologist attributes to a particular biological system. There are considerable problems involved in the realization of this apparently simple aim. Of central importance is the question of the land unit upon which evaluations are to be made, and there seem to be two main categories. In some cases the unit of study will be a habitat type of a land-use system, such as forest, moorland or orchard, and the objective will be to place several examples of a particular type on a scale of values or to evaluate the effects of modification of management within a particular example. In such cases the criteria for evaluation are best derived from the ideas of habitat conservation. The vertical stratification of the vegetation, the diversity of species, the areal extent and the nature of the perimeter, provide readily understood and easily measured parameters and there is a good measure of agreement among ecologists about their usefulness in this context. Rarity of the kind of biological system is also a useful criterion, since clearly if a woodland is the only one of its kind in an area, it is more valuable than if it is only one of several similar features.

In other cases the centre of interest will be in the landscape as a whole and the mosaic of elements of which it is made. Here the objective of evaluation will be to ascribe comparative values to land areas containing different mixtures of biological features and the unit of study will be an area, either chosen arbitrarily as a grid square on a map or in relation to some administrative or ownership boundary. Difficulties arise in such situations since there is no obvious way of placing such different features as ponds, streams and hedges on a comparable scale of value. There are also difficulties in integrating information about the ecological quality of individual habitat features with the quality of the land area as a whole. It is not easy to say, for example, how many ponds with scanty fauna and flora are equivalent to one with a well-developed community. Nor is it easy to make an objective statement about the relative value of a single large woodland and ten small pieces of woodland of the same total size. There is an element of subjective judgment involved in the selection of the criteria upon which judgments of the value of an area should be based. It is not clear whether universally applicable criteria are available, or whether each land area must be treated as a special case. There is little evidence to indicate whether a complete survey of a land area is more useful than some kind of random sampling method. Nor is it yet clear to what extent criteria derived from established ecological principles provide a better basis for value judgment than the collective views of experienced naturalists that a particular area of habitat is valuable from their point of view.

In evaluating habitats, it is possible to envisage a number of indices of ecological value in which a numerical notation is ascribed to habitat features on the basis of the number of vertical strata present in the vegetation and the number of plant and animal species present. Notations for extent and rarity are not difficult to devise. Such indices may be additive or multiplicative and can provide a concise and objective statement about the characteristics of a habitat. Evaluations for larger areas can be derived from a set of habitat evaluations by incorporating weightings for particular kinds of habitat according to the proportion of the land area which they occupy. There are many elements of uncertainty in the field of ecological evaluation and research is in its early stages. Nonetheless, ecologists have a responsibility to provide an input to planning processes. The precision of this input can only be improved by a process of successive approximation starting from the kind of working hypothesis outlined above.

(iv) *Creative conservation.* Recent years have witnessed a dramatic and progressive increase in the scale upon which man is capable of modifying the landscape. Reclamation of land from the sea, reservoir and motorway construction and new city development have created spheres in which conservationists have a twofold role. In some cases it will be desirable to influence the course of development in order to protect wildlife interest. Judgments will rest on both a knowledge of the ecological conditions of the development area and of their value in relation to sites of similar kind elsewhere. There will be a considerable premium upon the accuracy of the ecological information provided, since decisions about wildlife protection will need to be made in competition with other land uses. In other cases, developments of many kinds will provide opportunities for the creation of new wildlife interest. Motorway construction, land reclamation from the sea and the aftermath of extractive mining frequently leave large areas of land where it is desirable to create new biological systems for both amenity and wildlife conservation. In these situations the ecologist is required to provide information about the kinds of habitat most appropriate for a particular area and also to provide a prescription for creating them (Goodman, Chapter 16). Predictions about the kinds of habitat which a given area will support are relatively easy to make by analogy with the known relationships of biological systems with climatic and edaphic conditions. However, the creation of the systems presents greater problems. In some cases it will be acceptable to allow the natural processes of succession to take their course, in others it will be desirable to speed up or redirect these processes towards a specified aim. As Harper (1970) points out, the well-tried techniques of the agronomist and horticulturist have more to offer in this respect than has the ecologist. There is a considerable need for the kind of refined knowledge about the relationships between species composition, edaphic conditions and management for wild species of plants that is avaliable for grass mixtures in managed pasture. These aspects of conservation again present a field for important and fruitful research.

## REFERENCES

Clements, F. E. (1928). *Plant Succession and Indicators*, Wilson, New York, 577 pp.
Elton, C. S. (1935). *Animal Ecology*, 2nd edn., Sidgwick and Jackson, London, 209 pp.
Elton, C. S. (1958). *The Ecology of Invasions by Animals and Plants*, Methuen, London, 181 pp.
Elton, C. S., and Miller, R. S. (1954). The ecological survey of animal communities with a practical system of classifying habitats by structural characteristics, *J. Ecol.*, **42**, 460–96.
Harper, J. L. (1970). Grazing, fertilizers and pesticides in the management of grasslands, in: (eds.) E. Duffey and A. S. Watt, *The Scientific Management of Animal and Plant Communities for Conservation*, Blackwell, Oxford, pp. 15–31.
Lindeman, R. L. (1942). The trophic-dynamic aspect of ecology, *Ecology*, **23**, 399–418.
Margalef, R. (1969). Diversity and stability; a practical proposal and a model of interdependence, in: *Diversity and Stability in Ecological Systems, Brookhaven Symp. Biol.*, **22**, 25–37.
Moore, N. W. (1968). Experience with pesticides and the theory of conservation, *Biol. Cons.*, **1**, 201–7.
Tansley, A. G. (1929). Succession, the concept and its value, *Proc. Int. Cong. Plant Sci. (Ithaca)*, **1**, 677–86.
Tansley, A. G. (1935). The use and abuse of vegetational concepts and terms, *Ecology*, **16**, 284–307.

CHAPTER 7

# Conserving Genetical Variety

## R. J. BERRY

Under the heading of 'The Reasons for Conservation', Charles Elton (1958) pointed to six pieces of evidence which showed that simple ecological situations are less stable and more liable to violent fluctuations than more complex ones:

1. Mathematical simulation of the properties of food-chains and simplified laboratory experiments in very simple population systems show strong oscillations and often extinction.
2. If the habitat in these model situations is given additional structural properties so that prey can dodge and hide, there may be some lessening of this instability.
3. Natural habitats on small islands seem to be much more vulnerable to invading species than those on continents. This is especially true of oceanic islands which have small numbers of indigenous species.
4. Invasions and outbreaks of disease often happen on cultivated and planted land, i.e. in habitats and communities simplified in three main ways by man:
   (a) by the encouragement of crops of foreign plants that do not have a full fauna attached to them;
   (b) by growing these in a partial or complete monoculture;
   (c) by trying to kill all other species thought to be harmful.
5. Such outbreaks do not seem to take place in species-rich tropical forests.
6. Orchards not treated with insecticide achieve an ecological stability amongst their hundred or more species of animals. The explosions of pests in orchards have been due partly to new invasions from without, partly to the numerous accidents and interactions that afflict any animal community, but most importantly to the upsetting of the relationships between pests and their natural enemies through the differential effects of the poisons used to control pests.

Elton concluded that one of the chief aims of conservation should be the retention or replacement in the landscape of the greatest possible ecological variety. He called this the 'conservation of variety' and this has now become part of accepted conservation practice.

Yet there is another and less obvious meaning to the 'conservation of variety'. Just as agricultural practices have resulted in the simplification of ecosystems, so they have led to the selection and spread of a relatively small number of animal breeds and crop varieties. This concentration on a few types has led to questions being asked about the possible loss of valuable genes (i.e. ones for disease resistance or growth rate), particularly with the progressive destruction of the wild or primitive forms from which the economically important forms arose (e.g. Frankel and Bennett, 1970). Consequently, there is a need to consider the conservation of intra-specific or genetical variety, as well as the inter-specific sort discussed by Elton. This essay is concerned solely with genetical conservation: the problems and practice of the inter-specific (Eltonian) variety are those of ecology in general; the rules and limits combine the results of ecology with those of population genetics.

## IS GENETICAL CONSERVATION A REAL PROBLEM?

We generally assume that the genetical constitution of a population or species is to all extents fixed. After all, genetical change, being effectively synonymous with evolution, is usually said to be a geological not an ecological event. But this assumption is wrong: there are many known examples of rapid genetical change, many of them the direct or indirect result of man's activities.

### 1. Direct Consequences of Pollution

Undoubtedly the best known example of any recent genetical change is the spread of melanic forms of trunk-sitting, cryptically coloured moths over the last 120 years, involving over 100 species in Britain alone. This has happened only in areas where the fall-out from smoke pollution has changed the background upon which the moths sit (Kettlewell, 1961). Nevertheless, industrial melanics also occur in other groups: there is a melanic form of the spider *Salticus scenicus* (Clerck) confined to Stockport Gasworks, and one of *Arctosa perita* (Latr.) which seems to occur only on colliery spoil heaps in Warwickshire and Licestershire; and the melanic ladybirds which are also found are largely confined to industrial areas.

### 2. Pesticide Application

We are becoming increasingly aware of 'pest' species that develop an inherited resistance to chemical poisons: house-flies in different parts of the world have independently become less susceptible to DDT control, as have at least eight species of mosquitoes, including the more important carriers of malaria; reports have appeared of organophosphorus resistance in the house-fly, in several mosquito species, in blow-flies and in aphids; strains of mice and rats resistant to Warfarin are known from both Britain and Europe; penicillin-resistant staphylococci can be a major problem in hospitals, while resistant gonococci are aggravating social problems; and inherited resistance to myxomatosis in rabbits is believed to occur. This list could be extended considerably. In all cases, resistance appears to have arisen as a chance mutation which has been able to spread rapidly under conditions where an environmental change has produced strong selection against the normal susceptible form.

## 3. Incidental Results of Man's Activities

(a) New selection pressures can be set up with the release of unusual or new chemical substances into the environment. For example, there is a growing problem with the increasing introduction of new drugs, which may :

(i) be toxic to particular people (e.g. sensitivity to the antimalarial drug primaquine in persons lacking the enzyme glucose-6-phosphate dehydrogenase; or to barbiturates in sufferers from some sorts of porphyria);

(ii) produce potentially dangerous side-effects, such as interfering with steroid metabolism (as do chlorinated hydrocarbons in birds, since genetical variations exist in adrenal metabolism, the effects of DDT are likely to be subject to natural selection);

(iii) Cause chromosomal instability (e.g. fishing is now banned in parts of Sweden because of dissolved mercury, which is concentrated by fish to the extent that it acts as a breaker of chromosomes).

(b) The most drastic genetical changes produced by man are due to the 'founder effect' (Mayr, 1954), in which a small number of founders are introduced into a previously uncolonized habitat and increase in number as they occupy it. Since the founding members are extremely unlikely to carry the same alleles (i.e. different forms of the gene at any locus on a chromosome) in the same frequencies as in the ancestral population, the new population will differ genetically at a large number of gene-loci, effectively leading to 'instant sub-speciation' (Berry, 1967; 1969a). Founder events have undoubtedly had a marked, albeit largely unexplored, effect in evolution. One of the few situations described in detail concerns *Drosophila* spp. on the Hawaiian islands, where more than 650 species are recognized, only 17 being non-endemic. Studies of chromosomal inversions, supported by behavioural, biochemical and ecological investigations, have allowed the elucidation of many species relationships. The common pattern of speciation seems to follow when a population new to an island is established by a single founder individual from a nearby island, necessarily involving abrupt non-adaptive changes (Carson *et al.,* 1970). There is an abundance of accounts of differentiation from a parent stock following introduction into a new environment by man: for example, in the house sparrow (*Passer domesticus* L.) in North America after its deliberate introduction from Europe in 1852; in the long-tailed field-mouse (*Apodemus sylvaticus* L.) on the islands of the North Atlantic where it was inadvertently introduced by the Vikings on their colonizing voyages (Berry, 1969a).

(c) Finally, we are faced with the situation, already mentioned, in which farm animals and crops are increasingly drawn from a small number of 'improved' strains. This would not matter in the long run, were it not for the progressive destruction of the wild relatives of agriculturally important forms—both directly and through habitat 'improvement' in primitive areas. This process of 'genetic erosion' (Frankel, 1970) means that variations of economically important characters may be lost. Although new variation can be induced by mutagens, the rate of origin of new variation through recombination is so much higher than that of induced variation (Berry, 1972) that this is likely to remain a relatively crude and ineffectual technique for some time yet.

Once the possibility that genetical change can occur through man's activities is accepted, we are faced with the realization that the conservation of genetical variety needs to be taken seriously, and indeed the FAO, acting with the International Biological Programme, is taking steps to record and protect genetical resources in plants by seed collections and other means (Frankel and Bennett, 1970). We are concerned in this essay with the principles lying behind the aims of genetical conservation and not the methods, which have to be peculiar to different groups in different parts of the world.


## THE GENETICAL CONSEQUENCES OF CONSERVATION PRACTICES

The factors affecting the genetical constitution of a population of an animal or plant are summarized in Figure 7.1. Two agents (mutation, and immigration from a genetically different population) increase variation, and two (natural selection, and genetic drift in small populations) decrease it. Of these, immigration, natural selection and genetic drift are highly dependent on the environment as we normally understand it.

Conservation management very often involves the establishment of nature reserves, and as the environment changes around the reserve, the animals and out-breeding plants in the reserve will become increasingly isolated from their relatives in other parts of their species ranges. There will thus be a reduction in gene-flow (by migration) into the population, and a reduction in the number of individuals able to breed together. In fact, at least two of the four agents which affect gene frequencies are likely to be affected by this kind of common conservation practice.

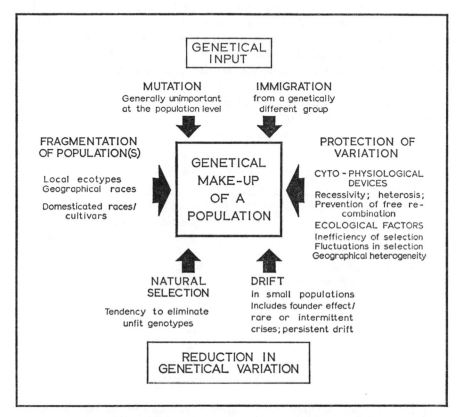

**Figure 7. 1.** Factors contributing to the genetical make-up of a population or group of populations. Note that all the factors affecting genetical constitution are influenced by the environment.

We now have to ask what will be the magnitude of the genetical forces which may be exerted by changes in immigration rates and population size? It is impossible to answer this question with certainty, because of the difficulty of predicting the outcome of interactions between poorly understood biological systems. The next section summarizes the state of knowledge about these; non-biologists may prefer to turn to the section on the Genetical Constitution of a Population, where some conclusions about the genetical make-up of individuals are re-considered.

## THE GENETICAL CONSTITUTION OF AN INDIVIDUAL

Until comparatively recently, diploid individuals were assumed to be homozygous at the great majority of their gene-loci for 'normal' alleles. Mutant genes in the process of elimination (or spread) by natural selection and a small proportion of gene-loci where differing selection pressures at different parts of the range or life-cycle allowed the persistence of more than one allele were thought to be exceptions (e.g. Ford, 1965). This simple (or 'classical') picture of population structure is now known to be very wrong. Electrophoretic techniques for the separation of proteins with different electrical charges have shown that most animals have more than one allele at about 10 per cent of their loci (Table 7.1) and that approximately a quarter of all loci in a population are similarly polymorphic. There is

**Table 7.1.** Protein (genic) variation in animals (based on Selander, 1970)

|  | Loci variable per population (%) | Loci heterozygous per individual (%) |
|---|---|---|
| *Limulus polyphemus* (King crab, a 'phylogenetic relic') | 25 | 5·7 |
| *Acris crepitans* (Cricket frog) | 14–23 | — |
| *Drosophila persimilis* | 25 | 10·5 |
| *D. pseudoobscura* | 42 | 12·3 |
| *Mus musculus* | 26 | 8·5 |
| *Homo sapiens* | 30 | 7·4 |

disagreement about whether this variation is retained in the population by selection for heterozygosis and the pleiotrophic action of the genes concerned, or whether it represents the accumulation of neutral mutations (*q.v.* Cook, 1971; Murray, 1972). All that need be said here is that every example where polymorphic variation has been studied in depth has shown the action of selective forces (e.g. Berry, 1971a), and that, as Fisher (1930) pointed out in the early days of population genetics, cumulative genetical differences will lead to phenotypic differences which will almost inevitably affect fitness (i.e. reproductive success) to some extent.

A second major change in our understanding of ecological genetics concerns the strengths of selection found in nature. Fisher (1930) and Haldane (1932) calculated the effect of selective intensities of 0·1 to 1·0 per cent and found that genetical change could result. However, these intensities have turned out to be too low in virtually every situation that has been studied (Table 7.2). Indeed, Haldane himself showed as early as 1924 that

**Table 7.2.** Intensities of selection in natural populations
(after Berry, 1971b, from many sources)

| Selection for: | % strength of selection |
|---|---|
| A. Directed selection (i.e. extreme phenotoype affected) | |
| Heavy metal tolerance of grasses on mine spoil heaps | 46–65 |
| Non-banded *Cepaea nemoralis* in woodlands | 19 |
| Melanic (*carbonaria*) form of *Biston betularia* in various regions of Great Britain | 5–35 |
| Spotted form in over-wintered Leopard frog (*Rana pipiens*) (*v* unspotted) | 23–38 |
| Unbanded water snakes (*Natrix sipedon*) (*v* heavily banded) | 77 |
| B. Stabilizing selection (i.e. intermediate phenotype favoured) | |
| Coiling in snails (*Clausilia laminata*) | 8 |
| Size and hatchability in duck eggs | 10 |
| Birth-weight and survival in human babies | 2·7 |
| Inversion heterokaryosis in *Drosophila pseudoobscura* | Up to 50 |
| Tooth variability (i.e. *de*-stabilizing selection) in *Mus musculus* | 21–26 |
| Shell variability in *Nucella lapillus* | 0–91 |
| Colour morphs in *Sphaeroma rugicauda* | 50+ |

the initial spread of the dark form of the peppered moth, *Biston betularia* L., in the Manchester area between 1848 and 1895 could only be accounted for by a 30 per cent disadvantage of the typical pale form over the melanic.

If we take together the amount of variation and the strengths of selection commonly found in populations it is not surprising that stabilizing selection (i.e. the elimination of phenotypic extremes) is apparently universal in nature. For example, 4·5 per cent of all babies born in London between 1935 and 1946 were still-born or died before 28 days, but only 1·8 per cent of average weight babies died.

The common dog whelk (*Nucella lapillus,* L.) experiences stabilizing selection of up to 90 per cent during life on wave-exposed shores, although whelks living on sheltered shores undergo no selection of this nature (Figure 7.2). There is a high correlation ($r \simeq 0·7$) between the amount of environmental stress (wave action) and the intensity of selection.

The easiest genetical way to achieve the situation of advantage of the mean or average over the extremes is for a heterozygote to produce a phenotype intermediate between two more extreme homozygotes. (This, incidentally, combines short-term uniformity in a stable environment with the

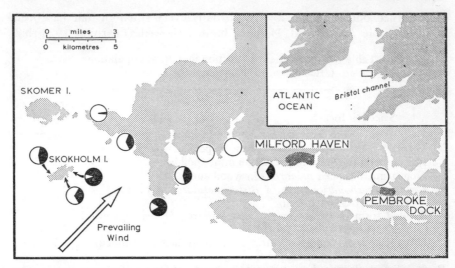

**Figure 7.2.** Stabilizing selection in the common dog whelk (*Nucella lapillus*). The proportion of black in each circle represents the difference in variance in a shell character between young and old members of the same population (=amount of selection). (Based on Berry and Crothers, 1968.)

possibility of long-term change.) In practice, most characters are controlled by alleles acting to increase the expression of the character and others acting to decrease it. In such a case, Fisher (1930) showed that selection will favour linkage between responsible loci, and also the accumulation of 'balanced' chromosomes with 'positive' and 'negative' alleles. The simplest situation to consider (Figure 7.3) involves two segregating loci $A,a$ and $B,b$ on the same chromosome, with $A,B$ acting in one direction and $a,b$ in the other (i.e. normal additive genes). Here the intermediate type can be either the attraction or the repulsion heterozygote, $AB/ab$ or $Ab/aB$. However, Fisher pointed out that the repulsion heterozygote ($Ab/aB$) will be favoured since it will be less likely than the attraction heterozygote, $AB/ab$, to produce zygotes giving the extreme phenotypes which are selectively disadvantageous. Any mechanism bringing about tighter linkage between the loci concerned (such as chromosomal inversion) will tend to spread.

This theoretical argument has been subjected to experimental test (mainly through selection experiments in *Drosophila*) by a number of workers (reviewed by, e.g., Lee and Parsons, 1968).

### Coadaptation

We have seen that there are four agents capable of changing the genetical constitution of a population (Figure 7.1). This simple fact was deduced by early mathematical geneticists from the Hardy–Weinberg principle (which

| PARENTS | | OFFSPRING | | | | | |
|---|---|---|---|---|---|---|---|
| | | FROM NON-RECOMBINANT GAMETES | | WITH RECOMBINATION IN ONE PARENT | | WITH RECOMBINATION IN BOTH PARENTS | |
| Chromosomes | Phenotypic score | Chromosomes | Phenotypic score | Chromosomes | Phenotypic score | Chromosomes | Phenotypic score |
| **REPULSION** | | | | | | | |
| 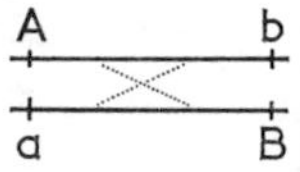 A—b / a—B (crossover) | 2 | Ab/aB | 2 | AB/aB | 3 | AB/ab | 2 |
| | | Ab/Ab | 2 | AB/Ab | 3 | AB/AB | 4 |
| 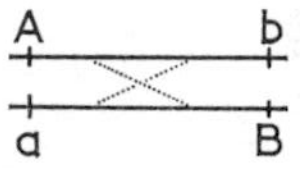 A—b / a—B (crossover) | 2 | cB/aB | 2 | ab/aB | 1 | ab/ab | 0 |
| | | aB/Ab | 2 | ab·/Ab | 1 | AB/ab | 2 |
| **ATTRACTION** | | | | | | | |
| 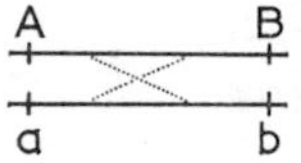 A—B / a—b (crossover) | | AB/ab | 2 | AB/Ab | 3 | Ab/Ab | 2 |
| | | AB/AB | 4 | AB/aB | 3 | Ab/aB | 2 |
| 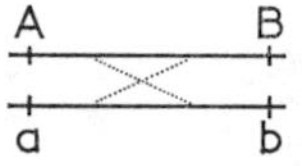 A—B / a—b (crossover) | | ab/ab | 0 | ab/Ab | 1 | aB/Ab | 2 |
| | | ab/AB | 2 | ab/aB | 1 | aB/aB | 2 |

**Figure 7.3.** Effect of linkage on the incidence of the extremes of manifestation of a continuously distributed variable. If AB produces a phenotypic effect of 1, and ab an effect of 0, then matings between two repulsion heterozygotes are most likely to produce non-extreme phenotypes.

states the relations between allele and genotype frequencies). They derived precise expressions for the relationships between the disrupting agents under a variety of conditions (see Crow and Kimura, 1970, *inter alia*). Unfortunately they were too simple in their biological thinking, since organisms are vastly more complicated than mathematical abstractions, and an individual is more than the sum of a series of discrete genes. Put another way, an individual has a genetical structure as well as a genetical content, and not every collection of alleles will produce a viable individual; in other words, the presence of some alleles in a population (and therefore in an individual) is dependent on the presence of others.

Perhaps the easiest genetical 'architecture' to understand is that involved in the modification and evolution of dominance and recessivity. The fact that dominance is a property of a character rather than a gene was argued in detail by Fisher (1930) and the first experimental test was made by Fisher himself in 1935 followed by Ford (1940). Ford selected for greater and lesser expression of the variable yellow *semilutea* form of the currant moth, *Abraxas grossulariata* L., and in four generations had 'made' the character almost completely recessive (with heterozygotes indistinguishable from the homozygous *lutea* form). He then crossed his selected heterozygotes back to the original stock and obtained offspring of the normal variable heterozygous type. In other words, the modifiers of dominance which were accumulated by the selection procedure were dispersed again so that dominance was broken down by changing the modifying genes, not by the *lutea* gene itself (see also Kettlewell, 1965).

Occasionally it is possible to identify the action of different genes contributing to natural variation. This has been done for the determinants of the pin-thrum polymorphism in the primrose, *Primula vulgaris* L., where different members of a linked group of loci control anther height, style length, pollen size, rate of pollen-tube growth and length of the papillae on the stigma; for the mimetic patterns in the African swallowtail butterfly, *Papilio dardanus*; and (less completely) for the colour and banding patterns of the shell in the snail *Cepaea nemoralis* (L). More often, it is only possible to conclude that the different components of a character complex are inherited as a unit (whether linked or not), which is to say that the gene-complex is coadapted (Cook, 1961).

## GENETICAL CONSTITUTION OF A POPULATION

There are a number of devices which act as a buffering or conservative force when a population is subjected to action which would otherwise cause genetical change (chapters 9, 10 in Mayr, 1963; see also right-hand side of

Figure 7.1). Conversely, there is a very fine dynamic equilibrium between environmental change and genetical adaptation.

## A. Conservatism

Selander and his co-workers (e.g. 1970) measured the amount of protein variation in populations of house mice, *Mus musculus* L., in Denmark in an area where the ranges of a dark-bellied form (*M.m. domesticus*) and a light-bellied form (*M.m. musculus*) meet with a narrow zone of intergradation which has been apparently constant in position for at least thirty years. Although the two forms are interfertile in the laboratory, the gene frequencies of isoenzyme variants (i.e. different forms of the same enzyme) on the two sides of the hybrid zone were very different to each other. Even more remarkable was the fact that the frequencies of the same variants in light-bellied mice from California (*M.m. brevirostris*), which were derived from light-bellied European mice, were more similar to the light-bellied Southern Danish ones than the Southern Danish were to the Northern Danish ones. Californian mice are fairly characteristic of mice from southern U.S.A. Despite the greatly different conditions in California to those in Europe, the genotype of these mice has remained astonishingly constant.

'Persistence of type' in this way does not need labouring. It is evident from most transplantation experiments where exotic forms are grown—and survive—among more normal ones.

## B. Fine Adaptation

In contrast, Dobzhansky (reviewed 1970) has shown that the frequencies of different inversions in the third chromosome of *Drosphila* species (especially *D. pseudoobscura*) in laboratory cultures depend on temperature, food, competition and degree of crowding, and that changes in the culture conditions lead to rapid and precise adaptation. From this it has been possible to show that inversion frequencies in wild-living populations are controlled by a complex of environmental variables which changes with season, altitude, competitors, and so on. A comparable situation in a mammal was shown by Berry and Murphy (1970) in house mice on the small Pembrokeshire island of Skokholm (Table 7.3). In this population there are two alleles at a locus which affects the physical characteristics of the haemoglobin molecule. During the summer, which is a time of rapid population increase and high juvenile mortality, the proportion of heterozygotes increases to about 60 per cent above the expectation on the Hardy–Weinberg equilibrium; whilst during the winter, when there is negligible breeding and considerable adult mortality, the proportion of heterozygotes decreases until in the spring there is approximately the expected number of heterozygotes. The different phenotypes seasonally change in frequency to maximize the

5

**Table 7.3.** Effects of seasonally varying selection at three loci in an island mouse population (data from Berry and Murphy, 1970)

|  |  | Hbb Excess of heterozygotes over expectation (%) | Es-2 Excess of heterozygotes over expectation (%) | Pep-C Heterozygotes in population (%) |
|---|---|---|---|---|
| Spring (March) | High adult mortality; no breeding | 12·9 | 52·4 | 13·2 |
| Autumn (September) | Low adult mortality; much juvenile death | 57·6 | 38·2 | 42·5 |

number of better adapted animals present in the population at any one time, and hence buffer the population against climatic fluctuations. This temporal change is directly analogous to geographical changes in gene frequencies in relation to air pollution in a species such as the peppered moth.

Thus we are faced with an apparently paradoxical situation: a local population is at once resistant to genetical change, and yet constantly changing as the environment fluctuates. Although we have already seen that the establishment of nature reserves may affect two of the four variation-controlling agencies (immigration and drift) (Figure 7.1), in fact a third agency (natural selection) in practice overrides them both and is more important in determining allele frequencies.

The classical study on this subject was made by Fisher and Ford (1947) on the scarlet tiger moth (*Panaxia dominula* (L.)) in an isolated small colony —theoretically the most favourable situation for drift to occur. They showed that the changes they observed in the frequency of an allele were too great to be explained by chance factors, particularly 'drift' when the number of individuals was reduced to a low level. In two other examples previously claimed to illustrate clearly the operation of drift—the speciation of the land snail *Partula* spp. on Moorea in the Society Islands and the distribution of banding and colour patterns in the field snail *Cepaea nemoralis* —field studies have shown the operation of selection (e.g. Clarke, 1968). A progressive change in inversion frequencies in *Drosophila pseudoobscura* over a 17-year period could be traced to no apparently relevant environmental change, but turned out to be correlated in time and space with an increase in DDT residues (Cory *et al.,* 1971). Put another way, the genetical constitution of a population cannot be *preserved* under conditions other than the sterility of a laboratory culture: even the first struggling towards domestication (some form of enclosure) involved selection for reproductive rates and (in animals) for docility (Berry, 1969b).

## GENETICAL RULES FOR CONSERVATION PRACTICE

An environmental change may be temporary or permanent—due to normal climatic fluctuations or to longer-term factors. This is likely to lead to a genetical disturbance which may or may not produce a lasting alteration in phenotype. For example, an increase in numbers in the meadow brown butterfly (*Maniola jurtina* (L.)) in Southern England in 1956 led to an increase in wing-spot variability, but by 1958 the previous pattern had been regained (reviewed by Creed *et al.*, 1970); a similar temporary population increase in a colony of the marsh fritillary (*Melitaea* (*Euphydras*) *aurinia* von Rott) led to a new wing phenotype even after numbers returned to normal (Ford and Ford, 1930). Without knowing all the modes of action and interaction of all the components of environment, phenotype and genotype, it is virtually impossible to forecast the genetical result of any environmental alteration. This leads us to our first generalization:

*any environmental change may produce a genetical change.*

However, we must qualify this to take account of the fact that selection is much more powerful than the other agents shown in Figure 7.1. This leads to the second generalization:

*adaptation is rapid and precise.*

It is, however, self-evident that adaptation is dependent on available variation. For example, the moth *Procus literosa* (L.) became extinct in Sheffield in its typical form early in the Industrial Revolution and only recolonized the area many years later when a melanic mutation occurred and spread (Kettlewell, 1957). Differences in genetical content are very clear cut when races of a species are genetically isolated and founded by a small

**Table 7.4.** % allele frequencies of some isozymes in house mouse population on different islands of the Shetland archipelago (Berry and Murphy, unpublished)

| | Es-2[a] | Es-5[b] | Trf[a] | Trf heavy variant | Trip-1[c] | Dip-1[c] | Hbb[s] |
|---|---|---|---|---|---|---|---|
| Mainland, south | 2·5 | 22·1 | 0 | 2·5 | 0 | 1·7 | 46·7 |
| Mainland, central | 20·2 | 10·5 | 1·7 | 6·0 | 20·0 | 10·2 | 76·3 |
| Papa Stour | 0 | 10·0 | 0 | 0 | 0 | 43·3 | 0 |
| Yell | 1·5 | 20·0 | 0 | 10·0 | 0 | 12·5 | 48·6 |
| Fetlar | 0 | 20·0 | 0 | 4·0 | 0 | 20·0 | 100 |

number of colonizers: Table 7.4 shows the frequencies of some alleles in samples of mice caught on different islands in the Shetland archipelago.

It is the question of the availability of genetical variation (or rather its loss, genetical erosion) that causes concern to plant breeders. Consequently it is encouraging that in terms of genetical markers like inversions,

*intra-population variation is large and resistant to loss.*

Some of the reasons for this are summarized on the right-hand side of Figure 7.1. In general they are not well understood: it is one of the chief current concerns of evolutionary and developmental geneticists to come to a better understanding of them. Nevertheless, genetical cohesion is an undoubted fact for even in a population subjected to rigorous and long-continued directional selection, considerable variation remains unused (e.g. Carson, 1967). The observation that forms at the edge of their range which are subjected to a varying environment have little variation in terms of genetical markers like inversions (e.g. Zohary and Imber, 1963) may represent nothing more than the adaptive loss of factors which reduce crossing-over and reduce phenotypic variation (Carson, 1958). It is extremely unlikely that any normal management procedures could significantly affect the amount of variation in a local population to the extent of making that population unable to respond to environmental change.

Related to the amount of variation present is the planning and management question of the optimum size of a conserved population. As so often happens, it is impossible to give a satisfactory answer. In forms which have been so reduced that an 'extinction–rescue' programme has to be designed (as with Père David's deer or the Hawaiian né–né) no particular problem seems to have been encountered. Indeed, there is some slight evidence that a population with a primary poverty of variability seems to acquire more. For example, the Skokholm mouse population, isolated since it was founded by a few individuals 70 years ago, nevertheless contains the same amount of variation as British mainland mouse populations (Berry and Murphy, 1970). Probably ecological factors related to population size may prove more important than genetical factors (e.g. Duffey, 1968).

Finally, it is as well to repeat that

*a local genotype cannot be preserved unchanged.*

Attempts at preservation such as in the 'gene-bank' at Whipsnade (Rowlands, 1964) may provide some alleles for study or possible introduction into a wild stock, but will certainly not preserve the whole genotype of the form in question. There is a cautionary tale in the attempt to improve the native turkey stock in Missouri by releasing commercially bred hybrid birds: the released birds proved inferior to the wild birds in every aspect of viability studied—brain, pituitary and adrenal size, and breeding success (Leopold, 1944).

## CONCLUSION AND SUMMARY

The genetical constitution of a population is a historical summation of all the previous environments of that population. Any management activity is therefore likely to produce genetical changes. On the whole these will be on a fairly small scale and genetical problems are most likely to arise through the elimination of forms that might be needed as contributions to domesticated races. However, it is hard to be specific about the magnitude of such problems. As yet we know too little about changes in gene frequencies with time to be able to predict the effect of any particular environmental change. All we can do is to state some general genetical principles for conservation practice:

1. any environmental change may produce a genetical change;
2. adaptation is rapid and precise;
3. intra-population variation is large and resistant to loss;
4. a local genotype cannot be preserved unchanged.

## BIBLIOGRAPHY

Baker, H. G., and Stebbins, G. L. (eds.) (1965). *Genetics of Colonizing Species*, Academic Press, New York, London, 588 pp.

Berry, R. J. (1972). *Teach Yourself Genetics*, 2nd ed., English Universities Press, London, 167 pp.

Ford, E. B. (1971). *Ecological Genetics*, 3rd ed., Chapman and Hall, London, 410 pp.

Frankel, O. H. and Bennett, E. (eds.) (1970). *Genetic Resources in Plants*, I.B.P. Handbook No. 11, Blackwell, Oxford, 554 pp.

Grant, V. M. (1963). *The Origin of Adaptations*, Columbia, New York, 606 pp.

Jones, D. A. and Wilkins, D. A. (1971). *Variation and Adaptation in Plant Species*, Heinemann, London, 184 pp.

Mayr, E. (1963). *Animal Species and Evolution*, Oxford, London, 797 pp.

Mettler, L. E. and Gregg, T. G. (1969). *Population Genetics and Evolution*, Prentice-Hall, Englewood Cliffs, N.J., 212 pp.

Sheppard, P. M. (1967). *Natural Selection and Heredity*, 3rd ed., Hutchinson, London, 192 pp.

Spiess, E. B. (ed.) (1964). *Papers on Animal Population Genetics*, Methuen, London, 513 pp.

Wallace, B. (1968). *Topics in Population Genetics*, Norton, New York, 481 pp.

Wilson, E. O., and Bossert, W. H. (1971) *Primer of Population Biology*, Sinauer, Stamford, Conn., 192 pp.

## REFERENCES

Berry, R. J. (1967). Genetical changes in mice and men, *Biol. Rev.*, **59**, 78–96.

Berry, R. J. (1969a). History in the evolution of *Apodemus sylvaticus* (Mammalia) at one edge of its range, *J. Zool. (Lond.)*, **159**, 311–28.

Berry, R. J. (1969b). The genetical implications of domestication in animals, in: *The Domestication and Exploitation of Plants and Animals* (eds.) Ucko, P. J. and Dimbleby, G. W., Duckworth, London, 207–19.

Berry, R. J. (1971a). Environmental mutagenesis in a genetical perspective, *Int. J. Environmental Studies*, **1**, 201–9.

Berry, R. J. (1971b). Conservation aspects of the genetical constitution of populations, in: *The Scientific Management of Animal and Plant Communities for Conservation* (eds.) E. Duffey and A. S. Watt, Blackwell, Oxford, 177–206.

Berry, R. J. (1972). Genetical effects of radiation on populations, *Atomic Energy Rev.*, **10**, 67–100.

Berry, R. J., and Crothers, J H. (1968). Stabilizing selection in the dog whelk (*Nucella lapillus*), *J. Zool.* (*Lond.*), **155**, 5–17.

Berry, R. J. and Murphy, H. M. (1970). Biochemical genetics of an island population of the house mouse, *Proc. R. Soc. B*, **176**, 87–103.

Carson, H. L. (1958). Response to selection under different conditions of recombination in *Drosophila, Cold Spring Harb. Symp. Quant. Biol.*, **23**, 291–306.

Carson, H. L. (1967). Permanent heterozygosity, *Evol. Biol.*, **1**, 143–68.

Carson, H. K., Hardy, D. E., Spieth, H. T., and Stone, W. S. (1970). The evolutionary biology of the Hawaiian Drosophilidae, in: *Essays in Evolution and Genetics* (eds.) Hecht, M. K., and Steere, W. C., North-Holland, Amsterdam, 437–53.

Clarke, B. C. (1968). Balanced polymorphism and regional differentiation in land snails, in: *Evolution and Environment* (ed.) Drake, E. T., Yale, New Haven, 351–68.

Cook, L. M. (1961). The edge effect in population genetics, *Am. Nat.*, **95**, 295–307.

Cook, L. M. (1971). *Coefficients of Natural Selection*, Hutchinson, London, 207 pp.

Cory, L., Fjeld, P., and Serat, W. (1971). Environmental DDT and the genetics of natural populations, *Nature* (*Lond.*), **229**, 128–30.

Creed, E. R., Dowdeswell, W. H., Ford, E. B., and McWhirter, K. G. (1970). Evolutionary studies on *Maniola jurtina* (Lepidoptera, Satyridae): The 'boundary phenomenon' in southern England 1961 to 1968, in: *Essays in Evolution and Genetics*, (eds.) Hecht, M. K., and Steere, W. C., North-Holland, Amsterdam, 263–87.

Crow, J. F., and Kimura, M. (1970). *An Introduction to Population Genetics Theory*, Harper & Row, New York, 591 pp.

Dobzhansky, T. (1970). *Genetics of the Evolutionary Process*, Columbia, New York, 505 pp.

Duffey, E. (1968). Ecological studies on the large copper butterfly *Lycaena dispar* Haw. *batavus* Obth. at Woodwalton Fen National Nature Reserve, Huntingdonshire, *J. appl. Ecol.*, **5**, 69–96.

Elton, C. S. (1958). *The Ecology of Invasions by Animals and Plants*, Methuen, London, 181 pp.

Fisher, R. A. (1930). *The Genetical Theory of Natural Selection*, Clarendon, Oxford, 272 pp.

Fisher, R. A., and Ford, E. B. (1947). The spread of a gene in natural conditions in a colony of the moth *Panaxia dominula* L., *Heredity* (*Lond.*), **1**, 143–74.

Ford, E. B. (1940). Genetic research in the Lepidoptera, *Ann. Eugen.*, **10**, 227–52.

Ford, E. B. (1965). *Genetic Polymorphism*, Faber, London, 101 pp.

Ford, H. B. and Ford, E. B. (1930). Fluctuation in numbers and its influence on variation in *Melitaea aurinia, Trans. R. Ent. Soc. Lond.*, **78**, 345–51.

Frankel, O. H. (1970). Genetic conservation in perspective, in: *Genetic Resources in Plants* (eds.) Frankel, O. H., and Bennett, E., Blackwell, Oxford, 469–89.

Frankel, O. H., and Bennett, E. (eds.) (1970). *Genetic Resources in Plants*, I. B. P. Handbook No. 11, Blackwell, Oxford, 554 pp.

Haldane, J. B. S. (1932). *Causes of Evolution*, Longmans Green, London, 235 pp.

Kettlewell, H. B. D. (1957). Industrial melanism in moths and its contribution to our knowledge of evolution, *Proc. R. Instn. (G.B.)*, **36**, 1–14.

Kettlewell, H. B. D. (1961). The phenomenon of industrial melanism in Lepidoptera, *Ann. Rev. Ent.*, **6**, 245–62.

Kettlewell, H. B. D. (1965). Insect survival and selection for pattern, *Science*, **148**, 1290–6.

Lee, B. T. O., and Parsons, P. A. (1968). Selection, prediction and response, *Biol. Rev. Camb. Phil. Soc.* **43**, 139–74.

Leopold, A. S. (1944). The nature of heritable wildness in turkeys, *Condor*, **46**, 133-97.

Mayr, E. (1954). Change of genetic environment and evolution, in: *Evolution as a Process* (eds.) Huxley, J., Hardy, A. C., and Ford, E. B., Allen & Unwin, London, 157–80.

Murray, J. (1972). *Genetic Diversity and Natural Selection*, Oliver & Boyd, Edinburgh, 128 pp.

Rowlands, I. W. (1964). Rare breeds of domesticated animals being preserved by the Zoology Society of London, *Nature (Lond.)*, **202**, 131–2.

Selander, R. K. (1970). Biochemical polymorphism in populations of the house mouse and Old-field mouse, in: *Variation in Mammalian Populations* (eds.) Berry, R. J., and Southern, H. N., *Symp. Zool. Soc. (Lond.)*, No. **26**, Academic Press, London, 73–91.

Zohary, D., and Imber, D. (1963). Genetic dimorphism in fruit types in *Aegilops speltoides*, *Heredity (Lond.)*, **18**, 223–31.

CHAPTER 8

# The Ecology and Conservation of British Lowland Heaths

CAROLYN M. HARRISON

## THE PROBLEM

Heathland communities which are dominated by species such as *Calluna vulgaris, Erica cinerea* and *Erica tetralix* occur widely throughout north-western Europe, but their distribution in southern England is a particularly fragmented one. Although this fragmentation is in part a reflection of the availability of suitable soil conditions, it is as much a function of the varying fortunes of heathland as an integral part of the local agricultural economy. In the past many heathlands afforded rights of grazing, turf cutting and collection of firewood for local commoners, and as such played an important role in farming practices. Until the mid-nineteenth century, therefore, extensive tracts of heath contributed to the landscape of southern England; but by the beginning of the twentieth century changes in land-use demands meant that the heathland acreage had embarked upon a decline which was to be intensified during the following decades. Heathlands were reclaimed for permanent pasture and arable land, for building land and forestry, for mineral extraction and military training. Nevertheless, a substantial proportion of the 70,000 acres of common land recorded for the southern counties between 1955 and 1958 (Denman *et al.*, 1967) remained as heathland. But where previously large extensive tracts of heath had existed now only small blocks, often of no more than 250 acres in extent, were the rule. These remaining heathlands represent a distinctive habitat for wildlife, and their scientific and educational value as wildlife refuges needs to be recognized at both the regional and national level. In addition the heathlands have considerable scenic value as the only tracts of wild vegetation in what is otherwise a highly urbanized landscape. In the face of a declining and fragmented acreage, the conservation of the remaining heaths has become a pressing problem; the more so since most of the southern heaths now fall within the

117

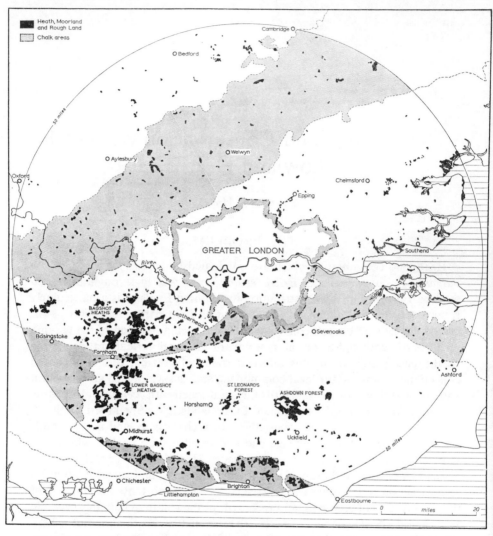

**Figure 8.1.** Heathland and roughland areas available within a fifty-mile radius of London and so easily accessible to the weekend motorist and to recreational pressure.

fifty-mile, day-trip zone of the London motorist (Figure 8.1) and many are now used for some form of recreational activity throughout the year (Wager, 1967). Against this background of land-use changes any rational approach to the conservation of heathlands needs to proceed from an examination of the nature of the resource itself (its structure and functioning) to an assessment of the different land uses which are compatible with maintaining it as a viable resource. Only then can formal management policies be designed which are based upon informed, scientific advice.

## THE NATURE OF THE RESOURCE

**Phytosociology**

The term heathland has come to embrace a wide variety of dwarf-shrub and herbaceous communities within its scope. It is generally used to describe Ericaceous communities located in lowland Britain, similar communities found in the upland areas being referred to as moorland (Tansley, 1939; Miller and Watson, Chapter 10). Floristically the two types are essentially similar and have many species in common, but on a small scale the floristic affinities of the lowland heaths lie with similar communities in continental and southern Europe, and those of the moorlands with communities of northern and montane Scandinavia (Gimingham, 1961; 1962). Within Britain, the floristic variation in lowland heaths reflects gross climatic differences associated with their geographical location. The communities of the Breckland have close similarities with the north German heaths, and contain many species which exhibit a continental distribution (Watt, 1971), but lack more oceanic species such as *Erica cinerea*. The heathland communities of the London Basin and the Weald show greater affinities with the heaths of Belgium and France: *Erica cinerea* is frequently co-dominant with *Calluna vulgaris,* and *Ulex minor* and *U. europaeus* are both constant members of the community. In comparison with the Breckland communities and those heathlands farther west in Dorset and Hampshire, these Wealden heathlands are rather floristically impoverished (Harrison, 1970). They are also areas subject to heavy pressure from recreational activities.

The heaths of Hampshire and Dorset are associated with the Tertiary sands and clays of the Bagshot beds and the widely distributed plateau and valley gravels. They possess a number of species which exhibit a westerly and oceanic distribution, for example *Erica ciliaris*, which is important in the wet-heath transition zone (Moore, 1962), and *Ulex gallii*, which replaces *Ulex minor*. In addition *Agrostis setacea* replaces *Deschampsia flexuosa*, which is important in the London Basin and Wealden heaths. Floristically these communities are similar to the more southerly and oceanic heaths of the Atlantic seaboard of Europe, particularly those of Britanny (Lemée, 1938). Their floristic richness is paralleled by a varied fauna which includes a number of rare species such as *Lacerta gracilis* and *Sylvia undata*.

A final group of heaths occurs in Cornwall on the Lizard peninsula, where the serpentine rocks confer a very distinctive character on the vegetation

(Coombe and Frost, 1956). Species such as *Schoenus nigricans* and *Erica vagans* are present, the latter having a further outpost in Ireland. Many of these heathland species in both the Dorset and Lizard heaths are at the northernmost edge of their range, and for this reason the heathland communities are of high scientific and educational importance.

## Local Variants

Superimposed upon this major floristic gradient between the more continental heaths on the one hand and the more oceanic heaths on the other are local variations in community structure associated with changes in topography and drainage conditions, with the ageing cycle of individuals and with past and present land-use history.

### Topographical Variants

Where the groundwater table is near to the surface the typical community of the dry heath gives way to a wet-heath community in which *Calluna vulgaris, Erica tetralix* and *Molinia caerulea* are dominant. Where the water table is permanently high this wet-heath community gives way to one in which bog species are important (Rose, 1957). Many of the southern heaths which are already designated as Local or National Nature Reserves and Sites of Special Scientific Interest (SSSI's) have been scheduled as such because of the scientific interest of these wet-heath and bog communities. For example, small depressions associated with former military activity and local flushes can harbour species which are locally rare in the south, such as *Narthecium osifragum, Eriophorum vaginatum, Lycopodium inundatum,* and may afford breeding places for insects such as dragonflies. These sites of high biological interest nevertheless depend for their survival upon a surrounding area from which acidic drainage waters flow, and here the dry-heath communities assume an important role which could easily be ignored, and a role which agricultural land could not perform.

### Cyclical Variants

In addition to the floristic variations associated with geographical location and local changes in the physical environment, the vegetation mosaic of a heathland also changes with the ageing cycle of individual plants. Watt's classic study of the four growth phases of *Calluna* and *Pteridium* (Watt, 1947) established that the competitive ability of a species was affected by the ageing process and subsequently Barclay-Estrup and Gimingham (1969) extended this work to illustrate how age also affected the biological productivity of the community and the local floristic structure of patches within the community (see also Miller and Watson, Chapter 10).

During the pioneer phase of growth of *Calluna,* which lasts for the first six to 10 years, its overall cover is low and the contribution of other species such as *Erica cinerea, E. tetralix* and mosses such as *Polytrichum commune* and *Funaria hygrometrica* is important. The building phase from seven to 15 years sees an increase in the cover and density of the *Calluna* canopy, and dry matter production falls from the figure of 1,200 kg/hr/yr for the pioneer phase on southern heaths, to 350 kg/ha/yr (Chapman, 1967). Litter production increases faster than decomposition so that an acid mor humus accumulates on the soil surface, and species accompanying *Calluna* at this stage are few on account of the dense shade. Some species which have a straggling habit, for example *Galium saxatile* and *Potentilla erecta,* do survive during the ensuing mature phase which lasts up to 25 years. This stage may also see the return of *Polytrichum spp.* and *Hypnum cupressiforme var. ericetorum.* The improvement in light conditions which results from the more spreading canopy of the mature *Calluna* is thought to be responsible for these floristic changes. During the final degenerate phase a well-defined gap appears in the canopy and the whole plant adopts a spreading habit as lateral branches become almost horizontal. Eventually a new individual becomes established in the dead heart of the old individual or springs up by layering of the lateral branches.

The mosaic structure of the community which would result from a number of individuals each at different stages in their life-cycle has important consequences for the whole ecosystem. For example, an increase in biomass with age means that more nutrients are taken out of circulation than are returned to the soil in annual litter fall. This is particularly the case with nutrients such as nitrogen and phosphorus (Chapman, 1967). Even so, the amounts of similar nutrients entering the system in precipitation may be sufficient to redress the balance and in the long term there is no reason to suspect that progressive nutrient depletion will take place for the system as a whole. However, if an annual burning regime is imposed on to this naturally conservative cycle, nutrient losses may not always be made good (Allen, 1964).

Micro-habitat conditions such as temperature, light intensity and moisture are also affected by the mosaic structure of the community and these changes affect the faunal composition of a site. On the whole, the differences are greatest between the young and degenerate phases on the one hand and the building and mature phases on the other (Gimingham, 1972), extremes being more typical of the former stages while the latter offer more equable conditions. Certain animals, for example lizards, appear to thrive best in old mature and degenerate heather (K. Corbett, personal communication), and decomposer organisms are also likely to vary with the different phases of primary production. A mosaic structure of individual plants of different ages is thus likely to increase the diversity of the plant and animal members alike.

*Biotic Variants*

The intrinsic causes of variation within heathland communities are frequently masked by extrinsic factors of change associated with man and his domestic animals, for heathland is a plagioclimax which is maintained by pressures of grazing and fire. The ecological status of the southern heaths as a plagioclimax has been recognized for some time (Tansley, 1939), although the antiquity of some of these heaths has only recently been appreciated. Dimbleby's (1962 and Chapter 18) evidence from the analysis of soil pollen buried beneath barrows led him to suggest that in lowland Britain present-day heathland communities occupy sites of former deciduous woodland. For example, a study of the heath community at Iping Common, Sussex (Keef *et al.*, 1965) showed that the site has been dominated until the end of the Boreal period (6000 BC) by an open deciduous woodland in which hazel (*Corylus*) was dominant. At the end of this period Ericaceous species entered and remained dominant up to the present day. The change from the woodland flora to an Ericaceous dominated one was attributed to the role of fire introduced either deliberately or accidentally by man. The subsequent continued dominance of *Calluna* could be attributed to a number of complementary factors: (i) to a climatic deterioration which on sandy soils would lead to the intensification of the podsolization process already initiated under a *Calluna* canopy; (ii) to grazing by domestic animals which would prevent scrub invasion particularly if used in conjunction with burning; (iii) to felling of any remaining woodland. Dimbleby's evidence was from a few selected sites, but the accumulated evidence from numerous palynological and archaeological studies suggests that many southern heaths are likely to have originated in the late Boreal and Atlantic periods as well as during the later periods of prehistoric agricultural expansion (Seagrief, 1959).

Other heathlands undoubtedly have a later origin, many at the time of the medieval clearances (Hoskins and Stamp, 1963), but once formed these and earlier heaths would have been maintained by grazing and the subsequent exercising of commoners' rights.

Grazing by domestic animals was frequently accompanied by burning in an attempt to improve the quality of the herbage, and this together with furze and bracken cutting would have prevented scrub invasion. With the decline of rural agricultural economies, heathlands have reverted to other uses and a recent survey showed that very few commoners now exercise their rights (Denman *et al.*, 1967). On the other hand, this survey showed that many heaths were now used for some form of recreational activity, and that while burning for increasing fodder has lapsed, other fires, generally result-ing from human negligence, still played a role in the heathland environment.

The use of heaths as public open space has a long history and the inter-vention of the state in 1865 by instituting the Preservation of Common and Open Space Act marked the confirmation of this role. The more recent increased mobility of London's population, however, has meant that all the southern heaths are well within the fifty-mile, day-trip zone of the weekend motorist, and even the most isolated of them are subject to some recreational use (Figure 8.1). Increased fire frequencies are often associated with a high level of use by the public, some heaths being burned two or three times during a year, giving little time during which the vegetation can recover. In other cases, scrub invasion is so far advanced on areas of former heathland that burning here tends to encourage fire-tolerant species such as gorse and birch. On the other hand, where burning is infrequent the structure of the community also changes in the direction of scrub. The present biological structure of the heathlands can therefore only be understood in the knowledge of their past land-use history and more especially in the knowledge of their modification by fire.

## THE EFFECTS OF FIRE ON THE ECOSYSTEM

### Effects upon the Mineral Cycle

The primary effect of the fire is to reduce the standing crop of the eco-system by the total or partial combustion of the above-ground parts. Most low-growing vegetation is consumed by the fire although trees and shrubs above 1–2 m high may survive. Survival will depend upon height above the ground of the lethal temperatures within the fire, which in turn depends upon a number of environmental factors. Wind speed and direction, moisture content of the standing crop and amounts of combustible material can all influence the temperature within the fire (Whittaker, 1961). Soil litter may be destroyed as well as living plant material but the depth of penetration into the soil by the fire is seldom more than a few centimetres. The majority of the plant nutrients are returned to the soil surface in the ash and can be readily absorbed by the green plants to be recycled through the plant litter. But the mineral budget associated with burning needs to be considered in more than these superficial terms and the amounts of minerals which may be lost from the system as a whole should be taken into consideration. Without firing, the normal nutrient cycle is maintained by the slow, gradual release of newly weathered sub-surface parent material, its uptake by the plants and its return to the soil in plant litter. Additional nutrients are received in the precipitation and through lateral soil water movement. In time, with the development of a state of dynamic equilibrium, nutrient inputs would equal outputs. The imposition on to this cycle of an irregular burning regime means that the system does not necessarily retain this balance especially over a period of time. Firing, while short-circuiting the release of minerals in a suitable form for plant uptake, also increases the losses of minerals from the system in a number of ways. Organic matter is directly volatilized and substances such as nitrogen and sulphur are lost as gases (Robertson and Davies, 1965). Other losses occur through direct oxidation while further losses are incurred through surface run-off, in the wind and through downward soil leaching. Over time these accumulated losses could mean that the normal slow replacement of minerals is exceeded and there is a decline in the amounts of plant nutrients available within the system.

### Effects on the Vegetational Structure

The result of progressive nutrient loss and frequent burning is reflected in the vegetational mosaic of the heathland, for although many heath-land species are fire tolerant they are not all equally so. Burning, by reducing the community to an even age, alters the competitive ability of species so that under repeated burning species other than *Calluna* and *Erica* may be more aggressive. For example, Watt (1955) established that the com-petitive ability of *Calluna* and *Pteridium* is affected by age and that burning is likely to favour *Pteridium,* since the rhizome is largely protected from fires and allows a more vigorous recovery than is the case with *Calluna.* On the southern heaths *Molinia* also appears to recover quickly after fire (Chapman, 1967) and *Juncus squarrosus* is also persistent. On the other hand, species such as *Galium saxatile* and *potentilla erecta* do not recover well and *Sphagna* species seem particularly vulnerable. The frequency of fires can thus determine which species contribute to the vegetation mosaic and their relative proportions. This in turn will control the recreational use which can be made of that community: bracken-dominated sites, for example, are of little use as picnic spots since the peak of the visitor season coincides with the peak of the growing season, while on the other hand a mosaic of *Calluna* and grass sites could fulfil this function more readily.

The most damaging aspect of fires is their frequency, so that heavily used sites which are likely to be burned more frequently than less accessible sites will show an observable difference in their vegetation mosaic. Fire-resistant species will be encouraged and the whole biological structure of the community altered. Given five or six years between burns a succession would normally take place which involves the colonization of bare ground by algae, mosses such as *Polytrichum commune,* and eventually higher plants such as *Erica cinerea* and *Calluna.* Even so, the overall percentage cover of the vegetation during these early years is quite low and fire-tolerant species such as *Ulex* and *Betula spp.* make good growth in response to a favourable seed bed and the lack of competition. In general, recovery rates of *Calluna* in the heathland environment are rather better than those in upland environments where older stands may not shoot from the old stools and regeneration is dependent upon seed establishment. Nevertheless, repeated burning of young growth on lowland heaths does appear to favour both grass forms and *Pteridium*.

## Other Changes in the Structure

The vegetation mosaic also changes in the absence of burning, notably in the direction of scrub invasion (Tansley, 1949). Observations made by the author on some West Sussex heaths (Harrison, 1969) and elsewhere in southern England suggest that there are two stages in the development of *Calluna* dominated sites at which tree seedlings may become established. These stages are closely conditioned by the growth phases of the dominant *Calluna*. When the cover of *Calluna* is low during the first five to six years after firing, both birch and pine seedlings take advantage of these environmental conditions. Growth may later become impaired as the shade cast by *Calluna* increases and as competition for minerals is increased (Carlisle and Brown, 1968). In addition, root exudates from *Calluna* may also play a depressive role on tree growth (Robinson, 1972). If the tree seedlings reach a height of about 1–2 m many will survive subsequent firing and will develop through a scrub stage and eventually to open woodland. A second stage of establishment can occur when *Calluna* enters upon the degenerate phase of growth when the plant is approximately 15 years old and when the canopy begins to open out again. Birch and pine appear to be able to take advantage of the increased light reaching the ground at this stage and can make good growth. If, therefore, it is thought desirable to prevent scrub invasion on existing open heathlands, a mosaic structure of areas of heather of different ages, with an adequate representation of the vigorous building phase, would ensure that seedling establishment is kept to a minimum. Prevention of scrub invasion may be an important consideration from the point of view of different land uses, for example hunting, model-aircraft flying and picnicking. It may also be important from the educational and scientific viewpoint.

So far little experimental work has been carried out on the potential use of fire as a management tool for lowland heaths, but one such study made by Nicholson (1968) on a Suffolk heath found that a single burning and mowing treatment of heather approximately 18 years old was sufficient to prevent the extension of fire-resistant species such as *Ulex* and *Pteridium* and to control the natural course of succession through to birch and pine woodland. On other heathlands a more frequent series of treatments may be desirable, particularly on those heaths where scrub invasion is well advanced, and burning and mowing could be supplemented by hand pulling or spot spraying. It is for reasons such as these together with the desirability of providing a scientific basis for the management of heathland communities that further study should be given to the effect of fire frequencies on the ecosystem as a whole.

## DEMANDS UPON THE RESOURCE

Moore's exemplary study (1962) of the land-use changes associated with the Dorset heaths clearly demonstrates the nature of the demands which are made upon the heathland resource. By a careful analysis of cartographic and field evidence Moore documented the changes in land use which led to the reduction of the heathland area to its present figure of one-third of the 1811 acreage. Demands come from the extraction of sand, clay and gravel from agriculture and forestry, from the military for training and from a range of recreational pursuits. The picture Moore draws for the Dorset heaths is typical of the southern heaths in general, and the process of attrition is a continuing one. Demands for forestry may have recently declined for the south as a whole, but further increases have come from the building and extractive industries.

Although there are some who would regard all of these land users as being equally damaging to the heathland resource, their relative destructiveness on the heaths varies and three groups of users can be distinguished on the basis of their compatibility with maintaining heathland communities. A first group includes those uses which completely destroy the resource, namely, reclamation for building land and permanent agriculture. Some heathland species might survive for a short time in gardens and hedges but the overall contribution as refuges will be very small. A second group includes those uses which involve a less complete change of use such as forestry, military training, mineral extraction and golf-courses. Heathland species may be able to survive for some considerable time within the new land-use pattern, although the number of suitable habitats included in the new pattern depends upon the intensity of use. For example, a commercial forestry plot managed on a sixty-year rotation will provide fewer habitats than an area used for military training on a few weeks a year. A third group includes non-commercial uses such as commons, Nature Reserves and Country Parks, which make few demands upon the resource.

Although this preliminary assessment does provide a useful means of comparing different land uses and their effect upon the heathland communities other factors need to be considered as well. Most land-use changes also involve an implicit alteration of the burning frequency. For example, users of the first group eliminate burning permanently, while users of group two may temporarily change the burning regime by taking active measures to reduce fire risks. Even users of group three may unwittingly alter the burning regime. In all these cases, therefore, the biological structure and hence the scientific, educational and aesthetic value of the site will be affected.

A further outcome of land-use changes is the fragmentation of the remaining heathland so that blocks become isolated from their neighbours by ever-increasing distances. This fragmentation has important repercussions for the breeding success of animals in particular, and Moore suggested that the declining population of the Dartford warbler in the south may be partly due to the decreasing availability of suitable habitats. Fragmentation not only affects animals, for the increasing edge-effect of small blocks also offers new opportunities for invasion by plant species alien to the heathland habitat. In these situations woody species such as *Rhododendron ponticum* are early colonizers along with birch and oak. In many cases scrub colonization is already so well advanced that even recourse to burning will not necessarily reinstate the typical heathland species, for example on many of the former heather tracts of Surrey.

## HEATHLAND CONSERVATION IN PRACTICE

From a consideration of Moore's observations and those of others (e.g. Denman *et al.,* 1967) it is evident that as the last reserve of uncommitted land in the southeast, heathlands will be subject to increasing pressures from a variety of land users and this demand will have to be met by a fragmented and declining acreage. Not the least of these demands will come from recreation. In the long term this may not be such a bad thing, for heathlands by their very nature are the product of a disturbed environment in which man has traditionally played an important part. The recreational use of heathlands may thus ensure their survival where other uses would not. Even so, the use of heaths as areas for recreation may not be wholly compatible with the maintenance of their essential biological interest. Increased visitor usage often brings with it an increase in burning frequency, and although there may be a point beyond which no further increase in fire frequency takes place, most heaths are likely to experience an overall increase in fires. For this reason the recreational use of heaths should be directed away from sites of special scientific and educational value, such as the wetter habitats, and might be encouraged in the least interesting, drier heaths of the London Basin and the Weald. In addition, some of the more wooded areas of former heathland might be felled or thinned to provide an alternative recreation resource in areas where existing heathlands are already under heavy pressure, as for example at Ashdown Forest in Kent and near Farnham in Surrey.

As a guide for those persons who are likely to be involved in considering planning applications which involve heathland areas, four points should be heeded:

1. Large blocks of heathland are likely to embrace a wide variety of habitats and will ensure a high biological and educational interest. At the same time they provide land managers with a viable management unit. Every effort should be made therefore to retain the larger blocks of heath in the south, but especially those in the more biologically interesting areas of Hampshire and Dorset.

2. Where heathland blocks are small (less than 250 acres), groups of adjacent communities should be considered for inclusion within a single management unit, such as a Country Park. On this basis, visitors could be encouraged to use one block for a few years while another might be allowed to recover.

3. Special attention should be given to changes of use which severely modify the burning frequency, both in the direction of increased and decreased burning. Provision of some form of burning management might be made a condition of planning consent, particularly in the case of military training and mineral extraction, for example.

4. In conclusion, it must be stressed that any effort to conserve heathlands will involve some positive management of the resource. Left in the casual hands of pyromaniacs or pyrophobes the character of the resource will change and with it the potential use which can be made of it, so that while the remaining heaths are scenically attractive and ecologically desirable they will only remain so if their management is invested in more formal hands.

## REFERENCES

Allen, S. E. (1964). Chemical aspects of heather burning, *J. appl. Ecol.*, **1**, 347–67.

Barclay-Estrup, P., and Gimingham, C. H. (1969). The description and interpretation of cyclical processes in a heath community. I. Vegetational change in relation to the *Calluna* cycle, *J. Ecol.*, **57**, 737–58.

Carlisle, A., and Brown, A. H. F. (1968). Biological flora of the British Isles: *Pinus sylvestris* L., *J. Ecol.*, **5**, 269–308.

Chapman, S. B. (1967). Nutrient budgets for a dry heath ecosystem in the south of England, *J. Ecol.*, **55**, 677–89.

Coombe, D. E. and Frost, L. C. (1956). The heaths of the Cornish Serpentine, *J. Ecol.*, **44**, 226–56.

Denman, D. R., Roberts, R. A., and Smith, H. J. F. (1967). *Commons and Village Greens,* Leonard Hill, London, 512 pp.

Dimbleby, G. W. (1962). The development of British heathlands and their soils, *Oxford Forestry Memoir,* **23**, Clarendon, Oxford, 120 pp.

Gimingham, C. H. (1961). North European heath communities; a network of variation, *J. Ecol.*, **49**, 655–94.

Gimingham, C. H. (1962). Biological flora of the British Isles: *Calluna vulgaris* (L.) Hull., *J. Ecol.*, **52**, 285–97.

Gimingham, C. H. (1972). *Calluna* heathlands: use and conservation in the light of some ecological effects of management, in *The Scientific Management of Animal and Plant Communities*, (eds.) Duffey, E., and Watt, A. S., Blackwell, Oxford, 91–103.

Harrison, C. M. (1969). The ecology of certain West Sussex heaths, Unpublished Ph.D. thesis, University of London, 405 pp.

Harrison, C. M. (1970). The phytosociology of certain English heathland communities, *J. Ecol.*, **58**, 573–89.

Hoskins, W. G., and Stamp, L. D. (1963). *The Common Lands of England and Wales*, Collins, London, 366 pp.

Keef, P. A. M., Wymer, J. J., and Dimbleby, G. W. (1965). A mesolithic site on Iping Common, Sussex, England, *Proc. Prehist. Soc.*, **31**, 85–92.

Lemée, G. (1938). Recherches écologiques sur la végétation du Pèrche, *Rev. gen. Bot.* **50**, 22-52, 94-114, 170-80, 222-43, 294-306, 359-72, 415-33, 489-500, 547-63, 615-28, 671-90.

Moore, N. W. (1962). The heaths of Dorset and their conservation, *J. Ecol.*, **50**, 369–91.

Nicholson, P. (1968). The use of heather burning as a management technique for a Suffolk heathland, *Trans. Suff. Nat. Soc.*, **14**, 7–10.

Robertson, R. A., and Davies, G. E. (1965). Quantities of plant nutrients in heather ecosystems, *J. appl. Ecol.*, **2**, 211–19.

Robinson, R. K. (1972). The production by roots of *Calluna vulgaris* of a factor inhibitory to growth of some mycorrhizal fungi, *J. Ecol.*, **60**, 219–24.

Rose, F. (1957). The importance of the study of disjunct distributions to progress in understanding the British flora, in *Progress in the Study of the British Flora* (ed.) Lousley, J. E., B.S.B.I., London, 61–78.

Seagrif, S. C. (1959). Pollen diagrams from southern England, Wareham, Dorset and Nursling, Hampshire, *New Phytol.*, **58**, 316–25.

Tansley, A. G. (1939). *The British Islands and their Vegetation*, Cambridge University Press, Cambridge, 930 pp.

Wager, J. (1967). Outdoor recreation of Common Land, *J. Town Planning Inst.*, **53**, 398–403.

Watt, A. S. (1947). Pattern and process in the plant community, *J. Ecol.*, **36**, 283–304.

Watt, A. S. (1955). Bracken versus heather, a study in plant sociology, *J. Ecol.*, **43**, 490–506.

Watt, A. S. (1971). Rare species in Breckland: their management for survival, *J. appl. Ecol.*, **8**, 593–609.

Whittaker, E. (1961). Temperatures in heath fires, *J. Ecol.*, **49**, 709–15.

# CHAPTER 9

# Woodlands: their History and Conservation

C. R. Tubbs

Woodland today occupies 4·4 million acres, or 8 per cent, of the land surface of Britain. This is similar to the woodland cover in such densely populated lowland countries as Denmark (10 per cent) and Holland (8 per cent) but significantly lower than Sweden (58 per cent) or West Germany (28 per cent). It is also a similar area to that occupied by urban and industrial development in Britain. Moreover, less than one-third of the woodland cover of Britain is now of native tree species and less still can claim continuity with the natural forest cover which confronted the Neolithic cultivators more than 4,000 years ago. Two-thirds of our woodland area have been established by deliberate planting, a practice which commenced during the latter part of the seventeenth century and which has culminated in the modern, massive operations of the Forestry Commission and forestry investment companies. The destruction of the natural woodland cover of Britain between Neolithic and Tudor times was remarkably complete and left little more than fragments of woodland much modified by long histories of cropping, casual exploitation or grazing.

## WOODLAND HISTORY

The process of woodland clearance in Britain has been described by many authors (Stamp, 1964; Pennington, 1969; Dimbleby, Chapter 18; Sheail, Chapter 19). Commencing in the Neolithic period, mainly on the lighter soils—classically, perhaps, the Wessex chalk—man's inroads into his woodland environment for tillage and pasture increased progressively during the succeeding prehistoric cultural periods. At the time of the Claudian invasion in AD 43, however, the densest human populations were still centred on the light soils and, indeed, even four centuries of Roman occupation saw little clearance of the heavy clay soils and had little impact on vast areas of upland Britain. It left Britain still a largely wooded country. Not until the

Anglo-Saxon and Scandinavian colonizations did the countryside begin to take on something of its modern appearance. Between the fifth and the eleventh centuries the assault on the woodlands became both widespread and intensive, both in upland and lowland Britain. In the lowlands much of the clay lands were cleared for arable farming and in the uplands the limits of permanent pastoral enclosure crept up the valleys and hillsides. By the Norman conquest a pattern of rural settlement had become established in England and Wales which has remained fundamentally unaltered to this day. Nevertheless it is clear from the Domesday survey of 1086 that in the eleventh century woodlands remained extensive. Indeed, as one commentator has remarked, the Domesday clerks, in seeking and recording their information, 'could not see the village except in many cases as encompassed by great stretches of wood, fen and heath' (Neilson, 1942).

Well before Domesday, woodland had achieved a definite economic value and place in the village economy. Various Anglo-Saxon documents—for example, the laws of Ine, promulgated in about AD 694—confirm its importance as a source of food for swine, and it is evident that its valuation at Domesday was based mainly on similar criteria. The actual entries in Domesday Book vary: sometimes they record that there was enough wood to support a given number of swine; sometimes that a given number of swine were returned as rent from the wood; and sometimes they record the actual extent of the woodland in the village in terms of approximate linear or area measurements. Interpretation in terms of modern units of measurement is fraught with difficulty, though the relative abundance of woodland has been successfully mapped for mots English counties by Darby and others and there can be no doubt that in 1086 woodland dominated the countryside much more than it has ever done since (Darby, 1950; 1952–67).

At Domesday the total population of England and Wales was probably less than $1\frac{1}{2}$ million people. It has been estimated that by 1348, on the eve of the Black Death, this had increased to about $3\frac{3}{4}$ millions (Russell, 1948). The population explosion gave rise to a considerable land hunger aggravated by the low productivity of farmland under open field systems and, especially in the lowlands where population was densest, open fields expanded and thousands of hamlets and farms managed in severalty came into existence, mostly at the expense of the woodlands and common grazings —themselves the result of woodland clearance. In a fascinating study of the history of settlement in the parish of Whiteparish in Wiltshire, which lay partly on the more open chalk, Taylor (1967) showed that from the nuclei of two Anglo-Saxon hamlets, settlement and cultivation expanded between the eleventh and mid-fourteenth centuries at the direct expense of both oak-wood and the open chalk grazings. 'The years between 1086 and 1350 saw the appearance of seven new farmsteads or hamlets, associated with one completely new open field system, probably 800 acres of assarts* in the Forest and 300 acres of enclosures on the Downs' (Taylor, 1967). The national hunger for more arable land terminated with the successive out-breaks of bubonic plague in the later fourteenth and early fifteenth centuries (assarting in Whiteparish more or less ceased after 1350), but the impetus of woodland clearance continued, especially in the uplands, under the pressure of an expanding sheep economy.

The beginnings of large-scale sheep farming in the uplands are associated with the monastic foundations of the twelfth and thirteenth centuries. The Cistercians in particular raised many of their great abbeys in the remote uplands, where there was ample space to graze their flocks and an abundance of exploitable natural resources such as minerals and timber. Monastic communities used large quantities of timber for construction and repair work and were frequently accused of illegal felling in the various Royal forests in which they had received grants of grazing and other common rights (Donkin, 1960). More importantly, the great abbeys such as Flaxley, Wenlock, Kirkstead, Fountains, Rivaulx and others amassed their wealth partly from the iron industry and therefore had to make considerable inroads into the remaining woodland for charcoal. Their sheep effectively prevented the cleared woodland from regenerating. In the fourteenth and fifteenth centuries both the Crown and numerous other landowners followed the lead of the monasteries in the exploitation of the uplands for sheep grazing and iron smelting.

Sheep grazing was not universal in the uplands, and over much of Wales and Scotland the Celtic cattle economy persisted throughout medieval (and later) times and developed, in Wales at least, into a considerable industry from the twelfth century onwards. The clearance of land for cattle pasture, together with the exploitation of the woods for the lead smelting industry, has been correlated with a phase of intensive woodland clearance indicated by pollen analyses from a number of Welsh sites (Moore and Chater, 1969).

In the lowlands, and especially in the Weald, the charcoal–iron industry was also making substantial inroads into the remaining woodlands by the dawn of the sixteenth century. Everywhere, the woodland which had once been so abundant was dwindling rapidly before the combined onslaught of pastoral agriculture and the industrial fuel industry, added to which the demands for domestic fuel and for timber for the construction of dwellings and ships were increasing rapidly in relation to the dwindling timber resources. The conflict between increasing demand for timber and diminish-ing resources became notorious in sixteenth- and seventeenth-century England and led to a succession of legal enactments (mostly ineffectual in

* The grubbing up of woodland and its reduction to pasture or cultivation.

application) aimed at woodland conservation (Wrigley, 1962, *inter alia*). On the industrial front the dilemma was particularly acute. The iron industry of the Weald, for example, could only expand without endangering its future to the point where its annual consumption of timber equalled the annual increment of new growth. The personal incentives to plant more woodland were weak, mainly because of the long-term nature of the invest-ment and competition from other land uses. The dilemma was ultimately resolved, as far as industrial processes were concerned, by the discovery of coal as a substitute for charcoal. The salt industry, for example, had largely gone over to coal fuel by the late sixteenth century, but for various technical reasons the iron industry did not completely free itself from dependence on charcoal until quite late in the eighteenth century (Ashton, 1963). For shipbuilding and for a variety of domestic and agricultural uses ranging from wood fuel to wattle hurdles wood remained essential. The shipbuilding industry in particular came close to crisis point many times in the late seventeenth and during the eighteenth century. Between 1727 and 1788 the size of the Royal Navy increased from 170,862 tons to 413,667 tons of shipping, and the long arm of the navy purveyor was reaching out from the yards at Plymouth, Portsmouth, Deptford, Woolwich and Chatham into any remote corner of England and Wales where mature oaks were to be found.*

### Early Woodland Management and Conservation

At least as early as the beginning of the thirteenth century the problem of satisfying the demand for wood from a diminishing resource prompted the deliberate conservation of some wood for profit. In Saxon and early Norman times woodland, almost by definition, was part of the commonable waste and was thus open to the grazing of domestic animals, which inhibited regeneration. The necessity, under these circumstances, for enclosing a wood after felling in order that it might regenerate first appears to have gained statutory recognition in an enactment of 1483, but enclosure for a period of at least three years after felling had already been practised widely, at least in the extensive Royal forests, for two centuries or more (Exchequer Records in the Public Record Office, Turner, 1901). Restric-tions on the quantity and kinds of wood which the villager might take from the common woodland have an even greater antiquity.

The method of management which emerged in medieval times was akin to a coppice-with-standards system. The felled woodland, or sometimes simply an area of ground which contained mother trees, was enclosed with a bank and an external ditch surmounted by a fence and/or a quickset

* *Eleventh Report of Commissioners to Enquire into the Woods, Forests, and Land Revenues of the Crown*, 1792, Appendix 23.

hedge, and the coppice so formed was left to regenerate itself. Since the felled area was seldom regular in shape, the coppices tended to have irregular boundaries, and where these are traceable on the ground today they contrast markedly with the rigid boundaries of modern plantations. Over much of the lowlands the success and rapidity of hazel regrowth from felled stools, assisted by the removal by felling of the overshading oaks, to which they had formed an understory, led to the deliberate management of hazel as a short-rotation cash crop, a light cover of oak 'standards' being encouraged to yield larger timber. The hazel coppice satisfied the industrial and domestic fuel markets and a variety of local manufacturing industries, whilst the standards provided timber for heavy construction.

In the uplands most of the relict oakwoods were coppiced, at least casually but more often systematically, by late medieval times, very largely for the charcoal fuel industry. The hazel understory, where it existed, appears to have been gradually eliminated, perhaps more by periods of intensive browsing than by any deliberate management policy. It is doubtful if by the beginning of the seventeenth century there remained more than a handful of upland oakwoods which had escaped the intervention of man. Wistman's Wood, one of the three pedunculate oakwoods in the centre of Dartmoor, may conceivably be an exception. Like many upland oakwoods, it has persisted in a clitter of boulders. Its oaks were described as ancient and wind-pruned into procumbent postures in 1620, and it has evidently not been exploited since: old, procumbent trees remain a feature of the wood, though younger generations of straight-stemmed oaks have arisen among them in comparatively recent times (Worth, 1953; Simmons, 1965; Courtney and Staines, 1971; Tansley, 1939). Black Tor Beare, another of the pedunculate oakwoods of the Dartmoor granite, was certainly felled, at least in part, in the early seventeenth century, and at least one writer has expressed the conviction that Piles Wood, the remaining wood of the trio, was also felled at some stage (Worth, 1953).

Even in the densely populated lowlands not all woodland came to be systematically managed as coppice. Many common woods survived, becoming much modified by grazing and the taking of wood in satisfaction of rights of common estovers.* Other woodland which might have some claim to continuity with the primary woodland cover survived in areas set aside originally for the conservation of deer and the pleasure of the chase, particularly some Royal forests such as the New Forest in Hampshire (Tubbs, 1969) and parks such as Mersham in Kent, Staverton in Suffolk and Moccas in Herefordshire; however, as Peterken pointed out in his admirable study of Staverton Park, it is often difficult to actually prove that the old woodland of today is not derived from secondary colonization following a very early

---

* The right to take necessary small timber.

and undocumented clearance (Peterken, 1969). Certainly some modern, apparently 'natural' woodland is secondary. For example, the extensive beechwoods of the West Sussex downs overlay the relics of prehistoric agriculture and may well represent Dark Age regrowth on the lighter soils of southern England which the Anglo-Saxons discarded in favour of the vales. By the eighteenth century the West Sussex beechwoods were being managed on a selective felling system and much of the timber was being exported through the port of Itchenor on Chichester Harbour.* Whether the beech high forest of West Sussex was, like much of that in the Chilterns, derived from medieval beech coppice (Roden, 1968), has yet to be established. Sadly, most of the West Sussex beechwoods which Watt knew have now been felled and replanted with conifers or conifer–hardwood mixtures: the old, uneven-aged forest has, save for small fragments, gone.

### Replanting

The planting era can be said to have begun with the Restoration, by which time woodland resources were at an all-time low. In 1668 the Crown took powers for the enclosure and planting of the Forest of Dean, the only limitation being that no more than 11,000 acres could be behind fences at any one time (Forestry Commission, 1959; Hart, 1966). In 1698 *An Act for the Increase and Preservation of Timber in New Forest* empowered the Crown to enclose and plant up to 6,000 acres at a time there, and though neither in the Forest of Dean nor the New Forest was the new policy pursued with sustained enthusiasm much planting was done, some of it at the expense of the remaining semi-natural woodland, which was destroyed in the process (Tubbs, 1969). Much of the early interest in forestry, however, focused on the enhancement of estate landscapes and it was not until after the 1720s that commercial planting on private estates gained momentum and then, to begin with, mainly in Scotland (Ferguson, 1956; Edlin, 1966). Between the late eighteenth and late nineteenth centuries a considerable area of woodland was planted, most of it on private estates, and though much was of conifer, in the lowlands much was also of oak, planted in the pious hope that wooden walls would remain the bastions of Britain when the seedlings reached maturity. A surprising amount of new hazel and chestnut coppice with oak standards was also established during this period, as a comparison between the first edition *Ordnance Survey* and the situation today in such counties as Hampshire and Dorset will confirm.

After the establishment of the Forestry Commission immediately after the First World War, afforestation took on a new dimension. Although the Forestry Commission received many of the old Crown woodlands from the Office of Woods, it started life with a comparatively small landholding. By

* Goodwood MSS in the West Sussex Record Office.

1971 it controlled nearly 3 million acres of land, of which 2,109,200 acres were either planted or awaiting planting (Forestry Commission, 1971). Most of the plantations established by the Commission between 1919 and 1971 were on upland sheepwalk. Many acquisitions, however, included woods of native deciduous species, and acquisition too often spelt their demise in favour of the faster growing conifers. Similar events have occurred in the private sector of forestry, though here the trend towards even-aged conifer monocultures has been to some extent countered by the desire of estate owners to leave the old coppices and other fragments of native deciduous woodland for the benefit of the shoot.

## CONSERVING THE PRESENT WOODLAND

From the viewpoint of historical ecology it is often convenient to think of the modern woodlands of Britain as belonging to four broad categories: first, woods which are known or can reasonably be inferred to have had a continuous history of tree cover for a very long period of time, perhaps since prehistoric times; second, woods of native species of trees and shrubs which have arisen by natural colonization of open ground during periods when grazing and cultivation have ceased; third, woods of native species which have been deliberately planted; and fourth, the plantations of non-native conifers which have been established since the eighteenth century.

### Woods with a Continuous History

From what has been said earlier, it can be seen that only a small proportion of British woodlands fall into the first category, but it is important to identify them because they are likely to be of special scientific and historical interest. It seems reasonable to suppose that the longer the history of woodland cover on a site, the richer its plant and animal communities will be. Woods with a continuous history of tree cover may still exhibit some of the structural and pedological characteristics of the rich forest ecosystem of Atlantic times, before man began to have a significant effect (Dimbleby, Chapter 18). It was said earlier that few woods had not been modified by man, and it was perhaps implied that they were thereby necessarily depleted of interest. Biological depletion may, however, be compensated for by an increase in historical interest, because long-established woods often reflect in their species composition, location, shape, and sometimes also their age structure, the rural economy of which they were part. They are cultural monuments in as valid a sense as are the towering ruins of the medieval abbey churches whose builders may have first enclosed and coppiced them.

Continuity of woodland cover in a particular locality over long spans of time is often difficult to prove, and because of the absence of documents is seldom possible once one passes further back in time than the eleventh century, save, perhaps, with the aid of soil pollen analysis (Dimbleby, 1961; 1967; Chapter 18). This technique has yielded valuable information about the history of a number of woods in the New Forest, some of which appear to have had a continuous history of woodland cover (though, of course, the relative proportions of the different tree species have changed) whilst others have proved, sometimes unexpectedly, to be secondary regrowth on heathland or abandoned arable fields (Dimbleby and Gill, 1955; Dimbleby, 1962). The relative floristic and faunistic richness of a wood will itself, however, indicate whether the wood is of respectable antiquity—though there are obviously elements of a chicken-and-egg situation in adopting this argument. Nevertheless, woodland which in the field is found to be biologically diverse can usually be given a reasonable pedigree from historical evidence.

In the field there are a number of definite pointers to the relics of the primary woodland. Primary woods are often characterized by uneven-aged stands of trees in which a biologically mature generation is present. Apart from the dominant oak, ash or possibly beech, other native species which were once relatively important woodland trees but are now of only local occurrence may also be present—notably Wych elm, *Ulmus glabra* and the native limes, *Tilia cordata* and *T. platyphyllos*. Successful tree regeneration at the present time may be inconspicuous because of the grazing pressure to which many primary woodland relics are now subject, especially in the uplands. A rich epiphytic flora of lichens and mosses and a rich invertebrate fauna—especially beetles—associated mainly with the older generations of trees are further indicators of antiquity. On intrinsically better soils the ground flora of the primary woodland is generally richer than in more recently established woods, though in fact most relict primary woods are on the poorer acidic soils where the ground flora is naturally impoverished.

Not all primary woodland will exhibit the characteristics outlined here. In southeast England most sites with a continuous history of woodland cover will have been managed as coppices since medieval times and little of their timber will have been allowed to reach biological maturity before being felled. Thus they will tend to have become impoverished of the epiphytic flora and invertebrate fauna associated with the older trees. On the other hand, many coppices are on relatively good soils and have a richer ground flora than most primary woods, as for instance in the ancient coppices of the East Anglian boulder clays.

Finally, in this brief survey of the characteristics of primary woodland, it is important to look at the soil profile, for this, if the woodland is a relic of the primary forest cover, is likely to have been less modified than on a site which has seen a phase of deforestation. At Staverton Park, for example, the soil beneath the old woodland of oak and holly is a leached brown earth, whilst the heathland nearby is on a humus-iron podzol (Peterken, 1969). A similar distinction between heathland and woodland soils on similar parent material is evident in many New Forest sites (Tubbs, 1969). Soil degradation has evidently been arrested by the persistence of the woodland.

We need look no further for reasons to justify the conservation of at least a sample of the primary woodlands than that they are part of the cultural heritage of Britain, at once both a link with the forest environment which faced our predecessors and a record of the ways in which they exploited some of the woods they suffered to remain uncleared. Such woodlands as those of the New Forest and the surviving medieval deer parks such as Staverton are of immense ecological and historical interest—their study lies at the meeting-place of the two disciplines—and can justifiably demand special attention from the conservation movement. It is the more startling, therefore, to find that no reasonably comprehensive inventory of localities exists, though the nucleus of one has gradually emerged over the past decade.

## Secondary Woods with Native Species

It is reasonable to view many secondary woods which have arisen naturally in a similar light to the primary woodland, and, indeed, it is in practice sometimes difficult to distinguish one from the other where they occur side by side. The secondary woods may be floristically and faunistically impoverished compared with primary woodland, but ecologically their development is often of great interest especially where, as on some New Forest sites, they may be reversing processes of soil degradation which have been associated with earlier woodland clearance and the subsequent dominance of heathland vegetation.

Many of our scientifically important woods are nature reserves. The Nature Conservancy has a fine series of upland oak and ash woods, many of which possess the characteristics of relict primary woodland. In the lowlands some of the ancient coppices and common woods are owned and managed by the Conservancy or by the county naturalists' trusts, whilst natural secondary woodland is well represented on a number of chalkland nature reserves. Other old woodland areas are protected by the ownership and enlightened management of some local authorities: Epping Forest and Burnham Beeches, for example, are managed by the City of London, and a number of important chalkland woods are managed by Hampshire County Council, some of them mainly as nature reserves.

Conservation organizations with limited resources are sometimes wary of acquiring woodland properties because of the management problems they often appear to pose. Many scientifically important woods exhibit little natural regeneration at present, either because the canopy is closed or because of the presence of grazing animals. Other woods appear to be comparatively even-aged and seem to offer long-term difficulties of regeneration. The conservation of coppice poses the most immediate difficulties because sufficient manpower must be available to cut the coppice on a reasonably short rotation if the ecology of the woodland is not to change fundamentally: the rich and colourful ground flora flourishes in particular under short-rotation coppicing. Most of the problems arising from apparent imbalances in age structure, however, tend to be less due to real difficulties than to the conventional forester's concept of natural woodland, which demands an even spread of age classes and an abundance of fresh natural regeneration. There is no ecological reason why, or evidence that, such a situation was normal in the primary forest cover. In woodland where the trees, or a proportion of them, are allowed a natural life span, which in the case of oak on a good site might be in excess of 400 years, gaps in age structure become irrelevant. Natural regeneration under 'natural' conditions is seldom prolific, nor need it be for the wood to perpetuate itself (Shaw, 1968). Thus, except in the coppices, policies of minimal management are often all that are needed in order to maintain the scientific, historical and, indeed, the aesthetic interest.

Nowhere, perhaps, is this lesson clearer than in the New Forest. The Forest contains the most extensive and finest ancient woodlands in lowland Britain, much of them with a well-established continuity reaching back into prehistory. Oak is generally dominant on the clay soils and beech on the lighter soils, with holly forming an understory to both: hazel has disappeared in historic times, evidently mainly as a result of grazing. The woods have a long and well-documented history of periodic exploitation balanced by periodic protection from felling, though grazing has been more or less continuous for some hundreds of years. Ancient, mature oaks and beeches are a conspicuous feature of the woods, but their age structure as a whole is varied and is related to past fluctuations in herbivore populations: whenever the numbers of deer and commoners' ponies and cattle fell, a phase of woodland regeneration took place. Since the late nineteenth century there has been a significant overall expansion of the woodland, though this has now long since ceased and natural regeneration is at present inconspicuous (Peterken and Tubbs, 1965). These 'ancient and ornamental' woodlands, so called, were given statutory protection from commercial management as long ago as the New Forest Act of 1877. The New Forest Act of 1949, however, made provision for their 'regeneration', and in the early 1950s there began a variety of ill-conceived and unnecessary attempts to do so. Despite evidence to the contrary (not least that obtainable from a walk in the woods), it was declared necessary to carry out widespread group fellings and replanting and, latterly, to open up the canopy in further areas by selective fellings. Fortunately, before irreparable damage occurred, a public outcry led to the cessation of this policy of unnecessary interference and, in view of public and professional scientific opinion and, indeed, of changing attitudes in the Forestry Commission, who are responsible for the woods, more rational policies of management will undoubtedly be adopted.

## Deliberately Planted Woodlands

The New Forest woodlands are relatively extensive—in excess of 8,000 acres—but most scientifically important woods are little more than tiny fragments of the original woodland cover and collectively represent only a tiny proportion of the existing woodland in Britain. Whilst it is important to conserve as much as possible of this heritage of woodland communities, it must be recognized that the large-scale conservation of our commoner and more widespread woodland flora and fauna can only be achieved in the much larger area of woodland planted in comparatively recent times, that is, in the third and fourth categories mentioned earlier. Here, too, there will be more scope for satisfying the public demand for recreation space, and ample opportunity to diversify the new conifer plantations in species and appearance to go some way to meeting the criticism that they are a visual affront.

All this has come to be recognized by the largest woodland owner in Britain, the Forestry Commission, and it was recognized long ago by many private owners. The recent review of Government forestry policy published gives the Forestry Commission a clear mandate in these fields (Forestry Commission, 1972). It also, incidentally, recognizes for the first time that there are social and economic disadvantages in continued massive upland conifer afforestation. 1972 also saw the publication of Steele's Forestry Commission booklet on wildlife conservation in woodlands (Steele, 1972). This describes clearly and concisely how the forester can improve commercial woodlands as habitats for plants and animals with comparatively little loss of production, essentially by resisting the temptation to tidiness and by retaining and encouraging native trees and shrubs and features such as dead and decaying timber, even if only in odd corners and along roadsides.

The widespread adoption of the guidelines laid down by Steele would go a long way towards enhancing the value of commercial woodlands as refuges for many elements of our native flora and fauna. It would be wrong, however, to think that this thereby absolves us from further concern over the destruction of our old deciduous woodlands, which is still taking place in order to create the commercial plantations. The economic scales are weighted heavily against the survival of deciduous woodland on many private estates and there are financial limits to the number of woods which

6

can be acquired and managed by conservation organizations or local authorities. The Forestry Commission is showing fresh concern for the conservation of native woodland on state property, but most of our native woodland is in private hands. If landowners are to be encouraged to maintain these woods then there will have to be financial incentives, possibly by allowing land owners to obtain tax relief for woodland of native non-commercial species in the same way that they can now claim for commercial plantations of alien conifers (Jeffers, 1972).

## REFERENCES

Ashton, T. A. (1963). *Iron and Steel in the Industrial Revolution*, 3rd edn., Manchester Univ. Econ. Hist. Series No. **2**, 265 pp.

Courtney, F. M., and Staines, S. J. (1971). Soils in the Wistman's Wood Forest Nature Reserve, *Quarterly J. Devon Trust for Nat. Cons.*, **3**, 109–14.

Darby, H. C. (1950). Domesday woodland, *Econ. Hist. Rev.*, 2nd ser., **3**, 21–43.

Darby, H. C. (ed.) (1952-67). *Domesday Geographies of England*, Cambridge University Press, Cambridge.

Dimbleby, G. W. (1961). Soil pollen analysis, *J. Soil Science*, **12**, 1–11.

Dimbleby, G. W. (1962). *The Development of British Heathlands and their Soils*, Oxford Forestry Memoirs, No. **23**, Clarendon, Oxford, 120 pp.

Dimbleby, G. W. (1967). *Plants and Archaeology*, John Baker, London, 187 pp.

Dimbleby, G. W., and Gill, J. M. (1955). The occurrence of podzols under deciduous woodlands in the New Forest, *Forestry* **28**, 95–106.

Donkin, R. A. (1960). The Cistercian setltement and the English Royal Forests, *Citeaux*, **11**, 1–33.

Edlin, H. L. (1966). *Trees, Woods and Man*, 2nd edn., Collins, London, 272 pp.

Ferguson, J. L. F. (1956). Forestry in Perthshire : Notes on past history, *Forestry*, **29**, 81–9.

Forestry Commission (1959). *Report of the Forest of Dean Committee*, HMSO, Cmnd. 686, London, 59 pp.

Forestry Commission (1971). *Fifty-first Annual Report and Accounts for 1970/1*, HMSO, London, 92 pp.

Forestry Commission (1972). *Forestry Policy*, HMSO, London, 15 pp.

Hart, C. E. (1966). *Royal Forest: A History of Dean's Woods as Producers of Timber*, Clarendon, Oxford, 367 pp.

Jeffers, J. N. R. (1972). Conifers and nature conservation, *Conifers in the British Isles*, Proc. 3rd Conifer Conference, Royal Horticultural Soc., London, 59–73.

Moore, P. D., and Chater, E. H. (1969). The changing vegetation of west-central Wales in the light of human history, *J. Ecol.*, **57**, 361–79.

Neilson, H. (1942). Early English woodland and waste, *J. Econ. Hist.*, **11**, 54–62.

Pennington, W. (1969). *The History of British Vegetation*, English University Press, London, 152 pp.

Peterken, G. F. (1969). Development of vegetation in Staverton Park, Suffolk, *Field Studies*, **3**, 1–39.

Peterken, G. F., and Tubbs, C. R. (1965). Woodland and regeneration in the New Forest, Hampshire, since 1650, *J. Appl. Ecol.*, **2**, 159–70.

Roden, D. (1968). Woodland and its management in the medieval Chilterns, *Forestry*, **41**, 59–71.

Russell, J. C. (1948). *British Medieval Population,* London, reprinted by Univ. of New Mexico Press, Albuquerque, N.M., 389 pp.

Shaw, M. W. (1968). Factors affecting the natural regeneration of sessile oak *Quercas petraea* in North Wales. 1, A preliminary study of acorn production, viability and losses, *J. Ecol.,* **56,** 565–83.

Simmons, I. G. (1965). The Dartmoor oak copses: observations and speculations, *Field Studies,* **2,** 225–35.

Stamp, L. D. (1964). *Man and the Land,* Collins, New Naturalist, London, 272 pp.

Steele, R. C. (1972). *Wildlife Conservation in Woodlands,* Forestry Commission Booklet, **29,** HMSO, 68 pp.

Tansley. A. G. (1939). *The British Islands and their Vegetation,* Cambridge University Press, Cambridge, 930 pp.

Taylor, C. C. (1967). Whiteparish: a study of the development of a forest-edge parish, *Wilts. Arch. & Nat. Hist. Mag.,* **62,** 79–102.

Tubbs, C. R. (1969). *The New Forest: An Ecological History,* David & Charles, Newton Abbot, 248 pp.

Turner, G. J. (1901). Select pleas of the forest, *Seldon Society Publications,* **13,** London.

Watt, A. S. (1924). On the ecology of British beechwoods with special reference to their regeneration, *J. Ecol.,* **13,** 145–204.

Worth, R. H. (1953). *Dartmoor,* reprinted by David & Charles, Newton Abbot, as *Worth's Dartmoor,* 1967, 523 pp.

Wrigley, E. A. (1962). The supply of raw materials in the industrial revolution, *Econ. Hist. Rev.,* **15,** 1–16.

# CHAPTER 10

# Heather Moorland: A Man-Made Ecosystem

G. R. MILLER and A. WATSON

The northern uplands of Britain are mainly treeless and covered with short vegetation which is mostly less than one metre in height. Many of these moors, and the lowland heaths of the south (Harrison, Chapter 8), are characterized by a predominance of heather (*Calluna vulgaris*), an ericaceous dwarf shrub. Its distribution extends from sub-arctic Scandinavia to the Mediterranean, and from Ireland to the Ural Mountains, where it grows in many different plant associations and occurs in various habitats from the sea coast to the hill tops.

*Calluna* flourishes particularly in eastern Britain and along the western seaboard of Europe from southern Scandinavia to northern Spain, where it dominates the vegetation of large areas, often in association with other dwarf shrubs. On the Continent, much of this land has been afforested or turned into highly productive farms, but this is less true of Britain and extensive heather moors remain in the east-central Scottish Highlands, north-eastern England and eastern Ireland. Here the acid and usually well-drained podzolic soils support a luxuriant growth of *Calluna* and in some places few other flowering plants occur. *Calluna* thrives less well in the cool moist climate and waterlogged soils of western Britain where it is merely one of several main constituents of the communities on blanket peat, including *Molinia caerulea*, *Trichophorum cespitosum* and *Eriophorum* spp. Only locally, on the best drained hillocks or slopes, is *Calluna* as vigorous and predominant as on the eastern heather moors.

Heather moorland covers roughly 0·8 million hectares in Scotland and 0·4 million hectares in England and Wales; there are also large tracts in eastern Ireland. Because most of the soils are freely drained and capable of economic exploitation, farmers, foresters and other land users have competed for this large area since the turn of the century. It is now recognized that moorland can make a significant contribution to the economy of our sparsely populated uplands and this has stimulated much research. As a result, probably more has been written about the origin, characteristics, management and potential for development of heather moorland than about any other kind of upland vegetation. Gimingham (1972) has thoroughly reviewed the literature and should be consulted for references to most of the original scientific papers.

## ORIGIN

Small areas of dwarf shrub heath have developed behind coastal sand dunes, on drained or drying bogs and, more widely, above the climatic tree limit. These apart, ecologists now generally accept that most heaths have arisen as a result of the destruction of woodland, but it is uncertain whether climatic change or human interference was the more important cause.

Many pollen analyses from various parts of Britain suggest that heath and bog vegetation extended and woodlands declined during the cool and wet Atlantic period beginning about 7,000 years ago (cf. Godwin, 1956). Nonetheless, northern Britain was still heavily forested when Neolithic men settled about 3000 BC. From this time onwards, however, forest destruction accelerated. At first, people practised a shifting agriculture close to the sea coast and on the drier slopes of the lower hills. By deliberately burning and felling, they made open spaces for growing crops and grazing livestock, used them for a short while, and then abandoned them for fresh ground. From about 500 BC onwards, human settlements became more permanent and forest clearance spread to poorer ground. The intensification and extension of primitive farming coincided with the onset of the cooler and wetter climate of the sub-Atlantic period. Together these factors not only destroyed woodland cover but also inhibited its regeneration.

By the end of the seventeenth century, a rapid expansion of agriculture and increasing demands for timber for buildings, boats, implements and charcoal had led to the almost complete destruction of natural woodland in England. Iron ore was taken north for smelting in Scotland but some of the more remote parts remained unscathed for a further 100 years.

Wherever soils are acid, *Calluna* was and still is abundant in open parts of pine, birch and oak woodland. Forest clearance would have allowed it to flourish, and the dwarf shrub vegetation of the scattered glades presumably spread and merged to form large stretches of heather moor. These open moors provided good free-range grazing for sheep and, in Scotland, stocks of hill sheep increased rapidly in the late eighteenth and early nineteenth centuries. Today grazing and burning ensure that tree seedlings are destroyed and that heather moor is maintained wherever there are acid, freely drained soils. On many moors, viable tree seed is now so scarce that even if burning and grazing were to cease there would not necessarily be an immediate reversion to woodland.

## VEGETATION AND ANIMALS

The predominance of *Calluna* and its influence on micro-climate and soils restrict the diversity of plant species on heather moorland. Several dwarf shrubs of the family Ericaceae are common but there are few other shrubs, herbs or grasses. There is, however, an abundant and varied bryophyte and lichen flora. Many of the characteristic species of heather moor also occur in woodlands, and this is sometimes cited as evidence that moors have been created by forest clearance.

The floristic composition of *Calluna*-dominated communities is related to regional differences in climate, soils, and past and present management. Gimingham (1972) has described and classified several heath associations. Using wider categories, McVean and Ratcliffe (1962) recognized the following three main associations where *Calluna* predominates below the tree line in the Scottish uplands:

(a) Dry heather moor (Callunetum vulgaris) comprises more or less pure stands of *Calluna* with a moss layer consisting largely of *Dicranum scoparium* and *Hypnum cupressiforme*. Small patches of abundant *Erica cinerea* and *Vaccinium* spp. may occur and this association includes the *Calluna-Erica cinerea* and some of the *Calluna-Vaccinium* heaths of Gimingham. Typically, this community occurs on podzolic soils, particularly iron–humus podzols.

(b) *Arctostaphylos*-rich heather moor (Arctostaphyleto-Callunetum) is an exact equivalent of Gimingham's *Calluna-Arctostaphylos* heath. It is a distinct variant of pure heather moor and contains a much greater variety of dwarf shrubs and herbs. Apart from *Arctostaphylos,* the herbs *Lathyrus montanus, Lotus corniculatus, Viola riviniana* and *Pyrola media* are frequent associates of *Calluna*. The association usually occurs on shallow, rather stony podzolic soils which lack a deep layer of raw humus at the surface.

(c) Damp heather moor (Vaccineto-Callunetum) occurs on steep, north-facing slopes and belongs to the *Calluna-Vaccinium* heaths recognized by Gimingham. *Vaccinium myrtillus* is abundant and may gain local co-dominance with *Calluna*. *Empetrum* spp. may also be present, and there is a conspicuous and deep layer of mosses, chiefly *Sphagnum capillaceum, Hylocomium splendens* or *Rhytidiadelphus loreus*. The association usually occurs on a deep layer of acid peaty humus—on drained or drying bog peat, on podzol rankers, or on peaty podzols.

Heather moorland supports distinctive animal communities, some of which have been described briefly by Pearsall (1950). Recent work has shown that the abundance of vertebrates on different moors is related to the type of underlying rock. Thus moors over base-rich rocks such as epidiorite support larger stocks of red grouse (*Lagopus lagopus scoticus*) than moors over acid rocks such as granite (Miller *et al.*, 1966; Jenkins *et al.*, 1967; Picozzi, 1968). This is also true of mountain hares, *Lepus timidus* (Watson *et al.*, 1973), and of several other species of mammal and bird, both herbivorous and insectivorous (Nethersole-Thompson and Watson, 1974). Less is known about the invertebrate fauna of moorland, and Cragg (1961) remains one of the best sources of information. More recently, studies for the International Biological Programme have concentrated on the complex communities of moorland invertebrates in plant litter and the soil (cf. Heal, 1972). Nevertheless, few quantitative data on moorland animals have been published and there are many opportunities for research. For instance, no one has determined if different types of moor support different communities or densities of animals, and even the habitat selection of common and conspicuous moorland birds such as golden plover (*Pluvialis apricaria*), curlew (*Numenius arquata*) and black grouse (*Lyrurus tetrix*) is little understood.

## LIFE HISTORY OF *CALLUNA*

During their life, *Calluna* plants change gradually in morphology and growth habit. These changes represent stages in physiological ageing that are reflected by differences in the plant's vigour and in its interaction with other species. This is an important consideration in deciding how best to manage heather moorland. There are four distinct phases (see Gimingham, 1972).

The 'pioneer' phase is one of establishment and early growth, either from seed or from buds at the base of charred stems remaining after a fire. The contribution that other species, including bryophytes, make to the plant cover is greatest during this period, which may last for 3–10 years. Plants next pass into a 'building' phase, which may last up to the age of about 15 years. During this period, *Calluna* develops a dense continuous canopy which suppresses bryophytes, lichens and other low-growing plants. From 15 to about 25 years, *Calluna* is in its 'mature' phase, when the plants are less vigorous and the central branches begin to spread outwards, so allowing light to penetrate to the ground. Bryophytes flourish and the lichen *Parmelia physoides* may begin to colonize the lower parts of the main branches of *Calluna*. Beyond about 25 years, these processes go further and plants become 'degenerate'. The central branches become heavily encrusted with lichens and eventually die, so leaving a space where bryophytes flourish and other species, including *Calluna* seedlings, may establish. Some of the outer branches of the moribund plant may become prostrate, root adventitiously, and continue growing with renewed vigour.

The rate at which one phase succeeds another varies. Where net growth is rapid, the plant ages quickly and may become degenerate when less than 20 years old. Conversely, physiological ageing is retarded when net growth is slow. Continual pruning, whether by clipping, grazing or wind blast, reduces net growth and so prolongs the period when the plant is physiologically young. Indeed, Grant and Hunter (1966) have shown that frequent clipping can maintain *Calluna* as a compact and vigorous plant, whereas unclipped plants of the same age become tall and spreading and lose vigour.

## ANNUAL PRODUCTION AND CHEMICAL COMPOSITION OF *CALLUNA* SHOOTS

Because it is difficult to measure accurately litter fall and increments of wood, there are few estimates of total above-ground production by *Calluna*. Forrest (1971), for example, found 168 g/m² on blanket peat in the Pennines, where *Calluna* covered 70 per cent of the ground. Some figures for net annual production, i.e. the mean annual accumulation of dry matter, have also been reported (e.g. Ballamy and Holland, 1966). However, most data are for the annual production of green shoots and flowers. This is easily measured and, in any case, is of greatest relevance to herbivores.

Production in the first few years after a fire is very variable and depends on how quickly the *Calluna* cover is restored. In contrast to the high production figures found on lowland heaths (Harrison, Chapter 8), Miller and Miles (1969) found only 24 g/m² in the first year after burning at a rapidly regenerating site in North-east Scotland, and only 5 g/m² where regeneration was slow. Such wide variations depend particularly on fire temperature, the age of the heather when burnt, soil type and grazing.

Estimates of the production of green shoots and flowers by *Calluna* in more or less closed communities vary from about 130 to over 300 g/m² (Table 10.1). Forrest's (1971) data were obtained from a *Calluna-Eriophorum vaginatum* blanket bog in the North Pennines, whereas the other figures all relate to heather moors in North-east Scotland. No doubt some of the wide variation in the values for mean production can be attributed to differences in altitude and in the cover of *Calluna* at the various study areas. However, the ranges of production measured on these areas are roughly comparable.

Some attention has been given to the effects of ageing and weather on *Calluna* production. Miller and Miles (1969) studied several stands of different ages with more or less complete *Calluna* cover and found that production did not vary appreciably up to 36–40 years. On the other hand, Barclay-Estrup (1970) concluded that production on an unburnt moor

**Table 10.1.**  Estimates of the annual production of green shoots and flowers by *Calluna* in more or less closed communities

| Source | National grid reference | Altitude (m) | *Calluna* cover (%) | Production (g/m²) Mean | Range |
|---|---|---|---|---|---|
| Miller and Miles (1969) | NO 702904 | 120–220 | 90 | 246 | 217–278 |
| Moss (1969)* | NO 253981 | 410–500 | 70 | 207 | 166–272 |
| | NJ 290905 | 340–410 | 70 | 161 | 123–193 |
| | NO 366928 | 300–460 | 70 | 226 | 202–251 |
| Barcay-Estrup (1970)† | NO 887952 | 107 | 41–94 | 316 | 141–442 |
| Forrest (1971) | NY 769331 | 550 | 70 | 130 | Not stated |
| Grant (1971) | NO 674777 | 215 | 51–82 | 139 | 86–205 |

\* Excluding data for Kerloch.
† Excluding data for pioneer heather.

reached a peak in the building phase at about nine years and thereafter declined. However, there was a parallel decline in the cover of *Calluna* and, if this is taken into account, there is no evidence of a decline in productivity until the degenerate phase is reached. Differences in climate between one moor and another might be expected to affect production. Indeed (using the figures from Table 10.1), there is a large, although not statistically significant, negative correlation ($r = -0.640$) between mean production and median altitude. Moreover, year to year variations in production at one site can be related to the weather during the growing season. Miller and Miles (1969) found that warm, dry, sunny weather between May and August favoured rapid growth and a high production of shoots; some 80 per cent of the observed variation in shoot production over five years could be accounted for by variations in summer weather. Flower production, however, was not related to summer weather.

Although different methods have been used, production from stands of pure *Calluna* is similar to that recorded from other types of upland vegetation. For example, by clipping at intervals during the growing season, Rawes and Welch (1969) found 202, 264 and 367 g/m² for swards of *Agrostis-Festuca, Nardus* and *Juncus squarrosus* at about 550 m in the north Pennines. However, data from a wide range of communities in Teesdale (Bellamy *et al.*, 1969) suggest that many spring and mire communities exceed these levels of production. Moreover, even the highest recorded production of *Calluna,* 442 g/m² (Barclay-Estrup, 1970), is far less than the estimates of 1,300 g/m² for pine woodland (Ovington, 1957) and 800 g/m² for birch woodland (Ovington and Madgwick, 1959). Although these data are from different parts of Britain and therefore are not strictly comparable, they suggest that one of the consequences of replacing woodland by moorland ecosystems might have been a decrease in the production of dry matter.

The content of major nutrients in *Calluna* shoots declines as the plant grows older. The greatest decrease occurs during the first four years after burning; thereafter there is little change up to 25 years (Figure 10.1). This pattern is particularly marked for nitrogen, phosphorus, potassium and magnesium, but not for calcium. However, Thomas and Dougall (1947) showed that, up to about seven years after burning, the decline in the content of nitrogen, phosphorus and calcium was balanced by an increasing yield of green shoots; thereafter the cover of *Calluna* was presumably more or less complete and they recorded a net decrease in the yield of nutrients per unit area. *Calluna* shoots have a high content of calcium and magnesium compared with other common moorland plants. However, this is not true of nitrogen and phosphorus, and *Calluna* is an exceptionally poor source of these important nutrients.

Both the quality and quantity of production from *Calluna* can be im-

proved by fertilizers. Phosphatic fertilizer will increase the phosphorus
content of the shoots but does not appear to affect growth on the podzolic
soils of heather moors (e.g. Miller, 1968). On the other hand, nitrogenous
fertilizer greatly increases both the growth and nitrogen content of *Calluna*
shoots (Miller, 1968; Miller *et al.*, 1970). Presumably leaching and rapid
uptake by the vegetation quickly exhaust the nitrate, because this response

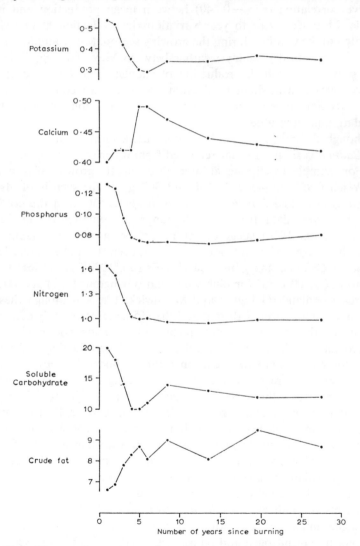

**Figure 10.1.** Changes in nutrient content (as a percentage of dry matter) of shoot
tips of *Calluna vulgaris* sampled in December after autumnal burning. The
figures show that most nutrients decline with increasing age of *Calluna*.

can no longer be detected three years after the fertilizer is spread. These findings support the view that the fibrous peat of heather moors has a greater deficiency of available nitrogen than of available phosphorus. In fact, phosphatic fertilizer does stimulate *Calluna* growth on the colloidal peats of western blanket bog, where phosphorus is acutely deficient (McVean, 1959).

## UTILIZATION

Traditionally, man has used heather moorland for free-range grazing by his domestic livestock and for sport. In the eighteenth and early nineteenth centuries, the black cattle industry flourished in the Highlands and many store cattle were exported annually to the south (Haldane, 1952). At this time sheep and goats were kept mainly for home use. However, the market for hill cattle eventually declined and many thousands of sheep were moved into the Highlands to replace them. By the 1830s sheep farming had spread to the Inner Hebrides and most Scottish hill grazings had been converted to sheepwalks. Although less profitable today than in its heyday, sheep farming still continues as one of the two main uses of heather moorland, and cattle are few or absent on most hill farms.

The other main use of heather moorland is for the shooting of red grouse, an endemic sub-species of the willow grouse (*Lagopus lagopus*). Red grouse are virtually confined to open moorland and presumably extended their range and became more abundant after the forests were destroyed. The birds had long been regarded as game, but no great importance was attached to them until about the middle of the nineteenth century. At that time many industrialists and merchants in the south were becoming affluent, road and rail links with the north were improving rapidly, and guns became more efficient. These developments combined to make grouse shooting a highly fashionable sport that was profitable to the landowner—and it has remained so up to the present day.

The practice of stalking and shooting red deer (*Cervus elaphus*) emerged at about the same time. Although red deer originally lived in open woodland, they have adapted to a more or less treeless environment in Britain. Because of their sporting value, the Victorians deliberately fostered large stocks on deer 'forests' (paradoxically these are mostly devoid of trees) until densities far exceeded those elsewhere in Europe. In recent years, many deer have been fenced out of their wintering grounds to make way for farming, afforestation and hydroelectric schemes. Often this was done without reducing deer stocks and the ousted deer then marauded farms and plantations. In 1959 the Red Deer Commission was established and, since then, landowners have taken bigger culls. Deer forests are mostly on high

**Table 10.2.** Human exploitation of the heather moorland ecosystem for secondary production

| Crop | Average density in spring (no./ha) | Biomass (kg./ha) | Production of young (no./ha/year) | Annual crop taken by man (no./ha) | (kg/ha) | Sources of data |
|------|------|------|------|------|------|------|
| Sheep | 0·30 | 13·6 | 0·24 | 0·24 | 5·7 | Cunningham et al. (1971); Eadie (1970) |
| Red deer | 0·089 | 6·1 | 0·015 | 0·014 | 1·1 | Red Deer Commission (1967) McVean and Lockie (1969) |
| Mountain hare | 0·16 | 0·43 | 0·50 | See note 2 | | Flux (1970); Watson et al. (1973) |
| Red grouse | 0·65 | 0·41 | 0·89 | 0·40 | 0·25 | Jenkins et al. (1963; 1967) |

1. These data are averages from a small number of study areas in north-east Scotland and so should not be interpreted too widely. For example, there are few sheep or hares in most of the Cairngorm Mountains.

2. Mountain hares are seldom exploited and so it is impossible to calculate a reliable figure for the annual crop. However, data from a few moors where hares are particularly abundant and where bag records are kept (Hewson, 1954) suggest that an average annual yield of about 0·7 kg/ha is obtained there.

ground or on westerly moors, where *Calluna* is less important in the vegetation than on the eastern grouse moors. Nonetheless, deer do seek shelter and forage on the lower heather moors, particularly in eastern Scotland in winter.

On many heather moors, *Calluna* is so predominant in the vegetation that there is little else for herbivores to eat. Thus cattle, sheep, deer and grouse, together with mountain hares, all depend to some extent on *Calluna* for food. Several workers have studied the diet and feeding preferences of hill sheep (e.g. Hunter, 1962; Martin, 1964), and all agree that *Calluna* is an important food at some time in the year. However, the preferences of sheep vary seasonally, depending on what other forage is available; for example sheep with access to *Agrostis-Festuca* grassland do not graze *Calluna* heavily in summer. Less is known about the feeding habits of hill cattle and red deer, but certainly both, like the sheep, may graze *Calluna* heavily in winter.

For both mountain hares (Hewson, 1962) and red grouse (Jenkins *et al.*, 1963), *Calluna* comprises nearly 100 per cent of the diet in winter and about 50 per cent in summer. Indeed, the almost total dependence of grouse on *Calluna* has been the subject of much research (e.g. Miller *et al.*, 1966; 1970; Jenkins *et al.*, 1967). It has been shown that (i) differences in the average number of red grouse breeding in spring on different moors are related to the quantity and quality of *Calluna* there, (ii) year to year changes in breeding stocks are related to weather-induced variations in the growth and dieback of *Calluna*, and (iii) breeding stocks can be increased by fertilizing and by burning the moor in small patches.

In general, herbivores are not abundant enough on heather moors to utilize fully the production from *Calluna*. During the first year or two after burning, hares and sheep may graze *Calluna* heavily but utilization otherwise seldom approaches the 60 per cent that is thought necessary to maintain *Calluna* in a productive and nutritious condition (Grant and Hunter, 1966).

Secondary production from heather moorland has received little attention. Table 10.2 provides a guide to the biomass and proportion taken by man as an annual crop. In fact, not all the production from sheep and deer can be validly attributed to heather moorland. In winter and spring, hill sheep are fed supplements and are allowed on to 'inbye' grass; and red deer seek much of their forage on the high heatherless plateaux during summer and on the grassy glen bottoms in winter. Thus the sum of the annual crops taken from each animal is certainly a gross over-estimate of the secondary production derived from *Calluna*. Despite this, the annual yield of about 7 kg/ha is very little compared with what can be cropped from more fertile land.

This low production from moorland herbivores provides part of the case for those who advocate forestry as a more efficient, productive and beneficial use of moorland. McVean and Lockie (1969) and Gimingham (1972) discuss this matter at some length. However, in an industrialized country the biological productivity of a land use is not usually regarded as being very important and, indeed, may be of no economic value in the short term. For example, on some moors red grouse give a far greater economic return than sheep, cattle, deer, hares or trees, although the biological production from each of these is usually greater. Tourism yields no biological crop at all, yet it can produce more revenue than all other land uses put together. Biological production is highly regarded only in a primitive, hunting type of economy although it is important for conservation in the long term.

## MANAGEMENT BY FIRE

Heather moorland is managed to ensure a continuing supply of nutritious food for the sheep, deer and grouse stocks that are exploited by man. Because there is usually insufficient grazing to maintain a short and vigorous sward, *Calluna* plants become tall and large amounts of dead and woody material accumulate. This excess production is most easily removed by periodical burning—virtually a crude method of pruning *Calluna*. If it is well done, burning can rejuvenate a stand of *Calluna* and provide a crop of rapidly growing and nutritious shoots that herbivores graze preferentially. On the other hand, bad burning can do irreparable damage.

The effects of fire on *Calluna* and its habitat have been much studied in recent years. This work has been reviewed by Miller (1964) and, more recently, by McVean and Lockie (1969) and Gimingham (1971; 1972). Aspects of practical management were considered by Watson and Miller (1970), and therefore only a brief summary of the main findings will be given here.

The practice of moor burning probably arose from the use of fire to clear the original forest cover. No doubt it was at first haphazard, as it still is in much of western Britain where burning is mainly for sheep and deer. However, in the east, many estates practise controlled rotational burning to maintain large grouse stocks as well. The aim is to burn patches of vegetation annually on a rotation such that each patch is fired once every 10–20 years. This is not always practicable, but on many moors there is a mosaic of 0·5 to 5 hectare patches of *Calluna*, varying from short young stands with nutritious shoots to tall stands which provide cover for the birds. When this management began in the second half of the nineteenth century, grouse bags increased greatly. In recent years, research has shown that grouse stocks are related to the age of the *Calluna* (Miller *et al.*, 1966), that bags are related to the number and size of fires (Picozzi, 1968), and that numbers can be increased experimentally by more than 50 per cent by burning small patches (Figure 10.2). Thus the regular burning of small patches is an essential part of grouse husbandry. Less is known about the

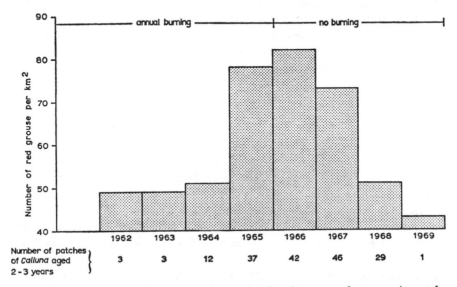

**Figure 10.2.** Changes in the breeding stock of red grouse after experimental burning of small patches of *Calluna* heathland each year from 1962-1965. The increase in the grouse stock three years after burning began, and the subsequent decrease after burning ceased, was closely correlated with changes in the availability of *Calluna* patches aged 2-3 years (data from Miller *et al.*, 1970).

effects of burning on sheep and deer. These animals live in groups and each individual moves over a large home range. By contrast, red grouse are territorial, living on a small defended territory in the late winter and spring. Thus in the west, large patches are deliberately burnt, often 20 to 40 hectares at a time and occasionally over 100 hectares. When this happens in the east—a rare and accidental event—no grouse at all may live on the burnt area and several years may pass before plant growth provides enough cover for them.

Burning is a drastic treatment which should be applied with care. Hot temperatures can kill *Calluna* and so prohibit vegetative regeneration from buds at the stem bases. It has been suggested that 500°C for 1 minute at ground level could be lethal, although in practice such hot temperatures appear to be rare. However, fires are generally hotter in old than in young heather, presumably because of the greater density of fuel, and vegetative regeneration is often sparse or even fails altogther after old heather is burnt. This failure is not due entirely to excessive heat but is associated with ageing.

Vegetative regeneration of *Calluna* is desirable because it results in rapid coverage of the ground after fire. It is best after burning in autumn and when the *Calluna* is aged 6 to 10 years; thereafter regeneration progressively declines with the age at which burning occurs. There appear to be two main causes of this: (i) the density of *Calluna* stems declines with increasing age and this reduces the number of sites from which regeneration can occur, and (ii) as the plant ages, the growing points from which the vegetative sprouts originate become gradually buried in secondary thickening. Thus the rapid vegetative regeneration of *Calluna* can be fostered by always burning before the heather enters the mature phase, by ensuring that the fire does not get too hot, and by burning in autumn rather than in spring. All this takes much planning and skill.

If vegetative regeneration should fail, there is usually ample *Calluna* seed available. Stands of pure *Calluna* produce annually, on average, 21,000 flowers per m²; since each flower may produce 20 to 32 seeds, about 0·5 million seeds per m² are released each year. Exposure to temperatures of 40 to 160°C for a few seconds hastens and improves germination but prolonged heat depresses it or is lethal. Regeneration from seed is much slower than vegetative regeneration because seedlings do not have ready-made root systems nor can they exploit stored food reserves. Vegetative regeneration can give almost complete cover of the ground within one or two seasons, whereas this may take six or more years with seedling growth alone. Slow regeneration weakens the dominance of *Calluna* and allows the spread or establishment of other, less desirable moorland species such as *Pteridium*, *Trichophorum* or *Nardus*. Thus regeneration from seed is best regarded as a supplement to vegetative regeneration rather than a substitute for it.

Several workers have noted that heavy grazing of the new shoots can seriously impede the regeneration of *Calluna*. This may happen particularly if only a few small patches are burnt in an area of predominantly old *Calluna*. Sheep in particular are known to congregate on such patches, but red deer, hares and rabbits (*Oryctolagus cuniculus*) may also nibble the fresh growth right down to ground level, so allowing less palatable plants to spread. Gimingham (1949) found that although moderate grazing hastened the development of cover by *Calluna*, heavy grazing (equivalent to a stocking of about 2·7 sheep per hectare for one year) was damaging to both *Calluna* and *Erica cinerea*. Apart from Gimingham's pioneer work, there have been no published experimental studies on the impact of grazing on the balance between different species of moorland vegetation. This is an important field that is worthy of further investigation, particularly the problem of interactions between burning and grazing.

To sum up, the carefully controlled burning of small strips and patches according to a planned rotation will ensure a continuing supply of rapidly regenerating, nutritious *Calluna* distributed in such a way as to be of maximum benefit to all herbivores. Fire can thus be a cheap and effective management tool. In reality, however, this ideal is seldom achieved because of bad weather, shortage of labour, statutory limitation of the burning season (Miller, 1964) and, above all, a lack of planning and determination on the part of many moor managers.

## Ecological Consequences of Burning

The most obvious consequence of burning is the presence of dense even-aged stands of *Calluna* over wide sweeps of hill ground. There is little doubt that repeated burning impoverishes the moorland flora. It favours the spread of fire-resistant species that are rhizomatous, tussocky, or able to regenerate rapidly from buds at the base of the stem. Examples are *Pteridium aquilinum, Molinia caerulea* and *Calluna* itself.

Most plant associations of heather moors contain few species compared with those in other habitats (McVean and Ratcliffe, 1962). Gimingham (1964) considered five main heath communities and ranked them from the 'species-rich', averaging 41 species per 4 m², to 'pure stands' of *Calluna*, averaging 13 species. He associated high floristic diversity with fertile soils but suggested that the impoverished flora of pure heather moors was due to burning as well as to poor soils.

Whereas burning in the relatively dry climate and poor soils of eastern Britain tends to result in a monoculture of *Calluna*, similar management elsewhere may eliminate it. Frequent burning along with heavy grazing may convert heather moor on the better brown-earth soils into *Agrostis-Festuca* grassland, and on poorer gleyed soils into *Nardus* grassland. Frequent burning favours *Molinia, Trichophorum* and *Eriophorum vaginatum* at the expense of *Calluna* on the poorly drained soils of western Britain and Ireland. *Molinia* is especially well adapted to resist fire and, once established, is difficult to eliminate (Grant *et al.*, 1963). It is a deciduous species and therefore—unlike the evergreen *Calluna*—valueless as winter grazing. As Miles (1971) pointed out, on the blanket bogs of northwest Scotland burning tends 'to increase further the dominance of *Molinia* at the expense of *Calluna*, thus reducing winter grazing and increasing the need to burn'.

Far less is known about the effects of burning on animals than on plants. No experimental data have been published except for red grouse (Miller *et al.*, 1970). There is anecdotal information about some other vertebrates and one of the best-documented cases is that of the greenshank (*Tringa nebularia*). This bird is confined to natural clearings or bogs in the boreal coniferous forest from Norway to east Siberia, except in Scotland. There, it occurs in large numbers in some boggy parts of the relict natural pine forest, but only after forest fires; numbers decrease as the trees and heather grow tall (Nethersole-Thomson and Watson, 1974). Over most of its Scottish distribution, the greenshank breeds on boggy moors where fire and heavy grazing keep the heather short and where many roots in the peat testify to the fact that forests used to grow there.

In recent years some research has been carried out on the possible loss of nutrients from the moorland ecosystem as a direct result of burning. It has been argued that, over a long series of fires, there may be a serious loss of nutrients in the smoke and in solution from the ash. This suggestion has stimulated much research.

Measurements of the potential losses in smoke have been made, for example, by Evans and Allen (1971). Their experiments indicated that losses by volatilization depended on the heat of the fire but were most severe for nitrogen, sulphur and carbon. Well over half of the original content of these elements in the vegetation can be lost, and smaller proportions of other elements may also be volatilized.

The fate of the nutrients deposited in the ash has also been studied (e.g. Allen *et al.*, 1969). Potassium salts are readily dissolved; but calcium and magnesium are less soluble and phosphorus occurs in a relatively insoluble form. However, the potential losses by leaching of rainwater down through the soil are reduced by the fact that nutrients are retained in the surface layer of organic matter. The degree of retention appears to be related to the thickness of the layer, and some leaching may occur in sandy soils with a thin $A_0$ horizon. These findings underline the need to ensure that combustion is not so fierce as to burn off the surface layer of humus, a point that is frequently ignored.

Several attempts have been made to draw up a balance sheet of nutrients within the heather moorland ecosystem, comparing the total losses that might result from burning and from the removal of animal crops with the total income from rain and atmospheric dust (e.g. Allen *et al.*, 1969). The results vary but all suggest that, with the possible exception of nitrogen, most losses appear to be made good during the interval between successive fires on the one area. Nonetheless this question cannot be considered as settled. It has yet to be shown that plants take up significant amounts of the nutrients contained in rainwater before they are lost by surface run-off or leaching. Indeed, Crisp (1966) has shown that large quantities of nutrients can be lost from a catchment in streamwater and by peat erosion. Further, it is necessary to clarify the status of nitrogen within the heather moorland ecosystem. The possibility of a continuing loss through burning is serious because nitrogen is essential to plant and animal nutrition; and the scarcity of available nitrogen in the soil is reflected by the great response of *Calluna* to nitrogenous fertilizer.There are sources of nitrogen other than rainfall but these have not been studied. For example, it is not known to what extent and under what conditions nitrogen might be derived by the mineralization of organic matter in moorland soils. Nor has anyone fully investigated the potentially valuable contribution of nitrogen from leguminous shrubs such as *Ulex* spp. and *Genista anglica.*

Burning may have undesirable effects on the physical properties of the soil. Peat that is frequently burnt develops a tough, rubbery skin which possibly reduces the penetration of moisture. The skin is due partly to physical changes in the peat and partly to the growth of algae and lichens such as *Lecidia uliginosa* (G. A. M. Scott, quoted by Gimingham, 1971). Soil erosion has also been associated with frequent burning (Warren, Chapter 3). However, as with certain other direct consequences of burning, the study of erosion has scarcely proceeded beyond the stage of description, association of events and speculation; virtually no experiments have been done.

One of the most important consequences of management by fire concerns the effects of the vegetation itself on the soil. Many of the species that are maintained by periodic burning produce fibrous litter which does not decompose easily. Deposition of litter by *Calluna* increases steadily with the age of the plant. Up to the mature phase at least, litter is shed faster than it is incorporated into the soil, and so large amounts accumulate at the soil surface. The thick layer of black peaty humus which is thus formed encourages podzolization of the soil. Grubb *et al.* (1969) have shown how *Calluna* bushes rapidly acidify the soils of chalk heath; they recorded that the pH of the top centimetre decreased from about 5·5 to about 4 within a decade. This acidification of the soil by *Calluna* has been attributed to inhibition of earthworms, shallow rooting, accelerated leaching and, most important, the removal of bases, particularly calcium (Grubb and Suter, 1971). Soil acidification promotes leaching, reduces the availability of bases, and inhibits nitrifying bacteria. Moreover, since *Calluna* and many of its associates are shallow-rooted species, leached nutrients deposited in the B horizon of podzols can no longer circulate within the ecosystem. Thus the monoculturing of *Calluna,* besides causing floristic impoverishment, also contributes to soil impoverishment.

## THE FUTURE

The future development of the British uplands in general, and of heather moorland in particular, has been much argued for over two decades (cf.

McVean and Lockie, 1969; Gimingham, 1972; James, Chapter 22). Some changes in land use have occurred and others may be imminent.

The traditional system of ranching hill sheep is relatively unproductive and is now uneconomic in so far as it is heavily subsidized by the State. Hence many people doubt the future of sheep farming in the uplands. It would be quite feasible to increase the output from hill sheep by fertilizing the existing vegetation, by creating more productive kinds of vegetation, or by closely controlling the grazing sheep. It is sometimes suggested that restocking with cattle might so improve upland vegetation that not only sheep but other animals would benefit. But there are great economic and practical difficulties in doing any of these things over wide areas of hill land. Therefore some experts urge that livestock husbandry should be intensified only on the most productive hill ground and that the poorer hills of the north and west should be abandoned to forestry, sport, recreation or, possibly, to deer farming. Some of these developments could encourage the spread of natural scrub and woodland.

Recently, planted woodland has encroached increasingly on to heather moors as foresters have overcome the technical problems of planting and growing trees on acid, infertile and sometimes waterlogged soils. Some welcome this as a return to a type of plant cover that better expressed the natural potential of this environment. However, afforestation almost invariably involves the substitution of one kind of monoculture for another: at present the exotics Lodgepole pine (*Pinus contorta*) and Sitka spruce (*Picea sitchensis*) are widely planted, although little is known about their impact on vegetation, animal life and, most important, on soils. Tree planting requires the long-term investment of large amounts of capital and so is mainly a State enterprise or a private one subsidized by the State. Because of the possible development of cheap substitutes, the future market for timber is uncertain and some economists doubt the profitability of afforestation, especially on poor soils or at high altitudes. However, forests can also cater for part of the rising demand for open-air recreation. Indeed, McVean and Lockie (1969) envisage three types of forest where (i) large amounts of low-quality wood are produced for pulping, (ii) high-quality timber is grown, and (iii) people pay for sport or other recreation.

However, woodlands can never satisfy all recreational needs. Many people like open spaces with unobstructed views and freedom to wander at will. This demand will always be served above the tree limit, but even at lower elevations open spaces are unlikely to disappear completely. Affluence in western Europe and North America will probably ensure that grouse shooting and deer-stalking will continue to prosper in the short term and that many open heather moors will survive. The game 'industry' earns foreign currency and contributes to the rates, local employment and viable human settlements in the uplands. On many estates, the income from the letting of the shootings exceeds the rentals from the hill farms (e.g. Airlie, 1971). Many other kinds of recreation are becoming popular in the uplands. Year by year more and more people go there to camp, walk, ski, watch birds and so on; and the purple heather moors of late summer are undoubtedly a big attraction for tourists. Already many landowners are worried that the influx of tourists from the cities on to heather moorland will damage their grouse-shooting interests and so reduce rents. These new conflicts in land use are adding to the deep-rooted antagonisms that already exist between foresters and hill farmers.

The creation of large tracts of heather moorland was fortuitous in that they were a by-product of man's exploitation of a 'natural' woodland ecosystem. No matter how profitable rough grazing and sport might be, clearly they cannot be justified either in respect of biological production or, because of the effects of *Calluna* on the soil, of environmental conservation. There is now a greater possibility of changes occurring than in the recent past. The development of new concepts in the management of hill sheep, a waning enthusiasm for large-scale afforestation and a rising demand for human recreation could result in a reversion to natural woodland on moors where grouse shooting is uneconomic. To some extent this might be welcomed as being beneficial to wildlife and to the land itself, but it must be monitored and controlled. Gimingham (1972) has warned of the need to ensure that representative examples of heather moor are preserved, not simply for recreation or amenity, but also for wildlife conservation, for educational use, and for scientific research.

## REFERENCES

Airlie, Earl of, (1971). Making full use of an upland estate, *Landowning in Scotland*, **142**, 3–6.

Allen, S. E., Evans, C. C., and Grimshaw, H. M. (1969). The distribution of mineral nutrients in soil after heather burning, *Oikos*, **20**, 16–25.

Barclay-Estrup, P. (1970). The description and interpretation of cyclical processes in a heath community. II, Changes in the biomass and shoot production during the *Calluna* cycle. *J. Econ.*, **58**, 243–9.

Barclay-Estrup, P., and Gimingham, C. H. (1969). The description and interpretation of cyclical processes in a heath community. I, Vegetational change in relation to the *Calluna* cycle, *J. Ecol.*, **57**, 737-58.

Bellamy, D. J., Bridgewater, E., Marshall, C., and Tickle, W. M. (1969). Status of the Teesdale rarities, *Nature* (Lond.), **222**, 238–43.

Bellamy, D. J., and Holland, P. J. (1966). Determination of the net annual aerial production of *Calluna vulgaris* (L.) Hull in northern England, *Oikos*, **17**, 272-5.

Cragg, J. B. (1961). Some aspects of the ecology of moorland animals, *J. Anim. Ecol.*, **30**, 205–23.

Crisp, D. T. (1966). Input and output of minerals for an area of Pennine moorland: the importance of precipitation, drainage, peat erosion and animals, *J. appl. Ecol.*, 3, 327–48.

Cunningham, J. M. M., Smith, A. D. M., and Doney, J. M. (1971). Trends in livestock populations in hill areas in Scotland, in *Hill Farming Organisation, 5th report* 1969-70, Edinburgh, 88–95.

Eadie, J. (1970). Sheep production and pastoral resources, in: *Animal Populations in Relation to their Food Resources*, (ed.) A. Watson, Blackwell, Oxford and Edinburgh, 7–24.

Evans, C. C., and Allen, S. E. (1971). Nutrient losses in smoke produced during heather burning, *Oikos*, 22, 149–54.

Flux, J. E. C. (1970). Life history of the mountain hare (*Lepus timidus scoticus*) in North-East Scotland, *J. Zool.* (Lond.), 161, 75–123.

Forest, G. I. (1971). Structure and production of North Pennine blanket bog vegetation, *J. Ecol.*, 59, 453–79.

Gimingham, C. H. (1949). The effects of grazing on the balance between *Erica cinerea* L. and *Calluna vulgaris* (L.) Hull in upland heath and their morphological responses, *J. Ecol.*, 37, 100–19.

Gimingham, C. H. (1964). The composition of the vegetation and its balance with environment, in *Land Use in the Scottish Highlands*, (ed.) L. D. Stamp, *Advmt. Sci.* (Lond.), 21, 148–53.

Gimingham, C. H. (1971). *Calluna* heathlands: use and conservation in the light of some ecological effects of management, in: *The Scientific Management of Animal and Plant Communities for Conservation*, (eds.) E. Duffey and A. S. Watt, Blackwell, Oxford and Edinburgh, 91–103.

Gimingham, C. H. (1972). *Ecology of Heathlands*, Chapman and Hall, London, 266 pp.

Godwin, H. (1956). *The History of the British Flora*, Cambridge University Press, Cambridge, 384 pp.

Grant, S. A. (1971). Interactions of grazing and burning on heather moors. 2. Effects on primary production and level of utilization, *J. Br. Grassld Soc.*, 26, 173–81.

Grant, S. A., and Hunter, R. F. (1966). The effects of frequency and season of clipping on the morphology, productivity and chemical composition of *Calluna vulgaris* (L.) Hull, *New Phytol.*, 65, 125–33.

Grant, S. A., Hunter, R. F., and Cross, C. (1963). The effects of muirburning *Molinia*-dominant communities, *J. Br. Grassld Soc.*, 18, 249–57.

Grubb, P. J., Green, H. E., and Merrifield, R. C. J. (1969). The ecology of chalk heath: its relevance to the calcicole-calcifuge and soil acidification problems, *J. Ecol.*, 57, 175–212.

Grubb, P. J., and Suter, M. B. (1971). The mechanism of acidification of soil by *Calluna* and *Ulex* and the significance for conservation, in: *The Scientific Management of Animal and Plant Communities for Conservation*, (eds.) E. Duffey and A. S. Watt, Blackwell, Oxford and Edinburgh, 115–33.

Haldane, A. R. B. (1952). *The Drove Roads of Scotland*, Nelson, Edinburgh, 266 pp.

Heal, O. W. (1972). A brief review of progress in the studies at Moor House (UK), in: *Proceedings IV International Meeting on the Biological Productivity of Tundra*, (ed.) F. E. Wielgolaski and T. Rosswall, Swedish IBP Committee, Stockholm, 295–305.

Hewson, R. (1954). The mountain hare in Scotland in 1951, *Scott. Nat.,* **66,** 70–88.

Hewson R. (1962). Food and feeding habits of the mountain hare *Lepus timidus scoticus* Hilzheimer, *Proc. zool. Soc. Lond.,* **139,** 515–26.

Hunter, R. F. (1962). Hill sheep and their pasture: a study of sheep-grazing in South-East Scotland, *J. Ecol.,* **50,** 651–80.

Jenkins, D., Watson, A., and Miller, G. R. (1963). Populations studies on red grouse, *Lagopus lagopus scoticus* (Lath.) in North-East Scotland, *J. Anim. Ecol.,* **32,** 317–76.

Jenkins, D., Watson, A., and Miller, G. R. (1967). Population fluctuations in the red grouse *Lagopus lagopus scoticus, J. Anim. Ecol.,* **36,** 97–122.

McVean, D. N. (1959). Ecology of *Alnus glutinosa* (L.) Gaertn. VII, Establishment of alder by direct seeding of shallow blanket bog, *J. Ecol.,* **47,** 615–18.

McVean, D. N., and Lockie, J. D. (1969). *Ecology and Land Use in Upland Scotland,* Edinburgh University Press, Edinburgh, 134 pp.

McVean, D. N., and Ratcliffe, D. A. (1962). *Plant Communities of the Scottish Highlands,* Nature Conservancy Monographs No. **1,** H.M.S.O., London 445 pp.

Martin, D. J. (1964). Analysis of sheep diet utilizing plant epidermal fragments in faeces samples, in: *Grazing in Terrestrial and Marine Environments,* (ed.) D. J. Crisp, Blackwell, Oxford, pp. 173–88.

Miles, J. (1971). Burning *Molinia*-dominant vegetation for grazing by red deer, *J. Br. Grassld. Soc.,* **26,** 247–50.

Miller, G. R. (1964). The management of heather moors, in: *Land Use in the Scottish Highlands,* (ed.) L. D. Stamp, *Adv. Sci., Lond.,* **21,** 163–9.

Miller, G. R. (1968). Evidence for selective feeding on fertilized plots by red grouse, hares and rabbits, *J. Wildl. Mgmt.,* **32,** 849–53.

Miller, G. R., Jenkins, D., and Watson, A. (1966). Heather performance and red grouse populations, I. Visual estimates of heather performance, *J. appl. Ecol.,* **3,** 313–26.

Miller, G. R., and Miles, A. M. (1969). Productivity and management of heather, in: *Grouse research in Scotland, 13th progress report,* The Nature Conservancy, Edinburgh, 31–45.

Miller, G. R., Watson, A., and Jenkins, D. (1970). Responses of red grouse populations to experimental improvement of their food, in: *Animal Populations in Relation to their Food Resources,* (ed.) A. Watson, Blackwell, Oxford and Edinburgh, 323–35.

Moss, R. (1969). A comparison of red grouse (*Lagopus l. scoticus*) stocks with the production and nutritive value of heather (*Calluna vulgaris*), *J. Anim. Ecol.,* **38,** 103–12.

Nethersole-Thompson, D., and Watson, A. (1974). *The Cairngorms,* Collins, Glasgow and London.

Ovington, J. D. (1957). Dry-matter production by *Pinus sylvestris* L., *Ann. Bot., (Lond.) N.S.,* **21,** 287–314.

Ovington, J. D., and Madgwick, H. A. I. (1959). The growth and composition of natural stands of birch. I. Dry-matter production, *Plant and Soil,* **10,** 271–88.

Pearsall, W. H. (1950). *Mountains and Moorlands,* Collins, New Naturalist, London, 312 pp.

Picozzi, N. (1968). Grouse bags in relation to the management and geology of heather moors, *J. appl. Ecol.,* **5,** 483–8.

Rawes, M., and Welch, D. (1969). Upland productivity of vegetation and sheep at Moor House National Nature Reserve, Westmorland, England, *Oikos,* Suppl. **11,** 7–72.

Red Deer Commission (1967). *Annual Report for 1966*, R. D. C. Edinburgh, 18 pp.

Thomas, B., and Dougall, H. W. (1947). Yield of edible material from common heather, *Scott. Agric.*, **27**, 35–8.

Watson, A., and Miller, G. R. (1970). *Grouse Management*, The Game Conservancy Booklet No. 12, Fordingbridge, 78 pp.

Watson, A., Hewson, R., Jenkins, D., and Parr, R. (1973). Population densities of mountain hares compared with red grouse on Scottish heather moors, *Oikos*, **24**, 225–30.

# Lowland Grassland and Scrub: Management for Wildlife

ERIC DUFFEY

## INTRODUCTION

Lowland grassland in Britain is essentially a man-made vegetation type which probably originated when early man cleared the forests for cultivation or for the grazing of his domesticated animals. Without continued intervention, the species composition of grasses and forbs would change and invasion by scrub would take place rapidly, followed by woodland.

During historical times it is likely that there have been many cycles of clearance and reinvasion, or even replanting, of woody species depending on the influences of wars, famine or disease. In some areas grassland cover may be very ancient, as for example on Celtic fields and prehistoric burial mounds, and even on some types of 'ridge-and-furrow', where ploughing has not taken place for many centuries. Elsewhere, on land of marginal fertility, grassland was ploughed up during periods of grain shortage but allowed to revert at a later stage. These factors, together with burning, cutting, grazing and manuring, have had profound effects on the composition of the sward and the status of the species present, while those species vulnerable to disturbance or with specialized ecological requirements have tended to become rare.

Nevertheless, in spite of intensive modification, unplanted grasslands qualify as semi-natural vegetation because, for the most part, they consist of native species of plants and animals which have established themselves by natural means. The extent of semi-naturalness is the criterion used to differentiate between the broad range of grassland and scrub types, mainly in lowland England, which are described in this chapter. Agricultural statistics distinguish only between (a) *permanent grass,* defined as more than seven years old, and therefore including planted grassland with few species, (b) *temporary or rotation grassland,* planted as part of an arable rotation lasting three to five years, and (c) *rough grazing,* including most of the rough

167

hill pastures in Britain, lowland heaths, moors and unenclosed commons. Of the 62 per cent of the total agricultural area of Britain under grassland, three-fifths is classified as rough grazing and is distributed mainly in the north and the west. In England and Wales there are over 10 million acres (4·1 million hectares) of permanent grass and $4\frac{3}{4}$ million acres (2 million hectares) of rough grazings.

In the eastern counties of England, less than 20 per cent of farmland consists of permanent pasture, while in the Midlands and in many of the southern counties, the proportion is between 21 and 40 per cent; in some parts of these areas, however, where the soils are heavy clays, the proportion is higher. Most permanent grassland is found in the western counties, where higher rainfall, poorer soil types and more rugged topographic features have influenced the pattern of agriculture.

In 1966 Blackwood and Tubbs (1970) surveyed unsown chalk grasslands in lowland England and found that downland had survived on only 3 per cent of the total area, the greater part (about three-quarters) being in Wiltshire. This is mainly because the Ministry of Defence owns large areas of Salisbury Plain, where military training has taken place since Napoleonic times. The 1966 survey was prompted by the rapid decline in permanent pasture on calcareous soils, during the 'Grow More Food' campaign of the 1939–45 War and the years that followed, with the result that much grassland and scrub was ploughed up and fen and marshland drained. After the War the Agricultural Acts of 1947 and 1957 provided guaranteed prices for all major farm products and increased the grants (first introduced in 1939) for reclaiming old pasture. There was therefore an increased incentive to convert grass to arable farming, particularly for cash crops such as barley (Munton, Chapter 21). The result of this process can be illustrated by reference to Wiltshire, where the 30,452 hectares of chalk grassland, found by Blackwood and Tubbs in 1966, were distributed between 529 separate sites, about 500 of which only averaged 20 hectares in area. Most of the surviving pasture is now restricted to steep scarp slopes, where the plough is unable to operate. The same trend can be found on the heaths and grasslands of the East Anglian Breckland, where in 1880 59 separate heathlands with an average area of 381 hectares were identified from the 6-inch Ordnance Survey map. In 1968 only 37 sites remained with an average size of 36 hectares, excluding the large area owned by the Ministry of Defence (Figure 11.1).

## TYPES OF LOWLAND GRASSLAND

### Calcicolous Grassland

This is one of the most distinctive grassland communities in Britain, occurring on calcareous soils ranging from the soft Cretaceous chalk to the

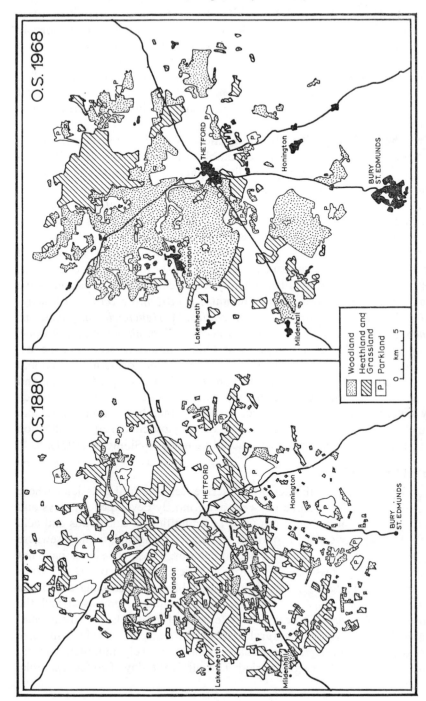

**Figure 11.1.** Maps of the Breckland of East Anglia showing extent of heathland in 1880 and in 1968. The large area in the north of the later map is the Stanford Practical Training area and includes much former farmland.

Oolitic (Jurassic) and hard Carboniferous limestones. Variants of these types can also be found on soils derived from igneous and metamorphic rocks, on the chalky boulder clays of Breckland and on calcareous sand dunes such as the machair of the islands off the Scottish west coast.

These soils generally have a relatively high pH varying from 5·5 to 8·4, a high available calcium-ion content and free calcium carbonate, and tend to be porous and dry, although drainage may be impeded when clay is present.

The chemical similarities between calcareous soils probably constitute the main factor responsible for the notably similar floristics of their grasslands. Certain species occur repeatedly in different grasslands, the following having a constancy value of 81 per cent or more: *Briza media, Festuca ovina, F. rubra, Carex flacca, Lotus corniculatus, Plantago lanceolata, Poterium sanguisorba* and *Thymus drucei*. The richest swards in terms of species numbers are types of chalk grassland: for example where the dominants are either *Festuca ovina, F. rubra* or *Carex humilis*, 40–45 species of flowering plants and mosses per square metre may be recorded (T. C. E. Wells, personal communication). Five other types of calcicolous grasslands have been distinguished according to dominants: (1) *Bromus erectus*, (2) *Brachypodium pinnatum*, (3) *Arrhenatherum elatius*, (4) *Helictotrichon pubescens*, (5) *mixed Gramineae*. *Festuca ovina, Brachypodium pinnatum* and *Bromus erectus* are also the main dominants on Oolitic limestone soils, but the last two become scarce on the Carboniferous limestone of northern England and of Wales, where they are on the northern edge of their range. Devonian and Magnesian limestones cover relatively small areas but the former, which only outcrop on the southwest coast of England, have several rare and distinctive plants. For a discussion on the phytosociological classification of calcicolous grasslands reference should be made to Shimwell (1971).

### Neutral Grasslands

Tansley (1939) used this term to describe 'semi-natural grassland whose soil is not markedly alkaline nor very acid, mostly developed on clays and loams', distinguishing them from grass communities on calcareous and acid soils. The majority occur in southern and eastern England, while elsewhere they are usually found below the 300 m contour. These grasslands have not yet been formally classified by phytosociological methods, but D. A. Wells (personal communication) has distinguished 14 divisions, using as criteria the constancy of groups of species to certain types of grassland and the occurrence of selected species characteristic of particular environmental conditions. Aspects of agricultural nomenclature are also retained in some cases because neutral grasslands have been extensively modified and exploited by man for a very long period. The survival today of so few examples of national importance for conservation is a result of their long and close association with agriculture and their suitability for 'improvement' (Figure 11.2).

The main types are characterized by their floristics, water regime and form of management. For example, the *Washlands* of East Anglia are long strips of land bounded on either side by artificial waterways and subjected to prolonged winter flooding so that agricultural use is restricted. The dominant plants are *Glyceria maxima* and *Phalaris arundinacea*, but generally these grasslands are botanically poor. *Flood meadows* are areas of permanent

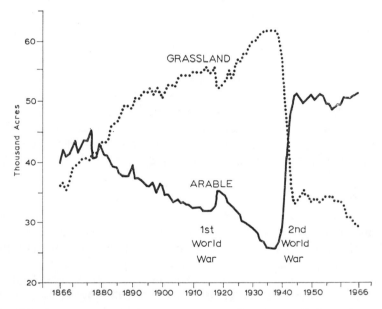

**Figure 11.2.** The decline of grassland in Rutland during and after the 1939–45 War. (Courtesy Leicester Museums.)

grassland situated on the broad floodplains of the upper Thames, south Midlands and parts of East Anglia. They are usually cut for hay and occasionally the aftermath may be grazed. The Yarnton and Pixie Meads in Oxfordshire are some of the best examples, having been managed as hay meadows for many centuries, and are rich in species without any one plant being dominant. The most frequently occurring grasses and herbs in flood meadows are *Alopecurus pratensis, Briza media, Agrostis stolonifera, Anthoxanthum odoratum, Cynosurus cristatus, Festuca pratensis, F. rubra, Holcus lanatus, Lolium perenne, Poa trivialis, Filipendula ulmaria, Sanguisorba officinalis, Silaum silaus, Thalictrum flavum* and *Ophioglossum vulgatum*. A few also retain rare and beautiful plants such as *Fritillaria meleagris* and *Leucojum aestivum*.

*Water-meadows* are of the flood type but were modified by man during the eighteenth and nineteenth centuries, when intricate systems of irrigation channels were constructed in order to promote early growth in the spring for sheep grazing. Few examples survive today, although similar irrigation systems are still widely used in many of the lower valleys of the Alps, where the meadows are cut for hay. The few which can still be seen in the Avon valley of Hampshire tend to be grass-dominant because the broad-leaved herbs are eliminated either by the use of herbicides or the application of fertilizers which stimulate grass growth.

A widespread and complex type is the *Ridge-and-furrow* pasture, mainly developed on soils with a high clay content, often with impeded drainage and usually low fertility. Management may consist of continuous grazing at low stocking rates or else a hay crop may be taken followed by grazing. The ridge-and-furrow surface topography of these grasslands is evidence of past arable farming, but a few of these fields surviving today are particularly rich in species and this seems to indicate that they have been managed as pasture for several centuries. Other variants of neutral grassland occur in northern England, Wales and parts of Scotland.

### Acidic Grasslands

Although very widespread throughout Britain, this type is best represented in the upland regions of Wales, Scotland and northern England, where hard, non-calcareous rocks such are granite, rhyolite, quartzite, acidic sandstones, schists, granulites and slates give predominantly acid and base-deficient soils with a pH range of 3·5 to 6. In lowland regions acidic grasslands tend to be very localized and occur with dwarf shrub communities on deep podsols developed on sands, gravels and clays of low fertility. In some areas, such as the Breckland sands, acidic grassland was maintained by extensive rabbit grazing which eliminated the ericaceous heath (Farrow, 1916; 1917), but after the myxomatosis epidemic in 1954 much of this was reinvaded by heather (Watt, 1960). In south and southwest England grasses are common on acidic heathland but are usually dominant only in open areas where grazing or burning occurs. The species most frequently found are *Festuca ovina, Agrostis canina, A. tenuis* and *Deschampsia flexuosa,* while *Agrostis setacea* may be locally abundant in certain areas.

For a detailed classification of upland acidic grasslands, reference should be made to McVean and Ratcliffe (1962) and King and Nicholson (1964). Other important types of lowland grassland which should be mentioned include the following:

(a) *Saltmarshes,* where *Puccinellia maritima* is widespread on the lower mudflats and often replaced by the vigorous *Spartina anglica.* In some coastal regions this type forms important grazing marshes. Near the upper limits of the tidal range, *Festuca rubra, Agrostis stolonifera* and several *Carex* species may occur to form a sward relatively rich in species.

(b) *Dune grasslands,* frequently maintained by grazing, are sometimes well developed on stabilized maritime sand dunes, and locally in wet dune slacks away from tidal influence. Dune meadows may be rich in species, especially where the calcium carbonate content of the sand is high, but areas of dune slack vegetation are seldom extensive, even on the west coast where the best examples occur.

(c) *Cliff-top grasslands* form a distinctive type whose variations are partly determined by the nature of the underlying rock and partly by the influence of salt-spray drift. On exposed rocky outcrops near the sea, *Festuca rubra* is abundant together with *Armeria maritima* and three species of *Plantago.* Where exposure is less, *Silene maritima, Sagina maritima, Sedum anglica* and *Cochlearia danica* also occur, while *Scilla verna, S. autumnalis* and *Erodium maritimum* may be locally frequent in the west. In some areas, where large colonies of seabirds breed or congregate by the cliff edge, the vegetation is greatly modified by the heavy deposition of nitrogenous bird droppings and the accumulation of discarded food material. A particularly rich variant of cliff-top grassland occurs on the serpentine rocks of the Lizard Peninsula in Cornwall, where a number of rare plants occur which are not found elsewhere in Britain (Malloch, 1972).

## THE GRASSLAND ECOSYSTEM

The wide geographical and altitudinal range of grasslands, and the influence of soil, climate, aspect and water regime, are all included in the range of life forms (Raunkiaer, 1934) which characterize the vegetation community. T. C. E. Wells (1973) classified 182 chalk grassland species according to these groupings (Table 11.1), showing that the majority were hemicryptophytes, and included species such as *Asperula cynanchica, Galium verum, G. mollugo, Carex flacca, Hieracium pilosella, Cirsium acaulon, Leontodon hispidus, Centaurea nigra* and *Carlina vulgaris.* Some 91 per cent of the 182 species were perennials and Wells suggests this as evidence that the grassland community evolved in relation to grazing. Those species best adapted to tolerate repeated defoliation, or with behavioural or structural devices for avoiding it, had been most successful in establishing themselves as permanent members of the community.

7

**Table 11.1.** The classification of 182 chalk grassland plants according to life forms (after Wells, 1973)

| | | | |
|---|---|---|---|
| Chamaephytes | 16 | (7·6%) | Woody or herbaceous plants with buds above ground level and below 25 cm |
| Hemicryptophytes | 123 | (66·7%) | Plants with buds at soil level or in the soil surface |
| Geophytes | 30 | (16·2%) | Herbs with perennating buds buried in the soil |
| Therophytes | 15 | (8·2%) | Plants which pass the non-growing season as seeds |

Vegetative means of reproduction are widely used by grassland plants when flower and seed production are prevented by grazing. Grasses spread by tillering, *Cirsium acaulon* by branching and rhizome growth, *Filipendula vulgaris* by woody tubers at the end of the roots and *Pulsatilla vulgaris* by the growth of lateral buds. Even when quantities of viable seed are produced, as in the case of *Pulsatilla,* seedlings are rarely found, possibly because germination conditions are often unfavourable. It is essential, however, for the small number of annuals which are constituents of the chalk sward to produce seeds in order to survive. If grazing is light during the period of flower production and the sward short and open, favourable conditions for seed production and germination can usually be maintained.

Longevity also seems to be an important characteristic of grassland plants. T. C. E. Wells (1967) has shown that individual plants of *Spiranthes spiralis* on the Knocking Hoe Nature Reserve (Figure 19.1, p. 293, in Sheail, Chapter 19) may be at least 22 years old, while the rate of increase of the population by vegetative multiplication was about 5 per cent per annum. From the data available he was able to postulate that the groups being studied could be more than 100 years old. Tamm (1948; 1972) suggests that some perennial herbs in meadows and woods may commonly live for 14–30 years, and in the case of a colony of *Primula veris* he produced evidence to show that the half-life of the population (time taken for half of the individuals to die) was likely to be about 50 years. Harper and White (1970) after studying the data of Rabotnov (1969) suggest that long life and vegetative reproduction are characteristics of meadow perennials and that establishment by seed is rare.

Most grasses show the highest rate of growth in the spring, with a reduced growth rate during and after flowering, although some have a secondary peak in late summer. Detailed information of growth curves is only available for a few species, but such data are of particular value in the control of dominants such as *Zerna erecta* or *Brachypodium pinnatum*. Cutting, or grazing and treading, during the period of most rapid growth is an effective means of reducing the competitive ability of these species. For example, when *Zerna erecta* in chalk grassland was cut three times per year, its above-ground yield was considerably reduced and it became less tussocky, allowing *Festuca ovina* to increase (T. C. E. Wells, personal communication).

## MANAGEMENT

Management for the maintenance of floristic diversity in grasslands must take all the above factors into account, but the practical means of achieving the objects of conservation usually depend on either cutting or grazing. These traditional techniques can be modified in various ways for nature reserve management. T. C. E. Wells (1971) compared these two treatments over a period of several years on experimental plots on chalk grassland and showed that the control of the fast-growing dominant grasses and the status of forbs in the community varied according to season of cutting and the depth of the soil (Figure 11.3). For example cutting in spring, or in spring and summer, were the most effective regimes for reducing the competitive powers of dominants, but because the growth of such plants is better on deeper rather than on shallower soils, more frequent cuts or more intensive grazing may be necessary.

Cutting is a non-selective treatment in which no nutrients are returned to the sward, whereas in grazing, in contrast, some dung and urine are recycled. In spite of this, the overall effects on floristic diversity of the two treatments have been found to be similar. Both regimes result in a short vegetation and prevent the development of litter so that dwarf species can persist and a balance is maintained between plants of different growth rates and structures. The season of cutting or grazing is important for management because defoliation will remove leaves, buds, flowers or seeds according to the phenological characteristics of the grassland species. For example, cutting in mid-May will remove the flowers and fruit of *Pulsatilla vulgaris* and so prevent seed production, but cutting in autumn will have a negligible effect on this species whereas it may influence others which flower later in the year. It is useful therefore to construct a phenological chart (T. C. E. Wells, 1971) for the important species in a sward so that an attempt can be made to predict the changes likely to occur following cutting or grazing at particular times of the year.

## THE FAUNA

The maintenance of the vast invertebrate fauna which is associated with the abundant food source found in grasslands is another important

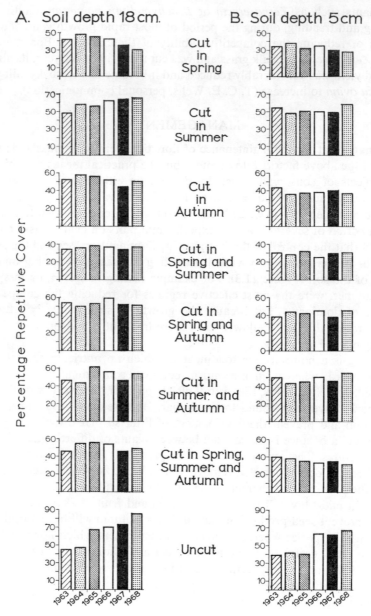

**Figure 11.3.** Performance of *Zerna erecta*, 1963–8, under 7 cutting treatments and in uncut controls. (Courtesy T. C. E. Wells.)

object for grassland conservation. The richness and diversity of these animal communities probably exceeds that of any other major 'ground' and 'field layer' types of vegetation with the exception of fens. The greatest range of species and the highest populations are usually found in old pasture where modifying influences such as grazing have been light, and the poorest faunas occur in temporary leys especially where grazing is heavy. There is even some evidence to suggest that hay-meadows tend to be poor in species, possibly because the more sensitive animals cannot tolerate the major change in the environment which takes place when the grass is cut and taken away. A well-developed sward structure and minimum disturbance is therefore of particular importance for the conservation of both the invertebrate fauna, the communities of which are stratified into vertical zones, and the vertebrate fauna such as rodents, which depend on vegetation cover and abundant food supply (Duffey, 1962a, b; Andrzejewska, 1965; Morris, 1971). The invertebrate fauna of chalk grassland has been particularly well studied in this respect and further information on the species which are associated with different types of sward can be obtained in Duffey and Morris (1966) and Morris (1967; 1968; 1969; 1971).

Almost every structural component of grassland plants is exploited by one or even many kinds of herbivorous invertebrate. The roots are eaten by the larvae of Lepidoptera and Coleoptera; the stems by these groups and by the larvae of Diptera; the leaves are eaten, mined, galled and sucked by larval and adult insects of several different groups; while the flowers, fruits and seed heads are also exploited.

Many insects are recognized as pest species of grassland, for example the larvae of Tipulidae (Diptera) and wireworms (Elateridae) which feed on grass roots, but experimental data on the influences of these activities on the performance and status of the plants in the sward are scarce. Work at the Grassland Research Institute (Hurley, Berkshire) on ryegrass leys and at Rothamsted (Hertfordshire) on old permanent pasture has shown that appreciable increases in yield were obtained when the invertebrate fauna were drastically reduced by pesticide treatment (Clements, 1971). In one case a difference in yield between treated and untreated plots of over 50 per cent was recorded six weeks after the application of an insecticide. Cantlon (1969) studied the seedlings of *Melampyrum lineare,* which is eaten by nymphs of the Katydyd (*Atlanticus testacius*) in Michigan woodlands. He showed that spring applications of the insecticide Aldrin, plus regular weekly applications in the first two years of a 50:50 mixture of Malathion and DDT to the foliage of plants, resulted in spectacular increases in the plant biomass. Similarly Foster (1964) showed that, when the seed of *Bellis perennis* was treated with a fungicide and an insecticide, there was a significant increase in establishment of the plant.

More is known about the effect on the invertebrate fauna of removing the aerial parts of plants by cutting or grazing. Morris (1971) showed that of seven species of insects recorded on *Centaurea nigra* in ungrazed grassland only one occurred on the same plant in grazed conditions (Figure 11.4). Three of the insects were species of Trypetid fly which breed in seed heads; three were leaf-feeding Coleoptera and Lepidoptera; and the seventh was an aphid which fed externally on the stem.

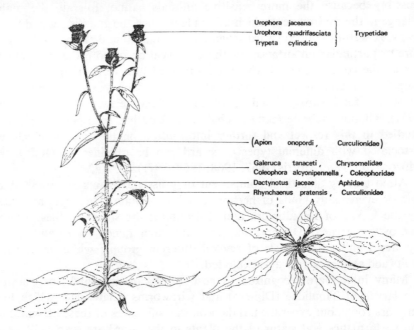

**Figure 11.4.** Hypothetical *Centaurea nigra* plants under grazed and ungrazed conditions, showing the phytophagous invertebrates recorded (larvae of *R. pratensis* not found), Barton Hills, Beds. (Courtesy M. G. Morris.)

Some plants appear to be adapted to periodic severe defoliage, as in the case of *Senecio jacobaea* whose leaves, buds and flowers are eaten by the larvae of the cinnabar moth (*Tyria jacobaeae*). Although no seed may be set during a season of high infestation, Dempster (1971) showed that the number of plants may increase greatly by growth from root buds. In spring, 1968, after complete defoliation by caterpillars in the previous year, five plants per metre square were counted. In the summer of 1968 a second defoliation occurred, and yet in spring 1969 the number of plants had increased to 68 per metre square. This type of response supports the suggestion of Morris (1969) that insects which feed on the leaves of grassland plants are less at risk than species which are dependent on buds, fruit and seeds.

Grazing or cutting not only removes the numerous small animal habitats in the upper layers of the vegetation but also results in a great change in the microclimate. Tall dense herbage protects the ground surface from high temperatures and sharp fluctuations and also maintains an equable humidity in the litter zone. A reduction in vegetation height, therefore, results not only in a loss of those faunal elements adapted to the structural character-istics of the upper zones (such as orb-web spiders, and flower- and seed-feeding insects) but also a fall in the number of species normally found in the moist conditions lower down in the sward. A well-formed litter layer has a complex assemblage of animals which feed on dead plants, or on the fungi, algae and bryophytes which grow on decaying material. Living with them are many other species which are parasitic or predatory. When the litter is trampled its structure is broken down, and the removal of tall vegetation by grazing exposes it to the drying action of the sun and wind. The fragmented particles are easily dispersed and the rich invertebrate community may be largely destroyed. The litter and its fauna are one of the most vulnerable microhabitats and show evidence of modification even when disturbance is comparatively slight. For example, Table 11.2 shows

**Table 11.2.** The influence of treading on the numbers of some invertebrate groups in grassland litter

|  | Control (means of 22 samples) | 10 'treads' during each of 12 months (means of 25 samples) |
|---|---|---|
| Annelida | 20·2 | 18·1 |
| Coleoptera | 80·1 | 12·8 |
| Araneae | 11·0 | 1·8 |
| Isopoda | 16·5 | 0·3 |
| Molluscs | 13·5 | 5·2 |
| Diptera larvae | 25·0 | 46·2 |

differences between the fauna of trampled and untrampled litter in an experimental grass ley. In this case trampling consisted of one tread by the foot of a 180 lb (75·3 kg) man twice per day for five consecutive days each month over the period of a year. The annual total of 120 treads would be considered very light trampling if measurements were being made of the vegetation response, but in this case it caused large changes in the fauna (cf. Goldsmith, Chapter 12).

These comments on the vegetation and fauna of grassland make it clear that management for zoological and botanical objectives must sometimes be achieved by different means. The short, open, grazed sward generally has the largest number of plant species, while the taller ungrazed or lightly grazed sward with a well-formed litter layer will be richer in animal life.

On lightly grazed areas, where there is selection by the grazing animal for certain species of grassland plants, a natural mosaic of short and taller vegetation will occur. Where this cannot be reproduced by the appropriate stocking density, management by a rotational system of grazing or cutting is the most appropriate procedure for ensuring that both botanical and zoological species diversity is maintained.

The invertebrate fauna is also known to be affected by season, as well as the intensity and duration of grazing. M. G. Morris (personal communication) has shown that spring and summer grazing depresses the numbers of some insect groups more than does autumn and winter grazing, although an annual treatment of any sort appears to result in some degree of impoverishment compared with no disturbance.

## GRASSLAND SCRUB

Almost any open habitat, whether grassland or bare ground, may be colonized by woody plants. The type of scrub which develops depends partly on the soils and existing vegetation and partly on the potential seed parents growing nearby. In southern England calcicolous grassland may be invaded by scrub mixtures which include hawthorn, juniper, hazel, privet, wayfaring tree, dogwood, buckthorn, yew, ash, beech, rose and bramble. Dry mesophilous grassland is colonized by hawthorn, blackthorn, oak, birch, elder, rose and bramble, while acidophilous grassland is favoured by gorse, broom, pine and birch. Many scrub species have brightly coloured fleshy fruits adapted for dispersal by birds, particularly the blackbird, song-thrush, mistle-thrush, redwing, fieldfare and the much less common waxwing. All these birds, except the last, feed regularly in open grassy places as well as on bushes, so that there is ample opportunity for them to spread the seed which is deposited in their droppings. Other woody species, such as field-maple and birch, are dispersed by wind, while larger seeds such as pine and oak may be moved to open areas by small mammals which feed on them. Squirrels are able to transport acorns, hazel nuts and beech mast up to 30 m, and oak regeneration may still be active 200 m from the seed source (Mellanby, 1968).

Initially the seedling utilizes the food material stored in the endosperm and is independent of the nutrient status of the soil, but the nature of the vegetation cover usually determines whether or not the young plant will survive. For example, juniper appears to need a habitat where there is little competition from other plants so that establishment is more frequently seen in relatively open areas such as abandoned arable land. Open ground situations are also necessary for the successful germination of yew and whitebeam, while gorse and birch germinate freely on land which has been burnt.

Juniper is one of the most interesting scrub plants because it is relatively local in southern England, where it occurs almost exclusively on the chalk, although in the north it tolerates a variety of soil types. Ward (1973) found that on some 250 sites in southern England once containing the species it is now extinct, although this is partly offset by her discovery of 121 sites on which it was not previously recorded. The decline is almost certainly due to changes in land use, particularly reclamation for agriculture. The few increases which have been recorded, for example the many young bushes on Porton Down, Wiltshire, date from the disappearance of rabbits after myxomatosis. In the absence of grazing, seedlings were able to establish on land not in agricultural use. Today the total population in southern England is estimated to be 81,200 bushes, distributed in 309 one-kilometre squares. About 25 per cent of this total occurs on Nature Reserves or Sites of Special Scientific Interest and so they have some degree of protection. However, the size of the colony may be of particular importance to the survival of the special juniper fauna. Ward (1972) has produced evidence to show that if a site is isolated from its immediate neighbours it should have at least 100 bushes if the full stenophagous fauna is to be maintained.

## REFERENCES

Andrzejewska, L. (1965). Stratification and its dynamics in meadow communities of *Auchenorhyncha* (Homoptera), *Ekol. pol. A.,* **13,** 685–715.

Blackwood, J. W., and Tubbs, C. R. (1970). A quantitative survey of chalk grassland in England, *Biol. Cons.,* **3,** 1–6.

Cantlon, J. E. (1969). The stability of natural populations and their sensitivity to technology, in: *Diversity and Stability in Ecological Systems,* (eds.) G. M. Woodwall, and H. H. Smith, *Brookhaven Symp. Biol.,* **22,** 197–203.

Clements, R. O. (1971). The effects of pesticides on the yield of cut and grazed swards, *J. Br. Grassld. Soc.,* **26,** 193.

Dempster, J. P. (1971). Some effects of grazing on the population ecology of the Cinnabar Moth, in: *The Scientific Management of Animal and Plant Communities for Conservation,* (eds.) E. Duffey and A. S. Watt, Blackwell, Oxford, 517–26.

Duffey, E. (1962a). A population study of spiders on limestone grassland. Description of study area, sampling methods and population characteristics, *J. Anim. Ecol.,* **31,** 571–99.

Duffey, E. (1962b). A population study of spiders in limestone grassland. The field-layer fauna, *Oikos,* **13,** 15–34.

Duffey, E., and Morris, M. G. (1966). The invertebrate fauna of the Chalk and its scientific interest, *Handbk. Soc. Promot. Nat. Reserves,* **1966,** 83–94.

Farrow, E. P. (1916). On the ecology of the vegetation of Breckland. II. Factors relating to the relative distributions of *Calluna*-heath and grass-heath, *J. Ecol.,* **4,** 57–64.

Farrow, E. P. (1917). In the ecology of the vegetation of Breckland. III. General effects of rabbits on the vegetation, *J. Ecol.*, **5**, 1–18.

Foster, J. (1964). Studies on the population dynamics of the daisy, *Bellis perennis* (L.), Ph.D. thesis, University of Wales.

Harper, J. L., and White, J. (1970). The dynamics of plant populations, *Proc. Adv. Study Inst. Dynamics Numbers Popul. (Oosterbeek)*, (eds.) P. J. den Boer, and G. R. Gradwell, Centre for Agricultural Publishing and Documentation, Wageningen, 41–63.

King, J., and Nicholson, I. A. (1964). Grasslands of the forest and sub-alpine zones, in: *The Vegetation of Scotland,* (ed.) J. H. Burnett, Oliver and Boyd, Edinburgh, 168–215.

Malloch, A. J. C. (1972). Salt-spray deposition on the maritime cliffs of the Lizard Peninsula, *J. Ecol.,* **60**, 103–12.

McVean, D. N., and Ratcliffe, D. A. (1962). *Plant Communities of the Scottish Highlands*, HMSO, London, 445 pp.

Mellanby, K. M. (1968). The effects of some mammals and birds on regeneration of oak, *J. appl. Ecol.,* **5**, 359–66.

Morris, M. G. (1967). Differences between the invertebrate faunas of grazed and ungrazed chalk grassland. I, Responses of some phytophagous insects to cessation of grazing, *J. appl. Ecol.,* **4**, 459–74.

Morris, M. G. (1968). Differences between the invertebrate faunas of grazed and ungrazed chalk grassland. II, The faunas of sample turves, *J. appl. Ecol.,* **5**, 601–11.

Morris, M. G. (1969). Populations of invertebrate animals and the management of chalk grassland in Britain, *Biol. Cons.* **1**, 225–31.

Morris, M. G. (1971). The management of grassland for the conservation of invertebrate animals, in: *The Scientific Management of Animal and Plant Communities for Conservation,* (eds.) E. Duffey and A. S. Watt, Blackwell, Oxford, 527–52.

Rabotnov, T. A. (1969). Plant regeneration from seed in meadows of the USSR, *Herb. Abs.,* **39**, 269–77.

Raunkiaer, C. (1934). *The Life Forms of Plants and Statistical Plant Geography*, Clarendon, Oxford, 632 pp.

Shimwell, D. W. (1971). *The Description and Classification of Vegetation*, Sidgwick and Jackson, London, 322 pp.

Tamm, C. O. (1948). Observations on reproduction and survival of some perennial herbs, *Bot. Not.,* **3**, 305–21.

Tamm, C. O. (1972). Survival and flowering of some perennial herbs. III, The behaviour of *Primula veris* on permanent plots, *Oikos,* **23**, 159–66.

Tansley, A. G. (1939). *The British Islands and their Vegetation,* Cambridge University Press, Cambridge, 930 pp.

Ward, L. K. (1972). Ecological studies on scrub, *Monks Wood Experimental Station Report 1969-71,* The Nature Conservancy, London, 55–7.

Ward, L. K. (1973). The conservation of Juniper. I, Present status of Juniper in southern England, *J. appl. Ecol.,* **10**, 165–88.

Watt, A. S. (1960). Population changes in acidiphilous grass-heath in Breckland 1936–57, *J. Ecol.,* **48**, 605–29.

Wells, T. C. E. (1967). Changes in a population of *Spiranthes spiralis* (L.) Chevall. at Knocking Hoe NNR, Bedfordshire, 1962–65, *J. Ecol.,* **55**, 83–99.

Wells, T. C. E. (1971). A comparison of the effects of sheep grazing and mechanical cutting on the structure and botanical composition of chalk grassland, in: *The Scientific Management of Animal and Plant Communities for Conservation,* (eds.) E. Duffey and A. S. Watt, Blackwell, Oxford, 497–516.

Wells, T. C. E. (1973). Botanical aspects of chalk grassland management, in: *Chalk Grassland. Studies on its Conservation in South-East England,* (eds.) A. J. Jermy and P. A. Scott, Kent Trust for Nature Conservation, 10–15.

# CHAPTER 12

# Managing Animal Populations

P. A. Jewell

## PRIMITIVE MANAGERS

The management of animal populations in order to conserve them is not a new concept or a new skill. The ancient laws of venery were codified for that purpose and the declaration of the Royal Forests in England in the eleventh century was an act to preserve the forest-dwelling deer for privileged hunters. These medieval practices must be seen, however, as simply one expression of man's awareness of the fact that animal populations can be manipulated for a variety of purposes: this awareness must have characterized the attitude of prehistoric hunters towards their prey, just as it does those of primitive hunters today.

A recent example of well-managed animal exploitation that has much in common with the modern practice of conservation is provided in Britain by the history of the sea-bird fowlers of St. Kilda (Fisher, 1952). Up to the end of the nineteenth century the St. Kildans lived in almost total isolation on their archipelago of Atlantic islands, 40 miles west of the Outer Hebrides: between 1760 and 1920 their numbers fluctuated between 80 and 100 persons. They subsisted primarily on the sea birds that nested (and still do nest) in great colonies on the islands and stacks. The populations of the staple species of sea birds are believed to have remained very stable throughout the period in question and are estimated to have consistently numbered 20,000 breeding pairs of fulmars (*Fulmaris glacialis*), 40,000 breeding pairs of gannets (*Sula bassana*), and perhaps a million pairs of puffins (*Fratercula arctica*).

Each species was exploited with an appropriate regard for its biology. The fulmar lays one egg and will not lay another if this is taken, so fulmars' eggs were not collected: similarly, adult birds that would nest were not killed because a maximum crop of young birds was required. Between 8,000 and 12,000 young birds were gathered just before they flew from their nesting ledges; this yielded an average of 115 fowls per person and left about half the young birds of the year to fly. The gannet responds to the loss of its first-laid egg by laying another, so from this species a large number of eggs were taken. The nests on one sub-division of the colony on Stac Lee, however, were not robbed and in this way some staggering of the dates on which the fledglings were ready to take was achieved. In their heyday the St. Kildans took at least 22,000 plump young gannets every year and they also took a number of adult birds on their arrival in spring. Gannet colonies are characterized by the presence of a great many idle birds, however (perhaps 20,000 at St. Kilda), so there is no lack of immediate recruits to the breeding population. Puffins were eaten but were also important as a source of feathers for trade; 89,600 birds are recorded to have been taken in the year 1876.

There is no reason to believe that any of these rates of cropping would have depressed recruitment to the breeding populations. The exploitation was closely controlled and the St. Kildans were careful not to disturb the birds except during the short periods of intensive collecting. No doubt the St. Kildans offered protection to the colonies from marauding seafarers who occasionally might otherwise have wrought havoc in them.

It is difficult to discern from the literature the extent to which peoples with an economy based on the hunting of mammals made any attempt to conserve the stocks of their prey. The Hazda, hunter-gatherers of Tanzania, apparently take whatever prey they encounter, be it a pregnant female antelope or any other category of the herd (Woodburn, 1968). It seems unlikely that the hunters adversely affect the populations of game animals, but like primitive hunters elsewhere the Hadza have had their best hunting grounds taken over by agriculturists or pastoralists and are now confined to areas that support relatively low numbers of game. Nevertheless, a Hadza hunter fulfills his need by spending an average of only two hours a day in hunting. The !Kung bushmen of Botswana are similarly efficient in their way of life and spend 12 to 19 hours a week actually gathering food (Lee, 1968). Only a part of this time, erratic in its incidence, is spent in hunting. Low hunting pressures by man would not be expected to have any regulatory effect on prey species unless the hunters were selecting a particular class of animals within the prey population. This does not appear to be their practice, although Laughlin (1968) suggests that hunters may avoid certain classes of animals for reasons of religious superstition or for conservation.

Unfortunately, little is known of the predator-prey relationships of peoples who were specialists in hunting large mammals and who depended on them as their main food resource. It has been suggested that man, as hunter, brought about the extinction of many species of very large mammals in the late Pleistocene (Martin and Wright, 1967). If this is true, then the hunters were evidently recklessly profligate of their resources. There is some evidence, on the contrary, that certain tribes of North American Indians had evolved an effective game conservation measure in the recognition of territorial boundary zones between tribal areas (Hickerson, 1965). These buffer zones provided a refuge for the virginia, or white-tailed deer, and were a reserve hunting area in lean times. We can only speculate that some societies of primitive hunters, despite the excesses of others, may have developed systems of controlled exploitation of prey that gave them a sustained yield and that amounted to management for conservation. When the process of management was taken further, and control was exercised over the prey herds, then sustained yields were certainly achieved, as exemplified by reindeer herders today (e.g. Sturdy, 1972).

Reindeer hunting provides a very important model of animal management with much relevance to conservation. In its modern form, however, this mode of animal exploitation exercises more complete control over the species than is desirable in management for wildlife conservation. Control includes selection of bulls and castration of excess males together with many other practices of husbandry. The model is of importance because it may provide a parallel for a phase of animal exploitation that was practised by prehistoric peoples before animals were shielded from the full effects of natural selection by domestication. Higgs and Jarman (1972) have elaborated the thesis that animal domestication was not an invention confined to the early Neolithic period but was a process that began much earlier, in the Pleistocene, and that in this process there arose a great variety of associations between animals and man with many kinds of exploitation patterns that were part of the overall economy of the peoples concerned. An example is provided by the economies of early Neolithic peoples in the Near East, where at Jericho (Clutton-Brock, 1971) and at Nahal Oren (Legge, 1972), great dependence was placed upon the gazelle. The slaughter pattern revealed by the remains of bones shows that a high proportion of immature animals were killed and this in turn suggests an ability to manipulate and manage gazelle populations. The question of how far domestication can be seen as a conservation measure will be discussed later.

## MANAGEMENT FOR A MARKETABLE PRODUCT

Whether or not a given form of management can be said to promote the conservation of a particular animal population depends upon the objective that the conservator has set. The circumstances may be so dire, as in the threatened extinction of an entire species, that any policy that permits the surviving animals to increase their stock becomes a proper objective of conservation. The Pribiloff fur seal provides an example of a species in which excessive hunting had caused the stocks to fluctuate erratically, making the economics of hunting unpredictable, and threatening the survival of the species (Peterson and Fisher, 1956). Pelagic sealing was stopped by government action in 1911 and the breeding population recovered. Hunting was then resumed on the basis of a limited annual take and the preferential killing of males. The world population now numbers about 2 million and the hunting regulations can be seen as an achievement in conservation. The primary aim of the regulations, however, is to give a sustained yield of a valuable commercial product, and the success in preserving the species must be qualified by the knowledge that the sex ratio of the adult populations is maintained in a severely distorted state. It is true that the social organization of fur seals, in which a single territorial bull collects and inseminates a large harem of females, lends itself to the cropping of 'excess' males, but the biological functions of these males are not known and their elimination must lead to an unnatural social structure and changes in the genetic composition of the stock. Despite these imponderables, nothing would be more gratifying to conservationists than to see the criteria that are applied to these seals applied to other hunted mammals in the sea, particularly the whales.

It is paradoxical that situations in which man acts as top predator and derives a sustained yield from prey populations are so healthy in their conservation prospects. The Saiga antelope in the Soviet Union, rescued from the brink of extinction (Bannikov *et al.*, 1961) and now a high-yielding commodity producer, is an outstanding example; red deer and grouse in Scotland are others. Wildlife biologists know very well, however, that predators play a constructive role in the regulation of natural populations (Pimlott, 1970). It is instructive to compare (Figure 12.1) two heribivore populations, in one of which (red deer) hunting control is exercised, while in the other (Soay sheep) predation is entirely absent.

These two populations were studied contemporaneously through the decade 1957 to 1968. Both populations subsist on islands off the west coast of Scotland, the red deer on Rhum in the Inner Hebrides (Lowe, 1969; 1971), and the Soay sheep on Hirta, in the more remote islands of St. Kilda (Jewell *et al.*, In Press). The deer were culled each year, one-sixth of the spring-counted adults being shot, and this imposed a much higher off-take than had been maintained previously. The take proved well judged, and the population was maintained at between 1,700 and 1,800 head. Moreover, the increased rate of culling reduced natural deaths in both stags and hinds by about 75 per cent (Lowe, 1969). The uncontrolled Soay sheep, by contrast, suffered drastic fluctuations of density. A crash from high numbers of between 1,300 and 1,600 occasionally wiped out half the population, to be followed by a cycle of rapid recovery (Figure 12.1). Mortality was conditioned entirely

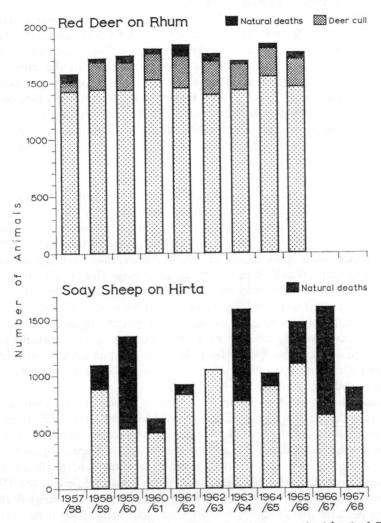

**Figure 12.1.** The fluctuations in numbers of red deer on the island of Rhum, and Soay sheep on the island of Hirta. Total numbers relate to an annual census each spring: most mortality occurred in the subsequent autumn (culling of deer, cross hatching) or winter (natural deaths in deer and sheep, solid black). In 1962–63 it appears that no sheep died: there were a few deaths in this winter but the errors of the censuses disguise them. (Data for red deer from Lowe, 1969 and for Soay sheep from Jewell *et al.*, In Press.)

by food shortage in the months of late winter. Mean annual mortality over the period of study was about 33 per cent.

In comparison, Pimlott's (1967) calculations of deer numbers in situations where the wolf is the effective predator show that wolves may take 37 per cent of the prey population. Here the wolves were important in preventing major eruptions and crashes of the deer population. In the absence of natural predators man renders a service to an herbivore population by taking a regular cull. It is possible to generalize from these observations, and state that if man does not assume the role of predator and cull the individuals surplus to the requirements of the population they have to die or be removed by some other means, as by road deaths, disease, poisoning, trapping or being shot as pests.

These examples allude to management by a balanced cull, but the selective effect of killing also needs to be mentioned. Carnivorous predators are efficient in removing sick and old animals from the prey population and in placing a high premium for survival on perfect physique and adaptive behaviour. In leaving no wounded prey, their role might be seen as humane. Man, on the other hand, as self-interested hunter, may adversely affect his prey's genetic propensities. In elephants the average size of tusks has fallen over the century (Brooks and Buss, 1962), probably occasioned, in part at least, by the elimination of large tuskers from the gene pool. Red deer may show a parallel situation, the abundance of stags carrying antlers with good points being adversely affected by trophy hunting. This is thought to be the case in Scotland, but Lowe (1971) failed to effect an improvement in the Rhum population despite the selective culling of stags with poor antlers over a period of nine years.

So far, the exploitation of single species in particular environments has been considered: this exploitation can lead to management practices that also comprise the most realistic conservation practices. But the very fact that a single species dominates the habitat (except in a special case such as that of the fur seal rookeries) is itself symptomatic of a situation far removed from natural. This shortcoming has been revealed in the Rhum study in that between 1957 and 1968 the average weight of stags declined by 7·3 per cent and hinds by 8·7 per cent, accompanied by a decrease in fecundity and the probable emigration of stags. It seems that, in the absence of sheep, cattle and burning, deer cannot keep the grazings open and a decline in productivity results (Lowe, 1971).

A community of herbivores in complex association with one another and the vegetation of their biome is nature's mode of exploiting primary production everywhere in the temperate and tropical zones. Such communities are severely localized in the modern world, but they exist in great variety and in some abundance in the diverse habitats of Africa. Almost

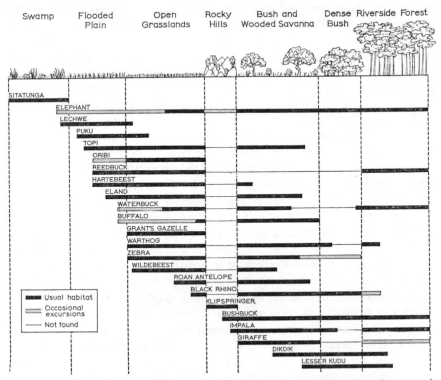

**Figure 12.2.** Environmental types in an African habitat showing the ways in which different species of large mammal exploit different parts of the habitat.

all these habitats are threatened, however, by the demands of agriculture, pastoralism or forestry. In some of these situations game cropping is seen to be a conservation measure (Riney, 1967). Great tracts of land in Africa are not available for the husbanding of domestic stock (cattle, sheep, goats and pigs) because of disease, aridity or unsuitable herbage. But these same areas carry a considerable standing stock of wild herbivores. Many pilot schemes have shown that these herbivores can be cropped on a sustained yield basis; outstanding examples are the Galana scheme in Kenya where elephant were a major resource and the Acholi scheme in Uganda that took buffalo, kob and other antelopes (Bindernagel, 1968). The costing of such schemes, as in the pioneering example of the Henderson Ranch (Dasmann, 1964), has shown that they are as high yielding as, but less expensive than, the ranching of cattle. But game cropping implies the organized and regular hunting of selected animals, and presents very great obstacles in the collection of animals, meat processing, meat preservation, marketing and veterinary control. As a mode of land use, however, game cropping has all the attractions of overall ecological soundness. A community of herbivores can use the primary production of a complex habitat more efficiently than one or two domestic species. The species that are members of the community are separated ecologically (Lamprey, 1963) and exploit and promote the diversity of the habitat (Figure 12.2). The maintenance of diversity is one of the aims of conservation and if game cropping permits a region to be useful to man, and to escape more drastic assault from him, then it is a form of management that the conservationist can countenance. Unfortunately, the productive potential of a mature long-term cropping scheme in Africa has never been realized, either for lack of the necessary capital expenditure, controversy over land use and hostility from agricultural and veterinary interests, or political upheaval. Pilot schemes have mostly been run in marginal areas that may have already suffered degradation from past abuse or that do not carry optimal animal populations for other reasons, and so cropping schemes remain as precarious conservation measures. It follows that cropping schemes are likely to be impressive economically where animal populations are superabundant. This is so, and leads to the irony that the most highly successful schemes have been conducted in national parks where the original intention was that animals should be immune from hunting. This facet of animal management will be returned to later.

One other form of managing animal populations that gives rise to a commercial product but is seen by some as a conservation measure needs to be mentioned: this is game farming, leading to new domestication. It would be practical to develop game cropping to the point at which considerable control was exercised over the meat-producing species. In South Africa, for example, the blesbok, *Damaliscus dorcas,* survives only on farms and in some nature reserves. The animals are shot on the farms, for sport and meat, and can be rounded up on the reserves into coralls for culling or translocation. The actual or potential degree of control is absolute. Similar potential is seen in the springbok, *Antidorcas marsupialis,* which is beginning to be farmed in South Africa. They are more tractable than most antelope and can be herded in paddocks 'enabling the farmer to exercise his rightful ownership' (Skinner, 1972), and with changes in the relative profitability of mutton and wool compared with venison, springbok farming could displace conventional animal husbandry over wide areas. Unlike the blesbok, the springbok still ranges freely in great numbers in south-western Africa. If the species become valuable for ranching, however, then it will fall under the shadow of inevitable change: it could cease to be conserved and become husbanded instead.

It is important to recognize that husbandry practices may lead to marked genetic changes, affecting appearance, conformation and behaviour, in the mammalian populations to which they are applied and changes of management practice could accelerate these effects. (Genetical constitution and the conservation of populations is discussed in illuminating detail by Berry in Chapter 7 and 1971.) Red deer have provided some examples above and illustrate other factors. If trophy hunting of stags is a primary objective, then the sex ratio of adults must be maintained at 1 : 1 and 20 per cent can be culled annually. If venison is wanted then no more than one stag to five hinds need be maintained, the annual calf production is greater and 33 per cent of the stock can be culled annually (McVean and Lockie, 1969). There have been proposals that red deer should be ranched and eventually domesticated (Bannerman and Blaxter, 1969). The manipulation of social structure, the castrating of males and the selection of tractable animals could then cause marked departure from the natural norm.

Finally, it must be emphasized that domestication is not a means of conserving an animal species. Wilkinson (1972), referring to the musk ox, maintains that domestication will help conserve it, but tamed and dehorned musk ox, selected for docility, improved conformation and the finest quivit (wool), must of necessity begin to depart in character from wild *Ovibos moschatus*. The new domestication of wild mammals is, of course, a development of great economic importance (Jewell, 1969; Wilkinson, 1972) with far-reaching implications for habitat maintenance and environmental conservation generally, but the species concerned will be transformed into domestic forms and will be farmed, not conserved. Cattle, domestic animals, are the most numerous of all large mammals in the world, but *Bos primigenius*, their wild progenitor, is extinct.

## MANAGING NATURAL COMMUNITIES

The areas that are set aside for wildlife conservation have been chosen because they represent functioning natural ecosystems. Ideally they comprise communities of plants and animals in balance, and exhibit maximum diversity. The fundamental importance of reserves is the protection they afford to integrated biological systems that have attained this state through processes of natural evolution. Reserves offer the opportunity to study animal species in an environment to which they have been adapted by natural selection; they exhibit productive processes and paths of energy exchange that have not been rendered defective by interference by man. This is the context in which the ecology of a species can be understood and which conservation aims to preserve.

Reserves and national parks, once they had been brought into existence, however, soon revealed an alarming instability and a propensity for following paths of distorted change. Herbivore populations might boom and crash;

some forms of vegetation could be damaged and depleted; a newly successful species could displace other members of the community. This internal disruption of the communities has raised the most exacting problems of management and revealed the paucity of our ecological understanding. Management has therefore had to be directed towards arresting deterioration rather than increasing diversity. The problems are starkly clear in African wildlife parks.

It is an inescapable fact that man as predator has been an integral component of all African (and indeed most other) wildlife systems. When hunting is necessarily prohibited in a park, one set of predator–prey relationships is disrupted. Animals with few enemies except man can proliferate unchecked. The hippopotamus in the Ruwenzon in Uganda provide an example. Along the shores of Lake Edward and the Kazinga Channel the density of hippopotamus had risen during the 1950s to up to 215 per square km. The surrounding area was grazed bare and bushes were encroaching on former grassland. In 1958 it was decided to cull the hippopotamus, breaking with the tradition of no shooting in the park. As part of the cull, and as an experiment, the hippopotamus were eliminated from one area, the Mweya Peninsula, and reduced in others. Subsequently, regular counts of animals and inspection of the vegetation showed that higher densities of other herbivores had replaced the hippopotamus and that the grazings had improved (Laws, 1968). The cull of the hippopotamus had provided a cropping scheme that was a notable success.

The elephant presents problems that are far more intractable and devastating in their effects than those created by hippopotamus. The rise in elephant density in parks has not been caused simply by decreased mortality rates and successful breeding of sedentary populations but has been exacerbated by the immigration into the parks of elephants that are harassed by man outside (Laws, 1969). Almost every park and reserve in East, Central and Southern Africa has developed an 'elephant problem'. The major effect is the destruction of trees and the rapid replacement of woodland by open grassland; regeneration is negligible. Elephant are not the sole agent, grazing by other large mammals and fire being important contributory factors (Spence and Angus, 1971), whilst changes in climate and soil salinity are also implicated (Western and Van Praet, 1973). Nevertheless, the elephant's effect, particularly in destroying mature trees, is the one most amenable to positive management action, and the reduction of elephant numbers has been carried out in some of the worst-affected areas. In Rhodesia and South Africa too this culling has provided the basis of economic meat production schemes.

It seems that in the present state of knowledge the carefully controlled culling of the largest herbivores is a necessary tool of wildlife management for conservation in Africa. Perhaps this is not surprising when it is recalled that meat-hungry man has been a major agent in manipulating their populations for half a million years. The total protection of animals in national parks creates very special problems that are peculiar to the present day.

Wildlife reserves and parks require land and must compete for it with every other form of land use. The maintenance of wildlife areas is a justifiable use of land for any nation because it represents a resource of multifarious values, both present and potential, but it has become increasingly expedient to expose wildlife reserves to another current use—recreation. The national parks in Africa show extreme examples of the impact of tourism on wildlife reserves partly because, on the one hand, the income they generate is a major (sometimes the major) component in foreign exchange earnings, whilst on the other hand the ecosystems of the reserves themselves, being in semi-arid tropical regions, are exceptionally fragile and vulnerable to damage. The numbers of visitors mount yearly: in 1968 there were 34,000 visitors to Kabalega National Park in Uganda; in 1970 there were 60,000. The small Nairobi National Park in Kenya, 115 square kilometres in extent, had 131,000 visitors in 1969/70 and they travelled in at least 26,000 cars.

The manner in which large numbers of vehicles travelling in a park affect animal populations is a subject that has rarely been documented and is little studied. In a pioneering report on the ecological significance of roads in national parks in South Africa, Pienaar (1968) showed that tracks, and even tarmac roads, when carefully sited, do not usually affect animals adversely. Effects can be different, however, when vehicles are not strictly prevented from driving off the tracks, as is the case in many East African parks. Here, the immediate impact is on soils and vegetation. Many parks, seen from the air, reveal a maze of car wheel marks. In places where lions, for example, can be seen on a kill the vegetation is often hammered by the vehicles of eager viewers. Eventually the damage caused by the habitat must reduce its carrying capacity for game.

A direct effect of tourists on animal populations has been observed in a few special situations. An example for herbivores is given by Walter (1969), who studied Thomson's gazelle in the Ngorongoro Crater in Tanzania and who considers that this species has declined in the area over recent years, since tourism became intensive. He measured the distance to which the gazelle could be approached before they were put to flight by humans. The closest approach could be made in a landrover to territorial male gazelles in areas much frequented by tourists. Female gazelles were shy and easily disturbed and were constantly frightened away from the male territories by vehicles, so failing to maintain their usual, high, reproductive rates.

A more severely disturbed animal population is seen in the crocodiles that inhabit the Victoria Nile in the Kabalega National Park in Uganda and that have long been the object of study by Dr. Hugh Cott. This is one of the few protected breeding populations that remain. On the Nile below the Falls 700 crocodiles were present in 1967; in 1968 only 534 were counted and this total was confirmed in 1969, but in 1972 only 241 were counted. It is difficult to account for this decline unless poaching is steadily reducing the numbers of adults, but equally alarming is the fact that relentless crocodile-viewing, from launches that ply regularly up and down to the Falls, is depressing recruitment to the stock.

Crocodiles have an elaborate courtship and pairing ritual which takes place in November and December. If excessively disturbed by boats the individuals may fail to breed or breed late, at a sub-optimal time. The eggs are laid in sand nests and covered by the female. Successful hatching (in March and April) depends on maternal care at the nest and, again, disturbance by launches, driving off the females, is fatal. The eggs are taken by monitor lizards, baboons, hyaenas and other predators. In addition the eggs are turned rotten by damp, and the wash from launches destroys many clutches, especially in years of high water levels. It is a situation that calls for determined action by management to conserve the crocodiles and yet retain the attraction that tourists come to see.

Perhaps management directed to the arrest of deterioration is the correct and only practicable strategy at the present time. A great deal of ecological research and new thinking is urgently required before stable wildlife communities can be maintained.

## REFERENCES AND BIBLIOGRAPHY

Bannerman, M. M., and Blaxter, K. L. (Eds.) (1969). *The Husbanding of Red Deer*, Rowett Research Institute, Aberdeen, 79 pp.

Bannikov, A. G., Zhirnov, L. U., Lebedeva, L. S., and Fandeev, A. A. (1961). *Biology of the Taiga*, Israel Program for Scientific Translations, Jerusalem, 252 pp.

Berry, R. J. (1971). *Conservation and the Genetical Constitution of Populations*, in: *The Scientific Management of Animal and Plant Communities for Conservation*, (eds.) E. Duffey and A. S. Watt, Blackwell, Oxford, 177–206.

Bindernagel, J. A. (1968). *Game Cropping in Uganda*, Uganda Game Department, mimeographed report, 200 pp.

Brooks, A. C., and Buss, I. O. (1962). Past and present status of the elephant in Uganda, *J. Wildlf. Mgmt.*, **26**, 38–50.

Clutton-Brock, J. (1971). The primary food animals of the Jericho Tell from the Proto-Neolithic to the Byzantine period, *Levant*, **3**, 41–55.

Cox, G. W. (1969). *Readings in Conservation Ecology*, Appleton-Century-Crofts, New York, 595 pp.

Dasmann, R. F. (1964). *African Game Ranching*, Pergamon, London, 75 pp.

Duffey, E., and Watt, A. S. (eds.) (1971). *The Scientific Management of Animal and Plant Communities for Conservation*, Blackwell, Oxford, 652 pp.

Field, C. R., and Laws, R. M. (1970). The distribution of the larger herbivores in the Queen Elizabeth National Park, Uganda, *J. app. Ecol.*, **7**, 273–94.

Fisher, J. (1952). *The Fulmar*, Collins, London, 496 pp.

Geist, V. (ed.) (In Press). *The Behaviour of Ungulates and its Relation to Management*, Calgary.

Hickerson, H. (1965). The Virginia deer and intertribal buffer zones in the Upper Mississippi Valley, in: *Man, Culture and Animals*, (eds.) A. Leeds and A. P. Vayda, American Association for the Advancement of Science, Washington, 304 pp.

Higgs, E. S. (ed.) (1972). *Papers in Economic Prehistory*, University Press, Cambridge, 219 pp.

Higgs, E. S., and Jarman, M. R. (1972). The origins of animal and plant husbandry, in: *Papers in Economic Prehistory*, (ed.) E. S. Higgs, University Press, Cambridge, 219 pp.

Jewell, P. A. (1969). Wild mammals and their potential for new domestication, in: *The Domestication and Exploitation of Plants and Animals* (eds.) P. Ucko and G. W. Dimbleby, Duckworth, London, pp. 101–9.

Jewell, P. A., Milner, C., and Morton Boyd, J. (In Press). *Survival in Isolation: the Ecology of the Soay Sheep of St. Kilda*, Athlone Press, London.

Lamprey, H. F. (1963). Ecological separation of the large mammal species in the Tarangire Game Reserve, Tanganyika, *E. African Wldf. J.*, **1**, 63–92.

Laughlin, W. S. (1968). Hunting: an integrating biobehaviour system and its evolutionary importance, in: *Man the Hunter*, (eds.) R. D. Lee and I. DeVore, Aldine, Chicago, pp. 49–55.

Laws, R. M. (1968). Interactions between elephants and hippopotamus populations and their environments, *E. Afr. agric. For. J.*, **33**, 140–7.

Laws, R. M. (1969). The Tsavo research project, *J. Reprod. Fert.*, Suppl. **6**, 495–531.

Lee, R. B. (1968). What hunters do for a living, or, how to make out on scarce resources, in: *Man the Hunter*, (eds.) R. B. Lee and I. de Vore, Aldine, Chicago, 36–48.

Lee, R. B., and DeVore, I. (eds.) (1968). *Man the Hunter*, Aldine, Chicago, 415 pp.

Leeds, A., and Vayda, A. P. (eds.) (1965). *Man, Culture, and Animals*, American Association for the Advancement of Science, Washington, 304 pp.

Legge, A. J. (1972). Prehistoric exploitation of the gazelle in Palestine, in *Papers in Economic Prehistory*, (ed.) E. S. Higgs, University Press, Cambridge, 119–24.

Lowe, V. P. W. (1969). Population dynamics of the red deer (*Cervus elaphus* L.) on Rhum. *J. Anim. Ecol.*, **38**, 425–57.

Lowe, V. P. W. (1971). Some effects of a change in estate management on a deer population, in: *The Scientific Management of Animal and Plant Communities for Conservation*, (eds.) E. Duffey and A. S. Watt, Blackwell, Oxford, 437–56.

Martin, P. S., and Wright, H. E. (eds.) (1967). *Pleistocene Extinctions: the Search for a Cause*, Yale University Press, New Haven, 453 pp.

McVean, D. N., and Lockie, J. D. (1969). *Ecology and Land Use in Upland Scotland*, University Press, Edinburgh, 134 pp.

Peterson, R., and Fisher, J. (1956). *Wild America*, Collins, London, 404 pp.

Pienaar, U. de V. (1968). The ecological significance of roads in a National Park, *Koedoe*, No. **11**, 169–74.

Pimlott, D. H. (1967). Wolf predation and ungulate populations, *American Zoologist*, **7**, 267–78. Also reproduced in G. W. Cox (1969). *Readings in Conservation Ecology*, Appleton-Century-Crofts, New York.

Pimlott, D. H. (1970). Predation and productivity of game populations in North America. *Trans. IX Internat. Cong. Game Biol., Moscow*, 63–73.

Riney, T. (1967). *Conservation and Management of African Wildlife*, FAO, Rome, 35 pp.

Skinner, J. (1972). The springbok: a farm animal of the future, *African Wildlife*, **26**, 114–5.

Spence, D. H. N., and Angus, A. (1971). African grassland management—burning and grazing in Murchison Falls National Park, Uganda, in: *The Scientific Management of Animal and Plant Communities for Conservation*, (eds.) E. Duffey and A. S. Watt, Blackwell, Oxford, 319–31.

Sturdy, D. A. (1972). The exploitation patterns of a modern reindeer economy in West Greenland, in: *Papers in Economic Prehistory*, (ed.) E. S. Higgs, University Press, Cambridge, 161–8.

Walter, F. R. (1969). Flight behaviour and avoidance of predators in Thomson's Gazelle (*Gazella, thomsoni*, Guenther, 1884), *Behaviour*, **34**, 184–221.

Western, D., and van Praet, C. (1973). Cyclical changes in the habitat and climate of an East African ecosystem. *Nature* (London), **241**, 104–6.

Wilkinson, P. F. (1972). Oomingmak: a model for man–animal relationships in prehistory, *Current Anthropology*, **13**, 23–44.

Woodburn, J. (1968). An introduction to Hadza ecology, in: *Man the Hunter*, (eds.) R. D. Lee and I. DeVore, Aldine, Chicago, 49–55.

# C   More Highly Modified Systems

CHAPTER 13

# River Management and Urban Flooding

## G. E. HOLLIS

### INTRODUCTION

Urban areas are absorbing a progressively greater proportion of the world's population. In the western world the urban expansion which is proceeding by suburban and new town development has brought with it many new problems, such as vehicle exhaust pollution and aircraft noise, and the old problems such as periodic flooding still persist. In Britain the nationwide floods of March, 1947 inundated Gloucester, Nottingham and Staines as well as many other urban areas; Lynton and Lynmouth were devastated by an Exmoor storm and subsequent flood during 1952 (Dobbie and Wolf, 1953); early 1953 saw the sea water inundation of large areas of the east coast, with Canvey Island and Tilbury being amongst the worst affected (Grieve, 1959); the autumn of 1960 saw five serious floods on the River Exe in Devon, and the extensive flooding of Exeter (Harrison, 1961); the West Country, the Mendips and Bristol were again subject to severe flooding during summer, 1968 (Hanwell and Newson, 1970), whilst in September of that year southeast England and particularly parts of the Great Ouse basin (Great Ouse River Authority, 1969), Kent (Taylor, 1972) and the lower Mole (Thames Conservancy, 1969) were severely flooded; houses in the Longlevens area of Gloucester were inundated in 1970 by the overflow of the Horsebere Brook (Severn River Authority, 1971) and more recently, the River Afan 'burst its banks' and flooded 502 houses in Port Talbot on November 12th and 13th, 1972 (*Guardian,* 13.11.72).

There are several factors which make this continued flooding of urban areas remarkable. First, Britain has had a very long history of settlement going back over 2,000 years. There is ample evidence that our forebears deliberately chose sites for villages which avoided floods (Dury, 1952). Second, Britain is one of the world's rich countries and has a high level of technology. Finally, the intensities of rainfall which occur over Britain are several orders of magnitude less severe than the global maxima (Rodda, 1970).

Why are we unable to manage our rivers so that we can protect our urban areas from flood damage? The factors which contribute to the problem are the nature of river flood hydrology, the economic factors which encourage urban development in riverine locations, the propensity of human organizations to undertake piecemeal flood alleviation schemes, and the frailty of the human mind. Each will be considered in turn.

## RIVER FLOOD HYDROLOGY

The controls of flood hydrograph characteristics have been categorized by Rodda (1969) as either permanent or transient (see also Kirby and Rodda, Chapter 5). The permanent controls include the morphology of the river basin, the planimetric layout of the drainage network and the characteristics of the individual channels. The transient factors are the storm characteristics, the rate of water loss by evaporation, the water storage capacity of the soil, bedrock, surface depressions and vegetation surfaces and the prevailing infiltration characteristics of the soils. Land use, in the form of cropping practices and impermeable surfaces, is said to be either transient or permanent. The rainfall–runoff relationship, therefore, varies spatially and temporally. Precipitation onto the earth's surface is translated into river flow by means of transfers between storages in the land phase of the hydrological cycle. As the rainfall continues, so the relative importance of interception, depression and soil storages declines, and more and more of the rainfall runs off to the river channel.

The size and capacity of natural channels is primarily determined by the magnitude and frequency of flood flows in the river. Independent work on major British rivers (Nixon, 1959) and on streams in the USA (Leopold *et al.*, 1964) has shown that river channels are adjusted to accommodate the flood which occurs about once every one or two years. Consequently, larger flows cause inundation of the area around the river. The floodplain, as the periodically flooded area is known, is usually underlain by sediments left behind by both previous overbank flows and the progressive movement of meanders and their associated point-bar deposits (Morisawa, 1968).

River conservation works and urban-orientated flood alleviation schemes must recognize the natural function of floodplain lands and realize that they are likely to be covered at least once every four or five years if nothing is done to disturb the natural situation.

## URBAN DEVELOPMENT

The second contributory factor to the flood problem in Britain is the siting of many of our major cities and towns on floodplains and river

PLAN

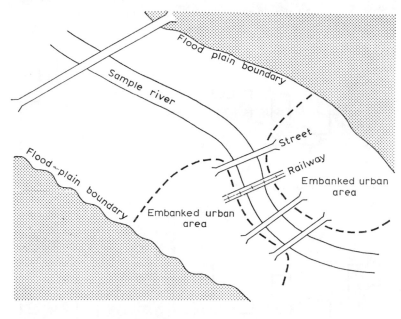

PROFILE

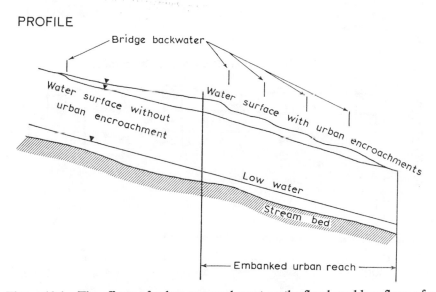

**Figure 13.1.** The effects of urban encroachment on the flood- and low-flows of a typical river. Floods become higher whereas low-flows are hardly affected. (After Dougal, 1969.)

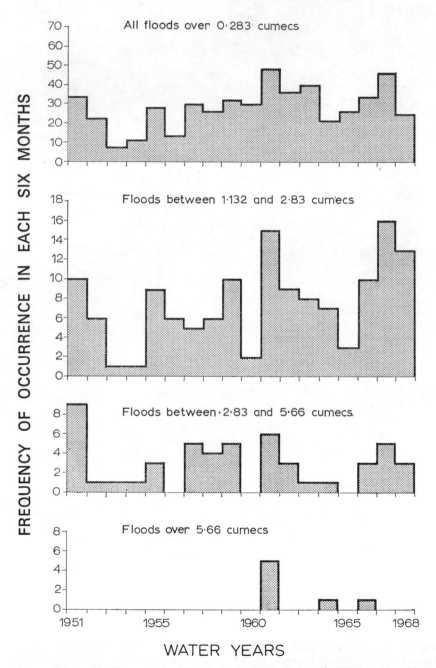

**Figure 13.2.** The frequency of floods in the Canon's Brook, Harlow New Town, Essex. The basin was progressively urbanized from 1953. This appears to be the reason for the increased incidence of summer floods.

# SUMMER (APRIL - SEPTEMBER)

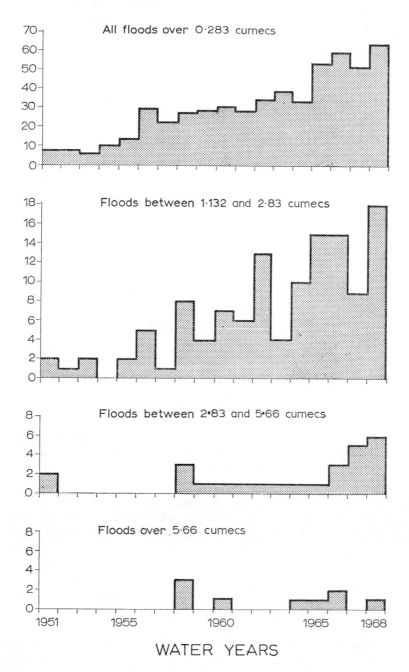

WATER YEARS

terraces. Nixon (1963) has illustrated the expansion of Nottingham into the Trent flood plain and Horner (1971) has shown the very considerable area of Greater London at risk from an overflow of the estuarine Thames. There were, and are, many good reasons for urban areas to be sited near rivers. Questions of defence, port activity, inland routes of communication and supplies of fresh water were no doubt in the minds of those who initially made settlements near rivers. Many early sites, however, though near rivers, were sited so that flooding was avoided; Horner (1971) showed for example

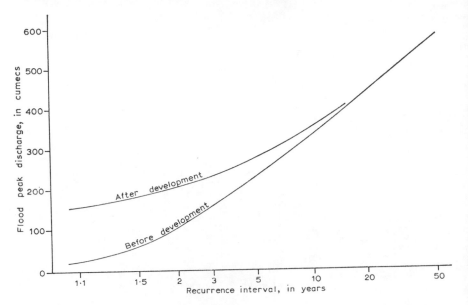

**Figure 13. 3.**  The hypothetical flood frequency curves for rural and urban areas. This suggests that larger floods are not affected by urbanization. (After Crippen and Waananen, 1969.)

that the City of London, which is largely coterminous with the Roman Londinium, is not liable to significant inundation by the Thames. It seems that our ancestors lacked only the foresight to see how their settlements would expand from the dry terrace sites to the neighbouring floodplains. Not only does urbanization on the floodplain increase the potential damage likely to result from flooding, but it also tends to raise the level of the flood. Moreover, urbanization in the drainage basin may result in an aggravation of natural flood problems downstream.

There is a tendency for urban areas to encroach on the river channel itself. The construction of bridges, wharves and embankments tends to constrict and impede the river so that the level of a flood is higher than it would have been without the encroachment (Figure 13.1). In the context of London, Bowen (1972) has suggested that the progressive increase in maximum Thames flood levels, from under 14 feet O.D. in 1791 to over 17·5 feet O.D. in 1953, has been almost wholly the result of the banking and walling which now lines the river.

The establishment of paved areas and other impervious surfaces in a catchment and the draining of these surfaces by a dense and efficient surface-water sewer system usually leads to an increase in the proportion of rainfall running off and also tends to decrease the time delay between rainfall and runoff. Seaburn (1969) used the unit hydrograph technique to show that flood peaks were increased by 2·5 times after the paving of 18 per cent of a 31-square-mile area of suburban New York. The frequency of floods, and particularly summer floods, has increased in the Canon's Brook since the construction of Harlow New Town began in 1953 (Figure 13.2). The effect of urbanization on floods of various magnitudes is not, however, entirely clear, for Crippen and Waananen (1969) have suggested that the hydrological functioning of a saturated catchment is probably little different from that of a paved basin (Figure 13.3). Indeed, floods with a return period of twenty years or greater are unaffected by urbanization in the Canon's Brook catchment.

## FLOOD ALLEVIATION AND ASSOCIATED CONSERVATION PROBLEMS

Most incursions of human activities on to floodplains are associated with some form of flood alleviation scheme. By definition, a flood alleviation scheme involves a conflict between man and nature, and as such it poses fundamental conservation problems with respect to the lives of the inhabitants, their cities, crops and water supplies, as well as the biological life of the river and its environmental quality. There is a great range of adjustments that can be employed by a society dwelling in a flood risk zone, but Nixon (1963) showed that whilst single schemes do exist, the majority of flood relief plans involve a mixture of techniques.

The most common response to the danger of flooding in the western world is the construction of engineering works. These works are of three basic types. Reservoirs or washlands can be created to store flood water, and so attenuate peak flows. Embankments or walls may be built to stop the water reaching the protected area, or the whole area may have its level raised by floodplain filling. On a much smaller scale, individual properties may be flood-proofed. Lastly, peak stages may be reduced by channel improvement such as diversion channels or by-passes, which increase flow velocities. White (1964, p. 25/113) suggests that 'experience shows that the construction and operation of engineering works to control flood flows may reduce or cut flows without necessarily reducing the threat to the health, safety and welfare of the community or the flood-damage potential. This may be because (1) while protection is given to life and property within a levee, new development takes place in unprotected areas; (2) while flood frequency and magnitude are reduced along the flood plain by channel improvements or reservoir operation upstream, new encroachments at lower levels cause greater threats to the public and greater losses, even though some floods are lower than formerly; or (3) the losses which occur when a levee is overtopped or channel capacity exceeded by a flow greater than the design flood are catastrophic and outweigh the benefits gained in other years'. In addition to White's criticisms, flood control works pose other environmental problems. Reservoirs and washlands occupy valuable land, and where the topography is subdued their area has to be considerable if sufficient storage is to be created. Moreover, flood-balancing ponds in urban areas tend to become filled with sediment as building activity disturbs the soil and renders it susceptible to erosion (Walling and Gregory, 1970). However, some flood storage schemes can be of positive benefit to amenity, as at Netteswell Pond in Harlow New Town which caters for ducks, model boats and landscaped picnic areas, or in the Ouse Washes in the Fens which provide an invaluable habitat for an extensive range of bird species. On the other hand, levees and walls may restrict access to the river bank and present landscaping problems if they are particularly high. The bed of the river may be raised by siltation so that, particularly during winter periods, the land level outside the banks is below even the base of the stream (Johnson, 1959). Modifications to channel geometry necessarily give the river an unnatural look. The River Crouch at Wickford is little more than a two-stage concrete flume (Nixon, 1963); and the Thames Conservancy propose to use four miles of heavy sheet steel piling in an 'improvement' scheme for the River Wey at Guildford (Anon, 1969). The enlargement of channels to conduct floods may result in very shallow flows during dry weather. Such conditions are undesirable for they may endanger fish and aquatic plants, expose shoals and banks which are quickly invaded by weeds which clog the channel during later floods, and increase the possibility of smells. These problems are usually tackled by the construction of either sluices or a narrow central channel to accommodate summer flows and a wide, stepped section with berms and revetments to contain floods. The River Tone through Taunton has been provided with such a multi-stage channel (Dobbie *et al.*, 1971).

Sewell (1969) suggests that some alternative responses to floods are the acceptance of loss, public relief, or emergency action. Few developed countries or individuals who have experienced a flood will accept a second loss without seeking a means for reducing future losses. Public relief, usually regarded as a right rather than a charitable gift, can only tend to encourage continued occupation of hazardous zones and therefore is not beneficial to society in the long term. Emergency action and flood fighting are useful measures which can reduce flood losses by between 5 and 15 per cent and they have no detrimental effects on the river. However, public investment in a flood warning system which is a necessary prerequisite for effective emergency action tends to encourage continued occupation of high-risk zones. It would appear, therefore, that whilst these measures, together with flood insurance (if it can be obtained), are alternatives to engineering works, in no way do they encourage the harmonious co-existence of river and city which should be the aim of any flood alleviation scheme.

The best method of maintaining a balance between river and city is by land-use planning and the zonation of floodplains. Such an approach aims to conserve the river channel and natural flow regime of the stream as far as possible and to prevent major loss or social disruption by keeping the urban area away from and above the river. Linsley and Franzini (1964) argue that 'zoning must pass the test of economic justification' and it must be shown that the benefits for a particular land use which are obtainable only on the floodplain are smaller than the costs of flood alleviation works. The zoning procedure might be preceded by an analysis of the rent-earning capability of the various land uses and their ability to pay the 'natural' tax of flooding (Sewell, 1969).

In practice, land use in Britain is in the hands of local authorities who have powers under the 1947 and subsequent Town and Country Planning Acts. Government Circulars in 1947, 1962 and 1969 (Ministry of Housing and Local Government, 1969) have 'drawn the attention of local authorities to the special importance of full consultation (with River Authorities) in respect of development in areas liable to flood or which might give rise to drainage problems'.

Areas liable to flood were defined by the Minister of Agriculture, Fisheries and Food in 1933, when in reply to the Medway Catchment Board, he defined, in the 'Medway Letter', areas which will derive benefit or avoid danger as a result of flood relief schemes. The 'Medway Letter line' includes all land 8 feet (2·4 m) or less above known flood levels in rural areas and no higher than flood levels in urban areas (Burton, 1961). This definition was taken up by the North Gloucestershire Sub-Regional Study (Collins *et al.*, 1970, p. 57), which stated 'in the valleys of the Severn and its tributaries, the 50 feet contour was regarded broadly as a reasonably safe lower limit for development. . . . The risk of inundation by flood water from the River Severn is the most important and decisive of natural restraints to the location of the new development.' The Milton Keynes Development

Corporation (1969) have identified those areas of the River Ouzel and Loughton Brook valleys which flooded in 1947 and have planned these areas as linear water parks.

Land-use zoning does, therefore, take place in Britain although it is not backed by absolute prohibitions on development. In some cases development is permitted in flood risk zones but usually these plans are subjected to a public inquiry first. Permissions may be given subject to flood control works being constructed, but as we have noted such works may only increase potential overall damage from a subsequent catastrophic storm.

In summary, it would appear that each of the adjustments to floods which have been considered have certain drawbacks. Some, like engineered flood control structures, may reduce the frequency of inundation but do not provide much protection from floods in excess of the design storm. Relief, welfare work and emergency action may help victims of floods, but in the long term they will be a subsidy for the occupant of the risk zone. Land-use planning minimizes the conflict between man and nature but may sterilize tracts of riverine land.

## HUMAN FRAILTY

The final reason given at the start of this chapter for continued flooding of urban areas in Britain, and elsewhere, was the frailty of the human mind. Following the seminal work of White (e.g. 1964) and his colleagues at Chicago, it is now widely appreciated that decision-makers base their decisions on the environment as they perceive it, not as it is. The action which results from the decision, however, is played out in the real world. White stressed that in floodplain management all possible courses of action should be reviewed, and the fact that this is not always undertaken is partly the result of the resource users' lack of total awareness of alternatives. Kates (1962), studying the conditions of knowledge under which floodplain resource decisions are made, found that the perceived probability distribution of floods was related to past knowledge and experience of floods, but that in many cases similar information and experience resulted in markedly different appreciations of the danger or of possible adjustments.

The basis of any evaluation of flood damage reduction measures must be a knowledge of the frequency and magnitude of floods. The professional land drainage experts can only base their 'objective' analysis on river-gauging records. Regrettably, only 560 stations were in operation in England and Wales in 1970, and only a handful of river flow records pre-date the formation of the River Boards in 1948. Consequently, the nation lacks a body of data from which precise estimates of the frequency of design floods can be made. Partly as a result of this, and also because of the long-held belief that 'the only true measure of the importance of a flood problem . . . is the amount of money the flooded people are prepared to pay in order to avoid floods' (Burton, 1961), British flood defence schemes are normally tailored to accommodate the greatest known flood. In practice, this means that floods before 1900 are rarely considered and that there are no national standards of frequency applied to the protection of different land uses on the floodplain.

## A CASE STUDY OF THE LOWER MOLE FLOODPLAIN

A review of the post-war management of the lower reaches of the River Mole in Surrey is an instructive illustration of the practical problems and pitfalls of floodplain planning in an urban setting. It shows not only the range of possible river flood conditions, but also the hazards of uncontrolled urban encroachment into floodplains and the fallibility of narrow engineering solutions to flood problems.

The River Mole rises in the Weald and drains northward to the Thames. Its 185 square-mile (479 sq. km) catchment includes Crawley, Gatwick, Horley, Reigate, Redhill, Dorking and Cobham. The floodplain of the lower Mole merges with that of the Thames and these flat riverine lands house the residents of East and West Molesey, parts of Esher and Walton, and include the Island Barn water supply reservoir.

The highest recorded flow of the Thames, which occurred in March 1947 after a snowy winter, caused flooding in parts of East and West Molesey and Thames Ditton (Figure 13.4b). In Molesey, however, as in the earlier flood of 1929, the flooding was largely confined to the open land of Hurst Park Racecourse. Between 1955 and 1958 the lower part of the Mole was subject to an improvement scheme (Dobbie *et al.*, 1971) capable of containing a flow of 2,300 cusecs (65·1 cumecs) which was 'considered to be the maximum likely to occur'. It can be argued that such optimism was founded more on the need to satisfy economic criteria than an appreciation of the hydrological realities. Moreover, the scheme probably gave the residents of the floodplain the impression that 'floods had been eradicated', when in fact the probable period between floods had only been lengthened.

In 1960, following an application for planning permission to build houses on the western end of the racecourse at Hurst Park, a public inquiry (Surrey County Council, 1960) heard evidence from the developers and objectors; flooding of the site and environs was a major issue. The developers proposed to raise the whole of the 1947 inundated area by 6 inches (15·2 cm) so that there was 'an ample safeguard for the future . . . [and protection from] . . . any further flooding of 70 houses' on the south side of the main road. The

loss of floodplain storage was expected to increase river levels by $1\frac{1}{2}$ inches (3·8 cm) but the developers offered to dredge the river to offset this.

Surrey County Council objected on the grounds that half of the land was liable to flood and that in 1948 and 1960 the Chief Engineer of the Thames Conservancy had exhorted them 'to prohibit all new building work on land subject to flood'. They also pointed to both the policy of the Ministry of Agriculture, Fisheries and Food, which was against floodplain development, and to the reference to flooding in the Minister's dismissals of other applications for development in the area. The Thames Conservancy, in an historical review of flooding since 1883, showed that the site 'had been flooded to some extent on an average once in 7 years'. The conservators objected in principle to 'any proposal which would restrict or obstruct the natural flood plain of the river', since filling of the whole floodplain of the Thames on the lines proposed would increase 'the peak flood levels by some 4 feet (1·2 m)'.

The Minister accepted his inspector's recommendations that development should be permitted on those parts of the western half of the racecourse which were not flooded in 1947, so long as it was raised by 6 inches (15·2 cm) by land filling. Pressure for more land for housing and the reservation of the eastern end of Hurst Park for open space, together with the fringe benefits of shops and a school, had clearly outweighed the pleas of the county planners and the Thames Conservancy. Building activity got under-way during the early 1960s.

'The exceptional (rain) falls on the 14th and 15th September (1968) . . . of 7 inches (17·8 cm) . . . in under 24 hours . . . in the Mole catchment to the east of Redhill' (Thames Conservancy, 1969) gave rise to a flow of 8,500 cusecs (240·7 cumecs) in the lower Mole and flooded 2,506 acres (10·2 sq. km), affecting 10,000 properties most of which were houses (Dobbie *et al.*, 1971). Figure 13.4(c) shows the area affected and reveals that not only was part of the Hurst Park Development under water but also most of East Molesey, including the post-war buildings. 'A rough estimate of the damage' was £1,300,000, and the 1968 flood's 'return period' might have been as low as 1 in 200, or as high as 1 in 1,000 years (Dobbie *et al.*, 1971).

In response to these 'disastrous floods', the Thames Conservancy ex-tended its flood warning system to the Mole (Thames Conservancy, 1969) and engaged consultants to examine the feasibility of improvements to the lower Mole. The proposed scheme is shown in Figure 13.4(d) (Anon, 1969). The scheme is designed to accommodate 8,500 cusecs (240·7 cumecs), which was the 1968 flow, and will cost an estimated £2,067,000.

The conclusions and questions which are prompted by this case study typify the problems which were discussed earlier. First, design floods, whether they are determined on a strictly statistical frequency basis or by reference to the greatest known flood, will be exceeded at some time in the future. Second, in spite of the provisions of planning acts and government circulars which call for consultations between river authorities and county planners, which numbered 1,267 in the case of the Thames Conservancy in 1971 (Thames Conservancy, 1972), there has been considerable encroachment onto floodplains. Third, the frailty of the human mind results in the necessity to implement a £2,067,000 flood relief scheme which will prevent £1,300,000 worth of damage once every 200 years or longer. Finally, the construction of considerable civil engineering works to 'prevent' floods gives a sense of security to floodplain dwellers and both reduces their vigilance and makes the refusal of planning permission for new buildings in the protected area more difficult. The future, therefore, does not hold the prospect of the elimination of urban flooding, but merely a reduction in the frequency of flooding and an increase in the severity of disasters when they do occur in our cities. Indeed, Nixon (1969) has stated, 'it is positively certain that there [will] be yet another disaster and it could well be two or three times the size of the 1947 floods'.

## REFERENCES

Anonymous (1969). £6m. scheme to prevent Surrey flooding, *Civil Eng. and Public Works Review*, Nov., 1089.

Bowen, A. J. (1972). The tidal regime of the River Thames; long term trends and their possible causes. *Phil. Trans. Roy. Soc. London, Series A*, **272**, 187–200.

Burton, I. (1961). Some aspects of flood loss reduction in England and Wales, in: *Papers on Flood Problems*, (ed.) G. F. White, Univ. of Chicago Dept. of Geography, Research Paper **70**, 203–28.

Collins, N. R., Downs, R. A., and Pullen, R. H. (1970). *North Gloucestershire Sub-Regional Study*, Gloucestershire County Council, 106 pp.

Crippen, J. R., and Waananen, A. O. (1969). Hydrologic effects of suburban development near Palo Alto, California, *U.S. Geol. Survey Open File Report*, 126 pp.

Dobbie, C. H., and Wolf, P. O. (1953). The Lynmouth flood of August 1952, *Proc. Instn. Civil Engrs.*, **2**, 522–88.

Dobbie, C. H., Prus-Chacinski, T. M., and Bowen, H. C. (1971). Flood alleviation works, *Civil Eng. and Public Works Review*, April, 383–90.

Dougal, M. D. (1969). Technique for developing a comprehensive programme for flood plain management, in: *Flood plain management: Iowa's Experience*, (ed.) M. D. Dougal, Iowa State University, Ames, Iowa, 53–78.

Dury, G. H. (1952). *Map Interpretation*, Pitman, London, 203 pp.

Great Ouse River Authority (1969). *Annual Report for the Year Ended 31st March 1969*, 68 pp.

Grieve, H. (1959). *The Great Tide*, Essex County Council, 883 pp.

Hanwell, J. D., and Newson, M. D. (1970). The great storms and floods of July 1968 in Mendip, *Wessex Cave Club, Occasional Publications* Series 1, No. 2, 22 pp.

Harrison, A. J. M. (1961). The 1960 Exmouth Floods, *The Surveyor*, **120**, 127–32.

Horner, R. N. (1971). The flood defence of London, *Civil Eng. and Public Works Review,* April, 393–5.

Johnson, E. A. G. (1959). Land drainage in England and Wales, in: *Design of Land Drainage Works,* (ed.) R. B. Thorn, Butterworths, London, 1–31.

Kates, R. W. (1962). Hazard and choice perception in flood plain management, Univ. of Chicago Dept. of Geography Research Paper 78.

Leopold, L. B., Wolman, M. G., and Miller, J. P. (1964). *Fluvial Processes in Geomorphology,* Freeman, San Francisco, 522 pp.

Linsley, R. K., and Franzini, J. B. (1964). *Water Resources Engineering,* McGraw-Hill, New York, 654 pp.

Milton Keynes Development Corporation (1969). The plan for Milton Keynes, *Tech. Supp.* No. 10, vol. 2, *Surface Water Drainage,* 61 pp.

Ministry of Housing and Local Government (1969). *Surface-water Run-off from Development,* Circular 94/69, 2 pp.

Morisawa, M. (1968). *Streams: Their Dynamics and Morphology,* McGraw-Hill, New York, 175 pp.

Nixon, M. (1959). A study of the bank-full discharges of rivers in England and Wales, *Proc. Instn. Civil Engrs.,* **12,** 157–74.

Nixon, M. (1963). Flood regulation and river training in England and Wales, in: *The Conservation of Water Resources in the United Kingdom,* Institution of Civil Engineers, London, pp. 137–50.

Nixon, M. (1969). Discussion following Land Drainage Section of the Future of our Rivers Symposium, *Assoc. of River Authorities Year Book,* 1969, 243–4.

Rodda, J. C. (1969). The Flood Hydrograph, in: *Water, Earth and Man,* Ed. R. J. Chorley, Methuen, London, pp. 405–18.

Rodda, J. C. (1970). Rainfall excesses in the United Kingdom, *Trans. Inst. Brit. Geog.,* **49,** 49–60.

Seaburn, G. E. (1969). Effects of urban development on direct runoff to East Meadow Brook, Nassau County, Long Island, New York, *U.S. Geol. Survey Professional Paper 627–B,* 14 pp.

Severn River Authority (1971). *Annual Report for this Year Ended 31st March 1971,* 69 pp.

Sewell, W. R. D. (1969). Human response to floods, in *Water, Earth and Man,* Ed. R. J. Chorley, Methuen, London, pp. 431–54.

Surrey County Council (1960). Report of the Public Inquiry into the Development of Hurst Park Racecourse, Mimeo. File no. 1088/40621/30, 32 pp.

Taylor, J. E. (1972). Sea defence, land drainage and water resources development in the Kent River Authority Area, *Assoc. of River Authorities Year Book 1972,* pp. 82–99.

Thames Conservancy (1969). *General Report for Year Ended 31st December 1968,* 24 pp.

Thames Conservancy (1972). *General Report for Year Ended 31st December 1971,* 31 pp.

Walling, D. E., and Gregory, K. J. (1970). The measurement of the effects of building construction on drainage basin dynamics, *J. Hydrol.* **11,** 129–44.

White, G. F. (1964). Flood plain adjustments and regulations, in: *Handbook of Applied Hydrology,* Ed. V. T. Chow, McGraw-Hill, New York, pp. 25–112; 25–124.

# CHAPTER 14

# Ecological Effects of Visitors in the Countryside

## F. B. GOLDSMITH

## INTRODUCTION

Ecological changes which result from increased levels of recreational activity are causing concern to those interested in and responsible for the management of semi-natural areas, particularly in western Europe and North America.

Recreation, in the context of this essay, is defined as informal leisure pursuits in the countryside (Countryside Recreation Research Advisory Group, 1970) and its effects are best examined in terms of a supply and demand model. The supply concerns the resource, which comprises the vegetation, the associated fauna and the underlying soil, whereas the demand consists of man's requirements for recreation and aesthetic quality. Problems arise because the characteristics of the resource are themselves affected by the type and intensity of demand. The first chapter of this book suggested that the area of interaction between cultural and natural systems is the central interest of the conservationist. Some contributions to this volume have concentrated upon the demands made on the countryside, whereas others, including this one, concentrate on the natural systems being exploited. In this essay, characteristics of the resource, types of sensitive areas, damage done by recreational activities and appropriate forms of management will be discussed.

The demand for recreation in the countryside continues to increase rapidly (Dower, 1965; Patmore, 1970). Although the number of holidays of four or more days in length may be levelling off, there is no such indication for day trips (Dower, 1972), and it is these which largely concern us here. Most visitors seek new landscapes with unusual features (good views, the land/water interface) or areas with provision for specific activities (such as skiing, sailing or photography). Very often the areas which offer such facilities are of high biological interest, as for example chalk grassland, coastal dunes or mountain tops, and there is a conflict between people who are more interested in the recreational experience and those who wish to protect biologically interesting vegetation and its associated wildlife. Recently a more general problem has become apparent: visitors damage the fabric of the areas they visit, and consequently reduce its amenity value and the level of recreational activity which the area can support. In terrestrial ecosystems, the damage is usually the direct result of human trampling, although other activities, such as ski-ing (Bayfield, 1971) and horse-riding (Perring, 1967), may have a more severe impact. Not all trampling is detrimental, since low levels of trampling may occasionally benefit the biological interest, for example on chalk grassland dominated by *Brachypodium sylvaticum* (Sankey and Mackworth-Praed, 1969).

## THE CONCEPT OF CAPACITY

There are several different types of recreation carrying capacity. The Countryside Recreation Research Advisory Group (1970, p. 2) distinguishes physical, ecological, economic and perceptual capacities:

'(a) Physical capacity: the maximum level of recreation use, in terms of number (of people, cars, boats, etc.) and activities that can be accommodated for the purpose(s) for which a particular facility was designed or issued. For example, the physical capacity of a car park can be said to be reached when all available parking spaces are in use. The term is normally applied to man-made facilities such as lavatories and restaurants, but it is also applied, for example, to lakes used for sailing of water ski-ing;

'(b) Ecological capacity: the maximum level of recreation use, in terms of numbers and activities that can be accommodated before a decline in ecological value, assessed from the ecological viewpoint;

'(c) Economic capacity: the maximum level of recreation use, in terms of numbers and activities that can be accommodated in an area which is also used for some non-recreation activity, before damage to that activity becomes economically unacceptable from the management viewpoint. The term can, for example, be applied to reservoirs used for boating and also for water supply, and to woodlands used for timber production and also for recreation;

'(d) Perceptual capacity: the maximum level of recreational use, in terms of numbers and activities, above which there is a decline in the recreation experience from the point of view of the participant. Different users could have a different view of the perceptual capacity of the same area according to their activity.'

These definitions, however, pose further problems. For example, how should ecological value be assessed? Burden and Randerson (1972, p. 440) state that 'the amount of use an area can receive without deterioration of the vegetation is dependent upon the declared management objectives for that site and the degree of "naturalness" it is felt necessary to preserve. Thus the same area might have a series of carrying capacities: a low level of recreational use which would preserve a rare, sensitive species; a higher one which would preserve an acceptable degree of flowering of a ground species; a higher one again which would preserve a complete grass cover; and yet a higher level in which a complete grass cover was dependent on artificial fertilization, seeding and watering. These considerations lead us to define carrying capacity as the maximum intensity of use an area will continue to support under a particular management regime without inducing a permanent change in the biotic environment maintained by that management.'

## CHARACTERISTICS OF ECOSYSTEMS

In order to assess the ecological consequences of recreational activities, it is necessary to consider the characteristics of ecosystems which determine their sensitivity and carrying capacity.

Ecosystems are complex, integrated, dynamic systems consisting of numerous components which can be considered under the headings: plants, animals, soil and climate (e.g. Tansley, 1939; Watt, 1968). The living components are dependent upon each other for energy which flows through the system, and for the cycling of nutrients. Competition between individuals and between species, seasonally induced changes, year-to-year fluctuations and complications due to behaviour give ecosystems an inherently variable character and a constantly changing structure. Whether or not ecosystems are highly integrated has been a matter of debate amongst ecologists; some (Clements, 1916) have even compared them with individual organisms, but this is now considered a rather extreme point of view (e.g. Raup, 1964). It is universally accepted, however, that ecosystems have enough cohesiveness to tolerate moderate levels of extrinsic change and to adjust to differing external conditions. They also have the unique characteristic of being capable of continuous and infinite self-replenishment due in part to the reproductive power of the component organisms.

The degree of natural stability inherent in an ecosystem depends upon the reference time scale from which it is viewed. If the reference interval were only one day, a groundsel (*Senecio vulgaris*) population in an abandoned field would appear stable. Conversely, for a reference period of a few millennia the North European Deciduous Forest Formation might appear relatively unstable. Plant and animal communities are in a state of constant flux, resulting from seasonal and other recurrent environmental and evolutionary changes, the immigration of plant propagules and the migration of animals, competition and behavioural effects. A community which shows a directional change over a relatively long time period is known as a succession. This is a natural process commencing with bare ground, or any other relatively simple state, and developing into a more complex and better-ordered condition. An understanding of the principal characteristics of succession is fundamental to the consideration of ecological carrying capacity. A generalized succession is represented diagrammatically in Figure 14.1. It is a continuous process, the various stages being identified as reference

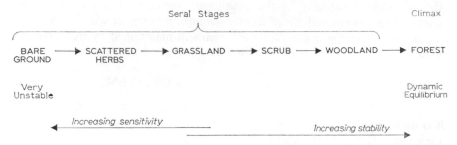

**Figure 14.1.** A generalized vegetational succession showing the relationship between seral stage, stability and intensity of management required to maintain a particular vegetation type.

points for the purpose of discussion only. The vegetation and associated fauna develop in terms of their species richness and structural complexity (degree of stratification in the vegetation and number of food-chain links) towards a relatively stable end-point known as the climax. Productivity (energy fixed per unit area per unit time) increases through the earlier stages and generally levels off towards the latter stages, whereas biomass (total carbon fixed or dry matter content) continues to increase regularly towards the climax. In the early stages the community is open, with a high proportion of bare ground, while the later stages are closed. Successions are often arrested at an intermediate stage by management as, for example, when a chalkland succession is arrested at a grassland stage by grazing or when a heathland succession is arrested by burning.

## THE SIGNIFICANCE OF SUCCESSION TO MANAGEMENT

The significance of successional theory to ecosystem management lies in the fact that many areas which are intensively used for recreation are sub-climax seral stages (e.g. sand-dunes, chalk grassland) and that larger management inputs are required to maintain a particular area at an early successional stage than at a later one. The earlier the stage in the sequence the more easily can it be destroyed and bare ground produced. Thus, in theory, forest is more resilient to damage than scrub, and scrub is more stable than grassland. However, this generalization must be interpreted in association with other properties of the system under study. The most important of these is that different plant growth-forms are more resistant to trampling than others. Plants with an apical bud at, near or below ground level are less likely to be damaged by trampling than plants with buds held aloft on delicate stems. Thus grasses in the vegetative state and herbs with a rosette of leaves, which are the main growth forms in grassland communities, are more resistant. The herb layer of a woodland is totally different, consisting of plants with their apical buds held well above the ground, and this community is consequently more vulnerable to damage from trampling.

The type of vegetation at a particular site will vary according to local climatic, edaphic or biotic factors. In some circumstances a climax vegetation may be particularly vulnerable to recreational activities. For example, mountain-top climax vegetation is comparable in resistance to relatively early successional stages at sea-level. The assessment of the sensitivity of vegetation must take into consideration:

(a) the position in a successional sequence;
(b) the proportion of the ground covered by tolerant growth forms;
(c) limiting environmental factors such as climate and nutrient-poor or physically unfavourable soils.

Thus the determination of vulnerability is not so simple that the ecologist can rank vegetation types in order of sensitivity, but it is possible to generalize about the types of habitat which are most vulnerable. These include coastal systems such as sand-dunes and salt-marshes which represent early successional stages and unstable substrata, montane habitats where the capacity for growth and self-recovery is reduced by the climate, systems with shallow or physically unfavourable soils such as chalk grassland (shallow), lowland heaths (nutrient-poor) and fens (excessively wet).

## DISTRIBUTION OF VISITORS

In order to manage a vegetation cover that is affected by large numbers of visitors it is necessary first to determine the distribution of the visitors and to analyse their motivation in selecting particular routes. The distribution can be determined using either mechanical or optical counters or indirectly using information supplied by the visitor on questionnaires.

Mechanical counters have been incorporated in steps or styles (Coker and Coker, 1972) and may be used in conjunction with data-logging devices. Bayfield (1971) has used a 'trampelometer' which consists of a row of nails connected by wire which are pressed into the vegetation by people's feet.

Optical methods include time-lapse photography as used on the Isles of Scilly (Goldsmith *et al.*, 1970; Coker and Coker, 1973) and light-sensitive (magic-eye) counters located at strategic positions.

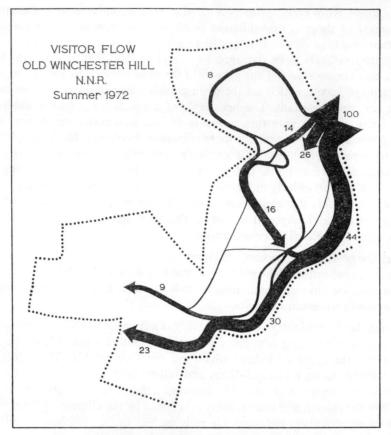

**Figure 14.2.** Outward visitor flows recorded by using questionnaire maps. The width of arrow is proportional to the number of visitors. (Reproduced by permission of Mrs. A. Coker.)

Questionnaire maps, again first used on Scilly, involve asking the visitor to indicate his route, stopping places, and the location of various activities on a map drawn on the questionnaire. This information can be used to determine distances travelled and preference for different vegetation types as well as the relative visitor pressure over an area (Goldsmith *et al.*, 1970). Coker has used this technique on Old Winchester Hill National Nature Reserve where it permitted the determination of mean outward and return visitor flow (Figure 14.2). But visitors find it more difficult to locate themselves in woods, and Gower (personal communication) has therefore used randomly selected numbers marked on trees and the visitor is asked to record the numbers seen. Thus there are a variety of simple techniques for recording visitor movements and these provide data which the recreation ecologist is able to use to relate to the distribution of ecological effects.

## EFFECTS OF TRAMPLING

The ecological effects of trampling and other activities have been reviewed by Speight (1973) and his conclusions may be summarized as follows:

(a) vegetation is bruised by trampling and most species are reduced in abundance or eliminated, although some species may increase in abundance; the height of the vegetation and its flowering frequency are reduced;

(b) the soil is compacted and its water-holding capacity reduced;

(c) animal life is disturbed and some species decline in number or move elsewhere.

Studies of the effects of trampling on vegetation have been conducted principally by Bates (1935; 1938; 1950), Wagar (1964), Bayfield (1971), Streeter (1971) and by the Conservation Course at University College London (Burden and Randerson, 1972; Coker and Coker, 1972; Goldsmith et al., 1970) and on fauna by Morris (1967) and Duffey (1967a).

There has been considerable discussion amongst ecologists about the effects of these activities on diversity and productivity. Confusion has arisen from misunderstandings about the meaning of the word diversity. It is important to distinguish between species diversity, which can be equated with richness, which is the total number of species (Williams, 1964), and habitat diversity, which concerns the variety of habitats as defined by a recognized system (e.g. the Society for the Promotion of Nature Reserves, 1969; Elton, 1966). Many different methods of calculating indices of species diversity have been proposed (Southwood, 1966; McIntosh, 1967), but no general agreement has been reached as to whether or not it is better to increase or decrease diversity, so that the answer to any particular problem must depend on the system under consideration. The assessment of ecological interest is a subjective and perplexing problem (Tubbs and Blackwood, 1971; Ratcliffe, 1971). In a particular area, it generally parallels species richness, but ecological change caused by recreational activities usually results in the disappearance of some species and the introduction of others. Unfortunately the species that disappear are usually the rare ones which are often, for that reason alone, considered the most important, whereas the introductions are considered undesirable by some ecologists because they are alien to that habitat. The net result is often the maintenance of, or only a slight change in, species richness.

A comparable difficulty is encountered if habitat diversity is considered. The assessment of ecological interest may be made on the basis of diversity, stability and rarity (Ratcliffe, 1971). But some areas are generally considered to have a high conservation value because they consist of extensive tracts of one habitat, in spite of the fact that they are deficient in habitat variety (e.g. Pennine moorland); if recreational activities in such areas produce new habitats, as along paths, then these activities increase diversity and so may be considered undesirable in that situation. In general, a wide variety of habitat types is considered desirable, but it is understood that the habitats must be biologically interesting and aesthetically pleasing.

It can be concluded that there is ambiguity as to the meaning of diversity and whether or not its increase is a desirable change. Moreover, there is no consistent relationship between recreational activities and the increase or decrease of diversity.

The status of a site is another important consideration. If the area is designated as a public open space whose prime purpose is recreation, the most important consideration is the effect of trampling on the aesthetic quality of the site. The loss of a few plant species will be unimportant, whereas bare eroding paths will be unacceptable. On a National Nature Reserve, however, the elimination of only one species as a result of recreation might be considered disastrous. Thus, trampling tends to reduce the number of plant species but the seriousness of this effect depends upon the values placed on this feature of the resource.

The effect of recreation on productivity is also the subject of considerable discussion which will continue in the absence of scientific evidence. Primary productivity is usually understood to mean the rate at which solar energy is fixed as dry matter per unit area per unit time. The overall effect of trampling is probably to reduce the rate of production, but it is likely that low levels of trampling intensity will stimulate growth and slightly increase production. This action would be comparable to the frequent mowing of grassland, which produces a greater bulk of herbage than an annual cut. However, from the nature conservation viewpoint, it is debatable whether increases in productivity are good or bad.


## RESEARCH ON ECOLOGICAL EFFECTS OF RECREATION

Much of the research on the ecological effects of recreation has been directed at the identification of the recreational carrying capacity of an area. Thresholds of acceptability, however, can be defined in a variety of ways, ranging from the state at which the aesthetic quality of the resource is reduced to the state from which recovery is impossible. The level of use that can be sustained will vary both with the inherent physical and ecological characteristics of the resources and with the type and timing of their use (Lloyd, 1970). Another major aim of research has been to identify species which will indicate different levels of pressure.

Research into changes in ecological patterns resulting from recreational activities has proceeded at a quickening pace. Speight (1973) refers to about fifty papers concerned with vegetational changes and twenty which record effects on animal life. Most of these record observations of a rather superficial nature and only a few describe specially designed experiments with detailed analyses of the resultant data.

The primary objective of much of current research is to monitor the changes taking place under increasingly intensive recreational activities in order to identify the stages at which different species disappear and ultimately the stage at which the vegetation cover completely disappears. Research with this objective must necessarily be long term in nature.

The major difficulties in conducting such research fall into three categories:

1. the difficulty of concurrently measuring both number of people and changes in the ecosystem;

2. the long time intervals over which changes often occur;

3. the lag between a change in the intensity of an activity and the resultant ecological effect.

Studies of both demand for recreation and effect upon the resource are complicated by the consideration of temporal and spatial scales of variation. Recreation demands vary in space, time, nature and intensity (Burton and Wibberley, 1967). Similarly the resource, that is vegetation, soils and fauna, varies in space and time and in terms of succession. But there is no necessary relationship between scales of recreational activity and scales of vegetational variation.

The range of scales of study form a continuum, but it may be useful to recognize three reference points.

1. *Large scale*: surveys to investigate recreation/vegetation relationships conducted, for example, to provide a basis for a recreational structure plan. These studies might concern an island, a National Park, or a city's park network and present results in map form at a scale of 1:25,000.

2. *Medium scale*: studies which involve the use of transects or quadrats to relate changes in species composition or loss of vegetation across paths or specific sites. Such investigations may aim to identify threshold values at which particular changes occur. This scale of study has been referred to as the 'path scale'.

3. *Small scale*: studies using designed experiments on turf or single plants under carefully controlled conditions for detailed measurement of

effects and capacity for recovery. For example, Bayfield's (1971) experiments using falling 'tamps' with Vibram soles and Coker's work with chalk grassland turfs (Figure 14.3).

The identification of different scales of study illustrates some important points:

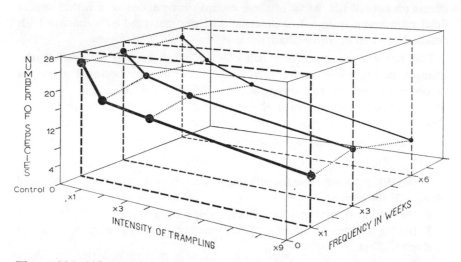

**Figure 14.3.** (Above) The effect of intensity and frequency of trampling on total number of species in chalk grassland. (Below) The effect of intensity and frequency of trampling on the percentage cover of *Carex flaca*. Both sets of data are from chalk grassland at Kingley Vale N.N.R. Sussex (both figures from Coker, A., unpublished).

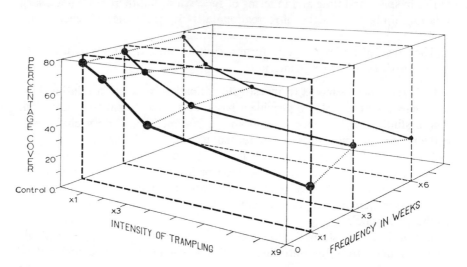

1. an increase in the scale of study results in an increase in the complexity of the system being investigated;

2. with increasing spatial scales of study it becomes increasingly important to determine the pattern of movement of visitors across an area and so the inclusion of information about the social system of the visitor becomes more important;

3. time and space scales are related in that the larger the spatial scale of study, the longer the time required for study (Harrison and Warren, 1970); for example, autecological studies last until the plant dies, path studies last for at least a year (minimum regeneration time), and large areas may require a socio-economic input which would probably involve both more research workers and a considerably longer period for study.

Most research studies have concentrated on spatial variation in recreational pressure and associated ecological effects. This is because it is very time-consuming to study changes on one site over a period of time. Such 'spatial' studies assume that the vegetation is in equilibrium with the pressure (Burden and Randerson, 1972) and place a premium on areas that are uniform in all respects except the level of recreation pressure. Studies of changes over a period of time are fewer but more meaningful (Burden and Randerson, 1972). Most studies on the ecological effects of recreation may be criticized, however, for assuming that if one state of affairs or event follows another the second event is necessarily caused by the first (Skellam, 1967).

One of the principal difficulties in conducting this type of research is the establishment of adequate controls. Transect studies across paths assume that there is a gradient of pressure from the centre outwards; other research projects involve diverting people to decrease the pressure on one area and to increase it on another. Whichever experimental design is adopted in the field it is unlikely to separate the effects of trampling from other supposedly normal activities such as grazing. It is for this reason that some workers have chosen to conduct research on experimental plots using factorial designs suitable for statistical analysis.

## MANAGEMENT

Recreational carrying capacity is affected by the kind of use, the time of year and the duration and intensity of the activity, and can be increased by management techniques directed either at the resource, such as by drainage or fertilizer application, or at the kind of use, such as by preventing ball games. Consequently it is impossible to assign to a site a single figure for its capacity. However, figures expressed in relative terms or qualified in some way are extremely useful to planners and managers of recreation areas and should remain a primary aim of research workers.

Species which will indicate different levels of pressure may be used to identify areas which are almost at their limit of tolerance. Huxley (1970) lists seven resilient species (*Agrostis tenuis, Cynosurus cristatus, Festuca pratensis, Lolium perenne, Poa annua, Poa pratensis* and *Trifolium repens*) but comments on the fact that these are restricted to lowland areas (less than 500 m). Consequently, in mountainous habitats, the regular use of a footpath soon results in bare ground. Similarly, because the seven species are light-demanding, they do not occur under woodland canopies and heavily used woodland trails are therefore rapidly denuded of vegetation. In open, lowland situations on neutral soils (pH 6–7), however, the absence of one, two, three or more of these species is likely to be correlated with increasingly frequent trampling, so that an observation that these species occur could be used to identify a threshold of capacity.

There are three strategies open to the manager of a site which receives intensive visitor use:

1. to manage the recreationists;
2. to manage the resource;
3. to manage both.

1. Management of the recreationist ranges from the use of physical barriers, such as fences and ditches, to more subtle approaches involving signposting, trails, alternative routes, and devices to attract people elsewhere ('honey-pots'). These attractions range from the provision of recreation facilities (car parks, refreshment huts, interpretation centres) to the designation of special areas such as country parks.

Sites can be developed as part of an overall plan to relieve pressure on more sensitive areas. Butser Hill in Sussex, for example, is partly developed to attract people away from the Nature Conservancy's chalk grassland reserves, and Northaw Great Wood in Hertfordshire to relieve pressure on the nearby Broxbourne Woods. Some areas are divided into zones with different intensities of use; for example, the area near the car park at Old Winchester Hill National Nature Reserve is used more intensively than the steep slopes beyond which support the more interesting chalk flora and fauna (Figure 14.2). Other areas, such as the coastal picnic site at Lepe, near Calshot in Hampshire, have been specially designed to attract and hold visitors (Runnicles, 1971). Activities in flooded gravel pits are also often zoned in both space and time, as at Cosgrove in Buckinghamshire. Small shallow pits with graded banks and convoluted perimeters are set aside as nature reserves, whilst boating and angling are accommodated elsewhere in the vicinity.

2. Management of the resource may involve the drainage of wet habitats or the application of fertilizer to promote growth and recovery of the vegetation. Ecologists have contributed little to this kind of management expertise, which is therefore based primarily on knowledge gained in municipal park management and agricultural practice and on advice from organizations such as the Sports Turf Research Institute. Management considerations of this kind should be related to the stage of succession represented by the vegetation of the area. If it is near the natural climax, the management inputs required will be very much less than if the vegetation corresponds to an early seral stage. Many areas that are intensively used for recreation represent early seral stages (e.g. sand-dunes) or arrested successions (e.g. lowland heath and chalk grassland). The maintenance of chalk grassland therefore requires a greater energy input, in terms of grazing or mowing, than does chalk scrub. Similarly, chalk scrub requires more frequent management than ashwood or yewwood. The advantage, however, of dealing with an early successional stage is that the alternatives open to the manager are greater. A lowland heath can be allowed to develop into birch, gorse, oak or hawthorn scrub, grassland or bracken. The ecologist understands very little about the factors that control these developments, but it is well known that once scrub is established it is very difficult to return to heather-dominated vegetation. The advantages of managing early successional stages apply also to chalk grassland and other arrested successions.

3. Management of both the resource and the recreationist involves the provision of such features as gravel paths (as in Epping Forest, Essex, for horses), catwalks (Holkham National Nature Reserve in Norfolk), steps (Beinne Eighe National Nature Reserve in Wester Ross), and mowing both to direct the visitor and to relieve pressure on the most sensitive areas. The characteristics and use of footpaths in the countryside have been discussed by Huxley (1970). Although paths often develop as a response to trampling, they also serve to attract and direct people. They can thus be designed and constructed to lead visitors away from biologically interesting or sensitive areas and to concentrate them on the more resilient substrata.

It may be concluded that whilst the rapidly increasing demand for recreation is now recognized, its effects have seldom been studied in a detailed and objective manner. Responsibility for this kind of research lies with national organizations such as the Countryside Commission, the Forestry Commission and the Nature Conservancy, as well as with the universities and landowners. Much of the monitoring required for specific sites could be carried out by local groups of naturalists under the guidance of advisors from one of the organizations referred to above. If this were done, indicators of undesirable effects might be recognized prior to the occurrence of unsightly and sometimes irreversible damage.

# REFERENCES

Bates, G. H. (1935). The vegetation of footpaths, sidewalks, carttracks and gate-ways, *J. Eco.*, **23**, 470–89.

Bates, G. H. (1938). Life-forms of pasture plants in relation to treading. *J. Ecol.*, **26**, 452–4.

Bates, G. H. (1950). Track making by man and domestic animals. *J. Animal Ecol.*, **19**, 21–8.

Bayfield, N. G. (1971). Some effects of walking and skiing on vegetation at Cairngorm, in : *The Scientific Management of Animal and Plant Communities for Conservation*, (eds.) E. Duffey and A. S. Watt, Blackwell, Oxford, 469–85.

Burden, R. F., and Randerson, P. F. (1972). Quantitative studies of the effects of human trampling on vegetation as an aid to the management of semi-natural areas, *J. appl. Ecol.*, **9**, 439–57.

Burton, T. L., and Wibberley, G. P. (1967). Outdoor recreation in the British countryside, *Studies in Rural Land Use, Report No. 5*, Wye College, University of London, 54 pp.

Clements, F. E. (1916). Plant succession: an analysis of the development of vegetation, *Carnegie Inst., Washington Publ.* **242**, 512 pp.

Coker, A. M., and Coker, P. D. (1972). Some practical details of the use of pressure sensitive counters, *Recreation News Supplement*, **7**, 14–7.

Coker, A. M., and Coker, P. D. (1973). A single method of time-lapse photography for use in recreation studies, *Recreation News Supplement*, **8**, 31–8.

Countryside Recreation Research Advisory Group (1970). *Countryside Recreation Glossary*, Countryside Commission, London, 47 pp.

Dower, M. (1965). Fourth wave: the challenge of leisure, *Civic Trust*, **5**, 68 pp. (Also *Architects Journal*, January 20th, 1965.)

Dower, M. (1972). Amenity and tourism in the countryside, in: *The Remoter Rural Areas of Britain*, (eds.) J. Ashton and W. H. Long, Oliver and Boyd, Edinburgh, 74–90.

Duffey, E. (1967a). An assessment of dune invertebrate faunas in habitats vulnerable to public disturbance, in: *The Biotic Effects of Public Pressures on the Environment*, (ed.) E. Duffey, Nature Conservancy Monks Wood Symp., No. **3**, 112–20.

Duffey, E. (ed.) (1967b). *The Biotic Effects of Public Pressures on the Environment*, Nature Conservancy Monks Wood Symp. No. **3**, 178 pp.

Elton, C. S. (1966). *The Pattern of Animal Communities*, Methuen, London 432 pp.

Goldsmith, F. B., Munton, R. J. C., and Warren, A. (1970). The impact of recreation on the ecology and amenity of semi-natural areas: methods of investigation used in the Isles of Scilly, *Biol. J. Linn. Soc.*, **2**, 287–306.

Harrison, C. M., and Warren, A. W. (1970). Conservation, stability and management, *Area*, **2**, 26–32.

Huxley, T. (1970). *Footpaths in the Countryside*, Countryside Commission for Scotland, Perth, 51 pp.

Lloyd, R. J. (1970). *Countryside Recreation: The Ecological Implications*, Lindsay County Council, Lincoln, 125 pp.

McIntosh, R. P. (1967). An index of diversity and the relation of certain concepts to diversity, *Ecology*, **48**, 392–404.

Morris, M. G. (1967). Insect collecting with special reference to nature reserves, in: *The Biotic Effects of Public Pressures on the Environment* (ed.) E. Duffey, Nature Conservancy, Monks Wood Symp. No. 3, 20–4 .

Patmore, J. A. (1970). *Land and Leisure*, David & Charles, Newton Abbot, 332 pp.

Perring, F. H. (1967). Changes in chalk grassland caused by galloping, in: *The Biotic Effects of Public Pressures on the Environment*, (ed.) E. Duffey, Nature Conservancy Monks Wood Symp. No. 3, 134–42.

Ratcliffe, D. A. (1971). Criteria for the selection of Nature Reserves, *Adv. of Sci.*, 27, 294–6.

Raup, H. M. (1964). Some problems in ecological theory and their relation to conservation, *J. Ecol.*, 52 (Suppl.), 19–28.

Runnicles, G. (1971). Lepe car parking experiment, *Recreation News Supplement*, 4, 22–5.

Sankey, J., and Mackworth-Praed, H. (1969). Headley Warren Reserve in 1968, *The Surrey Naturalist, Ann. Report* for 1968.

Skellam, J. G. (1967). Chairman's summing-up and general discussion, in: *The Biotic Effects of Public Pressures on the Environment*, (ed.) E. Duffey, Nature Conservancy Monks Wood Symp. No. 3, 173-8.

Society for the Promotion of Nature Reserves (1969). Biological Sites Recording Scheme, *S.P.N.R. Conservation Liaison Committee Technical Publication*, 1, 41 pp.

Southwood, T. R. E. (1966). *Ecological Methods*, Methuen, London, 391 pp.

Speight, M. C. D. (1973). Ecological change and outdoor recreation, *Discussion Papers in Conservation No. 4*, University College London, 35 pp.

Streeter, D. T. (1971). The effects of public pressure on the vegetation of chalk downland at Box Hill, Surrey, in: *The Scientific Management of Animal and Plant Communities for Conservation*, (eds.) E. Duffey and A. S. Watt, Blackwell, Oxford, 459–68.

Tansley, A. G. (1939). *The British Islands and Their Vegetation*, Cambridge University Press, Cambridge, 930 pp.

Tubbs, C. R., and Blackwood, J. W. (1971). Ecological evaluation of land for planning purposes, *Biol. Cons.*, 3, 169–72.

Wagar, J. A. (1964). The carrying capacity of wildlands for recreation, *Forest Sci. Monog.*, 7, 24 pp.

Watt, K. E. F. (1968). *Ecology and Resource Management: A Quantitative Approach*, McGraw-Hill, New York, 450 pp.

Williams, C. B. (1964). *Patterns in the Balance of Nature and Related Problems in Quantitative Ecology*, Academic Press, London, 324 pp.

# CHAPTER 15

# Ecological Effects of Pesticides

N. W. MOORE

## PESTICIDES—A NEW ECOLOGICAL FACTOR

Pesticides are chemical substances used by man to control those living organisms which are inimical, or are believed to be inimical, to his interests. Most are poisons insofar as the target species are concerned: but the term pesticide is also used to cover chemosterilants and growth inhibitors. In Britain we associate pesticides principally with agriculture and horticulture, although they are also used widely in food storage and for the protection of wood and wool and other fibres. In many countries they are also applied very extensively to control vectors of disease and in forestry. Today pesticides are used throughout the world in a wide range of habitats—mainly in agricultural and urban environments, but also in natural or semi-natural ones such as forests, rangelands, inland and coastal marshes, lakes and even deserts. The more persistent compounds disperse into all environments, including those which are never sprayed, notably the oceans and polar regions. This means that most life on the earth comes into contact with pesticides, and therefore nowadays they must be taken into account in all ecological studies; although there are still many ecosystems where their effects are likely to be negligible.

Pesticides have been used on a small scale for centuries, but they have only become an integral part of agriculture, preventative medicine and forestry during the lifetime of many of the readers of this book. Most modern pesticides are entirely novel organic substances, and so until recently no species has had previous experience of them in its evolutionary history. Their particular interest lies in the fact that they are a new environmental phenomenon.

Research on the ecological effects of pesticides concerns many applied biologists working on agricultural and conservation problems, and it should also be of great interest to a wide range of workers concerned with theoretical aspects of ecological and evolutionary biology.

## THE EFFECTS OF PESTICIDES AND THEIR STUDY

Usually the biocidal effects of pesticides have been discovered empirically —by screening a vast number of compounds which happen to be available to industry. No pesticide has been especially designed to deal with a particular pest, and therefore it is not surprising that a list of pesticides covers a wide range of heterogeneous substances, both inorganic and organic, naturally occurring and synthetic, and that none are specific to target species. The most commonly used pesticides today are synthetic organic substances, and many of these are fairly selective. For example most herbicides have low toxicities to animals, several kill mono-cotyledonous weeds but not dicotyledonous ones and *vice versa,* and many insecticides have very low toxicities to mammals and birds. Of course all pesticides are toxic to some species or they would not be used.

Studies of pesticide effects emphasize the importance of studying cause and effect at different levels of integration and the need to relate the results at different levels to each other. Most studies have concerned physiology and autecology, but an increasing number are being carried out at lower and higher levels—on the cell and the ecosystem. Some, but not enough, work has been done to integrate toxicology and population dynamics.

Much information exists on the acute oral and dermal toxicity and on the chronic toxicity of pesticides to laboratory mammals, because this is required for registration schemes designed to protect the human operator and consumer and also livestock. Pesticides frequently have multiple pathological effects; in some cases the primary mechanism is quite well known, as in the large family of organophosphorous insecticides which act by inhibiting cholinesterase. In others, such as DDT, the mechanism is not known, but knowledge of biochemical mechanisms is not usually necessary for understanding population effects. On the other hand, studies on the toxicology of pesticides are essential for this purpose, because if we are to determine the effects of a pesticide in the field we must understand the toxicological significance of the doses which organisms in the population are likely to receive. The single dose administered orally which kills 50 per cent of the experimental population of laboratory animals (the acute oral LD50) is the most widely used yardstick, but since organisms in the field are subject to stresses additional to those provided by the pesticide, the investigator into field effects must also have information about sub-lethal toxicological effects, especially when they involve reproduction or behaviour. The fundamental question for the agricultural and conservation biologist is: what effect does the pesticide have on the population? While the investigator is generally concerned with one particular species, or a small range of species in the ecosystem, no species lives in isolation, and so the species studied must be considered in relation to others within the ecosystem.

Predators always occur at lower numbers than their prey, and therefore, together with other species whose populations are small, they tend to be at greater risk from pesticides than abundant species. For the same reasons, they tend to recover more slowly from the effects of pesticide applications. In addition, predators are at a further disadvantage when they feed upon resistant prey species which have accumulated residues of pesticides in their fat. Thus the general effect of pesticides, like other pollutants, is to reduce species diversity, and through the differentially severe effects on predators they also allow an increase in the numbers of resistant phytophagous and saprophagous species. Hence pesticides tend to increase productivity at the lower trophic levels and to lessen it at high ones. Their effects on the productivity of whole ecosystems have been little studied but are likely to vary.

Pesticides affect a given species in the field both directly and indirectly. Direct effects are those due to the lethal or sub-lethal toxicity of the pesticide to the organism itself. Indirect effects are due to the toxicity of the pesticide to other species in the ecosystem which affect the organism, notably competitors, predators and prey. Ultimately, population numbers of a species reflect both direct and indirect effects and their interaction. Unless all the individuals in the population are killed by the pesticide its effects are likely to be complicated and difficult to unravel.

Two special methodological difficulties arise in studies on pesticide effects in the field. First, one often needs to know the toxicological effects of a pesticide on a species which cannot easily be kept or bred under laboratory conditions, and therefore one can only make inferences from laboratory species. Scientists working in medical research have the same problem. Unfortunately, even closely related species can vary considerably in their response to the same chemical, and so extrapolations from toxicological studies on laboratory species to wild species can rarely be exact and may be misleading.

The second difficulty concerns experimental studies of populations. It is quite easy to carry out a controlled experiment on the effects of a pesticide on species with very dense populations, for example soil animals, but it is practically impossible to do such experiments on animals with widely dispersed populations, for example birds of prey. Conclusions on pesticide effects on these species have to be based on circumstantial evidence derived from rigorous observations on different responses to different pesticide situations in the field, and must be related to basic knowledge of the biology of the species.

## SOME ECOLOGICAL EFFECTS OF PESTICIDES ON
## ORGANISMS IN CROPS

No study has been made of all the effects of a pesticide application to a crop, but studies of pesticide effects on parts of the crop ecosystem give valuable insights into the processes involved. Two examples are given below.

In a series of papers, Dempster (1967; 1968a, b, c) described the interrelationships between the Cabbage White butterfly, *Pieris rapae,* and other species in a crop of Brussels sprouts, and the effects of DDT upon them. He found that *Pieris* larvae were preyed upon by beetles, harvestmen and birds and were parasitized by Hymenoptera and Diptera. They also suffered from a fungus and a granulosis virus. He constructed life tables for three generations of *Pieris* and found that there was a mortality of about 90 per cent between egg and pupal stages, that over half of this mortality occurred during the first two larval instars, and that it was due mainly to the ground beetle *Harpalus rufipes* and the harvestman *Phalangium opilio.* Birds took about 20 per cent of the larvae and their predation was only important during the last two larval instars. The effects of parasites and disease were insignificant. Bad weather had little effect on mortality, but it did affect the fecundity of *Pieris.*

DDT is a broad-spectrum insecticide of unusual persistence. Its concentration on the crop itself decreases as the sprayed leaves expand and new unsprayed ones develop. On the other hand, it remains concentrated in the soil, especially if it is ploughed in. Therefore, direct effects on animals living on the crop and on weeds are likely to be less than those on animals living partly or wholly in the soil. Dempster found that the numbers of the ground beetle *Harpalus rufipes,* millipedes, centipedes and arachnids decreased. DDT gave a good initial control of *Pieris,* but eventually caused an increase in the populations of this and other species, notably Cabbage aphids, Collembola and the ground beetles *Trechus quadristriatus* and *Nebria brevicollis.*

The initial decline of *Pieris* was clearly due to the action of the pesticide (Figure 15.1). The subsequent increase of the species was due to immigrants laying eggs after the crop had been sprayed and to reduce predation on the larvae emerging from these eggs by *Harpalus rufipes* and *Phalangium opilio,* because these ground-living species had been particularly severely affected by the spray. DDT not only caused death, but also reduced the rate of feeding of those beetles which had survived treatment. Similarly, the increase of Collembola appeared to be due to deleterious effects on their predators. The increase of *Trechus* and *Nebria,* two species which appeared to be comparatively resistant to DDT, was probably due to the increase of

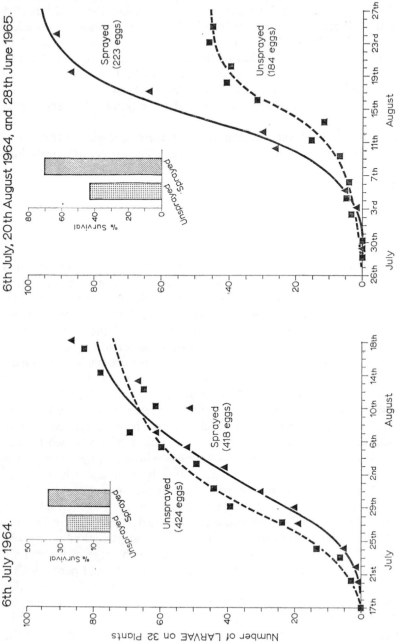

**Figure 15.1.** An illustration of the differential effects of DDT on crop and soil fauna. *Pieris* lives on crops; spraying with DDT to control it is effective for only a very short period in the first year (A). Because the soil-living predators of *Pieris* are affected by residuals in the soil, *Pieris* in fact increases markedly after repeated spraying (B). (After Dempster, 1968a.)

the Collembola on which they fed. Many of the species feeding on the crop were able to recolonize it from surrounding areas, but the persistence of DDT in the soil prevented successful recolonization by ground-living species. As a result, the effects of DDT on the predators of *Pieris* continued to operate long after the application of the insecticide and enabled *Pieris* to increase even more in the second season (Figure 15.1). This admirable study illustrates the interplay of direct and indirect effects of an insecticide and the complexity of effects due to differential toxicity and differential persistence.

Herbicides are used very extensively, but their ecological effects have been much less studied than those of insecticides. The farmer uses herbicides in order to reduce competition between crop and weed and to ease the handling of the harvested crop. Plants vary in their sensitivity to different herbicides: the use of one herbicide eliminates some species of weed, but enables other more resistant species to flourish. For example, growth regulating herbicides like MCPA have greatly reduced the population of the poppy in eastern England, but indirectly have caused a great increase in the population of the wild oat. Herbicides have caused conspicuous changes in the weed flora of countries like Britain, and these in turn must have caused great changes in the populations of phytophagous invertebrates and hence in predators and parasites dependent upon them. The recent work of Potts (1970; 1971) on the population dynamics of the grey partridge throws light on some of the changes which occur in cereal crops.

The grey partridge is a game bird of considerable economic importance, and much is known about the fluctuations in its numbers in Britain from game bag reports made during the last century. These show that its numbers have always fluctuated considerably, but that in recent years there has been a continuous general decline of a kind not previously described (Figure 15.2), the causes of which have been the subject of Potts' work. The partridge is essentially an herbivorous species which is preyed upon by a number of birds and mammal species as well as by man, and it is subject to a range of diseases. Mortality of young chicks was found to be the key factor in controlling the short-term variations of partridge populations. The chicks require high-level protein diets at an early stage of their development, and they obtain them largely from insects. Exceptional mortality was found to be due to a combination of two factors—shortage of insect food (mostly caused by inclement weather in April and May) and poor weather in June and July. Cold wet weather increased the need for food, this lengthened the search for it, and, if insects were not easily available, increased the danger of heat loss while the chicks were searching.

The decline of the partridge in recent years was found to be due to the combination of below-average seasons, especially cold springs, and changes in cereal growing. One of these changes was the use of herbicides, which was shown to cause a 70 per cent reduction of the biomass of the insects living on weeds, and the other was the reduction in undersown leys, which support the over-wintering state of the leaf-eating sawflies whose larvae are a particularly important food for young partridges. Other factors were not insignificant in some cases: if predators, especially carrion crows, stoats and weazels were controlled, and if grass strips were left to provide alternative

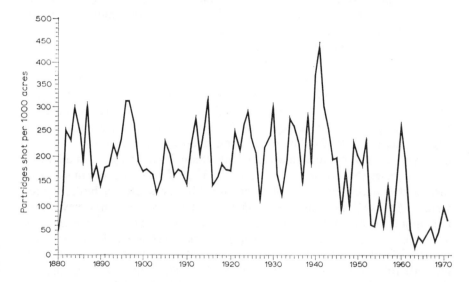

**Figure 15.2.** Grey partridge numbers per 100 acres on 20 'best' estates; figures from game bag records. The recent general decline appears to be due to a number of changes in cereal growing practices such as the introduction of herbicide sprays, and the abandonment of undersown leys. (After Potts, 1971.)

food, shortage of food in the crop and bad weather had less harmful effects. In this case the use of herbicides of low toxicity has had important indirect effects not only on the invertebrate fauna, but also on a vertebrate species which is dependent on the invertebrates for a short time in its life history. This very promising study is still in progress; a recent report on it strongly suggests that outbreaks of cereal aphids are correlated inversely with species diversity, and that arthropod faunas with a high diversity have a larger proportion of entomophagous individuals. As so often happens, a thorough autecological study on a wild species throws light on other aspects of the ecosystem, and has profound economic implications.

## SOME ECOLOGICAL EFFECTS OF PESTICIDES ON ORGANISMS
## LIVING OUTSIDE THE SPRAYED AREAS

A small number of pesticides are broken down so slowly that they have time to spread outside the areas of application; if they have deleterious effects they can be classified as environmental contaminants. Some persistent pesticides, notably the dipyridyl herbicides paraquat and diquat and the triazine and substituted urea herbicides, remain bound up in the soil and do not appear to be released under normal circumstances; they seem to have little effect on the environment. Those which cause most concern as environmental pollutants are fat-soluble organochlorine insecticides, notably DDT and the cyclodienes aldrin and dieldrin, and the organomercury fungicides. These compounds or their stable metabolites break down so slowly that they become transported throughout the world in air, water and in organisms. Their high fat solubility allows them to become concentrated in animal bodies and hence they get passed from prey to predator. Chemical analyses of persistent organochlorine insecticides in British birds and their eggs in the early 1960s showed that, on average, predators which fed on other vertebrates contained more pesticides than did herbivorous and insectivorous species (Moore and Walker, 1964). Thus if persistent organochlorine insecticides were having an effect on any bird populations, birds of prey were most likely to show these effects, and accordingly they have been the subject of much research in Britain, the United States and elsewhere. The studies of Ratcliffe, Prestt, Jefferies, Lockie and others have been particularly illuminating because so much background information is available about the species which they studied. The initial studies showed that two fish-feeding species, the great crested grebe and the heron, two bird-feeding species, the peregrine and the sparrowhawk, and two species which fed on both mammals and birds, the kestrel and the golden eagle, contained residues of DDE (the principal metabolite of DDT) and dieldrin which were above the average found in British birds as a whole. The responses of the six species differed greatly, a fact which underlines the danger of making sweeping generalizations about pesticide effects from particular instances.

The great crested grebe increased despite the introduction of pesticides: the lethal and sub-lethal effects on individuals which occurred locally were more than compensated in this case by some feature in the environment which favoured the general increase of the species. This feature was almost certainly the great increase in gravel extraction in post-war England, which produced numerous waterfilled pits, which provide a very suitable habitat for the species (Prestt and Jefferies, 1969).

Herons and their eggs have been found to contain higher levels of dieldrin and DDE on average than any other wild bird investigated. Eggshell thinning and abnormal breeding behaviour which caused males to throw eggs and young out of the nest were observed in heronries in districts subjected to particularly high persistent organochlorine insecticide contamination. Nevertheless, because this species will readily lay replacement clutches, the breeding success of the colonies was not reduced beyond the point at which replacements were available to compensate 'normal' adult mortality. Despite considerable pesticide contamination in recent years the population has remained remarkably steady since 1928, when the first censuses were made of this species under the auspices of the British Trust for Ornithology. All declines recorded in the heron population of England and Wales have

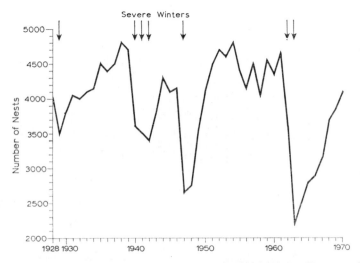

**Figure 15.3.** Occupied Herons' nests in England and Wales showing the effects of severe winters and the absence of a distinct long term trend. (After Prestt, 1970.)

followed abnormally severe winters (Figure 15.3), but numbers have recovered to about 4,500 pairs within a few years after each decline. So, in this species, despite severe sub-acute effects and some acute ones, the breeding population has remained unaffected by pesticides (Milstein *et al.*, 1970; Prestt, 1970).

The golden eagle population has not been affected by acute poisoning by persistent organochlorine insecticides. However, eggshell thinning and a decline in the number of pairs rearing young from 72 per cent to 29 per cent occurred in those areas where the species fed extensively on carrion sheep which had been dipped in dieldrin. In the eastern Highlands of Scotland, where eagles are known to feed on grouse and hares, the species bred normally and eggshells were of normal thickness. The golden eagle is a long-lived species, but eventually the inability to replace natural losses in the western Highlands would have probably caused the species to have died out had the use of dieldrin for sheep dipping continued. Restrictions on the use of dieldrin as a sheep dip were made in 1966, and since that date the dieldrin content of eagle eggs has declined, the eggshells have become thicker and the reproductive success of the species in western Scotland has returned to normal. In the eastern Highlands, where the eagles did not acquire significant amounts of dieldrin, reproduction remained normal throughout the period of observation (Lockie *et al.*, 1969; Ratcliffe, 1970).

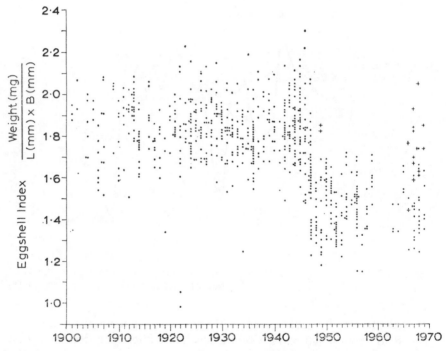

**Figure 15.4.** Changes in the eggshell index (relative weight) of eggs of the peregrine falcon in Britain. The start of the decline coincides with the introduction of DDT in the late 1940s. (After Ratcliffe, 1970.)

Ratcliffe showed that eggshell thinning in peregrines and sparrowhawks coincided with the introduction of DDT in the late 1940s (Figure 15.4). Nevertheless, the peregrine population was increasing at this time as a result of the protection being reimposed after wartime persecution, when it had been reduced in order to protect carrier pigeons used by the armed forces.

The remarkable population decline in this normally very stable species, which still affects it to a considerable degree, did not start until the late 1950s; it coincided with the introduction of aldrin and dieldrin as cereal seed dressings, and was almost certainly due to peregrines eating pigeons containing large but sub-lethal residues of these substances. The eating of only three such pigeons would be necessary to cause death. Since the restriction on the use of aldrin and dieldrin seed dressings in 1962 the peregrine has made a slow recovery except in areas where its prey is still contaminated. Thus in this species persistent organochlorine insecticides caused both acute and sub-acute effects, but only the acute effects had a serious effect on the population (Ratcliffe, 1972). The peregrine is one of the very few cosmopolitan bird species, and it is interesting to note that in the United States the decline of one of its races (*Falco peregrinus anatum*) appears to be largely due to sub-lethal effects of DDT (Hickey, 1969). The histories of the sparrowhawk and kestrel are similar to those of the peregrine: both showed sub-lethal and acute effects, the latter being the main cause of the declines. In both species recoveries in reproductive success and population numbers were recorded after restrictions had been made on the use of aldrin and dieldrin.

The research briefly summarized above is based on four types of information: first, chemical analyses of pesticide residues in birds and eggs, and secondly, toxicological studies on several species which showed the range of acute toxicity of DDT, DDE and dieldrin to birds, and demonstrated that these substances could have sub-acute effects, including eggshell thinning, at levels encountered in the field. Third, field studies were made on the feeding habits and behaviour of the birds concerned, and fourth, total or sample population counts were conducted. Unfortunately, crucial controlled experiments on a bird of prey population are impracticable and have not been attempted in Britain. Nevertheless, if all the evidence from the four sources of information is carefully related, very little doubt remains that the unprecedented declines of some birds of prey in Britain were due to the use of persistent organochlorine insecticides, and their subsequent partial recoveries were due to partial restrictions on the use of these substances. In Britain, acute effects of the very toxic persistent organochlorine insecticides aldrin and dieldrin appear to have been much more important than sub-lethal effects of these substances or DDT, which is much less toxic. In the United States, on the other hand, where DDT was used much more extensively, the sub-lethal effects of DDT and its metabolites have been more important. An extreme case is that of the brown pelican. High levels of DDT in some colonies of this species have caused the birds to lay 'shell-less' eggs and so have caused total reproductive failure (Keith *et al.*, 1970; Blus *et al.*, 1972).

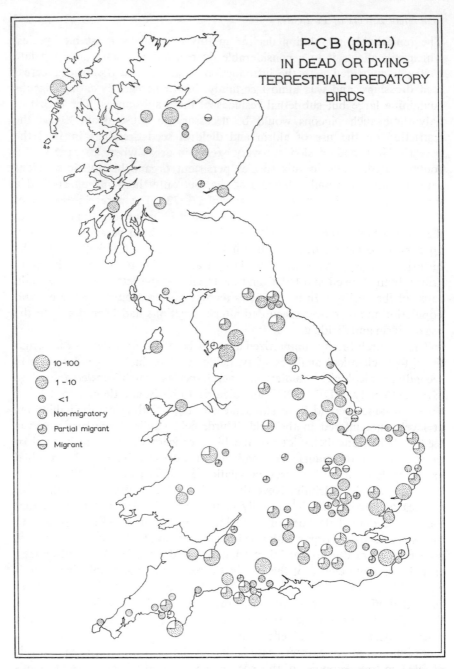

**Figure 15.5.** P-C.B. residues in dead or dying birds, 1966–68. The map shows the widespread occurrence of P-C.B.s in areas well away from their industrial sources and the higher levels found in the more resident birds. (After Prestt *et al.,* 1970.)

## THE EFFECTS OF POLYCHLORINATED BIPHENYLS
## AND OF PESTICIDE IMPURITIES

Brief mention should be made of the polychlorinated biphenyls (PCBs), which have similar characteristics to insecticides like DDT. PCBs were invented before DDT and are used for a wide range of different purposes in many industries. Like DDT, they have a very low solubility in water, a high solubility in fat, and are very persistent in the environment. Despite their long history of use, their presence in the environment was not recorded until 1966. Subsequent studies (e.g. Prestt *et al.,* 1970) showed that they were present in terrestrial, freshwater and marine environments. The presence of PCBs in raptorial birds in Great Britain is shown in Figure 15.5. Laboratory studies showed that they had low acute toxicities to mammals and birds, but recent work indicates that they can have measurable biological effects at low concentrations (Jefferies, personal communication).

There is no evidence to suggest that PCBs have had serious effects on the population of any organism, although it is quite conceivable that they could have effects. PCBs were found in large amounts in the livers of guillemots which died in the Irish Sea Bird Disaster in 1969. Studies on the causes of this event are inconclusive, but they suggest that PCBs were only of secondary importance as a cause of death. The incident was important, since it drew attention to the general problem of industrial pollution of the sea. When it had been shown that PCBs were widely distributed in the environment, Monsanto, the principal manufacturer of PCBs in the US and UK, withdrew those uses of PCBs whose entry into the environment could not be controlled. Nevertheless, PCBs are very persistent substances and so are likely to remain in the environment for some time, but their levels should decline as the result of this action.

In recent years many organisms have come into contact with several new environmental contaminants at the same time, notably organochlorine insecticides, organomercury fungicides (Saha, 1972) and PCBs. Very little is known about the effects of combinations of these compounds. Research on their effects has caused governments and industry to keep a closer watch on other substances which have similar physical and chemical characteristics in case they are, or might become, significant environmental contaminants.

A rather different environmental problem is provided by pesticide impurities. Many pesticides contain small amounts of these; usually they are less toxic than the pesticide, or the amounts are too small to have biological effects. An exception is the dioxin impurity of the herbicide 2,4,5-T. This impurity is much more toxic than the herbicide. There is laboratory and field evidence which shows that it can cause teratological effects. An unusually impure form of 2,4,5-T was used in defoliation campaigns in Vietnam, and this drew attention to the hazards of pesticide impurities. Little is known of the ecological effects of dioxins, of other pesticide impurities, nor indeed of many of the metabolites of pesticides.

## IMPLICATIONS OF RESEARCH ON THE USE AND CONTROL OF PESTICIDES

The studies of birds of prey which were described above are important for conservation biology, but they have a much wider significance because they show that the ordinary use of fat-soluble persistent pesticides can affect populations of non-target species living outside the areas of application. When Moore (1965) showed that fish-feeding seabirds contained appreciable quantities of persistent organochlorine insecticides there was justifiable concern that these pesticides could damage the living resources of the sea. Thus, while man derives great benefit from pesticides he is also threatened by some of them. The threats are indirect rather than direct : human casualties due to pesticides are negligible compared to the lives saved by their use in preventative medicine; on the other hand, man's protein resources in the form of freshwater and marine fish may be threatened by some of the pesticides used to protect plant crops on the land. In some cases crop protection is being made more difficult, more expensive and more uncertain by the same pesticides. All these secondary disadvantages of pesticides can be greatly reduced by their more scientific use.

Ecological studies of the kind mentioned in this chapter raise important questions about the use and control of pesticides. Research and practical experience in the field have both shown that the use of any pesticide is likely to raise problems. This does not mean that pesticides should not be used, but it does indicate that if pesticides are to be used effectively in the future more account must be taken of their effects on non-target species. Otherwise new pests are likely to be produced by alterations in competitive and prey/predator relations caused by the continuous use of broad-spectrum pesticides; and resistant strains of pest are likely to be created through natural selection. The snags of pesticides can be greatly reduced by using them as sparingly as possible, in particular by refraining from 'insurance spraying', by using persistent compounds as little as possible, and by developing more specific pesticides. Unfortunately, short-term economic pressures frequently prevent farmers from undertaking these commonsense measures, and chemical firms and agricultural advisers from supporting them.

The protection of consumers, contractors, domestic animals and wildlife from the deleterious effects of pesticides largely depends on assessments of risks which are based on acute and chronic toxicity tests. Insofar as direct effects on man are concerned, the procedure can be made to work efficiently simply by applying a large safety factor, but for animals in the field where many individuals are in contact with acute and sub-acute doses and indirect effects are important, overall effects cannot be predicted from toxicological studies alone; frequently the important effect is due to the combination of a pesticide and some other deleterious environmental factor. Therefore, insofar as effects in the field are concerned, the correct appraisal of a pesticide's value and its hazards must depend on field experience. Most of the predictions about pesticides which were based on toxicological tests and a limited number of field trials, have stood the test of time, although in the important, but exceptional cases of the persistent organochlorine insecticides and the organomercury fungicides, restrictions have had to be placed on their use as the result of experience in the field.

Most of the research on pesticides has been done to increase their value in agriculture, forestry and preventive medicine, to ensure their safety to man, and to reduce harmful side effects to wildlife, including species such as fish which are important to man as food. Perhaps because of these practical considerations the extraordinary fundamental interest of pesticide effects is often overlooked. The speed with which resistant strains are selected and the delicacy and complexity of the competitive relationships which have been demonstrated by the use of selective pesticides are particularly notable. Pesticides are potentially valuable as tools in ecological research: for example the insecticide dieldrin has been used to dissect an ecosystem in order to test a hypothesis about the ecological role of a constituent species (Davis *et al.*, 1969). If more selective pesticides were invented, they would become much more useful for such purposes. Conservation biologists have hitherto been mainly concerned with discovering means of avoiding the harmful effects of pesticides, but some work has already been done which shows that herbicides can be useful as conservation management tools, principally in preventing scrub regrowth in plagioclimax grasslands (Moore, 1968). Similarly, introduced mammals which have become pests in vulnerable ecosystems on small islands could be reduced or eliminated by the judicious use of rodenticides.

The need for pesticides will increase so long as increases in the human population and raised standards of living cause an increased demand for higher outputs per hectare. If full use is to be made of pesticides, and if serious hazards to the environment are to be prevented, we need to understand their complicated effects much better than we do today. The necessary research must be interdisciplinary and is likely to be scientifically rewarding. Conservation of man and of wild organisms is, and should be seen to be, complementary.

## BIBLIOGRAPHY AND REFERENCES

Blus, L. J., Gish, C. D., Belisle, A. A., and Prouty, R. M. (1972). Logarithmic relationship of DDE residues to eggshell thinning, *Nature (Lond.)*, **235**, 376–7.

Cooke, A. S. (1973). Shell thinning in avian eggs by environmental pollutants, *Environ. Pollut.*, **4**, 85–152.

Davis, B. N. K., Moore, N. W., Walker, C. H., and Way, J. M. (1969). A study of millipedes in a grassland community using dieldrin as a tool for ecological research, in: *The Soil Ecosystem,* (ed.) J. G. Sheals, *Systematics Assoc.,* London (Publ. No. **8**), 217-28.

Dempster, J. P. (1967). The control of *Pieris rapae* with DDT, I. The natural mortality of the young stages of *Pieris, J. appl. Ecol.*, **4**, 485–500.

Dempster, J. P. (1968a). The control of *Pieris rapae* with DDT. II. Survival of the young stages of *Pieris* after spraying, *J. appl. Ecol.*, **5**, 451–62.

Dempster, J. P. (1968b). The control of *Pieris rapae* with DDT. III. Some changes in the crop fauna, *J. appl. Ecol.*, **5**, 463–75.

Dempster, J. P. (1968c). The sublethal effect of DDT on the rate of feeding by the ground-beetle *Harpalus rufipes, Entomologia exp. appl.*, **11**, 51–4.

Fryer, J. D., and Evans, S. A. (eds.) (1970). *Weed Control Handbook Vol.* I, *Principles,* Blackwell, Oxford, 494 pp.

Fryer, J. D., and Makepeace, R. J. (eds.) (1972). *Weed Control Handbook Vol.* II, *Recommendations,* Blackwell, Oxford, 424 pp.

Hickey, J. J. (ed.) (1969). *Peregrine Falcon Populations: their Biology and Decline,* University of Wisconsin Press, Madison, Milwaukee, 596 pp.

Keith, J. O., Woods, L. A., and Hunt, E. G. (1970). Reproductive failure in Brown Pelicans on the Pacific coast, *Trans. N. Am. Wildl. Conf., 35th,* 56-63.

Lockie, J. D., Ratcliffe, D. A., and Balharry, R. (1969). Breeding success and organo-chlorine residues in Golden Eagles in West Scotland, *J. appl. Ecol.*, **6**, 381–9.

Martin, H. (ed.) (1964). *The Scientific Principles of Crop Protection,* 5th Edn., Edward Arnold, London, 376 pp.

Martin, H. (ed.) (1973). *Pesticide Manual,* 3rd Edn., British Crop Protection Council, Droitwich, 535 pp.

Mellanby, K. (1970). *Pesticides and Pollution,* 2nd Edn., Collins, New Naturalist, London, 221 pp.

Milstein, P. le S., Prestt, I., and Bell, A. A. (1970). The breeding cycle of the Grey Heron, *Ardea,* **58**, 171–257.

Moore, N. W. (1965). Environmental contamination by pesticides, in: *Ecology and the Industrial Society: a Symposium of the British Ecological Society, Swansea, 1964,* (ed.) G. T. Goodman, Blackwell, Oxford, 219–37.

Moore, N. W. (ed.) (1966). Pesticides in the environment and their effects on wildlife, *J. appl. Ecol.*, **3** (Suppl.), 311 pp.

Moore, N. W. (1967). A synopsis of the pesticide problem, in: *Adv. Ecol. Res.* **4**, 75–129.

Moore, N. W. (1968). The value of pesticides for conservation and ecology, in: *Some Safety Aspects of Pesticides in the Countryside,* (eds.) N. W. Moore and W. P. Evans, Joint ABMAC/Wild Life Education and Communications Committee, London, 104–8.

Moore, N. W., and Walker, C. H. (1964). Organic chlorine insecticide residues in wild birds, *Nature, Lond.*, **201**, 1072–3.

Moriarty, F. (1969). The sublethal effects of synthetic insecticides on insects, *Biol. Rev.*, **44**, 321–57.

Muirhead-Thomson, R. C. (1971). *Pesticides and Freshwater Fauna*, Academic Press, London, 248 pp.

Potts, G. R. (1970). Recent changes in the farmland fauna with special reference to the decline of the Grey Partridge, *Bird Study*, **17**, 145–66.

Potts, G. R. (1971). Agriculture and the survival of partidges, *Outlook on Agriculture*, **6**, 267–71.

Prestt, I. (1970). Organochlorine pollution of rivers and the Heron (*Ardea cinerea* L.), *Pap. Proc. Tech. Meet. int. Un. Conserv. Nat. nat. Resour.*, *11th, New Delhi, 1969*, **1**, 95–102, I.U.C.N., Morges.

Prestt, I., and Jefferies, D. J. (1969). Winter numbers, breeding success, and organochlorine residues in the Great Crested Grebe in Britain, *Bird Study* **16**, 168–85.

Prestt, I., Jefferies, D. J., and Moore, N. W. (1970). Polychlorinated biphenyls in wild birds in Britain and their avian toxicity, *Environ. Pollut.*, **1**, 3–26.

Ratcliffe, D. A. (1970). Changes attributable to pesticides in egg breakage frequency and eggshell thickness in some British birds, *J. appl. Ecol.*, **7**, 67–115.

Ratcliffe, D. A. (1972). The Peregrine population of Great Britain in 1971, *Bird Study*, **19**, 117–56.

Rudd, R. L. (1964). *Pesticides and the Living Landscape*, Faber and Faber, London, 320 pp.

Saha, J. G. (1972). Significance of mercury in the environment, *Residue Rev.*, **42**, 103–63.

Stafford, J. (1971). The Heron population of England and Wales, 1928–1970, *Bird Study*, **18**, 218–21.

# CHAPTER 16

# Ecological Aspects of the Reclamation of Derelict Land

G. T. GOODMAN

## DEFINITIONS

In this chapter. *derelict land* means 'land so damaged by industrial or other development that it is incapable of beneficial use without treatment'. This is the definition adopted by the British government when administering the Acts of Parliament which refer to derelict land; it includes mineral extraction sites such as quarries or opencast (stripmine) workings, spoil heaps or other waste tips, sites of dilapidated buildings, land damaged by subsidence and land which has become neglected or unsightly in other ways. All these categories are regarded as derelict *only if they are disused and abandoned*. Land in active use for any purpose is excluded from the definition.

The term *disturbed land* is used for any of these land categories where there is at least some current usage, however small, or when this land is subject to special planning conditions for further industrial or other development. This may include after-treatment such as infilling, levelling, revegetation or other reclamation work. The term is also used to include any unsightly or other industrially affected land subject to the General Development Order, which exempts from planning control any land which was used under the categories already mentioned prior to July 1948. For convenience, derelict and disturbed land when considered together are referred to as *damaged land*.

Some authorities distinguish between the terms reclamation (for some specific new use), rehabilitation (visual improvement), restoration (to its former use) and renewal or redemption (returning land to flexible re-use planning). Because these words have sometimes been used as synonyms, they will be used here interchangeably and in the broadest sense. Thus, 'reclamation' is used to cover all aspects of the process which stimulate the

re-use of damaged land. Since the emphasis in this chapter is on the ecological aspects of reclamation, the main interest will be the primary stage
of renewal, namely, the redevelopment of a cover of soil and/or vegetation.

## EXTENT OF DAMAGED LAND

Most countries have broadly similar types of damaged land, although the
proportions of each type depend on the particular kinds of minerals which
have been extracted and the urban-industrial wastes which have been
produced. The acreage varies greatly according to the degree of industrialization, urbanization, population density and size of the country. It is,
however, an oversimplification to judge the impact of damaged land by its
acreage alone, for the basic criterion for assessment should be its effect on
people, a point which will be discussed later.

Statements about damaged land in Britain are not very informative unless
they can be compared with the situation in some other urban-industrial
countries, but such comparisons are hindered by inadequate statistics. The
land classification criteria upon which returns of damaged land are made
are not the same in different countries, and indeed the difficulties of establishing uniformity are very great even from county to county within Britain.
One must be very doubtful about the usefulness of the statistics of damaged
land until much more objective and quantitative classification and measurement criteria have been developed.

The United States Department of Agriculture has calculated that by
January 1st, 1965, some 3,187,800 acres (0·14 per cent of the US land area)
had been disturbed after surface and stripmine operations. Of these, about
two-thirds (2,040,600 acres, or 0·09 per cent of US land surface) required
some form of reclamation. Although these figures do not include land
affected by subsidence, areas of dilapidated buildings, etc., they do at least
serve as some basis for comparison. In the United Kingdom, estimates of
derelict land are collected by the local authorities; by January 1st, 1968,
the figures for England and Wales were respectively 92,643 acres and
19,785 acres. The amounts said to justify treatment were, as for the American figures, approximately two-thirds of the total (56,841 and 13,272 acres,
respectively). Adding to these figures the total estimated by the Scottish
Development Department for October, 1966 (15,000 acres) gives a grand
total for mainland Britain (excluding Northern Ireland) of 127,428 acres.
This does not differ much from a later estimate accepted by the Hunt Committee (1969) of 130,000 acres. Ongoing surveys may show there to be
142,000 acres.

The American and British totals cannot be usefully compared until an
acreage for disturbed land is added to the British figure. From surveys
carried out within their counties, several planning officers have suggested

that if disturbed land were included, the acreage would double. Thus, a figure often quoted for derelict and disturbed land in Britain is 250,000 acres (0·44 per cent of the land surface). Assuming that about two-thirds of this total requires treatment, it can be estimated that approximately 165,000 acres need reclamation.

Although the total American acreage is more than ten times greater than that for Britain, these figures show that the United States has about one-third of the British figure for the damaged land per unit area of ground. Added to this, the gross population density of Britain is roughly eleven times greater than that of the United States (1 person per acre and 1 person per 11 acres, respectively). Thus the impact of damaged land per head of population is likely to be about thirty times greater in Britain than in the United States.

This picture might be altering rapidly if the rates of production and clearance of damaged land were widely different in the two countries or if marked changes in population density were occurring. On the basis of returns to the United States Department of the Interior for 1964, the rate of loss of land to strip and surface mining was an estimated 153,000 acres annually (about 5 per cent of the total 3·2 million acres referred to earlier). Of this, probably about 100,000 acres annually would need some form of reclamation. We have no figures for current reclamation rates in the United States.

In Britain, Wibberley (1959) has estimated that the annual gross loss of land to mineral extraction is 12,000 acres (about 5 per cent of the 250,000 acres total referred to earlier). Probably about two-thirds of this would need some form of treatment. If half of this treatable land is classed as derelict and half as disturbed, this gives 4,000 acres per annum as the rate of production of derelict land in Britain, a figure close to the Civic Trust's estimate (believed by some to be conservative) of 3,500 acres per annum (Civic Trust, 1964). From these estimates it would seem that both America and Britain will double their acres of damaged land during the next twenty years or so unless reclamation begins to balance or overtake production. In Wales, where a special effort was made after the Aberfan disaster, reclamation of 'derelict' land has been running at an average of 5 per cent per annum since November 1966, when the Derelict Land Unit of the Welsh Office commenced operations (Derelict Land Unit, 1971). Both Scotland and England are currently also reclaiming this figure, so that as a whole reclamation is now overtaking production.

## IS DAMAGED LAND A PROBLEM?

Planners and successive governments have recognized that derelict land is so repellent to potential developers that it remains unused. The following unattractive properties are common to most derelict land wherever it is found:

1. Complex ownership. Nineteenth-century industry was frequently in the hands of small businesses who usually occupied only an acre or two of land which often passed by inheritance into obscure or unknown ownership. The problems of amalgamating these small parcels for an overall development plan often present the greatest single difficulty in the process of reclamation which, under these circumstances, may take years to start or even be impossible.

2. Complex surface levels. Tipping of industrial wastes or excavation of minerals creates very uneven ground, and the earth moving required to produce a uniform level for subsequent development is very costly.

3. Tips. These may be more or less mechanically unstable and, if they are not freely drained, may slide as did the Aberfan tip on October 21st, 1966, when 144 people were killed. Tips revegetate very slowly, if at all, and are therefore subject to wind, water and frost erosion. Blown dust from tips can be a health hazard and a nuisance near housing. Wind-blown chemical constituents, particularly non-ferrous metals, and the noxious gases which may be emitted after spontaneous combustion (hydrogen fluoride, sulphur dioxide and carbon monoxide) may be a health hazard or affect crop yields and livestock over a wide area. Sediment from tip drainage may be a danger to fish and wildlife or may block and pollute watercourses and contaminate drinking water. Tips are very unsightly, a particularly important drawback in urban areas, as it is a commonly held view that this kind of disamenity encourages other unsightly land uses.

4. Flooding. Tipping, excavation and subsidence above deep mines frequently give rise to drainage and water-quality problems.

5. Poor access. Many nineteenth-century industries were served only by canals and railways which are now unusable. Good road access is one of the most important factors stimulating the relocation of industry, and local authorities are understandably reluctant to make the costly decision to build a road solely in the hope of attracting industry to a derelict area.

6. Absence of services. Electric power, mains water and sewerage are frequently absent from such areas and are costly to install.

7. Poor housing. Early industry was served by cheap labour which was poorly housed close to its place of work. The still commonplace rows of back-to-back terraced houses pose costly problems of slum clearance.

8. Industrial ruins. No legislation exists to prevent the dilapidation of abandoned works, and many unused chimney stacks and roofless buildings still occupy derelict land, adding to clearance costs.

9. Absence of vegetation. Derelict land was in many cases occupied by industries producing sulphurous fumes or toxic solid and liquid wastes at a time when pollution legislation was more permissive than it is today. This frequently led to the death of vegetation and the subsequent removal of topsoil by sheet and gully erosion. In addition, mineral-extractive industries often produce heavily compacted, toxic or nutrient-poor spoils as a result of surface or opencast mining. These are so inimical to plant establishment and growth that recolonization, if any, is slow. Dust-blow from bare substrates and flooding from flashy run-off are attendant problems.

These nine characteristics create a situation which often attracts 'dereliction industries' such as scrap-yards, burning yards and rag-and-bone yards. All these nuisances combine to inhibit other uses of the land, which then becomes neglected, unsightly and unused. This lack of use only serves to reinforce the already repellent nature of the area and the depressive effect often spreads to adjacent land, so that nearby property prices fall and rateable values are adversely affected (Barr, 1969). This often leads in turn to a reduction in public services such as road repairs, drainage maintenance, refuse collection and a general slowing down of developmental turnover. Planners often estimate that one acre of true dereliction may generate ten acres of 'grey zone' around it.

The seriousness of these disamenities is obvious; nobody would willingly live or work in such conditions. But if the amount of damaged land that needs treatment in Britain is only about 0·3 per cent of the total area, why does it merit attention out of all proportion to its size? The area affected is insignificant when it is compared with the area of naturally occurring land of little commercial value such as mud-flats or moorland. The reason for its importance is that a large proportion of the damaged land occurs in and around heavily populated cities and conurbations. Every acre of derelict or disturbed land near a large town is a far greater disamenity than thousands of similar acres in some remote, uninhabited place.

Successive governments have produced legislation in an attempt to cure the problem of derelict land. Under various Acts (e.g. Local Government Act, 1966; Local Employment Act, 1972), grants of between 50 and 85 per cent of the cost of clearance and treatment of derelict land are available to eligible local authorities. There were stipulations that growth of employment. housing or industry should be stimulated as a result. The National Parks and Access to the Countryside Act, 1949 and the Countryside Act (1968) include provisions for the reclamation of derelict land inside National Parks or Areas of Outstanding Natural Beauty. The Civic Amenities Act, 1968, lays the responsibility on local authorities to replace trees and clear litter, old cars, etc. Reclamation has not been encouraged in the past except where failure to do so would jeopardize public safety, deter industrial development, employment or housing. These constraints have now been relaxed.

To qualify under the relevant Acts, the land must be brought into public ownership (although local authorities are often very reluctant to use powers of compulsory purchase when owners are unwilling to sell). A clearance and reclamation scheme is then submitted to central government agencies for approval. Clearance usually entails the removal of old buildings, the filling of holes or the contouring of waste-heaps. Where a clear-cut after-use exists for housing or industry, new roads, services and buildings can be started immediately. If after-use is for agriculture, forestry or amenity, some form of revegetation is necessary. On the other hand, it is very common to find a local authority who merely wishes to remove the derelict land because it is an eyesore. There will be no planned after-use although the authority may hope eventually to sell the cleared site to a developer. Planning officers in counties with large amounts of derelict land know from experience that developers want high-quality sites; old industrial sites are not taken up even when development and occupation costs are minimized, but it is a common experience that after clearance and reshaping, a 'cosmetic' cover of vegetation placed on the land dramatically improves the chances of the site being sold for re-use. Sites so treated are usually redeveloped in such a way that although not all the grass or trees planted may be permanent, the future use of the area is properly regulated by modern planning control. The earlier dereliction or industrial squalor need not be repeated. It is thus very important to recognize that, apart from any direct value revegetation might have in terms of agriculture, forestry or amenity, it also has an important 'priming' role in stimulating the urban or industrial re-use of land. It appears to restore to damaged land a flexibility of re-use which it had lost through dereliction.

## THE RATE OF RECLAMATION

If derelict land presents so many serious disamenities, and generous government grants exist to clear it, why is it still on the increase in many places when it is obviously in the public interest to reclaim it? The following are the main features which inhibit reclamation:

1. Lack of a financial incentive by the developer or local authority.
2. Lack of a clear after-use for the land, if reclaimed.
3. Procedural or administrative difficulties.
4. Lack of technical expertise in reclamation procedures.

In practice, the inhibitory factors usually have this order of importance, but it can be demonstrated that whereas the first and third items could change in favour of reclamation in the space of a year or so, the fourth item could take a carefully organized 10 to 20 year programme to remedy (where, for example, effective revegetation techniques are unknown).

1. *Finance.* In general, developers will only restore a derelict site when it is the cheapest and most convenient choice, since otherwise they would be attracted to 'easier' sites elsewhere. On the other hand, public concern about environmental problems has made the clearance of derelict land a minor political issue and the major political parties have promised 10-year targets for the clearance of dereliction (*Hansard*, 1971). In the past, reclamation has been very low on the list of government budgetary priorities and has been one of the first items to be dropped during any period of economic stringency. More recently, government policy has been in sympathy with clearance and substantial increases in grants in aid have been forthcoming. Thus, although in the past it may have been necessary to demonstrate clearly in cost/benefit or other economic terms the social value of reclamation, this is at present unnecessary as other motivations for clearance already exist. Even so, many local authorities find it difficult or impossible to raise the 15–50 per cent balance required from them under the relevant Acts, even where the existence of rate equalization grants reduces this percentage still further.

2. *After-use.* Derelict land is less likely to attract a prospective developer, so that when no intention to use the land exists it is regarded as a low priority by planners who are hard-pressed in other directions.

Formerly, under the various Acts, reclamation for amenity was discouraged unless employment prospects would be favourably affected or unless the land was a hazard. However, interpretation of the Acts has been liberalized in the last few years so that reclaimed land can now be used as amenity open space until a favourable development presents itself.

3. *Procedural difficulties.* Many small local authorities or those with great pressure on their resources find it difficult to go through the complete process of planning a reclamation application and applying for government aid. That this is a real problem has been amply demonstrated by the great success of the Welsh Office's Derelict Land Unit, who have been able to offer guidance to local authorities seeking advice on such matters.

4. *Technical expertise.* Many widely different kinds of technical expertise are necessary when reclamation work is undertaken. The immediate problem is getting the land into public ownership so that it may qualify for grant aid. This legal process is well understood. The next problem is to remove old buildings, regrade the land using earth-moving equipment, and drain it and these too are problems well understood by civil engineers.

Revegetation techniques do not have such reliable results, and the maintenance of grass or trees in good health is even more difficult to guarantee. Where good soil already exists there are only minor problems, but where no soil is present or where the physical or chemical features of the ground are inimical to plant growth, real difficulties of plant establishment and maintenance arise. The resulting failure may be more repellent than the original dereliction. Large sums of money have already been spent on inadequate revegetation of difficult sites and it may be seriously questioned whether we could competently revegetate them all without incurring prohibitive costs, even if enough money suddenly became available to clear them.

## THE IMPORTANCE OF REVEGETATION

The problems already discussed provide the basic motivation for all reclamation work. They have been dealt with at some length because although they may be well understood by the planning authorities who deal with derelict land they are rarely within the experience of the agronomists, ecologists, foresters or soil scientists who are able to make a real contribution to the technology of revegetation. The problems encountered in revegetating tip wastes, slags and rubble have not been intensively studied by applied scientists mainly because of this lack of understanding. Neither have the problems been studied as problems in pure science, although the special plant–soil relations of difficult substrates are likely to put some of our existing theoretical knowledge into a new perspective (see, however, Goodman *et al.*, 1965; Hilton, 1967). When both pure and applied scientists appreciate the practical and theoretical relevance of such studies, there is little doubt that a great deal more research will be carried out and rapid progress made.

If some form of building development is planned for the land after reclamation, no revegetation is required, although selected areas may be set aside for amenity landscaping. If, on the other hand, it is intended to return the reclaimed land to farming or forestry, restoration to a fairly high standard of productivity is essential. At present, this can only be carried out on a rather limited range of largely innocuous substrates, because we do not fully understand the techniques of generating proper soils on 'difficult' spoils, wastes or other substrates whose physicochemical nature tends to inhibit soil-forming processes and plant growth.

In many cases, no clear-cut after-use for the damaged land exists and reclamation is carried out with the intention of removing eyesores and generally improving the chances of eventual re-use of the land for any purpose. Under these circumstances revegetation is essential as a holding operation to prevent any wind and water erosion which might occur after clearance and levelling have been completed, and to give a visually attractive effect. The great variety of physicochemical problems encountered on 'difficult' substrates which receive this 'cosmetic' treatment unfortunately makes for a high rate of failure. Failure may be outright, or, more commonly, good germination or establishment is succeeded by a decline of the green vegetative cover after a year or two. This tendency to failure is often aggravated by the fact that the local authority, which needs to stimulate the redevelopment of a site and fully appreciates the catalytic role of 'cosmetic' revegetation, does not know where to obtain the best technical advice. The plant–soil problems met with on these difficult sites are often quite outside the normal experience of horticulture, agriculture or forestry and require the accumulation of special experience and expertise not yet fully possessed by any professional group.

All damaged land, however toxic, could be improved immediately if sufficient money were available to cover it with a deep layer ($\frac{1}{2}$–3 feet) of good soil followed by routine grass or shrub planting. The cost of this treatment is far too great in most cases, often being well in excess of £1,000 per acre. This emphasizes the fact that the whole problem of effective treatment is one of finding acceptable revegetation at the lowest possible cost per acre. In spite of this, soiling frequently has to be used, the rate of treatment being controlled by the rate at which enough money becomes available to buy, transport and spread topsoil on the difficult sites.

The view is often expressed that the technical problems of revegetating damaged land are not worth serious scientific investigation to find inexpensive methods, since crude and costly treatments will serve the purpose because dereliction is a once-and-for-all problem and once the 'backlog' is cleared the scale of the ongoing problem would not merit an expensively acquired technology. However, it is generally acknowledged that the demand for a wide variety of minerals in Britain will increase during the next two decades. In many cases, these are likely to be exploited by opencast rather than deep mines. Extraction sites may have to be close to large towns to minimize haulage costs to building sites, of sand and gravel, for example, or in countryside of high environmental value, for example where the non-ferrous metals are concerned. This will mean that extraction and restoration will have to be planned in advance as one continuous operation in order to minimize undesirable side-effects. Added to this problem are the increasing amounts and variety of dumped urban-industrial wastes which need burial and coverage. There also appears to be a growing public reluctance to accept our old urban and industrial landscapes left as relics from the industrial revolution of the nineteenth century. This latter problem arises when new motorways are routed through such landscapes or when new towns are built in them. Coupled with population growth and the loss of land to housing, industry and roads, all these factors combine to promote an attitude which favours intensive land use and turnover. Landscapes formerly exploited for one purpose can be quickly cleared, reshaped if necessary, and re-used for another. This dynamic approach to land use may well be the future pattern in any intensively settled country. It demands the development of effective revegetation technology for a wide range of difficult substrates.

## A SURVEY OF REVEGETATION PROBLEMS

Several bibliographies on the reclamation of derelict and disturbed land exist for various parts of the world (e.g. Whyte and Sisam, 1949; Limstrom, 1960; Knabe, 1957–8; Bowden, 1961; Funk, 1962; Ministry of Housing, 1963; Civic Trust, 1964; Drlik and Stys, 1964; Knabe, 1965; Vyle, 1966; Oxenham, 1966; Barr, 1969; Commonwealth Bureau of Pastures and Field Crops, 1971; Newcastle-upon-Tyne University, 1972; Goodman and Bray; 1974).

Revegetation procedures, to which these works refer, can be classified into three groups, or the various combinations of them:

1. The acceptance of the poor site conditions as they are and the attempt to plant pioneer species with a high tolerance of the inimical conditions. This approach is often carried out by trial and error.

2. The attempt to incorporate a soil amendment into the substrate (such as organic matter, lime, nitrogen, phosphorus, or potassium fertilizer, or innocuous waste) to ameliorate the poor conditions. This may involve some chemical site analysis.

3. Planned exploitation to bury any harmful waste under a surface layer of least harmful waste. This involves preliminary geo-chemical analysis and careful operation-planning.

The motivation of the early work was generally to restore damaged land to agriculture or forestry. Later attempts were made to remove eyesores, improve visual amenity or to create leisure areas. Revegetation was also undertaken as a safety precaution to stabilize banks or prevent wind and water erosion. Some of the most recent work recognizes the catalytic role of a *temporary* cover of grass, trees or shrubs in stimulating the re-use of waste land, bringing it back into the mainstream of planning and development.

A feature of much of the early work was its pragmatic nature. It was often carried out by people who clearly saw the social or economic need for it but lacked the technical expertise to do it properly, either because this did not exist at the time or because it was outside their skills as planners or civil engineers. Early restoration sites were often treated like gardens or fields and planted with mature horticultural specimens or agricultural grasses which demanded very good site conditions. Trial and error demonstrated the need to be more selective about the choice of species and to use young stock. The importance of some form of soil amendment soon became evident, usually lime and/or nitrogen, phosphorous or potassium fertilizer. Eventually, commonly occurring substrates, such as coal waste, ironstone waste or pulverized fuel ash, were recognized to pose their own distinct problems. This led to several empirical trial plantings of various trees and shrubs to discover whether certain species could be regarded as generally more successful on certain wastes than on others. The now familiar list of trees and shrubs emerged as more or less satisfactory on wastes. These included: *Alnus glutinosa; A. incana; Betula pendula; B. pubescens Hippophae; rhamnoides; Larix decidua; L. leptolepis; Pinus nigra* s.sp *laricio; Populus robusta; P. tremula* and hybrids; *Robinia pseudoacacia; Salix* spp.; *Ulex europaeus;* and many more. In the same way, a list of successful grasses and legumes emerged, including the grasses *Agrostis stolonifera, A. tenuis, Dactylis glomerata, Festuca rubra, Lolium perenne, Phleum pratense* and *Poa pratensis,* and the legumes *Lotus corniculatus, Medicago lupulina, Trifolium hybridum, T. pratense* and *T. repens.*

Three features of these lists are noticeable: (a) the high proportion of nitrogen-fixing species which appeared successful; (b) no one species was always successful on all types of substrate; (c) virtually all the species tried were of stock already in use in agriculture, horticulture or forestry. From this is can be concluded that (a) not surprisingly, most wastes were probably nitrogen-deficient; (b) each type of waste did not always possess the same grouping of plant-inhibitory factors; (c) no attempt had been made to regard wastes as special soil environments unparalleled by conditions prevailing in agriculture, horticulture or forestry. This is still true today, although where special problems exist, it is natural for sustained empirical attempts to be made to cover over particular spoil tips or waste dumps. But the chances are small that a careful scientific analysis will be made of physico-chemical factors inhibiting plant growth on particular substrates prior to restoration. This latter approach may appear to be somewhat academic at the outset, but in the long run it will be far more effective in solving revegetation problems. The classic example of this is the work carried out by Leeds University in collaboration with the Central Electricity Generating Board on pulverized fuel ash (Holliday *et al.,* 1958; Hodgson, 1968). Thus, although the great majority of work has been 'substrate-orientated', there are a few good examples of 'inhibitor-orientated' work. It is to be hoped that the numbers of these will increase in the future.

# Table 16.1

Substrates in U.K.

| | | 1 | 2 | 3 | 4 | 5 | 6 | 7 | 8 | 9 | 10 | 11 | 12 | 13 |
|---|---|---|---|---|---|---|---|---|---|---|---|---|---|---|
| I. | Brick clay pits | − | − | ++ | + | − | ++ | ++ | + | ++ | − | + | + | + |
| II. | China clay waste and pits | + | − | ++ | + | − | − | ++ | ++ | ++ | − | − | ++ | ++ |
| III. | Coal mine waste (deep mine and opencast) | ++ | ++ | ++ | + | ++ | + | ++ | ++ | ++ | + | + | ++ | ++ |
| IV. | Domestic refuse | − | ++ | − | + | ++ | ++ | − | + | − | − | ++ | − | − |
| V. | Ironstone waste | + | − | ++ | + | + | ++ | ++ | ++ | + | − | ++ | + | ++ |
| VI. | Metal-mine wastes | + | + | − | − | ++ | − | ++ | ++ | ++ | + | − | ++ | ++ |
| VII. | Peatland stripping | − | + | − | ++ | +++ | ++ | + | + | + | − | − | ++ | ++ |
| VIII. | Pulverized fuel ash | − | − | − | + | +++ | − | +++ | +++ | + | + | − | − | + |
| IX. | Quarry stone pits and waste | − | − | ++ | ++ | − | +++ | ++ | ++ | +++ | + | ++ | + | ++ |
| X. | Sand and gravel workings | − | − | + | ++ | − | − | ++ | ++ | + | − | + | + | + |
| XI. | Slate and shale wastes | ++ | − | ++ | + | − | − | ++ | ++ | +++ | ++ | +++ | ++ | ++ |
| XII. | Smelter slags and wastes | + | + | + | + | ++ | − | ++ | + | + | + | ++ | ++ | ++ |
| XIII. | Wastes from chemical factories | + | − | − | − | ++ | + | + | + | ++ | − | − | ++ | ++ |

Arabic numerals refer to the physical and chemical substrate factors which inhibit plant growth:

1, Instability of substratum; 2, Spontaneous combustion of waste; 3, Steep slopes on tips and excavations; 4, Periodic flooding and water stress; 5, High levels of potentially toxic elements; 6, Compaction and cementation of substratum; 7, Extremes of surface temperature; 8, Wind turbulence, wind erosion and 'sand blasting' effects; 9, Low nutrient status; 10, Excessive stoniness and absence of fine, soil-forming material; 11, Broken, uneven surfaces; 12, Sheet and gully erosion; 13, Absence of soil micro-organisms and soil fauna.

++ Inhibitory factor very pronounced
+ Inhibitory factor present
− Inhibitory factor negligible or absent

## PHYSICAL AND CHEMICAL FACTORS INHIBITING PLANT GROWTH

It is possible to identify the thirteen principal physical and chemical phenomena which are inimical to plant growth and to obtain some idea of their importance in each substrate (Table 16.1). The arabic numerals in the Table refer to the physical and chemical properties of the different substrates which in various combinations tend to inhibit germination, establishment, growth or persistence of vegetation. Other substrates encountered in the UK are: abandoned railway tracks, old airfields, military installations and other stretches of concreted ground, and these can still be a problem in some places. The list is common to most other countries, which in addition may have problems from phosphate mine waste, oil-soaked land, saline soils or sea-bed soils.

## OTHER PROBLEMS

During the preceding discussion, attention has been drawn to our lack of knowledge in several important areas of the subject. One striking omission in the literature is the absence of any work following up the long-term performance of a planting scheme and recording any natural successional changes in its vegetation structure. The work of Gemmell (1971) in recording the changing species composition of grass-swards established on smelter wastes is a useful start. But we are still mainly at the stage where the primary problems of establishing any sort of green cover on bare wastes predominate over the secondary problems of maintenance and management. Despite this, there is a real need for planned follow-up studies to begin as soon as the vegetation is established.

The enormous amount of empirical work on planting trials, often inadequately recorded, must give way to work on the analysis of those physical and chemical factors and their interactions which are likely to inhibit plant growth on any damaged site. This predictive approach is bound to be the most effective in the long term and it is hoped that the consideration of inhibitory factors as suggested here will pave the way for a more general recognition of its value.

## REFERENCES

Barr, J. (1969). *Derelict Britain*, Pelican, Penguin, Harmondsworth, 240 pp.
Bowden, K. L. (1961). *A Bibliography of Strip-mine Reclamation 1953–60*, Uni. Mich. Dept. of Conservation, Ann Arbor, 13 pp.
*Civic Amenities Act* (1968). H.M.S.O., London, Ch. 69.
Civic Trust (1964). *Derelict Land,* The Civic Trust, London, 71 pp.
Commonwealth Bureau of Pastures and Field Crops (1971). *Reclamation and Revegetation of Industrial Waste Land,* Annot. Bibl. no. 1249, Hurley, Berks.

*Countryside Act* (1968). H.M.S.O., London, Ch. 41.

Derelict Land Unit (1971). *Derelict Land in Wales: The Activities of the Welsh Office*, Welsh Office Cardiff, 13 pp.

Drlik, R., and Štýs, S. (1964). Asanace a rekultivace uzemi postizenych uhelnou těžbou, *Státní Vědecká Knihorna Ōstravě* (CSR), Rada II, cis, 370.

Funk, D. T. (1962). *A Revised Bibliography of Strip-mine Reclamation*, Cent. St. For. Expt. Sta. (Misc. Release 35), Columbus, Ohio, 2 pp.

Gemmell, R. P. (1971). The ecological behaviour of species—populations of grasses susceptible and tolerant to heavy metal toxicity, Ph.D. Thesis, University College Swansea, 164 pp. + 72 appendix.

Goodman, G. T., and Bray, S. (In Press). *Ecological Aspects of the Reclamation of Derelict and Disturbed Land: an Annotated Bibiography*. Natural Environment Research Council, London.

Goodman, G. T., Edwards, R. W., and Lambert, J. M. (Eds.) (1965). *Ecology and the Industrial Society*, British Ecological Society Symposium, 5, Blackwell, Oxford, 395 pp.

*Hansard* (1971). House of Lords, 17 November 1971, Vol. 325, no. 8, pp. 661–743.

Hilton, K. J. (Ed.) (1967). *The Lower Swansea Valley Project*, Longmans, London, 329 pp.

Hodgson, D. R. (1968). *The Growth of Plants on Pulverised Fuel Ash*, National Congress on PFA Utilization, Central Electricity Generating Board, London, 6 pp.

Holliday, R., Townsend, W. N., Hodgson, D. R., and Wood, J. W. (1958). Plant growth on 'Fly Ash', *Nature (Lond.)*, **176**, 1079–80.

*Industrial Development Act* (1966). H.M.S.O., London, Ch. 34, 36 pp.

Knabe, W. (1957–8). Beitrage zur Bibliographie uber Wiederrurbarmachung von Bergbauflachen (Bibliography on reclaiming mined areas), Wizzen, Z. Humboldt—University Berlin, 7, no. 2, 291–304.

Knabe, W. (1965). Observations on world-wide efforts to reclaim industrial waste land, in: *Ecology and the Industrial Society*, Ed. G. T. Goodman, R. W. Edwards and J. M. Lambert, Blackwell, Oxford, 395 pp.

Limstrom, G. A. (1960). Forestation of strip-mined land in the Central State, *U.S.D.A. Agric. Handb.*, **166**, pp. 74.

*Local Employment Act* (1972). H.M.S.O., London.

*Local Government Act* (1966). H.M.S.O., London, Ch. 42.

Ministry of Housing and Local Government (1963). *New Life for Dead Lands*, H.M.S.O., London, 30 pp.

*National Parks and Access to the Countryside Act* (1949). H.M.S.O., London.

Newcastle-upon-Tyne University (1972). *Landscape Reclamation*, Vols. 1 and 2, I.P.C. Science and Technology Press, Guildford, 100 pp.

Oxenham, J. (1966). *Reclaiming Derelict Land*, Faber and Faber, London, pp. 204.

Vyle, C. J. (1966). *A Collection of References on Landscape Reclamation*, Dept. of Town and Country Planning, Landscape Reclamation Research Project, University of Newcastle upon Tyne, 15 pp.

Whyte, R. D., and Sisam, J. W. B. (1949). *The Establishment of Vegetation on Industrial Waste Land*, Commonwealth Agricultural Bureaux Joint Publication, no. 14, 78 pp.

Wibberley, G. P. (1959). *Agriculture and Urban Growth*, Joseph, London, 240 pp.

Part II   Demands and Responses

A   Historical Perspectives

# CHAPTER 17

# Chronicling Soil Erosion

### C. VITA-FINZI

The modifications in the system of which man is the
instrument do not, perhaps, constitute so great a devi-
ation from previous analogy as we usually imagine...
CHARLES LYELL, *Principles of Geology*

If it is to be beneficial, soil conservation must hinge on a correct diagnosis
of the prevailing or impending ills. The classic symptoms of soil degradation—declining yields, sheetwash and gullying—do not invariably reflect
human mismanagement of the land. Though useful in identifying areas in
need of attention, they can be interpreted correctly (and hence rendered
amenable to correction) only if detailed, individual case-histories are
available.

The latter part of such histories may be provided by documentary sources
and eyewitness accounts. With luck, these will also touch on the climatic,
vegetational and land-use patterns that held at different times, whereupon
an attempt can be made to interpret the physical evidence. But beyond the
period of record, both erosion and the circumstances that led to it have to
be traced from indirect evidence. The doubts that attend any historical
reconstruction are thereby compounded; yet they are justified by the conversion of a narrative measured in decades or centuries into one which
reckons in millennia, and by the inclusion within the narrative of periods
during which human intervention differed markedly in scale and character
from that of today. The gain in time perspective is useful in establishing
how far modern erosion departs from its former levels; glimpses into prehistory are essential to an assessment of the influence of man on the distribution and severity of erosional processes.

The task of chronicling erosion is relatively simple where the soils in
question either are alluvial in origin or have been redeposited by fluvial
action. This is by no means fortuitous. Man has long occupied river plains,
and in so doing has endowed them with the artifacts and hearths needed for

the erection of detailed alluvial chronologies (Vita-Finzi, 1969a). Moreover, the ease with which fluvial sediments are attacked by running water, and which renders them sensitive to human influence no less than to other sources of hydrological and vegetational change, helps to provide the stratigrapher with detailed sequences and ample exposures. He may therefore be forgiven for viewing (say) a gully which cuts through several layers of alluvium, each of which represents a period of erosion elsewhere, with something less than disapproval.

This chapter attempts to illustrate some of the methods employed in the construction of alluvial chronologies and considers the implications the chronologies may have for soil conservation. No *a priori* distinction is drawn between normal and accelerated rates of erosion, or between natural and man-induced phenomena. Strahler (1956) has already reviewed some of the difficulties that arise in deciding what is and what is not the normal state of affairs, and accordingly employs 'accelerated' simply to mean a very considerable increase in the rate of erosion or aggradation. Yet it is probably too late to free the term from the connotation that responsibility for the increase lies with man; what is more, the physical criteria proposed by Strahler for identifying accelerated erosion, such as a change towards coarser texture in alluvial deposits or the presence of steep-walled channels cut into fine-grained soils, are poor substitutes for more direct evidence and in any case often lend themselves to alternative explanations. The use of 'natural' to exclude human activity became inexcusable in 1859, when the *Origin of Species* was first published; its retention, though perhaps convenient, obscures the many parallels between the effects of man and of other species on the land, to the possible detriment of conservation practice.

## ALLUVIAL CHRONOLOGIES

It is unusual for different parts of a river to erode or aggrade in concert. The forces at work, and the resistance of the rocks to them, vary from place to place; moreover, changes undergone by one reach are likely to influence its neighbours, as when material eroded in a headwater is deposited further downstream. Given time, however, a unifying trend may become apparent: for example, gully development at the headwaters coupled with aggradation downvalley may ultimately lead to a general decrease in channel gradient. The recognition of such a trend may in turn throw light on the underlying mechanism: in the above example, this might turn out to be an increase in the peak flow experienced by the stream. And even if an explanation remains elusive, local phenomena will now be seen in better perspective.

The stratigrapher in search of such trends has two main concerns: to recognize the processes that have been at work, and to specify the periods during which they were dominant. Further information can be obtained by combining the physical evidence with that of chronology: rates of deposition, for example, may be calculated by dividing the volume of sediment in a particular reach by the time taken for its accumulation.

A major problem remains that of deciding the extent to which the record is to be subdivided. Like other fields, stratigraphy has its lumpers and its splitters, so that, for example, the aggradational phase of one worker will rank in the eyes of another as a complex alternation of erosional and depositional episodes. And even when the degree of refinement is agreed upon, drawing the boundaries is rarely straightforward. To quote the code of practice prepared by the American Commission on Stratigraphic Nomenclature (1961, Article 5), 'the boundaries of stratigraphic units are placed at sharp contacts, or may be fixed arbitrarily within zones of gradation. Both vertical and lateral boundaries are based on the lithologic criteria that provide the greatest unity and practical utility.'

The units that are ultimately identified need to be dated. On occasion, all that is possible is to establish their relative age. Where archaeological or organic material is present, however, quantitative dating may be feasible, as it will be for those forms and deposits that are represented in successive maps, air photographs and field descriptions. Whatever the method of dating, its limitations need to be evaluated. For example, artifacts which have been washed into a deposit will only yield a maximum date for the overlying material. Again, contamination by living plants means that many radiocarbon (C14) dates based on samples from shallow depths are too 'young', whereas the converse is true of tufas laid down by water from older limestones.

These and other technical problems can be allowed for in drawing conclusions from the evidence; in contrast, dates that stem from inferences regarding the origin of the sediments are more difficult to assess and also detract from the freedom with which the record can be translated into environmental terms. The dating of terraces by reference to the former sea-levels to which they were allegedly graded, or in terms of their position in a sequence of terraces which supposedly corresponds to an accepted climatic chronology, falls into this category. Similarly, when the current phase of erosion comes to be ascribed to land misuse, the temptation is strong to date all such features to the period in question. Yet, as Leopold and Miller (1954, pp. 79-80) discovered in Wyoming, 'vertical walls of alluvium, completely bare of vegetation . . . need not represent erosion in the past 70 years, as a first glance might lead one to surmise'. As it happens, some of the gullies had probably formed before AD 1200.

This leads us to the question of correlation in general. The term is often used to imply a vague equivalence between two units or events (Vita-Finzi,

10

1970), and it is helpful to specify whether time or rock correlation is intended. That they are often incompatible is clear from what has been said about the progressive nature of aggradation or erosion. A particular deposit or surface generally differs in age from place to place, or, in stratigraphic parlance, it is time-transgressive. Hence the recognition of regional 'events' or phases involves a greater or lesser degree of fudging, a harmless exercise provided the alleged synchroneity is known to be approximate. To correlate between river basins raises similar problems, with the added difficulty that lithological or erosional units cannot be traced directly. The need for quantitative dates is here all the more pressing, as similar features or sequences need not have formed simultaneously. Nevertheless, the assumption that they did often serve as a useful working hypothesis which subsequent work can be designed to test.

The importance of a detailed chronology is equally clear once we turn to the task of interpreting the evidence. Recent years have witnessed marked advances in our understanding of fluvial action, and hence in the confidence with which its products can be translated into hydrological terms (Rigby and Hamblin, 1972). To go further, and account for the onset of a particular hydrological situation, requires a detailed knowledge of the many strands that make up a basin's history. The task of the alluvial geologist now becomes that of specifying to his colleagues in botany, archaeology and other related fields which portions of their own data are in greatest need of elaboration.

## EPIRUS

The problems outlined above were much in evidence during an attempt to reconstruct the erosional history of Epirus, in northwestern Greece, although the first step—that of subdividing the alluvial deposits of the area into major sedimentary units—was facilitated by the close correspondence beween the morphological and sedimentological evidence.

The valleys of Epirus are floored by two alluvial surfaces (Figure 17.1), the higher underlain by coalescing fans up to 50 m thick, the lower forming a terrace trenched by the modern streams to a maximum depth of 5 m. The fans consist of poorly sorted and bedded sediment, ranging in texture from clay to coarse subrounded gravel, and strongly coloured by red iron oxides; the terrace is composed predominantly of grey, silty alluvium with horizons of rounded pebbles. A strong erosional unconformity separates these two sedimentary bodies, and another separates the older of them (the 'Red Beds') from the underlying Tertiary and Mesozoic rocks. The simple twofold scheme appears to be violated at only two points, in one by a localized tufa deposit underlying the Red Beds, and in another by a lens of clayey material separating the Red Beds from the younger deposit. The two fills also lend

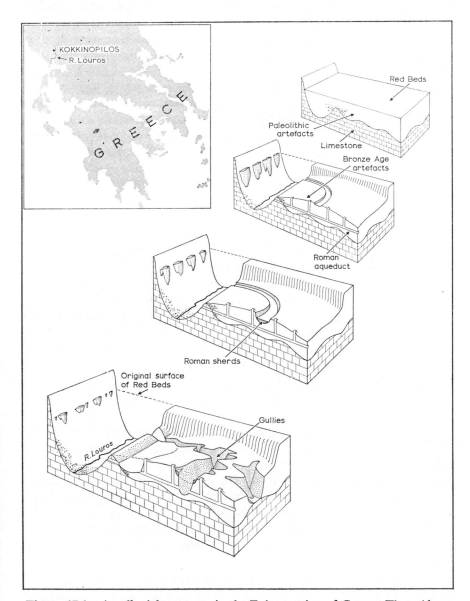

**Figure 17.1.** An alluvial sequence in the Epirus region of Greece. The evidence indicates active erosion and deposition over the past 22,000 years at the very least. The most probable control has been climatic rather than anthropogenic.

themselves to internal subdivision on the basis of lithology, but the results are rarely consistent for more than a few metres along the stream.

Dating was based on archaeological methods; fortunately, several C14 determinations were available for the stratified Palaeolithic sites that furnished the reference material. The Red Beds yielded Middle and Advanced Palaeolithic artifacts which range in age from over 40,000 to 11,000 years (Higgs and Vita-Finzi, 1966). Most of this material had been washed into the alluvium; at the site of Kokkinopilos, however, excavation showed that the Middle Palaeolithic (Mousterian) artifacts were restricted to the base of the deposit and the Advanced Palaeolithic artifacts to its upper horizons (Dakaris *et al.,* 1964). As the Advanced Palaeolithic industries go back at least 22,000 years ago, there can be little doubt that Red Bed deposition had begun before this date. A Neolithic ditch which was cut into the Red Beds near Ioannina, and which presumably postdates the close of aggradation, has given a C14 date of 7,380 years ago.

To judge from the evidence of Roman structures, the ensuing phase of stream downcutting and gully development continued after classical times until it was supplanted by renewed aggradation. In many valleys the resulting (younger) fill contains Roman pottery; at the sites of Rogous, on the Arta Plain, there is evidence to suggest that deposition had ceased prior to Turkish occupation. Hence, as in other parts of the Mediterranean Basin (Vita-Finzi, 1969b), the current phase of downcutting and gully development has been in operation during the last two or three centuries at most.

The sequence is in itself instructive. The Red Beds reflect severe upland erosion during Palaeolithic occupation of the area; moreover, although C14 dates are still insufficient for estimates of the rate at which this erosion operated, the evidence to hand shows that its cumulative effect greatly exceeded the erosion represented by the younger fill, especially when we take into account the important contribution made to this deposit by material eroded from the Red Beds. The intervening phase of downcutting may well have been accompanied by further interfluve erosion, but, to judge from its current equivalent, most of the sediment then carried out to sea was the product of channel erosion. In other words, the barrenness that characterizes upland Epirus appears to date in large measure from over seven millennia ago.

The processes responsible for this barrenness led to the concentration of soil, formerly to be found in pockets and hollows, into large units in the valley bottoms. What is more, alluvial deposition meant the addition of gravel, with a corresponding increase in permeability of the soils. The trend was accentuated during medieval aggradation by the selective removal of clay in favour of the silt and sand fraction (Vita-Finzi, 1971). Finally, the alluvium acquired a flat surface, more or less sloping in the case of the Red Beds and almost horizontal when it came to the younger fill.

Soil erosion thus emerges as both an ancient phenomenon and one that has been substantially favourable to the agricultural potential of Epirus (Hutchinson, 1969). The qualifying term 'potential' is used advisedly, as there would be no gain without some technological adjustment. The herdsman is unlikely to view the removal of upland soils with favour. Again, the lowland soils often needed irrigation or drainage before fulfilling their promise; the Arta Plain, for example, which is underlain by the younger fill, became a major citrus-producing area only after it was drained in the early part of the present century (Admiralty, 1945).

The need remains to account for the major subdivisions of the succession. The Red Beds reflect deposition in alluvial fans by ephemeral streams, coupled with frost weathering in the mountainous areas. This finding accords with the pollen record of the Ioannina area, which indicates the prevalence of cold, dry steppe conditions between about 35,000 and 8,000 years ago (Bottema, 1967; Butzer, 1972). The role of man during this period was negligible, even if the traditional picture of a hunting and gathering economy is broadened to take into account the probable use of fire in the hunt and the likelihood of human migratory patterns closely linked with those of the exploited herd animals (Higgs and Vita-Finzi, 1966; Higgs *et al.*, 1967); the hydrological and thermal conditions required by the physical record can be satisfied only by a climatic explanation.

Certain features of the pollen spectrum for the latter part of the last 10,000 years could be taken to indicate biotic disturbance by man (Bottema, 1967), but, as the outcome was at most to confer a selective advantage on Kermès oak (*Quercus coccifera* L.), the physical consequences can hardly have been serious. There is also circumstantial evidence for widespread devastation in post-Hellenistic times (Hammond, 1967, p. 43), but, as we have seen, this is not supported by the stratigraphic record. One of the items cited as evidence of soil erosion during this period is the sediment that buried the Greek theatre of Dodona, but it consists of material laid down during the medieval phase of stream aggradation and, like its counterparts elsewhere in Epirus (and like the Red Beds that preceded it), reflects a stream regime indicative of a change in the seasonal distribution of rainfall. What is more, throughout Epirus, devegetation, unwise cultivation and other human activities at the present day have merely accentuated linear erosion and stream incision (Harris and Vita-Finzi, 1968); the loss of good land as a consequence of agricultural activities has been small, and the practice of terracing has if anything tended to reduce the risks of erosion in soils which are inherently unstable (Hutchinson, 1969). In brief, erosion, far from being a modern or even a historical phenonemon, has been the rule in this part of Greece for at least 22,000 years, and this by virtue of climatic controls.

## RATES OF EROSION AND DEPOSITION

The next step in the analysis of an alluvial sequence is to evaluate the speed at which soil removal and redeposition operated at different times. The younger fill of Epirus, though volumetrically dwarfed by the Red Beds, may well have accumulated more rapidly; the current wave of erosion could emerge as being more aggressive than any which preceded it.

Rates of erosion or of aggradation are generally expressed as means, for example in terms of the tonnage of sediment yielded by a square kilometre of catchment in a year. Consequently they will obscure the range of values attained from one year to the next during the period on which the mean is based, and it becomes desirable to keep the periods as short as possible. Some of the pioneering studies in this field, such as that by Leopold and Miller (1954) cited earlier, were limited by the need to found age determination largely on stratigraphic correlation with adjoining areas. A later investigation in New Mexico benefited from a C14 determination near the base of one of the fills under review and the presence, both in and on it, of artifacts whose age could be specified to within 50 years or less (Miller and Wendorf, 1958); in Iowa, the progress of sedimentation and erosion has been traced in great detail thanks to numerous C14 dates, early surveys and the refined measurement of the volume of material involved in each episode (Ruhe and Daniels, 1965). An extreme illustration of what is occasionally attainable is the work of Larrabee (1962), who was able to specify with the help of historical documents the twelve days in 1862 and 1864 within which a stratified silt with a thickness of 1 m was laid down at Harpers Ferry.

The rates that now prevail can be derived from various sources, among them the extent to which features of known age (such as tree roots or walls) protrude from an eroding soil or have been buried by sediment. In some areas, notably the United States, gauging stations can supply information on suspended stream load. The speed with which reservoirs have silted up is an indirect measure more widely applicable and with the added advantage of incorporating bedload transport. Burdon (1951) has demonstrated its value in his work on Cyprus. There remains the problem of making the rates which relate to aggradation compatible with those that apply to periods of stream incision. In their Wyoming study, Leopold and Miller (1954) calculated annual rates of sediment production from the basin by multiplying the rate at which each alluvial fill had been deposited by three, this being the ratio between the volumes of suspended load and of material being deposited in the middle reaches of the Rio Grande. The results could then be compared with values for modern streams in the midwest and the southwest of the United States.

As the authors freely acknowledge, calculations of this sort are fraught with many possible sources of error. The results given in Table 17.1 are

**Table 17.1**

**E. Wyoming:** sediment production from the basin in acre-feet/square mile/year (Leopold and Miller, 1954)

| | |
|---|---|
| Kaycee fill (2500–400 BC) | 0·90 |
| Lightning fill (AD 1400–1850) | 0·40 |
| Modern streams in midwest | 0·11–0·39 |
| Modern streams in southwest | 0·56–1·10 |

**Tesuque Valley, New Mexico:** sediment production from the basin in tons/year/ square mile (Miller and Wendorf, 1958)

| | |
|---|---|
| High-terrace alluvium (250 BC to AD 1200–1250) | 1,620–2,448 |
| Low-terrace alluvium (AD 1250–1440 to 1880) | 993–1,244 |
| Modern tributaries of upper and middle Rio Grande | 425–2,340 |

**Iowa:** slope erosion in inch/year (Ruhe and Daniels, 1965)

| | | |
|---|---|---|
| Side valley, Adair County | 4850 BC to AD 1840 | 0·006 |
| | AD 1840 to present day | 0·06 |
| Side valley, Harrison County | AD 150–1700 | 0·31 |
| | AD 850–1700 | 0·44 |
| | AD 1850–present day | 0·20 |

*Note*

Although the units of measurement have been left in their original form, all the dates are given in BC/AD. As some of them are based on C14 determinations and others were expressed in ' years ago ', they must be regarded as very approximate. It should be noted that AD 1840 and AD 1850 in the examples from Iowa refer to the date of settlement in each of the basins.

therefore to be treated with caution. Yet, at the very least—that is to say, by ignoring the post-settlement tenfold *decrease* in the rate of slope erosion in Adair County, Iowa—they provide a useful corrective to the belief that soil loss in recent decades has been unusually rapid. To assume that 'human interference' produces high sediment yields (Douglas, 1967) is no more warranted than to use present-day rates in reconstructing those of the past.

## DISCUSSION

The contention that human activity does not necessarily promote erosion is endorsed by studies which are based on techniques other than alluvial history or which refer to environments other than those already considered. In a part of Guatemala, for example, Cowgill *et al.* (1966) found that, despite over 4,000 years of agricultural exploitation, there was no sign of an increase in erosion rate 'that could be interpreted as disastrous'. In California, Veihmeyer (1951) found that the substitution of grass for trees and brush following burning in experimental plots did not accelerate run-off or erosion. In the Queen Elizabeth National Park, Bishop (1963) concluded that gullying is the natural process under which the steep slopes are gradually being eliminated and stabilized, although he stressed the possibility that animal populations and human activities might trigger such gullying where the natural balance is already precarious.

Such findings are not incompatible with concern for the serious soil erosion that is widely prevalent nor with a willingness to indict man where this is apposite. At the same time, they could on occasion lead to a change in the aims of the conservationist. Stamp (1961, p. 23) has pointed out that 'In recent decades too much attention has been paid to attempts, sometimes futile, to prevent erosion, while the equally vital question of building-up lands with eroded material has been negected'. He goes on to cite in illustration the use of dams in the north Indus Plain to impound water-borne sediment, to which may be added the extensive application of this technique to northern Tripolitania in Roman times (Vita-Finzi, 1960). Blind enthusiasm for conservation measures can be as wasteful as fatalism, and judicious reference to the history of soil erosion is often of help in steering a middle course.

## ACKNOWLEDGMENT

The fieldwork cited in this essay was made possible by a grant from the Nuffield Foundation.

## REFERENCES

Admiralty (1945). *Greece: v. 3*, Naval Intelligence Division, Geographical Handbooks, London, 587 pp.

American Commission on Stratigraphic Nomenclature (1961). Code of Stratigraphic Practice, *Bull. Am. Ass. Petrol. Geol.*, **45**, 645–60.

Bishop, W. W. (1963). Gully erosion in the Queen Elizabeth National Park, *Uganda J.*, **26**, 161–5.

Bottema, S. (1967). A Late-Quaternary pollen diagram from Ioannina, north-western Greece, *Proc. prehist. Soc.*, **33**, 26–9.

Burdon, D. J. (1951). The relationship between erosion of soil and silting of reservoirs in Cyprus, *Jour. Instn. Water Engrs.*, **5**, 662–85.

Butzer, K. W. (1972). *Environment and Archaeology*, 2nd edn., Methuen, London, 703 pp.

Cowgill, U. M., Goulden, C. E., Hutchinson, G. E., Patrick, R., Raček, A. A., and Tsukada, M. (1966). The history of Laguna de Petenxil, *Mem. Conn. Acad. Arts Sci.*, **17**, 126 pp.

Dakaris, S. I., Higgs, E. S., and Hey, R. W. (1964). The climate, environment and industries of Stone Age Greece: Part I, *Proc. prehist. Soc.*, **30**, 199–244.

Douglas, I. (1967). Man, vegetation and the sediment yields of rivers, *Nature, (Lond.)*, **215**, 925–8.

Hammond, N. G. L. (1967). *Epirus,* Clarendon, Oxford, 847 pp.

Harris, D. R., and Vita-Finzi, C. (1968). Kokkinopilos—a Greek badland, *Geog. J.*, **134**, 537–46.

Higgs, E. S., and Vita-Finzi, C. (1966). The climate, environment and industries of Stone Age Greece: Part II, *Proc. prehist. Soc.*, **32**, 1–29.

Higgs, E. S., Vita-Finzi, C., Harris, D. R., and Fagg, A. E. (1967). The climate, environment and industries of Stone Age Greece: Part III, *Proc. prehist. Soc.*, **33**, 1–29.

Hutchinson, Sir J. (1969). Erosion and land use: the influence of agriculture on the Epirus region of Greece, *Agric. Hist. Rev.*, **17**, 85–90.

Larrabee, E. McM. (1962). Ephemeral water action preserved in closely dated deposit, *Jour. sedim. Petrol.*, **32**, 608–9.

Leopold, L. B., and Miller, J. P. (1954). A postglacial chronology for some alluvial valleys in Wyoming, *U.S. Geol. Surv., Water-Supply Paper* **1261**, Washington, 90 pp.

Miller, J. P., and Wendorf, F. (1958). Alluvial chronology of the Tesuque valley, New Mexico, *J. Geol.*, **66**, 177–94.

Rigby, J. K., and Hamblin, W. K. (eds.) (1972). Recognition of ancient sedimentary environments, *Soc. Econ. Paleontologists and Mineralogists, Spec. Pub.*, **16**, 340 pp.

Ruhe, R. V., and Daniels, R. B. (1965). Landscape erosion—geologic and historic, *J. Soil Wat. Conserv.*, **20**, 52–7.

Stamp, L. D. (1961). Introduction to *A History of Land Use in Arid Lands,* UNESCO, Paris, 17–24.

Strahler, A. N. (1956). The nature of induced erosion and aggradation, in: *Man's Role in Changing the Face of the Earth* (ed.) W. L. Thomas, Chicago University Press, Chicago, 621–38.

Veihmeyer, F. J. (1951). Hydrology of range lands as affected by the presence or absence of brush vegetation, *Internat. Ass. Scient. Hydrol., Brussels 1951,* III, 226–34.

Vita-Finzi, C. (1960). Roman dams in Tripolitania, *Antiquity*, **35**, 14–20.

Vita-Finzi, C. (1969a). Fluvial geology. In: *Science in Archaeology,* (eds.) D. Brothwell and E. Higgs, Thames and Hudson, London, 135–50.

Vita-Finzi, C. (1969b). *The Mediterranean Valleys,* Cambridge University Press, Cambridge, 140 pp.

Vita-Finzi, C. (1970). Time, stratigraphy and the Quaternary, *Scientia, Bologna,* **105**, 725–36.

Vita-Finzi, C. (1971). Heredity and environment in clastic sediments: silt/clay depletion, *Bull. geol. Soc. Am.*, **82**, 187–90.

# CHAPTER 18

# The Legacy of Prehistoric Man

## G. W. DIMBLEBY

In examining a plant community with a view to its conservation it is important to realize just how much its pattern has been dictated by human activities over an immensely long period. The evidence for this is a reminder of just how much a part of the ecosystem we ourselves are, and conversely how much it is part of our own social history.

The vegetational history of Britain through the post-glacial period is well established, very largely from the evidence of pollen analysis combined with radiocarbon dates from strategic levels (Pennington, 1969; Godwin et al., 1957), and while the sequence of events is not difficult to describe for many parts of the country (particularly the highland zone, in which suitable deposits occur more abundantly), it is not so easy to find good evidence to explain the changes in terms of ecological factors. How much was due to climatic change (and what was the time lag?), how much was due to soil maturation, and how much was due to man? Some botanical evidence can be obtained from earlier interglacial deposits, which are in the main free of human influence, and it is reasonable to conclude that, had man not been present in Britain in the post-glacial, even at this stage of the temperate interlude, the whole of Britain would have been under deciduous forest, excepting specialized habitats such as mountains over 2,000 feet, fens and marshes, tidal lands, etc.

The extent to which the present landscape contrasts with this is itself a measure of how drastic has been the influence of man. Despite the weight of historical evidence in the landscape it would be wrong to imagine that this has all happened mainly in historical times, when the means to change the landscape were more effective and the populations were greater. Indeed, there are extensive areas of this country, such as the chalk downs and some areas of moorland, which have probably changed little in the last 2,000 years, having been cleared and developed—sometimes ruined—in the period of agriculture preceding the Roman occupation. Moreover, the hand of man was probably having some effect on the landscape even before agriculture was brought to Britain. This was not on a wide scale, for it is often barely detectable in pollen sequences, but in certain habitats the effect of Mesolithic man can be detected. Simmons (1969) has demonstrated this for the higher areas of Dartmoor and the North York Moors, and there is archaeological evidence that some of our southern heaths were created in the Boreal period (Keef *et al.*, 1965) and have remained treeless ever since. In general, however, the land was forest-covered through the Atlantic period and it was not until the latter half of the 4th millennium BC that the first inroads of agriculture were manifested. When they did appear, they were surprisingly widely distributed and not noticeably orientated towards the Continent (Clark, 1965), some of the earliest dates coming in fact from Ireland (Smith *et al.*, 1971).

The impact of agriculture was not always followed by a permanent change in the vegetation. The early clearings were not extensive, and as in many other 'swidden' systems they were allowed to revert to forest, a process which may have happened several times. Land was cleared for both arable and pastoral purposes (Turner, 1965), the former occurring mainly on the uplands and the latter on the lighter and lower ground. These clearances were often followed by soil degradation of one sort or another and this, combined with the continued ecological pressures exerted through the use of fire and through grazing, resulted in the progressive retreat of the forests. In some areas the uplands were largely deforested by the Bronze Age, and by the Iron Age the intensification of agriculture in such places gave non-arboreal pollen/arboreal pollen ratios in the peat deposits of the time comparable with those of pollen analyses of modern sediments (Hayes, 1967). Hazel became the most widespread woody species, presumably along the valley forest-margins, in holts, and in protected places. It gradually declined through Roman and subsequent periods and did not reach its present-day low levels until the end of the medieval period. The heavier soils in the valley remained clothed in forest and were not cleared until the introduction of the iron plough by the Romans (Darby, 1956; Bowen, n.d.).

Whilst it is not strictly accurate to say that prehistoric man determined the character of much of our landscape today, it can be said that by bringing about major changes in the landscape he did cast a shadow before him. For instance, once the acidic uplands had been extensively cleared of forest, potential future land use was almost predetermined. Regrowth of trees, if it could occur at all, was very slow, so restoration of soil fertility scarcely took place, whereas the cleared land was directly usable as rough grazing, and this has remained its use till today, despite changes in the flora and often in the type of stock raised. At the same time, extensive open areas of this type are a fire risk, and in any case fire is regularly used to promote new growth for the grazing stock, so that, apart from the deleterious effects of fire on the fertility of the soil, it effectively prevents the establishment of woody vegetation. Similar connections exist between other types of countryside as seen today and their origin in prehistoric time, though the historical details can be quite different. In chalk country, for instance, cereal agriculture was probably a major feature of the prehistoric period (Simpson, 1971), particularly in the Bronze and Iron Ages (Evans, 1973), and it has recurred from time to time since, interspersed with long periods of pastoralism during which the characteristic chalk downland flora that we prize so highly was able to develop.

It is often not appreciated that our so-called 'heritage' of the beautiful and interesting chalk flora is really an artifact. In the primeval condition of this country the chalk and limestone hills would have been forested and the specialized communities of light-demanding plants of the so-called 'chalk flora' would have been very restricted in their occurrence. As we are seeing today, their full development demands short grazed turf; even the post-myxomatosis tall growth of upright brome (*Zerna erecta*) has reduced this flora drastically. Prehistoric man would have contributed to our heritage of interesting plants not only by creating conditions which enabled them to reach such an abundance, but also by adding to their number of species. It is difficult today to say which species are truly native and which were introduced into this country by man. Sometimes the palaeobotanical record can tell us which were here before the immigrations of agricultural man. Some of the weeds of arable land, for instance, were present in the Late-glacial (Godwin, 1956). They are plants which cannot tolerate competition from established vegetation, especially if it is light-excluding forest, and it was not until man eliminated this overhead competition that such plants were able to come into their own. Examples are the plantains (*Plantago lanceolata, P. major* and *P. media*), knotgrass (*Polygonum aviculare*), the buttercups (*Ranunculus acris* and *R. repens*) and the dandelion (*Taraxacum officinale*). But apart from this effect, agricultural man must have brought new species into the country, some deliberately, some accidentally. All our staple cereal crops were, of course, introduced. Wheat and barley were domesticated in the Near East from wild grasses alien to Western Europe (Zohary, 1969), whereas oats and rye came into cultivation through being successful weeds in arable fields, both being domesticated before reaching this country. With the seed of these crops must have come the seed of some of the weeds of cornfields, as discussed in some detail by Salisbury (1964) and Godwin (1956), who list species that were probably introduced into the country at critical periods from the Neolithic onwards. Among Neolithic arrivals were charlock (*Sinapis arvensis*) and fumitory (*Fumaria officinalis*); in the Bronze Age came red deadnettle (*Lamium purpureum*) and poppy (*Papaver rhoeas*), whilst among the Romans' gifts to Britain were such familiar pests as ground elder (*Aegopodium podagraria*) and the sow-thistles (*Sonchus asper* and *S. oleraceus*). Not only were such plants introduced, but they were spread by man's movement across the country. We tend to underestimate this movement, but the identification of the sources of the stone of which Neolithic axes were made shows that men moved very great distances. Even if such movement were by specialist craftsmen and traders and not by the general mass of the population, this could have been a means of spreading plants. Salisbury suggested that the Roman roads provided pathways of movement, introduced plants establishing themselves on the verges of the aggers and being carried great distances by the traffic in much the same way that weeds spread along our railways today. The fact that in Roman times the horses were not iron, but consumed vegetation, no doubt added to the effectiveness of the dispersal.

In suggesting that much of our heritage of plant life is perhaps more artificial than natural I do not in any way wish to denigrate its interest, but there is a sense in which the glamour and fascination of this flora detracts from other aspects of our heritage. It is doubtful, for instance, whether there is any woodland in its natural state now left in Britain. There are small areas, in the New Forest, East Anglia, Scotland and perhaps a few other places, where woods exist today on land that has been wooded since the prehistoric period and perhaps even before man started practising agriculture. Such woods are indeed a priceless heritage and should be rigorously protected against any form of exploitation or—equally damaging—well-intentioned management (Dimbleby, 1971). We have lost forever the unbroken forest which stretched from one end of the country to the other and created within itself a stability which enabled it to develop its ecological richness. The fragmented woods of today do not represent true forest conditions; nevertheless they contain a great deal of information about the past, much of it completely unstudied. Nor does our concept of gnarled trees represent the form of the dominants of the primeval forest; these would have been tall, straight and unbranched up to the crown (Dimbleby, 1967).

Perhaps more important than the changes that prehistoric man brought about in the vegetation were the changes he produced in the soil. Evidence of this comes from various sources. Indirect evidence may come from the succession of vegetation recorded by the pollen analysis of peat-bogs, lake muds and other stratified deposits; the replacement of deciduous forest by *Calluna* heath, for example, not only indicates a change from forest to open conditions, but also a change to more acidic soil (Godwin, 1944). Analyses of lake muds, for example the work of Mackereth (1965) on Windermere, have also indicated changes in the soil conditions of a catchment area, and these in turn have been tentatively correlated with successive periods of land use from the Neolithic onwards. Similar changes can often be inferred from the pollen analysis of mineral soils, especially acid ones (Dimbleby, 1961a). Here the pollen is progressively washed down into the soil, giving a broad separation of pollen of different ages. Not only may this reveal changes of plant communities, but the way the pollen is distributed may give a clue to soil changes. Havinga (1963) has shown how the pollen in a soil containing soil-mixing animals may be so mixed that the age pattern is destroyed, but as the soil was acidified, causing these animals to disappear, a new stratified pattern appeared superimposed on the background of earlier mixed pollen. In many soil profiles the pollen record does not date back as far as the primary deciduous forest, but begins with Zone VIIb* hazel woodland. The reason for this is probably that in the primary woodland the pH is too high (pH>*ca.* 5·5) for the good preservation of pollen, but that as a result of deforestation the acidity increased and the pollen record began.

Acidification of the soils on base-poor parent material would have been brought about by a number of processes all acting to the same end. The destruction of deep-rooting trees would curtail the enrichment of the surface of the soil by bases brought up from the deeper layers. The use of fire would release nutrients in the form of readily soluble salts, some of which would inevitably be lost in drainage, especially in soils poor in colloids. The taking of crops and of animal produce would deplete the soil reserves to an extent probably greater than would be controlled by any manurial practices used by prehistoric man. And as the soil degraded, the vegetation which came in—bracken, heather, etc.—would itself produce a more acidic humus type of soil than the original mixed deciduous forest and so continue the process. The increased fire hazard offered by such ecosystems has, as we have seen, ensured that the processes of soil degradation have often been continued up to the present day: in some moorland areas the land is now suffering severe erosion—what happens is that the equilibrium of the soil/ vegetation system finally collapses. It is often assumed that such drastic deterioration must have been brought about by climatic change, but there is no reason to believe that there is any other cause than the continuation for some 4,000–5,000 years of those processes first initiated by prehistoric man, though climatic deterioration such as that at the end of the Bronze Age would have intensified a process that was already well advanced.

So far only the indirect evidence for soil changes following prehistoric man's impact on the landscape has been mentioned, but there is also abundant direct evidence. All over the British Isles there are earthworks left behind by people from Neolithic, Bronze Age, Romano-British and Roman

* A pollen diagram covering a long period of time shows a succession of phases, each with its characteristic pollen composition. Such phases are called pollen zones (see, Godwin, 1956).

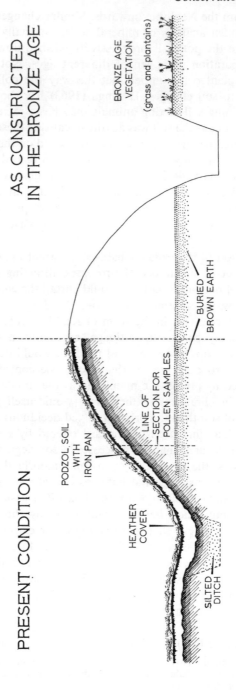

SECTION OF A BRONZE AGE BARROW

PRESENT CONDITION

PODZOL SOIL
WITH
IRON PAN

HEATHER
COVER

LINE OF
SECTION FOR
POLLEN SAMPLES

SILTED
DITCH

AS CONSTRUCTED
IN THE BRONZE AGE

BRONZE AGE
VEGETATION
(grass and plantains)

BURIED
BROWN EARTH

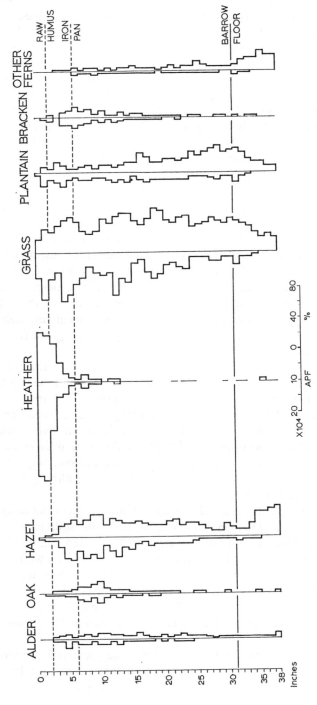

**Figure 18.1.** Diagrammatic representation of a Bronze Age barrow, showing condition at the time of construction and today. The histogram shows the pollen distribution through the mound (APF=absolute pollen frequency (grains/gm); %=percentage of total pollen plus fern spores).

times and later. Apart from the fact that there are sometimes heavy concentrations of round barrows on land which today is too poor for agricultural use, beneath the earthworks themselves the old land surface is frequently preserved and we can actually see and study the contemporary soil profiles (Figure 18.1 and Dimbleby, 1962). They may not be in a completely natural state. For instance, in some cases the old soil has been truncated by land use or by erosion; and allowance has to be made for the influence of the overlying material, which varies according to its thickness and its physico-chemical composition. Nevertheless, a buried soil profile is always instructive, and when it is augmented by additional information based on organic remains associated with the land surface, a convincing ecological picture can often be built up. These other remains vary according to the nature of the site. On calcareous soils the evidence comes from charcoil, land mollusc shells and bones; on acid soils charcoal is also preserved, but pollen is the most important source of evidence. In conditions where aerobic decomposition has been restricted—mainly waterlogged situations, or under massive earth works such as Silbury Hill—other forms of organic remains may be found remarkably well preserved. Pieces of leaf and plant stem, seeds and exoskeletons of Coleoptera may be present in considerable quantity and may be of great ecological significance. It is a surprising fact that plant remains extracted from such situations may still be green (e.g. moss from Wilsford Shaft near Stonehenge).

One of the lessons to be learnt from buried soils is that the process of degradation, whilst undoubtedly a long one, has not been an even one, for there have been periods when the changes were rapid. For instance, studies on the North York Moors (Dimbleby, 1962) showed that soils in all stages from acid brown forest soils to thin iron-pan soils could be found under round barrows of the Middle Bronze Age period. In one case leached and unleached profiles were found under one barrow, suggesting that the development of a bleached $A_2$ was a rapid progress although the B horizon seemed to take much longer to mature.

It can also be demonstrated that early land use was frequently associated with soil erosion (Dimbleby, 1961b; 1972). Chalk soils in particular were susceptible. Not only are the buried profiles often remarkably shallow, suggesting truncation, but dry valleys are often choked with many feet of topsoil has been washed off the surrounding hills. The pottery and mollusc remains found in these deposits show that they were largely laid down during the prehistoric period, though later deposits may overlie them. Lynchets, too, are probably evidence of soil movement during prehistoric farming.

Earthworks and old field systems should be preserved wherever possible in nature reserves. They hold information that we can get from no other source (Tubbs and Dimbleby, 1965; Dimbleby and Speight, 1969). It is even possible to detect differences in phosphate in the soil dating back to the original use of prehistoric fields (Hatt, 1931), and old plough marks may also be preserved (Evans, 1971) which pose some puzzling problems about early methods of arable farming.

Finally, it is important to emphasize the value of conserving ancient woodlands wherever they can be found, for the impact of early man can be traced with some completeness and the resulting increase of soil acidity demonstrated (see also Tubbs, Chapter 9). It is sometimes argued that the effect of man was merely to hasten a process which was taking place anyway, and it is undeniable that acidification is part of the natural process of soil maturation through the post-glacial. This has been elegantly demonstrated by Iversen (1969), who has made effective use of a relict wood, the forest of Draved in Denmark, which he showed to have a forest floor with an $A_0$ horizon dating back to prehistoric times. Nothing quite comparable to this is known to exist in Britain, but it is my belief that we also have ancient stands which could be made to reveal their ecological and pedological history. By their very nature, archaeological sites are always man-modified, so we have to look to other sources for information about the conditions before man took over. Ancient woodlands are one such source; they offer the possibility of establishing the soil/plant relationships of the primary forest and revealing the processes of soil maturation which may have been taking place. It is of fundamental importance, especially in forestry, to know whether there was ever a balance between vegetation and soil; or whether the acidification was progressive and inevitable, even without the intervention of man (Dimbleby and Gill, 1955).

Ancient woodlands are standards against which we can measure the changes which have taken place in the countryside. We are aware that great changes have taken place, and we suspect that over much of Britain these changes have been accompanied by ecological degradation of vegetation and soil. But unless we have some standard by which to compare the present we cannot do more than guess at the past, and in particular we cannot disentangle anthropogenic influences from normal developmental processes. Though none of these woods is now in a completely natural state since they are inevitably degraded to some extent, they may contain a record of their own history, and in any case they are much nearer to the virgin state than any other communities we have today. We need to conserve fragments of not only the recent past but also those rare remnants of the far distant past.

## REFERENCES

Bowen, H. C. (n.d.). *Ancient Fields*, British Association for the Advancement of Science, London, 80 pp.

Clark, J. G. D. (1965). Radiocarbon dating and the expansion of farming culture from the Near East over Europe, *Proc. prehist. Soc.*, **31**, 58–73.

Darby, H. C. (1956). The clearing of woodland Europe, in: *Man's Role in Changing the Face of the Earth*, (ed.) W. L. Thomas, University of Chicago Press, Chicago, 183-216.

Dimbleby, G. W. (1961a). Soil pollen analysis, *J. Soil Sci.*, **12**, 1–11.

Dimbleby, G. W. (1961b). Transported material in the soil profile, *J. Soil Sci.*, **12**, 12–22.

Dimbleby, G. W. (1962). Development of British heathlands and their soils, *Oxford Forestry Mem.*, **23**, 120 pp.

Dimbleby, G. W. (1967). *Plants and Archaeology*, Baker, London, 187 pp.

Dimbleby, G. W. (1971). The ancient and ornamental woods of the New Forest, *Ecologist*, **1** (9), 16–18.

Dimbleby, G. W. (1972). The impact of early man on his environment, in: *Population and Pollution*, (eds.) P. R. Cox and J. Peel, Academic Press, London, 7–13.

Dimbleby, G. W., and Gill, J. M. (1955). The occurrence of podzols under deciduous woodland in the New Forest, *Forestry*, **28**, 95–106.

Dimbleby, G. W., and Speight, M. C. D. (1969). Buried soils, *Adv. Sci.*, **26**, 203–5.

Evans, J. G. (1971). Habitat change on the calcareous soils of Britain: The impact of Neolithic man, in: *Economy and Settlement in Neolithic and Early Bronze Age Britain and Europe*, (ed.) D. D. A. Simpson, Leicester University Press, Leicester, 27–73.

Evans, J. G. (1973). *Land Snails in Archaeology*, Seminar Press, London, 436 pp.

Godwin, H. (1944). Age and origin of the 'Breckland' heaths of East Anglia, *Nature*, **154**, 6.

Godwin, H. (1956). *History of the British Flora*, Cambridge University Press, Cambridge, 384 pp.

Godwin, H., Walker, D., and Willis, E. H. (1957). Radiocarbon dating and postglacial vegetational history: Scaleby Moss, *New Phytol.*, **147**, 352–66.

Hatt, G. (1931). Prehistoric fields in Jylland, *Acta Archaeol.*, **2**, 117–58.

Havinga, A. J. (1963). A palynological investigation of soil profiles developed in cover sand, *Meded. Landbouwhogeschool Wageningen*, **63**, 1–93.

Hayes, R. H. (1967). The Chambered Cairn and adjacent monuments on Great Ayton Moor, North East Yorkshire. *Scarborough & District Archaeol. Soc. Res. Rept. No.* **7**, 44 pp.

Iversen, J. (1969). Retrogressive development of a forest ecosystem demonstrated by pollen diagrams from fossil mor., *Oikos Suppl.*, **12**, 35–49.

Keef, P. A. M., Wymer, J. J., and Dimbleby, G. W. (1965). A Mesolithic site on Iping Common, Sussex, England, *Proc. prehist. Soc.*, **31**, 85–92.

Mackereth, F. J. H. (1965). Chemical investigation of lake sediments and their interpretation, *Proc. Roy. Soc. B.*, **161**, 295–309.

Pennington, W. (1969). *The History of British Vegetation*, English Universities Press, London, 152 pp.

Salisbury, Sir E. (1964). *Weeds and Aliens*, 2nd edn, Collins, London, 384 pp.

Simmons, I. G. (1969). Evidence of vegetation changes associated with Mesolithic man in Britain, in: *The Domestication and Exploitation of Plants and Animals*, (eds.) P. J. Ucko and G. W. Dimbleby, Duckworth, London, 113–19.

Simpson, D. D. A. (1971). *Economy and Settlement in Neolithic and Early Bronze Age Britain and Europe*, Leicester University Press, Leicester, 186 pp.

Smith, A. G., Pilcher, J. R. and Pearson, G. W. (1971). New radiocarbon dates from Ireland, *Antiquity*, **45**, 97–102.

Tubbs, C. R., and Dimbleby, G. W. (1965). Early agriculture in the New Forest, *Adv. Sci.*, **22**, 88–97.

Turner, J. (1965). A contribution to the history of forest clearance, *Proc. Roy. Soc. B.*, **161**, 343–54.

Zohary, D. (1969). The progenitors of wheat and barley in relation to domestication and agricultural dispersal in the Old World, in: *The Domestication and Exploitation of Plants and Animals,* (eds.) P. J. Ucko and G. W. Dimbleby, Duckworth, London, 47–66.

# CHAPTER 19

# The Legacy of Historical Times

JOHN SHEAIL

In selecting plant communities for conservation and in deciding on management policies for them the conservationist needs to make close reference to the past in order to understand the character and composition of wildlife communities and wilderness areas today. When were they established, and how were they affected by man's use and management of the land? It is also relevant to ask how man regarded wildlife and wilderness areas in the past. How did he perceive the land and its natural resources? The study of the natural environments of the past, and the evolution of the present patterns, is frequently described as historical ecology, whose value in the field of conservation is discussed in this chapter.

## SURVIVAL OF COMMUNITIES

Nature reserves are usually created in order to protect their wild plant and animal communities from current and future changes in land use and management. For example the nature reserve in the Minsmere marshes of Suffolk is kept flooded in order to preserve the rich and varied birdlife and the Royal Society for the Protection of Birds has taken a lease in order to prevent the land from being reclaimed. The Nature Conservancy acquired 150 hectares of Yarner Wood in Devon in order to safeguard one of the few surviving examples of sessile oakwood within the Dartmoor National Park. These acquisitions were deliberate attempts to protect areas from contemporary and future economic pressures since the conservationist is trying to preserve living ecosystems which are in effect relics of the past, and which would be destroyed if the prime use of the areas ceased to be nature conservation.

Conservation is necessary not simply because the communities are long established—the interest is not entirely antiquarian—but frequently there is a coincidence between the age of the communities and their floristic richness. Devils Dyke in Cambridgeshire was constructed between the fourth and eighth centuries and has remained ever since an 'unploughable artificial habitat'. John Ray recorded finding the bloody cranesbill *Geranium, sanguineum,* on the Dyke in the 1650s, and today the plant survives, together with the pasque flower, *Pulsatilla vulgaris,* the spotted cat's ear, *Hypochoeris maculata,* and the lizard orchid, *Himantoglossum hircinum.* These rare and distinctive species cannot withstand disturbance by ploughing and they are extremely slow in colonizing new areas. The pasque flower, for example, occurs on only 27 sites in England, on all of which there is no evidence of ploughing in historic times, and it has become extinct on 25 other sites where ploughing has occurred (Wells, 1968). Thus in the study of these species, and of floristically rich grasslands in general, the botanist must often go to the relics of an earlier land-use system.

Attempts to measure the relationship between the age of the community and floristic richness have found, for example, that hedgerows established in medieval times are more likely to be richer than those planted during the 'enclosure period' of the eighteenth and nineteenth centuries (Hooper, 1971). In a study of 227 hedges in the midland counties, Devon and Lincolnshire, the number of species present in a length of 27·3 m increased by about one per century. There was a correlation coefficient of $+0·85$ and the regression equation for predicting the age of the hedge came to $X = 110Y + 30$, where $X$ represented the age of the hedge in years and $Y$ the number of species per 27·3 m of hedge. The absolute number of shrub species will vary according to whether one or more were planted when the hedge was established: for example there was a tradition of planting mixed hedges in Shropshire.

## ORIGINS AND AGE OF COMMUNITIES

It is important to find out when plant communities were first established. In a few cases this is relatively easy, as, for example, on the south coast of England where, during Christmas 1839, nearly 80 million tons of Chalk and Upper Greensand became detached from 0·8 km of cliffline between Axmouth and Lyme Regis (Arber, 1940). The fall was caused by prolonged rainfall which had washed out much of the Foxmould Sands from beneath the Chalk and had converted the remainder into a quicksand. There was little effort to reclaim the displaced farmland on the former cliff-top, and the site of 322 hectares has now been declared a National Nature Reserve in order to protect the plant and animal communities which have evolved since that date.

More usually the communities have been established over a longer period of time, and it is difficult to distinguish the effects of natural processes from man-induced changes. The sand dunes and saltings of the Saltfleetby–

Theddlethorpe National Nature Reserve in Lindsey on the east coast, for example, have formed over the last seven centuries, largely as a result of coastal accretion (Robinson, 1970). The twelfth to fourteenth centuries were usually stormy, and large quantities of glacial material were swept on to

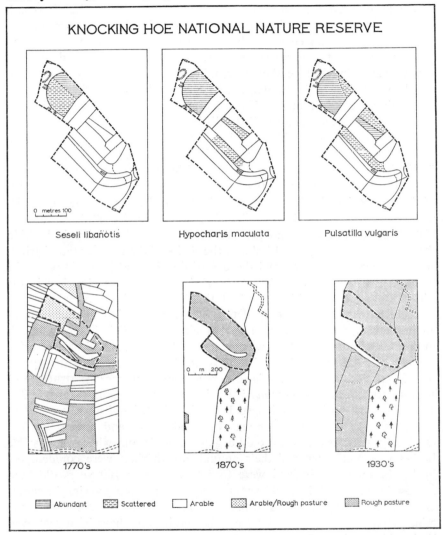

**Figure 19.1.** Knocking Hoe National Nature Reserve, Bedfordshire, showing the distribution of various species as related to past land use patterns. The land use patterns for the 1930s and 1870s are taken from the Land Utilization Survey and Ordnance survey respectively, and that for the 1770s is from an original estate map in the Bedfordshire Record Office. (Biological data supplied by T. C. E. Wells.)

the shoreline, to form storm beaches on which blown sand accumulated as dunes, reaching a height of 15·2 m in some places. Up to this time, the Withern Eau flowed into the sea at the north end of the present-day reserve, but gradually the mouth became silted up and in the 1340s the stream was artificially directed northwards into Saltfleet Haven. During the nineteenth century, extensive tracts of saltmarsh were reclaimed for pasture and, as part of this work, an enclosure bank was constructed south of Saltfleet. This had the effect of accelerating accretion and a new line of dunes was formed, parallel with the earlier system. The two formations are 45 m apart, and between them a freshwater marsh has developed, which is today of outstanding biological interest. Thus, as in many coastal situations, human and natural processes cannot easily be distinguished.

There is frequently a wide variation in the age of the communities on a reserve, reflecting differences in past land use. The reserve at Knocking Hoe, Bedfordshire (Figure 19.1), was established in 1958 and the annual report of the Nature Conservancy of that year described the site as ' a small relict' of the former downland: 'The turf is thought to be of very ancient origin, and has probably remained undisturbed by cultivation at least through historic times.' In fact, the greater part of the site has been ploughed within the last 300 years. Figure 19.1 shows the limits of the reserve, the distribution of three plant species, and the use of the site and its environs in the 1930s, the 1870s and the 1770s. Parts of the reserve were ploughed in the mid-1950s and resown with a cocksfoot, timothy and white clover mixture.

There have been attempts to determine the age of individual plants as an indication of the minimum age of their habitat. This is most difficult in the case of grasslands because no way has been discovered of measuring the age of herbaceous plants, but it is much easier to assess the age of 'woody species', as for example in a recent study of the age structure of juniper scrub, *Juniperus communis* L., in southern *England* (Ward, 1973). The age of the bushes was judged by their height, basal girth, amount of annual growth of shoots, amount of dead wood and foliage colour. Obviously, these features are only a general guide and whenever possible bushes were cut down and their annual growth rings were counted. No bushes in southern England were found to be over 100 years old, and frequently bushes of 70 to 90 years of age were found growing in stands of dead and dying bushes. The presence of such specimens indicates the minimum age of the community, since the scrub would have been destroyed if ploughing had occurred. The bushes may also suggest the pattern of land management at the time of their establishment and up to the present day, for there is evidence that germination and seedling growth tend to occur where there is bare ground, with little competition from other vegetation, and with no intensive shading. Seedlings and young plants will die if they are grazed by rabbits, deer, sheep or cattle. These juniper bushes character-istically occur in even-aged stands, which may indicate that only rarely has the habitat been relatively open and free of grazing animals. It is rare for all age-classes to be present, except on such steep slopes and shallow soils as cliff faces and quarry walls. In this example it can be seen that judicious use of field data can reveal a wealth of information about past land use.

## NATURE OF HISTORICAL EVIDENCE

Evidence gained in the field can frequently be supplemented and corrobor-ated by that obtained in old books and papers found in libraries, record offices and private archives. The grounds of the National Nature Reserve at Aston Rowant, for example, are shown on a sixteenth-century map of Lewknor in Oxfordshire (1)* to have had grazing on the chalk pasture of the scarp and crest of the Chilterns when the sheep were not needed for manuring the arable fields of the scarp-foot zone. An agreement drawn up in 1765 between the 11 principal farmers of Lewknor expressly forbade the ploughing-up of the sheep-walks (2), but this policy was modified in the nineteenth century, when farmers used greater quantities of fertilizer and became less dependent on sheep manure. The first edition of the Ordnance Survey 1:2,500 map suggests that by the 1870s most of the present-day reserve was under pasture, but significantly the lower slopes had been ploughed along with most of the rest of the chalk grassland.

Although old books and manuscripts are a valuable source of information, the ecologist should be aware of their limitations. Few printed books identify the use and management of individual fields and open spaces: for example, the Board of Agriculture report for Oxfordshire, published in 1813, contains an excellent description of the grasslands of the county (Young, 1813), but it is quite impossible to deduce the use and management of individual meadows which are of interest to the botanist today. Frequently, the ecolo-gist finds there are no extant documents for a field although plenty for a neighbouring one; he should beware of assuming they were managed in a similar manner because the better-documented sites tended to belong to the more progressive farmers who compiled and kept written records. It is worth noting that many landowners, occupiers and labourers were illiterate and so extremely unlikely to leave detailed accounts of the land they knew so well, and even those who could write were very selective as to what they recorded. Frequently, they distinguished between different tree species

---

* (1), (2), etc., are references to documentary sources listed at the end of the chapter.

because the value of the timber varied, but few recorded the presence of such plants as the snakes-head fritillary because this was hardly relevant to the economic well-being of the estate. Wherever possible, every effort should be made to check the information gained from documentary sources. The enclosure award for Great Raveley, Huntingdonshire, dated 1778, does not indicate woodland on the site of the present-day reserve of Raveley Wood (3). This may indicate that the woodland did not exist, but it is equally likely that the surveyor omitted the information since it was not essential to the purpose of his map.

In a recent study of two National Nature Reserves in Holme and Woodwalton Fens, Huntingdonshire, information was obtained from a variety of sources. A local landowner wrote a general account of the area in the first half of the nineteenth century (Heathcote, 1876), and William Wells (1860; 1870) described how over 1,250 hectares of peatland were drained and reclaimed for arable farming between 1842 and 1870. The Ordnance Survey prepared large-scale maps of the area in 1887, 1902 and 1926, which identify in a stylized manner the distribution of pasture, scrub and woodland. More detailed maps may be compiled from the Tithe Commutation Survey of the 1840s and the Land Use Survey of the 1930s, which indicate the use of each field and open space in the area. There is an estate map of 1777 which includes the site of Holme Fen (4), and both reserves are shown on a land use map prepared for agricultural purposes in 1917 (5). There are a few valuable references in the estate papers of local landowners, for the documentation of the Holme Wood estate contains leases for land in Holme Fen before drainage took place (6), and records have been kept of the personal recollections of men who lived or worked in the area during their youth. Mr. Maidment, for example, was employed in the 1870s in establishing plantations on two parts of the present-day reserve at Holme Fen (7). Several naturalists made reference to the distinctive flora and fauna of the undrained fen, and their published papers and manuscript notes describe the species found growing in the peat fen and marsh grasslands. The Society for the Promotion of Nature Reserves acquired parts of Woodwalton Fen from 1919 onwards, and the records of the Society contain field reports which have become valuable historical records.

These references make it possible to distinguish the salient features of the sites over the last 200 years. Both reserves were fenland pastures during the eighteenth and early nineteenth centuries, but parts of the Holme Fen reserve were sown with wheat during the period 1850 to 1870 after the land had been drained, allowing farmers to cultivate the fenland soils with little risk of their crops being flooded. Significantly, however, landlords and farmers did not succeed in reclaiming all the fenland during the nineteenth century. A small part of Holme and Woodwalton Fen may not ever have been cultivated, and the more marginal agricultural soils reverted to pasture by the turn of the century. Belts and groups of trees, mainly birch and alder but including oak, Norway spruce, Scots pine and Japanese larch, were planted. Holme Fen was used as a pheasant covert, and this phase in land use prevented the fenland species from being eliminated by ploughing. The plant communities on Woodwalton Fen were affected by the extraction of peat: A. J. Wilmott commented in the early 1900s on how the rare and distinctive *Viola stagnina* flourished on the remains of the most recent peat workings, where there was less competition from other species. During this century, the sites have been influenced by considerable improvements to the drainage of neighbouring farmland and the consequent fall of the water-table, which have encouraged the spread of scrub species and the decline of the characteristic fenland plants. Today both reserves are surrounded by arable land and they are not truly representative of the fenland environ-ment of 150 or more years ago. It can be seen that they are much modified relicts of the past.

## CHANGES IN LAND USE AND MANAGEMENT

Many reserves contain species which are not otherwise found in the neighbourhood, and if the vegetation of the reserves were destroyed there would be little or no chance of these species recolonizing the area. It is relevant to ask how long they have occupied such an isolated position. At Knocking Hoe in Bedfordshire, for example, it is clear from Figure 19.1 that there was no pasture land adjacent to the site of the present-day reserve in the 1870s, although some of the cultivated land had reverted to pasture by the 1930s. A wider study of the heathlands of east Dorset and west Hampshire was undertaken in the late 1950s, and their distribution was compared with that shown on the first Ordnance Survey maps of those counties, surveyed in 1811 (Moore, 1962). The earlier survey was, of course, much less accurate, and the definition of heathland may have varied from one surveying party to another, and from that adopted in the more recent survey. Bearing these qualifications in mind, the area of heathland appears to have fallen from 30,000 hectares in 1811 to about 10,000 hectares in 1960, and the previously continuous areas of heath were fragmented into over 100 pieces of at least 4 hectares. It is difficult to measure in precise terms the effects of these changes on species composition because there are almost no quantitative data on the plants and animals of the earlier period. In order to overcome this difficulty, a study was made of the persistence of those species which are thought to be characteristic of the heathland com-munities of Dorset. It was found that such species as *Erica tetralix*, the grayling butterfly, *Eumenis semele*, and the stonechat, *Saxicola torquata*, occurred on areas which were grazed, but were absent from mature conifer plantations and cultivated land. There was evidence that fewer characteristic species were present on the more isolated fragments of heath.

It is possible for a plant community to remain undisturbed by ploughing or afforestation, and yet change completely in its structure and composition owing to a change in management. For this reason, the ecologist wants to know how regularly the meadows were mown, the pastures grazed, the coppicewood cut, or the sedge beds harvested. If it is hard enough to obtain this information for the present day, it is even more difficult to find the data for the past. Although many farmers made a note of the crops planted in each field, they rarely recorded the duration and intensity of grazing in the pastures. In view of these problems, the grassland botanist is often interested in the flora of the commonable meadows, or Lammas lands, where the incidence of grazing and mowing was strictly regulated; these sites were generally used in a uniform manner over a long period of time, and detailed records have been kept. The grassland was subdivided every year and each farmer was responsible for harvesting the hay crop on his allotment. Animals were excluded from the commonable meadow during this period, but on August 12th, or some other fixed date, the hay had to be removed and the livestock were admitted. The animals of each commoner were allowed to graze the entire meadow, irrespective or how the hay rights had been awarded. This complicated system of management made it possible for many people to share the valuable grasslands, but it also tended to inhibit any further changes or improvements in the use of the sites. The meadows were never ploughed, and apart from an occasional application of farmyard manure fertilizers were rarely applied.

Former management practices have had such a profound influence on plant and animal communities that they are frequently the most convenient means of classification. Alluvial grasslands, for example, may be subdivided into three categories (Wells, 1969). A *flood-meadow* is a river meadow which is naturally flooded whenever the river is in spate, and can be distinguished from a *water-meadow* which was drained and flooded at the discretion of the farmer, by means of a system of weirs and hatches, carriers and drains. The number of plant species in the grasslands probably declined under the impact of controlled flooding, efficient drainage, intensive grazing and the annual harvest of hay (Sheail, 1971). The third category of alluvial grasslands, the *washlands,* was artificially created in an attempt to control winter flooding on the lower stretches of such rivers as the Nene and the Ouse in the East Anglian fens. The floodwaters which would have flowed across the potentially fertile floodplains were diverted into linear washlands, bounded by high embankments, which acted as reservoirs until the level of the river water had fallen; on the Ouse the washes are 33·6 km long and up to 0·8 km wide. The frequently flooded grasslands are famous for their wildfowl and for such plants as the bur marigold, *Bidens cernua,* the Marsh stitchwort, *Stellaria palustris,* and the great spearwort, *Ranunculus lingua.* At first, the washland was occasionally flooded by seawater, but under the acts of 1756 and 1812 earthworks were constructed which excluded seawater, and this has caused the decline of such maritime species as *Aster tripolium* and *Scirpus maritimus*—indeed the former plant has not been recorded since the turn of the century.

Such studies of former management practices help to elucidate the current trends in plant communities. In a recent survey of the unenclosed woodlands of the New Forest, three distinct generations of trees were identified, dating from the periods 1663 to 1764, 1858 to 1923, and since 1938 (Peterken and Tubbs, 1965). A study was carried out to see whether these periods coincided with a reduction in the grazing pressure of herbivores. Since there is a marked variation in the impact of the different types of herbivore, the population figures were expressed in 'feeding units', so that five units represented a pony, three units a deer and one unit a cow. Unfortunately, the data are scanty and often the figures are only crude estimates, but nevertheless it was found that the browsing pressure fell to 0·28 units per acre (0·4 hectare) between 1884 and 1893, when there were signs of regeneration throughout the unenclosed woodlands. It rose to 0·40 units per acre between 1760 and 1850, when there is no evidence of regeneration. Today, the grazing pressure is 0·37 units per acre, which generally permits regeneration in open conditions but prevents it in woodland. The relationship between regeneration and grazing pressure is highly complex, but clearly all regeneration would cease if the current pressure increased.

## MAN'S ATTITUDE TOWARDS WILDLIFE AND LANDSCAPE

There is little evidence in historical records before the Victorian period of a concern for wildlife and wilderness areas *per se*. In 1851, the *London Illustrated News* produced a feature on the drainage of Whittlesea Mere and the reclamation of the Huntingdonshire fens (Bede, 1851). Far from regretting the loss of amenity and natural history interest, it regarded the project as a fine example of contemporary enterprise, for the loss of distinctive and irreplaceable wildlife and scenery was thought to be small compared with the expected profits from the cultivation of the area. It was only later in the century, when the fields proved less profitable than expected, that some observers began to question the wisdom of the changes that had occurred. Pell (1899) described the site of the former lake as 'a dreary flat of black arable land, with hardly a jack snipe to give it a charm and characteristic attraction'.

The only circumstances in which men tried to protect wildlife and the natural ecosystem were when they felt their livelihood and well-being were being endangered. Thus, Parliament tried to regulate the use of timber as an industrial fuel in the sixteenth century. 'Iron mills and furnaces' made such heavy demands on woodland for fuel that there was often a local shortage of domestic fuel and timber for building purposes. The Elizabethan parliaments (8) tried to regulate these demands by forbidding, for example, the cutting of trees for iron-smelting within the vicinity of navigable rivers, but the measures largely failed because they proved impossible to enforce.

Landowners attempted to conserve the natural resources of their estates by drawing up leases in which they ensured that their tenants would leave the land as productive as it was at the outset of the lease. This was demonstrated by a lease of 1653 for a stretch of the river Ouse in Huntingdonshire which was owned by the Borough of Godmanchester (9). The bailiffs of the Borough forbade the tenant to use fishing nets with a small mesh so that immature fish would not be caught and the value of the river would not decline. The tenant had to clear the water of excessive weed, maintain the banks and protect the osier beds which supplied the willow for basket-making. He had to assist the bailiffs in looking after the swans and take part in the annual census. In this way, landowners sustained the value of their property and, incidentally, the richness and diversity of wildlife.

Although most land was managed for sustenance and profit, some landowners tried to enhance the appearance of their estates by preserving, adapting and replacing the vegetation according to their tastes in landscape design. The fifth Earl of Abingdon converted part of his estate at Wytham, Oxfordshire, into an ornamental park. 'The original pattern of semi-natural woodland, common and farm fields was added to or overlaid by a new design of curved belts and patches of trees' (Elton, 1966). The establishment and management of these parkland areas extended over many decades and generations. Often, landowners found that amenity planting was compatible with commercial afforestation. William Salvin, a landowner in Durham, recorded how he felled many of the trees planted by his grandfather in the seventeenth century and proudly recalled that there was no damage to the appearance of the parkland since every tree was replaced by a new sapling (10).

The ecologist must be careful in accepting the usual distinction between domesticated and wild animals, because the terms often refer to the ownership of the animals rather than how they actually lived. Frequently, domestic stock received little support from farmers during a hard winter and there were heavy losses of lambs when grass growth was delayed in spring, while on the other hand many so-called wild species received some measure of support. The sum of £20 was spent on providing hay for the deer of Cranborne Chase, Windsor, in 1706 (11), and the rabbits of Knebworth Warren, Hertfordshire, were given browsewood during the 1720s (12) in order to prevent the animals from starving during hard winters. Some sportsmen became fine naturalists while in pursuit of their quarry. Lubbock (n.d.), in a pamphlet on hare-coursing, advised beginners to learn as much as possible about the ways of the animal. They should follow the tracks of the hare in the snow and watch how the animals behaved in high winds. The pursuit of these wild animals for food and sport must have had a profound effect on their distribution and abundance. Figure 19.2 illustrates the widespread interest in fox-hunting: it indicates the places 'where the hounds met' during the 1840s. There were over 1,200 centres in that part of lowland England and the huntsmen made sure there were plenty of healthy foxes to chase through the countryside. The landowners on the Northamptonshire–Huntingdonshire border, for example, cooperated with one another in the 1860s in providing sufficient fox-earths and coverts for the animals (13).

In general, the natural resources of the countryside were carefully husbanded, but there were exceptions. Cornish (1824) criticized the way in which weirs were often built across streams and rivers without any regard for the fish which annually passed upstream for spawning. He wrote (p. 14):

' It was painful to see the millions of salmon-roe which strewed the sandbanks of the Dart in the rideway below Totnes Weir; the old fish could not pass the weir, and when the natural season arrived they were compelled to shed their spawn where they could. The whole proved abortive; for, as those sand-beds were dry at low water, and the sand shifted with the tides and the floods, the pea was uncovered and lay so thick upon the surface, that a man could not put his foot on the sand without crushing a hundred to pieces at a time.'

From the late nineteenth century onwards, there was a great increase in the number of people visiting the countryside for recreation and study. It became easier for town-dwellers to visit rural areas for a day or longer periods: the cover design of various Ordnance Survey maps of the 1920s illustrated this trend, showing a rambler exploring the countryside, map in hand, with cyclists and a car passing on a nearby road. Gilmour (1972) has described how 'top hatted Victorians' travelled by train to the Lizard or Teesdale in search of unusual plants or insects. This had two effects. There were reports of colourful wild flowers being 'picked excessively' by the public, and of excessive numbers of specimens being collected by botanists and entomologists, consumed by the collecting passion. On the other hand, more and more people became aware of the decline of species and the loss of communities through changes in land use and management.

11

Their concern was expressed through the formation and growth of many
natural history societies and field clubs, which had the protection of wildlife
as one of their objectives. The Royal Society for the Protection of Birds
was the first body entirely devoted to wildlife preservation, and it obtained

WHERE THE FOXHOUNDS
MET IN THE MID
19th CENTURY

miles

**Figure 19.2.** The extent of fox-hunting in the mid-nineteenth century. The hunts
deliberately enucouraged and conserved foxes for their sport (Data from *Hob-
son's Fox Hunting Atlas* (J. and C. Walker) London, 1850, 42 maps).

its royal charter in 1904. The protection of wildlife was part of a broader
concern for scenery and sites of architectural and archaeological interest,
which led to the foundation of the National Trust for Places of Historic
Interest and Natural Beauty in 1895. It was realized that the only way to
ensure the safety of a site was to acquire the land and manage it accord-

ingly. The Trust fulfilled an extremely valuable role in proving that a well-directed voluntary body could achieve this. In 1912, the Society for the Promotion of Nature Reserves was founded, primarily to help the Trust and local groups in the selection and purchase of land, and, towards this end, a list of about 250 areas 'worthy of protection' was compiled in 1915. But relatively little was achieved owing to the lack of finance to meet the cost of acquisition and management.

Meanwhile, the invention of new processes created new and often unexpected hazards to wildlife. This was clearly seen with respect to the combustion engine and the use of mineral oil. The people of the Scilly Isles were used to shipwrecks and made use of the objects washed up on the beaches, but in 1907 a new kind of wreck occurred. The ship *Thomas W. Lawson* sank and oil escaped into the sea as its tanks burst on the rocks. Many birds and rabbits on the island of Annet died on the beaches, killed by the oil (Mothersole, 1910). The risk of oil pollution increased as the number of oil-fired ships rose and oil tankers became more common. There was concern for holiday beaches and fishing grounds during the 1914–18 war and in the following years. The R.S.P.B. publicized the effects of oil on sea birds, and Lord Montagu described to the House of Lords in 1922 how swans and mullet had died in the Solent and Beaulieu river (14). The first Oil in Navigable Waters Act, designed to curb pollution, was passed in 1923.

Most people prefer to lead an urban way of life in a rural setting, and this became increasingly possible following improvements to passenger rail services and road transport. C. J. Cornish discussed the trend in a book *Wild England of Today and the Wild Life in it* published in 1895. He described the spread of houses across the 'pine and heather country' of Surrey, Berkshire and Hampshire, inhabited by people attracted by the scenery of that area. He wrote (p. 77):

> 'The villas follow the line of the sand as closely as collieries follow the line of the coal. Even the outlying and detached wastes, which, until recently lay barren and uninhabited among the Surrey hills, or Hampshire commons, are parcelled out and covered with substantial houses.'

Cornish warned that the area of heath and pine was limited, and that the buildings and people would destroy the amenities which had originally attracted the inhabitants to the area. There was a similar dilemma along parts of the coast. Fields on top of the cliffs and overlooking various bays were acquired for building purposes. Vaughan Cornish (1935) estimated that there were about 500 miles (804·5 km) of cliffed coastline in England: the average frontage of a modest villa was 22 yards (20·1 m), so that 40,000 villas could be built along the top of the cliffs. He noted that 160,000 houses were built in England during the six months ending March 31st, 1935 and that there was a grave risk of the entire length of cliffline being built over within a few years. It was not a question of protecting the countryside from 'vandals' but of preserving it from people who wanted to live within it and enjoy the amenity and atmosphere of the landscape more fully.

Agriculture was the most ubiquitous form of land use, and as early as 1929 E. J. Salisbury warned the Addison Committee (1931) of the harmful effects of new forms of land use and management on the native fauna and flora of the countryside. He estimated that one-sixth of the flora was extinct or had declined in one or more counties. But little heed was taken of these warnings. Most commentators regarded farmers as the traditional custodians of the landscape, protecting amenity and sustaining wildlife as a by-product of their husbandry. The Scott Committee (1942) on rural land use observed that the landscape which townspeople liked to see was essentially an agrarian landscape, and that if farming ceased there would be a serious loss of amenity. The Huxley Committee (1947) on nature conservation rejected any idea of a clash of interests between nature conservation and agriculture. There would be little profit in cultivating areas which were proposed as nature reserves, and the ploughing up of pastures during the 1939–45 war was regarded only as a temporary phenomenon. A. G. Tansley (1945) remarked that 'it is scarcely probable that the extension of agriculture will go much further, for the limits of profitable agricultural land must have been reached in most places'. This attitude towards the future of agricultural development influenced the content of much of the post-war legislation, and little or no attempt was made to regulate such changes as further reclamation and afforestation. Farmers do not have to notify the planning authorities that they intend to plough up old pasture or install under-drains: this does not constitute a change of land use in a legal sense although it can have a profound repercussion on the amenity and wildlife interest of an area. Local Authorities do not have the powers nor opportunity to intervene and protect Sites of Special Scientific Interest or Areas of Outstanding Natural Beauty from this kind of change. The significance of changes in agriculture and forestry was recently demonstrated in a survey of twelve grassland sites (Grubb *et al.*, 1969) studied by Adamson and Tansley in the 1920s: when visited in the late 1960s, nine of them were under cultivation and two were afforested. Changes on this scale were not envisaged during the late 1940s, and consequently the administrative machinery and legislation conceived in that period have proved in many respects inadequate.


## CONCLUSION

In order to conserve them, we must know how plant and animal communities have evolved. The historical ecologist can help by assessing the age of the communities, the chronology of development, and the relative importance of natural processes and human influence. He can demonstrate how changes in human outlook and concern have affected wildlife and amenity. The results of these enquiries into the past will help to place in perspective the problems of managing the natural environment of today.

## REFERENCES

Addison Committee (1931). *The Report of the National Park Committee* (chairman C. S. Addison), Cmd. 3851, HMSO, London, 131 pp.
Arber, M. A. (1940). The coastal landslips of south-east Devon, *Proc. geol. Ass.*, **51,** 257–71.
Bede, C. (1851). The drainage of Whittlesea Mere, *Illustrated London News*, 26 April, 1851 (supplement).
Cornish, C. J. (1895). *Wild England of Today and the Wild Life in it*, Seeley, London, 310 pp.
Cornish, Vaughan (1935). The cliff scenery of England. *Geog. J.*, **86,** 505–11.
Cornish, J. (1824). *A view of the present state of salmon and channel-fisheries*, Longman, Hurst, London, 217 pp.
Elton, C. S. (1966). *The Pattern of Animal Communities*, Methuen, London, 432 pp.
Gilmour, J. (1972). How our flora was discovered, in: *Wild Flowers*, (eds.) J. Gilmour and M. Walters, Fontana, London, 22–44.
Grubb, P. J., Green, H. E., and Merrifield, R. C. J. (1969). The ecology of chalk heath, *J. Ecol.*, **57,** 175–212.
Heathcote, J. M. (1876). *Reminiscences of Fen and Mere*, Longmans, London, 134 pp.
Hooper, M. D. (1971). Hedges and local history, in: *Hedges and Local History*, National Council for Social Service, for Standing Conference for Local History, London, 6–13.
Huxley Committee (1947). *Conservation of Nature in England and Wales*, Report of the Wildlife Conservation Special Committee (chairman J. S. Huxley), Cmd. 7122, HMSO, London, 139 pp.
Lubbock, H. J. (n.d.). *Hints on Hare Hunting*, 16 pp.
Moore, N. W. (1962). The heaths of Dorset and their conservation, *J. Ecol.*, **50,** 369–91.
Mothersole, Jessie (1910). *The Isles of Scilly*, Religious Tracts Society, London, 244 pp.
Pell, A. (1899). *The Making of the Land in England—a Retrospect*, Murray, London, 27 pp.
Peterken, G. F., and Tubbs, C. R. (1965). Woodland regeneration in the New Forest, Hampshire, since 1650, *J. appl. Ecol.*, **2,** 159–70.
Robinson, D. N. (1970). Coastal evolution in north-east Lincolnshire, in: *Geographical Essays in Honour of K. C. Edwards*, (eds.) R. H. Osborne, F. A. Barnes, and J. C. Doornkamp, Department of Geography, Nottingham, 62–70.
Scott Committee (1942). *Report of the Committee on Land Utilisation in Rural Areas* (chairman Lord Justice Scott), Cmd. 6378, HMSO, London, 138 pp.
Sheail, J. (1971). Formation and maintenance of water-meadows in Hampshire, *Biol. Conserv.*, **3,** 101–6.

Tansley, A. G. (1945). *Our Heritage of Wild Nature,* Cambridge University Press, Cambridge, 74 pp.

Ward, Lena K. (1973). Conservation of juniper. I. Present state of juniper in southern England, *J. appl. Ecol.,* **10,** 165–88.

Wells, D. A. (1969). The historical approach to the ecology of alluvial grassland, in: *Old Grassland,* Monks Wood Experimental Station, Nature Conservancy, Symposium, **5,** 62–7.

Wells, T. C. E. (1968). Land use changes effecting *Pulsatilla vulgaris* in England, *Biol. Conserv.,* **1,** 37–43.

Wells, W. (1860). The drainage of Whittlesea Mere, *J. R. agric. Soc.,* 1st series, **21,** 134–53.

Wells, W. (1870). On the treatment of the reclaimed bog-land of Whittlesea Mere, *J. R. agric. Soc.,* 2nd series, **6,** 203–8.

Young, A. (1813). *General View of the Agriculture of Oxfordshire,* Sherwood, Neeley & Jones, London, 362 pp.

## MANUSCRIPT SOURCES

1. All Souls College archives, Lewknor map, 1598.
2. Oxford Record Office, MSS He VI/4.
3. Huntingdon Record Office, Enclosure Award, Great Raveley.
4. Huntingdon Record Office, land book of estates of William Wells.
5. Huntingdon Record Office, copies of original maps.
6. Huntingdon Record Office, documents of Wells estate.
7. Nature Conservancy, management report.
8. Statutes of the Realm 1558–9, 1 Elizabeth, c. 15; 1580–1, 23 Elizabeth, c. 5;
9. Huntingdon Record Office, Borough of Godmanchester documents.
10. Durham Record Office, D/Sa/E 731.
11. Berkshire Record Office, D/EN 013.
12. Hertfordshire Record Office, 46606.
13. Huntingdon Record Office, Manchester MSS, Box 10b, 24.
14. Hansard, Parliamentary debates, Commons, vol. 156 (1922); Lords, vol. 50 (1922).

# B  Demands on the Countryside

# CHAPTER 20

# A Changing Countryside

Joan Davidson

## INTRODUCTION

Like wilderness, the concept of countryside is elusive; its meaning varies with the experience, taste and mood of the individual. Yet for most people, it is something precious to be safeguarded, not only from the physical intrusion of towns, but also from the superficiality of urban living. Country-side resources of wildlife, fine landscape and remoteness are valued even when they are not used; rural life—apparently so genuine—offers simplicity and permanence. This is a simple and perhaps romantic view, but neverthe-less a popular one which is reflected in many spheres of public and private action: in much of the conservation movement; in continued support for Green Belts and National Parks; and in the lively resistance to developments of all kinds in the countryside.

But how realistic is this traditional view?

This chapter explores some of the ways in which the British countryside has changed over the last two decades, the conflicts of interest these changes have generated and the problems and opportunities which face those whose decisions will shape the countryside of the future.

## THE COUNTRYSIDE AND PLANNING*

The popular view of a rural environment as distinct and different from the town has permeated planning thought for more than three decades. The 1947 Town and Country Planning Act introduced, for the first time in Britain, the mechanisms of development planning and control by which land could be allocated for the use thought best suited to it. Yet the countryside was very largely excluded from this system. It was designated 'white land' on development plans with the negative policy 'that existing uses should

* 'Planning' in this chapter refers to the statutory activity of town (and country) planning unless otherwise qualified.

remain for the most part undisturbed'. Almost all agricultural and forestry practices were exempt from planning control and there was a strong belief that, left alone and protected from urban encroachment, the countryside would take care of itself.

There was justification enough for this view. After the war, planners were rightly preoccupied with rebuilding shattered towns and cities. Moreover, the problems of rural Britain were identified by the Scott Committee (Ministry of Works and Planning, 1942) and others in terms not of the need for planned change, but for protection: from the encroachment of ugly, inefficient ribbon development, for the rural community, and, most of all, for a revitalized farming industry.

Despite the lack of involvement of *town* planners, whose interests have been, and over much of the country still are, confined to urban environments, powerful *resource* planning agencies with their own legislation and finance have shaped the use and appearance of the countryside since the war. The Ministry of Agriculture with its persuasive planning system of guaranteed prices, grants and advisory services has guided the development of an agricultural industry highly efficient in technical and economic terms (Munton, Chapter 21). The Forestry Commission has continued its afforestation programme especially in the uplands. The Nature Conservancy has acquired more National Nature Reserves in its efforts to conserve a range of representative British habitats (Blackmore, Chapter 27).

The situation of the fifties was therefore neat and simple: there were development planners for the towns and resource planners for the countryside, each acting independently of the other.

## CHANGING DEMANDS

Few in 1950 could anticipate the way conditions would change within the countryside and outside it. The growth of population (instead of a forecast decline) and the evolution of a more affluent, space-demanding and mobile society had obvious implications for the planning of towns; the effects on the countryside were less sudden, but nevertheless significant. One thing was clear: it was no longer possible to treat the two environments as distinct, even though substantial differences remain.

Two groups of new demands have been placed upon the resources of the countryside: those arising within the rural environment and economy, and those associated with changes in urban society. Other chapters in this section describe some of the changes generated within the countryside. Munton (Chapter 21), for example, discusses recent developments in agriculture, which have undoubtedly brought to many rural areas the most significant changes in function and appearance, and James (Chapter 22) looks at developments in the uplands. Many of the direct and indirect implications of urban growth for the countryside—including the demands for more building land, for airports, roads, more mineral working and water conservation schemes and the social changes of commuter and holiday villages—have been well documented in a number of recent papers, especially those by Bracey (1970), Clout (1972), Green (1971) and Smart (1968). It would be misleading to summarize, in so short a space, all the economic, social and environmental consequences of these changes. But a brief discussion of the development and implications of outdoor recreation will serve as an example of the changes and allow some reappraisal of the validity of continuing to treat the countryside as a separate entity and to plan the use of its resources in isolation.

**Leisure in the Countryside**

Leisure activity is not a new phenomenon in the countryside. Traditional sports of hunting and shooting have been part of the rural scene for centuries. But the activities of city dwellers were limited until recently, principally by lack of time and money and especially by lack of mobility.* In 1949, when the National Parks and Access to the Countryside Act was framed, the major issue was not so much to provide more outdoor recreation facilities (although this was a provision of the Act) but to ensure protection of the finest scenery. Because the demand for countryside recreation was small, and of a kind simply requiring more access to private land rather than tourist and recreation facilities, impacts upon the rural environment and economy were almost negligible.

Since the mid-fifties, however, and especially during the sixties, participation in leisure pursuits of all kinds has increased rapidly. Casual family activities, such as picnics and pleasure motoring associated with holidaymaking and day trips, show the greatest growth; it is these activities that have brought new conflicts—and also benefits—to the countryside. Not only are more people using rural areas for leisure purposes, but they are travelling further (aided by road improvements as well as the spread of car ownership) and spending longer there. At the same time as a greater 'quantity' of the rural environment is sought, there is increasing concern for its quality: the protection of fine scenery, wildlife and historic resources, and remote areas. Others argue that the countryside must still support an expanding agricultural programme, continued commercial timber production, extensive water conservation schemes, more mineral working and the many other demands of an urbanized industrial nation. The consequences of increased leisure activity, therefore, go beyond the more immediate observable conflicts of

* The changing pattern of leisure activity and the reasons for it were well described by Patmore (1970).

crowded beaches or congested traffic, to affect nearly all rural interests in many different ways (Hookway and Davidson, 1970).

There are obvious conflicts between visitors and the traditional rural enterprises of farming and forestry, expressed in terms of damage to crops, trees and machinery, disturbance of stock, pollution of water supplies and the host of other consequences of intended, or more often, unwitting trespass. The growing use of second homes brings other problems. Property values in those rural areas which are attractive and easily accessible from conurbations have risen dramatically, forcing some local residents to search elsewhere for accommodation, and exacerbating the difficulties of areas already experiencing a declining population.

The effects of increasing use of the countryside for leisure are therefore social as well as economic, and in this way they encourage a hardening of attitudes and further resistance on the part of country people to the claims of urban visitors. But the conflict may not always be one way. Some of the activities of mineral operators and reservoir engineers as well as farmers and foresters can lead to dramatic changes in scenery and loss of public access. Then there are the smaller-scale changes of hedgerow clearance, the felling of copses and draining of wet areas which often lead to an overall reduction in the variety of landscape, which, in many areas, is its particular value.

There are more subtle environmental consequences of recreation, resulting from the heavy use of fragile habitats: the erosion of dunes, lake margins and some grasslands (Goldsmith, Chapter 14; Lindsey County Council, 1970). Without management or rehabilitation, these areas not only become unattractive for recreation, but less valuable as wildlife refuges and for ecological research and teaching.

But not all the implications of increased leisure activity are damaging. Quite apart from the intangible benefits to health and mental well-being which accrue to a more leisured population, recreation and tourist developments have brought substantial economic benefits to some rural communities and may yet mitigate the effects of economic stagnation in others. Moreover, increased leisure activity in the countryside has been associated with a growing concern for environmental conservation, and has provided a stimulus for the care of historic buildings and the creation of new reserves for wildlife. Unique opportunities are offered for more imaginative interpretation of the countryside and illustrations of what practical land management and conservation entail.

### Conflicts of Interest

Here, then, is one example of how demands upon the countryside, unforeseen in 1949, have led to change and conflict. A discussion of other demands (developments in agricultural practice and building, afforestation, commuting from the towns and villages of a city region, the expansion of extractive industries or even the strengthening of interest in wildlife conservation) would show, in a similar way, the many conflicts of interest that exist. It would also show the inadequacies of the legislative, organizational and financial measures developed in the forties to integrate the demands of the seventies in a satisfactory way.

The 1947 planning system is powerless to resolve many rural conflicts, with its lack of control over the operations of major land activities and its emphasis upon land *use* rather than land *management,* for it is the management of resources in the countryside—the day-to-day operations of farming or the way in which recreation areas are organized—rather than the simple classification of use as 'agriculture' or 'leisure' which is important (Hookway, 1967; O'Riordan, 1971).

The policies of the national parks legislation, providing for the protection and development of only 9 per cent of the countryside (Figure 20.1), cannot cope with recreation pressures felt almost anywhere within 20–30 miles of a large town. Even the policies of the Countryside Act which encourage the development of country parks and picnic sites (Davidson, Chapter 24) do not solve all the problems. Although new single-purpose recreation areas will obviously meet some of the present demands, they are probably still too few; they may increase trespass and road congestion rather than reduce them; they cannot be reached by everyone, nor do they offer the variety of leisure opportunities that some people want (Zetter, 1971). Recreation, certainly of the informal kind, cannot be contained within a handful of sites scattered across the countryside; it requires the secondary use of other suitable land like forests, reservoirs and hill grazings. In a similar way, it is no longer feasible to imagine that wildlife can be protected in National Nature Reserves or Sites of Special Scientific Interest alone; the viability of most protected species depends upon conservation measures being adopted, to a varying degree, throughout the countryside.

The existence of powerful rural interest groups working for agriculture, forestry, nature conservation, water supply, even recreation, each pursuing independent policies to meet single-purpose objectives, emerged with increasing clarity during the three 'Countryside in 1970' conferences held in 1963, 1965 and 1970, and more recently at the Stockholm conference on the Human Environment (Department of the Environment, 1972). In preparatory work and in conference discussion, coordination of purpose and method was accepted, but the ways of achieving it were less obvious.

It is true that some improvements in legislation and the organization of resource-planning agencies followed the first and second 'Countryside in 1970' conferences: water conservation was rationalized; the 1968 Transport

**Figure 20.1.** The extent of protected areas of the countryside in England and Wales. (Based on a map made by the Department of the Environment and updated in May, 1973.)

Act allowed for the rehabilitation and amenity use of redundant commercial waterways; the Ministry of Agriculture began to expand its advisory services to farmers, including an amenity component. In 1966, the Government published a White Paper on leisure (Ministry of Land and Natural Resources, 1966) and its proposals, which were adopted in the 1968 Countryside Act, go some way towards solving recreation problems. The Act also requires all public bodies to look at the rural implications of their work. The 1968 Town and Country Planning Act, following the recommendations of the Planning Advisory Group (1965), has introduced a system of structure and local plans which allows planners new opportunities not only to be involved at all in the countryside, but also to make a more positive contribution towards the planning of it (Mercer, Chapter 26; Smart, 1968).

Yet, in practice, integration has proved elusive. Few of the improvements of the sixties have lasted. The system of 29 River Authorities advised by the Water Resources Board established in 1963 is now replaced by ten Regional Water Authorities and a National Water Council. The advisory services of the Ministry of Agriculture have been curtailed, while the failure of the Rural Development Boards is a further example of opportunities lost for a more comprehensive treatment of the problems of upland Britain. Wibberley (1970), Dower (1972) and others have argued that differences of opinion on how the countryside should be planned have hardened since 1970, and that sectional interests grow stronger.


INTEGRATED RESOURCE PLANNING

New powers, new organizations, even new sources of finance, it seems, are not enough. It is for a workable method of rural resource planning that the need exists, and more important still, for an attitude of real commitment on the part of rural interests to the resolution of their conflicts.

Some pointers to the way in which integration might be achieved were given in early, multidisciplinary studies of specific problem areas like the Broadland report (Nature Conservancy, 1965) and the work of the Land Use Study Group (Department of Education and Science, 1966). The first showed the advantages of involving all major interests in the plan-making process; the second suggested a method (using discounting) by which the claims of rival interests might be evaluated. But both studies had few detailed, feasible policies, and were vague on methods of implementation. Yet their approach was an attempt to tackle the realities of countryside conservation: the harmonization of resource interests with the minimum of conflict.

## The East Hampshire Study

A more recent study in East Hampshire (Hampshire County Council, 1968) provides a better example of what rural conservation means and how it might be practised. The East Hampshire Area of Outstanding Natural Beauty (Figure 20.1), a tract of some 150 square miles of chalk downland east of Winchester, is an area of prosperous arable farming. With its rolling, often well-wooded appearance, this is attractive countryside, suitable and popular for a variety of informal recreation activities. For the present, the intensity of use is not high, apart from the concentration points at Old Winchester Hill (a National Nature Reserve) and Butser Hill; but the potential for increased recreation pressure is clearly there, as accessibility from London to the south and west continues to improve, and more especially, as the city region of South Hampshire grows. Wildlife interest over much of the area is limited by the poverty of natural habitats on land so intensively farmed, but there are valuable enclaves of chalk grassland, river valleys, and beech hangars on the scarp slopes.

Many aspects of rural policy-making—on settlements, communications, mineral working—had already been decided in previous work by Hampshire County Council before the conservation study began. The East Hampshire team* was therefore free to concentrate upon the present and future interactions between five major resource interests—agriculture, forestry, recreation, wildlife and landscape conservation. For each of these interests the A.O.N.B. was zoned according to differences in character and value. There was speculation by those representing each interest on the likely future changes that would take place—for example, the increasing intensification and specialization of agriculture; the expansion in volume and variety of recreation activity; or the growth of interest in wildlife conservation.

Present clashes of interest and the likely conflicts resulting from further developments in the major activities of agriculture and recreation were explored. The acceptability, to each of the five interests, of activities such as chemical spraying, field drainage, tree felling, the introduction of horticultural uses, footpaths or country parks was gauged.

The results of this analysis were synthesized in the generation of 'policy zones' (delineated on grounds of resource quality) within which certain activities were considered to be more or less acceptable and for which, therefore, policies of promotion or restriction might apply. In some zones,

---

* Composed of officers of five public bodies: Hampshire County Council, National Parks Commission (now Countryside Commission), Nature Conservancy, Forestry Commission and the Ministry of Agriculture.

for example, where landscape or ecological values were high, it was suggested that priority should be given to these interests; measures such as planting in field corners were to be encouraged, while practices damaging to the ecological interest—hedgerow clearance, for example—were to be restricted. Elsewhere, in zones of high agricultural quality, it was accepted that recreation activities might need to be curtailed, if not wholly diverted to areas of poorer farming. For some zones, where values were high for several interests and direct policy conflicts could be anticipated, more detailed studies were recommended. This applied particularly to those areas where novel methods of implementing policies were advocated: where restrictions and positive action were sought not simply through development control or by public ownership, but perhaps through the use of management agreements (Hookway, 1967).

Inevitably, there were weaknesses in the approach and methods of the East Hampshire exercise. The resource evaluation techniques suffered from varying degrees of subjectivity, and were not suited to direct comparison. But some headway was made with the evaluation of ecological interest, based upon a field survey of the rarity and diversity of habitats in the A.O.N.B. The assessment of future demands, however, was crude, especially for recreation, on which considerable progress has been made elsewhere since 1968 (Countryside Commission, 1970; Rodgers, 1972). The statements of acceptability were based upon broad value judgments; given more time, more skills, these might have been verified by some more rigorous analysis of costs and benefits.

In many ways the planning problems tackled by the East Hampshire team were simple: large areas of policy-making were already decided, and although conflict did exist between interests which would probably intensify in future, the problems were not intractable. Studies have since begun in other, very different rural environments, such as Sherwood Forest (Nottinghamshire County Council, 1973) and in the North Pennines (Countryside Commission, 1972) where—in the latter case especially—social issues seem to be far more prominent and rather more tangible conflict exists between the needs of local communities and those of visitors and preservationists. In the rich lowland farming areas typified by East Hampshire, conservation implies protection of the remains of a semi-natural landscape substantially altered by recent and rapid changes of land management especially in agriculture. By contrast, conservation in the uplands, and most of all in National Parks, will depend much more upon establishing viable social and economic structures as a prerequisite for recreation, landscape, and wildlife conservation policies. This theme of 'protective' and 'development' planning has been explored by Wibberley (1970) and others (for example, Robinson, 1972).

## The Future of Resource Planning

Despite the limitations of simplicity, the East Hampshire Study has raised a number of crucial issues for integrated resource planning. Moreover, as the first example of a piece of rural *district planning* in the style of the 1968 and 1972 Town and Country Planning Acts, the problems of method and policy-making experienced in East Hampshire continue to face those preparing new-style plans. This is evident from the rural sections of a number of recent plans and studies, not only at local level, but also at the scale of county structure plans and sub-regional studies. Four issues seem especially important to the development of integrated planning, and with it the successful implementation of positive policies for rural conservation.

Firstly, a good deal of work remains to be done on techniques of resource evaluation (e.g. O'Connor, Chapter 6); on the generation of policies and evaluation of them—all progressive fields in urban planning, but barely introduced in rural studies.

Secondly, quite apart from the process of plan-making, the kinds of policies proposed for the use and management of countryside resources need to be far more positive. The policies contained in a number of recent plans for rural areas still imply a fairly negative view of the rural environment, not greatly different from the traditional 'white land' notion held in 1947. The prevailing rural strategy, with notable exceptions (Cheshire County Planning Department, 1971; South Hampshire Plan Advisory Committee, 1972), is to preserve the countryside against the town, by careful siting of new urban growth and stringent controls on all development. But this is to ignore the kind of conflicts that arise *within* the countryside between major rural interests, and the potential values of closer integration between urban and rural activity. The resolution of conflicts requires positive land management policies at all scales, from the introduction of new wildlife habitats on farms and in forests to increase wildlife diversity (Barber, 1970) to large-scale landscape treatments—the reclamation of dereliction, lake building and extensive tree planting, as Fairbrother (1970) suggests for her 'green–urban' fringe environments.

Thirdly, the implementation of these policies may require more subtle tools in addition to those of protective zoning, development control and public ownership with which planners are familiar. The influence of planners upon the way in which rural resources are used may be improved rather than resisted by offers of technical information and advice, the promotion of voluntary codes of practice (perhaps with financial support from public funds) and by participation in more formal agreements for the management of land (Countryside Commission, 1973). The Countryside Commission's Upland Management Experiment in the Lake District has demonstrated how far farmers can be persuaded (with financial help) to undertake landscape and recreation improvements (Countryside Commission, 1971). Such measures will demand a greater commitment of public funds and manpower, but most of the powers already exist.

Finally, the role of the physical planner in the countryside, and his relationship with other resource planners, needs to be clarified. Certainly, if policies are to involve activities and practices over which the planner has limited or no statutory control, then the preparation of plans for rural areas cannot be his task alone: those affected by the policies should be part of the planning team. There are already successful examples of co-operation between landowners and the local planning authority in plan preparation (Leonard Manasseh, 1969), but the wider implications of public participation in the planning of rural areas have yet to be explored.

Perhaps the most valuable outcome of the East Hampshire study and subsequent work structured in a similar way has been the demonstration of how different disciplines can work together: how, for example, ecologists —whose contribution appeared as uncertain as that of sociologists a few years ago—can be used in the planning process.

## CONCLUSIONS

This chapter began with a description of the traditional, somewhat romantic view of the countryside as a changeless backcloth to urban growth. But this is far from reality. As the example of recreation activity has shown, considerable change has taken place in recent years; new conflicts have arisen among a widening group of rural interests. The East Hampshire exercise was an attempt to react positively to a changed countryside. The increasing number of rural studies as part of recent development plans is a welcome indication of the growing interest of planners and others in rural issues. But the mood is still one of cosy optimism, a concern to resolve present conflict rather than to anticipate the future. To conserve any environment so that as many as possible of the demands upon it may be satisfied presupposes some vision of what the future might be. This requires a good deal more thinking than has been evident so far about the agencies and nature of potential change: the implications of the Common Agricultural Policy for Britain; the effects of inflation on land ownership and management; new industrial demands for water and minerals; social changes in the pattern of work and leisure.

The countryside has altered considerably over the last two decades; the changes in future may be very much more dramatic.

## ACKNOWLEDGMENTS

I am grateful to my husband, John Davidson, to Adrian Phillips and to Professor Gerald Wibberley for helpful comments on this paper.

# BIBLIOGRAPHY AND REFERENCES

## General

Barber, D. (ed.) (1970). *Farming and Wildlife*, Royal Society for the Protection of Birds, Sandy, 93 pp.

Bracey, H. E. (1970). *People and the Countryside*, Routledge and Kegan Paul, London, 310 pp.

Clout, H. D. (1972). *Rural Geography: An Introductory Survey*. Pergamon, London, 206 pp.

Fairbrother, N. (1970). *New Lives, New Landscapes*, Architectural Press, London, 397 pp.

Ministry of Works and Planning (1942). *Report of the Committee on Land Utilisation in Rural Areas (Scott Report)*, HMSO, Cmnd. 6378, London, 138 pp.

## Leisure in the Countryside

Countryside Commsision (1970). *The Demand for Outdoor Recreation in the Countryside*, Report of a seminar held in London, January 1970, Countryside Commission, London, 59 pp.

Hookway, R. J. S., and Davidson, J. (1970). *Leisure: Problems and Prospects for the Environment*, Countryside Commission, London, 32 pp.

Lindsey County Council (1970). *Countryside Recreation: The Ecological Implications*, L.C.C., Lincoln, 125 pp.

Ministry of Land and Natural Resources (1966). *Leisure in the Countryside*, HMSO, Cmnd 2928, London, 15 pp.

Patmore, J. A. (1970). *Land and Leisure*, David and Charles, Newton Abbott, 332 pp.

Rodgers, H. B. (1972). Problems and progress in recreation research: a review of some recent studies, *Urban Studies* **9**, 223–8.

Zetter, J. A. (1971). *The Evolution of Country Park Policy*, Countryside Commission, London, 10 pp.

## Rural Planning and Management

Countryside Commission (1970). Focus on rural resource planning, *Recreation News Supplement*, **2**, 47 pp.

Countryside Commission (1971). *Fourth Report*, HMSO, London, 70 pp.

Countryside Commission (1972). *Fifth Report*, HMSO, London, 52 pp.

Countryside Commission (1973). *Landscape Agreements*, Countryside Commission, London, 15 pp.

Department of Education and Science (1965). *Report of the Land Use Study Group: Forestry, Agriculture and the Multiple Use of Rural Land*, HMSO London, 110 pp.

Department of the Environment (1972). *Sinews for Survival, Report on Natural Resources for the United Nations Conference on the Human Environment, Stockholm*, HMSO, London, 74 pp.

Dower, M. (1972) Who plans the countryside? *Town and Country Planning*, **40**, 252–4.

Green, R. J. (1971). *Country Planning*, Manchester University Press, Manchester, 123 pp.

Hookway, R. J. S. (1967). The management of Britain's rural land, *Report of Proceedings, Town and Country Planning Summer School*, Royal Town Planning Institute, London, 63–75.

O'Riordan, T. (1971). *Perspectives on Resource Management*, Pion Press, London, 183 pp.

Planning Advisory Group (1965). *The Future of Development Plans*, HMSO, London, 62 pp.

Robinson, D. G. (1972). Comprehensive development, in: *The Remoter Rural Areas of Britain*, (eds.) J. Ashton and W. H. Long, Oliver and Boyd, Edinburgh, 215–224.

Smart, A. D. G. (1968). Rural planning in the context of the city region, *Report of Proceedings, Town and Country Planning Summer School*, Univ. of Manchester for Royal Town Planning Institute, London, 34–38.

Wibberley, G. P. (1970). Rural planning in Britain—protection or development? *Journal of the Town Planning Institute*, **56**, 285–8.

## Planning Studies

Cheshire County Planning Department (1971). *Policy for Rural Cheshire*, Cheshire County Council, Chester, 34 pp.

Hampshire County Council, (1968). *East Hampshire A.O.N.B.: A Study in Countryside Conservation*, H.C.C., Winchester, 62 pp.

Leonard Manasseh and Partners (1969). *North West Solent Shore Estates: Study and Plans*, Leonard Manasseh, London, 75 pp.

Nature Conservancy (1965). *Report on Broadland*, Nature Conservancy, London, 98 pp.

Nottinghamshire County Council (1973). *Sherwood Forest Study*, Nottinghamshire County Council, Nottingham, 14 pp.

South Hampshire Plan Advisory Committee (1972). *South Hampshire Structure Plan*, Hampshire County Council, Winchester, 317 pp.

# CHAPTER 21

# Agriculture and Conservation in Lowland Britain

R. J. C. MUNTON

During the past forty years non-agricultural users of the countryside have asserted with increasing vigour their own views as to how it should be managed. As differences of opinion between these interests and those of the farming community have emerged, so views have sharpened and opinions hardened. Until recently these differences have been articulated most clearly in the context of upland Britain, where the claims of farmers to the exclusive management rights over land have been successfully challenged and the principle of multiple use has been generally accepted. During the remainder of this century attention seems likely to focus on lowland Britain, where a different problem presents itself. Here population densities are higher, outdoor recreational demands more immediate and agriculture more intensive and more profitable. The industry's ability to accommodate the demands of recreationalists and conservationists is circumscribed by its high level of capital input and the need to make the most effective use of its investments. As a result, land management practices which are inimical to other countryside interests are frequently practised. One writer has gone so far as to say that 'Intensive farming cannot tolerate tourists, too much is at risk; it would be as unthinkable as letting a crowd of rubbernecks run riot in a power station' (Bonham-Carter, 1971, p. 163). The same might have been said about conservationists.

Even if Bonham-Carter's statement is considered to be an over-generalization, it does pinpoint the nature of the problem. Always assuming that some kind of intensive agriculture aimed at meeting a substantial proportion of our food requirements will be encouraged in Britain by governmental assistance, the multiple use of farmland would seem an unsatisfactory solution (see also Wibberley, 1971). In any event, in the long term a more positive approach towards rural land-use planning than at present would seem essential, especially as, in the short term at least, it is reasonable to anticipate a further intensification of agricultural practices as farmers respond to the financial rewards offered by the high level of product prices that generally prevail under the Common Agricultural Policy of the European Economic Community.

## GENERAL LAND-USE CONSIDERATIONS

There are two schools of thought concerned with environmental conservation and food supplies whose views presume quite different goals and management practices for Britain's farmers. One school of thought points to the world population explosion and the possibilities of a future world shortage of food (see, for example, Bramley, 1965). This observation leads to the view that Britain should at least maintain, if not increase, its present level (50–60 per cent) of self-sufficiency in food production. Agricultural land should therefore be strictly conserved from loss to other uses and the agricultural industry encouraged to become more intensive in its methods.

Others question the economic sense of government support for British agriculture and the long-term validity of a policy that encourages land management practices opposed by other countryside interests (see, for example, Cheshire and Bowers, 1969). It is argued that farmers should be made to face world market competition in agricultural products and, in some areas, be financially encouraged to maintain an aesthetically interesting and ecologically diverse farming landscape. Needless to say, proponents of this view consider a future shortage of food unlikely, at least for those nations able to buy on the world market. Whilst a majority of agricultural economists would endorse this assessment of world food supplies, most also expect a further intensification of farming practice in Britain as a result of Britain's entry to the European Economic Community. In the light of these expectations it is necessary, therefore, constantly to review our attitudes towards the rate of transfer of farmland to non-agricultural uses, particularly to urban activities, and to monitor the natural environment in order to avoid any undesirable long-term ecological effects caused by modern farming methods.

Despite the concentration of urban land uses in some regions of Britain, as high as 35·6 per cent in Southeast England and 28·7 per cent in Northwest England (Best, 1965), the land-use pattern of lowland Britain remains dominated by rural land uses and by agriculture in particular. Nevertheless, the rate of transfer of land from rural to urban uses has caused concern, although the actual rate has been shown to be less than many agricultural land conservationists had feared (Best, 1968; Best and Champion, 1970). Strict planning controls since World War II have reduced the rate of transfer from 24,500 hectares per annum in the latter part of the 1930s to an average of 15,500 hectares per annum between 1945 and 1965. It has been estimated, however, that the physical productivity of this land averaged 70 per cent above the national norm (Wibberley, 1968), and awareness of this has led to a number of attempts to assess the effects of future land transfers on the total productive capacity of Britain's farmland. Working on the assumption that a further loss of 783,000 hectares (about 5 per cent of land surface of the United Kingdom) of farmland to urban uses can be expected by the year 2000 (Best, 1964), then a recent study suggests that anticipated increases in agricultural productivity should be sufficient to make good the loss of output from this land, cater for an increased population at the present level of self-sufficiency, and could even leave a small surplus of rural land for non-agricultural uses (Edwards and Wibberley, 1971).

These conclusions rest on two further important assumptions. First, that the best agricultural land will be protected from urban encroachment and a protective policy towards agricultural land in general will be adopted. Planners will have to be responsible for the implementation of such a policy, as the market mechanism places agricultural interests at a considerable disadvantage when compared with urban interests on the urban–rural fringe. Second, that the current rate of increase in agricultural productivity will be maintained over the next thirty years. There is little evidence at present to suggest that the necessary further increases in productivity in the livestock sector will not be forthcoming, since livestock production systems are still absorbing the technological developments of the last fifteen years. However, yield increases in the arable sector have suffered several setbacks in recent years and it remains to be seen whether this is only a temporary situation. Clearly, a further intensification of production methods will be required if the additional demands of a larger population with a higher real income are to be met from a smaller agricultural acreage. Whilst this should not provide insuperable technological difficulties (Cooke, 1970), it will heighten the conflict of interest in the countryside.

Modern farming methods may be endangering the long-term biological productivity of certain environments. The kind of farming practices included in this category are the abandonment of traditional crop rotations leading to the breakdown of soil structure and even to soil erosion (Warren, Chapter 3) in some arable farming areas, the overstocking of poorly drained grassland and the addition of persistent pesticides (Moore, Chapter 15). Some of these issues are discussed later in this chapter. To meet rising costs farmers have intensified their farming systems by cropping their land more intensively and stocking their grassland more heavily. Intensification and specialization have been made possible by a number of important technological developments, including new cereal varieties that give higher yields, mechanization of arable farming, correct additions of inorganic fertilizers, herbicides and pesticides, new storage possibilities for arable crops and commercial development of intensive livestock production using factory farming methods. The adoption of many improvements has been facilitated by the extension of electric current to almost all farms, whilst an improved financial use of these innovations has resulted from the introduction of new farm business methods.

The increase in productivity which has resulted from these technological innovations is considerable, amounting to approximately 2·5 per cent per annum over the last twenty-five years. Not only have yields been raised but farmers are now able to grow crops on soils where previously they would not have been contemplated, as with barley on thin chalk downland soils for example, and poor permanent pastures have been drained, ploughed and their new ley swards heavily stocked. The long-term ecological effects of some of these decisions were not immediately apparent and the initial success of the innovations in cutting costs and raising output and incomes led some farmers to overestimate the control that they had acquired over their environment. New disease, weed and soil structure problems have, however, emerged. Their emergence can, in part, be attributed to a changing farm economic situation resulting from a shift in government policy. For the last fifteen years farmers have had to absorb most cost increases, such as those attributable to the new technology itself and to rising land prices, higher interest rates and inflation, whilst the guaranteed prices of many farm products have been held constant in real terms. In order to maintain the same level of return as previously on their greater capital investments farmers have sought economies of scale largely through intensification and specialization, so placing new and greater ecological pressures on their land resources.

## AGRICULTURE IN BRITAIN

The importance of agriculture to the British economy has been in decline over a long period of time. By the mid-nineteenth century agricultural production, excluding the value added by ancillary agricultural industries, represented only 17 per cent of Britain's Gross National Product, and this proportion had fallen to 6 per cent by 1911–13 and to a mere 3 per cent by 1966–68 (Coppock, 1971). Only 3 per cent of the nation's work force is now employed in agriculture.

In contrast to most other members of the European Economic Community, the influence of farming interests on national politics in Britain is small (Self and Storing, 1962). At the local level in rural areas, however, landowners exert considerable influence over land-use planning decisions through their ownership of certain rights to land. Moreover, as a result of the agreement struck between farmers and the Government during the Second World War, the farming industry acquired a degree of bargaining power over its economic future that was not enjoyed by previous generations of farmers.

The strength of this bargaining power should not be overestimated, since the industry has to respond largely to the wishes of the Government. Nevertheless, it has given farmers the opportunity continually to present their case and to make the most of a relatively secure, if not particularly lucrative, financial situation. Under the 1947 Agriculture Act the Government agreed to support product prices at a level which would provide reasonable living standards for all those employed in the industry as well as an acceptable level of return on the capital invested in it. At this time the Government's objective was to produce food at almost any price. The industry demonstrated a considerable ability to respond to price guarantees and new technological developments, and by the mid-1950s a number of products were being over-produced. Overproduction resulted in a change of emphasis in policy in the late 1950s a change which led towards efficient rather than maximum production. The subsequent drive towards efficient agricultural production has been tempered by policies, such as the Small Farmer Scheme, aimed at disadvantaged groups within agriculture, although this may have kept inefficient producers in business (McCrone, 1962). It was not until the end of the 1960s that there was any explicit attempt to assess the role of agriculture in anything but food production terms. Limited moves have now been made by the Countryside Commission to explore and encourage the recreation potential of farming in scenically attractive areas (for general discussion see Phillips and Roberts, 1973), but a more general rural land-use assessment of marginal farming areas has not been encouraged by the present Government's axing of the Rural Development Boards which were to have operated in Central Wales and the North Pennines.

The financial security intended for agriculture in the price support programme has bred an air of confidence and farmers have been prepared to plan ahead and to enter into long-term investment programmes. Equally important, bankers and other providers of agricultural credit, as well as machinery producers, fertilizer manufacturers and food processors, have shared in this confidence, and through their combined research and investment have created new farming opportunities. Farm incomes have increased and the proportion directly attributable to government support has fallen, although in real terms the increase has not been dramatic, particularly when the enormous amount of capital invested in the industry in recent years is taken into account. In 1971, for example, net farm income averaged only £2,405, and this figure includes management and investment income as well as a measure of the value of the labour output of the farmer and his wife (HMSO, 1972).

In the late 1960s the total capital assets of British agriculture were assessed at £11,000 million, of which £8,000 million represented the value of land (Thomas, 1970). The remaining £3,000 million was largely made up of investments in machinery, buildings and stock, although the amount per acre varied widely between farming types, being generally greatest on arable cash-cropping farms and lowest on hill farms. Land prices are obviously critical to the total figure. During the first part of the 1950s they had averaged between £50 and £60 per acre. Since then they have risen rapidly to reach £195 per acre by 1969, £300 per acre by the end of 1971 and £750 per acre by the end of 1972. Price increases during the 1960s took place against a background of rising interest rates which required new purchasers of land to farm intensively merely to meet the interest charges on their loans. The substantial price increases of the last couple of years can only be partly attributed to the land's present earning capabilities in agricultural use. They also reflect the capitalization into higher land values of the higher farm incomes expected to result from Britain's entry into the European Economic Community, and the increased interest of non-agricultural concerns in agricultural land at a time of inflation and uncertainty on the stock market. Land is seen as a safe investment with a high capital appreciation potential. The effect of the enormous and increasing absolute differential in value between farmland prices (say £750 per acre) and urban development prices (say £20,000 per acre, with prices in excess of £100,000 per acre in parts of Southeast England) also cannot be overlooked. Perhaps as much as £1,000 million per annum is now entering the pockets of urban-fringe landowners, and even allowing for taxation and alternative investment outlets, a substantial proportion of this sum is being reinvested in land away from the immediate urban fringe, so pushing up rural land prices in general. This is because current taxation legislation permits the avoidance of capital gains tax at 45 per cent provided the proceeds of a land sale are reinvested in land within three years.

Agriculture is over-capitalized. The small size of most farm businesses means that insufficient internal scale economies are available to make the most economic use of the new capital-intensive innovations. In an attempt to meet this difficulty farmers are desperately seeking more land, often further inflating the price, and farm size has steadily increased in recent years. Cooperation has become increasingly commonplace, usually between the operators of medium- as opposed to small-sized farms. Farmers have also reduced the number of enterprises on their farms, and intensified them, and by so doing have created less flexible management situations. Investment in a specialized farming system makes it difficult to adapt in the short

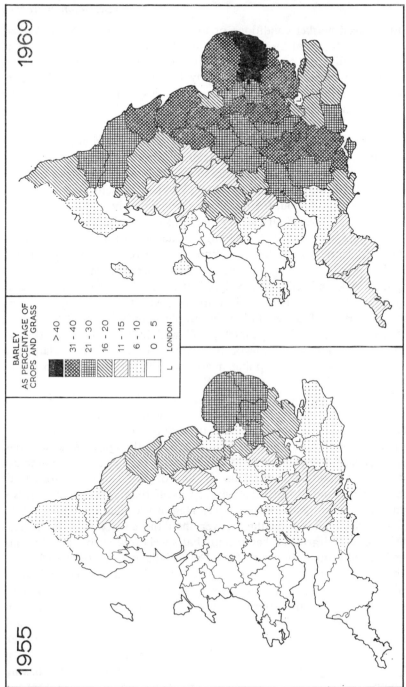

**Figure 21.1.** Changes in Barley Acreage in England and Wales, 1955–1969. Statistical Source: Agricultural Statistics 1955/6 and 1969/70 for England and Wales. Ministry of Agriculture, Fisheries and Food, HMSO, London 1957 and 1971.

term to changed market conditions or to respond to unexpected ecological difficulties. The financial loss that often results from the limited opportunities for the realization of fixed assets with a change from one specialized farming system to another has led many farmers to press on with their existing systems in the hope that their difficulties will prove to be short-lived or that new technological innovations will arrive to resolve their problems.

A rapid expansion in arable acreage took place in Britain during the 1960s so that by 1969 over 50 per cent of all farmland was in arable use. This expansion was largely attributable to the doubling of the barley acreage to more than 5·1 million acres by 1969. Yield improvements of over 30 per cent during this period, the development of intensive livestock systems based on barley as a feedstuff and the mechanization of barley growing have been largely responsible for this expansion, despite a fall in real terms in the guaranteed price of barley. The enormous increase in barley acreage obscured a decline in the acreage of oats, mixed corn and potatoes during the 1960s and reduced the significance of a 10 per cent increase in acreage and 40 per cent increase in output of wheat. The barley crop has become the basis of a revolution in arable farming. Traditional crop rotations consisting of three years ley followed by three years of cereals or two years ley and four years of cereals have been steadily replaced by almost continuous barley cropping, made possible by the addition of in-organic fertilizers, herbicides and pesticides.

An increase in barley acreage since 1955 has been recorded in every county in England and Wales (Figure 21.1). Increases have been least in upland, western Britain and greatest in counties on the margin of the traditional arable farming area of East Anglia. Although Suffolk now has the highest percentage yield of farmland in barley (41 per cent), the greatest increases were recorded in the East Riding of Yorkshire, Hertfordshire, Nottinghamshire and Northamptonshire. Casual observation also suggests that the chalk downlands of Wiltshire, Hampshire and Berkshire would record an even higher percentage cover than the county of Suffolk. The expansion in cereal growing has meant that specialized arable farming has replaced mixed farming in parts of the East Midlands and southern Britain and that mixed farming has become well established in the traditional grassland farming areas of the northwest, southwest and the Welsh Border. Nevertheless, the overall pattern of an arable east and grassland west of England and Wales remains (Figure 21.2; Coppock, 1971). Dairying is still concentrated in the mid-west of England and southwest Wales, and livestock rearing in the wetter upland areas. The total number of cattle has risen slowly, but with higher productivity per head and with increased stocking rates output of livestock produce per grassland acre has risen sharply.

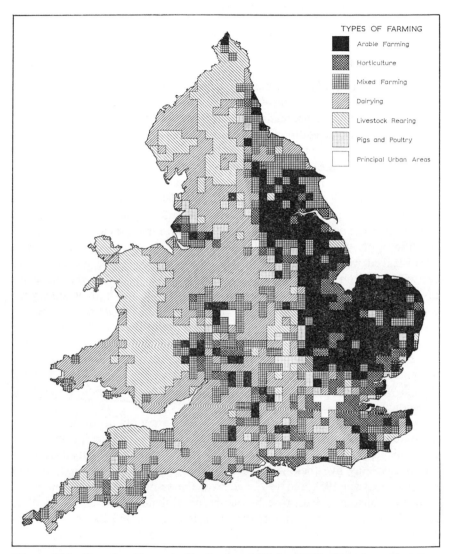

**Figure 21.2.** Farming Types in England and Wales, 1965. (Based on Church *et al.*, 1968.)

Intensive factory farming methods have been specially in evidence in pig and poultry production but have also influenced beef production (barley-beef) and to a lesser extent dairying (zero-grazing).

## SOME EFFECTS OF MODERN FARMING PRACTICES

The trends towards intensification and specialization in modern farming practice have been responsible for the creation of a number of ecological issues of concern to conservationists. The best known of these are problems associated with the addition of persistent pesticides and their effects on wildlife (Moore, Chapter 15), the pollution and eutrophication of freshwaters, and the increasing mechanization of farming practices. Mechanization has been partly responsible for widespread hedgerow removal in eastern England, and for loss of soil structure and a deterioration in soil drainage conditions in some arable farming areas. Despite the use of pesticides and herbicides, the farmer is unable to control certain diseases and weeds under conditions of intensive arable farming. Herbicides have controlled most broad-leaved weeds easily enough but wild oats, couch and meadow grass are widespread in continuous cereal growing areas. Likewise, the incidence of fungal diseases increases in wheat and barley crops if they are grown continuously and *Rhynchosporum* in barley can be serious in wetter growing areas. The incidence of disease varies considerably from season to season, suggesting that farmers have only limited control over its occurrence once traditional cropping rotations have been abandoned. A return to traditional rotations is not economic in most farming situations even though yields may be reduced by 25 per cent or more by disease and weed infestation.

In order to sustain intensive farming greater amounts of inorganic fertilizers are required than were traditionally added, especially as it is no longer economic to cart and spread farmyard manure and as many farms no longer have any livestock. Additions of nitrogenous fertilizers rose by 150 per cent between 1957 and 1967 and over the same period fertilizer input, valued at constant prices, rose by one-half (Midland Bank, 1968). In 1966, 590,000 tons of nitrogen, in nutrient equivalent terms, 435,000 tons of phosphate and 382,000 tons of potash, as well as six million tons of lime, were added by farmers in the United Kingdom (Coppock, 1971). This represented a 450 per cent increase over additions made in the 1930s and has undoubtedly been encouraged by a fertilizer and lime subsidy, although this has been recently withdrawn. Leaching from the soil of excess nitrogen in particular has led to freshwater eutrophication and algal blooms as, for example, on parts of the Norfolk Broads. Similar pollution problems have faced water authorities where farmers, instead of returning farmyard manure to the fields, have allowed it to seep into the drainage system (Weller, 1967).

The mechanization of British agriculture has led to a new farming landscape, especially in eastern Britain. In areas of continuous arable farming, where field boundary maintenance for livestock control purposes is no longer relevant, large fields, often over 100 acres in size, have been created to meet the working needs of large machines. Large fields now predominate in cereal farming areas, and the removal of hedgerows, which are costly to maintain but provide shelter for livestock and reduce the blowing of soils, has been facilitated by a government subsidy, although this too has been recently withdrawn. The arguments of recreationalists and conservationists (see, for example, Hooper and Holdgate, 1968) that the removal of hedgerows does nothing for the beauty of the landscape, minimizes cover for wildlife and reduces the biological diversity of the countryside have had little effect on the majority of landowners, even though this diversity might help to control pests and diseases in farm crops. Hedgerow removal adds workable area to the farm, as do the clearance of copses and the drainage of long-established floristically rich permanent pastures, and supports the drive towards a more intensive use of agricultural land resources. However, nature conservationists and agriculturists have shown that modern farming practices and the provision of suitable habitats for wildlife can be accommodated on the same farm, and a successful national conference at Silsoe (Barber, 1970) has been followed by more local case studies (for example, Dorset Naturalists Trust, 1970).

Soil structure problems have also appeared in parts of Britain as a result of the intensification and mechanization of arable farming. The extent and severity of these problems became apparent during the wet autumn and winter of 1968–69, when arable land had to be left fallow because of the poor drainage conditions resulting from a loss of a satisfactory soil structure. The Government then set up a special advisory committee to look into the problem (Ministry of Agriculture, 1970; see also Batey and Davies, 1971). The committee's conclusions support the view that machinery had been used inadvisedly on wet soils in an effort to meet crop cultivation schedules. Problems are most severe where continuous cropping has led to a low organic matter content in the soil, where annual rainfall is in excess of thirty inches, where late harvested crops, such as sugar beet and Brussels sprouts, necessitate the use of machinery on the land late in the autumn, and where soils have textures dominated by fine sands, silts or heavy clays. Compaction and panning occur on heavy soils and surface instability, leading to crusting, on fine sands and silts. Generally, soils in traditional arable farming areas in eastern England, because of low rainfall amounts and their medium textures, have not been badly affected, and it is those regions that

12

have only recently experienced intensive arable farming, such as parts of the East Midlands and the clay soil areas of Warwickshire, that are in greatest difficulty. The report also noted the problems of poor drainage and high grassland stocking rates in western Britain. Soil problems have been eased by direct sowing techniques into the stubble of the previous crop, so removing the need for ploughing and other cultivations. Intensified agriculture also introduces problems of soil erosion, particularly by wind (Warren, Chapter 3).

## REFERENCES

Advisory Committee on Agriculture, Forestry and Land Management (1970). *Agriculture, Forestry and Land Management,* Report presented to the Standing Committee of The Countryside in 1970 Conference, Report **1,** 39 pp.

## CONCLUSION

The purpose of this chapter has been to point out some of the implications for rural planning and the natural environment of a continued intensification of agricultural practice in Britain (for further discussion see Report of the Advisory Committee on Agriculture, Forestry and Land Management, 1970). As total investment in specialized production systems increases, so the cost to, and the length of time necessary for, the industry to readjust its practices becomes greater. Most farmers are aware of the potential ecological dangers of some contemporary farming practices, and many would like to introduce farm management programmes based on long-term ecological considerations, but individually, they feel unable to reverse current farming trends without satisfactory financial recompense from government sources. A similar situation has been observed in the United States, where rising land prices and interest rates have reduced the farming community's commitment to soil conservation measures (Held and Clawson, 1965). At present, the great majority of farmers are too concerned with making immediate ends meet to contemplate the possible long-term ecological effects of their actions, which may be resolved by technological developments anyway. The withdrawal of financial support to agriculture, as a means of encouraging extensive farming, is not the answer, as the resulting bankruptcies and run-down rural landscapes would be socially undesirable, aesthetically unattractive and not necessarily ecologically more interesting and balanced. It is almost inevitable, therefore, that unless rural land use is positively zoned in the future, both on a local and a regional scale, with agriculture being accredited different goals in different locations, then current trends will lead to severe conflicts of interest between farmers, recreationalists and conservationists.

Barber, D. (Ed.) (1970). *Farming and Wildlife—a Study in Compromise*, Royal Society for the Protection of Birds, and Farming and Wildlife Advisory Group, Nature Conservancy, Sandy, Beds., 93 pp.

Batey, T., and Davies, B. D. (1971). Soil structure and the production of arable crops, *J. Roy. Agric. Soc.*, **132**, 106–22.

Best, R. H. (1964). The future urban acreage, *Town and Country Planning*, **32**, 350–5.

Best, R. H. (1965). Recent changes and future prospects of land use in England and Wales, *Geog. J.*, **131**, 1–12.

Best, R. H. (1968). Extent of urban growth and displacement in post-war Britain, *Urban Studies*, **5**, 1–23.

Best, R. H., and Champion, A. G. (1970). Regional conversions of agricultural land to urban use in England and Wales, 1945–67, *Transactions of the Institute of British Geographers*, **49**, 15–32.

Bonham-Carter, V. (1971). *Survival of the English Countryside*, Hodder and Stoughton, London, 240 pp.

Bramley, M. (1965). *Farming and Food Supplies*, Allen & Unwin, London, 131 pp.

Cheshire, P., and Bowers, J. (1969). Farming, conservation and amenity, *New Scientist*, 3rd April, 13–15.

Church, B. M., Boyd, D. A., Evans, J. A., and Sadler, J. I. (1968). A type of farming map based on agricultural census data, *Outlook on Agriculture*, **5**, 191–6.

Cooke, G. W. (1970). The carrying capacity of the land in the year 2000, in: *The Optimum Population for Britain*, (ed.) L. R. Taylor, Academic Press, London, 15–42.

Coppock, J. T. (1971). *An Agricultural Geography of Great Britain*, Bell, London, 345 pp.

Donaldson, J. G. S. and Donaldson, F. (1969). *Farming in Britain Today*, Penguin, London, 340 pp.

Dorset Naturalists Trust (1970). *Farming and Wildlife in Dorset*, DNT, Poole, 94 pp.

Edwards, A. M., and Wibberley, G. P. (1971). An agricuutural land budget for Britain, 1965–2000, *Wye College Studies in Rural Land Use*, No. **10**, 120 pp.

Held, R. B., and Clawson, M. (1965). *Soil Conservation in Perspective*, Johns Hopkins University Press for Resources for the Future Inc., Baltimore, 344 pp.

HMSO (1972). *Annual Review and Determination of Guarantees*, HMSO, Cmnd 4928, London, 37 pp.

Hooper, M. D., and Holdgate, M. W. (eds.) (1968). *Hedges and hedgerow trees*. Monks Wood Experimental Station Symposium **4**, The Nature Conservancy, 104 pp.

McCrone, G. (1962). *The Economics of Subsidizing Agriculture*, University of Toronto Press, Toronto, 189 pp.

Midland Bank (1968). *Britain's Agriculture Today*, Midland Bank, London, 32 pp.

Ministry of Agriculture, Fisheries and Food (1970). *Modern Farming and The Soil*, Report of the Agricultural Advisory Council on Soil Structure and Soil Fertility, HMSO, London, 119 pp.

Phillips, A., and Roberts, M. (1973). The recreation and amenity value of the countryside, *J. Agric. Econ.*, **24**, 85–98.

Self, P., and Storing, H. J. (1962). *The State and the Farmer*, Allen and Unwin, London, 251 pp.

Thomas, H. A. (1970). Capital intensity in agriculture, *Agriculture*, **77**, 13–14.
Weller, J. (1967). *Modern Agriculture and Rural Planning*, The Architectural Press, London, 442 pp.
Wibberley, G. P. (1968). Pressures on Britain's rural land, in: *Land Use or Abuse*, Report of the 22nd Oxford Farming Conference, Oxford, 3–15.
Wibberley, G. P. (1971). European Conservation Year 1970 in relation to agriculture and forestry, *J. Roy. Agric. Soc.*, **132**, 13–17.

# CHAPTER 22

# Land Use in Upland Britain—An Economist's Viewpoint

GWYN JAMES

Interest in a rational approach to the use of land in Britain is of fairly recent origin. It has long been accepted that land has two major uses—rural and urban—and that the demand for land for urban development would grow over time. But the use of rural land has been traditionally thought of almost exclusively in terms of agriculture, and any demand for the use of rural land by non-agricultural interests has been strongly, sometimes violently, but always consistently opposed.

## THE THEORY OF LAND USE

From a technical standpoint, land of a given type may be suitable for a variety of uses. Land in a water catchment area may be used exclusively for water conservation; it could, however, be afforested or grazed. Indeed, it could be used for all three purposes simultaneously. Likewise, land scheduled for recreational use could be partly afforested and this might enhance its amenity value and improve its recreational potential. The forest could, if properly managed, be used simultaneously for commercial timber production. Which use, or combination of uses, is to be preferred? If a rational use of land is to be achieved, society must accept three basic principles:

1. Farmers have no sacrosanct right to the use of land, any more than other individuals or occupational groups wishing to develop land for non-farm purposes. The reason that over 80 per cent of the total land acreage of Britain is currently used for agricultural purposes is historical, and should not influence decisions concerning the future use to which the land should be put.

2. Non-agricultural activities or interests have a legitimate right to acquire land in rural areas and this right must be recognized and catered for.

3. If these two principles are accepted, the third follows axiomatically. It is that the right to use land for any purpose and by any individual or institution (i.e. state or private) must be proved. This involves the selection and use of criteria by which the claims of alternative activities for a given area of rural land can be measured.

If society's declared objective is the rational use of rural land, by which is meant a proper sharing of such land between the variety of alternative land-using activities, by what criteria should the respective claims of these activities for land be assessed?

Is a policy which provides employment opportunities for 100 workers and their families in a rural area more, or less, rational than one which provides employment opportunities for only 50 workers and their families?

Is the conservation of 100 million litres of water a year a more, or less, rational form of land use than the production of 500 tonnes of lamb or beef?

Is the growth of trees in hill and upland areas more, or less, rational than the development of leisure or recreational facilities?

These questions mirror many of the nebulous motives which influence the use of land, and highlight the criteria which governments and private landowners adopt in formulating policies of land use. Basically, the use to which land in any country may be put is a function of environmental factors such as climate, topography, aspect or soil. Such factors, however, often permit a variety of activities which present the owner with a difficult choice. How then is the investor, government, private institution or individual to make an effective choice between these alternative land-using activities?

In seeking a criterion by which an objective comparison can be made between the claims of a variety of activities for the use of a given area of land, the economic implications of these alternative activities provide society with its best measuring rod. This is not to imply that social, strategic or political issues are irrelevant or unimportant, but rather to suggest that these factors are ancillary to economic efficiency or resource use and that, in consequence, their influence should be subordinated to that of economic performance. Two main reasons support this thesis. First, economic analysis of the use of land under alternative activities enables society to make valid comparisons between *quantifiable* objectives whose end products are heterogenous. It enables society, for instance, to compare the use of a given area of land producing 1,000 cubic metres of timber with the use of similar land producing 200 tonnes of beef. More importantly, economic analysis can even permit an evaluation of *non*-quantifiable objectives, which are often subjective in character and are consequently incapable of direct evaluation.

How does one, for instance, assess the amenity value of a forest or the employment value of agriculture or water conservation? This can only be achieved objectively by the use of economic analysis. Consider as an illustration, amenity value, which is probably the most subjective, and hence the most non-quantifiable, of all the factors that determine the use of land. Assume that, in an effort to provide amenity in rural areas, the Forestry Commission, or a private landowner, pursues a policy of mixed planting rather than one which concentrates on a single species. If the net income from the single species is £20 a hectare, while that from the mixed plantation is only £15 a hectare, the cost of amenity can be evaluated at £5 a hectare. This represents the opportunity cost* to society of beauty, and it is surely important that society is aware of the net cost involved in pursuing non-monetary objectives?

The second reason why the economic criterion is both acceptable and necessary in respect of land use is this. The use of land, for any purpose, brings into being relationships which themselves are economic in character. Land is traditionally a natural factor in production, it is limited in quality relative to demand and is specific in location. It is therefore an economic good which possesses value. But the use of land automatically incurs the use of other scarce, valuable goods (labour and capital), and the combined use of these three inputs results in the production of commodities (food, timber, water, pleasure) which themselves are economic in that they are scarce relative to demand and possess a value. In other words, the use of land by any activity implies the use of an economic good, in association with other economic goods, to produce another economic good. In view of the economic relationships which the use of land evokes, it seems both reasonable and logical to suggest that the assessment of the claims of alternative activities to the use of a given area of land should, at least initially, be made on the basis of their respective efficiencies in the use of the economic goods incurred. This would give society an objective measurement of which activity, or combination of activities, makes the 'best' use of land.

Land whose economic return under a given use is assessed to be zero would be marginal *under that use*; if its economic return is negative its use would be sub-marginal. Using the economic criterion alone, therefore, decisions relating to land use would be confined to those activities (or combination of activities) whose return was super-marginal. On occasions, the resultant 'best' use of land might need to be modified or adjusted to meet other socially more desirable ends. But society would then be in a position to assess the opportunity cost of pursuing less 'profitable' goals

---

* Opportunity cost is defined as the reward that is sacrificed by not pursuing the most profitable alternative.

requiring the use of land, and should accordingly be able to make its choice on a more informed basis than would otherwise have been the case.

## COMPETITION FOR LAND USE

Competition for land use between alternative uses occurs when the total supply of land available is less than that required by the various uses in aggregate, to produce that quantity of products necessary to meet the demands of the market. It may be inferred from this that if the total supply of land available in a country is equal to, or exceeds, the aggregate requirements of the individual uses, there will be no competition between these uses for land. The requirements of the farmer, forester, water engineer, recreationist and conservationist would then all be fully met. Under such conditions the economist would lose his franchise, for the land itself would lose its scarcity value and its use, in consequence, would have no economic meaning. The economic problems associated with the allocation of *scarce* resources between alternative uses would not exist.

But land is not a homogeneous product. The total physical supply of land in a country comprises a wide variety of land types, each of which reflects differences in soil characteristics, aspect, moisture, temperature, topography and location. These particular attributes determine the suitability of land for specific uses. Climatic influences might attract the forester to an area, but repel the farmer; soil conditions or topography in another area may encourage livestock farming but be unsuitable for arable cropping. The physical and environmental attributes of many areas can equally meet the requirements of a variety of different activities. The total supply of land in a country, therefore, will only equal or exceed the total demand for land if there is available an adequate supply of land of use-types in the place required by all the potential users. In the real world this ideal situation rarely, if ever, exists and in consequence competition between uses for a specific type of land builds up, even in those countries where the total physical supply of land is abundant.

The situation is further complicated by the pattern of population distribution in most countries, and the natural and understandable inclination of man to concentrate his productive activities as near as possible to the market, in an effort to minimize transport costs. The growth of large conurbations in most countries has concentrated a large part of the total demand for the products of land in relatively few major markets. Competitive pressures for the use of land are greater in and immediately around these population centres than in more distant areas, where land of comparable, and often higher, quality may be readily available. There is, for instance, a seemingly inexhaustible physical supply of land in Australia; yet competition between alternative uses for land is as keen and the problems of allocation as pressing in and around the major cities as in West European countries, where the total supply of land is so much less.

In considering the strength of competition for the use of land between alternative activities, one must not be misled by an abundance of physical acres. Supply implies a use concept, which is a function not only of physical quantity but also of quality. Barren or waste land which has no use value does not constitute a part of the total land supply of a country, although such land is included in the aggregate physical acreage.

In recent years, the demands for the use of rural land in Britain, particularly in upland areas, have increased and they will continue to do so in the future as population grows. Additional land is required by the Forestry Commission to meet its planting programmes; water undertakings need more land to meet the requirements of an increasing urban population and of growing industry; there is an increasing awareness of the scientific value of specific areas and a complementary desire to schedule such areas as nature reserves; more land is required for recreational purposes to give people the opportunity to enjoy their leisure in rural surroundings.

## NON-MARKET BENEFITS

A non-market benefit is defined as a benefit emanating from an investment project for which no market price exists. It is therefore impossible to evaluate it directly in money terms. Non-market benefits are invariably intangible, but not all intangible benefits are necessarily of a non-market character. The pleasure enjoyed by a visitor to a commercially operated national park is intangible, but inasmuch as an admission fee is charged it is a market benefit.

If investment decisions involving alternative forms of land use are to be made in as rational a manner as possible, it is necessary that as many as possible of these non-market benefits should be included in the analysis. This implies the objective quantification of such benefits and the inclusion of them in the economic analysis alongside the other tangible priced benefits. Objections to any attempt to evaluate the non-market benefits of investment projects are usually made on the basis that such an evaluation is either undesirable or is difficult. The major problem associated with intangible non-market benefits is that, in many instances, they have been traditionally available free, as a result of which a philosophy has developed that they are incapable of reflecting the willingness of users to forego other commodities of value in order to enjoy them. Evaluation of such benefits questions the validity of this philosophy. It may be unconventional to do so but it is not undesirable. It is certainly true that evaluation is difficult, but it does not necessarily follow that evaluation is impossible. In some instances, evaluation may indeed be impossible—for instance, in respect of cultural or nationalistic or even mystical values. But the fact that the evaluation of some non-market benefits is impossible is not sufficient reason not to attempt the evaluation of other such benefits.

A variety of approaches can be adopted to evaluate non-market benefits (Sinden, 1967). Measurement may be attempted in purely physical terms, either on a quality basis or on a quantity basis. A subjective, qualitative evaluation of the benefits of recreation or of hunting can be made on the basis of high-, medium- or low-density use, or of good, moderate or poor sport. Some of the non-market benefits of a highway construction scheme may be evaluated on a quantity basis in terms of the likely savings in road deaths per million car kilometres. Alternatively, as a first approximation, a subjective monetary value may be assigned to the non-market benefit, but a more precise approach is to assess any actual or potential cash flows associated with the benefit. This may be attempted in terms of the cost of providing the benefit; the gross volume of business generated by the activity, through the additional expenditure incurred by those who use the project; or by using the 'value-added' approach, by which the difference between the gross expenditure of the activity and the costs of the raw materials, or semi-finished products, which are incorporated in the final product is assessed.

## The Use of Demand Curves

These methods can be criticized, however, on at least two major grounds. First, there is a lack of any generally accepted reasoning underlying any of the methods. More specifically, all the methods display an inbuilt need to identify some physical manifestation of the intangible benefit, which itself is capable of monetary assessment. Second, none of the methods are based at all closely on the principle that the economic value of the benefit is related to the willingness of a consumer to obtain it. A very definite correlation can be observed between the willingness of people to pay for a commodity and the quantity of that commodity that is demanded, and this applies equally to a physical good and to intangible services or experiences. As with any other good or service, as the price that consumers are required to pay for recreation or amenity or pleasure increases, the quantity demanded would be expected to fall. The demand analysis approach has consequently been used in a number of different forms over the past decade to obtain an objective measurement of the non-market value that might be associated with land-using activities.

Attempts to establish derived demand curves to evaluate non-market benefits have been based on three different approaches:

(i) The market price that would be charged if the resource was managed under private enterprise is identified and the intensity of consumer demand is related to this price. The major weakness of this approach is the difficulty of identifying a privately managed activity that is identical in type to that activity under review.

(ii) Consumers may be approached directly through questionnaires, and asked to relate their possible use of the resource to a range of prices. This approach has been used quite extensively and successfully, and is generally accepted by economists as a legitimate method of constructing a derived demand curve (Knetsch and Davis, 1966; Shafer, 1964). In all the researches that have used this method, the willingness of the consumer to pay for the benefit accruing from the resource was found to be related significantly to expected variables such as income, acquaintance with the area, quantity of leisure time available, personal idiosyncrasies, and so on. The total value of the non-market benefit will be a function of aggregate demand at the 'assumed' price, so that it can be varied by the analyst merely by manipulating this assumed price, and this again introduces a subjective element into the analysis and weakens considerably its use as an acceptable method.

(iii) The third approach attempts to overcome the problems inherent in any attempt to 'assume' a price for the benefit. It makes an assumption that the 'price' paid by consumers of the benefit is equal to the actual costs that they incur in obtaining the benefit. In practice, such costs largely comprise the cost of travel incurred by consumers. The cost of travel has therefore been adopted as a measure of the 'price' consumers are prepared to pay to enjoy the non-market benefits of a variety of land-using activities, including recreation, pleasure and amenity.

The 'travel cost' approach was pioneered by Hotelling (1949) and has been variously developed and adapted over the years by Trice and Wood (1958), Clawson (1959), Knetsch and Davis (1966) and Clawson and Knetsch (1967).

Two main points emerge from the above discussion. First, not all non-market benefits are capable of quantification or of monetary evaluation, either directly or indirectly. Second, in those instances where such non-market benefits are capable of quantitative and ultimately monetary assessment, there is no 'best' method which should be used in every instance. In some instances a quantitative assessment of the benefits is possible, but no direct money values are available. Subjective values may be sufficient as an approximation of the value of the benefits. In other instances a purely qualitative assessment may be adequate, especially if the purpose of the analysis is merely to rank similar projects and no absolute assessment is needed or no comparative assessment of heterogenous projects is required.

But even where the non-market benefit can be measured and evaluated directly, no single 'best' method exists. In these instances, however, the more acceptable methods are those that are based on willingness to pay. This would restrict the choice largely to the use of demand curves or the opportunity cost approach.

There is one last point. None of the methods by which non-market benefits might be evaluated are perfect; all have their weaknesses and their merits. Hence, the absolute magnitude of the assessed benefit which results from their use may be either undervalued or overvalued, and consequently incorrect decisions would result. On this basis, the justification for attempting any evaluation of non-market benefits emanating from land-using activities will depend on how much less imperfect the subsequent decisions in respect of land use might be when compared with decisions based solely on vague, arbitrary and often contradictory notions of the social values ascribed to such benefits. In other words, the defence of attempting to evaluate non-market benefits is not that such evaluations remove all errors from the decision-making process, but that they reduce the degree of error that might otherwise occur.


## THE PROBLEM OF CHOICE

Another issue of concern to the economist in his assessment of the use potential of rural land revolves around the practical problems associated with such an analysis. Four separate problems arise: the choice of area within which the assessment of land use is to be made; the choice of objectives; the choice of methodology by reference to which the financial calculations are made; the choice of criteria by which the relative claims of alternative activities to the use of land are assessed.

### The Choice of Area

A word which is currently in fashion in political circles in Britain is 'regionalism'. Goverment has, of recent years, been occupied in making decisions on the regional level. The development of the Northeast Region and the growth of Rural Development Boards were examples of this cult. The hills and uplands of Britain have a natural regionalism about them; their location is specific to given regions and there is therefore a serious danger of considering the use of these hills and uplands on a regional basis —a danger which has not been sufficiently foreseen in the past and which, in consequence, has led to an irrational use of land in these areas. Economists need not be concerned about the size of the area whose use is under review: it may be a large region covering a number of administrative countries (such as Mid-Wales, the Pennines or the Highlands and Islands of Scotland) or it may be as small as a farm. But the size of the area under review is of relatively secondary importance, except insofar as a large area may make the analysis more complicated. What is important is that in assessing the use to which land within a given area is put, the area, regardless of its size, must be homogeneous in respect of those factor combinations which influence its productivity under the activities being examined—these factors include soil type, rainfall, altitude, temperature, aspect and other physical features. The combination of these factors may vary considerably throughout an area, giving rise to distinctive patterns of land-use types: the whole area may be currently used for agricultural purposes, but the type of agriculture practised may differ considerably from one part to another. In some parts fat lamb production may predominate, while in others the production of store lambs may be the only possible system of sheep management. Dairying may be the dominant enterprise in another part and beef production elsewhere. Hence, it is often necessary to break down a given, natural region into smaller units, each representing a homogeneous use type. Small areas may be sufficiently homogeneous in themselves, but it should never be assumed that smallness is synonymous with homogeneity. Often it is necessary to break down an individual farm into separate parts, each representing a distinctive type of farming.

The effect of these local physical and climatic differences, however, is not limited to agriculture, but influences other activities. In forestry, the choice of species, the rate of timber growth, the cost of operations, the quality (and value) of the felled timber, are all affected by differences in soil quality, altitude, aspect and rainfall. In some areas, recreation means mountaineering or sailing; in others, pony-trekking, hiking or camping. Such differences, within broad categories of activities, in effect create separate, distinct activities and may thereby exert a considerable influence on the use potential of land.

In considering the area, the existing broad pattern of land use should, as a starting point, be broken down into a systematic pattern of homogeneous uses. Since agriculture is invariably the 'sitting tenant' in hill and upland areas, this will mean the classification of farming according to type: hill-sheep farming, livestock rearing, mixed livestock, and so on. The analyst should then impose on the area under review, classified in respect of its current land use, the alternative uses to which the area could, from a technical standpoint, be put. These alternative uses should likewise be classified into homogeneous groups, as shown in Figure 22.1.

Consider a hypothetical example, by which a decision needs to be made as to whether a thousand-hectare upland farm should be afforested, or whether its recreational potential should be exploited. The objective, in this instance, is not necessarily to determine whether the *whole* farm should be retained in agriculture or be afforested or be developed for recreation, but rather to ascertain what parts of the farm, if any, are better suited to afforestation or to recreation than to agriculture. This is not, therefore, a straightforward comparison between agriculture, forestry and recreation, but one between specific types of agriculture and specific types of forestry and specific types of recreation. Unless such a classification of the potential uses of an area,

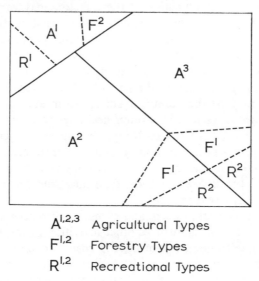

$A^{1,2,3}$   Agricultural Types

$F^{1,2}$   Forestry Types

$R^{1,2}$   Recreational Types

**Figure 22.1.** An hypothetical area classified into homogeneous land use activities. For discussion see text.

or a farm, is undertaken, it would be concluded, irrationally, that the *whole* area or farm should remain in agriculture or be transferred to forestry or used for recreation, whereas *parts* of the area or the farm characterized by a distinctive type of forestry may be economically more attractive than the type of farming practised there, while other parts, characterized by a different type of forestry, may be economically less attractive than the current type of agriculture. Referring to Figure 22.1, it may be found, for instance, that whereas F2 is more profitable than A2, A3 is more profitable than F1. Likewise, R2 may be more profitable than A2, but less profitable than A3. Decision makers, in the past, have been prone to falling into the trap of regarding agriculture in hill and upland areas in Britain as a homogeneous activity, and on the evidence of general farm surveys have arrived at one or other of two conclusions in respect of land use: either, the financial results from farming are such that no alternative activity could possibly compete effectively, which means therefore the retention of the land in agricultural use; or, the financial results from farming are such that any other activity must surely be a better economic prospect, which means that the area should be afforested, flooded or developed for recreation. In other words, conclusions have been arrived at by a process of deductive reasoning; the claims of the alternative uses to which the land has ultimately been put have not been proved objectively.

## The Choice of Objectives

The choice between alternative forms of land use will be influenced by the objective that the landowner is seeking. If the objective is profit maximization, then the form of land use (or combination of uses) with the highest net income potential should be adopted; if, on the other hand, the principal objective is the maintenance of rural population, the decision between alternative activities will be made on the basis of their respective employment potentials. The objectives that are pursued by the private landowner are naturally subjective. He is not necessarily concerned about national priorities or interests, but is influenced by his own private or family needs. His overriding requirement is, normally, income, but this objective is often modified by other personal foibles such as an interest in shooting, a desire to enhance or maintain the amenity value of his property, and so on. The state, on the other hand, can adopt a more impartial view of land use; it can, and often does, subject personal and individual interests to those of society at large. As such, its objectives tend to differ from those of the individual.

### National Objectives

A major national objective in Britain over the past decades has been a desire to provide employment opportunities in rural areas. It is often claimed that this objective invariably favours forestry rather than other activities in hill and upland areas, in that it employs more men per hectare, and generally per unit of investment. In assessing the employment potential of forestry, two points are relevant. First, it is incorrect to generalize about the higher labour requirements of forestry compared with other forms of land use. Forestry employs more labour per unit of land only in marginal agricultural areas, which would, of course, be characterized by extensive sheep and cattle farming. If the average size of farms is large in these areas (as in parts of North Scotland), the relative employment potential of forestry is greater than in areas where the average size of farm is small (as in Mid-Wales). Second, even in marginal agricultural areas, the higher employment requirements of forestry are confined to the establishment years of the forest-life; thereafter, labour requirements for maintenance are low. Unless therefore a rotation is arranged that allows continued planting and establishment, on an annual basis, the long-term employment potential of forestry will be disappointing.

Another national objective is to create social amenities in rural areas. This is closely associated with the employment objective, as new jobs in an area mean that additional families are attracted to that area. In consequence, viable communities may result which create a demand for schools, shops, recreational facilities, transport services and public utilities which, when provided, revitalize the social life of the area and provide additional amenities for tourists. The Forestry Commission has in the past, for instance, built completely new villages in upland areas of Britain, such as Llwynygog in Montgomeryshire, Llandulais in Breconshire and Dalavich in Argyllshire. Current policy, however, is to try to graft new houses for forest workers on to an existing village, in an attempt to bring new life to villages suffering from an ageing population.

From time to time, the desire of national government to increase the production of a commodity, and hence alter the pattern of rural land use, is influenced by economic considerations relating to the country's overall balance of payments situation. In such circumstances, production will be encouraged of that commodity (food, timber or tourism) which will save imports to the greatest value.

Britain is still very largely dependent on imports for its supplies of timber and timber products, and although much of it is obtained from soft currency areas, any considerable increase might have to come from dollar areas. Clearly, therefore, future increases in the supply of home-grown timber would be very desirable from a national standpoint, particularly if such increases could be achieved at relatively low costs. However, Britain is also dependent on imports for approximately a half (by value) of its total food supplies; increases in the supply of home-produced foods, particularly those which reduce its dependence on dollars, would also be very desirable.

Different views have been expressed by economists about the importance of balance of payments considerations. McCrone (1962, pp. 74–83) for instance, questioned the contribution of agriculture to the balance of payments even in the immediate post-war years, when the 'dollar shortage' was most critical. He pointed out that the increase in the output of home agriculture replaced overseas supplies from the sterling, rather than the dollar, area; that in consequence Britain eventually had a current balance of payments surplus with the rest of the sterling area which became an embarrassment through the serious effects it produced on the ability of these countries to purchase British exports. The effect of the expansion of domestic agricultural production on the 'dollar gap' was negligible because, for various reasons, the imported supplies which came from the dollar area could not be replaced by increased home production. McCrone concluded, 'indeed, if account is taken of the imports of feeding stuffs which have come from the dollar area as a result of the increase in home livestock production, the contribution may even have been negative during some of the years of the dollar shortage'.

Moore and Peters (1965) attempted to measure agriculture's *net* contribution to the overall balance of payments, and concluded that although the contribution was positive it was considerably smaller than that suggested by the leaders of the industry.

Other objectives that have influenced national decisions in respect of rural land use include strategic considerations, relating to an overdependence on imported supplies of essential commodities, notably food and timber; the need to earn a commercial return on the investment of national capital in land; and the desire to develop recreational facilities in rural areas to meet the increasing demands for leisure from a growing urban population.

*Private Objectives*

A national policy geared towards the attainment of any of the above objectives does not directly motivate the private landowner in his choice of activity; but the private use of land can be influenced indirectly by nationally inspired measures. Changes in the level of production grants, adjustments to taxation allowances, variations in the level and volume of guaranteed prices, improved credit facilities or the creation of assured markets can all, indirectly, affect the plans of private landowners and lead to a pattern of land use more closely related to the attainment of national objectives than might otherwise be the case.

There are, nevertheless, a number of objectives which are associated more with the private landowner than with the nation and which, individually or collectively, determine the pattern of land use on private farms or estates. Perhaps the most insistent is the need to manage the property on a commercial basis, to earn sufficient income each year to meet current expenditure charges, or to earn as high a return as possible on capital investment. Other private objectives include a need to provide shelter for livestock and the desire of estate owners to create and maintain recreational facilities within the estate.

On occasions, however, the freedom of the individual landowner to implement a pattern of land use related to the attainment of any of these objectives is limited by factors completely outside his control. Many farms on private estates, for instance, are situated within the boundaries of National Parks, where a policy towards afforestation might mean that land which from an estate standpoint would be better used under trees has to remain in agriculture. Again, the security of tenure currently enjoyed by tenant farmers is another restricting factor that must be taken into account by private land-owners in replanning land use on their estates. Lack of sufficient capital often prevents a landowner from pursuing a particular objective, while the need for an annual cash flow of income limits the freedom of the owner to plan his property according to his natural desires. These restrictions are common to the majority of private landowners, and it seems that it is the restrictions, rather than the objectives, that determine the pattern of land use on most private estates.

**The Choice of Methodology**

One of the most critical differences between alternative land-using activities concerns the length of their respective production cycles. For instance, land devoted to agriculture yields a fairly immediate return (agricultural crops are typically of one year duration) whereas, at the other extreme, the return on forest land is virtually nothing for almost 20 years after planting, and is not fully realized for perhaps 50 years or more. Hence, a profit calculation based on the straightforward difference between annual gross revenues and expenditures (as is customary in assessing the economics of agricultural production) is a meaningless indication of the relative economic values of activities with widely differing production cycles and cash flow patterns.

To overcome this 'time factor' effect, it is necessary to absorb into the calculations time as a cost of production (the cost of waiting) by discounting all items of revenue and expenditure incurred over the life of the longest activity under review, and to relate the resultant 'net discounted margin' to a similarly discounted margin calculated over a similar time period in respect of the other activities. Discounting thereby enables the analyst to assess the 'present worth' of any long-term investment. In effect, it implies answering two questions:

(a) On the expenditure side, how much money would an investor need to set aside today (at a given rate of discount) to finance an expenditure of £X in Y years' time?

(b) On the revenue side, what is the worth or value today of an income of £X which an investor will earn in Y years' time (at a given rate of discount)?

Consider, as an example, an investor who intends to spend £20 in 15 years' time and expects to receive £40 in 30 years' time from this investment. What is the present net value of his investment, if both his expected expenditure and revenue are discounted at 5 per cent? Let $X$ = expenditure and $Y$ = income, then:

$$\text{Net Present Value (N.P.V.)} = \frac{Y}{(1 \cdot 0p)^n} - \frac{X}{(1 \cdot 0p)^n}$$

where $p$ = discount rate and $n$ = year in which income is received and expenditure is incurred, respectively.

If this simple illustration is extended to a situation within which, during the course of one productive rotation, a series, or flow, of incomes is received, and a flow of expenditures is incurred regularly, the net present value of the activity will be determined by the equation:

$$\text{N.P.V.} = \sum \left( Y^0 + \frac{Y^1}{(1 \cdot 0p)^1} + \frac{Y^2}{(1 \cdot 0p)^2} + \cdots \frac{Y^n}{(1 \cdot 0p)^n} \right) -$$

$$\sum \left( X^0 + \frac{X^1}{(1 \cdot 0p)^1} + \frac{X^2}{(1 \cdot 0p)^2} + \cdots \frac{X^n}{(1 \cdot 0p)^n} \right)$$

where $Y$ and $X$ represent incomes and expenditures respectively, earned in, and incurred in, given years (0, 1. 2. . .) up to and including year $n$, all of which are discounted at $p$ per cent (Hiley, 1956).

Thus, both revenues and expenditures are brought to a common period of time (the present) as a means of overcoming the different time elements involved in different productive processes. Net present value is therefore dependent upon three variables—the rate of discount, the timing of the cash flows and the magnitude of the cash flows. The net present value of a given sum of money, invested in a given year, will be smaller at a high than at a low discount rate. It will also be smaller, at a constant discount rate, if the investment is deferred until a later date, unless the magnitude of the deferred investment can be enlarged sufficiently to offset the increased costs of waiting. Accordingly, the choice of discount rate is crucial to the assessment of the relative profitability of alternative activities whose patterns of income and expenditure flows differ over time and are of predetermined magnitudes.

Several factors can influence a landowner's choice of discount rate. First, it may be governed by the prospective rate of return from the most efficient alternative use to which the owner's resources may be put, for example investment or spending within the owner's current business, which in agriculture might be in livestock or cereal production or in forestry might be in timber management or wood processing. Here the relevant rate is the anticipated annual rate of return from these activities or the owner's borrowing rate, whichever is less, after allowing for risk. Another alternative is investment outside the owner's present business, as occurs when farmers contemplate forestry and foresters contemplate investment in the securities of some outside borrower, such as industry or commerce. Here the rate that governs is the prospective yield from the alternative investments. Still another alternative is spending for personal consumption. The rate here should equal the owner's rate of 'time preference'; in other words, the premium he places on current consumption in preference to its postponement.

The selected discount rate may also be affected by various fringe benefits that may accompany the income from various alternative activities. For the owners who are in a position to enjoy these benefits, the guiding rate of discount applicable to the activity is lowered. Consequently, activities that confer fringe benefits upon the owner need not yield so high a return as otherwise in order to compare favourably with alternative investments. Fringe benefits may include taxation allowances to certain specified investors, or they may merely represent non-monetary gains of a subjective nature, such as love of the countryside.

The owner's discount rate may also be influenced by his judgment of the related risks (and uncertainties) involved in his present business compared with the alternative objects of investment or spending. In general, the risks associated with forestry appear to be higher than those in agriculture. Broadly, they fall into two categories—the risks of physical loss, resulting from fire, pests and storms, and the risks of declining prices or rising costs. The latter concern the farmers as well as the forester, but in this respect agriculture is more flexible than forestry in that the farmers can change from one enterprise, or one system of farming, to another more quickly and at less cost than can the forester. Agriculture, in fact, is far more adaptable to changing economic conditions than forestry. The higher the risks, the higher should be the discount rate—that is, the more the enterprise has to earn in order to be comparatively attractive.

Finally, the selected discount rate should be modified by any extra costs incurred in transferring funds from one investment to another. A shift of investment from one activity to another may subject the investor to an extra income tax beyond that which would be involved in the absence of the shift. In such a situation, the selected discount rate should be lowered, reducing thereby the required rate of return by the percentage of the extra tax.

For land-using activities it appears to be traditional that lower average and marginal rates of return are accepted than, for example, among public service industries. This can be accounted for, in the main, by the fringe benefits associated with land ownership which cannot readily, if at all, be valued in money terms: for instance, social prestige, the presence of sporting facilities, love of the countryside, or the security of land as an investment. Individual owners may, therefore, adopt lower discount rates than the market price of capital. The state, on the other hand, can and often does subject economic achievement to social needs and, as an alternative to using the long-term government borrowing rate, adopts as a social discount rate either the social time preference rate or the social opportunity cost rate.

In view of the differences inherent in assessing 'correct' discount rate for use in the analysis, a better approach is to assess the economic use potential of rural land using a range of discount rates. This approach serves two further purposes. First, it indicates the effect of different discount rates on the profit potential of the individual activities; second, it enables the effect of possible future changes in the money market on the calculation of profitability to be assessed.

## The Choice of Criteria

Benefit-cost analysis, which incorporates all the methodological issues raised in the preceding section, throws up three criteria by which the worthiness of prospective investment projects can be evaluated:

1. Net Present Value (N.P.V.), which is gross discounted benefits ($B$) less total discounted costs. The costs include both the capital costs of establishing the project ($K$) and the annual operating costs incurred ($O$).

2. The Benefit-Cost ratio ($B/C$), which can take either of two forms:

$$\text{(a)} \quad \frac{B}{K+O} \quad \text{or} \quad \text{(b)} \quad \frac{B-O}{K}.$$

3. The Internal Rate of Return (I.R.R.) which represents that discount rate at which the difference between $B$ and $K+O$ is zero; that is, the discount rate at which N.P.V. is zero.

Unfortunately, these criteria are not mutually exclusive and their use, in practice, can give rise to problems of divergent rankings, as shown in Table 22.1.

**Table 22.1.** A comparison of two projects and three criteria

| Project | A | B |
|---|---|---|
| Cash flow in year 1 | −1 | −1 |
| 1 | +0 | +2 |
| 2 | +4 | +1 |
| N.P.V. @ 10% | 2·31 | 1·65 |
| $B/C$ ratio @ 10% | 3·31 | 2·65 |
| I.R.R. | 100% | 141% |
| Ranking with I.R.R. | 2nd | 1st |
| Ranking with N.P.V. and $B/C$ | 1st | 2nd |

The question that arises therefore is which criterion should be used? The answer is perfectly straightforward: that criterion should be used which maximizes whatever is desired to be maximized, or minimizes whatever is desired to be minimized. In other words, problems of choice in respect of land use are resolved not by questioning the criteria themselves, but by determining what are the maximands or minimands* and any associated constraints (normally a capital constraint) built into the analysis. The situation in respect of maximands is summarized in Table 22.2.

**Table 22.2.** Maximands for investment criteria

| Criterion | Maximand | Discount rate | Constraint |
|---|---|---|---|
| N.P.V. | Net benefits | External | — |
| $B/C$ | Net benefits per £ invested | External | Fixed capital $(K+O)$ |
| $B-O/K$ | Net benefits per £$K$ | External | Fixed $K$ only |
| I.R.R. | Compound rate of return over costs | Internal | — |

The selection of maximands or minimands is the prerogative of the investor—whether he is a private individual, a public corporation or a government agency.

All present value criteria are influenced by the discount rate selected. The higher the discount rate, the smaller will be the present value criteria. On the other hand, the I.R.R. is independent of the discount rate selected. By definition, it is that discount rate which equates the present value of the benefits with the present value of the costs of the project. If, therefore, the investor is concerned about the future level of gains or losses, his maximand is the present value of the investment. Under these circumstances, the I.R.R. is the wrong criterion to adopt, and one or other of the present value criteria must be selected. The choice will depend on what objective the investor wishes to maximize. He may wish to maximize income, in which case the appropriate criterion will be N.P.V. This is invariably the maximand of farmers, who are more concerned with total income than with return on capital, even in those instances where capital is the most limited resource. Alternatively, the investor may wish to maximize his return on capital, in which case the benefit-cost ratio is the appropriate criterion. If total capital $(K+O)$ is fixed, the benefit-cost ratio will be of the form $B/K+O$; where establishment capital only is in fixed supply, the appropriate form of the benefit-cost ratio will be $K/B-O$.

But an investor may have a minimand as his objective, in which case neither of the above value criteria are suitable. Consider, for instance, a

* A maximand relates to an objective that is to be maximized; a minimand implies that the objective is to be minimized.

farmer with a debt burden of £5,000 who wishes to redeem his debt in the least possible time, i.e. his objective is a minimand. He has two alternative projects available (A and B) with streams of annual discounted net profits (at say 10 per cent) as follows:

| Year | 1 | 2 | 3 | 4 | 5 | 6 | 7 | 8 | 9 | 10 | Total |
|------|---|---|---|---|---|---|---|---|---|-----|-------|
| A (£) | 3,000 | 2,000 | 2,000 | 2,000 | 2,000 | 2,000 | 2,000 | 2,000 | 2,000 | 2,000 | 21,000 |
| B (£) | 2,000 | 2,000 | 3,000 | 5,000 | 5,000 | 4,000 | 5,000 | 4,000 | 5,000 | 4,000 | 39,000 |

Given this situation, all present value criteria will favour B, as will incidentally the I.R.R. criterion. But all these would be inappropriate, because they do not comply with the investor's objective to redeem his debt in the minimum possible time. Project A clears the debt in two years; project B takes three years. Project A will therefore be selected.

The I.R.R., on the other hand, is appropriate as a criterion under one, and only one, condition—where the maximand is the rate of growth of assets, and all benefits can be reinvested in other projects to yield a return not less than the I.R.R. In this case, the time preference of the investor, or his social discount rate, is of no relevance, since there is no choice between consumption or reinvestment at different points in time, but rather a determination to plough back all benefits and achieve, at the termination of the project's life, as large a stock of assets as possible.

## EMPIRICAL EVIDENCE

For illustrative purposes, two areas in the hills and uplands of mid-Wales have been selected; within each, agriculture has been compared with forestry (James, 1964). First (area 1), an area characterized by livestock rearing situated in Radnorshire, about 10 miles south of Rhayader and adjacent to the urban parish of Llandrindod and lying within the boundaries of Coed Sarnau Forest. Second (area 2), an area characterized by hill-sheep farming, situated in Merionethshire between Dolgellau in the south and Trawsfynydd in the north, Ganllwyd in the west and Llanuwchlyn in the east. The area forms part of Coed-y-Brenin Forest, one of the largest state forests in Wales. The financial results of the economic assessment of agriculture and forestry in these two areas are presented in Tables 22.3 and 22.4, showing the situation facing the private owner and the nation, respectively.*

The conclusions to be drawn from this exclusively economic analysis are as follows. In the Radnorshire area, forestry, both to the private owner

---

* Costs and returns to the nation do not include production grants or price subsidies.

**Table 22.3.** The profitability of forestry and livestock rearing in mid-Wales (Radnorshire)

### (i) *To the private owner*

| | 3% | | 5% | | 7% | |
|---|---|---|---|---|---|---|
| | Agriculture | Forestry | Agriculture | Forestry | Agriculture | Forestry |
| N.P.V. (£ per acre) | 23 | 147 | −30 | 50 | −51 | 11 |
| Capital (K+O) (£ per acre) | 48 | 61 | 48 | 51 | 48 | 43 |
| B/C ratio B/K+O | 0·48 | 2·41 | Neg. | 0·98 | Neg. | 0·26 |
| I.R.R. % | Agriculture 3¼ | | | Forestry 8 | | |

### (ii) *To the nation*

| | 3% | | 5% | | 7% | |
|---|---|---|---|---|---|---|
| | Agriculture | Forestry | Agriculture | Forestry | Agriculture | Forestry |
| N.P.V. (£ per acre) | −67 | 112 | −88 | 17 | −102 | −19 |
| Capital (K+O) (£ per acre) | 51 | 95 | 51 | 84 | 51 | 74 |
| B/C ratio B/K+O | Neg. | 1·18 | Neg. | 0·20 | Neg. | Neg. |
| I.R.R. % | Agriculture ¼ | | | Forestry 5¼ | | |

**Table 22.4.** The profitability of forestry and hill sheep farming in mid-Wales (Merionethshire)

*(i) To the private owner*

|  | 3% Agriculture | 3% Forestry | 5% Agriculture | 5% Forestry | 7% Agriculture | 7% Forestry |
|---|---|---|---|---|---|---|
| N.P.V. (£ per acre) | −19 | 12 | −15 | −15 | −13 | −2 |
| Capital $(K+O)$ (£ per acre) | 24 | 52 | 24 | 43 | 24 | 37 |
| B/C ratio $B/K+O$ | Neg. | 0·23 | Neg. | Neg. | Neg. | Neg. |
| I.R.R. % | Agriculture Neg. | | Forestry $3\frac{1}{2}$ | | | |

*(ii) To the nation*

|  | 3% Agriculture | 3% Forestry | 5% Agriculture | 5% Forestry | 7% Agriculture | 7% Forestry |
|---|---|---|---|---|---|---|
| N.P.V. (£ per acre) | −32 | −11 | −23 | −37 | −15 | −42 |
| Capital $(K+O)$ (£ per acre) | 25 | 76 | 25 | 65 | 25 | 57 |
| B/C ratio $B/K+O$ | Neg. | Neg. | Neg. | Neg. | Neg. | Neg. |
| I.R.R. % | Agriculture Neg. | | Forestry $2\frac{1}{4}$ | | | |

and to the nation, is to be preferred to livestock rearing. Here a transfer of land from its present use (farming) to an alternative use (forestry) would be economically justifiable. In the Merionethshire area, characterized by intensive hill farming, both agriculture and forestry are economically un-attractive, except private afforestation at a discount rate less than $3\frac{1}{2}$ per cent. In fact, subsidized agriculture in this area incurs a loss even before any interest charge on borrowed capital is levied.

To what use, therefore, should such land in the hills and uplands be put? Two alternative approaches are possible. The causes of the low productivity of land under the stated activities can be identified, and attempts made to remedy them. Alternatively, the possibility of using such land for other purposes can be explored.

## Low Productivity

The data presented in Tables 22.3 and 22.4 are based on the current systems of farming practised in the areas, allied to the present structure of farms. While farmers in the upland areas of Britain may be severely restricted in their choice of system, an intensification of their present system may sometimes be possible through reclamation. Moreover, the size of holding may be increased through a rational, deliberate policy of farm amalgamation. There are often practical limitations to the reclamation of upland areas, and to the amalgamation of one farm with another. While it may be possible to improve the viability, and hence the competitiveness, of some farms through an intensification of their present use, and while one farmer may fortuitously manage to acquire a neighbouring farm and run both as a single amalgamated holding, it is unrealistic to generalize and suggest that such remedies are always and inevitably successful. There will remain instances where, even after reclamation and amalgamation, the economic returns from agriculture would still be insufficiently attractive to merit the investment of either national or private capital. The same situa-tion might also apply in respect of afforestation. In other words, such land is sub-marginal under farming and forestry.

## Alternative Uses

In such instances, to what use can, or should, the land be put? This question can be viewed from two directions. First, the ancillary, imponder-able benefits that accrue from the use of land under given activities can be considered. To the nation, the most important of these benefits are the employment potentials of various activities, particularly in the remoter upland areas, the recreation potential of the hills and uplands and, more recently, the conservation of flora and fauna. The non-economic benefits enjoyed by the private owner include shooting and sporting facilities, the psychological appeal of land ownership, and so on. These benefits may be so important to, or so highly valued by, the landowner that an activity that appears to be economically unattractive may still be considered worthwhile. Such a conclusion does not invalidate the economic conclusions derived from a purely financial comparison of the alternatives. Rather, as has been shown earlier, the economic assessment may be instrumental in measuring the real cost of these non-market benefits.

Second, in those instances where land is governed solely by economic considerations, or where the real cost of pursuing non-economic objectives is greater than the value attributed to them by the landowner, it is important to realize that land use, even in hill and upland areas, is not confined exclusively to agriculture or forestry. The use of the hills and uplands is not the prerogative of the farmer or the forester. Although such areas may not be required for urban development or industrial use, rural land is needed especially for water conservation purposes and the provision of recreation. Where the topography and climate is suitable (as it is in many parts of the hills and uplands of Britain), such marginal and sub-marginal agricultural and forestral land could be scheduled as water-gathering grounds to meet the growing demand of industrial and urban centres. In other cases, where the investment of resources in both agriculture and forestry is uneconomic, the national advantages of an area—geographical, environmental, topographical, physical—may be exploited through its recreational development. Other areas in the hills and uplands might be better protected than used, and be designated as nature reserves, within which flora and fauna are conserved together with the natural beauty of the area.

## BIBLIOGRAPHY AND REFERENCES

Anon (1966). *Report of the Land Use Study Group—Forestry, Agriculture and the Multiple Use of Rural Land,* H.M.S.O., London, 120 pp.

Clawson, M. (1959). *Methods of Measuring the Demand for and Value of Outdoor Recreation,* Resources for the Future Inc., Washington, D.C. (Report No. **10**), 36 pp.

Clawson, M., and Knetsch, J. L. (1967). *Economics of Outdoor Recreation,* Resources for the Future Inc., Washington, D.C., 328 pp.

Daiute, R. J. (1966). Methods for determination of demand for outdoor recreation. *Land Economics,* **42**, 327–38.

Devine, E. J. (1966). The treatment of incommensurables in cost-benefit analysis, *Land Economics,* **42**, 383–7.

Gregory, G. R. (1965). An economic approach to multiple use, *Forest Science,* **1**, 6–13.

Hiley, W. E. (1956). *Economics of Plantations,* Faber and Faber, London, 216 pp. (Chapter 3).

Hotelling, H. (1949). The economics of public recreation, in: *An Economic Study of the Monetary Evaluation of Recreation in National Parks,* The Prewitt Report, U.S. Dept. of the Interior, Washington, D.C.

James, P. G. (1964). *An Economic Analysis of Land Use in Mid-Wales under Agriculture and Forestry,* unpublished Ph.D. thesis, University of Wales.

James, P. G. (1965). An economic appraisal of the use of hills and uplands for forestry and agriculture respectively. *The Farm Economist,* **10,** 497–506.

Knetsch, J. L. (1963). Outdoor and recreation demands and benefits, *Land Economics,* **39,** 387–96.

Knetsch, J. L., and Davis, R. K. (1966). Comparisons of methods for recreational evaluation, in: *Water Research,* (eds.) A. Kneese and S. Smith, Resources for the Future Inc., Washington, D.C.

Lessinger, J. (1958). Measurement of recreation benefits: a reply, *Land Economics,* **38,** 369–70.

McCrone, G. (1962). *The Economics of Subsidising Agriculture,* George Allen and Unwin, London, 189 pp.

Moore, L., and Peters, G. H. (1965). Agriculture's balance of payments contribution, *Westminster Bank Revew Quarterly,* 32–7.

Peters, G. H. (1970). Land use studies in Britain: a review of the literature with special reference to applications of cost-benefit analysis, *J. Agric. Econ.* **12,** 171–214.

Prest, A. R., and Turvey, R. (1965). Cost-benefit analysis: a survey. *Econ. J.* **75,** 683–735.

Robinson, W. C., Clawson, M., Lee, I. M., and Moore, A. L. (1962). Economic evaluation of outdoor recreation benefits. *Study Report* **24,** Reports to the Outdoor Recreation Resources Review Commission.

Shafer, E. L. (1964). The photo-choice method for recreation research, *Research Papers, U.S. Forest Service,* Washington, D.C., No. **29,** 10 pp.

Sinden, J. A. (1967). The evaluation of extra market benefits: a critical review, *World Agricultural Economics and Rural Sociology Abstracts,* **9,** 1–15.

Trice, A. H., and Wood, S. E. (1958). Measurement of recreation benefits, *Land Economics,* **34,** 196–207.

Wennergen, E. B. (1964). Valuing non-market priced recreational resources, *Land Economics,* **43,** 112–16.

Wood, D. F. (1961). The distances-travelled technique for measuring value and recreation areas: an application, *Land Economics,* **37,** 363–9.

CHAPTER 23

# Wilderness

T. HUXLEY

## INTRODUCTION

During the summer of 1972, Scottish listeners to Radio 4 could hear a series of programmes entitled 'They Sought the Wilderness'. My listening was incomplete but those which I did hear consisted of interviews with people who had chosen to emigrate from the more crowded parts of Britain so as to live and work in places remote from cities. I particularly recall an interview with a young couple living in Harris because during the course of my work I had chanced upon their studio home and brought back to mine one of their paintings. Thus it so happened that the circumstances of one of these allegedly wilderness-seeking interviewees were known to me, yet not once throughout the whole of that Hebridean day—a day which had included a walk up Clisham, the highest point in the Outer Isles—did the idea of wilderness occur to me.

From the foregoing, in the context of this Introduction, one might draw two conclusions. Either I am the wrong person to write about wilderness, being insensitive to it, or it is an idea which has different meanings for different people. Naturally, I choose the latter and would go so far as to surmise that even for those parts of the world which are judged true wilderness by all who would write about them, there are probably a few people for whom the idea has no meaning because such places are where they derive their living for at least some part of each year. Aldridge (1969) has developed a similar thesis in an historical context, tracing the origin of the word from the idea of a place where wild beasts dwelt, and from his thinking we may conclude that the growth of the wilderness concept has paralleled the increasing urbanization of man, so that for ever more people remote places are assumed to be wilderness and not simply unknown to them.

The corollary of this general introductory point is that for those who believe in wilderness it must exist somewhere. Thus, the writer about

361

wilderness is required not only to identify what bits of the world he is mainly writing about but also the geography of the believers. And because my global experience of both is insecure outside Britain, I must eventually lead discussion towards considering attitude to wilderness in this country, yet hope that the conclusion may have more general significance. So, in the context of Britain, let me begin by confessing that although I am in agreement with Phillips (1972) that wilderness no longer exists in these islands (I regard the coastal exceptions suggested by Simmons (1966) as irrelevant), nevertheless many do think it does. For them wilderness has such strong attractions that even when all rational evidence points to the contrary, they will yet strive to attach the word to parts of their surroundings. Thus the exercise for this practitioner of (wilderness) conservation is to try to be sensitive to other people's needs—even if one's scales of value differ—and this is really what the theme of this essay is all about.

## THE MEANING OF THE WORD

Discussion must begin with semantics; here is Darling and Eichhorn (1969, p. 73):

> 'Wilderness is another of those words which have suffered some erosion or derogatory change of connotation through the years. The Oxford English Dictionary derives the word from Old English, possibly wild-deer-ness, but the plain definition is wild, uncultivated land, uninhabited by human beings but occupied by the wild animals. Webster says "a tract of land or a region (as a forest or wide barren plain) uncultivated and uninhabited by human beings ... an empty or pathless area ... a part of a garden devoted to wild growth". Through history the tendency has been to think of a cultivated place as being better or more acceptable than a wild one; then an untended garden became a wilderness in common parlance; and finally the politicians gathered the word into their fevered vocabulary to signify the state of being out of power. Webster, at least, has lifted the word from an utter abyss by speaking of a part of a garden devoted to wild growth.'

The positive need for wilderness was enlarged upon by Darling in his 1969 Reith Lectures (1970, p. 57):

> 'The ecologist sees the decline of the great natural buffer of wilderness as an element in our danger. Natural wilderness is a factor for world stability, not some remote place inimical to the human being. It is strange that it has been so long a place of fear to many men and so something to hate and destroy. Wilderness is not remote or indifferent, but an active agent in maintaining a habitable world, though the co-operation is unconscious.'

Thus, Darling makes the global case for wilderness: for the healthy metabolism of space-ship earth some parts must not be manipulated by men for any purpose but must be left to the natural cycles of change and decay for the ecological well-being of the whole.

So much for one man's view of the subject. Another reference point is the Wilderness Act of 1964. In that year, on September 3rd, the 88th Congress of the United States of America made law a Wilderness Act 'to establish a National Wilderness Preservation System for the permanent good of the whole people, and for other purposes'. The Wilderness Areas so designated were to be administered 'for the use and enjoyment of the American people in such manner as will leave them unimpaired for future use and enjoyment as wilderness, and so as to provide for the protection of these areas, the preservation of their wild character, and for the gathering and dissemination of information regarding their use and enjoyment as wilderness'. The word is defined as follows (United States Congress, 1964, pp. 1–2):

> 'A wilderness, in contrast with those areas where man and his own works domi-nate the landscape, is hereby recognized as an area where the earth and its com-munity of life are untrammeled by man, where man himself is a visitor who does not remain. An area of wilderness is further defined to mean in this Act an area of undeveloped Federal land retaining its primeval character and influence, without permanent improvements or human habitation, which is protected and managed so as to preserve its natural conditions and which (1) generally appears to have been affected primarily by the forces of nature, with the imprint of man's work substantially unnoticeable, (2) has outstanding opportunities for solitude or a primitive and unconfined type of recreation, (3) has at least five thousand acres of land or is of sufficient size as to make practicable its preservation and use in an unimpaired condition, and (4) may also contain ecological, geological, or other features of scientific, educational, scenic or historical value.'

## OBJECTIVES

In commenting on this definition, Darling and Eichhorn (1969, p. 75) make the interesting observation that 'the act does not allow itself to be bogged down by any scientific criterion of wilderness, and wisely. In general a wilderness area will appear in essentials to be unaltered by man, but the act recognizes that secondary forest or grassland may still attain to wilder-ness quality.' The authors continue: 'Happily, elimination of mining is envisaged. Management so far as it is necessary, will be permitted, but there will be no rules of management. All of this seems to us wise and far-seeing.' Well, when a world expert of the calibre of Darling speaks thus, who are we to question his judgment? Yet one does wonder! Although the cessation of mining may be a long-term aim, the Act stated that nothing in it 'shall prevent within national forest wilderness areas any activity, including pros-pecting, for the purpose of gathering information about mineral or other resources' (section 4(d)(2) p. 5), including the use of heavy equipment. That such activity should be carried out 'in a manner compatible with the preservation of the wilderness environment' may create problems in practice, problems paralleled by allowing (in certain circumstances) 'prospecting for water resources, the establishment and maintenance of reservoirs, . . . power projects, transmission lines, and other facilities needed in the public interest, including the road construction and maintenance essential to development and use thereof, upon his [the President's] determination, that such use or uses in the specific area will better serve the interests of the United States and the people thereof than will its denial' (section 4(d)(4) p. 6). The grazing of livestock is also permitted where established prior to 1964, and in addition permanent roads and commercial enterprises necessary to meet minimum requirements for the administration of the area for the purposes of the act, including measures required for emergencies involving the health and safety of persons within the area.

From the distance of Britain, it is difficult to judge the effectiveness of these measures, except in the broadest context of political recognition of the wilderness concept. Certainly the provisos and exceptions permitted in the Wilderness Act would, if translated direct to these isles, provide only for a form of legislation potentially too widely open to differing interpretation. Permissible exceptions such as measures required for emergencies involving the safety of people in a wilderness area bring swiftly to mind the prolonged publicity in 1968 and 1969 over proposed improvements to the Camasunary track, leading to the Cuillin Hills in Skye, 'considered by many to be one of the finest examples in Western Europe of unspoilt, wild landscape in which many have found quiet recreation for more than a century' (Countryside Commission for Scotland, 1969, p. 11). I have little doubt that far more public monies were expended in arguments as to whether the track should be improved than by the Army in doing the work, which included construction of a footbridge at Coruisk. Within a year the bridge 'collapsed in severe weather' and the Second Report of the Countryside Commission for Scotland (1970, p. 17) goes on to state 'In the meantime the collapsed structure is being removed. We are glad that this matter is being considered in a cordial atmosphere of co-operation between representatives of the interested parties.' We may be amused in retrospect at the weakness of the bridge or the strength of the weather and at the official mirror which reflects cordiality from smiles that hurt, but a kind of pain still lingers on: the chilling knowledge that strong voices can carry through acts to reduce the danger element of wilderness, because danger is unquestionably a countryside resource which may need to be conserved.

At this point let us retrace our steps to the Darling/Eichhorn observation concerning the wise lack of scientific criteria in the Wilderness Act definition. Is it fair to paraphrase this by saying the Act is wise not to be too precise? Setting aside the point that legislation about land use is often

imprecise and thus the wisdom of imprecision as much accidental as pur-
posive, nevertheless clearer guidelines may be thought desirable than 'untrammeled by man' and 'primeval character', should the time ever come
in Britain when wilderness areas are to be designated under statute. Some
years ago I wrote:

> 'Today to try to resurrect the concept of wilderness areas would be a retro-
> grade step, if by that term is implied an ideal striving after a primitive land. If,
> however, a new concept of wilderness is to be multiple land use in which the
> primary aim is low density recreation, then are we not dealing with a manage-
> ment problem about a type of land which is only an extreme condition of one
> or more existing categories of land, e.g. low intensity agriculture? Indeed in
> Britain, as wilderness in the primitive sense no longer exists, it must chiefly
> be a concept of the mind and a way of looking at the countryside.
>
> Regarded thus, wilderness must fulfil certain minimum qualifications related
> to our five senses, many of which are measured in terms of absence; for
> example the absence of people—except a few companions—the visual absence
> of too much obvious evidence of man's activities such as post and wire fences
> or hill drainage and, perhaps most important of all, the absence of the sight,
> sound and smell of the internal combustion engine. Positive qualities must be
> a sense of distance, literally distant views, and a variety of natural sights and
> sounds' (Huxley, 1965, p. 1).

## WILDERNESS AND PEOPLE

One must confess that, in re-reading the above written before hearing
Darling's Reith Lectures, it strikes one as being a mite too sectional in
outlook, too limited to that interpretation of wilderness 'as a place where
such men as can should spend their forty days alone or with a companion'.
Darling went on:

> 'I do not wish to dwell on this aspect because the fulfilment of it is the privilege
> of the few and I have an uneasy feeling deep down that we should not burden
> the wilderness with this egocentric human purpose. The wilderness does not
> exist *for* our re-creation or delectation. This is something we gain from its
> great function of being, with the oceans, part of the guardianship of the world
> in which we have come so recently to be a denizen' (1970, p. 85).

How one admires the strength of these ideals! Yet this is where, on a practical plane, one may be forced to depart from them. Some twenty years ago
I recall Charles Elton asking a group of his research students, meeting
informally for discourses on conservation in Britain, 'Do rotifers have
rights?' My reply was that they did not—at least for all practical purposes
—that only people had rights to meet with rotifers. By the same token, while
one may deeply envy Darling's high striving and the beauty of his writing,
it seems to me that the 'very egocentric human purpose' which he uneasily
abjures must be the touchstone of the public servant charged (overtly or
not) with wilderness conservation.

13

Indeed, in the British context, I would go further and say that in this country wildlife conservation as an objective of wilderness selection is generally of secondary consideration to parameters measured according to the five senses of man, and that for most of us we shall find more meat in the oft-quoted paper by Wagar on 'The Carrying Capacity of Wild Lands for Recreation' (1964), in which, as is clear from the title, at most a human purpose, if not an egocentric one, is the dominant theme. The point may be brought home by a further quotation from Darling and Eichhorn (1969, p. 75) where they dispute an 'arbitrary limitation' set by the US National Park Service that wilderness should exclude those areas which might be in sight or sound of civilization. They write:

> 'All of us might prefer it that way but it could be too harsh a definition. An island in Florida Bay serving as a nesting site for roseate spoonbills and other water birds could be excluded for such a reason, whereas, as long as the public does not go ashore, such an island is essentially a wilderness.'

Fine for the birds! Fine, too, for non-exploring man, happy that the wilderness exists somewhere out there, though he never seeks to prove it. One succumbs to the temptation to paraphrase Ronald Knox (n.d.):

> 'There once was a man who said "Yes!
> I am sure there is true wilderness;
> Let Congress designate
> And the people vacate
> And my proof is as sound as a guess." '

In truth, is not the idea of wilderness for birds imputing to a form of life a concept which we can never know if it shares? Only visiting men, some privileged ecologists perhaps, can test the island's wilderness quality and for them we may be sure it will be enhanced by a little sea mist curtaining the distant shore.

## MARGINAL CASES

The landscape architect practising the gospel of containment is touching upon the same theme. By planting enclosing spaces so as to exclude that which jars (and perhaps leading the eye to long views which do not) he can create a pleasance of formality or wild abandon. Landform, natural or contrived, can achieve a similar end, and what better example can be given of the former, in the medium scale, than Holyrood Park in Edinburgh? Here, totally surrounded by a city of 450,00 people, lie 880 acres of mostly steep land between 125 and 822 feet above sea level. But it is not the splendid views from Arthur's Seat, Dunsapie and Salisbury Crags that locate Holyrood Park at one end of the long gradient leading to wilderness, rather it is the shadowed depths and craggy heights of Hunter's Bog, passing through which—especially on a blustery winter's day—the walking spirit can swiftly fly to memories of places more perfectly wild.

A recent report on the nearby Pentland Hills makes the same point:

> 'We regard this long cleft between the hill ranges as one of the most important recreational features of the area. If the Pentlands consisted of one single spine of hills, all the views would be outwards and would partly overlook the sprawling mass of Edinburgh and its satellite towns. Although these views contain much of interest—on a clear day the northern panorama has few equals anywhere in Britain—the foreground is full of reminders of urban weekly turmoil. The long interior valley, enclosed by the hills, provides an essential sense of remoteness where for an hour or so daily cares can be forgotten. It will be important not to do violence to the peace of this inner valley in formulating proposals for recreational activities' (Pentland Hills Technical Group, 1972, p. 8).

In a later part of the same report, the authors describe this inner valley as a 'wilderness management area', a name borrowed from the recreation resource classification devised by Travis and his colleagues for the Clyde area (Travis, 1970) which in its turn was modified from the Outdoor Recreation Resources Review Commission's (1962) classification developed in the United States.

These two Scottish examples of highly modified landscapes, examples which could be repeated in one form or another in dozens of places throughout lowland Britain, are introduced for the specific purpose of making readers face up to the realization that any wide-ranging discussion of wilderness in Britain is bound to include tracts surely excluded by those who equate wilderness with remoteness from cities rather than a sense of remoteness which their visually containing properties may yet possess.

## TESTS OF THE WILDERNESS THRESHOLD

Let us pause here for a few moments and think a bit more about the role of our five senses in judging wilderness quality. Sight is clearly the most complex sensor of wilderness because the perceived landscapes will be weighed by such different scales of acquired knowledge. Earlier the point was made that wilderness is landscapes without obvious evidence of man. But who judges what is obvious? Everyone may agree that a necklace of pylons is obvious; a depressed tree line, however, or secondary woodland with beech and sycamore may powerfully signal 'Man!' only to a few. Yet this is the difficulty. The average user of the purer wilderness types may tend to be more knowledgeable, more acutely aware of man's subtle imprints than the average user of modified, quasi-wilderness. Thus a graph of acceptability probably has a geometric form when one plots numbers of people appreciating wilderness against a wilderness-type scale ranging from highly modified to totally 'untrammeled'.

For sound, the graph may be a similar geometric progression, if less pronounced. The sound of an engine, whether from a vehicle or chain saw, must always be intrusive and diminishing to the wilderness quality; worse still the transistor radio (with no distinction between Bach and bop!). The threshold of sensitivity is less clear, however, when we try to plot bird song as our measure. Are the deep notes of raven and chattering of peregrine one or several octaves removed from the 'gobak, gobak' of grouse? We know these signs could be unreliable: that some peregrine stoop close to highly trammeled landscapes while all grouse are not the inhabitants of a simplified (heather moor) habitat managed for the Glorious Twelfth.

But for smell, taste and feel, positive and negative wilderness elements may be less dependent on expert knowledge and experience than on more generally accepted stimuli. Thus, one may oppose the smell of hydrocarbons from a refinery against the perfume of bog myrtle, the taste of salt air and mountain springs against the city grime, or the feel of polished banisters against the abrasive texture of gabbro. But what of that distinctive smell of the Hebrides in high summer from peat smoke and machair? Does peat smoke signal man in general or specifically primitive man? The question is not posed in jest. Some wilderness administrator of the future might be required to decide whether peat fires must be burnt in wilderness-type areas!

The foregoing crude analysis of wilderness criteria based on our five senses may seem silly to some readers because exceptions come so easily to mind which fracture the simplistic logic of what is being attempted. Furthermore, the hesitant distinction being made between different curves of wilderness appreciation may be as much a general reflection of man's physiological sensory abilities (when comparing, say, sight and smell) as of the more or less increased sensibilities of people who venture into wilderness. But the validity of the point is surely not in doubt that our understanding of the cultural, ecological and agricultural land-use history of a landscape can heighten or impair our more strictly physiological perception of wilderness, and thus in selecting wilderness areas (or wilderness-type areas, which is all that can now be identified in Britain) it must be recognized that criteria will be tougher for remote areas than those close to centres of population.

## SELECTION OF WILDERNESS AREAS

In moving on to the problem of selection, it is convenient to begin with a passage from the report of Study Group Number 9 (1965), that historic collection of representatives and individuals who met under the chairman-ship of Professor Sir Robert Grieve to report on planning and development in Scotland for the 1965 conference on the Countryside in 1970. Regarding wilderness they wrote (p. 12):

'The group considered that there is a strong case for certain areas being safe-guarded as "wilderness" areas. These would be remote areas where the in-trusion of man and man-made things would be at an absolute minimum—above all, the vehicle would be excluded. Entry beyond a certain point should be only for those prepared to carry their requirements for travel on their backs; they should be areas where human self-reliance could be tested. Such re-servations might be, for example, the Fada-Fionn area lying between Loch Maree and Little Loch Broom (some 115 square miles), or a part of north-west Sutherland which has a population of only four persons per square mile. Surveys have shown that only 4% of these areas are suitable for forestry by reason of their barrenness; however, they are by no means absolute deserts and require a degree of land management. It has been proved abroad that a buffer zone, provided with simple facilities, is required to safeguard such "wilderness" areas. These areas and their facilities can never "pay" and because they are desirable elements in any United Kingdom countryside policy, special arrange-ments will have to be made.'

At the time the report was published, it seemed that the Group's most important implicit observation was to be derived from their hesitant placing of wilderness in quotation marks. Yet for those faced with the real possi-bility of attempting to put these proposals to the test, the last sentence may be the major stumbling block. Place rather than finance is, however, our present concern and it is noteworthy that both areas suggested by the Study Group were also identified by the Scottish Countryside Activities Council when they debated the same question four years later.

Roughly, the seven areas suggested by SCAC were (i) the Ben Hope/Ben Loyal area in Sutherland, of 50 square miles; (ii) an area between Lochs Lurgainn and Assynt including Suilven on the borders of Sutherland and Wester Ross, of 90 square miles; (iii) the area between Little Loch Broom and Loch Maree in Wester Ross, amounting to about 200 square miles; (iv) some 50 square miles encompassing the Cuillins of Skye; (v) Ben Nevis and the Grey Corries eastwards to Loch Treig, about 110 square miles; (vi) the Ben Alder district of 120 square miles; and (vii) a 50 square mile area east of Loch Etive in Argyll.

Because the SCAC report is unpublished, I do not propose to comment in detail on these suggestions for wilderness designation in a part of Britain. Comparison between this bold attempt by SCAC and another survey is, however, fair. In the Cairngorm Area Report (1967) there is a map of 'remote areas in Scotland' where the criterion of remoteness is a straight line distance more than five miles from public roads. (A longer measure was not used because, according to the report, there is no place on mainland

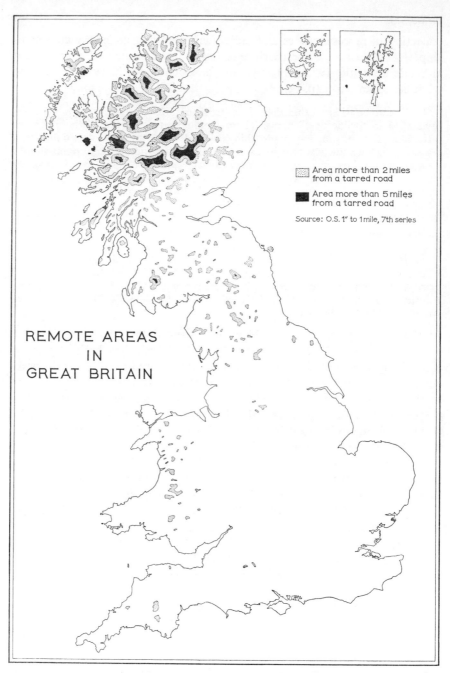

Area more than 2 miles
from a tarred road

Area more than 5 miles
from a tarred road

Source: O.S. 1″ to 1 mile, 7th series

REMOTE AREAS
IN
GREAT BRITAIN

**Figure 23.1.** A map of 'remote areas' in the British Isles compiled and drawn at University College London from the latest one inch maps issued by the Ordnance Survey. Disagreements with other maps of remoteness may appear where tarred roads as shown are newer than the base maps or where they are not open to the public. The map emphasizes the importance of the few remote areas south of the border.

Scotland more than ten miles from a public road.) The interesting point is that in comparing the 'remote areas' map with the SCAC map we find remarkably little agreement. No part of four of the SCAC proposals are remote according to the five-mile criterion and only one comprises a substantial proportion of land so described. Thus, although 'having a high degree of isolation from main roads' was a SCAC criterion of wilderness, the areas actually selected seem hardly to stand this test. Perhaps this is because SCAC distinguishes between main roads and public roads.

Figure 23.1, drawn using only the information on the 1in. Ordnance Survey map, illustrates the extension of the Cairngorm wilderness concept to the rest of Britain. It shows how common 'remote' areas are in Scotland and how rare in England. This may itself be an argument for the conservation of these areas.

There is one other point about the SCAC report which one should mention, not to introduce a quibble, but because it illustrates further the way in which attitudes to wilderness continually intrude into any discussion of the subject. The report added certain criteria to those of Study Group No. 9, in particular that the selected areas should have marked aesthetic appeal in addition to remoteness and that they should have a wide variety of flora and fauna. But wilderness, whatever other emotions it may stimulate, need not necessarily be thought beautiful—which is what aesthetic considerations are about—and stressing biological diversity is superimposing a present-day nature conservation bandwagon (most laudable in itself) on to a type of landscape which should certainly encompass desert situations in both high and low latitudes where ecological conditions and consequently biological diversity may be severely limiting. More important, however, the SCAC report recognized certain operational management problems, for example: 'to deny what are now regarded as normal amenities (e.g. electricity) to isolated pockets of population, simply because they happen to be what is otherwise "wilderness", would be totally unjust'.

Other suggestions for wilderness areas have been made in Britain, some published, some still the subject of informal discussions. Their analysis would, however, tell us little new in principle about where wilderness is found, and the reader will rightly conclude my own view that British wilderness is where one feels oneself to be in a wild place, according to the sensibility of one's particular experience and knowledge on a global or local scale. That we should strive for some more rational and selective approach is right, and it is right too that we should continue the dialogue in the public forum, embracing thinking about wildscape (Coleman, 1970) as well as wilderness. Where my doubts lie is in the expectation that much concrete action will take place, for example by legislation on the American pattern.

## THREATS AND MANAGEMENT

Finally we come to the remaining two questions to which the Editors invited answers: what threats are posed to wilderness and what should its management be? The two are linked, of course, because it is axiomatic that much management is the disarming of threats. Thus, in broad terms the answer is that threats are factors tending to diminish wilderness quality and management is comprehended by those actions aimed at deflecting the diminishing trends. A check list of management prescriptions could therefore be as long as the list of factors requiring to be negatived: no roads, no vehicles (even for rescue), no domesticating afforestation, power lines, reservoirs, noticeboards, and so on. Most significant of all, and most despairing to those for whom inaction is anathema, the chief management prescription should almost certainly be no designation as wilderness. This is the real crux of the matter, deeply uncomfortable and uncomforting though it may seem. Although for purposes of regional development planning (for recreation, communications, power supply, and so on) we need to recognize the concept of wilderness as a positive element in land-use apportionment, many people in densely crowded countries such as Britain are coming to regard the national designation of wilderness areas as the first step to their destruction. If Britain possessed true wilderness—in a global context—state-owned, uninhabited and lacking in existing vested interests, then designation could be justified. But no such areas exist; for all practical purposes, the whole of the country is under some form of positive land use and therefore any scheme for wilderness management will have to be dovetailed into a wider type of multipurpose plan. Thus, in conclusion, I see wilderness management as part and parcel of any hierarchical management scheme aimed at low intensities of use and action wherein the solutions, such as deflecting buffer zones, will be similar in principle whether we are dealing with near primitive or highly modified wilderness types. Snyder (1966) has made the same point, although he called modified wilderness by the simpler name of 'back country'.

## SUMMARY

Here, then, in the context of Britain, is a summary of my views:

1. True wilderness no longer exists.

2. Thus, designation of wilderness will probably never reach the statute books.

3. Nevertheless, the wilderness concept is a valid objective both for debate and as a tool in land-use planning.

4. In practice, its definition involves a human egocentric purpose.

5. But that purpose will describe a gradient of acceptability as it is weighed in finer or coarser balances of personal experience and sensitivity.

6. This gradient of personal acceptability will often coincide directly with a relationship to accessibility.

7. Threats to wilderness are all those factors which diminish the wilderness quality of a particular place.

8. Management is that activity which removes and deflects the diminish-factors; this is the ideal.

9. In practice, management will generally have to accept an uneasy compromise involving multipurpose use.

## ACKNOWLEDGMENTS

It is a pleasure to thank colleagues in the Countryside Commission for Scotland for helpful criticism of the manuscript and also Robert Aitken of the Geography Department of Aberdeen University, who is currently writing a thesis on wilderness. I am particularly grateful to W. H. Murray, OBE, Chairman of the Scottish Countryside Activities Council, for his kind permission to refer to their unpublished report. The views expressed are, of course, my own and should not be assumed to imply the policy thinking of my employers.

## BIBLIOGRAPHY AND REFERENCES

Aldridge, D. (1969). *Wildlife Parks as Interpretive Media,* The Countryside Commission for Scotland, Perth, 26 pp.

Coleman, A. M. (1970). The conservation of wildscape: a quest for facts, *Geog. J.,* **136,** 199–205.

Countryside Commission for Scotland (1969). *First Report,* for period 1.4.68 to 31.12.68, CCS, Perth, 18 pp.

Countryside Commission for Scotland (1970). *Second Report,* for period 1.1.69 to 31.12.69, CCS, Perth, 42 pp.

Darling, F. Fraser (1970). *Wilderness and Plenty,* (The Reith Lectures, 1969), British Broadcasting Corporation, London, 88 pp.

Darling, F. Fraser, and Eichhorn, N. D. (1969). *Man and Nature in the National Parks,* 2nd edition, The Conservation Foundation, Washington, 80 pp.

Huxley, T. (1965). *Wilderness Areas,* Paper No. 21 considered by Study Group No. 9 (Planning and Development in Scotland) for 'Countryside in 1970' Second Conference, 2 pp.

Knox, R. J. (n.d.). Knox's verse has been widely published, e.g. in Cohen, J. M., and Cohen, M. J. (1960), *The Penguin Dictionary of Quotations,* 672 pp. as follows:
    'There once was a man who said "God
    Must find it exceedingly odd
    If he finds that this tree
    Continues to be
    When there's no-one about in the quod".'

Nash, R. (1967). *Wilderness and the American Mind,* Yale University Press, New Haven, 256 pp.

Outdoor Recreation Resources Review Commission (1962). *Report to the President and to the Congress,* United States Government Printing Office, 245 pp.

Pentland Hills Technical Group (1972). *Pentland Hills: Conservation and Recreation,* Report and Draft Recommendations, Midlothian County Council, Edinburgh, 66 pp.

Phillips, A. A. C. (1972). *Conservation Planning in North America,* The Countryside Commission, London, 30 pp.

Simmons, I. G. (1966). Wilderness in the mid-twentieth century United States of America, *Town Planning Review,* **36,** 249–56.

Snyder, A. P. (1966). Wilderness management—a growing challenge, *J. Forestry,* **64,** 441–6.

Study Group No. 9 (1965). *Planning and Development in Scotland,* A Preparatory Study for the 'Countryside in 1970' Second Conference, The Royal Society of Arts, London, 28 pp.

Technical Group on the Cairngorm Area of the Eastern Highlands of Scotland (1967). *Cairngorm Area,* HMSO, Edinburgh, 78 pp.

Travis, A. S. (1970). *Recreation Planning for the Clyde,* Firth of Clyde Study Phase 2, The Scottish Tourist Board, Edinburgh, 278 pp.

United States Congress (1964). *Wilderness Act,* Public Law, 88–577, 88th Congress, S.4, September 3, 1964.

Wagar, J. A. (1964). *The Carrying Capacity of Wild Lands for Recreation,* Forest Science—Monograph, **7,** 24 pp.

# C   Organizing Conservation

# CHAPTER 24

# Countryside Conservation: Some National Perspectives

J. M. DAVIDSON

## INTRODUCTION

There is a long history of concern for the protection and creation of fine landscapes in Britain. The eighteenth-century landowners who redesigned their large estates for the benefit of subsequent generations were farsighted in their individual creative efforts, but state intervention in landscape matters came relatively late in Britain. It began in the blitz of legislation which followed the war and has continued with intermittent additions to the statute book and the growth of a number of specialist organizations. This chapter is concerned with some aspects of national policymaking in the related fields of landscape conservation and recreation planning; it discusses the structure of organizations in central government and the work of some of them, notably the Countryside Commission.

In the decade after the war, two Acts were especially important in securing the foundation of a national programme of rural conservation. The 1947 Town and Country Planning Act, which came, in part, as a response to the haphazard building developments of the 1930s, imposed controls upon most forms of development. It also required local authorities to prepare development plans in which they could designate areas of special landscape value where these controls would be more vigorously applied. Two years later, the National Parks and Access to the Countryside Act introduced special measures of protection for the areas of finest scenery. The designation of National Parks and Areas of Outstanding Natural Beauty was prompted not only by the desire of some people, notably Dower (1945) and Hobhouse (National Parks Committee, 1947), to see high-quality landscapes protected and enhanced, but also by the demands of an articulate minority who sought public access to private land. In response, the Act encouraged park authorities to make access agreements, and if necessary access orders, to overcome the resistant attitude of many landowners. It also gave park authorities the powers, backed by Exchequer finance, to provide facilities for the fairly limited amount of outdoor recreation activity needed at that time. The National Parks legislation therefore had two principal aims: landscape conservation and provision for recreation, even though the emphasis—in need and in practice—was clearly on the former.

Conditions since 1949 have changed dramatically. Landscapes within National Parks, as well as outside them, are now threatened by developments of many kinds: the expansion of agriculture and forestry operations; new water conservation schemes; more mineral working; road improvements; pressures for commuting and second homes; and the intensification of outdoor recreation activity. At the same time, there has been growing public interest in the quality of the rural environment and a concern for its protection, and this concern is expressed not simply for those areas of the finest scenery like the National Parks which are subject to landscape designations, but for the countryside as a whole.

## CO-ORDINATION OF RURAL POLICIES

The 'Countryside in 1970' conferences held between 1963 and 1970 provided important arenas for discussions of the ways in which the countryside had changed since the war and the conflicts which had been generated between the main rural interests. Papers and discussions at the second conference revealed two major needs: for more cooperation between those rural activities and industries which, like agriculture, strongly influence the visual appearance and ecological values of the countryside; and for more specific provision near towns for informal outdoor recreation.

On the first issue, a variety of improvements have followed the conferences including, for example, agreement on a pesticides safety precautions code of conduct (Moore, Chapter 15); the introduction of new powers (in the Civic Amenities Act) for the care of trees in the environment; the extension of amenity advice to farmers from the Ministry of Agriculture; and an increased amenity consciousness in public organizations like the Forestry Commission and the Central Electricity Generating Board. Despite an abortive attempt to house many government departments and agencies concerned with environmental matters under one ministerial roof (The Ministry of Land and Natural Resources), successive governments have attempted to improve the co-ordination of policies on environmental matters by departmental restructuring. A Secretary of State for Local Government and Regional Planning was introduced in 1969 with responsibilities for overseeing the work of the Ministries of Transport and of Housing and Local Government. The creation of the Department of the Environment in 1970, which now has responsibilities for housing, planning, local government, roads and transport, water conservation, historic buildings, sport and physical recreation, country-side matters and nature conservation, has been generally welcomed as a significant improvement in the Government's approach. Yet although several

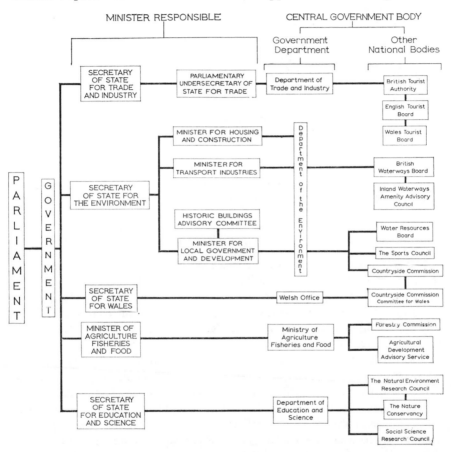

**Figure 24.1.** The structure of government organization for the rural environment in England and Wales. Adapted from a chart made by the Countryside Commission (March 1973).*

potentially conflicting rural interests are now within this department, co-ordination of policies on the development and conservation of rural resources remains difficult to achieve, partly because the Ministry of Agri-

* Changes in the Nature Conservancy's status are outlined by Blackmore, Chapter 27. The Water Resources Board will cease to exist in April 1974. The National Water Council will now liaise between the new Regional Water Authorities; the Water Space Amenity Commission will advise them on recreation and landscape matters.

culture, and to a lesser extent the Department of Trade and Industry, the Department of Education and Science and the Ministry of Defence, operate outside this policy-co-ordinating framework (Figure 24.1). As agriculture continues to adopt new methods, often with large-scale consequences for the landscape, it is likely that the need for closer harmony between agricultural and environmental policies will become more apparent. Even so, the evolution of 'super Ministries' may not be as effective in achieving greater harmony as the broadening of aims and interests within existing ones, and within those agencies of central government with direct or advisory responsibilities for the management of rural land, such as the Forestry Commission and the Nature Conservancy.

Moves to improve the co-ordination of rural policymaking in central government have been paralleled in local government in a number of ways, principally by the creation of County Countryside Committees. Various commitee structures have been adopted, and in some cases the new arrangements allow many different interests to express their views upon rural policies and to promote action in neglected areas.

## THE COUNTRYSIDE ACT

Government response to the growing concern about rural amenity and the problems of outdoor recreation during the early 1960s came in 1966 with the White Paper 'Leisure in the Countryside' which preceded the Countryside Act of 1968 (Ministry of Land and Natural Resources, 1966). The Act requires that 'every Minister, government department and public body, in exercising their functions under any enactment, shall have regard to the desirability of conserving the natural beauty and amenity of the countryside' (Section 11, Countryside Act, 1968). This may be a bland expression, as yet of unproven efficacy, but it is nonetheless evidence of a recognition of conflicts and a legislative attempt to resolve them. More positive powers were given to the Forestry Commission and statutory water undertakers to widen their interests by providing for outdoor recreation on their holdings.

Two provisions of the Countryside Act were especially important: the powers given to local authorities and others to set up country parks and picnic sites, and the reorganization of the National Parks Commission as the Countryside Commission, a new agency charged with keeping under review all matters relating to the conservation and enhancement of natural beauty of the countryside of England and Wales and the provision and improvement of facilities for the enjoyment of the countryside. The Countryside Commission is now the principal branch of central government concerned with landscape and recreation, although as Figure 24.1 shows, many agencies have some responsibility in one or both of these fields. The Commission's duties are, for example, similar in some respects to those of the Sports Council, but by careful discussion and agreement overlap is avoided: the Commission concentrates on informal recreation in the countryside, the Sports Council has responsibility for physical recreation and sport in town and country.

As in the 1949 Act, the provision of outdoor recreation opportunities is seen to be complementary to the policies for conservation of natural beauty. There is concern to protect the countryside for people to enjoy: no-one would deny that recreation is probably the strongest *raison d'être* for landscape conservation. But the provision of facilities for visitors (by local authorities, the Forestry Commission, water suppliers and others) is also seen as a means of protecting vulnerable areas—especially National Parks—from damaging pressures and safeguarding the rural economy from disturbance. Thus, while there is an obvious potential conflict between the protection of landscape and the promotion of outdoor recreation in this country, as abroad (Simmons, Chapter 25), policies for both can be interdependent.

The powers of the Countryside Commission in both recreation and amenity are mainly advisory, not executive. It performs its duties by advising on the planning and administration of National Parks, by recommending the payment of Exchequer grant aid for a range of local authority recreational schemes and landscape protection measures, by providing information to the public about the countryside, and by carrying out a programme of research and experiments upon which much of this advice is built. The Commission can provide technical and financial assistance to the private sector, as well as to local authorities, for schemes which contribute to the purposes of the Countryside Act.

Although the Commission has only limited executive powers, its advisory remit is wide and the organization occupies a unique position in relation to the development of central and local government conservation policies for the countryside. The rest of this chapter is concerned with three important areas of its concern—the National Parks, the coast and the remaining countryside—in which policymaking is adjusting to the emergence of new problems.

## NATIONAL PARKS

Ten National Parks, covering 9 per cent of England and Wales, have been designated since the National Parks and Access to the Countryside Act was passed in 1949. The parks have special administrative arrangements: two (the Peak and the Lakes) have joint planning boards, while other parks are administered by special park planning committees of the county council and also, where a park is part of several counties, by a joint advisory committee. These park authorities are locally constituted, though a proportion of their members are nationally nominated.

Since 1949, the park authorities, advised by the Countryside Commission and (on its recommendation) helped financially by Exchequer grants, have undertaken a wide range of work. They have made agreements with landowners to secure greater public access to private land; they have provided recreation facilities and warden services; and they have enhanced the landscape by such measures as tree planting and eyesore clearance.

Yet, it is in the National Parks that perhaps the greatest problems now exist of matching the dual objectives of landscape conservation and provision for recreation. This has not always been the case: in the decade after their designation, when car ownership was less common and motorways still on the drawing board, satisfying the leisure demands of motorists was not a major problem for park authorities. The limited staff and financial resources available could be focused on the problem of controlling major intrusive developments and securing additional access for walkers. Today, although most people would still accept the importance of development control in National Parks, the emphasis in recreation provision has changed significantly from making access agreements to providing for parking and picnicking. Even so, in most parks, provision for the new demands is admitted to be inadequate (Countryside Commission, 1971). The view of many park authorities is that as much informal car-borne recreation as possible should be catered for outside the parks, although certain areas within them will undoubtedly remain extremely popular even if sufficient counter-attractions are provided outside. Parts of most parks, especially those like the Peak District, on the edge of large urban areas, are experiencing such heavy pressures from visitor use that their character and value is in danger.

A further problem in National Parks arises from the pace and nature of landscape change brought about by land-use pressures within them. In spite of the skills of development control officers, and the strengthening of public support for the idea of resisting intrusive developments, the present procedures do not provide an adequate mechanism for conserving many traditional upland landscapes. These are often subject to alteration by practices over which there is only limited statutory control: open hills are encroached by scrub when sheep cease to graze them; and their lower slopes may be fenced and improved, or even ploughed. More obvious changes have been caused by large-scale afforestation in the uplands, often in monotonous, single-species blocks unsympathetic to the land form. In all parks, voluntary consultation agreements, designated to limit planting to those areas where it can more easily be accommodated, operate between the park authority and forestry interests. But the success of these arrangements has been variable. They have not curtailed the effects of some afforestation schemes which, as in the case of Langsrothdale in the Yorkshire Dales, may have severe effects upon the park scenery. The reaction to these threats has been increased pressure from some organizations (including the Countryside Commission) for the extension of planning control to large-scale commercial forestry operations.

The parks suffer other pressures which are also difficult to control, such as mineral excavations, power stations and water catchment schemes. Some changes, as in the case of a properly landscaped reservoir to which there is full public access, may not always be a disadvantage; but it is difficult to reconcile acceptance of the scale of operations which might, for example, be envisaged if opencast copper mining were to be introduced to Snowdonia (Dower, 1972) with the general goal of protecting characteristic landscapes and retaining a sense of remoteness. Even so, where questions of national economic need and a possible improvement in local employment are raised, it is difficult to argue the counter-case for the total exclusion of these developments from National Parks. There is an urgent need to investigate alternative policies which might improve local prospects for steady employment and higher incomes.

A major problem derives directly from the curious concept of National Parks in this country. These areas are neither 'national', for they are locally administered, nor are they like normal parks, for they are mainly in private ownership and house a quarter of a million people. There is a growing realization that local interests have not been given adequate weight in National Park planning. Stringent control of development has imposed costs on local residents while it may have denied them increased opportunities for employment. Farmers, for example, have not been actively encouraged to participate in recreation and tourist developments which could supplement their incomes. In addition, local residents may be forced out of the housing market by second-home seekers and—for some parks—by commuters. In addition to the need to resolve these conflicts between visitors and long-established residents, the park authorities are faced with administrative difficulties and costs. Most park authorities find it difficult to raise sufficient revenue, even with Exchequer aid, to meet the considerable costs of National Park administration. Contributing authorities often resent the use of local finance to meet visitors' needs.

Moreover, it can be argued that insufficient advice on administration and some aspects of policy has been available from central government. It is true that the National Parks Act 1949 established the National Parks Commission to keep under review the developments in each park, and to recommend Exchequer grant aid for certain tasks undertaken by local authorities, but no detailed or consistent central policies have been advocated, still less enforced, and very few specialist staff have been recruited locally: only one park—The Peak District—has its own chief officer, the others are serviced on a part-time basis by county planning staff. Those parks which lie in more than one county face particular problems of unco-ordinated planning.

## Review of National Park Policy and Administration

Faced with these growing problems in National Parks, the Government appointed in 1971 a Review Committee, under the Chairmanship of Lord Sandford, to enquire into their purposes and planning. At the same time discussions were held between the County Councils Association and the Countryside Commission into the more urgent problem of devising new administrative arrangements for the parks in the light of proposals for local government reorganization.

The administrative reforms for National Parks, which will take effect on April 1st, 1974, leave the two existing Boards for the Peak and Lake District National Parks unchanged. In the other eight parks, even when more than one county council is involved, the park will be run by a single executive committee and many planning powers will be delegated to this committee. The legislation requires that each Park Authority, in consultation with the Countryside Commission, appoint a National Parks Officer to serve the committee. Although no details are known of the future financial arrangements, the Government have promised to bear the 'lion's share' of the cost of running the National Parks. In response to the inadequacies of present planning and management policies, the Government have also decided that each park will have a plan which should provide the necessary strategic guidelines for the conservation of resources, the zoning of different intensities of use, and for traffic management. The hope is also that interpretative programmes will be developed on a far wider scale than exists at present.

The report of the Sandford Committee will provide much-needed policy guidance to the new authorities and their officers on how conflict in National Parks might be resolved. Without anticipating the findings of the committee, it is possible to speculate on some solutions. One can, for example, argue a case for stronger government resistance to pressures for intrusive development in the parks, especially when the development is proposed by a public body. Much thought needs to be given to the ways of regulating changes in farming and forestry practice so that characteristic landscapes do not disappear. While it may be desirable and feasible to bring large-scale afforestation schemes within the scope of planning control, it will be less appropriate to treat farming operations in this way. Management agreements with landowners, incorporating payments for work done in the interests of landscape and recreation by the park authority, may prove to be more successful and general powers are being sought (Countryside Commission, 1973). These measures will undoubtedly require most park authorities to play a more positive role in managing the environment of National Parks. Although much will be achieved by agreement with landowners, it seems likely that more public acquisition of land is essential if the purposes of the parks are to be secured. If farsighted decisions are taken to bring some of the 'heartlands' of National Parks into public ownership or quasi-public ownership by the National Trust, then these areas at least would correspond much more closely to the existing international definition of National Parks (see Simmons, Chapter 25), and only in this way would it be true to look upon them as both 'national' and 'parks'.


## THE COAST

The coast has for long been the most popular destination for British holidaymakers: more than 70 per cent of all holidays taken in this country by British people are spent at the seaside. Since the war the coast has achieved added significance as an area for outdoor recreation, but many of the new pressures have been felt outside established resorts on stretches of unspoiled coastline such as headlands, dunes and estuaries. Such areas are well suited to meet new recreational demands, but the consequences of unplanned and unmanaged expansion of activity have been congestion, erosion and disturbance of other interests, especially wildlife.

Fearing that too much of the coast was being spoiled by development and uncontrolled use, the Minister of Housing and Local Government in 1966 asked the then National Parks Commission to carry out a study of the coast of England and Wales in conjunction with all maritime local planning authorities, and also with the Nature Conservancy, the Sports Council and the British Travel Association* (Ministry of Housing and Local Government, 1966). The findings of this study showed that 25 per cent of the coast of England and Wales was substantially developed in 1966, while 63 per cent was protected by planning policies with a strong presumption against allowing additional development. But the analysis in the final report (Countryside Commission, 1970) shows that there was often a big difference between the intentions of planning authorities as expressed in their policy statements and their performance in terms of development permitted on the ground. What was needed, in the Commission's view, was a much firmer commitment to the principles of conservation along the undeveloped

* Now the British Tourist Authority.

coast, especially the most beautiful stretches. They recommended the designation of 34 areas as 'Heritage Coasts' within which stringent policies of development control would apply and positive steps would be taken to manage the environment so that recreation could be encouraged but not allowed to destroy the natural attractions.

With some reservations, the concept of Heritage Coasts has been endorsed by the Government. Local authorities have been asked to proceed with their definition in consultation with the Countryside Commission and to prepare, as soon as possible, interim policies for the conservation and use of protected areas (Department of the Environment, 1972). Eventually, the boundaries of Heritage Coasts, and policies for their conservation, will be incorporated in structure plans.


## THE COUNTRYSIDE

A major increase in government involvement in landscape conservation and outdoor recreation *outside* the National Parks was introduced by the Countryside Act of 1968. It is true that a second tier of nationally designated areas—Areas of Outstanding Natural Beauty—have given, since 1949, an added protective status to some of the most beautiful stretches of country-side and coast which did not qualify, on various counts, for recognition as National Parks (Figure 20.1, p 314, Chapter 20). Moreover, in those areas around major cities in which Green Belt policies apply, open land has been retained which is substantially free from development. But the principal achievement in both these nationally recognized zones—AONBs and Green Belts—has been negative: the land has not been built upon, but despite many good intentions to the contrary, little has been done significantly to improve the appearance of the landscape, and there has been a considerable amount of landscape decay (Thomas, 1970; Hall, 1973). Many intrusive developments have occurred by a process of attrition, where, for example. developers probe the defensive armour of the Green Belt planning author-ities and win development applications on appeal. Other detrimental visual changes are the result of land management decisions—for example, to fell trees, or increase field size—which have been taken by individual farmers in response to government requests and economic pressures to improve farming efficiency. Some agricultural changes reflect the insecurity and trespass difficulties facing farmers on the fringes of towns.

Areas of Outstanding Natural Beauty were not designated in order to increase opportunities for public recreation: the provisions of the 1949 Act include neither powers nor incentives for local authorities to provide facilities for visitors. The emphasis in these areas has been on landscape conservation: development control policies have generally been more stringently applied than elsewhere in the countryside and some additional grants have been available for tree planting and the removal of eyesores. For Green Belts, an implied intention of government policy has been that amenity would be protected and enhanced. Many have argued that such protected urban fringe areas should also provide recreational outlets for city dwellers. But in practice, as Thomas (1970) has shown, the amount of land in recreational use in the Metropolitan Green Belt is less than 6 per cent of the total area, and only 3 per cent is publicly accessible. The rest is in private open space in the form of golf courses, tennis courts, and playing-fields for the use of schools, universities or the employees of industrial companies.

Most of the countryside, of course, has not had the benefit of nationally approved designations like AONB or Green Belt. In the so-called 'white land' of development plans, the main goal of planning has been to retain existing uses in an undisturbed state, and many county plans are still drafted in these terms. But the development plan system has now been reorganized following the recommendations of the Planning Advisory Group (1965). The effect of the new planning system introduced by the Town and Country Planning Acts of 1968 and 1971 has been to provide an opportunity for the inclusion, in a statutory plan, of policies on all relevant environmental issues. Moreover, landscape and recreation have received more attention from local planning authorities since the Countryside Act extended to the whole countryside the landscape grants which were formerly restricted to Areas of Outstanding Natural Beauty, and introduced powers and finance for the provision of country parks, picnic sites and camping and transit caravan sites.

### Country Parks and Picnic Sites

The concept of country parks was first proposed in the 1966 White Paper 'Leisure in the Countryside' (Ministry of Land and Natural Resources, 1966) as a means by which townspeople out for a day in the country could find a place to stop and picnic in attractive rural surroundings. Before publication of the White Paper, the Government had been presented with some evidence, and more pressure from interest groups, on the shortage of open space near towns where visitors to the countryside, mainly motorists, could spend their leisure time. No one was able to quantify the existing demand, nor the shortfall of supply, let alone forecast future needs. What was apparent was the growing anxiety expressed by the farming community, landowners, naturalists and others about the damage which was being caused to their interests by increasing numbers of visitors. Existing open spaces were eroded and made unsightly by heavy visitor pressure (Goldsmith, Chapter 14); farmers, especially on the urban fringe, suffered damage to their crops and stock from trespass and farm gates were blocked by parked cars. Wildlife was disturbed by trampling, noise and fire. People who valued the quietness and solitude of the National Parks saw the steadily rising number of car-borne visitors as a threat to the essential character of these areas.

Under the Countryside Act, local authorities are given powers to establish country parks, picnic sites and places for campers and caravanners to stop overnight. These provisions are intended to make additional land available for recreation and reduce the pressures on agricultural land, nature reserves and National Parks. Substantial Exchequer grant aid towards the costs of land acquisition and site development and the operation of warden and litter collection services is available from the Department of the Environment (and the Welsh Office) on the recommendation of the Countryside Commission.

The concept of country parks is by no means fixed, although it is intended that they should be areas of countryside, usually greater than 25 acres in extent (Countryside Commission, 1972a), set aside exclusively or predominantly for informal recreation. By September 30th, 1972, 84 country parks had been recommended for grant aid by the Countryside Commission and approved for grant by the Department of the Environment or the Welsh Office; a further 29 schemes were awaiting approval from Departments. A total of 86 picnic sites had been approved for grant and a further 65 recommended for approval (Countryside Commission, 1972b). The distribution of approved schemes is shown in Figure 24.2.

When the currently approved country park schemes have been implemented, nearly 25,000 acres of countryside will be available for public use, although this figure includes a substantial acreage of land used for recreation *before* the Countryside Act was passed and subsequently included in designated country parks. Approved expenditure on the 66 local authority schemes had reached £2 million by September, 1972, while over £300,000 had been approved for the 18 privately run parks which the Commission had grant aided under Section 5 of the Countryside Act. Even so, the distribution of parks and picnic sites is patchy (Figure 24.2), although it would be dangerous to draw too many inferences from the pattern which is emerging. The unevenness of the response from local government to the incentives provided by the Act reflects not only variation in the demand for countryside recreation but also differences in the amount of land to which the public already have access, the quality of agricultural land, the relative wealth of the local authorities, and, perhaps most important of all, the strength of the committee and staff organization for planning and management within local authorities. In counties like Cheshire, Durham, Hampshire, Lancashire and Nottinghamshire, special teams have been set up

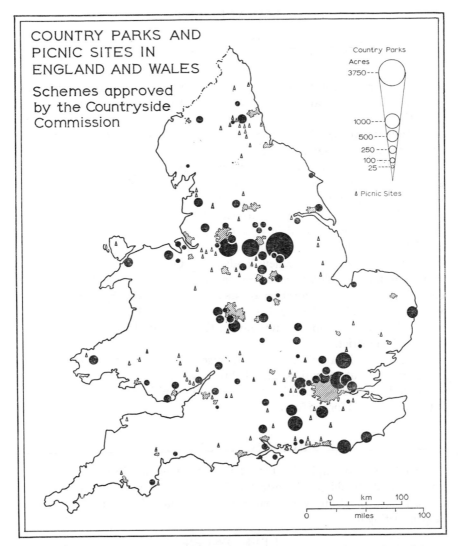

**Figure 24.2.** The distribution of country parks and picnic sites. Adapted from maps and statistics for September 1972. (Countryside Commission 1972b.)

within the orbit of the County Clerk, the Planning Officer or the Land Agent to conceive and implement countryside recreation schemes. The record of these authorities clearly indicates the importance which councillors and officers attach to the provision of recreation opportunities and the value of having appropriate technical expertise in the authority.

## MANAGEMENT

This chapter has been concerned mainly with the designation of land for the purposes of landscape conservation and informal recreation provision. It is, however, increasingly being realized that it is not enough merely to zone land for particular purposes: both within and outside designated areas it is necessary to embark upon programmes of management if conservation objectives are to be secured. The Countryside Commission, and other organizations, are seeking to take a lead by initiating research on landscape and recreation management issues.

A number of common and widespread problems have been identified for study. For example, there is much concern about the visual appearance of the new agricultural landscapes that are emerging (Munton, Chapter 21). Research sponsored by the Countryside Commission is seeking to record changes that have occurred in selected areas in lowland England, identify possible future changes if existing trends continue and find out the reaction of farmers to proposals for new landscapes. On the subject of recreation, two continuing problems are the management of recreational traffic in the countryside and the restoration of surfaces worn away by pressure from visitors (Goldsmith, Chapter 14). The Commission have sponsored work into both of these problems, notably in the Goyt Valley (Miles, 1972) and in the Lake District.*

These are only a selection of the research and experimental projects being carried out at national level, but new ideas are clearly essential if an attractive countryside with a range of opportunities for public enjoyment is to be conserved for the future.

## ACKNOWLEDGMENTS

I would like to emphasize that the views expressed in this chapter are my own and should not be attributed to the Countryside Commission. I would like to thank my wife, Joan Davidson, and Adrian Phillips for their help in writing it.

## REFERENCES

Countryside Act (1968), HMSO, London, 62 pp.
Countryside Commission (1970). *The Planning of the Coastline*, HMSO, London, 95 pp.
Countryside Commission (1971). *Reform of Local Government in England and Wales—National Parks* (Longland Report), Countryside Commission, London, 47 pp.

* For others see Research Register No. 6, Countryside Commission, 1973; for the Commission's own research programme see the *Annual Report* for 1972.

Countryside Commission (1972a). *Policy on Country Parks and Picnic Sites*, Countryside Commission, London, 8 pp.

Countryside Commission (1972b). *Fifth Report*, HMSO, London, 52 pp.

Countryside Commission (1973). *Landscape Agreements*, Countryside Commission, London, 15 pp.

Department of the Environment (1972). *The Planning of the Undeveloped Coast*, HMSO, Circular 12/72, London, 5 pp.

Dower, J. (1945). *National Parks in England and Wales*, HMSO, Cmnd. 6628, London, 57 pp.

Dower, M. (1972). The Smile of Sir Val Duncan, *Town and Country Planning*, **40**, 510–12.

Hall, P. (1973). Anatomy of the Green Belts, *New Society*, **23**, 9–12.

Miles, J. C. (1972). *The Goyt Valley Traffic Experiment*, Countryside Commission and Peak Park Planning Board, London, 114 pp.

Ministry of Housing and Local Government (1966). *The Coast*, HMSO, Circular 7/66. London, 4 pp.

Ministry of Land and Natural Resources (1966). *Leisure in the Countryside*, HMSO, Cmnd. 2928, London, 15 pp.

National Parks Committee (1947). *Report* (Hobhouse Report), HMSO, Cmnd. 7121, London, 134 pp.

Planning Advisory Group (1965). *The Future of Development Plans*, HMSO, London, 62 pp.

Thomas, D. (1970). *London's Green Belt*, Faber and Faber, London, 248 pp.

# CHAPTER 25

# National Parks in Developed Countries

I. G. SIMMONS

## THE NATIONAL PARK CONCEPT

The resource management policies of many developed nations include among their different types of protected ecosystems areas of land and water designated as National Parks.

The denomination of such parks arises from the desire to set aside particular areas of terrain from production in the conventional economic sense and to designate these as protected areas. Conservation of wildlife, of individual plant and animal species, or more commonly of assemblages of species, of habitats and groups of habitats, are often a major reason for their setting up and subsequent management. The needs of education and research are another function of such areas, since unaltered or little manipulated ecosystems provide reference points. There is also their capacity as wilderness areas used for back-country recreation, usually on foot or with the help of horses or mules, together with the symbolic, cultural and ecological values of terrain which is virtually unaltered by human activity.

The preservation of entire landscapes which are particularly valued is another concern of National Park management. Such landscapes are frequently natural but they may also be cultural, in which case there are generally some productive uses. The last major use is that of outdoor recreation, where the park is the setting for informal activities in a rural setting, the most popular of which are driving, walking, swimming and bicycling.

Of the various goals for management, outdoor recreation presents the developed countries with the strongest and most easily quantifiable social demand. Of the possible management aims for National Parks, outdoor recreation is the most akin to production in the conventional economic sense; the more so because of all the alternatives it is the most easily priceable. Because of their outstanding qualities of interest and beauty, National Parks are special magnets for recreationists and the number of visitors to them has been doubling every 6 to 7 years since the 1950s. There is thus considerable scope for conflict between recreation and the other, protective, roles of National Parks, leaving aside the demands for productive uses in some of them, and these disharmonies will form the main theme of this essay.

## Criteria for Selection

A feature common to the selection of National Parks in most countries is that it is undertaken by the national government. The criteria used, however, are not necessarily constant through time: at some periods the demands for recreation may be paramount, at others the desire for the protection of landscapes and ecosystems may be the dominating feature.

In the USA, for instance, one of the founding fathers of the National Parks system, Steven Mather, intimated that the parks should contain scenery of a supreme and distinctive quality with some natural features so extraordinary or unique as to be of national interest or importance, and further that the system should not be lowered in standard, dignity or prestige by the inclusion of areas which expressed in less than the highest terms the particular class or kind of exhibit which they represented (Ise, 1961). In the USA, these criteria are little changed today except in language (National Parks Service, 1967a).

Likewise in Canada, the overall purpose of the system has been stated to be the preservation of the Canadian heritage: this somewhat indefinable concept is amplified by criteria which develop the notion that a National Park must be an outstanding example of the best scenery in the nation or must possess unique scenic, geographical or geological features of national interest, or have outstanding examples of fauna or flora, again of national interest, or must provide outstanding opportunities for non-urban forms of outdoor recreation in superb surroundings. The parks must be large enough to support indigenous flora and fauna and it is desirable that part of the park should be suitable for recreational purposes and for the provision of appropriate services (National and Historic Parks Branch, n.d.).

In England and Wales there is no public domain, but this did not prevent John Dower, in his Report (1945) which was largely the foundation of the 1949 National Parks and Access to the Countryside Act, from defining National Parks as extensive areas of relatively wild country in which the characteristic landscape beauty is strictly preserved, in which access and facilities for enjoyment are amply provided, and in which wildlife, buildings and places of historic interest are preserved. He also maintained, and this principle has been enshrined in legislation and management, that farming, rural industries and afforestation should continue to function.

The theme of the inclusion of cultural phenomena, particularly ancient buildings, in National Parks is also carried through in the National Parks of Japan. Here, a long tradition of the harmony of man and nature (not now evident in many parts of those densely populated islands) is expressed in the criteria for selection of National Parks in which areas distinguished by superlative scenic beauty are accompanied by cultural relics that blend with nature (National Parks Association of Japan, 1966).

Together with examples from other countries, these examples of national policies have been incorporated by IUCN into criteria which must be satisfied if the area is to be included in the *U.N. List of National Parks and Equivalent Reserves*. Most importantly, it must have protected status in which the legislative machinery exists to preserve the park from resource development, although where only a part of a park is under strict protection, as with Daisetsuzan National Park in Hokkaido (Japan), it may still qualify for inclusion in the list. Secondly, there must be 'minimum superficies'. This does not preclude from the list parks which are subject to manipulation and management policies, but it does exclude such areas of terrain as have permanent inhabitants and on-going programmes of resource development. The National Parks of England and Wales, therefore, are not included, although some of the National Nature Reserves of the UK qualify on the grounds of their supposedly natural status (Simmons, 1969). Thirdly, there must be effective enforcement of status, and conditions are laid down for the wardening, expenditure and boundary establishment, all of which must be seen to be enforced (Harroy, 1969; IUCN, 1971).

**Management for Protection**

The critical first phase in the history of a National Park is protection from economic development, and this is enshrined in many legislative acts, whether it be complete protection from all forms of activity such as grazing, mining, building of roads and the development of water storage facilities, or partial protection involving the acknowledgment of the compatibility of some production provided that its ecological and aesthetic effects are consciously minimized. In areas where National Parks have been created upon terrain formerly used for economic yields, particularly timber extraction, it has not always been possible to persuade the agency concerned with lumbering to cease their more obvious practices, such as clear-felling; thus in Japanese parks such as Nikko National Park and the Shikotsu-Toya National Park in Hokkaido, clear-felling has been a cause of some contention between the Forest Agency and the National Park Agency. Similarly, in the Krkonose National Park in the northern Bohemia region of Czechoslovakia, clear-felling has been permitted after the designation of the area as a National Park and is a source of conflict in management policies. In the National Parks of England and Wales, most economic activities, including wholesale landscape change by agricultural reclamation of moorland or afforestation, are permitted. This is partly because the legislation exempts agriculture and forestry from the development controls which are a major feature of the 1949 Act, and partly because it was always intended that the ordinary everyday activities included in the National Park should continue. Activities such as the building of roads and the extraction of minerals have all continued, subject only to cosmetic landscaping.

A second phase is the protection of ecosystems and landscapes within areas of National Park status. There exists here the dichotomy of management technique, which may be expressed as *laissez-faire* versus manipulation. *Laissez-faire* management is rarely successful because the boundaries of the natural ecosystem do not usually coincide with the legal limits of the park; therefore if the managers desire to protect either rare or typical biota then it is unusual to find that they are components of an ecosystem confined to the protected area. The simplest example is of an insect which is a part of the natural ecosystem within the park but which becomes a pest in ecosystems manipulated for economic yield outside the park area. Examples are to be found in the Gypsy Moth and the Spruce Budworm in the coniferous forests of the western cordillera of the USA. The problem for the park manager is then whether he should continue to manage for a pristine set of ecosystems or whether he is to be accused of providing the source area for pests that damage the economic resources of peripheral forests. Again, the role of fire in natural ecosystems has been little understood, and efficient, indeed ruthless, fire suppression has been a feature of park management. In the case of the sierra redwood (*Sequoia gigantea*), suppression of fire has led to the shading out of the seedlings of this rare species by other coniferous forest taxa, and hence a lack of regeneration. The discovery that light burning was a normal feature of the forest ecosystem has led to the introduction of prescribed burning as a management technique in such places as King's Canyon–Sequoia National Park and Yosemite National Park in California, and regenerative levels have been improved.

In summary, we may say that unless a National Park is very large and has been subject to practically no manipulative influences before its designation, it is unlikely that its purpose will succeed unless some management operations are undertaken with the object of stabilizing some of the ecosystems.

A third phase is the restoration of ecosystems and landscapes which were disturbed by economic use prior to emparkment. This process is obviously not much employed in cultural landscapes, but in the National Parks of England and Wales, the enhancement of landscapes by the removal of eyesores such as military installations and relics of former periods of industrial activity is provided for, and indeed encouraged by, the financial structure of the legislation.

Elsewhere there have been attempts to reconstruct a natural environment in which certain elements of the biota which had been eliminated, either deliberately or accidentally by management for economic gain, are restored. We may quote the examples of woodland management in the High Tatras National Park of Slovakia, designed to restore the multiple-dominance mixed forest of the middle and lower slopes of the mountains which had been regulated as a virtually single-species unit, and the reintroduction of animals which had either been hunted out or had been victims of habitat change. The reintroduction of the wolf in parts of Europe is an example of this, as is the reintroduction in 1968 of the caribou into Cape Breton Island National Park in Nova Scotia.

There are two reasons for these planned reversions. There is firstly the need for increasing scientific knowledge of ecosystems both of the present and the past, and this is allied to a desire for a better understanding of the principles of ecosystem management which might enable the reintroduction of species, and secondly there is increasing public concern in the developed countries that ecosystems and landscapes should be maintained in a wild condition and with high biotic diversity. The sentimental, total-preservationist attitudes of the past are giving way to an increasing willingness to accept management as a feature of National Parks.

### Management for Development

Of the several kinds of development which can take place within National Parks, recreation is generally held to be compatible with protection. The role of recreation is usually enshrined in most acquisition and management legislation and regulations and is often accorded equal status with protection. It is held to be ethically right in the sense that it is no use having National Parks if people cannot enjoy them. The apotheosis of this idea was probably in the slogan used in the USA in the 1950s and 1960s: 'Parks are for people.'

An early phase of tourist-oriented development existed in some places before the parks attained the full flowering of their present conceptual basis. There are instances of development of resorts, particularly at hot spring areas in the Rocky Mountains of Canada, and in many parts of Japan where luxury resorts, along with roads, railways, hotels and golf courses, have eventually become an integral part of large National Parks.

The major phase of development has been under the impetus of the demand for outdoor recreation facilities in the industrial countries in the post-1945 era. Because of the generally wild areas in which National Parks are situated, statistics of visitor numbers are often of doubtful validity

14

except as general guides. On this basis we may note that in 1971 Shenandoah National Park in Virginia, USA, recorded 2·4 million visits, Yosemite National Park California), 2·4 million, and Yellowstone National Park (Wyoming–Montana–Idaho), 2·1 million. The total National Park system of the USA (which includes National Monuments, National Recreation Areas, and some historic sites) received around 200 million visits in 1971 (National Parks Service, 1972). According to Wager (1965), the increase in visitors to National Trust properties in Britain in the decade 1952–62 was 50 per cent, and overnight visitors to National Forest Parks increased 130 per cent (no statistics are collected for the National Parks). The annual average increase in the developed countries has been in excess of 10 per cent, rising to approximately 15 per cent in Japan, thus testifying to the popular appeal of the attractions that the parks have to offer.

The demand thus exhibited made itself felt in the landscapes of the parks in many ways. Since one of the triggers of the outdoor recreation explosion is the possession of the private automobile, then the provision of roads, petrol stations and all the infrastructure associated with road transport, on a vastly greater scale than hitherto, has been the most noticeable effect. Park managers have been led to construct roads into formerly wild areas of the parks in order to spread the existing load, and thus of course have created even greater demand for the future. Following the existence of the visitors has been the creation of numerous facilities for their accommodation and comfort. Urban-type developments create urban problems of the disposal of solid wastes and sewage, and the contamination of air (Yosemite Valley may have a smog problem in summer); camp sites in forests permit no regeneration of trees and sites on grass are quickly reduced to a quagmire in wet conditions.

In some National Parks whole townships have been established. At Banff and Jasper (Alberta, Canada), for example, the permanent human population is above 3,000, not unexpectedly creating demands for facilities of an altogether urban kind.

All these developments have been thought to have followed the right course of events for National Parks, either because the existing facilities were crumbling under the strain of increased demand or because it was thought good to enhance the use of the National Parks by the public: even in 1971 the Canadian government was mounting holiday travel campaigns based on National Parks as if they were commercial resorts.

In the last few years there have been distinct signs of a retreat from this maximum phase of development. Public opinion expressed through vocal citizen groups is swinging in favour of wildness and the holding down of development. Examples of this will be discussed in succeeding sections of this essay.

## SOME EXAMPLES

In the National Parks of industrial countries, protection and development appear as divergent trends in spite of attempts to combine them by zoning. In this section the management of some National Park systems will be examined in the light of their dominant trends since inception.

### The United States of America

The National Parks system of America contains several elements, such as National Monuments, National Recreation Areas and National Historical Sites, besides the National Parks. The first US National Park, Yellowstone, also the first in the world, was created in 1872. The National Parks Service was set up in 1916. There were, in December 1971, 38 National Parks with a total area of about 6 million hectares, nearly all of which is Federal land. They were strongly concentrated in the west, where the scenic and biotic resources are most valued, and where economic uses for the land are not so competitive, though by no means absent. Unlike lower-grade recreation areas, the distribution of the parks is not related to population concentrations in any way. The number of National Parks is supposed to be complete by the 100th anniversary of the founding of Yellowstone.

In the pre-1940 years development of the parks was confined to a few roads and trails, together with accommodation facilities of varying degrees of splendour, from permanent canvas camps through to wooden cabins and luxury hotels like the Ahwahnee in the Yosemite Valley. The justification for such developments was that the 1916 Act made enjoyment of the parks a legal purpose of their management and that at that time they were in rather inaccessible places.

Fraser Darling and Eichorn (1967) contend that the years 1935–40 were probably the peak of achievement and enjoyment of the National Parks: visitors could gain the experience of the National Parks that had been the goal of the founders of the movement, and there was much less pressure than at present from other visitors and cars. The post-1945 boom brought pressure to bear on facilities, including roads, of an altogether new dimension and the response of the parks service was a 10-year (1956–66) programme entitled 'Mission 66' to open up more of the parks and enlarge visitor facilities. This was a self-feeding spiral because more development led immediately to increased numbers of visitors.

Mission 66 was mostly for people rather than for parks, and the retreat from development was symbolized by the Leopold Report (Leopold, 1963), in which the parks policy to date was said to have been too heavily weighted in favour of visitors rather than the park resource, and which proposed a management goal to preserve these 'vignettes of primitive America'. In a remarkable redirection of aims, the Service adopted a new classification (National Parks Service, 1967b; 1967c) for their entire system in which the major part of the National Parks is classified as 'natural areas' and management plans have been formulated on an ecosystem basis (Reid, 1968). De-development is being undertaken, so that, for example, private cars are being excluded from Yosemite Valley and being replaced with shuttle minibuses, to be followed by the removal of built structures to a service area outside the gates. Eventually even camping will be outside the park itself. At Yellowstone, it is planned to reduce the developed zone from 5 per cent to 2 per cent of the park area. The master plans for each park are now becoming public documents, and under pressure of vocal public opinion more wilderness proposals under the authority of the National Wilderness Preservation Act of 1964 (Huxley, Chapter 23) are being submitted to the Congress. These events chronicle a strong retrocession of development which currently makes the US National Parks probably the most protected in the world; undoubtedly the most important factor in the changes of policy has been the shift in public opinion due to increased awareness of environmental matters.

## Canada

The prototype for Canadian parks was the Banff Hot Springs Reserve, established on 2,600 hectares of land near Banff Station (Alberta) in 1885. In 1887 this was expanded into a 67,340 hectare Banff National Park; the system has grown slowly to its present size in which 27 parks cover a total area of 12·8 million hectares of which 72·5 per cent is in the very wild terrain of the north. The organization of a managing agency came with the National Parks Act of 1930, and it is its aim to acquire 30–55 new parks in the next 30 years (Nicol, 1969). So far, all the parks except one are on Federal land: the exception is Forillon where the land is on a 99-year lease from the province of Quebec.

The development of Canadian National Parks has taken place under the same pressures as those of the USA, mitigated only by the smaller population of Canada, although the 'overflow' from the US National Parks finds Canada especially appealing. Commercial development was encouraged in the parks to attract tourists into areas otherwise economically marginal and some Canadian National Parks function also as regional parks for nearby cities: Elk Island National Park is used for summer weekends by Edmontonians, for example, and Banff National Park for winter sports by the denizens of Calgary. Likewise, Prince Edward Island National Park is largely a beach area for local residents. Development pressures are still high, as shown by the proposal to alter the visitor facilities at Lake Louise in Banff National Park by removing the old hotel development (a relic of the grand days of railroad travel) and replacing it on a different site with a multi-purpose resort area to be known as Village Lake Louise, to cost $30 million, 50 per cent of which would be owned by Imperial Oil Ltd. This proposal was strongly opposed by the organizations which spearhead the antidevelopment movement for National Parks (National and Provincial Parks Association of Canada, 1972), and was rejected by the Minister in July 1972.

The decision to formulate park master plans and then to submit them for approval by public hearings has produced a movement strongly in favour of protection rather than increased development. Such development as is undertaken will be confined to clearly defined zones in the parts where they will not offend, aesthetically or visually, the scenic and ecological values of the region.

## Japan

The National Park Law of 1931 resulted in the creation of 12 National Parks by 1945. In 1957 it was replaced by the National Parks Law, which added the categories of Quasi-National Parks and Prefectural Parks. There are now 23 National Parks covering 1·9 million hectares, which is about 5·3 per cent of Japan. Land ownership is 62 per cent by the state, 17 per cent by local authorities and 21 per cent by private owners (Senge, 1969). Since it is the valleys which are mostly in individual hands, and the upper forested slopes which are state-owned, usually as National Forest, development is commonly under private control. The zoning system of the parks admits to 32 per cent of the system as 'ordinary zone' in which no development controls are applied beyond those voluntarily accepted at the behest of the park authorities, such as restrictions on building height. Indeed, the government encourages development in such zones, with loans for *ryokan* (Japanese inns), hotels and other visitor facilities: there are about 400 public lodgings in the National Parks built with government funds in return for a controlled price.

The visitor pressure which brings about considerable development is inexorable, since large numbers of Japanese visit the cultural features of many parks (such as the Kasuga shrines at Nikko) as well as venture away from the roads. Parks such as Nikko and Fuji-Hakone-Izu are very close to Tokyo, and Shikotsu-Toya is close to a large proportion of the population of Hokkaido. The ubiquity of cheap public transport in Japan means that most of the National Parks are within weekend range of most of the population (excepting Hokkaido, but those who can afford to fly can be there in one and a half hours from Tokyo), and those near central Honshu are available for day use by 60 million people. The result is an immense urbanization of the settlements and routeways in the parks. Winter use of the parks is also gaining strength as skiing gains hold on a population whose disposable incomes are rising rapidly.

Protection from development exists in the creation of the Specially Protected Areas for nature preservation, which comprise 8·8 per cent of the National Parks, and Special Areas, where industrial (but usually not commercial) activity can be controlled, totalling 59·2 per cent of the park area. At Nikko National Park the Specially Protected Area has been enlarged to form a wilderness area in which only walking is allowed, and no developments are permitted other than simple huts for the night in the middle of the two-day round. Usage is currently at half a million a year.

A major trend towards protection is the commencement in 1971 of a funded programme to buy up private holdings in National Parks, especially where these are in critical areas. Its progress depends simply upon the amount of money the Diet will provide. A straw in the wind is possibly provided by the insistence of the Environment Agency that one of the chairlifts built in a Specially Protected Area of the Shikotsu-Toya National Park for the 1972 Winter Olympics must be removed now that the games are finished.

### England and Wales

Eleven National Parks totalling about 9 per cent of the surface of the two countries were established in the years following the 1949 National Parks and Access to the Countryside Act and have experienced relatively little development for public enjoyment. On the other hand, the Act provided strong measures of development control and the authorities have given priority to their implementation. Finance for recreational development has also been in short supply since such uses of money are the first to be culled in every financial crisis, of which there has been no shortage since 1949 (Darby, 1963; Johnson, 1971). However, several long-distance footpaths, of which the Pennine Way is the best known, have been established and numerous lay-bys and picnic sites constructed. Most noticeable are the car parks designed to relieve pressure on narrow roads or in small villages such as Hawkshead in the Lake District National Park. They are invariably accompanied by public toilets, thus becoming known in the trade as 'park 'n' pee facilities'.

The development control measures have been quite firmly applied and have aroused considerable opposition from local residents since they restrict, *inter alia,* the building of new houses and the conversion of old structures, and regulate the spread of caravan sites. Nevertheless, they generally enjoy public support since they are also applied to potential eyesores and sources of land dereliction. On the positive side, the Countryside Commission has carried out experiments in traffic control, such as the exclusion of cars from the Goyt Valley in the Peak District National Park. There is as yet no formal zoning of National Parks, but since the Town and Country Planning Act of 1968 requires local authorities to produce structural (broadscale) and local (more detailed) plans for their areas, then it is conceivable that zoning could be applied under the aegis of a local plan (Mercer, Chapter 26). These plans will be public documents.

England and Wales differ from the other examples, therefore, in having the balance of their trends on the side of protection; whether more development is to come of whether the prevailing trend will even increase their degree of protection is not yet foreseeable, particularly since a government committee is (in 1972) reviewing the whole future of the National Parks.

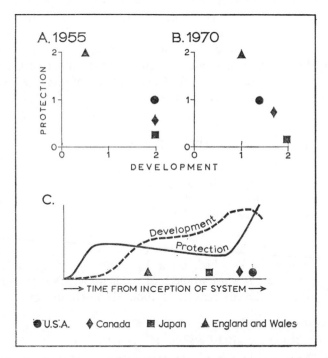

**Figure 25.1.** A schematic model of the balance between protection and development in the National Park systems of four countries plotted for 1955 and 1970, and on a metachronous time scale.

## Comparisons

A comparison of the outcome of the tension between protection and recreational development can be made by plotting these two measures against each other (Figure 25.1). The measures are entirely subjective esimates. Figure 25.1(a) shows the suggested situation for 1955 when the recreation surge had fully developed and was strongly affecting park management programmes; England and Wales remain staunchly protectionist with little development for recreation. Some movement away from the mid-development cluster is seen in Figure 25.1(b): the USA and Canada more towards greater protection, though with still adequate emphasis on development; Japan continues as highly developed; and England and Wales move towards greater development.

Figure 25.1(c) attempts to plot the trends of both development and protection (again in subjective units) through a metachronous 'time from inception'. Each country is placed along the graph at a point appropriate to its balance of development and protection: the result is that the systems are arranged from youngest to oldest, suggesting perhaps that there is a definite set of 'growth phases' of parks in which one or other management trend is dominant. (Here the curves are analogous to the balance of photosynthesis and respiration during the lifetime of an annual plant, for example.) More work is needed, both in the shape of objective measures of development and protection and of examination of other systems, to see if these conclusions can be substantiated.

## IMPORTANCE OF THE NATIONAL PARKS

Possibly the most important role of these wild areas in developed lands is their symbolic value, providing a sense of 'otherness' or the 'of the wild beyond' where man has not yet been a force; or in Luten's (1967) terms 'wilderness as helmsman', functioning as an inertial reference point of a cybernetic nature for man's activities. Such a capacity is hard to define, measure and price, but finds its way to the surface in the political espousability of National Parks which generally transcends party loyalties: the setting up of a system is a useful piece of publicity which enables a government to say that it is keenly concerned about the environment.

### Social Importance

In the developed countries wildlife is valued *per se* and National Parks inevitably form one of the larger reservoirs for biota, especially large mammals. The parks are thus outdoor biological gardens where the bird, beast or flower may be observed and recorded in either its natural habitat or a little-altered version of it. Natural populations can also be trimmed of surplus members to reintroduce them to areas from which they have disappeared.

Outdoor recreation is, without doubt, the most important current social role of National Parks. The difficulties which it can cause in management goals and programmes have been discussed and it is now becoming clear that de-emphasis of the recreational use of the National Parks is coming about and other resources are being developed to take some of the strain off National Parks in this regard. We may quote the Country Parks of England and Wales (Davidson, Chapter 24), National Recreation Areas, State and Regional Park systems in the USA, some Provincial Parks in Canada and Prefectural Parks in Japan as examples of resource development with outdoor recreation as a primary aim. Nevertheless, the increase of recreational demand, together with even slow increases in population (which mean high absolute numbers in nations like England, Japan and the USA), coupled with the high values put upon their qualities, mean that pressure upon National Parks for recreation will continue for the foreseeable future.

**The Wilderness Function**

Completely wild areas are important in constituting a pool of genetic diversity in their biota. The necessity for such a reservoir is discussed in another chapter (Berry, Chapter 7) and will not be elaborated here, except to emphasize that it is one of the objectively scientific reasons for National Parks.

Another part to be played by ecosystems is to act as regulators of the $CO_2/O_2$ balance of the atmosphere. Large National Parks with a high rate of productivity are clearly a component of the mechanism which keeps the element cycles, of which these gases are a part, in working order. In a broader perspective, they are part of the mosaic of different types of ecosystems to which Odum (1969) has drawn attention. In nature, there are simple ecosystems which may have, for a time, high biological productivity; and complex systems whose productivity may be lower but which are stable and buffered by their diversity against catastrophic change. Man's use of the world's resources has obliterated some ecosystems, and transformed others into highly productive simple systems yielding desired crops over a short period, i.e. modern intensive agriculture. Other systems are multi-purpose, like many forests in the developed countries. If the biosphere is to remain stable and hence continue to maintain the life-support systems upon which our species depends, then the complex stability-enhancing systems must also form part of the pattern. Obviously National Parks, and particularly the parts of them which are little altered, are part of these protective ecosystems and as such are essential to our future. In this, as in other ways demonstrated here, it is difficult to underestimate the importance of National Parks to the nations of the developed world.

**Acknowledgments**

I should like to thank those bodies which have made it possible to visit other countries and collect information, especially the American Council of Learned Societies, NATO, and, most recently and most generously, the Winston Churchill Memorial Trust. Personal communications made on such visits account for the unattributed material in this paper.

## REFERENCES

Darby, H. C. (1963). British National Parks, *Adv. Sci.*, **20**, 307–18.

Darling, F. F., and Eichorn, N. (1967). *Man and Nature in the National Parks: Reflections on Policy*, The Conservation Foundation, Washington DC, 80 pp.

Dower, J. (1945). *National Parks in England and Wales*, HMSO, London, Cmnd. 6628, 57 pp.

Harroy, J. P. (1969). The development of the National Park movement, in: *The Canadian National Parks: Today and Tomorrow*, (eds.) J. G. Nelson and R. C. Scace, University of Calgary Studies in Land Use History and Landscape Change, National Parks Series No. **3**, pp. 17–34.

Ise, J. (1961). *Our National Park Policy*, Johns Hopkins Press for Resources for the Future Inc., Baltimore, 701 pp.

IUCN (1971). *U.N. List of National Parks and Equivalent Reserves*, Hayez, Brussels, 601 pp.

Johnson, W. A. (1971). *Public Parks on Private Land in England and Wales*, Johns Hopkins Press for Resources for the Future Inc., Baltimore, 136 pp.

Leopold, A. S. (1963). *Wildlife Management in National Parks*, US Dept. of the Interior Advisory Board on Wildlife Management, Washington, DC, 23 pp.

Luten, D. B. (1967). Resource quality and the value of the landscape, in: *Natural Resources: Quantity and Quality*, (eds.) S. Ciriacy-Wantrup and J. J. Parsons, University of California Press, Berkeley, Los Angeles, pp. 19–34.

National and Historic Parks Branch, Department of Indian Affairs and Northern Development (n.d.). *National Parks Policy*, Government of Canada, 32 pp. (Dates from late 1960's.)

National Parks Association of Japan (1966). *National Parks of Japan*, Tokyo, 38 pp.

National Parks Service, U.S. Department of the Interior (1967a). *Criteria for Selection of National Parklands and National Landmarks*, US Govt. Printing Office, Washington, DC, 31 pp.

National Parks Service, U.S. Department of the Interior (1967b). *Administrative Policies for Natural Areas of the National Park System*, US Govt. Printing Office, Washington, DC, 63 pp.

National Parks Service, U.S. Department of the Interior (1967c). *Administrative Policies for Recreation Areas of the National Park Systems*, US Govt. Printing Office, Washington, DC, 64 pp.

National Parks Service, U.S. Department of the Interior (1972). *Public Use of the National Parks, December 1971*, US Govt. Printing Office, Washington, DC, 9 pp.

National and Provincial Parks Association of Canada (1972). Village Lake Louise, *Park News*, **8**, 2–20.

Nelson, J. G., and Scace, R. C. (eds.) (1969). *The Canadian National Parks: Today and Tomorrow*, University of Calgary Studies in Land Use and Landscape Change, National Parks Series No. **3**, Calgary, 1027 pp.

Nicol, J. I. (1969). The National Parks movement in Canada, in: *The Canadian National Parks: Today and Tomorrow,* (eds.) J. G. Nelson and R. C. Scace, University of Calgary Studies in Land Use History and Landscape Change, National Parks Series No. 3, Calgary, 2 vols., 35–52.

Odum, E. P. (1969). The strategy of ecosystem development, *Science,* **164,** 262–70.

Reid, N. J. (1968). Ecosystem management in the National Parks, in: *Proceedings 33rd N. American Wildlife and Natural Resources Conference,* 160–9.

Senge, T. (1969). The planning of National Parks in Japan and other parts of Asia, in: *The Canadian National Parks: Today and Tomorrow,* (eds.) J. G. Nelson and R. C. Scace, University of Calgary Studies in Land Use History and Landscape Change, National Parks Series No. 3, Calgary, 706–21.

Simmons, I. G. (1969). On National Parks and cultural landscapes, in: *The Canadian National Parks: Today and Tomorrow,* (eds.) J. G. Nelson and R. C. Scace, University of Calgary Studies in Land Use History and Landscape Change, National Parks Series No. 3, Calgary, 738–41.

Wager, J. (1965). Known demands for outdoor recreation, *The Countryside in 1970,* 2nd conference, Royal Society of Arts, London, Paper No. **6,** 21 pp.

# CHAPTER 26

# The Role of the Local Government in Rural Conservation

## Ian Mercer

'To conserve' is a transitive verb—one has to conserve something. We seem to have fallen into a habit during the last decade of using the word 'conservation' alone, as though it was something itself—a process parallel with other well-understood generalizations like education or engineering. Conservation almost became a subject at school during 1970, alongside Greek and Woodwork, and the thought that one might pass examinations in it, and possibly drop it at 16 and begin to live, is clearly ridiculous, but a risk as long as the word is used alone. This misguided use of the word, and more important, of the idea, has coloured much of the layman's thinking, and has led to unfortunate generalizations about an amorphous range of people now collectively called conservationists. For the purposes of this essay, therefore, it is necessary to state that we are discussing the conservation of resources—and more particularly the conservation of environmental quality as a basic resource for human health and happiness.

Local government in England and Wales is at this moment facing gigantic reorganization, and substantial internal shifts in responsibility, particularly with regard to the environment. This affects what it is possible to say about its role in the conservation of the environment, so that this essay can only be a general discussion of its present role and its potential.

The decisions and actions of a Local Authority fall into three categories as far as the environment is concerned. There are, firstly, positive works such as the construction and modification of roads, the erection of buildings of all kinds, and many other minor engineering works. All of these affect the environment, and some may indeed enhance it in that they allow the removal of structures, the reclamation of dereliction, or even for directional persuasion, such as by the provision of information centres.

There is, secondly, a group of decisions and legislative acts which regulate activities in the environment. Most of them come under the general heading of 'planning'—although this word like so many basically sound English words is now also sadly misused. The Local Authority becomes the Local *Planning* Authority in this situation, and with this hat on, actually regulates its own positive actions, as well as those of all other members of the community, with the notable exception of the Crown and its agents. This last fact leads to some strange environmental anomalies. The Post Office, for example, is a Government Department not subject to planning control, whereas the Electricity Authority, as a statutory undertaker, *is* subject to that control. Both bodies erect poles in the landscape and string wires between them, materially affecting the scene, and in some cases the use of the land beneath. Even if the Planning Authority were to recognize that only one set of poles would serve both purposes in a particular case, there might be great difficulties in effecting such a logical economy.

Thirdly, there is the group of activities which are probably best called persuasive. They fall in a wide spectrum, from discussion with landowners leading to changes in their own management policies, to that massive persuasive system we call 'education'. Somewhere between these extremes lies the growing function of the Local Authority as a catalyst which receives increasingly vociferous public opinion, sorts it, rationalizes it, and forges it into some constructive action. Public participation—in the continuing sense rather than only at election time—is thus to be considered part of the local government operation in this context. These three groups are not, of course, entirely distinct, and the overlap between them is, in some cases, considerable.

## POSITIVE WORKS

The use of certain positive works by Local Authorities for conservation was made easier by the Countryside Act, 1968, and by the influence on local government of that great persuasive broadside—the 'Countryside in 1970' movement (1970). This latter, with regal backing and a crescendo in 1970 itself, brought about the beginning of a change of attitude to the landscape, wildlife and the quality of rural living and human experience in the country. Some examples of this change can be seen from the Devon experience.

### Urbanization Schemes

Local authorities sometimes plan large extensions of urban areas. On the northeastern edge of Plymouth such a proposal involved the laying out of 1,250 acres of former farmland as an industrial and residential estate. It was hoped to create a new community, and it was thought that the potential quality of the life of that community would be enhanced by the careful retention of certain components of the existing landscape which could, properly integrated, allow continuing biological connection and interchange between the plant and animal communities of the new estate and the surrounding country. Plymouth City Corporation called in the Devon Trust for Nature Conservation, whose newly appointed Conservation Officer produced a biological plan for the whole new estate (Figure 26.1; and Smith and Wheeler, 1970).

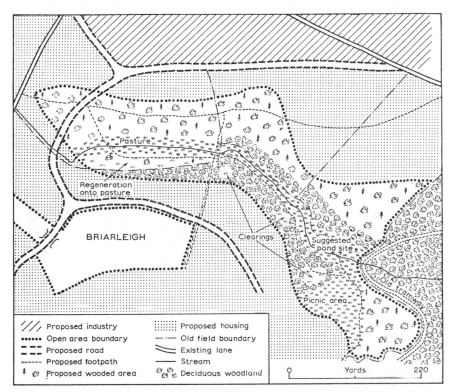

Legend:
- ⁄⁄⁄ Proposed industry
- •••••• Open area boundary
- ‗ ‗‗ Proposed road
- ------ Proposed footpath
- ✝ ✧ Proposed wooded area
- ⁝⁝⁝⁝ Proposed housing
- —·— Old field boundary
- ⌇⌇ Existing lane
- —— Stream
- ✧✧✧ Deciduous woodland

Labels on map: Pasture, Regeneration onto pasture, BRIARLEIGH, Clearings, Suggested pond site, Picnic area, Old tramway

Yards 0 — 220

**Figure 26. 1.** A part of the plan for nature conservation in the Estover Estate, Plymouth, showing existing and planned areas of semi-natural vegetation and projected areas for housing and industry around the Mainstowe Valley site. (After Smith and Wheeler, 1970.)

The plan introduced the Planning Authority to such things as biological corridors, nature-trails and a butterfly garden as permanent parts of the development, and the City Council accepted and approved the report. Individual industrial developments within the estate then called on the Trust to advise them on the integration of their lands into the whole scheme.

## Country Parks and Picnic Sites

County and District Councils have been empowered since 1949 to create and manage various areas for public recreation in the countryside. In the

Countryside Act, 1968, these powers were widened, and more positive guidance has since been forthcoming from the national level. Thus the local authority can now make positive efforts to enhance the visitor's enjoyment of the landscape, and at the same time, by providing sites which are planned, executed and managed for concentrated human use, alleviate pressures which might otherwise be directed at inappropriate, low-capacity, or eco-logically fragile sites. Near Ottery St. Mary in East Devon, 25 acres of scarp slope, acquired urgently to preserve a viewpoint in the face of afforestation proposals, have been developed by the County Council as a picnic site, with interconnecting circular trails through a number of different plant communities, geological outcrops and observation points.

### Roadsides

Devon has 6,500 miles of unclassified roads, and a few hundred miles of principal and trunk roads. The County Surveyor has been persuaded that the mileage of verge and hedgebank associated with this network is a valuable visual, ecological, and indeed a business asset to a county which is dependent upon visitors for a major part of its income. He has set up a working party including the National Farmers' Union, the Country Land-owners Association, the Devon Trust for Nature Conservation, the County Federation of Women's Institutes, the Dartmoor Preservation Association, the Community Council and others to report on the management of this linear asset. It is hoped to inject a new attitude to the planned management of all these much-observed verges and at the same time to designate vital verges as of special importance from scientific or visual points of view. The management of special verges may well be entirely placed in the hands of specialists. These moves, and the ensuing debates, actually influence all matters handled by the officer or committee in question, and, from this concern for existing roadsides, attitudes to new verges are altered. Planting and management proposals become more sensitive, and the quality of the landscape in this small respect is improved (Stevenson, 1973).

### Tree Planting

Finally, the Local Authority can have a direct effect upon visual amenity in the landscape by removing eyesores, and by planting trees and other plants. In the latter case, all authorities hold land themselves for public services, such as road verges, and in the case of County Councils, as small-holdings. Tree planting, and the retention of existing single trees, has been encouraged on council-occupied and leased land for some time. Some authorities now spend considerable sums annually in providing trees and the necessary fencing materials to any landowner in return for a manage-ment agreement in perpetuity for the trees in question. This is a positive move to counter the loss of hedgerow timber and small copses in the face of the development of intensified agriculture (Munton, Chapter 21).

## PLANNING AND REGULATING

We have in Britain what is probably the most comprehensive and highly developed system of land-use planning in the world. With certain minor exceptions, it covers all land in both town and country, and most kinds of development including material changes in the use of land and buildings and civil engineering operations. Legislation on the subject has evolved through a long series of Acts beginning with the Housing, Town Planning, etc., Act, 1909, but it is now for the most part consolidated in the Town and Country Planning Act of 1971 (Davidson, Chapter 24). The central features of the system are:

(a) the development and structure plans which show, in broad terms, the purposes for which land is intended;

(b) control of development in detail by the granting or refusal of planning permission.

### Planning Authorities

The Town and Country Planning Act of 1962 designated County and County Borough Councils in England and Wales as the 'Local Planning Authorities' responsible for administering the Act subject to the overall responsibility vested in the then Minister of Housing and Local Government and the Secretary of State for Wales. In certain circumstances a Joint Planning Board (representing two or more County or County Borough Councils) could be set up as the Planning Authority. This has been done in the case of two of the National Parks.

County Councils have until now, with the consent of the Minister, been able to delegate planning control and its enforcement to County District Councils. Any County District (outside the National Parks and the metropolitan areas) whose population exceeds 60,000 has been entitled to claim delegated powers as of right. The majority of County Councils have exercised this power, although the degree of delegation varies. Most delegation agreements contain a provision that requires that decisions on planning applications must be agreed with an official of the County Council before they are issued, or, in the event of disagreement, that they are referred to a joint committee of the District and County Councils. It is not unusual for agreements to reserve major proposals for development for the decision of the County Council. In most cases the delegation of powers of development control to County Districts follows a similar pattern in the National Parks and in other areas of high landscape value.

From April 1st, 1974, new District Councils will handle development control as of right, and will also be responsible for local plans (of towns, villages, etc.), County Councils will produce the structure plans for the counties, and will deal with proposals thought to be of county-wide importance.

## Development Plans

Every Planning Authority must prepare a development plan, soon to be known as a 'structure plan', which must indicate the manner in which it proposes that the land should be used, whether by development or not, and the stages by which development should be carried out.

### Control of Development

The 1971 Act provides that planning permission shall be required for any development of land. Development is defined as the execution of any building, engineering, mining or other operations in, on, over or under the land; or the making of any material change in the use of buildings or land.

A number of operations are excluded from the definition of 'development'. Of these the more important are:

> The use of any land for the purposes of agriculture or forestry, including the use of any associated building; changes of use within a class included in the Use Classes Order (see below) for example, a change of use from dairy farming to horticulture; works carried out by a highway authority for the maintenance or improvement of a road on land within the boundary of the road.

Proposals for certain kinds of development must be advertised in the local press before application for planning permission is made; these include sewage disposal works, refuse tips, slaughterhouses, public lavatories, theatres, cinemas and bingo saloons or other buildings for indoor games. In all other cases the Planning Authority is at liberty to take whatever steps it thinks necessary to ensure that it is sufficiently informed to take the right decision. In many cases the Authority will be able to decide on the application from its own local knowledge. In others it may consider it advisable to advertise the proposal in the press in order to ascertain local opinion, including that of local amenity and civic societies. It is for the Planning Authority to decide, in the light of all the circumstances, whether or not such consultations are desirable.

In dealing with an application for planning permission a planning authority must have regard to the provisions of the development plan, and to any other material considerations. It must also take into account any representations it may have received.

In the case of certain kinds of development the Planning Authority must consult other Authorities before coming to a decision. It must, for example, consult the Department of the Environment before allowing development affecting a trunk road, or the National Coal Board in the case of an area in which the Board have an interest. The Secretary of State for the Environment has power to direct the Local Planning Authority to refuse permission if the proposal would adversely affect the road traffic situation, or to impose conditions on the grant of permission. In all other cases the Authorities consulted can only advise the Planning Authority, and although the advice need not be taken, it usually is.

There are three important Statutory Instruments affecting countryside planning. First, the Use Classes Order, 1973, classifies users of land which are similar for planning purposes, and declares that a change from one use to another within the same class shall not be construed as development and shall not need planning permission.

Secondly, the General Development Order serves two main purposes: to set out the procedure for dealing with planning applications; and to give a blanket permission for certain classes of development.

Article 3 of the order gives planning permission for the classes of development for which no application for planning permission need be made. There are 23 of these classes, including small extensions to dwelling houses, temporary uses of land, the erection of farm buildings (subject to an upper limit of 5,000 square feet ground area), development by statutory undertakers (electricity sub-stations, underground gas mains, signal boxes, etc.), the deposit of colliery waste on land previously used for that purpose, road works on land adjoining an existing highway, small extensions to industrial buildings, and minor development by Local Authorities (bus shelters, lamp standards, etc.).

Article 4 of the order enables the Minister, or a Local Planning Authority, subject to the approval of the Minister, to direct that the permission granted by the Order should not apply to a particular development and/or a particular area. Where a direction has been made, planning permission is required for any specified development.

The Landscape Areas Special Development Order, 1950, applies to certain specified areas of natural beauty and provides that development for agriculture or forestry which is permitted under the General Development Order shall, in these areas, be subject to a condition enabling the Local Planning Authority to control the design and external appearance of any buildings.

Local Planning Authorities may make preservation orders for trees and woodlands in the interests of amenity. Such orders, when confirmed by the Minister, prohibit felling, topping and lopping except with the consent of the Authority (penalty for contravention £50), and may make provision for replanting.

## National Parks, Access and Natural Beauty

The National Parks and Access to the Countryside Act, 1949, gave to Local Planning Authorities in England and Wales additional powers to preserve and enhance the natural beauty of their areas, and added powers to provide facilities for its enjoyment. The Act also gave them power to

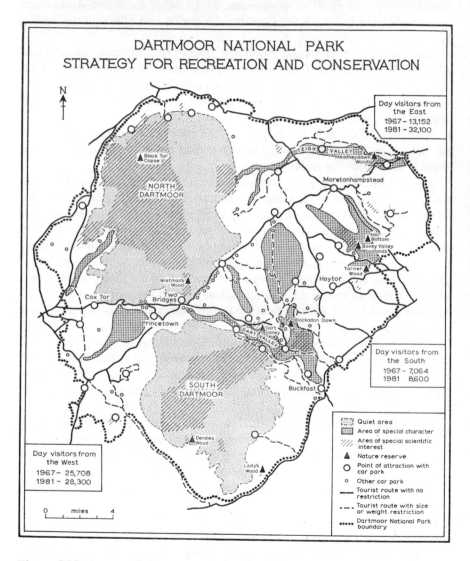

DARTMOOR NATIONAL PARK
STRATEGY FOR RECREATION AND CONSERVATION

N

Day visitors from
the East
1967 – 13,152
1981 – 32,100

Black Tor
Copse

NORTH
DARTMOOR

TEIGN VALLEY
Meadheydown
Woods

Moretonhampstead

Mill
Bottom
Bovey Valley
Woodlands

Yarner
Wood

Wistman's
Wood
Cox Tor
Two
Bridges          Haytor

Blackadon Down
Princetown
DART VALLEY
Dart
Valley

Day visitors from
the South
1967 – 7,064
1981   8,600

SOUTH
DARTMOOR          Buckfast

Quiet area
Area of special character
Area of special scientific
interest
Nature reserve
Point of attraction with
car park
Other car park
Tourist route with no
restriction
Tourist route with size
or weight restriction
Dartmoor National Park
boundary

Dendles
Wood

Day visitors from
the West
1967 – 25,708
1981 – 28,300

Lady's
Wood

0        miles        4

**Figure 26.2.** A part of the structure plan for Dartmoor National Park showing projected developments for recreation and nature conservation. (After Devon County Council, 1973.)

improve derelict land, to plant trees, shrubs and grass, to provide access facilities on open land by agreement, order or purchase of land, to make byelaws for such 'access land', to appoint wardens to secure compliance with the byelaws and to help the public in general, and to provide facilities for accommodation, meals and refreshments along long-distance paths. As an example of the kind of local government planning in a National Park, Figure 26.2 shows the current plan for Dartmoor.

In areas designated by the 1949 Act as being Areas of Outstanding Natural Beauty or National Parks, approved expenditures incurred in the exercise of the powers just listed are eligible for a 75 per cent exchequer grant payable by the Department of the Environment (or the Welsh Office) after consultation with the Countryside Commission (Davidson, Chapter 24). In the case of the creation and maintenance of the long-distance paths, a 100 per cent grant is payable in all areas of England and Wales.

In the National Parks, Planning Authorities have, in addition, powers with similar grants to provide car parks and camp and caravan sites, to secure access to waterways and to improve these for sailing, boating, bathing or fishing; and such improvements of waterways could also attract a 100 per cent grant.

The Countryside Act in 1968 revised slightly and extended greatly the effect of the National Parks Act. It also introduced the idea of 'Country Parks' as specific areas of recreational land (Davidson, Chapter 24), and gave Ministers power—if they wished to take it—to make orders requiring farmers of rough grazing land to give notice of intentions to change the surface. Most significantly, it enjoined that 'In the exercise of *their functions relating to land* under any enactment, every minister, government department and public body shall have regard to the desirability of conserving the natural beauty and amenity of the countryside' (Countryside Act, 1968, Sect. 11). This puts a particular onus with regard to the landscape fairly and squarely on local government, among others. The Act also created the Countryside Commission, with duties which include consultation with the Local Planning Authority and 'in cases where special problems are raised or special skill is needed, to notify the local planning authority or other appropriate body, and on application, make available to the local planning authority or other public body the servants or consultants of the Commission'. The Countryside Act, 1968, thus drew central government and the Local Authorities together in a more concerted effort on behalf of the natural and semi-natural landscape, and the manipulation of people within it.

## Nature Conservation

So far this discussion of planning has concerned itself with people, land use, 'natural beauty' and the rather impertinent idea that men might 'enhance' it. Wildlife or 'nature' has not been specifically mentioned, but 'natural beauty' is dependent upon living systems, and must, for its maintenance, depend upon the conservation of natural systems.

The 1949 Act created the Nature Conservancy for this purpose; it was to work side by side with the then National Parks Commission (Blackmore, Chapter 27). It also designated various statutory land-use categories on behalf of wildlife, with National Nature Reserves as the elite members of a rather short hierarchy. The Local Authorities were given the power to create Local Nature Reserves, although the number of Local Nature Reserves in existence is pathetically small. This is partly because Local Authorities, in 1949, and immediately after, did not normally number ecology among their skills. Pressure was not exerted to persuade them of the need of reserves since the Nature Conservancy, at least, was busy carving out its own niche on the national scene. It is now clear that government priorities and budgets on the national scale do not run to wildlife conservation at the local level, so that the maintenance of animal and plant populations and locally significant habitats must be carried out by local bodies. To date this has been the self-imposed task of voluntary bodies, mainly the County Trusts for Nature Conservation, but there is a limit to voluntary effort, both in time and money. The community is enriched by the voluntary aspect of the effort, but if the task is as vital as most thinking people believe, then this particular conservation operation will have to be more formal, and set in the priority list of environmental care and maintenance at the right level. Local government, of course, does take account (in its development plans) of Sites of Special Scientific Interest as designated by the Nature Conservancy (Blackmore, Chapter 27), and consultation about their management does take place, but the 'protection' afforded is of the most slender kind.

National Nature Reserves are owned or leased by the Nature Conservancy, Local Nature Reserves by the Local Authority, and others by trusts or individuals. Their protection is comparatively easy in our present land-tenure system. On the other hand, those areas of land designated as being of significance in relation to aesthetic or recreational qualities—often sizeable areas such as National Parks—have no such simple protective covering: while called 'national', they are administered locally; and while called 'parks', they remain almost wholly in the occupation of private individuals or bodies. The Local Authority carries the responsibility for their administration and maintenance with few powers that are unique to the situation, little support from other arms of government, local or national, and often heartfelt opposition from occupiers and owners of the designated land. Vociferous and articulate would-be conservationists, with only opinions and no responsibilities, are variously a help and a hindrance in this difficult and ill-supported task.

Many of the problems besetting our modern affluent society are to be found within the National Parks. We live in a landscape organized by Anglo-Saxons, while valuing our political freedom and our democratic processes at least as highly as our environment. It is here that the ways in which conservation can inhibit the freedom of the individual are most obvious, for the seeker after one social freedom erodes that of another. This is the point at which the discussion should pass from regulation by the Local Authority to its persuasive role.

## PERSUASION

The persuasive role of the Local Authority for conservation falls into two quite separate areas: formal and informal. In the sphere of formal education the Authority has a statutory function to perform, for it administers and accounts for the state education system within its area, concentrating on children to the age of 18, but also pursuing further education through colleges of education, polytechnics and various forms of instruction for voluntary groups. The Local Authority in this context becomes the Local Education Authority, and derives much of its power direct from specific national statutes, and not solely from the Council itself.

The actual front-line business of educating is carried out by teachers, who are perhaps the most independent employees of the Local Authority, remote from its policy-making heart. Nevertheless, through a system of advisors, teachers' centres and *ad hoc* working parties, it is possible for educational policies to be conveyed to the school and the individual teacher. Thus the views of the Education Committee, its Chairman or the Chief Education Officer, if strongly enough held, can influence the teaching operation. The Authority can therefore use the education system as the main weapon in its management armoury by passing the ideas on to schools. But the Authority with such a will—and none yet exists—faces resistance at every step, from business organizations and the individual, and as long as vote-catching remains the incurable disease of democracy such resistance is likely to prevail. But the battle must be won, since education of the right kind—whatever that may be—is, to many, the only answer to the task of producing a citizenry equipped with sufficient ecological literacy to underpin the democratic process (e.g. Crookall, 1973).

Many teachers are already motivated by a concern for the environment, although few of them are well equipped to teach about it. There is all the difference in the world, however, between the activities of the odd teacher or even a few teachers and the acceptance by administrators, teachers' organizations and the teaching body at large that conservation is as vital as reading, writing and arithmetic, and needs to be pursued as urgently.

If a start is to be made in environmental education, then no better part of the curriculum exists for its introduction than in that group of topics which has so far failed to be enlivened in school, namely local government, the management of the local environment, the conservation of the local landscape, local resources, and the local community (Newbould, Chapter 28).

Outside formal education the Local Authority's persuasive function is not statutorily derived nor is it necessarily seen by all Authorities as an important operation. Statutory backing for informal persuasion does, however, exist—especially in respect of the local environment. Various Acts of Parliament provide for the making of *agreements,* for example for management and access, and such agreements must depend upon persuasion. Most National Park Committees have—sometimes after long years of discussion and argument—persuaded the Forestry Commission, and in their turn timber growers, to make voluntary afforestation agreements. Currently such ideas are also being discussed for agricultural reclamation in upland areas. During 1970 many local conferences about environmental concern were mounted by local governments (e.g. Devon County Council, 1971). In a democracy, central government is bound to attempt persuasion before legislation, and thus it does encourage the Local Authority in these persuasive efforts.

The persuasion of one party to behave in a conservation-minded manner is one thing, but to persuade two—probably opposed—parties of the rightness of a particular course of action, near to neither's original navigational estimate, is quite another. In the last decade a great voluntary 'conservation' movement, latent for 100 years, has arisen with persuasion as almost its only weapon. While it aims a few of its broadsides directly at those whom it recognizes as environmental villains, it attempts, more often, to operate by persuading the Local Authority into particular action against such villains. The Authority then becomes almost a judge, or ombudsman, in this triangular, pseudo-legal setting, in which conservation criteria may be substituted for 'the law'. While this might be seen as a reasonable function for the Authority, it clearly erodes its available time and energy, and thus possibly militates against more positive resource-conservation achievement. In such situations the Local Authority inevitably finds itself doing a double persuasion act, attempting to bring the operator's policies and public opinion towards each other in some environmental compromise which epitomizes conservation in this context. The great weakness in this process is the lack of ecological knowledge among the elected members of an Authority, and the short-fall in available expertise in the official ranks at the level at which advice is proffered to these members. A few Local

Authorities have appointed ecologists to 'assist' those who derive their status from statute or professional qualification. Some of these new appointees are called 'conservation officers'. In rural matters these officers tend to be advisors, not conservators, whereas in urban contexts, in contrast, there are 'conservation areas' to be managed positively. The risk in such appointments is that, alongside a surveyor and an educator, a conservation officer might be thought to conserve—as something separate and specialized —when in fact the need is to persuade all other officers to behave in a particular way *vis-à-vis* the environment.

Government at all levels has now sown the seed for the provision of balanced advice about the environment within its own ranks. This is important since, as Julian Huxley says, evolution for the human species is now cultural and social rather than organic, and in this evolutionary process government is the major instrument of adaptation.

## REFERENCES

Countryside Act (1968). HMSO, London, 62 pp.

Countryside in 1970 (1970). *Reports,* Nature Conservancy, London.

Crookall, R. E. (chairman) (1973). *Schools and the Environment,* South-western Group of Local Education Authorities, Dorset County Council, Dorchester, 88 pp., and *Devon Trust for Nature Conservation Journal.*

Devon County Council (1971). *Man and the Devon Environment,* chairman J. E. Packer, Devon County Council, Exeter, 56 pp.

Devon County Council (1973). *Dartmoor National Park Development Plan,* Devon C.C., Exeter, 30 pp.

Smith, L. P., and Wheeler, F. G. (1970). *A Nature Conservation Plan for an Urban Development, Estover Estate, Plymouth* (Abstract), Devon Trust for Nature Conservation, Exeter, 17 pp.

Stevenson, R. B. (1973). *The Management of Devon's Roadsides,* Devon County Council, Exeter, 8 pp.

# CHAPTER 27

# The Nature Conservancy: its History and Role

M. Blackmore

Anyone who begins to study the organizations that play a part in managing the British countryside may well feel puzzled when he tries to unravel their respective roles. Apart from private owners, the bodies (both official and voluntary) that have an interest in rural land are so numerous, and their activities so varied, that the seeker of information can easily lose his way. The needs which the land itself serves are equally varied, but if one considers all the interested groups and the main land-use practices it becomes apparent that the planning of a proper balance between the demands made on the countryside and its capacity to sustain them is a pervasive element in the aims of most of these bodies. Management of this kind, which is conservation in the broad sense, seeks to integrate as many interests as possible, and is now a widely accepted part of overall planning policy.

## ORIGINS OF NATURE CONSERVATION

Nature conservation illustrates the gradual evolution and development of modern attitudes. From Saxon times onwards (Sheail, Chapter 19) rural land was usually treated as an asset to be exploited for profit or enjoyment (often both) without conscious regard for the long-term effects on natural organisms that served no obviously 'useful' purpose. The great landowners of the seventeenth and eighteenth centuries recognized the value of planting trees to provide timber for houses and ships or to improve the landscape of their estates, while game was reared for sport and also because it added variety to the table. But the notion that wild plants and animals could be a source of instruction or enjoyment in their own right, or that they ought to be protected as part of a natural heritage, claimed only a few adherents. The earliest of these seems to have been Charles Waterton (1782–1865), the squire of Walton Hall in Yorkshire, who was the first landowner to manage his property as a sanctuary for wildlife. He made shelters for nesting birds and kept boats off his lake for part of the year in case they disturbed wildfowl. Dogs were not allowed to run loose, shooting was forbidden, and all wild creatures except rats were protected. Most of Waterton's contemporaries, including his fellow proprietors, regarded him as a harmless eccentric, which in many ways he was. They ignored his precepts as being altogether too revolutionary and uneconomic as a way of running a country estate; but within fifty years of his death a new generation of conservationists began working on similar lines and on a more ambitious scale. Voluntary bodies such as the Royal Society for the Protection of Birds (founded in 1889), the National Trust (1895) and the Society for the Promotion of Nature Reserves (1912) owe much to Waterton's efforts, but it is doubtful if their founders realized to what extent they were following in his footsteps. Neither they nor their successors have given this enthusiastic country squire his due as a pioneer of nature conservation, and his reputation as a naturalist rests mainly on the fact that he wrote a successful, though quaint and discursive, book about his explorations in the jungles of South America (Waterton, 1825).

The voluntary conservation bodies expanded what Waterton had begun. In 1899 the National Trust, for example, started to acquire parts of Wicken Fen in Cambridgeshire as a private nature reserve, and from 1919 the Society for the Promotion of Nature Reserves did the same at Woodwalton Fen in Huntingdonshire. Neither of these areas, nor similar ones that followed soon afterwards through the initiative of private bodies, enjoyed statutory protection from adverse development; they were nature reserves in fact, but not in law. During the first three decades of the present century the State did little to support the movement, which was still very much a minority interest. Despite the ravages of the Industrial Revolution, with its legacy of wholesale destruction and dereliction, society in general showed a casual attitude to the countryside, where further changes were beginning to make themselves felt between the two world wars. Drainage of agricultural land, improvement of roads as a necessary consequence of the motor car and—most significant of all—new factories and housing estates, often built by speculators with little or no regard for environmental planning, pointed to a future which threatened to destroy nature unless man could learn how to co-exist with it. By the end of the 1930s it was becoming clear that the task of safeguarding scientifically important sites was too great for voluntary effort to tackle alone.

## Nature Reserves Investigation Committee

In June 1941 the Society for the Protection of Nature Reserves convened a conference to discuss the place of nature conservation as part of national planning after the war. Three meetings were held that year and the participants came to certain general conclusions about the need to establish and manage different types of countryside as nature reserves under public control. A short memorandum to this effect was sent to the Prime Minister and other Ministers in charge of departments concerned with land use (Society for the Promotion of Nature Reserves, 1941) and in 1942 Sir William Jowitt, who was then chairman of a ministerial committee dealing with the problems of reconstruction, invited the conference to appoint an appropriate body that could advise the Government in more detail. Prompted by this official encouragement, the conference immediately set up a Nature Reserves Investigation Committee, with a network of regional sub-committees, to make a survey of important sites in England and Wales. It later formed a special sub-committee to advise on geological features needing protection.

Between March 1943 and December 1945 the Nature Reserves Investigation Committee issued three reports containing lists of sites with recommendations for their selection and management (Society for the Promotion of Nature Reserves, 1943; 1945a, b). Among them were 47 suggested National Nature Reserves chosen purely on their scientific merit. Although the committee made no detailed proposals for administering such areas, it envisaged the creation of a 'central authority' with full executive power to select, control and manage them.

## National Parks

Meanwhile a separate campaign was gathering its forces in Britain to influence the future use of the relatively wild and unspoilt countryside that had a mainly aesthetic appeal. The followers of this movement (whose origins can be traced back to several voluntary organizations) wanted to protect the beauty of the landscape and to promote recreation and enjoyment in selected areas. Although different in emphasis from the concept of nature reserves, the idea of National Parks complemented the aims of nature conservation.

In May 1945 the Dower report (Dower, 1945) was presented to Parliament 'for information and as a basis for discussion'. Its author supported the principles of nature conservation already put forward, but he wanted to see them applied more widely than the Nature Reserves Investigation Committee had proposed. He suggested that a special Government body (to be called the Wild Life Conservation Council) should be created to deal nationally with the problem and that its main functions should be advisory, educative and co-ordinative. While agreeing that National Nature Reserves were a necessary part of a countrywide policy for nature conservation, Dower believed that those within the proposed parks (and preferably others outside) should be administered by a single authority, the National Parks Commission, who would be advised by local experts and enthusiasts. He considered this to be a matter of practical convenience outside the parks and to be essential within them. Unless the Commission was made responsible for such reserves he did not think that a proper balance and interrelationship could be maintained between the objectives of nature conservation and the other main aims of the parks, namely the preservation of landscape, the protection and improvement of farming, and the development of access and recreational facilities.

A National Parks Committee was formed in July 1945, with Sir Arthur Hobhouse as its chairman, to consider the Dower Report. Because parts of it raised issues of a scientific nature, the committee decided in August to appoint a Wild Life Conservation Special Committee under the chairmanship of Dr (now Sir) Julian Huxley to advise it not only on the recommendations for wildlife conservation in National Parks but also on any other cognate measures that seemed desirable or necessary as part of a national policy.

## A Biological Service

The Special Committee agreed that the National Parks Commission should be responsible for the day-to-day management of nature conservation within the proposed parks, but it found a practical difficulty in the argument that the Commission itself should control National Nature Reserves. In its report (Cmd. 7122, Ministry of Town and Country Planning, 1947) the Special Committee concluded that the surveying of suitable areas for National Nature Reserves, and the research and management to be carried out in them, called for a high degree of scientific knowledge and skill which the National Parks Commission alone would not be able to provide effectively. An independent 'Biological Service' was therefore needed to implement a system of National Nature Reserves and to advise generally on nature conservation.

Much of the preliminary work of selecting proposed National Nature Reserves had been done by the Nature Reserves Investigation Committee, to which the Special Committee acknowledged its debt; but it added several other areas to the list, making a total of 73 sites which contained about 70,000 acres.

Meanwhile the Scottish National Parks Committee and the Scottish Wild Life Conservation Committee, which had been appointed early in 1946 to examine similar matters in Scotland, came to the same general conclusions about the need for National Parks and National Nature Reserves and the appropriate bodies to control them. Their recommendations were issued in two reports: Cmd. 7235 and Cmd. 7814 (Department of Health for Scotland,

1947; 1949). The latter contained 24 sites as proposed National Nature Reserves (also covering 70,000 acres) which, like those in England and Wales, were regarded as the minimum requirement.

Those who are interested in the development of official interest in nature conservation may wonder why the Government came to take these initiatives within a relatively short time after many years of neglect. Max Nicholson (Director-General of the Conservancy from 1952 to 1966) has made the tart comment that wartime suspension 'of the normal British mechanisms for ensuring inaction' had a beneficial effect on progress (Nicholson, 1970).

## CREATION OF THE NATURE CONSERVANCY

Official committees were not the only bodies pressing for a Biological Service; the Royal Society and the British Ecological Society (1943) had also urged this need. The consensus of opinion was that the new organization should be predominantly scientific so that it could not only fulfil executive duties but also undertake the complex ecological research on which successful conservation depended.

In April 1948 the Government announced its acceptance of the principles put forward in the reports of the Special Committees and on March 23rd, 1949 it created the Nature Conservancy by royal charter as a new research council, the ultimate responsibility for which was given to the Committee of the Privy Council for Agricultural Research and Nature Conservation.

The Conservancy's functions, as defined in the charter, were:

'to provide scientific advice on the conservation and control of the natural flora and fauna of Great Britain; to establish, maintain and manage nature reserves in Great Britain, including the maintenance of physical features of scientific interest; and to organise and develop the research and scientific services related thereto'.

The charter nominated the initial membership of the Conservancy, which was to consist of not more than 18, nor less than 12, members who were to be appointed at all times 'on account of their scientific qualifications or interest in matters connected with nature conservation'. It also enabled the Conservancy to hold money and property and to appoint staff. Moreover, it required a Scottish Committee to be appointed for the purpose of furthering the objects of the charter in Scotland.

## STATUTORY POWERS

For the proper discharge of its responsibilities the Conservancy needed additional powers and these were given to it by the National Parks and

Access to the Countryside Act, passed in December 1949. Much of this Act
dealt with National Parks and the duties of the National Parks Commission,* while Part III covered nature conservation and the Conservancy.
Because of the initial close association between the two movements, now
launched on their independent paths, it was perhaps fitting that their
statutory powers should be defined within a single piece of legislation.

Although the Act as a whole did not apply to Scotland (where the proposals for National Parks were dropped), the provisions relating to nature
conservation included that country. Under its charter the Conservancy could
already own or lease land, and section 16 of the Act gave it the additional
power to make agreements with landowners and tenants so that areas not
actually held by the Conservancy could be managed as National Nature
Reserves and enjoy the same protective status. Such agreements were to
run with the land in the same way as forestry dedication covenants made
under the Forestry Act of 1947. This arrangement allowed full cooperation
between landowners and the Conservancy, including the sharing of costs
for putting management plans into effect and the payment of compensation
for restrictions specified in the agreement.

In creating the Conservancy as its instrument for a national policy to
conserve nature, the Government had to deal with several problems. For
example, it was necessary to know what changes were taking place in the
distribution and numbers of native wild animals and plants. Some of the
changes were 'natural' in the sense that they were the result of alterations
over which man had little or no control, such as climate; others were due
to deliberate human actions which could be altered if necessary. It is
important to distinguish the separate causes.

The science of ecology which had developed rapidly during the first half
of the present century showed that the pattern was complicated and dynamic.
Some of the factors were already understood but many others still had to
be discovered. In order to practise effective nature conservation it was
therefore necessary to form groups of skilled scientists to study the problems and find the answers. The result of this approach was that the Conservancy's three main tasks of research, practical conservation (applied
ecology) and the provision of advice were organized under various teams
whose knowledge and experience could be freely exchanged and made
available to others.

### Early Progress

Immediately after its creation the Conservancy began to survey and
acquire many of the areas which the Wild Life Conservation Special Committee and others had proposed as National Nature Reserves. This was

* Renamed the Countryside Commission in 1968.

relatively easy in the uplands of Scotland and northern England where several large tracts of scientifically interesting wild and semi-wild land were available. Beinn Eighe National Nature Reserve in Wester Ross (10,450 acres) was purchased in 1951 and Moor House National Nature Reserve in Westmorland (10,000 acres) followed in 1952. In the southern lowlands, where competing uses and pressures for development were often intense, the Conservancy found it more practicable, as a rule, to concentrate on securing fairly small areas. Although it made significant progress, the results in terms of acreages declared in southern England were somewhat disappointing during the early years, and acquisitions there have tended since to be rather piecemeal.

It was not until 1954 that the first National Nature Reserves were established by agreement. These were at Bridgwater Bay, Somerset, at Havergate Island, Suffolk, and in three areas of the Cairngorms, Inverness-shire. Purchase or lease had previously proved to be a quicker way of securing reserves, but as the third method became more widely understood and appreciated by landowners the areas in this category increased significantly. For several years more than half the total acreage has been managed under agreements. (See Table 27.1.)

Table 27.1. Acreage of National Nature Reserves as at December 31st, 1972

| | Owned | Leased | Nature Reserve Agreement | Total | No. of National Nature Reserves |
|---|---|---|---|---|---|
| England | 15,993 | 21,798 | 25,902 | 63,693 | 65 |
| Scotland | 54,001 | 5,291 | 132,920 | 192,212 | 40 |
| Wales | 3,457 | 10,240 | 8,790 | 22,487 | 29 |
| Total | 73,451 | 37,329 | 167,612 | 278,392 | 134 |

The distribution and relative size of British National Nature Reserves is shown in Figure 27.1

## HOW RESERVES ARE CHOSEN

National Nature Reserves are chosen to protect geological sections, landforms, habitats and associations of plants and animals rather than individual species. The main aim is to maintain samples of the most interesting kinds of vegetation in Britain together with their associated animals. The sites are in many different parts of the country and show how assemblages of plants and animals vary in accordance with different rocks, soils and climates. Areas rich in species or habitats are generally preferred to more

15

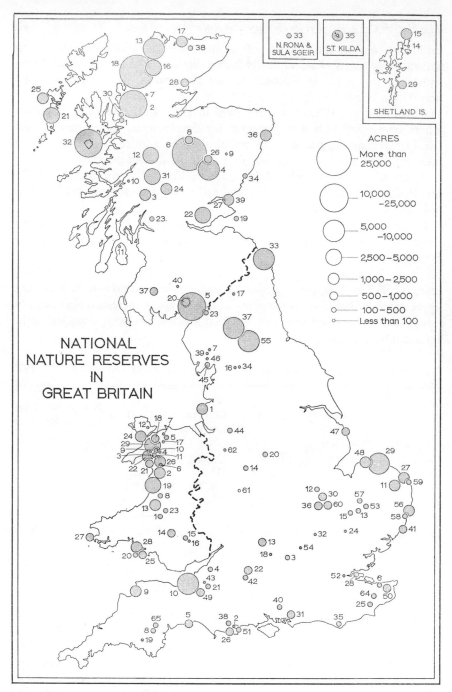

**Figure 27.1.** National Nature Reserves in Britain. The size of each circle is proportional to the acreage of the reserve. Most of the reserves are in the south, but the largest reserves are in Scotland. See acompanying table for Reserve names and acreages. The reserves shown are those declared to December 1972.

## SCOTLAND

| Map number | Name | Acreage |
|---|---|---|
| 1 | Allt nan Carnan | 18 |
| 2 | Beinn Eighe | 10,507 |
| 3 | Ben Lui | 925 |
| 4 | Caenlochan | 8,991 |
| 5 | Caerlaverock | 13,514 |
| 6 | Cairngorms | 64,118 |
| 7 | Corrieshalloch Gorge | 13 |
| 8 | Craigellachie | 642 |
| 9 | Dinnet Oakwood | 33 |
| 10 | Glasdrum Wood | 43 |
| 11 | Glen Diomhan | 24 |
| 12 | Glen Roy | 2,887 |
| 13 | Gualinn | 6,232 |
| 14 | Haaf Gruney | 44 |
| 15 | Hermaness | 2,383 |
| 16 | Inchnadamph | 3,200 |
| 17 | Invernaver | 1,363 |
| 18 | Inverpolly | 26,827 |
| 19 | Isle of May | 140 |
| 20 | Kirkonnell Flow | 383 |
| 21 | Loch Druidibeg | 4,145 |
| 22 | Loch Leven | 3,946 |
| 23 | Loch Lomond | 624 |
| 24 | Meall nan Tarmachan | 1,142 |
| 25 | Monach Islands | 1,425 |
| 26 | Morrone Birck-Wood | 557 |
| 27 | Morton Lochs | 59 |
| 28 | Mound Alderwoods | 659 |
| 29 | Noss | 774 |
| 30 | Rassal Ashwood | 209 |
| 31 | Rannoch Moor | 3,704 |
| 32 | Rhum | 26,400 |
| 33 | Rona and Sula Sgeir | 320 |
| 34 | St. Cyrus | 227 |
| 35 | St. Kilda | 2,107 |
| 36 | Sands of Forvie | 1,774 |
| 37 | Silver Flowe | 472 |
| 38 | Strathy Bog | 120 |
| 39 | Tentsmuir Point | 1,249 |
| 40 | Tynron Juniper Wood | 12 |

## ENGLAND

| Map number | Name | Acreage |
|---|---|---|
| 1 | Ainsdale Sand Dunes | 1,216 |
| 2 | Arne | 9 |
| 3 | Aston Rowant | 259 |
| 4 | Avon Gorge | 156 |
| 5 | Axmouth/Lyme Regis Undercliffs | 793 |
| 6 | Blean Woods | 164 |
| 7 | Blelham Bog | 5 |
| 8 | Bovey Valley Woodlands | 180 |
| 9 | Braunton Burrows | 1,492 |
| 10 | Bridgwater Bay | 6,076 |
| 11 | Bure Marshes | 1,019 |
| 12 | Castor Hanglands | 221 |
| 13 | Cavenham Heath | 376 |
| 14 | Chartley Moss | 104 |
| 15 | Chippenham Fen | 193 |
| 16 | Colt Park Wood | 21 |
| 17 | Coom Rig Moss | 88 |
| 18 | Cothill | 4 |
| 19 | Dendles Wood | 73 |
| 20 | Derbyshire Dales | 158 |
| 21 | Ebbor Gorge | 101 |
| 22 | Fyfield Down | 612 |
| 23 | Glasson Moss | 143 |
| 24 | Hales Wood | 20 |
| 25 | Ham Street Woods | 240 |
| 26 | Hartland Moor | 637 |
| 27 | Hickling Broad | 1,204 |
| 28 | High Halstow | 130 |
| 29 | Holkham | 9,700 |
| 30 | Holme Fen | 640 |
| 31 | Kingley Vale | 351 |
| 32 | Knocking Hoe | 22 |
| 33 | Lindisfarne | 7,718 |
| 34 | Ling Gill | 12 |
| 35 | Lullington Heath | 155 |
| 36 | Monks Wood | 387 |
| 37 | Moor House | 9,956 |
| 38 | Morden Bog | 367 |
| 39 | North Fen | 4 |
| 40 | Old Winchester Hill | 151 |
| 41 | Orfordness/Havergate Island | 555 |
| 42 | Pewsey Downs | 188 |
| 43 | Rodney Stoke | 86 |
| 44 | Rostherne Mere | 378 |
| 45 | Roudsea Wood | 287 |
| 46 | Rusland Moor | 58 |
| 47 | Saltfleetby/Theddlethorpe | 1,088 |
| 48 | Scolt Head Island | 1,821 |
| 49 | Shapwick Heath | 546 |
| 50 | Stodmarsh | 402 |
| 51 | Studland Heath | 429 |
| 52 | Swanscombe Skull Site | 5 |
| 53 | Thetford Heath | 243 |
| 54 | Tring Reservoirs | 49 |
| 55 | Upper Teesdale | 8,593 |
| 56 | Walberswick | 1,211 |
| 57 | Weeting Heath | 338 |
| 58 | Westleton Heath | 117 |
| 59 | Winterton Dunes | 259 |
| 60 | Woodwalton Fen | 514 |
| 61 | Wren's Nest | 74 |
| 62 | Wybunbury Moss | 26 |
| 63 | Wychwood Forest | 647 |
| 64 | Wye and Crundale Downs | 250 |
| 65 | Yarner Wood | 372 |

## WALES

| Map number | Name | Acreage |
|---|---|---|
| 1 | Allt Rhyd-y-Groes | 153 |
| 2 | Cader Idris | 969 |
| 3 | Coed Camlyn | 157 |
| 4 | Coed Cymerau | 65 |
| 5 | Coed Dolgarrog | 170 |
| 6 | Coed Ganllwyd | 59 |
| 7 | Coed Gorswen | 33 |
| 8 | Coed Rheidol | 107 |
| 9 | Coed Tremadoc | 50 |
| 10 | Coedydd Maentwrog | 169 |
| 11 | Coed-y-Rhygen | 68 |
| 12 | Cors Erddreiniog | 78 |
| 13 | Cors Tregaron | 1,898 |
| 14 | Craig Cerrig Gleisiad | 698 |
| 15 | Craig-y-Cilau | 157 |
| 16 | Cwm Clydach | 50 |
| 17 | Cwm Glas Crafnant | 38 |
| 18 | Cwm Idwal | 984 |
| 19 | Dyfi | 3,974 |
| 20 | Gower Coast | 116 |
| 21 | Morfa Dyffryn | 500 |
| 22 | Morfa Harlech | 1,214 |
| 23 | Nant Irfon | 336 |
| 24 | Newborough Warren/Ynys Llanddwyn | 1,566 |
| 25 | Oxwich | 564 |
| 26 | Rhinog | 1,478 |
| 27 | Skomer Island | 759 |
| 28 | Whiteford | 1,932 |
| 29 | Y Wyddfa (Snowdon) | 4,145 |

uniform sites, and the reserves as a whole are planned to include the habitats of as many different plants and animals as possible. When rare species occur on National Nature Reserves their protection is one of the tasks of management.

National Nature Reserves have sometimes been called 'living museums', a description which is apt in some but not all respects. Museum specimens are displayed in artificial surroundings and, whereas a group of exhibits may illustrate affinities and relationships, they are generally static. On a reserve change and ecological succession occur constantly and, although management may arrest, control or guide them in certain directions, the process is inevitably dynamic. Reserves are therefore of great scientific and educational value because they show the interactions between living organisms and the processes of growth and decay which continually produce new situations and combinations.

### Management

The successful management of National Nature Reserves depends on an adequate understanding of the ecology of the species and communities they support. In the early years of the Conservancy not enough was known about environmental factors and their interaction with species because ecology was then a relatively new branch of biology so that much of the management was inevitably empirical. The Conservancy has always appreciated the need for intensive long-term and short-term research in order to provide a better scientific foundation for its management and advisory tasks. After many years of effort facts are gradually emerging and guiding the development of new management techniques, even though much remains to be learnt before some of the problems can be resolved. This process of ecological enquiry and experiment makes the National Nature Reserves 'outdoor laboratories' in a real sense.

Conditions and problems vary from site to site but, generally speaking, the aims and techniques of management fall into several well-defined categories. They include the control of water levels (vital for conserving bogs and fens); the prevention of undesirable plant successions (for example those leading to the invasion of scrub on open grassland); the control of animal populations, especially pest species; the diversification of habitats; the prevention or reversal of degenerative changes caused by excessive human pressures; the controlled burning and grazing of grasslands, heathlands and moorlands; and the creation of the right conditions for the regeneration of woodlands. Some or all of these factors (and often many others) have to be considered on most National Nature Reserves. They are set down in detailed management plans which summarize the existing conditions and indicate the methods whereby these can be perpetuated or altered if desired.

## SITES OF SPECIAL SCIENTIFIC INTEREST

Because there are many places of scientific interest that could not be established as National Nature Reserves, section 21 of the National Parks and Access to the Countryside Act gave the Conservancy a duty to notify planning authorities of any area which, 'not being land for the time being managed as a nature reserve, is of special interest by reason of its flora, fauna or geological or physiographical features'. There are about 3,200 Sites of Special Scientific Interest. Should proposals be made for development within them, the planning authority must inform the Conservancy before granting permission so that its views can be taken into account.

There are advantages and weaknesses in this system. Faced with the prospect of opposition, a potential developer may abandon or modify his proposal and the scientific interest of a site may thus be preserved. But many Sites of Special Scientific Interest can be ruined by actions that do not constitute 'development' within the meaning of the Act. Drainage, forestry and ploughing are examples, and such threats can be averted only through negotiation and persuasion, the success of which depends on the goodwill and co-operation of owners. Fortuately there are many who value the scientific features of their property, but the inducement to improve the commercial yield of land is always present and frequently conflicts with its management for nature conservation.

## RESEARCH

Much of the Conservancy's research is directly related to specific management problems. Investigation into the ways in which the animals and plants of chalk grasslands respond to different grazing and mowing systems, and studies of the conditions under which tree seedlings can establish themselves in old woodlands, come into this category. Other research, like work on the population dynamics of grouse or the social organization of ant colonies on southern heaths, is more fundamental.

The professions and skills represented among the staff of the Conservancy are extremely varied. In the Research Branch teams of botanists, zoologists and soil scientists study the main types of habitat such as coasts, lowland heaths and grasslands, agricultural land, woodlands, mountains, moorlands and wetlands (e.g. Tubbs, Chapter 9; Miller and Watson, Chapter 10; Duffey, Chapter 11). When necessary these scientists can call on the help of colleagues including those working on surveys, biometrics and the geographical sciences.

For many years the Toxic Chemicals and Wildlife Section at Monks Wood Experimental Station, near Huntingdon, has studied the effects of pesticides on wildlife, and as a result of this work the Conservancy has urged consistently, with marked success, that the more harmful products should be controlled (Moore, Chapter 15). Since 1968 the section's research has been extended to include the detection and analysis of polychlorinated biphenyls (PCBs) and heavy metals, particularly lead and mercury, in several species of birds. The Biological Records Centre (also based at Monks Wood) records the distribution and numbers of British plants and animals. Professional scientists and amateur naturalists outside the Conservancy take part in these surveys, which now cover major plant groups and several animal groups as well.

## ADVICE

The task of giving advice cannot be assigned to any specific group or team in the Conservancy. Staff in the Conservation and Research Branches are often asked to advise on ecological problems which are referred to them by government departments when considering land reclamation, barrages and other development schemes, by local authorities, for example when planning the management of open spaces for recreational use, by voluntary conservation trusts, and by private landowners and other individuals. The Conservancy's staff in both branches is composed mainly of botanists and zoologists who have received ecological training during their degree courses and, in many cases, during postgraduate research in Britain or overseas. They are in a position to provide an enormous fund of ecological knowledge and experience derived from several countries.

The demand for advice has grown rapidly as pressures on the countryside have increased and, although the Conservancy must always give priority to areas in which it has a specific interest (such as National Nature Reserves and Sites of Special Scientific Interest), it cannot treat them in isolation. What affects one area directly may often have indirect consequences for another, and constant liaison by the Conservancy with numerous other bodies enables it to propose ways of satisfying conservation requirements that will harmonize or avoid conflict with other interests.

Recognizing the need to foster in every citizen an understanding of man's natural environment and his place in it, as well as the need for trained environmental specialists, the Conservancy has given special attention to advice and support in the educational field. In 1960 it established a Study Group on Education and Field Biology (1963) and, also in 1960, it helped

University College London to establish its Diploma Course in Conservation (now the M.Sc. Conservation Course). In March 1965 it organized the 'Countryside in 1970' Conference on Education at the University of Keele, and in 1968 it took a leading part in establishing the Council for Environmental Education (Newbould, Chapter 28).

The Conservancy works closely with universities, with Her Majesty's Inspectorate of Schools, with local education authorities, and with numerous educational bodies such as the Field Studies Council, the National Association for Environmental Education (formerly the National Rural Studies Association) and the Youth Hostels Assocation. In particular, it advises on the management of land for field studies, as well as making some of its reserves available for this purpose.

## ORGANIZATIONAL CHANGES

For the first sixteen years of its existence the Conservancy was an independent research council, but in 1965, when the Government created the Natural Environment Research Council by royal charter as part of the reorganization of civil science, the Conservancy became a component body (officially a committee) of the Council, to which all the statutory powers hitherto belonging to the Conservancy were transferred under the Science and Technology Act of 1965. Since this Act was passed the Conservancy has continued to exercise these powers as the executive agent of the Council.

## POSTSCRIPT

Since the above account was written (in December 1972) various changes have occurred as a result of the Nature Conservancy Council Act, 1973. This abolished the Nature Conservancy and replaced it with an independent statutory body known as the Nature Conservancy Council. Its members are appointed by the Secretary of State for the Environment in consultation with the Secretaries of State for Scotland and Wales.

The new Council is responsible for National Nature Reserves in Great Britain and for notifying Sites of Special Scientific Interest. It advises Ministers on nature conservation policies and on how other policies may affect nature conservation. It is also a source of ecological knowledge and advice for all those who are interested in the natural environment or whose activities may affect its scientific interest.

In order to discharge its functions the Nature Conservancy Council commissions and supports research, much of which is done by the Natural Environment Research Council. The Nature Conservancy Council may itself undertake relevant research that cannot be done appropriately elsewhere, but the research stations that formed part of the Nature Conservancy remain with the NERC, and will be known collectively as the Institute of Terrestrial Ecology.

## ACKNOWLEDGMENTS

I am grateful to Mr. Philip Oswald, head of the Nature Conservancy's Interpretative Branch, for reading my manuscript and making several helpful suggestions. Miss S. M. Penny, the Nature Conservancy's Librarian, has also helped greatly by providing copies of documents referred to in the text.

## REFERENCES

British Ecological Society (1943). *Nature Conservation and Nature Reserves*, Report by a committee of the British Ecological Society, Cambridge University Press, Cambridge, 38 pp.

Department of Health for Scotland (1947). *National Parks and the Conservation of Nature in Scotland*, Report by the Scottish National Parks Committee and the Scottish Wild Life Conservation Committee, Cmd. 7235, HMSO, London, 72 pp.

Department of Health for Scotland (1949). *Nature Reserves in Scotland*, Final Report by the Scottish National Parks Committee and the Scottish Wild Life Conservation Committee, Cmd. 7814, HMSO, London, 34 pp.

Dower, J. (1945). *National Parks in England and Wales,* Cmd. 6628, HMSO, London, 37 pp.

Ministry of Town and Country Planning (1947). *Conservation of Nature in England and Wales,* Report of the Wild Life Conservation Special Committee (England and Wales), Cmd. 7122, HMSO, London, 139 pp.

Nicholson, E. M. (1970). *The Environmental Revolution: a Guide for the New Masters of the Earth,* Hodder and Stoughton, London, 366 pp.

Society for the Promotion of Nature Reserves (1941). Conference on Nature Preservation in Post-war Reconstruction, Memorandum No. **1,** 8 pp.

Society for the Promotion of Nature Reserves (1943). Conference on Nature Preservation in Post-war Reconstruction. *Nature Conservation in Great Britain,* Report by the Nature Reserves Investigation Committee, Memorandum No. **3,** 25 pp.

Society for the Promotion of Nature Reserves (1945a) Conference on Nature Preservation in Post-war Reconstruction. *National Geological Reserves in England and Wales,* Report by the Geological Reserves sub-Committee of the Nature Reserves Investigation Committee, Memorandum No. **5,** 42 pp.

Society for the Promotion of Nature Reserves (1945b) Conference on Nature Preservation in Post-war Reconstruction. *National Nature Reserves and Conservation Areas in England and Wales,* Report by the Nature Reserves Investigation Committee, Memorandum No. **6,** 79 pp.

Study Group on Education and Field Biology (1963). *Science Out of Doors,* Longmans, London, 240 pp.

Waterton, C. (1825). *Wanderings in South America, the North-West United States, and the Antilles in 1812, 1816, 1820 and 1824. With original instructions for the preservation of birds etc. for cabinets of natural history,* J. Mawman, London, 326 pp.

CHAPTER 28

# Conservation in Education

P. J. NEWBOULD

## INTRODUCTION

Since most conservation objectives and decisions will have to be realized through the political or democratic process, a major educational exercise will be necessary to enable the public to arrive at its own assessments; and a more specialized but smaller educational exercise will be needed to help those charged with carrying out more specific conservation practices.

It is convenient to treat conservation in education under three major headings—the education of the land-linked professions, that is of the professionals or practitioners; education in the formal sense of school, college or university, and including the continuing education of adults; and thirdly, on-site education in the form of countryside centres, nature trails, planning enquiries, etc.

## EDUCATION OF THE LAND-LINKED PROFESSIONS

Almost all the professions bear in some way on the man–resource–environment relationship. The role of teachers is apparent in the next section, doctors have an important role in family-planning services and thus in implementing population policy as well as in the monitoring of environmental health, and the profession of environmental lawyer has recently emerged in the United States, allowing private citizens or, more usually, pressure groups to take out lawsuits against polluters and other environmental 'criminals'.* However, we are more concerned here with the professions involved in the planning, management and development of land, air, water and wildlife resources.

Planning, and the implementation of plans, is increasingly becoming a team activity, in which the planner himself may be the conductor or

* There is now a group in Britain, called the Solicitors' Ecology Group, c/o the Law Society's Hall, 113 Chancery Lane, London.

437

orchestrator of a team (a concept developed by Nicholson, 1964). Depending on the precise task in hand, the team may include engineers, architects, quantity surveyors, economists, sociologists, ecologists or landscape architects. It is important for the specialists to be able to communicate with one another, and since the manipulation of resource systems is essentially an ecological problem ecology should form the basis of communication. It is easier to add new material such as ecological knowledge to the training of such people than to jettison old material from their courses, but it is not easy to specify the precise nature of the ecological content that should be inserted into a course. Ecologists have not always been helpful in this respect, often seeming to be prepossessed with 'natural' systems such as the Amazon basin or the Carpathian mountains to the exclusion of the simplified systems found in Hyde Park or the Weald of Kent.

**Ecological Concepts**

The central concept in current ecological thought is the ecosystem, a complex of plants and animals together with the soil or water they inhabit and the microclimate they create. All the component parts of an ecosystem are closely interrelated and a change in one may cause changes in all the others. A crop may be taken from the ecosystem, as in agriculture or forestry where the function is economic, or the ecosystem may have an entirely protective function, as in some nature reserves, water catchment or amenity areas. A basic understanding of ecosystems is important to all those involved in their manipulation, and can be obtained from many excellent texts (e.g. Odum, 1971). The laws of thermodynamics set firm quantitative limits to their functioning and these limits, together with the results of careful study of current processes, allow a small amount of prediction of the consequences of particular types of management.

The ecosystem is but one example of the systems analysis approach, based on the precise, often quantitative, definition of the elements (components), states and interrelationships of a system, which can be applied to a great variety of environmental and social systems.

The ecosystem is the fundamental concept useful to planners and the like, for although there is plenty of cookery-book horticultural information on what will grow where, the basic requirement is more for communication between different specialists than for encyclopaedic ecological knowledge.

*Action*

What then needs to be done? The training of new entrants to the land-linked professions needs a greater component of environmental, ecological, conservation-oriented education, based on the understanding of the eco-system concept. Those already practising in the land-linked professions might benefit from short refresher courses, conferences and so on. Recommendations of this type were accepted in Britain by the 'Countryside in 1970' Conference in 1965, and were taken further by the professional and technical services liaison committee which reported to the third Countryside in 1970 Conference (1970) which led to the establishment of PICG (Professional Institutions Conservation Group), now changed to PICC (Professional Institutions Council for Conservation). This group includes some 18 professional institutes as full members and about 40 societies, government departments, research councils and so on as corresponding members. Its draft terms of reference include two which are especially relevant in the present context, viz.

to encourage the inclusion of conservation in appropriate professional and academic qualifying courses;

to promote lectures and short courses for the better understanding of conservation by the professions and the public.

To this end PICC* has already established a working party on Education for Conservation.

Postgraduate, usually M.Sc., courses at universities on conservation, ecology or environmental resources have attracted a number of students with, or on their way to acquiring, professional qualifications. The Certificate in Environmental Studies course given by Southampton University attracted a number of students who were practising in one or other of the land-linked professions. This is a part-time extramural course extending over three years of which the first year is a preliminary or qualifying course and the final year is mainly devoted to project work. A number of the project dissertations produced by the first group of students were real blueprints for action in particular local areas and have already influenced the actual course of events. Similar courses are available in London (Certificate of Proficiency in Ecology and Conservation) and Liverpool (Diploma in Environmental Management). The Department of Forestry at Edinburgh University changed its title to Forestry and Natural Resources, modifying the training of foresters and bringing forward a new profession of resource manager.

An alternative strategy is to insert environmental education prior to the professional training. Thus the conservation content of many geography and biology degree programmes is increasing; a list of some of the more explicitly environmental degree programmes is set out in Table 28.1. The most exciting and useful combination of environmental education and professional training is that provided by the University of Wisconsin, Green

* Further information about this important new group can be obtained from the Royal Institution of Chartered Surveyors (12 Great George Street, Parliament Square, London SW1P 3AD).

**Table 28.1.** Some courses with environmental relevance in the UK (not intended as a comprehensive list)

---

*First-degree (undergraduate) courses, mostly 3 (or 4) year courses for B.Sc.*
Orthodox or long-established subjects such as biology, geography, geology, town planning, agricuture, and horticulture are not listed.

| | |
|---|---|
| Environmental science | East Anglia, Lancaster, Salford, Southampton, Ulster, Plymouth Polytechnic (CNAA) |
| Ecology | Edinburgh, Ulster, Hatfield Polytechnic, Liverpool Polytechnic (CNAA) |
| Resource Management, Wildlife and fisheries management | Edinburgh |
| Environmental Engineering | Loughborough, Strathclyde |
| Civil engineering and environmental studies | Swansea |
| Soil science | Aberdeen, Newcastle, Nottingham, Reading |
| Oceanography | Liverpool, Bangor, Swansea |
| Human ecology | Ulster, Huddersfield Polytechnic (CNAA) |
| Human sciences | Oxford, Surrey |
| Technological economics | Stirling |
| Environmental health | Aston |

*Postgraduate M.Sc. or diploma courses, mostly 1 year duration*
Conventional and professional courses as in aspects of town and country planning, landscape architecture, architecture, civil engineering, the social sciences, geology, geophysics, agriculture, horticulture or forestry are not listed.

| | |
|---|---|
| Geochemistry or economic applications thereof | Leeds, Leicester, Newcastle, Aberdeen, Oxford, Imperial College |
| Hydrogeology | University College London, Birmingham |
| Meteorology or similar | Birmingham, Imperial College, Reading, Bangor |
| Applied geomorphology and natural resources | Sheffield |
| Integrated land resources survey | Reading |
| Natural resource survey | Sussex |
| Environmental resources | Salford |
| Environmental conservation | Heriot-Watt |
| Environmental planning | Nottingham |
| Environmental design | Newcastle |
| Environmental control and resource utilization | Strathclyde Reading |
| Environmental pollution control | Leeds |

---

*(continued)*

**Table 28.1.**—*continued*

| | |
|---|---|
| Urban conservation | Heriot-Watt |
| Ecology | Bangor, Aberdeen, Durham |
| Conservation | University College London |
| Recreational land management studies | Reading |
| Recreation management | Loughborough |
| Landscape ecology, design and maintenance | Wye College |
| Soil science, Soil biology | Newcastle, Oxford, Reading, Aberdeen, Nottingham |
| Oceanography and other aspects of marine science | Southampton, Bangor |
| Applied hydrobiology | Chelsea |
| Biology of water management | Aston |
| Water resource technology | Birmingham |
| Water resource technology | Dundee |
| Freshwater biology | Liverpool |
| Water resources | Newcastle |

Bay, where the School of Professional Studies runs courses in managerial systems, various aspects of social services, teacher training and mass communication. These can be combined with course units such as 'Ecology', 'Environmental Science' or 'Economics'. The prospectus for this university points out that every field of study and every profession has a social responsibility as well as a technical expertise. Too many universities emphasize the latter and forget the former. The other distinctive feature of the UWGB courses is the communiversity approach, the university working in, and helping to solve, community problems and involving students in the process, and members of the community becoming actively involved in campus life. Somewhat similar degree programmes are available in the Division of Environmental Studies at the University of Waterloo in Ontario.

The boldly conceived, imaginative Environmental University has much to commend it. It seems highly desirable but equally inconceivable that there should be such a university in Britain. Increasing central control by the Department of Education and Science through the University Grants Committee and the educational conservatism of existing universities both serve to prevent it. Employment demands are as yet insufficient to dictate it, though Nicholson (1971) maintains 'that at every level, voluntary, governmental, scientific and professional there is an acute shortage of men and women suitably educated to handle with success even the existing volume and complexity of environmental problems, let alone these which will surely confront us before 1975'.

## CONSERVATION IN GENERAL EDUCATION

The need for limitation of population growth and of *per caput* demand on resources is outside the scope of this book, but even apart from this the alternative society prescribed in the Blueprint for Survival (*Ecologist*, 1972) or deriving from 'the Stabilised World Model I' of the *Limits to Growth* team (Meadows *et al.*, 1972), would need social, political and economic reform beyond the wildest imaginings of politicians. The educational system must train a generation which is able to assess the type of reforms needed and to implement those which seem necessary. This objective differs only in degree from the education to accept the sort of conservation objectives and decisions spelt out in earlier chapters of this book. Reform of the educational system is vital, especially if Meadows and his colleagues and the *Ecologist* are correct in the time-scale of their diagnoses. The British Prime Minister for the year 2020 may well be starting his or her primary school career now.

### Science Out of Doors

A study group was set up by the Nature Conservancy in 1960 to look at the role of field studies in education. Its report, *Science Out of Doors* (Study Group on Education and Field Biology, 1963), provided a good baseline which described the situation as it was in Britain in the early 1960s and demonstrates the enormous progress made since that time. It suggested that most children of primary school age have a considerable interest in nature which is subsequently killed by the educational system, particularly at 'O' and 'A' levels.* Great diversity was found between different schools in the amount of field study carried out. Available facilities for field studies were outlined, including a list of more than 80 field centres of one type or another.

*Science Out of Doors* was followed by the Keele Conference on Education (Nature Conservancy, 1965), a part of the 'Countryside in 1970' operation. The report of the Keele conference concluded with portentous resolutions, and indeed there has been a rapid growth in field studies, field centres, nature trails and general conservation education since that time. But this particular line of development, based on nature study and the natural sciences, and encouraged strongly by the Nature Conservancy, seems at times rather genteel and almost irrelevant in the face of population growth, resource shortage and the problems of the Third World.

* In England and Wales, most children take, at the age of 15 or 16, the Certificate of Secondary Education (CSE). A minority take the General Certificate of Education, Ordinary Level ('O' level), and may go on at age 17 or 18 to take the Advanced Level ('A' level).

The social science theme in environmental education, well typified in the views frequently expressed in the *Bulletin of Environmental Education,* may be less scientific but it is certainly more angry and does make a strong impact.

A major outstanding difficulty is the bridging of the social science/natural science gap. This is probably best done by field projects, outside the class-room, where this gap seems less real and where different specialists are confronted with the same, real, problem.

Two alternative strategies are available for the incorporation of conservation in general education. The study of the relationship between man and his environment, including his resources, could be introduced into the curriculum as a new subject called either 'Conservation' or 'Environmental Studies', or the entire curriculum could be restructured around the man–environment relationship.

## Environmental Studies as a Subject

The first alternative is exemplified by the Hertfordsire 'A' level environmental studies syllabus (Carson, 1971), which is divided into four sections:

1. processes and systems of the natural environment and the limits of the resources base;
2. the ecosystem;
3. the interaction of man and the environment;
4. environment conflicts and planning—a field study.

Another example can be found in the Wiltshire 'A' level environmental studies syllabus, which consists of three parts:

1. the local and national environment;
2. man's management of the environment;
3. field study.

Both these syllabuses bridge the natural sciences/social sciences divide, particularly in their field studies. The Hertfordshire scheme also concentrates strongly on the energy theme. It is interesting to note that the Hertfordshire environmental studies syllabus has aroused a fair amount of opposition, partly on the grounds of its excessive breadth and insufficient depth and partly because it cuts across existing 'A' level subjects such as geography and biology.

These 'A' level syllabuses are only one symptom of an upsurge of environmental studies at all levels in schools. A conference in Hertfordshire in 1971 discussed the role of environmental studies in the all-ability school (Hertfordshire County Council, 1972). CSE and 'O' level syllabuses dealing with environmental studies are well suited to Mode 3 CSE examinations, where the papers are set and marked internally by a school and are moderated externally. The National Rural Studies Association has recently changed its title to 'The National Association for Environmental Education' (1972) and is actively discussing and promoting environmental studies.

The environmental studies/conservation theme is also developed in a number of university degree programmes listed in Table 28.1. These vary as their titles indicate in the degree of breadth and generality and in their depth. In Sweden the Office of the Chancellor of Swedish Universities has decreed that there shall be introductory environmental courses, available as an option in every Swedish university, equivalent to ten weeks full-time study but often given in the evening. Students in some UK universities have asked for similar courses and it is encouraging to find students increasingly commenting on course content, often in the search for relevance.

## Man–Environment Relationship as a Theme

The second alternative, that of redesigning the whole school curriculum around the man–environment relationship, is more radical and would take longer to achieve, though it is clearly more satisfactory in the end. History becomes the time dimension of the man–environment relationship, Geography the space dimension. Physics and Chemistry represent attempts at detailed scientific description of the environment. Mathematics allows quantification of either human activities or environmental systems. Ecology and related aspects of biology allow description of the biological environment and man's interaction with it. Language allows the study of different cultures and life styles. Art and Music also represent different perceptions of the environment related to different modes of communication. Domestic science describes the man–environment relationship at the household level; Social Studies can enlarge this to the community level.

Education would become a process of learning about the real world and how to live in it, instead of being based on nineteenth-century abstractions from that world. Relevance would be perceived by the pupils, providing a motivation which is currently lacking. A good deal of this real-life education would have to take place outside the classroom, and some methods of achieving this are discussed below in the section dealing with on-site education.

Massive reorientation of teachers would be required; colleges of education and university education centres could achieve this for new teachers, and refresher or in-service training courses would be needed by teachers already 'in post'. An example of such a course is found at the University of Reading School of Education, where a one year full-time Diploma in Environmental Studies in Education caters for experienced teachers.

**Educational Resources**

The confidence of teachers should be improved by a new abundance of supporting resources such as the on-site facilities offered by field centres, countryside centres and educational nature reserves, and a range of books, films, filmstrips, slides, wallcharts, simulation games and other teaching aids which can be brought into the classroom. Some lists of resources are suggested in the Appendix to this chapter. Teachers' centres, both in universities and elsewhere, may help to familiarize teachers with the resources available and their use.

## ON-SITE EDUCATION

The theme of learning outside the classroom is also the basis of on-site education, which conveys environmental or conservation information and ideas about sites or areas to people living in them, using or visiting them. This has the dual advantage that the education is completely specific to a local topic studied at first hand and that the section of the public receiving the information have a specific interest. On-site education can there include, at one extreme, participation in the planning process by way of a planning enquiry (Skeffington Report, 1969), the activity of community development associations as exemplified by Stocksfield in Northumberland (Stocksfield Neighbourhood Development Association, 1972), or protest groups, and at the other extreme the passive activities involved in nature trails, motor trails (e.g. Exmoor National Park Committee, 1970), farm trails, town trails, countryside centres or local museums.

### Nature Trails and Related Techniques

Self-guiding nature trails are of two main types: those where all the information is contained in a leaflet and only numbers are set out in the ground or those where the information is set out on display boards, although the two methods can be combined. Both types are fully described in the nature trail booklet produced by the Nature Conservancy (1968).

Nature trails were almost unknown in Britain before National Nature Week in 1963. The British Tourist Authority (1972) now publish a list of 345 nature trails in Britain, and there are a good many more that never get on the list. Nature trails impart environmental information and ideas to that section of the public interested enough to follow them. Properly used, with preparation and follow-up, they are a valuable educational tool for school parties. They also represent an important management tool, concentrating public impact (see Goldsmith, Chapter 14) along a particular route and imparting important conservation principles. An extension of the idea of a pedestrian nature trail is a car trail. Town trails are less well known but are likely to prove important educational tools in the future

(Carter, 1971). They could be readily available to a much larger proportion of the population and can more easily combine social, historical and environmental material. The prime example is the Leicester town trail devised by Wheeler and Waites (1972) of the Leicester College of Education.

Highly diverse natural environments are not needed for such nature education. Indeed, the Glasgow Parks Department has become a major force in the environmental education of schoolchildren, and such on-site education can help to check vandalism. The forest plots planted in the lower Swansea valley to improve industrially derelict land thrived once they had been adopted by schools.

Nature trails illustrate the conflict that exists between field study and conservation, for excessive study of a delicate habitat may damage it and the collection of a rare species for study only serves to make it more rare. The general problem of field studies is covered by the Outdoor Studies Code.* The main headings of the code are set out in Table 28.2. The more

**Table 28.2.** Outdoor Studies Code

**Care / conduct / conservation**
Plan and lead excursions well
Take safety seriously
Choose and use your area carefully
Respect ownership
Think of other users of the countryside
Leave the area as you found it
Avoid disturbing plants and animals
Do not collect unnecessarily
Safeguard rare species
Give no one cause to regret your visit

specific problem of the collection of wild plants is set out in the Code of Conduct for the Conservation of Wild Plants.†

However, the sparing collection of above-ground parts of common plant species may produce an educational benefit without any ecological harm. Conservation is for man, and total prohibition on the visiting of nature reserves or on the collection of specimens might stultify its objectives.

## Field Centres

The Field Studies Council, founded in 1943 by the late F. H. C. Butler as the 'Council for the Promotion of Field Studies', has established in

* Available from the Field Studies Council, 9 Devereux Court, Strand, London WC2.
† Available from the Honorary General Secretary, Botanical Society of the British Isles, c/o Department of Botany, British Museum (Natural History), Cromwell Road, London, SW7.

Britain a pattern of field study centres unrivalled anywhere else in the world. Either purpose-built or adapted from country mansions, these field centres take 50–70 students at a time, usually for one week; most commonly they provide a course on field-oriented biology or geography, but their programmes include many more specialized courses, e.g. on spiders, mosses, outdoor painting, soils or achaeology. In 1971 the nine FSC centres provided a total of 15,347 student weeks.

The distinctive features of the FSC centres include :

1. good laboratory and library facilities;
2. the warden and his assistants (usually three) are all scientifically qualified and combine management of the centre with teaching the courses;
3. a small but growing element of research;
4. many of the centres function as local conservation centres, or biological records centres;
5. some own a little of their own working ground but all are dependent on the goodwill of local landowners.

The FSC functions as a coherent whole, develops definite policies on courses, conservation and other topics, avails itself of the advice of many distinguished scientists, and increases its teaching coverage by short-term exchanges of its own staff from one centre to another. It is an independent organization but originally received a grant from the Ministry of Education. It now receives an indirect subsidy from local education authorities, who pay the fees of the pupils attending its courses.

There have recently been two important developments in the work of the Council (Field Studies Council, 1968). The Council, with the Countryside Commission, has set up the Pembrokeshire Countryside Unit, which functions as an information centre and provides evening lectures and guided day and half-day courses in the field for the general public. A second experiment, in co-operation with the Corporation of London, is the Epping Forest Conservation Centre, which is a day centre and receives school parties for the day but does not provide residential accommodation. Situated close to London, it will allow more children to experience its facilities than would have been the case with a residential centre. It also functions as a local information centre.

The pattern of the FSC has been widely followed—though not, as yet, bettered. There are now more than 200 residential field centres in England and Wales run by local education authorities, charitable trusts and various other organizations. The Youth Hostels Association has provided special facilities for field study groups at certain of its hostels, appropriately located. In general there has been much more emphasis in Britain on residential centres than on day centres.

**Countryside Centres**

A new generation of countryside centres is now appearing which stress information rather than education, insofar as the two are separable. A conference held in the University of Leicester (1969) reviewed several types of these centres. A variety of sponsors such as the Nature Conservancy, the Countryside Commission, various County Naturalists' Trusts, the Royal Society for the Protection of Birds, the Forestry Commission and, in one instance, a commercial concern are all involved in running countryside centres of some sort.

Some National Park Authorities are making considerable use of mobile information centres, which are usually specially adapted caravans. Another emerging pattern is represented, for example, by the co-operation between the Lake District National Park and the University of Newcastle Extra-Mural Department in running guided tours and evening lectures in the Lake District during the tourist season. The New University of Ulster Adult Education Department has similarly run programmes of talks and tours, during the summer, related mainly to the environment and history of the spectacular north coast of Antrim and Londonderry.

In fact 'interpretation' in the broadest sense is a boom industry at present, fitting in well with increased affluence, leisure and mobility. Some general supervision may be desirable to ensure that the education and conservation content of the information peddled is accurate and in harmony with the general use and conservation of the countryside. Information and nature trails are both powerful management tools.

**Volunteer Groups**

The twin concepts of the formal educational system extending out of the classroom and of on-site education may come together in the work of various voluntary groups, which consists typically of groups of young people who carry out some conservation task such as scrub clearance and learn about conservation as they work.

A number of organized schemes are available which involve school-children as groups or individuals in projects involving environmental education. These include the joint National Rural and Environmental Studies Association (as it then was)/Nature Conservancy Hedgerow Project, the Forestry Commission Scheme whereby schools can adopt forestry plots, the Countryside Commission Rights of Way Survey, several projects organized by the Royal Society for the Protection of Birds (see Taunton, 1968) and various species-distribution surveys, such as of frogs or hedgehogs, most of which are organized by the Nature Conservancy's Biological Records Centre. The Countryside Commission launched an ambitious scheme in which schoolchildren recorded changes in the countryside and, even more courageously, terminated it when they found the recording was not accurate enough for the purpose. The report of this project (Countryside Commission, 1971) is useful both as a blueprint and as a warning.

The British Trust for Conservation Volunteers runs the Conservation Corps, which has the longest experience of this type of work in Britain. The role of these Conservation Corps groups was reviewed by a Countryside Commission Report (1972), and their role as environmental pressure groups as well as a labour force is strongly recommended in the *Report on the Role of Voluntary Organisations and Youth in the Environment* Stevenson, 1972), which formed part of the UK submission to the Stockholm Conference. The report urges local authorities to take more explicit responsibility for education outside the classroom.

A number of universities have conservation action groups, ranging from left-wing activist groups of the talk-shop type to gangs of muscular young men and women of the Conservation Corps type. The National Union of Students have inaugurated a conservation project which seeks to co-ordinate the activities of conservation groups in universities and colleges all over the UK. While most Conservation Corps activities are rurally oriented, Community Serice Volunteers (1972) have produced an Action Plan which aims to persuade schoolchildren and others to get out into the local urban community and do things, and in some respects to 'stir it up'.

## CONCLUSION

The educational problem in conservation is so urgent, and the educational machine so innately conservative, that we must not neglect any of the approaches described in this chapter. In the brave new world of the twenty-first century, the distinctions between living, learning and education will be blurred. The 'medium will be the message', the world the classroom, and the pupil the teacher. Citizens and members of the professions will both need and receive an education which continues through life and their education will mainly occur outside the classroom in 'real-life' situations. The environmentally aware citizenry produced by these processes will be better able to participate in its own democracy. This may seem a very utopian vision, but unless it can be achieved the conservation practices outlined in the earlier chapters of this book have little chance of being implemented, for there will be a shortage of both expertise and political support.

## APPENDIX. EDUCATIONAL RESOURCES: A GUIDE TO GUIDES

DELTA—*Directory of Environmental Literature and Teaching Aids*—is compiled by Carol Johnson and Jacqui Smith of the Council for Environmental Education, The School of Education, Univ. of Reading, 24, London Road, Reading RG1 5AQ. It contains sections on books, films, filmstrips and slides, posters, study kits, games and work cards and it will be updated from time to time.

*Guide to Resources in Environmental Education*, July 1972 by P. S. Berry, mimeographed by the Reading and District Branch of the Conservation Society (and available from the author, c/o Reading College of Technology, Kings Road, Reading, Berks.). It includes sections on books, periodicals, films, filmstrips and slides, games, study kits, wallcharts, speakers, broadcasts, examination syllabuses, degree courses and organizations.

*A Directory of Lectures in Natural History and Nature Conservation* is produced by the Council for Nature, Zoological Gardens, Regents Park, London NW1 4RY.

*An Environmental Directory* produced by the Civic Trust (17, Carlton House Terrace, London SW1Y 5AW) lists 220 organizations concerned with amenity and the environment and details the services each organization can provide.

Carson, S. McB. (compiler) (1971). *Environmental Studies: the construction of an 'A' Level Syllabus*, National Foundation for Educational Research (The Mere, Upton Park, Slough, Bucks., SL1 2DQ), contains an extensive section listing resources useful in the teaching of the syllabuses outlined.

*Nature Trails in Britain*—available from the British Tourist Authority, 64 St. James Street, London SW1A 1NF. The 1972 edition listed 345 trails with details.

*Directory of Centres for Outdoor Studies in England and Wales* is published by the Resources Committee of the Council for Environmental Education and available from the Field Studies Council, 9 Devereux Court, Strand, London, WC2. Lists 200 centres.

*Environmental games* are reviewed in the *Bulletin of Environmental Education*, **13**, for May, 1972. The *Bulletin,* which is a cornucopia of ideas and sources for environmental education, is published by the Town and Country Planning Association, 17 Carlton House Terrace, London, SW1.

*The Ecology Box* and its supporting handbook are produced by the Ontario Institute for Studies in Education at the request of the Canadian Commission for UNESCO. For details write to Ecobox, 252 Bloor Street West, Toronto 181, Ontario, Canada.

## REFERENCES

British Tourist Authority (1972). *Nature Trails in Britain*, British Tourist Authority, London, 38 pp.

Carson, S. McB. (compiler) (1947). *Environmental Studies: the Construction of an 'A' Level Syllabus*, National Foundation for Educational Research, Slough, 158 pp.

Carter, G. (1971). Urban nature trails: pupils and parks, *Your Environment*, **2**, 66–8, 77.

Community Service Volunteers (1972). *The Action Plan*, Community Service Volunteers, London, 24 pp.

Countryside Commission (1971). *Changing Countryside Project: A Report*, Countryside Commission, London, 206 pp.

Countryside Commission (1972). *The Use of Voluntary Labour in the Countryside of England and Wales,* Countryside Commission, London, 37 pp.

Countryside in 1970 (1970). *Report 14. Professional and Technical Services,* Nature Conservancy, London, 23 pp.

*Ecologist* (1972). *Blueprint for Survival,* first published by the *Ecologist,* January 1972, 1–43. Now available in Penguin, London, 173 pp.

Exmoor National Park Committee (1970). *Countryside Trails by Car,* Exmoor National Park Committee, Taunton, 20 pp.

Field Studies Council (1968). *Outdoor Studies Code,* Field Studies Council, London, 6 pp.

Hertfordshire County Council Education Department (1972). *Environmental Studies in the All-Ability School,* Hertfordshire. County Council, Hertford, 62 pp.

Meadows, D. H., Meadows, D. L., Randers, J., and Behrens, W. W. III (1972). *The Limits to Growth,* Potomac Earth Island, London, 205 pp.

National Association for Environmental Education (1972). *Environmental Education 1972/3,* Heinemann, London, 70 pp.

Nature Conservancy (1965). *Proceedings of the Conference on Education, Keele, March 1965,* Nature Conservancy, London, 43 pp.

Nature Conservancy (1968). *Nature Trails,* Warne, London, 22 pp.

Nicholson, E. M. (1964). Orchestrating the use of land, *New Scientist,* **22,** 350–1.

Nicholson, E. M. (1971). Environment—a challenge to education, *British Ecological Society Bulletin,* **2,** 3–6.

Odum, E. P. (1971). *Fundamentals of Ecology,* 3rd edn., W. B. Saunders, London, 574 pp.

Skeffington, A. M. (chairman) (1969). *People and Planning, Report of the Committee on Public Participation in Planning,* HMSO, London, 72 pp.

Stevenson, D. (chairman) (1972). *50 Million Volunteers, A Report on the Role of Voluntary Organisations and Youth in the Environment,* HMSO, London, 104 pp.

Stocksfield Neighbourhood Working Party (1972). *An Experiment in Democracy,* Stocksfield Neighbourhood Working Party, Mountview Terrace, Stocksfield, Northumberland, 32 pp.

Study Group on Education and Field Biology (1963). *Science Out of Doors,* Longmans, London, 240 pp.

Taunton, J. (1968). *Bird Projects for Schools,* Evans, for the Royal Society for the Protection of Birds, London, 39 pp.

University of Leicester, Departments of Adult Education and Museum Studies (1969). *Countryside Centres, 1969 Conference Report,* University of Leicester, Leicester, 23 pp.

Wheeler, K., and Waites, B. (1972). The Leicester Town Trail, *Bulletin of Environmental Education,* Town and Country Planning Association, London, August-September, 28 pp.

CHAPTER 29

# The Economics of Conservation

ALAN CODDINGTON

## INTRODUCTION

There are two broad areas in which the problems of managing natural resources may be illuminated by the application of economic principles.

The first case is where activities of production or consumption have undesirable environmental side-effects which although incidental to those who are pursuing them may nevertheless interfere with the quality and availability of natural resources, particularly 'common property' resources like the atmosphere and waterways. This is a case which economists have discussed under various headings such as 'spillover effects', 'neighbourhood effects' and 'external effects' or 'externalities'. It is essentially a situation in which individuals, in the course of their economic activities, exert an effect on others that is not mediated by the workings of a market. Unlike the processes of exchange which markets can accommodate, these influences of individuals on one another are neither mutual nor voluntary, and as such may be taken to represent disturbances on, or distortions of, the workings of a market-based economic system. It is not the mere existence of a side-effect of production or consumption that creates an externality, but rather the absence of any trading arrangements with regard to the effect. If, for example, property rights exist such that payment must be made for the right to allow the side-effect, the activity would then become *internal* to the market system, and there are other ways, too, as we shall see, in which side-effects may become 'internalized'. The discussion of this type of situation leads to a consideration of questions of pricing arrangements and the definition or establishment of property rights.

The second type of case I wish to discuss here is that of resource depletion, seen not as a problem of reducing the *use* of resources, but of reducing the *consumption* associated with their use. This is a straightforward enough idea, and calls for no further introductory comments except as regards the economic concept of a resource. In economics, a resource is thought of not in physical but in value terms. Thus, whether something is or is not a resource, and its value if it is one, is not a matter of its nature or inherent characteristics alone, but depends on circumstances such as the current state of technical knowledge (uranium was not a significant resource until the technology of nuclear fission was developed), current tastes or fashions (the tobacco plant was not a significant resource until the taste for smoking it became widespread), or the distribution of income and wealth (a resource which is more intensively used in the production of luxury goods would lose value if income and wealth were distributed more equally—the sturgeon as a source of caviar might be an example).

## EXTERNAL EFFECTS

In economic terms, cases of environmental disruption may often be seen as situations in which the costs of firms or individuals do not take into account the external costs imposed on others by their activities. Oil tankers may operate more cheaply by discharging their waste at sea, but this imposes costs on others—in terms of despoiled beaches, for example—which are not reflected in the oil company's accounts. The textbook case of such 'externalities' is the factory chimney which showers smoke and soot on the surroundings, creating social costs which are not reflected in the private costs of the factory owner. What is cheap for the individual may not be cheap for society as a whole; the same is true of benefits.

### Taxation and Subsidy

From the perspective of economics, we are led to ask how we may modify individual incentives in the cases where the pursuit of self-interest is leading to environmental deterioration. The classic way of modifying allocative patterns by way of individual incentives is by taxation or subsidy, where, for example, activities which impose 'external' environmental damages are taxed, and those which cause environmental improvements are subsidized. Ideally the tax on the output of the factory having a smoky chimney should accurately reflect the external costs imposed by the smoke, so that the *effective* costs of the factory are brought into line with the overall social costs that it imposes, and this, in turn, should mean that pursuit of self-interest after the tax is imposed will lead to the same behaviour as would follow from the pursuit of the social interest. In this way, the allocation of resources could be changed in a way involving lower production where there is external environmental damage, and higher production where there is external environmental improvement. In each case, production will be changed until a further decrease, say in output, would involve a greater loss of revenue than the gain in avoiding the costs of production, including the imposed tax.

An obvious objection to such a policy is that one cannot know all the external costs involved, the problems being not only the practical ones of collecting and processing the information, but the formidable conceptual one of how such things are to be valued. My view is that the nature of these conceptual problems means that it would not be worth making great efforts with elaborate methods for measuring social costs, since this could only lead to spurious precision.

A further complication is that what one needs to know in order to devise the system of taxes and subsidies is not the external costs in the existing situation, but rather what they would be in the 'corrected' situation, since these will be equal to the taxes that are actually paid. In other words, what one needs to know is not the external costs as they are, but what they would be in the hypothetical corrected situation. There are both practical and conceptual obstacles to designing such a system. But the fact that we cannot get things perfectly right does not mean that we cannot try to make a modest improvement.

There is nothing in this policy that stipulates how the yield of the taxes should be spent: they are simply being used to influence allocation. While the policy has a correcting influence on *currently* generated environmental effects, however, it takes no account of the backlog of previously generated deterioration. Therefore, although this does not follow from the economics, it would appear sensible to treat the yield of the tax as a fund for the restoration of already existing environmental deterioration. To underline the fact that the principle of 'making the polluter pay' for the deterioration he causes is concerned with economic and not moral considerations, it should be pointed out that as far as allocation is concerned, one could just as well use bribery as taxation. A suitable bribe made conditional on curtailing output would have the same incentive effect as the previous tax on output. If the external effect were worth correcting, then, from a social point of view, the bribe would be worth making—it would be less than the reduction achieved in social costs. This does not, of course, constitute a realistic policy since it obviously violates our notions of equity. Indeed, the idea of being paid for not producing something seems uncomfortably like the mad logic of *Catch 22* where someone was reputed to have made a fortune by not growing alfalfa.

### Compensation

In contrast to a taxation policy, there is an alternative policy which may at first look superficially very similar to it. This is a policy of compensation, which requires that all victims of external effects be compensated for the cost imposed (and, conversely, if the reverse effects were important, they should pay for any external benefits received). It might be thought that this would have the same effect as imposing a tax to cover the external costs, except that here we are specifying how the tax will be spent, namely, to compensate the victims.

Whereas both the taxation and compensation policies have the same effect on the incentive of the producers of the external costs, the compensation policy differs in having an additional effect on the incentives of the victims. It has been argued that this additional effect has adverse consequences from an economic point of view, for if people were to be compensated *in full* for the smoke nuisance, say, their incentive to locate themselves away from the smoke would be weakened. The allocative approach takes the quite dispassionate view that what is to be avoided is not smoke itself, but smoke and people in the same place; and that, if it is cheaper to have people elsewhere than to have the factories elsewhere, then that is what is 'better'. If it were cheaper to have the people elsewhere, the compensation policy would nevertheless mean that it is the factory, not the people, which has the incentive of move, and for this reason the policy can be criticized on allocative grounds. Even where compensation is feasible, it may be extremely costly to administer. It is estimated that processing the claims for damage compensation caused by a fleet of Concordes would require a department as big as the Inland Revenue.

### Taxation vs. Compensation

But all this appears very hard-headed. That the individuals who suffer the smoke should also be the ones to uproot seems grossly unfair, especially if the people were there first. This hard-headedness stems from the economists' habit of treating allocative questions (what should be produced) as separate from distributional questions (who should get what is produced). Rather than spending any energy on trying to humanize economics, however, I am going to discuss the pros and cons of these policies in practice.

First, the taxation policy assumes that there is a definite relationship between the output of an industry and the external environmental costs it imposes, so that by reducing output one causes a definite, predictable reduction in external costs. But if we take the case of spillage from oil tankers, it is not at all clear that there is such a definite relationship, except perhaps in the case where the tankers refine the oil on board and jettison the waste *en route*. What is required is a disincentive to *spill* oil rather than a disincentive to *carry* oil, and the compensation policy seems much better adapted to provide this. One can avoid having to rely on a definite relationship between output and external costs, however, simply by regarding the tax as being levied on the degree of utilization of the environment rather than on the output itself. In other words, it is quite permissible to ignore output, and concentrate instead on the use which is being made of environmental resources in producing that output. Although this involves no change in principle, it does entail a shift of focus. It leads us to consider the development of pricing arrangements for what would otherwise be treated as free goods. This is a theme we shall return to.

The theoretical objection to compensation is that, if the oil company must compensate Eastbourne or Torquay Council for oil washed up on their beaches, then Eastbourne and Torquay have much less incentive to keep out of the way of the oil! It is obvious that this objection has force only to the extent that the victims have any choice in the matter. On the other hand, there are practical objections to compensation, which are far more serious. In order to carry out the policy, one must be able to identify those inconvenienced, detect the damage, ascertain its extent and assess its cost, as well as identifying the culprit. If the effects are dispersed, or the damage is spread thinly over many people, or if there is an intermingling of effects, it will just not be feasible to unscramble the individual compensations nor impute them to the appropriate culprits. Imagine, for example, trying to compensate for pesticide damage.

Let us return to the previous example of oil tankers. Although from an economic point of view the problem is merely to keep the oil away from the people, from an environmental point of view one really wants to keep the oil away from the water. The former objective would perhaps be quite adequate if our use of the environment was well within its assimilative capacity, so that if we could keep the various wastes out of people's way they would be degraded by natural processes. We must, however, operate on the principle that in a physical sense everything goes somewhere. When the environment is overloaded, keeping oil and people apart does not solve the problem, it merely gains time.

The policies so far described would involve changes not only in the levels of outputs, but also in the methods or techniques by which they are produced. Suppose there are various pesticides which as traces in food are harmful to people in varying degrees; or various types of throwaway cup or bottle some less easily degradable than others. Then, by either the taxation or the compensation policy, there would be an incentive to switch towards the forms which impose the lower external environmental costs as reflected in either the taxes or the compensations.

So far, all this has taken a more or less static view of things: we have been concerned with improving the allocation of resources, taking into account external (unpaid) costs with a given state of technical knowledge. But technical knowledge is not stationary: it develops in a way which can be influenced by producers' decisions. From a more dynamic viewpoint, therefore, the major importance of these policies may be the incentives they provide for induced technical change. If there were a tax on long-lived disposable cups, for example, this might provide some inducement for producers to develop a viable bio-degradable plastic.

## Pricing Environmental Use

The discussion so far has assumed that cases of environmental disruption are to be interpreted as instances of external costs—where private and social interests diverge. There are, however, other ways of looking at the matter. One can adopt the approach that what is happening is in part a case of ill-defined property rights, or the absence of pricing arrangements for the appropriate resources. One could accordingly see the natural environment of clear property rights to, for example, waste-disposal facilities productive inputs such as water and oxygen. These services and inputs are available free of charge. But to treat a resource as free when it is in fact scarce, and therefore valuable, results in its over-utilization: that is to say, a misallocation. On this line of argument, what is required is the establishment of clear property rights to, for example, waste-disposal facilities where ownership may be vested in governments, or even in international bodies. The establishment of suitable property rights in these cases may constitute an alternative way of 'internalizing' the environmental costs. With policies of taxation or compensation, the costs are brought within producers' considerations by imposing actual charges; with this policy the costs themselves are brought within producers' considerations by extending property rights to encompass the resources involved.

Having established property rights, the next step in this policy would be the introduction of pricing arrangements of some form. One wants to achieve prices which will lead to conditions of demand consistent with the capacity of the environment. The extreme form of this policy would be merely to establish property rights, and then allow a free market to take care of pricing on the assumption that the individuals involved can be trusted to take account of the new 'internalized' costs. This is the sort of thing that is happening in the case of North Sea oil, except that there is no reason to suppose that the environmental costs are being internalized by the property rights and markets that are being set up.

Alternatively, the pricing arrangements may be administered so that charges are calculated on the basis of considerations of environmental capacity. This policy would be much like the establishment of parking meters. Before their introduction, road space (for parking) was being treated as a free good even though it was scarce, and at the zero price there was clearly an excess demand for it. The pricing of parking facilities did require some technical innovation in the form of parking meters, but the system does bring demand closer into line with existing capacity. Similarly with waste-disposal facilities and environmental inputs, the pricing arrangements would require some technical ingenuity. There is also the question of *what* exactly is to be priced. In the case of waste disposal, schemes have been tried in which biological oxygen demand (BOD) is used as the criterion for charging. This is not entirely satisfactory since a measure of the demand for oxygen to degrade organic matter is insensitive to the presence of toxic inorganic substances which constitute much of the pollution problem.

Such schemes leave outstanding problems of the policing and administration of the arrangements. The question is: can one devise a technical arrangement which is foolproof—or rather, cheatproof—which rules out, or detects with considerable reliability, illicit free use of environmental resources?

These two approaches—the earlier one based on external cost and the later one based on 'free goods'—are not at all inconsistent. In the first one the effluent from a factory is seen as imposing an external cost on society; in the second one the effluent is seen as making free use of a scarce resource, namely 'waste-disposal facilities'. Insofar as property rights can be defined for this resource, and pricing arrangements devised, the previously imposed costs cease to be 'external'—they are not internal to the provision of waste-disposal facilities. Whether the problem of external costs can be transferred in this way depends on whether the appropriate property rights are legally definable, and whether the technical prerequisites of a pricing arrangement can be devised. In other words, could one invent an ' effluent meter ' to fulfil the same sort of function as a parking meter?

To propose taxation, compensation or pricing does not mean that one or other policy is being advocated for every environmental problem. Whether any one of them is worth implementing will depend on the circumstance of the individual case. There will, of course, be cases where direct controls in terms of environmental standards will be called for. Even given that the requisite legislation were produced, we must still enquire what individuals' incentives would be in regard to the choice between compliance and violation. Firms or individuals faced with legislation that prohibits or regulates some activity still have the choice of violating the regulation in the knowledge that they must accept the penalty if they are detected. This raises the question of the policing and enforcement of the prohibition. The incentive to comply can be increased either by increasing the penalty for violations or, more realistically, by tightening up the policing of the regulation and so increasing the chance of detection. This can be a costly business, and a guarantee of certain detection may be simply impossible.

## RESOURCE DEPLETION

Resource management is not simply a matter of preventing the use of natural resources, for this would bring depletion processes to a complete halt and the only point in having resources is to use them. To refrain from using them now is to make them available for some future use, so that the rate at which the use of resources should proceed depends on what balance we wish to strike between the present and the future. More now means less in future, which includes the future beyond our own lifetimes. Such balances cannot be struck on the basis of economic calculations alone, but involve an irreducible moral component. What should we hand down to posterity: a plentiful stock of resources or an appalling mess? Of course, society as a whole is quite free to say 'What did posterity ever do for me?' and continue in its prodigal way. Even to the extent that the future arrives within our own lifetime, we may, individually and collectively, discount it as heavily as we please. Such behaviour may be myopic, and to the extent that the economy merely reflects our collective myopia, we cannot accuse it of malfunctioning. Another possibility is that each of us would like to see a lower collective rate of resource depletion, and would be willing to accept his or her own share of the consequences, provided everyone else did the same. However, each of us correctly takes his or her own contribution to be imperceptible and so sees no point in making personal gestures of sacrifice.

The fact that resources command a price means that producers have an incentive to economize on their use; even if a producer owns the resource in question, he still forgoes alternative uses of it by using it up in production, or selling it at its market price, and in that sense it still costs him something. The fact that we regard the depletion of a resource as undesirable means that we do not regard the market price as an adequate reflection of its scarcity.

The principal ways of curbing resource depletion, other than simple abstinence, are: recycling of materials; increasing the lifetime of durable goods; and substituting renewable for non-renewable resources. Each of these means is subject to qualifications which will now be discussed.

### Recycling

Recycling is the retrieval and re-use of waste products, by-products and materials which have been embodied in commodities. It is evident that a great deal of recycling goes on already (especially for metals, for example iron retrieved from scrapped cars), reflecting the fact that such processes are often worthwhile from a purely commercial point of view. There has, however, been a move away from the recycling of containers, with disposable plastic replacing returnable glass bottles, and the encouragement of the throwaway mentality.

The point to be made here is that there are materials which, although not worth recycling from a commercial point of view, may still be worth recycling from a social point of view, for the commercial calculation does not take into account the social costs of not recycling materials such as disposal and pollution costs, nor does not allow for prices of raw materials

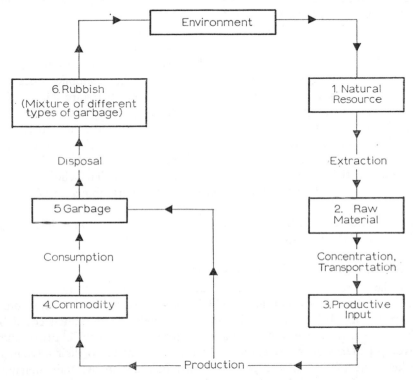

**Figure 29.1.** The movement of resources through the economic system.

which do not adequately reflect the social costs of using them up. It does not follow that from a social point of view all materials should be recycled, for against the advantages must be set the 'unscrambling' problem—the costs in terms of energy and other materials used up in separating the various wastes and getting them into a re-usable state. Next to nothing is known, however, about the economics of recycling. It is important to know which of the materials that are not commercially recycled would nevertheless be, from the broader viewpoint, worth recycling. It will very likely be the case that the answers will depend on the scale of the operation, and on

16

the degree of development of the recycling industry. In particular, there may be economies of processing new and recycled materials, since the major costs are likely to be those of collection and centralization, which will not be a great deal more expensive for subsequent materials once the organization for the first one is established. It may be possible to make out a case for the subsidization of an 'infant' recycling industry to allow its development to a scale or degree of organization at which it becomes socially worthwhile or even commercially viable. In her stimulating and heterodox book *The Economy of Cities,* Jane Jacobs (1970) introduced the idea of 'the city as a mine' and was generally optimistic about the possibilities for the spontaneous development of a recycling industry.

Another question which arises with recycling and the formulation of policies to encourage it is this: at what stage in the economic process is recycling best carried out? This issue is illustrated in Figure 29.1, which is a scheme showing the stages through which materials pass as they are transformed and transported in the course of economic activities. The question arises as to whether recycling could be more efficiently introduced at stage 5, 6, or even at the post-dispersal stage, when the residuals of economic activity have returned to the environment. The choice in any particular case will involve a trade-off between 'unscrambling costs' (which may be reduced by recycling from the earlier stage, 5) and collection and transportation costs (which may be reduced by recycling from a later stage, where materials have already become fairly centralized).

## Increasing the Lifetime of Durable Goods

If the increase in the lifetime of goods required proportionally more resources than inputs, nothing would be gained, so that the method must be based on a belief that the durability of goods is less than it could be with present resource inputs. Various firms within one industry may develop patterns of tacitly collusive behaviour, it being to their advantage to keep the lifetime of the product down in order to maintain demand. There are fairly well-known examples where techniques for increasing product durability without proportionate increases in cost have variously been disregarded or suppressed—paints, nylon stockings and car coatings spring to mind.

The relative durability of goods may, to the extent that consumers are well informed, be reflected in relative prices. A longer-lasting shirt will, other things being equal, command a higher price. But an increase in the *general* durability of goods would not be reflected in the general price level, which is determined by other things.

This line of reasoning has led to the questioning of the significance of aggregates like GNP, and to the idea of correcting such figures in certain ways. But once one starts making corrections in this way there is no obvious place to stop. Making sensible corrections to a ludicrous number is obviously not a sensible thing to do. My own opinion is that the best thing to do with GNP is to ignore it.

### Substituting Renewable for Non-Renewable Resources

The idea of substituting renewable for non-renewable resources calls for little comment. The sort of things I have in mind as renewable resources are solar energy, hydro-electric energy and the energy of the tides. Of course, such processes are often 'uneconomic' and renewable resources themselves have limits to what they will yield. But what is 'economic' and where the limits are depend on the state of technical knowledge, and, since the direction of research and development is something over which men exercise some control, what is or is not economic is not a fact of nature. Heavier than air flight was, and would remain, uneconomic if it were not that its obvious military applications brought an enormous public subsidy to finance the research and development. So, in a world of technical change, one cannot think of economic efficiency in purely static terms. Some processes are born efficient, others achieve efficiency, but still others have it thrust upon them.

## CONCLUSION

In considering the whole question of curbing the consumption of resources, one is faced with the problem that we are not prevented by lack of technical knowledge from achieving this, but rather by our inability, as a society, to cope with the repercussions. This is to say that within the existing framework of institutions, the goal of conservation conflicts with other social goals, most notably with that of full employment. The policies we have been considering would have an effect not only on the allocation of resources between alternative uses, as intended, but also on the overall employment of resources, including the employment of labour. And although, conventionally, economics treats allocation and employment as two quite separate branches of study, and even as quite distinct problems, it remains the case that when it comes to the implementation of practical policies, the employment effects of allocation policies will be a salient, if not a decisive, consideration.

Whether this conflict between conservation and employment is as sharp as some people have presented it is another question. In any event, to present economic policies directed towards the goal of conservation while ignoring their effects on employment is to consign one's analysis to political irrelevance. And if it is true, as it seems to be, that the conflict is unavoidable

16*

within the framework of existing institutions, then it follows that conservation itself is not a technical, nor even an economic, but an institutional problem (see Kennet, Chapter 30).

It is not that we do not know how, in principle, to achieve a given level of consumer satisfaction with a lower input of resources. It is that we do not have economic institutions which are capable of coping with the employment effects of such shifts. Even if it were technically possible to satisfy consumer needs with a lower input of resources, and hence employment, it would not, with existing institutions, allow an across-the-board reduction in the working week (or an increase in holidays). Rather, it would have an uneven impact: total unemployment for some and an unaltered situation for others. It is generally accepted that work is unpleasant at the margin. But the trouble is that what is marginal for the economy is not marginal for some individuals concerned. The problems go deeper. For there is no point in, for example, increasing the physical durability of commodities if their effective lifetime will be determined by the pressures of fashion, planned obsolescence, routine style changes, etc., which seem necessary, under the existing system, to maintain aggregate demand and employment.

The system of distribution in which a large class of propertyless individuals are dependent for a livelihood on selling their labour on the market has been traditionally attacked as being exploitative and inhuman. A less dramatic but possibly more telling defect than the system's alleged lack of humanity is its lack of versatility when faced with situations such as the need to conserve. It cannot be over-emphasized that the problem of implementing conservation is institutional and political.

## BIBLIOGRAPHY AND REFERENCES

Baumol, W. J. (1965). *Welfare Economics and the Theory of the State*, Longmans Green, London, 212 pp.
Boulding, K. E. (1970). *Economics as a Science*, McGraw-Hill, New York, 157 pp.
Coddington, A. (1970). The economics of ecology, *New Society*, April 9, 595–7.
Coddington, A., and Victor, P. A. (1972). Economics/ecology, *Your Environment*, **3**, 16–39.
Jacobs, Jane (1970). *The Economy of Cities*, Cape, London, 268 pp.
Kapp, K. W. (1950). *The Social Costs of Business Enterprise*, Harvard University Press, Cambridge, Mass., 287 pp.
Mishan, E. J. (1967). *The Costs of Economic Growth*, Staples Press, London, 190 pp.
Pigou, A. C. (1952). *The Economics of Welfare*, Macmillan, London, 876 pp.

CHAPTER 30

# The Politics of Conservation

WAYLAND KENNET

A politician sees the conservation of natural resources as part of a wider scene. He perceives it as an important part of the complex of issues which would present itself to him as 'conservation' or 'environment' in general, and this would be not only because his electors and the press and television tend to consider it in this way, but also because there are in fact attributes, conflicts, and social and economic institutions which are common to all parts of this larger complex. The conservation and rational management for the different and sometimes conflicting uses of natural resources has much in common with the conservation and rational management for multiple use of the whole physical environment, including the urban structure and heritage, as well as the mineral resources of the planet: the industrial metals, fuels such as oil, coal and uranium, and the building materials such as clay, sand and gravel.

A politician also has to relate his perceptions and policies to two other factors for which room could not have been found in this book: population and wealth. He has to think at every turn about the rate of increase of his base population (a phrase to which I return) and of other populations, the ways in which it is migrating internally, the rate at which it is becoming richer or poorer, the changes which can be foreseen in any of those rates, and the changes which cannot, but which must be surmised.

The base population of a politician is that which keeps him in business. For a local councillor it is his ward or parish; for an MP his constituency; for a minister his country. Unless he contents them, he will be thrown out, and thus be able to content neither them nor anyone else. But the true interest of every voter is often, indeed usually, wider and more complex than that voter knows. Therefore politicians are accustomed, almost without thinking, to seek to reconcile the interests of their own base populations, as the latter may perceive them, with those of other populations.

465

# THE HISTORY OF ENVIRONMENTAL CONCERN IN
# POLITICS

The machinery for reconciling conflicting interests in the conservation field has grown up slowly over a very long period. The medieval and Rennaissance air pollution laws were true examples of conservation legislation; they forbade the subject to burn soft coal in city centres on pain of various punishments (death, in one case) because of what we should now call its deleterious effects on public health and amenity. They regulated the conflict between those who objected to having to burn dearer fuel and those who objected to stink, dirt and coughs, and in doing so they conserved a renewable resource, namely clean air. But they were autocratic in genesis, and have left little mark on our institutions and procedures.

Probably the first conservation laws to be democratically made were the series of laws controlling the taking of turtles which were passed by the Assembly of Bermuda in the first half of the seventeenth century. Democratic conservation law in this country stems perhaps from the clean water legislation of 1848, which was passed after the carrying mechanism of cholera was first identified in Soho. After some controversy, Parliament gave government the power and the money to insist on the laying of safe water mains and sewers. The conflict in this case was regulated by a redistribution of well-being from those who now paid higher rates and taxes to those who now no longer risked dying of cholera. The beginning of democratic air pollution law in this country was the Alkali Act of 1863: 'an act for the more effectual condensation of muriatic acid in alkali works'. This was a true reallocation of well-being between the generality, who now had to pay more for soap and glass, and the much smaller class of those who lived close to chemical works and now no longer had to suffer coughs and bronchitis from the hydrochloric acid.

Each of these two seminal enactments has given rise to a characteristic institution. The 1848 law gave rise to the local authority employee we know as the Public Health Inspector, and the 1863 law gave rise to the central government employee we now know as 'Her Majesty's Alkali and Clean Air Inspector'.

The Public Health Inspector may be regarded as the prototype of the local government official who, armed with powers given him by Parliament, but acting on the instructions of local councillors directly elected by the people, advises on the solution of so many of our conservation conflicts, and often enforces the solution when it has been found. The Alkali Inspector may be regarded as the prototype of the central government employee, the man from Whitehall, fulfilling the same sorts of functions but under the direction of a minister responsible to the national Parliament, consisting of members elected by the wider base population. The fact that the Alkali Inspectorate is at present a weak body, more inclined to listen to the industrialists it exists to discipline than to the representatives of the people it exists to protect, is an historical accident, and does not make it an invalid prototype or example.

The National Park Planning Officer springs remotely from the Public Health Inspector, and the Countryside Commissioner from the Alkali Inspector.

## ADVICE AND THE MECHANICS OF POLICY-MAKING

Such are the instruments of local and central government available to the politician. How shall he use them? The place of party advantage in his thoughts will at present be secondary, since conservation is in general an area of secondary party conflict. (A primary party conflict is one where the two parties think opposite things should be done, and blame one another's general direction. A secondary conflict is one where they agree what should be done, and blame only one another's way or rate of doing it.) So he will turn his thoughts to deciding what solutions to particular environmental conflicts are most just. If he can bring about social justice, it will automatically do his party good.

First, he must know what the issues are. Unless, as is seldom the case, he has come to political office straight from the discipline concerned (botany, soil mechanics, oceanography, or whatever) he needs advice. He will get it from reading, from those whose job it is to advise him, and from other sources. A local councillor will be advised mainly by his own council's officers; a minister will have a wide range of statutory and non-statutory bodies to advise him, and he will be able to set up more if he feels the need. In the conservation field, from the Royal Commission set up in 1969 downwards, the central advisory bodies are numerous and highly expert. But a minister will still be wise to go wider for his advice. If he is not himself an expert, neither will he know the experts, even by reputation, and there is an element of play-safe in the civil service which will always tend to suggest advisors who are unlikely to propose far-reaching or troublesome reforms. So unless he wants to limit his pace to that natural to the bureaucracy, he must get his own sources of independent advice, by going to interest groups and pressure groups, and by himself reading the technical and semi-technical press. Once he thinks he has the feel of the situation he will, in this field as in others, want to proceed on two levels. The first level is general policy. In what direction should the government or council of which he is a member be pointing in this matter? The second is the particular; how shall he settle his daily dozen of individual conflicts?

The most important function of any politician is legislation for, unlike
a speech, a law lasts, and unlike a case decision it affects everyone; that
is why it can only be made by the representatives of everyone, in Parliament.
The actual day-to-day drudgery of power in this field, as in others, consists
of working out 'what may wash in the House' and what does not stand a
chance, of trying it out in private on a few interested members, then taking
it through the eleven parliamentary stages that every bill must go through,
and at eight of those stages trading amendments and improvements with
those of one's own party who are not convinced and with those of the
opposition party with whom they make common cause. It is a fairly widespread delusion, among those whose life does not bring them close to it,
that the House of Commons has little power, or less than it used to have.
The delusion is even shared by some of its members, who do not always
distinguish between their own failure to get the House to do what they want
and the supposed failure of the House to get the Government to do what
it wants. But the delusion is not shared by anyone who is or has been a
minister.

In matters of conservation, the political content of which is entirely concerned with the distribution or redistribution of well-being in the use
of limited resources, the law cannot lay down in detail what shall be done;
it can only lay down who shall decide what shall be done, and when, and
what they shall take into account, and what evidence they shall hear before
they do decide. Conservation decisions in this country are now overwhelmingly taken by elected ministers and councillors, and not, for instance, by
judges, or the military, or capital or labour, or any other politically irresponsible agency; and it is the job of the politician to ensure that this continues
to be so.

Inevitably many of the detailed decisions affecting conservation, which
run into thousands in the country each day, cannot be taken by ministers
or councillors in person. But none are (or should be) taken without a
thorough knowledge of the claims and wishes of all concerned, and all are
taken by persons who are appointed by ministers or councillors, directly
responsible to them, and through them to Parliament or the council as a
whole. If the appointed and employed people take unwise or unpopular
decisions, they will not last long; it is also part of the work of a minister or
local authority committee chairman to keep patting the administrative
machine into shape, by discussions and policy notes, by commendations
and reprimands in private, and very occasionally by a demotion or dismissal
which, while it is not conspicuously done, cannot but be publicly visible to
those who are interested.

That is the general rule. But it is interesting that there is one class of
decisions affecting conservation which are taken in another way; that is,

decisions whether and where a new reservoir shall be built. Until recently these usually went by private bill procedure, which means that each House of Parliament decides as a whole, after considering the report of a committee of its own members. On these occasions, the minister concerned has no more power than any other member of the House. His opinion may carry special weight, but it is still only an opinion, not a judgment or decision. Parliament has recently turned against this way of doing things, and is increasingly passing reservoir decisions to the executive, retaining only the general power it has over all planning and conservation decisions: the power to fire the minister. This brings reservoirs into line with other classes of decisions.

## RECENT CHANGES IN CENTRAL GOVERNMENT IN RESPONSE TO ENVIRONMENTAL PROBLEMS

The increasing tendency in Parliament to wish the executive to take more and wider-ranging decisions, of which reservoir decisions are an example, must make the politician re-examine the executive structures to see that they are in the best possible condition to take them. In fact, the branch of the executive mainly responsible for conservation has recently been subjected to a major shake-up and re-amalgamation; the way the Department of the Environment came into existence is an interesting example of how the executive structures come to be changed.

Throughout the 1960s public opinion followed (about a decade behind) a great professional increase in ecological understanding. This increase occurred more in America than here, because America was in a worse mess than Britain from the uncontrolled ravages of industrialism and the industrialization of agriculture. Pollution control in Britain was at that time in the hands of a dozen separate ministers, which put any co-ordinated national plan out of the question. Though Britain was cleaner than America, that was only because we had had control mechanisms for longer; the dispersal of control was as bad here as it was there. Also during the 1960s, successive Ministers of Housing and Local Government (who had inherited the powers of the old Ministers of Town and Country Planning) proposed improvements in the land-use planning system to Parliament, and operated the improved system Parliament from time to time allowed them. Each successive revision in the system made it more 'democratic'; that is, allowed more and more people, on more and more occasions, to make their opinion felt before decisions were taken. More was published, more was justified, more opinions and advice were sought. The Ministry of Housing and Local Government was, towards the end of the sixties, in a state of convulsive democracy.

But this democracy applied only to private development; government development was exempt. If it was a question of a road or a telephone exchange, a new prison or barracks, then the citizen might as well whistle his opinion to the four winds for all that the big battalions would hear. The roads were built by the Minister of Transport and the telephone exchanges, prisons, barracks, etc., by the Minister of Works, and they did not 'come under' the Minister of Housing and his planning law. There were repeated attempts to set up joint planning staffs between the Ministries of Housing and Transport, but all were defeated by entrenched bureaucracy.

By late 1967 or 1968, the public concern about environmental pollution and about government development being above the law made it at last inevitable that government should overhaul its structures and reform them if that was needed. The overhaul took some time, and it was not until the autumn of 1969 that the reforms were ready to go into effect. The main reform was the institution of a new overlord minister in the Cabinet, called the Secretary of State for Local Government and Regional Development. To help him and the government machine at all levels in the task of environmental improvement, the Government in due course set up three new organs. First was the Royal Commission on Environmental Pollution, with a small and powerful membership, and a position of unchallengeable independence, as all Royal Commissions have, not because they are not set up by the Government, but because the Government cannot prevent them publishing their reports. It was the only permanent Royal Commission set up by the Labour Governments of 1964-70, and it has fulfilled its function well, choosing areas which the Government ought to tackle urgently and telling it how to tackle them. Partly to support the Royal Commission, partly to co-ordinate all anti-pollution work within government, including international negotiations, and partly to assist the Secretary of State directly, there was also set up a Central Unit on Environmenal Pollution, staffed by scientists from the relevant disciplines. And lastly, alongside the Clean Air Council, which had been on the whole a success during the preceding fifteen years, a new Advisory Council on Noise was set up.

The office of Secretary of State was the most important innovation. Until then, the Minister of Housing had been in the Cabinet and the Ministers of Transport and Works, though not in the Cabinet, had been full ministers; that is, they came under no Cabinet minister. They quite specifically and ardently did not, as we have noticed, come under the Minister of Housing (and Planning). In October 1969 the Minister of Housing was himself removed from the Cabinet and all three ministers were subjected to the 'co-ordination' of the new Secretary of State for Local Government and Regional Development. Each was left with his own independent statutory functions, but he had no access to the Cabinet, and thus to money, except through the new Secretary of State. The arrangement was an improvement, but it contained built-in tensions and was never meant to be more than a stopgap.

The real plan was that the statutory functions themselves should all, by order of Parliament, be passed 'upwards' to the new Secretary of State, who would thus be in undoubted control of the whole field; both the statutory powers of decision and the access to money through the Cabinet would be his alone. He would be assisted by three subordinate ministers who would correspond more or less to the former Ministers of Housing and Local Government, of Transport, and of Works. But one does not do away with independent ministers during an election campaign, and the final amalgamation was held over until the forthcoming general election should have taken place.

In June 1970, when there was a change of government, the incoming party, in a display of confidence that everything done in the last six years had been wrong, reverted to the original arrangement. The office of the co-ordinating Secretary of State was abolished, the Minister of Housing returned to the Cabinet, and the three separate ministers again went their separate ways. Some inexpert conservation decisions were taken during this period. The most noticeable was the permission given for a giant brewery to be built at Samlesbury in Lancashire; it ruined a beautiful and well-loved landscape, which is in short supply in lowland Lancashire.

But it was not long before the factors which had led the former government to decide on an amalgamation came to the attention of their successors, and the amalgamation scheme was produced from a drawer and implemented. Thus came about the office of Secretary of State for the Environment, which its first holder used to declare co-ordinated all environmental functions better than the arrangements in any other country. This is possibly true. On the other hand, it does not control all the government functions concerned with the environment. It does not control the pollution of the sea by ships or underwater pipelines; that is the province of the Secretary of State for Trade and Industry, as are aircraft noise and air pollution by aircraft exhausts. It does not control pollution of food and farmland by the wrong use of pesticides and drugs; that is for the Minister of Agriculture. It does not control the conservation of fish or animal stocks; fish are for the Minister of Agriculture, wild animals for the Home Secretary. Nor does it control land drainage and the prevention of flooding from rivers, for that too falls to the Minister of Agriculture. It is not generally known that this last minister is responsible for preventing the flooding of London, or that the threat of such a flood is, after nuclear war or accident, the greatest physical threat at present facing the British people. All in all, it may be necessary for yet more functions to be taken into the

Department of the Environment, particularly those which, like the control of aircraft noise, at present rest with the departments responsible for the economic development of the industry concerned.

## THE NATURE OF DECISIONS

The actual decisions the politician makes each day on conservation usually have the form: how much wealth for whom, and how soon? In recent years, the decisions have overwhelmingly removed wealth from the private individual or firm, and transferred it to the generality of citizens; they have also tended to the realization of potential wealth later rather than sooner. They have tended, to use the economists' jargon, to re-internalize externalities, laying the cost of clean air, water, soil, or whatever it may be, on the producer of the industrial or agricultural product or service, and thus in due course on the consumer, and removing the cost from the taxpayer, who formerly had to pay (for instance) for the medical treatment of those who suffered from the dirty water, etc.

But any decision which increases the internal costs of private industry in one place without equally increasing them in all places distorts the framework of competition in general, and reduces the short-term efficiency of the enterprises in the place concerned, thus risking local unemployment. And if there is one thing a voter hates more than being polluted, it is being unemployed.

The politician has therefore to seek to relate the rate at which he transfers costs away from the public and on to the enterprises in question to the rate at which they are being transferred on to other, comparable and competitive enterprises. This is true at local level, where a decision to impose conservation measures on industrial production will tend to deter industry from investing in plant in the area where that decision is in force. On the international level the situation is the same; the modern multinational corporations enjoy very wide freedom to invest where they think fit, and especially where the national government will give them what they regard as favourable conditions, or realistic concessions from the full rigour of law, whether fiscal, monetary, labour or environmental.

The different rates at which local councils introduce conservation measures can be regulated through the mechanisms of central government. The different rates at which nation states do the same cannot be regulated by any supranational mechanism, since none exists. It is for that reason that the United Nations Council for Environmental Programmes, set up after the 1972 Stockholm Conference, and its attendant Secretariat are so important. This new member of the UN family is to begin the task of dreaming up the international arrangements which will correspond to those by which national governments are accustomed to regulate the divergences among their own local authorities. The work will last for many decades, but it is clearly one of the tasks on which the future of mankind depends.

## WHAT CHANGES ARE NECESSARY?

Within this global task, the main day-to-day duty of the national politician in office is to keep his own legislative framework up to date with change. To do this, he must try to foresee what changes will next be needed. The changes extraneous to the political and legal system itself which most regularly impose change upon it are ideological, technological, demographic and economic. It has a famous-last-words ring, but I do not believe that change in popular ideology is going to impose change on conservation law in the near future. The prescriptions of the conservation pressure groups are an order of magnitude less informed and constructive than their descriptions. Commoner and Ehrlich in the United States, and the 'Blueprint for Survival' group in this country, have analysed the friction at the interface between social and ecological systems with insight and vigour; but the social remedies they prescribe are the work of beginners indeed, and until they or others delve into social and political reality with the care they have devoted to ecological reality, it is not 'conservationism' which is going to change society.

Technology is changing and must change our legal and social systems all the time. People keep inventing things, for instance hovercraft, or doing things, for instance giving antibiotics to healthy calves, about which there is no law, and a law has to be invented to match. But in a field where so much is done at the level of individual decisions between conflicting interests, the perpetual updating of the system to keep pace with technology is probably more a matter of bringing young faces into the administrative machine than of anything else.

### The Demands on the Land

Population and wealth, on the other hand, are, if they continue to increase, going to turn our system upside down. Our land-use planning system, which is the framework for most of the decision-making on conservation, was founded in its present form only a quarter of a century ago, and it has been increasingly democratized; that is to say, more and more types of decisions may only, by law, be taken after all the world and his wife have had their say. At the same time, both population and individual wealth relentlessly grow. They do so at rates slower than those prevailing in most countries of the world, but then our average per capita income is already much higher than that of most countries in the world, and our population density is higher than any, except city states such as Hong Kong and Singapore.\* More wealth means a demand for more land per head; not only for material production, but also for education, health and leisure. And more heads mean a demand for more land, whatever the wealth.

These two trends have recently combined to create a rise in land prices which is the sharpest Britain has ever experienced, and perhaps is sharper than any ever experienced anywhere. British people do not move house often, so it will be some years before even half the people have personally met this price rise. But when a sizeable proportion of the people have met it, the land price explosion will be recognized as a national disaster.

The land price explosion has its effects on conservation through the planning system. The progression is as follows. There is and always has been an unregulated economic conflict between different claimants who may wish to put a given piece of land to the *same use*. My house or yours on this land? That question is settled by money. When the conflict is not between different people aiming at the same use, but between people or sets of people each of whom desires a *different* use, the question is not settled solely by money; it is settled also by law and involves planning applications, decisions, refusals, variations, appeals, hearings and enquiries.

Among the uses which may be claimed for a piece of land is of course 'conservation', whether conservation pure and simple for the good of the people or the advance of science, or, on the other hand, the introduction of conservation factors into the management of the land, in such a way that it does not yield as high a short-term financial return as it would have done without them. The recent and continuing price explosion will thus make it more difficult for conservation values to withstand profit values, and conservationists must look to their defences within the planning system.

When we add to the increasing population and increasing wealth the increasing democracy we mentioned before, the situation becomes even more acute. If the private individual has a right to make his views heard before a small planning decision (housing on these fields, or conservation?) then he naturally must also have the right to make them heard before the big decisions on which the smaller ones depend. These are the so-called structure plans which, under the 1968 Planning Act, the new local authorities are now drawing up and which must be approved by the Secretary of State for the Environment after a public enquiry or run of enquiries. Only one of these plans has yet come to the 'participation' phase; that is the Greater London Development Plan, into which a public enquiry sat from 1969 to 1972. But in time the 44 new top-tier local government authorities will no doubt all have to subject their draft structure plans to three year enquiries. During the same period, 1969–72, there was

\*England and Wales: 324 persons per sq km., Netherlands: 319, Belgium, 317. (*UN Demographic Handbook*, 1970)

also the Roskill Commission enquiry into the timing and location of the Third London Airport. Both the London Plan and the Roskill enquiries heard hosts of witnesses, and handed in gigantic reports to the Government. Neither the cost of the enquiry into the Greater London Development Plan nor the content of its report is known as I write. But the Roskill Commission cost a million and a quarter pounds, and said that the airport should be built soon, and built in the Vale of Aylesbury, because an impeccable cost-benefit analysis showed that was the best time and the best place. The Government rejected the advice and the analysis on which it was grounded, and decided the airport should be at Foulness instead. The million and a quarter pounds had been wasted.

## POLITICS AND THE RESOLUTION OF CONFLICTS

The task of thinking up a way of avoiding such waste in future is a daunting one, and has hardly yet begun. But a politician will naturally look to politics for the way forward. The Roskill Commission itself was only set up when the first choice of the government of the day, namely Stansted in Essex, had run into difficulties in Parliament. It is interesting that it was not the House of Commons which blocked a great airport at Stansted in 1967, it was the House of Lords. When the minister in charge of the matter in the House of Lords reported that (1) the House would almost certainly throw out an order designating Stansted, (2) in his opinion the country would agree, (3) the House of Commons, which had approved Stansted, would be made to look like a pack of sheep, and (4) the attempt which was at that time being made to reform the House of Lords would be wrecked, the then Leader of the House of Commons took the point, and the Stansted order was pigeonholed. It had been the opinion of the minister responsible in the House of Lords all along that, of all the places which had been studied (and many had), Foulness was on general social and political grounds the only one which would work. Nevertheless, the Roskill Commission was set up, reported the preference of its majority for the Vale of Aylesbury, and saw its work dismissed. It may well be that as technological complexity, population and wealth continue to grow, so democracy will increasingly have to be exercised, not by sifting evidence and opinions, but by requiring the responsible person to get on with it. If the day comes when there is no room in the hall for all the qualified instrumentalists, we shall have to revert to the time-, money- and sanity-saving procedure of hiring a single pianist and, when we don't like the tune, shooting him.

# Author Index

Citations in the text are shown in ordinary type, precise references to publications are in bold type. Cross-references between chapters are also shown.

477

# Subject Index

*Entries with italic page numbers refer to important discussions of the topic.*

Public impact, *see* Recreation
Public ownership, 256, 317
Public participation, 410
*Puccinellia maritima, 173*
Puffins, (*Fratercula arctica*), 185
*Pulsatilla vulgaris* (pasque flower), 174, 175, 292, 293
*Pyrola media,* 147

Queensland, 59, 66, 68
*Quercus* spp. (oak), invasion of heath and grassland, 127, 180, 297
  pollen diagram, 285
  replanting, 136, spp. 138, 140
  standards in coppice, 135
*Q. coccifera,* 273 (Kermès oak)
Questionnaires, 221, 222, 343

Rabbits, 101, 172, 181, 295, 301, 303
Radnorshire, 355, 356
Railways, 282
Rainfall, 42, 201, 202
Ramblers, *see* Walkers
*Rana pipiens* (Leopard frog), 105
*Ranunculus acris* (buttercup), 281
  *repens,* 281
  *lingua* (great spearwort), 299
Rarities, conservation, 6, 96, 219, 223, 292, 317, 432, 446
Rats, resistance to Warfarin, 101
Recessivity (genes), 108
Reclamation, 97
  damaged land, 251–63, 318
  from fen, 296
  from saltmarsh, 294
  upland, 358
Recreation, economics, 342–4, 346–7, 393
  in National Parks and wilderness areas, 365, 367, 378, 382, 393–4, 397–8, 400–3
  in woodlands and forests, 141, 162
  management, 227–9, 313, 412, 416, 445
  measurement, 221–3, 225
  on grassland, 171, 222
  on heathland, 118, 122–3, 126, 127
  on moorland, 153, 156, 162–3, 358–9
  planning, 311–2, 313, 316–7, 337, 387–8, 390, 411–2

Recycling, economic, 9, 460–2
  natural, 175
Red beds, 270–3
Red deadnettle (*Lamium purpureum*), 281
Red deer, *see Cervus elaphus*
Red Deer Commission, 153–5
Redemption, *see* Reclamation
Redwing, 180
Refresher courses, 439
Regeneration (vegetation), coppice, 134–5
  grazing effects, 134, 138
  in woodland, 140, 141
  on moorland, 146, 149, 158
Regionalism, 344
Regional Parks, U.S.A., 405
Regional Planning, Secretary of State, 378
Regional Water Authorities, 59, 315
Rehabilitation, *see* Reclamation
Reindeer management, 187
Relevance, 444
Remoteness, 309, 367, 369, *370*
Renewal, *see* Reclamation
Reproduction, pesticide effect, 234
Reserves, *see* Nature reserves
Reservoirs, amenity, 97, 312, 363, 383
  function, 207–8, 298
  politics, 469
  recreation, 218, 313, 383
  siting, 274
Resources (natural)
  depletion, 453, 460–4
  economics, 2, 316–7, 318, 340, 442, 453–4, 460, 463, 464
  management, 4, 318–9, 438, 439–41, 460
  marine, 246
  non-renewable, 3, 5, 463
  politics, 465, 468
  renewable, 3, 4, 5, 9, 463
Restoration, *see* Reclamation
Return period, *48,* 59, 207, 214
Rhayader (Radnor.), 355
Rhine Delta, 59
Rhodesia, 194
*Rhododendron ponticum,* 127
Rhum (N.N.R.) (Scotland), 188, 189, 190, 431
*Rhynchosporium* (barley disease), 332